Fletcher Benton

AN AMERICAN ARTIST

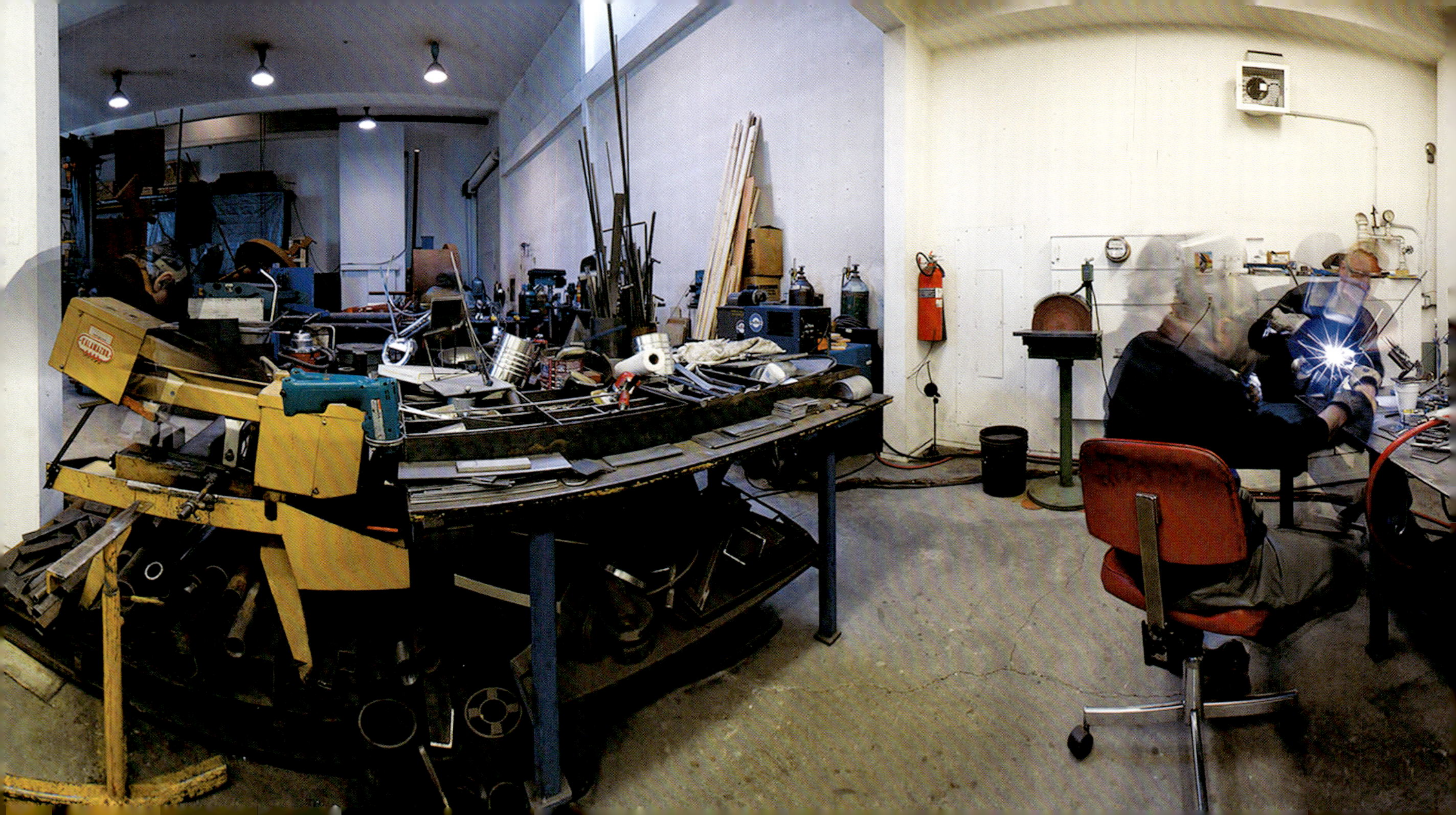

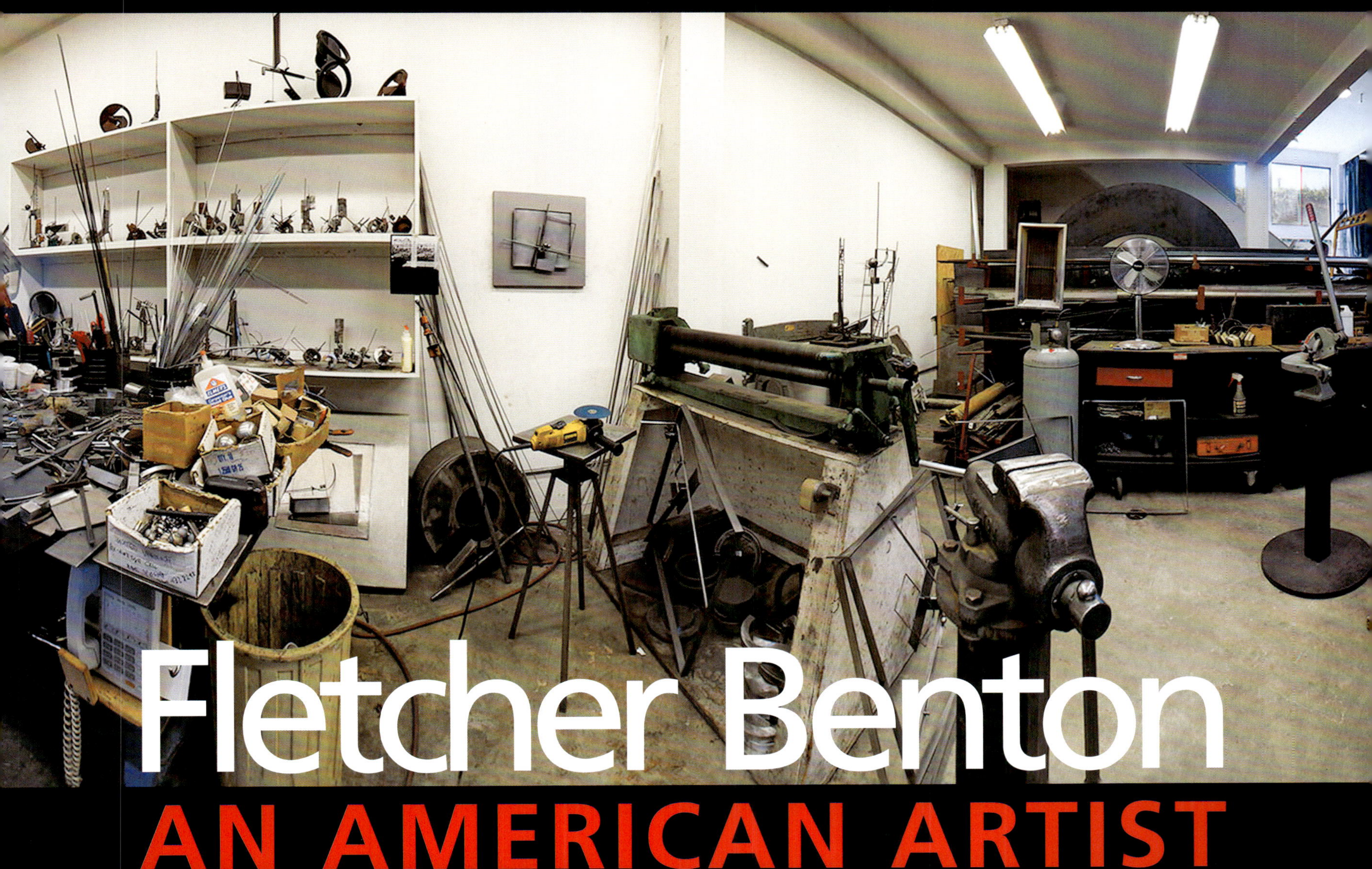

Fletcher Benton

AN AMERICAN ARTIST

Acknowledgments

It is a very special privilege for me, at this time in my life and career, to have Hudson Hills Press publish the books *Fletcher Benton: An American Artist* and *Fletcher Benton: The Kinetic Years*. The work that has gone into these projects has at times been intensive and exasperating. Michael Roby, who is involved in all phases of my studio operations, has relieved me of many time-consuming tasks. I can't thank him enough for his unselfish involvement at the studio and for shepherding these two books through to completion. Mark Ong of Side By Side Studios, who I might add did my very first book for Harry N. Abrams in 1990, agreed to design these two books. You're the best, Mark. In every major project like this, there are the tedious details and mechanical finals. Francee Ricarte, you did a splendid job. Monja Merkel assisted in researching the projects—thank you. I would also like to express my gratitude to The Board of Directors of The International Sculpture Center for honoring me with the 2008 Lifetime Achievement in Contemporary Sculpture Award. Finally, I want to thank, above all, my lovely wife, Bobbie, who has had to deal with me. I'm a lucky man.

First Edition

Published in the United States by Hudson Hills Press, LLC
P.O. Box 205, 3556 Main Street, Manchester, Vermont 05254

Distributed in the United States, its territories and possessions, and Canada by National Book Network, Inc.
Distributed outside of North America by Antique Collectors' Club, Ltd.

Publisher and Executive Director: Leslie Pell van Breen
Production Manager: David Skolkin
Designer: Mark Ong, Side By Side Studios
Production Director: Michael Roby
Production Assistant: Francee Ricarte
Production Assistant: Monja Merkel
Copy Editor for "Creating the Truth": Elisabeth Beller
Composition: Mark Ong and Susan Riley
Proofreader: Judith Higgins
Printed and bound by Tien Wah Press Pte Ltd
Founding Publisher: Paul Anbinder

Manufactured in Singapore.

Library of Congress Cataloging-in-Publication Data

Fletcher Benton : an American artist. -- 1st ed.
p. cm.
Essays by Carter Ratcliff, Collette Chattopadhyay and Jolei Leisegang.
Includes bibliographical references.
1. Benton, Fletcher, 1931---Criticism and interpretation. I. Ratcliff, Carter. II. Chattopadhyay, Collette. III. Leisegang, Jolei. IV. Benton, Fletcher, 1931-
NB237.B4348F59 2008
730.92--dc22
2008048852

ISBN 13: 978-1-55595-296-9

Contents

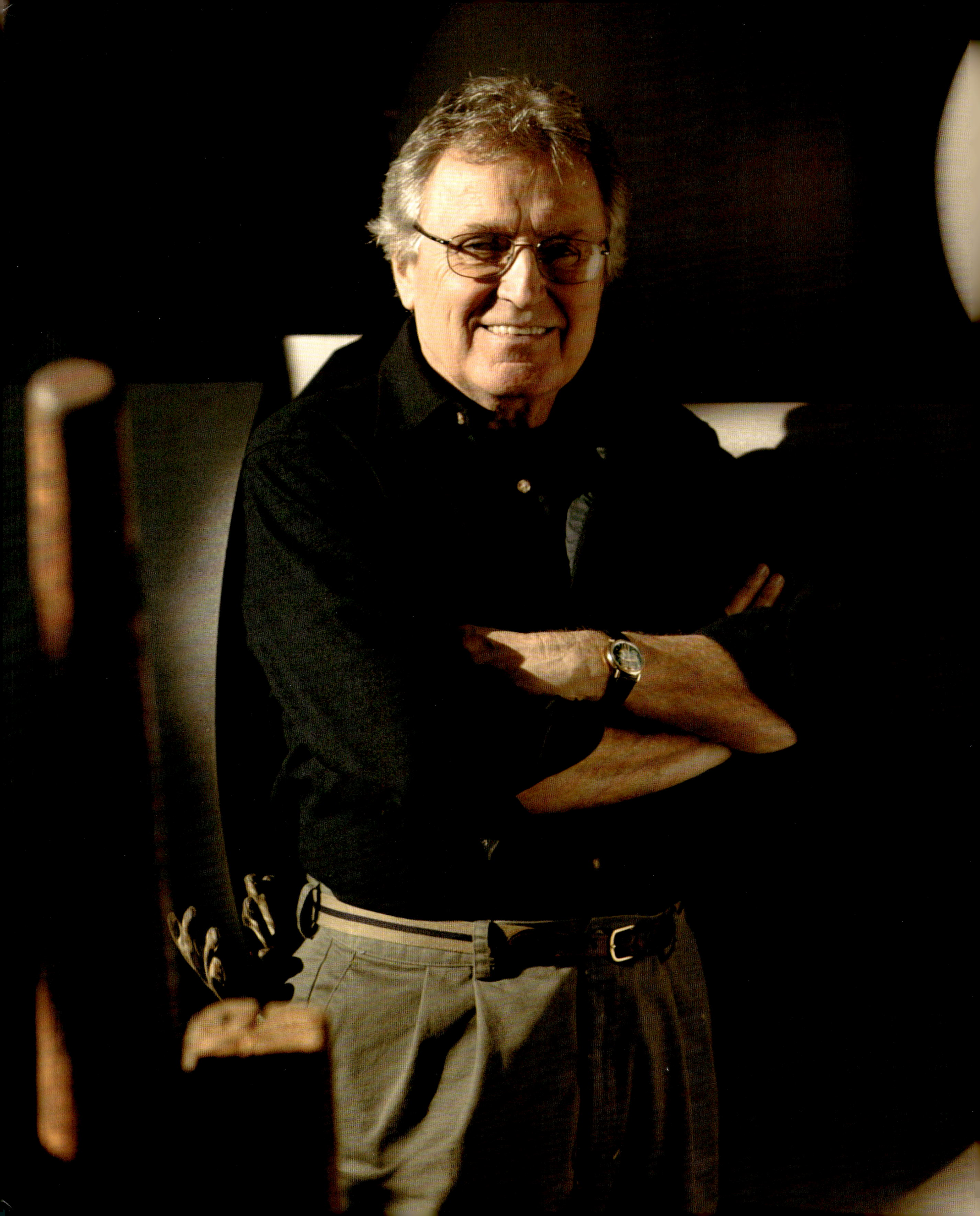

Fletcher Benton: The Purpose of Harmony

Carter Ratcliff

Fletcher Benton's *Folded Circle T*, 1999 (see page 1), is more than large. It is monumental, which means that it has a presence greater than its physical bulk would suggest. Yet it is delicately articulated. From a certain angle, it appears to be tilting forward in anticipation, as if to greet any viewer who might be approaching. Nonetheless, it is absolutely still. Seeing Benton as a maker of delicate monuments, an artist of animated stillness, one might conclude that he deals in paradox. But it is truer to see him as unifier, an artist who reconciles apparent opposites.

Over twelve feet high and as solid as a rock, *Folded Circle T* is a daunting presence, but only until some subtlety catches your eye and you move in for a closer look. Then the wariness induced by this object's monumental weight becomes a delight in details, which Benton balances with all the care—and calm bravura—of a tightrope walker placing one foot in front of another. Close-up, even the large, blocky folds in this *Folded Circle* have the crisp, immaterial precision of lines drawn on a sheet of drafting paper. Solid steel acquires a sort of friendliness, and you begin to see lush, elusive colors in the rusted Cor-ten surface of *Folded Circle T*.

Though Benton never defies his materials, he often brings out unsuspected aspects of their nature. It is as if he induces brute matter to join him in elaborating the

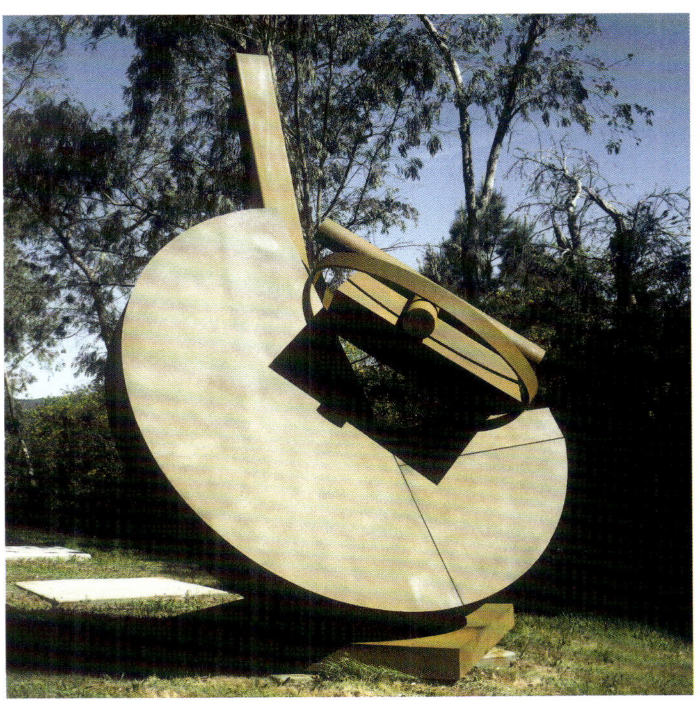

Folded Circle T

1999, Cor-ten steel
12 x 9 x 9 feet
366 x 274 x 274 cm

possibilities of form. In *Folded Circle T*, a sizable wedge rests in the notch created by the fold. The "T" of the title rests on this wedge—or stretches out on it like a bather on a beach towel. An abstract artist, Benton has no fear of the figurative motifs we read into his sculptures. Still, a motif of this sort is never the rationale for a form, and it is incumbent on us to look past the allusion to a sunbather to something more important: the position of the "T," which has been precisely calculated to anchor the wedge in its precarious place. Echoing the circle that serves this sculpture as a basic axiom, a ring ties wedge and "T" to the larger configuration.

Often the degree of disparity within a single work is extreme. *Plane to Edge: 2 Balls*, 1997, shows Benton's familiar contrast of the circular and the straight, the planar and the spherical. The quick, vertical ascent of the central slab contrasts sharply with the leisurely, lateral drift of the forms clustered around this sculpture's ring. Further, these elements range from the very small to the very large. By staking out extremes, Benton implies every gradation in between. Thus he presents a concise invocation of all the disparity, all the difference, there is. Having invoked the world, he finds equally concise ways to suggest the reconciliation of its differences. Concision is a form of wit, and Benton's is endlessly resourceful. His placements of small elements often have the tone of elegant, insightful one-liners. When medium-size forms assemble, one thinks of fast-moving repartee. And when he ascends to monumentality, his wit is that of a logician finding new and surprising solutions to long-standing problems.

Mediating between extremes, Benton charges matter with meaning. This is what sculptors always have done, although, until recent times, they intended their forms to look like something familiar—more often than not, a human anatomy. In the long perspectives of history, the possibility of abstract sculpture looks quite new and rather shocking. Though we have gotten used to the idea of abstraction, the very idea of nonfigurative sculpture remains mysterious. If a sculptor's forms resemble nothing in particular, how can they mean anything at all? There is a hint of an answer in my remarks on *Folded Circle T*: abstract forms make allusions to human forms and to other things, notably the forms of architecture and landscape. These should never be overlooked. In making sense of an abstract sculpture, however, we must focus, first and last, on the relations between its disparate shapes. We must see how the sculpture is put together, how it works, what is going on internally. And when we have seen that, we will begin to see what the sculpture has to do with the external world.

After the *Folded Circle* sculptures came *Folded Squares*. Among the first is *Folded Square Alphabet Q*, 1979 (see page 2). Every sculpture has a physical premise, the chunk of matter from which all else follows. The premise of this sculpture could not be simpler: a rectangular slab of steel just over eight feet high. Simplicity became complexity as Benton cut into the slab with an Oxy/Acetylene torch. Sweeping incisions allowed him to fold out large shapes: a disc, a ring, and a flange-like protrusion that inflects these circular forms with the hint of a Q's tail. Though it conjures up a letter of the alphabet, *Folded Square Alphabet Q* invites a thoroughly visual reading. And scanning is useless. The viewer must circle the sculpture slowly, watching its forms shift. From certain angles, the void in the slab and the second void of the ring stand in opposition to the solidity of the disc. From other angles, ring and disc are complementary, fitting together almost like pieces of a puzzle, and one glimpses—or intuits—the pristine simplicity of the original slab.

Painted bright blue, *Folded Square Alphabet Q* is, for all its complexity, a crisply defined presence. Beginning with geometrical givens of the kind one understands in a glance, Benton elaborated them until he had achieved the

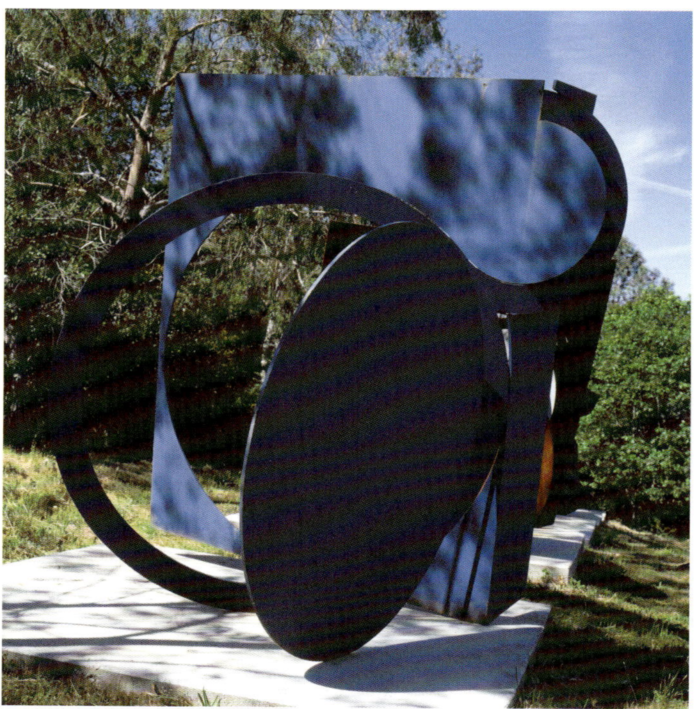

Folded Square Alphabet Q
1979, painted steel
98 x 84 x 91 inches
249 x 213 x 231 cm

sort of clarity one discovers only in the course of attentive looking. Tracing a *Folded Square*'s visual rhymes, half rhymes, and reversals, one watches the internal coherence of the sculpture emerge. Alert for the moment when that coherence feels complete—the "Ah-ha" moment—the attention zooms in on the work of art. This narrow focus is natural, yet it often prevents us from seeing that the search for coherence renders not only the sculpture but also our seeing more coherent. Noticed or not, this shared clarity gives us one of our chief motives for looking at art.

In *Folded Square Alphabet U*, 1980 (see page 3), the first fold turned a flat slab into a right-angled slab. So far, Benton had left the simplicity of the original form almost intact. Suddenly, matters became complicated. Cutting a wide, looping ribbon from one side of the folded slab, he bent and rolled it downward to form a U-shape. He formed another by cutting a thin loop from the outer edge of the thicker one, and then bending it out and upward. At first, one hardly notices that the two "U"s are variations on one another. The lower, wider one serves as a prop to give this tilted piece its look of stability. Cantilevered into the air, the upper, thinner "U" is simply part of the superstructure that the lower "U" must stabilize—or so it appears until one sees how precisely Benton has balanced the thrusts and counterthrusts of these curving shapes. Whatever stresses gravity imposes on the lower "U," it hardly looks strained, and the upper "U" seems to levitate, relieving the entire sculpture of its weight. Thus the sculpture finds a coherence independent of its literal weight.

Soon after *Folded Square Alphabet U* came *Folded Square Alphabet F*, 1982. Five years later, Benton reprised the theme in *Folded Square Alphabet F—Phase II* (see page 3). With its circular opening, this sculpture recalls the circular forms of *Folded Square Alphabet Q*, a sculpture from the beginning of the series. There are even closer affinities between *Folded Square Alphabet Q*, from 1979, and *Folded Square Numerical 6* (see page 3), which Benton made in 1995. In the realm of Bentonian form, time passes, as it must; yet it is forever circling back on itself, as the artist recapitulates with variations the landmarks of earlier seasons. These temporal patterns are imaginary, yet they are strong. To look from one of Benton's sculptures to the next and the next is to sense their immersion in currents of invention that have flowed from the late 1970s to the present. Earlier, Benton dealt in actual motion. Until 1973, he was a kinetic artist.

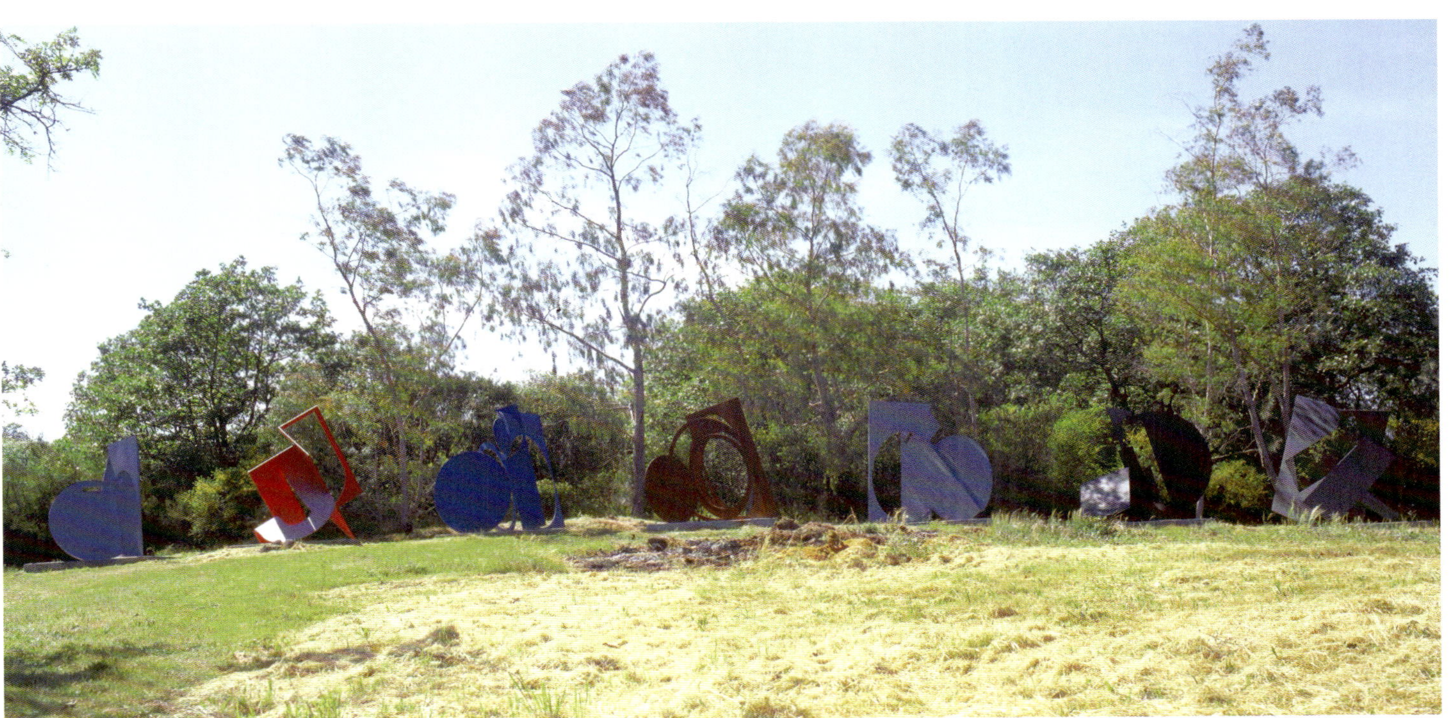

Folded Square Alphabets
1979–1995, painted and rusted steel
Napa, California

(from left to right)
Folded Square Alphabet F–Phase II
Folded Square Alphabet U
Folded Square Alphabet Q
Folded Square Numerical 6
Folded Square Alphabet T
Folded Square Alphabet G
Folded Square Alphabet F

Born in Jackson, Ohio, in 1931, Benton received his B.F.A. in painting from Miami University, in Oxford, Ohio, in 1956. By the late 1950s, he was living in San Francisco, painting and teaching would-be painters at the California College of Arts and Crafts, in Oakland. He exhibited his work widely in Bay Area galleries and museums. A relentless experimenter, he carved figures from balsa wood and attached them to the surface of his canvases. These led to more figures, freed from the canvas now, and set in motion by small, battery-powered motors. Nude and female, one of them swung on a trapeze. Another rode a unicycle. Painted bright pink, their pubic hair and nipples were indicated by dabs of black and red paint. Scheduled for a show at San Francisco's Gump's Gallery, in 1959, they offended the director of the gallery, and the exhibition was canceled.

Benton continued to motorize his forms, which were now abstract. In 1964 the Esther Robles Gallery, of Los Angeles, presented the first exhibition of his kinetic works. Soon he was swept into a movement the international scope of which he had not, until then, suspected. Among the liveliest developments of the 1960s, kinetic art was not entirely unprecedented. Naum Gabo set *Kinetic Constructionist No. 1* in motion in 1920. Moreover, Gabo and other Constructivists—like the Futurists before them—called for art that would exploit all the resources of modern technology. But it was not until after the Second World War that works of kinetic art began to proliferate in Europe, Latin America, and the United States. By the '60s, kineticism was an art-world rage, a rival to Pop and Op Art. Never at a loss for a variation on his first motorized abstractions, Benton quickly found himself in the front ranks of the kinetic artists. As the 1960s ended, the demand for his work had given him a career on the international exhibition circuit.

Benton abruptly stopped making kinetic art in 1973, for he had realized that his success was having a double effect. The first was obvious: the greater the demand for new works, the more prolific he became. The second, subtler effect was the exhaustion inflicted by the frenetic pace of his career. Kinetic art puts form through relentlessly repetitive cycles, and Benton may have felt trapped in the patterns of motion he had invented. Possibly, he was not physically worn down so much as imaginatively depleted. In any case, he abandoned kineticism as quickly as he had embraced it. To become a sculptor was to embark on a new path, which once again brought him international recognition. During the past quarter-century, he has had a succession of solo exhibitions at galleries and museums in the United States and Europe. Moreover, he has carried out a succession of major public commissions here and abroad.

In a 1989 interview with the art historian Paul Karlstrom, Benton said, "The *Folded Square* and *Folded Circle* works were my first steps outside of the kinetic world."[1] He set himself a problem: to begin with a two-dimensional "given," a flat slab of steel, and find his way into "the three-dimensional world." The rules were strict. There was to be no "adding to or subtracting from. . . . All I could do was cut, fold out, and redesignate the parts." Though the given, whether circle or square, would remain, it would be transformed. From simplicity would come complexity, yet nothing would be sacrificed. No matter how monumentally intricate a *Folded* sculpture might be, it never obscures the original slab in all its clarity.

Recently, Benton described the steps that lead to a *Folded Square* sculpture. On a three-by-three-inch portion of an index card, he draws a letter or a number. Then he cuts out the drawn form, bends and folds it, and glues in into a new, three-dimensional configuration. Next, he and his studio crew transpose this shape into steel. From the start, he resisted the temptation to delegate the execution of full-scale pieces to outside fabricators. As he says, "I'm a builder." During his kinetic phase, he was obsessed with perfect surfaces, and that obsession may be all that stayed with him as he reinvented himself as a sculptor. Refusing to leave even the smallest matter of construction or finish to outsiders, he insists on overseeing every detail of a sculpture's fabrication. When he says that he is a builder, he means, in part, that he wields a metal worker's tools. Of course, that is not all he means.

Traditionally, sculpture was carved from wood or stone or cast from metal. In modern times, sculptors borrowed the methods of modern manufacturers: torch cutting, bolting, welding. These borrowings from the factory floor changed the nature of the sculptural object. Though ancient statues were sometimes made from several chunks of marble, the seams are subtly hidden, and the effect is of a stone figure as organically unified as a living body. Far from hiding its joints, a modern, fabricated sculpture puts them on display. Yet we are not being invited to see the object as disjointed. Rather, the sculptor hopes that his explicit articulation of his forms will make us conscious of the tensions between parts and the whole. Further, this clarity encourages us to trace the steps in the sculptor's struggle to resolve those tensions.

As Benton often says, each of his sculptures results from a series of decisions. Starting with elemental forms, his givens, he works his way toward a harmony comparable to that of an ancient statue—comparable but not the same, for Benton is not a biomorphic sculptor. Though the proportions of a *Steel Watercolor* may evoke a standing figure, he never tries to mimic the form of a living organism. Like those of the Constructivists, Benton's geometries are frankly assembled, built, constructed. Unlike those artists, he writes no manifestos setting forth utopian goals and promising that clarified form will one day reveal transcendent truths. For Wassily Kandinsky, Naum Gabo, and other Constructivists active early in the 20th century, geometry had the quasi-religious aura of the absolute. For Benton, it offered the most compelling possibilities available to a kinetic artist who wanted to step into three-dimensions. Geometric form, he believed, would give him freedom.

Over the years, Benton has extended the *Folded Square* series to include all twenty-six letters of the alphabet, A to Z, and the cardinal numbers, zero to nine. There are several ways of understanding this thoroughness. First, we could see it as evidence of Benton's affection for—and sensitivity to—the shapes of letters and numbers. As a teenager, he was apprenticed to a sign painter in his hometown. Learning the trade with ease, he quickly found all the work he wanted. Though Benton has always made a sharp distinction between sign painting and fine art, he notes that a sense of proportion is crucial to both. Furthermore, the forms he mastered as a young sign painter gave him, as a mature artist, an indispensable repertory of basic forms—and, as the *Folded Square* sculptures show, the negative forms of letters and numbers are just as important to him as the positive ones.

Given Benton's history, one still might ask why he felt compelled to transform every last letter of the alphabet and every number, zero to nine, into a *Folded Square* sculpture. A further answer to that question is that he wanted to make the transition from kinetic art to sculpture as decisive as possible. To recite the alphabet is to begin a process and bring it through to a clear and obvious point of completion. By making sculptures from the shapes of all twenty-six letters, Benton carried out that process at a monumental scale. Moreover, he did the same with the numbers, another ready-made set of forms. Thus he made the move from kinetic art to the three-dimensions of sculpture in a deliberate, systematic way, and he did it not once but twice.

Because kinetic sculpture is sometimes considered a form of sculpture, we should note that, for Benton, it was an extension of painting: a way to animate the static shapes of paint on canvas. He has said, on occasion, that painting is an illusory, elusive medium. This is an admiring, not a disparaging, description, yet he wanted more control over his art than he felt he could have as a painter. Kineticism, he may have felt, would give him that control. By mechanizing shapes and colors, he exchanged the impalpable ambiguities of pictorial art for actual, predictable patterns of motion. Eventually, those patterns became too predictable. As I've suggested, he moved from two dimensions to three in search of freedom.

Among David Finn's photographs of Benton's work is a panoramic shot of eight *Folded Square* sculptures. Often Finn moves around a sculpture with his camera, approaching for close-ups, stepping back for full views. With his unfailing sensitivity to the personalities of individual works, he enacts for us the experience of responding to sculptural form. With this *Folded Square* panorama, he gives us something different: a family portrait of one of Benton's major series. He gives us, as well, a glimpse of the sculptures' setting. Since 1971, Benton has been installing sculptures on his property in Napa Valley, California. As several of Finn's photographs show, this is wine country. Beyond the vineyards rise tree-covered mountains. Benton's sculptures look as if they are at home in this landscape, and yet a viewer familiar with the art—and the ideology—of the early 20th century might be nagged by a question. Why has an heir of the Constructivists installed his art amid all this rural beauty?

Those artists were urban. So is Benton—or, at any rate, his sculpture more than holds its own amid the glass and steel towers of the contemporary city, as he demonstrates with *Double Folded Circle*, 2002 (see page 6), which stands in front of the S. Mark Taper Imaging Center, Cedars-Sinai Medical Center, Los Angeles. Yet he never identifies his geometrical forms with the scientific and technological ethos of the modern metropolis, as the early Constructivists did. "The plumb line in our hand, eyes precise as a ruler, in a spirit as taut as a compass, we construct our work as the universe constructs its own, as the engineer constructs his bridges, as the mathematician his formula of the [planetary] orbits," declared the Constructivists Naum Gabo and Antoine Pevsner, in their "Realistic Manifesto" of 1920.[2]

Though Benton has all the studio expertise he needs, he does not submit his art to "the engineer's esthetic," as the architect Le Corbusier called it. Nor does he seek the unity of art and science invoked time and again in the manifestos of Gabo, Pevsner, and the other Constructivists. Having inherited their geometry, Benton endowed it with new sympathies. Where his Constructivist predecessors tried to

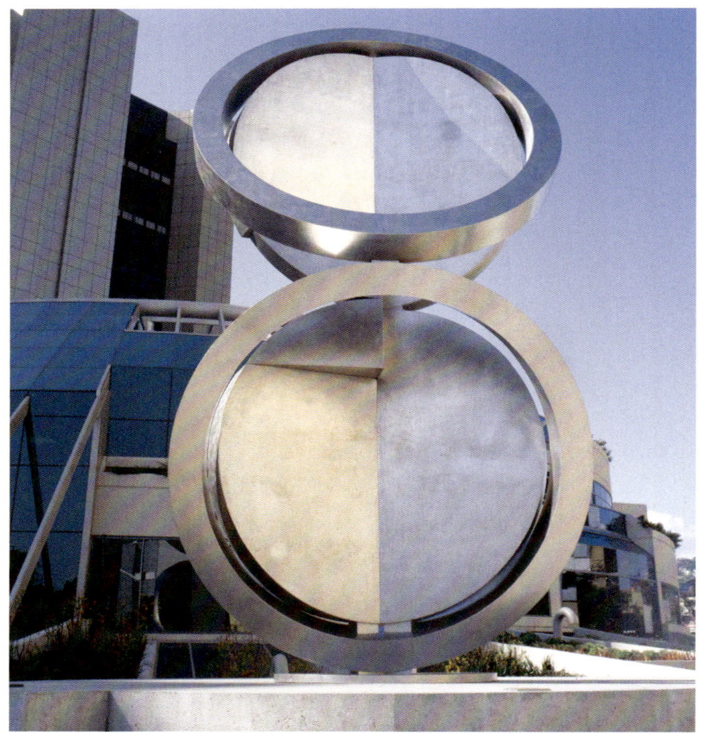

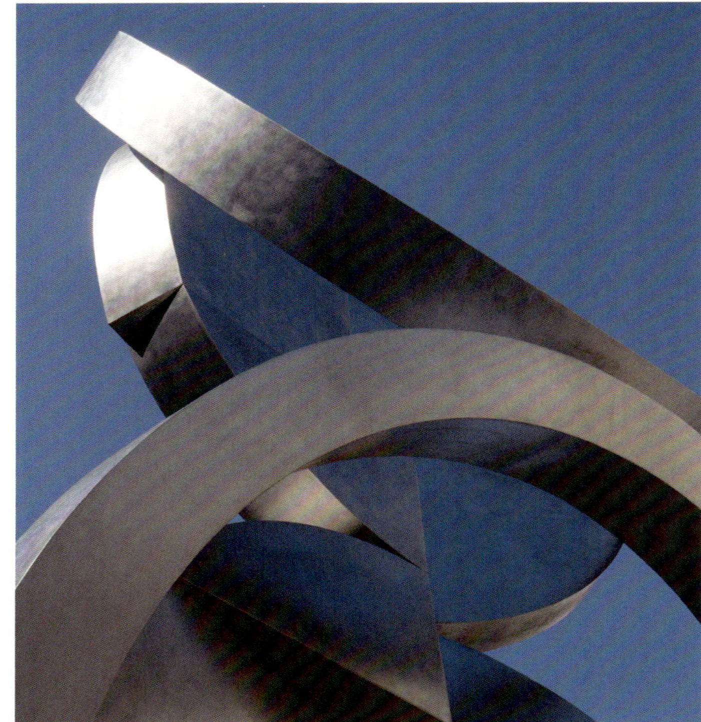

Double Folded Circle
2002, 316-L stainless steel
H: 30 feet
H: 914 cm
Cedars-Sinai Medical Center, Los Angeles

ally their structures with those of machinery and with laboratory models of physical matter, Benton seeks affinities with musical form. Thus he sees his elementary forms as notes, which he composes "with timing, with repetition, with beat, with all the things that go into music."

To quote this comment of Benton's is not to suggest that we ignore either the elegant engineering of his art or its compatibility with mathematical and scientific styles of clarity. He is, after all, a geometric sculptor. His forms invoke grids, crystals, and the structural logic of architecture. Yet he appeals to none of that as a justification for his art. The Constructivists of the 1920s and '30s promised that their affinities with scientists and technologists would give art the power to perfect the world. Those promises were never kept and, in the aftermath of the Second World War, utopian prophesy ceased. As an artist of a later generation, Benton is impatient with the idea that art can better the world in a programmatic way. Art, he feels, is not a means to an end. From simplicities he builds complexities, self-sufficient forms that provide a self-justifying pleasure. Art is an end itself, which seems simple enough. Yet the pleasure of Benton's art is endlessly complex, in ways that we are just beginning to glimpse.

In 1982 he made *Pole Drawing 1* and *2* (see page 7). One "Drawing" is blue, the other red. Each appears in a metal frame, which is raised about three feet off the ground by a metal pole. Literally speaking, these are not drawings at all, but clusters of flat forms confined to a single plane—like shapes on a sheet of drawing paper. Instead of paper, there is empty space, and so, as thin as it is when viewed from the side, *Pole Drawing 1* and *2* count as a sculpture. The chief form in the blue "Drawing" is the circle, or disc, that rests near the upper end of the tilted horizon line marked by a thin strip of steel. A wedge holds the disc, or sun, in place—not in fact, of course, but according to the improvised logic of this exuberant configuration. In practical fact, each element is welded into its place, which seems to have been determined by the gravitational force of the large blue form.

In the red "Drawing," the disc is split into halves that are stacked to produce a somewhat wobbly vertical form. Here it is not easy to say which shape dominates. Maybe neither of them does. Yet here, as in the blue "Drawing," coherence

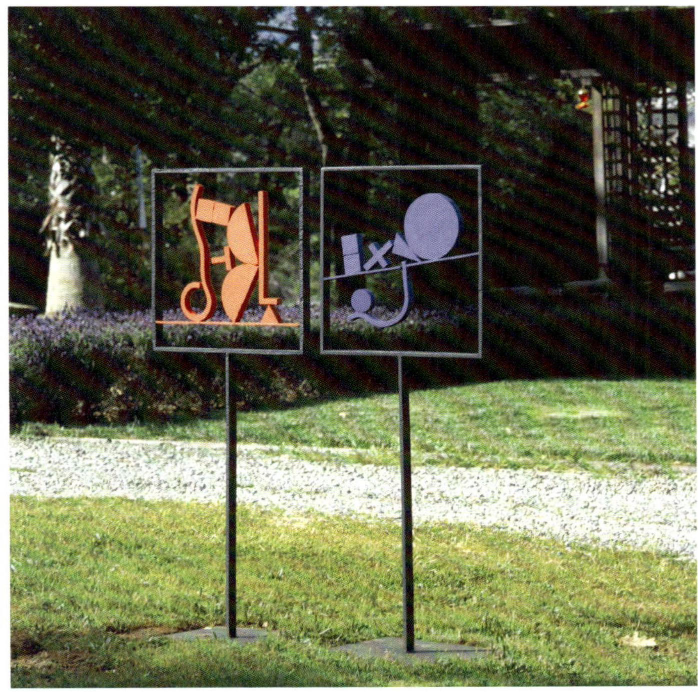

Pole Drawing 2 (left)
1982, painted steel
60 x 23 x 17½ inches
152 x 58 x 44 cm

Pole Drawing 1 (right)
1982, painted steel
60 x 23 x 17½ inches
152 x 58 x 44 cm

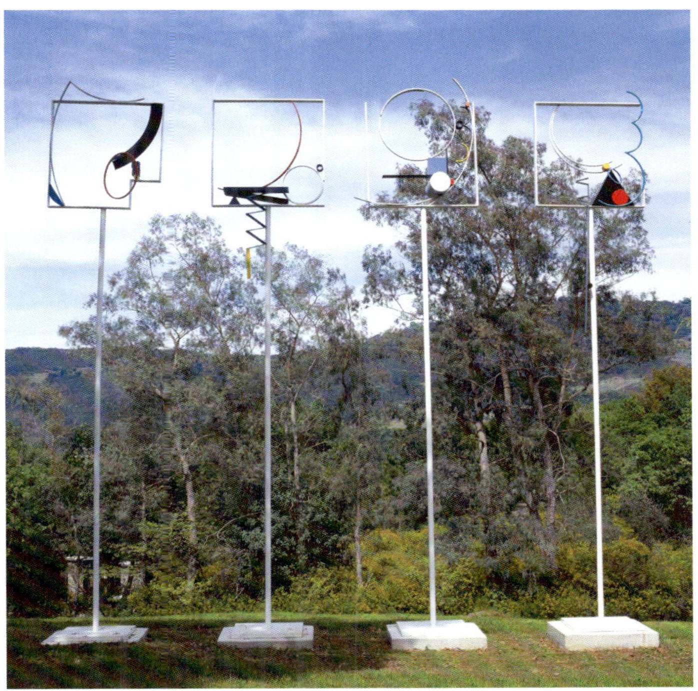

Four Pole Pieces
1990, painted steel
H: 24 feet
H: 732 cm

wins out. Some of the red forms are slightly jittery or a bit precariously balanced, yet calm prevails overall. *Pole Drawing 1* and *2* face in two directions at once: toward Benton's past as a painter and into the sculptural future that, by 1982, he had already entered. In 1990 he made *Four Pole Pieces* (see page 7). Taller than *Pole Drawing 1* and *2*, this refined quartet is even more reminiscent of works on paper. Many of the elements in these *Pole Pieces* are as thin as pencil lines, and Benton has arranged them within their frames with an almost total disregard for gravity. In three of the four *Pole Pieces*, however, the frames are either open or irregular. In the fourth, a zigzag form reaches outside the frame. Thus Benton defies the standard, foursquare enclosure basic to painting and drawing. Though they flirt with pictorial possibilities, these slim works occupy three dimensions. Furthermore, their compositions of curves and zigzags, discs and cubes and triangles, look like silhouettes of other, more expansive sculptures.

The year he made *Pole Drawing 1* and *2*, Benton launched a series of *Steel Watercolors*. Like the *Pole Pieces*, these sculptures can be seen as silhouettes, yet they occupy more space. *Steel Watercolor: Falling Rings*, 1984, is a bright red flourish of straight lines and circles. At roughly the midpoint of this nearly eleven-foot-tall sculpture, Benton placed a cylinder—in other words, a circle expanded into three dimensions. This is the fulcrum of the piece, the form around which all the others find their equilibrium. Above, an angled rod points upward, its ascent accentuated by a row of small, evenly spaced triangles: allusions to the teeth of a ratchet, perhaps. Attached to the end of the rod is a large circle broken along its upper edge by an extrusion. Sharply pointed, it reaches upward at an angle opposite from—and complementary to—the angle of the rod.

The cylinder-fulcrum rests on a short horizontal bar that makes a sudden right angle and extends downward almost to the ground. Like the pole in a *Pole Piece*, this vertical element serves as the backbone of *Steel Watercolor: Falling Rings*. A pair of smallish rings hovers at the point where the right angle occurs. Another ring of the same size appears at the bottom of the sculpture, where the supporting pole meets the two blocky forms resting on the thin slab of a pedestal. These rings give the sculpture its name, which is fitting. It is natural to see these forms as falling. Yet it is just as natural to see them as sailing upward. Benton balances his forms with a precision that relieves them of their metallic weight. For vision, the rings levitate, suspended between falling and ascending. The prevailing red reinforces this anti-gravitational effect, even if it can't quite persuade us to see this sculpture as streaks of color in the air.

When major forms intersect, smaller ones—wedges, cylinders, blocks—often mark the occasion. Though these elements sometimes look like structural necessities, Benton could get by without them—but only if he were a designer, not a sculptor. The necessities that matter to him are visual, not utilitarian, and he can never know in advance what they are. Sculptural imperatives cannot be stated as axioms. The sculptor must discover them experimentally, as he works. Once he has settled on a few large forms—a sculpture's basic premises—Benton looks for the overall structure that will bring them into harmony. Smaller forms can have the function of exclamation points, emphasizing some subtlety of organization. Slowing vision, so that the sense of resolution doesn't arrive too quickly, they can work like commas or even semi-colons.

Benton's small forms are not all analogous to marks of punctuation. Some have the grammatical task of shaping the relationship between larger forms. For example, in *Steel Watercolor #81–Phase III*, 1985 (see page 312), a small disc separates—or joins—two long lines that swoop down from the top of the sculpture. It is important to see that this disc appears where it does because Benton decided that it would, not out of any merely practical necessity. The disc could have been a simple strut or brace. It could have been eliminated altogether. Yet it belongs precisely where it is, displaying precisely the form it does, because it gives formal coherence to the interplay between the two swooping lines. As small as it is, this disc establishes—or at the very least reinforces—the terms on which this *Steel Watercolor* works as a sculpture.

The key to the disc's success is its concentrated circularity. Like a visual shock absorber, it mediates the force of the careening, angled line. And the smoothly curving line is drawn to it as if it were a dense star. Its effect on both lines, the smooth and the angled, is to focus their lithe, springy energy. *Steel Watercolor #81–Phase III* is a taut, muscular presence—its vertical zigzag suggests both rib cage and backbone—and of course the disc I've been discussing is not its only point of sculptural intensity. Wherever large forms meet and negotiate their differences, Benton introduces at least one other smallish form to bring the negotiations into focus—as Finn's close-up images show us. When the photographer moves back, to show a sculpture in full, we see that none of these incidents is local. Each takes all the others into account, and thus the work is resolved.

In the early 1980s, not long after he began to work in three dimensions, Benton embarked on a series he called *Balanced/Unbalanced*. The title is ironic, for all the sculptures that bear it are thoroughly balanced. Yet the irony is not absolute, for in every case Benton preserved a degree—or perhaps just a reminder—of precariousness. In *Balanced/Unbalanced U*, 1980, a pair of thick cylinders rests on top of the "U" form. At first glance, they seem to have tumbled into a dubious position. Will they settle and possibly fall? The more one looks, the clearer it is that Benton has placed the cylinders so that they offer a stable, even stately response to the monumental curve of the "U" that supports them. Balanced, they nonetheless invite us to imagine how little would have to change for them to lose their balance and crash to the ground.

Building reminiscences of collapse and chaos into his sculptures, Benton helps us see what it is to create formal order: from physical contingency, he builds aesthetic necessity. What keeps Benton's sculptures alive is his disinclination to let necessity look ponderous. Thus he teases balance with hints of unbalance. He puts the fate of large forms in the hands, so to speak, of much smaller forms. He lets balls roll away from the sculptures to which they belong. He plays sober, weighty blocks off against thin, soaring—even flighty—curves and zigzags. And so he shows us that there is nothing inevitable about sculptural necessity. It must be won from the forces of mundane disorder, and once the victory is achieved, it must be achieved again.

Benton has said, "Sculpture is real, in space . . . . There's nothing illusionary about it." The contrast is with painting. An object depicted or evoked by a painter—by Benton himself in his early years as an artist—appears in a fictive space that we cannot enter. A sculpture is a solid object in our space. This much is clear and undeniable, yet Benton's compositions present us with puzzles of their own—not the ambiguities and illusions of painting but complexities of a sculptural kind. As precise and tangible as an element in a *Steel Watercolor* may be, it is not always obvious why it has the shape and placement it does. And when, with sufficient looking, one sees the sculptural logic at work, one may not be able to convey one's understanding. Visual intuitions can be nearly impossible to transpose into language. In fact, this is a sign of Benton's success: his art is so powerfully visual that, finally, we can only talk around it. So we turn to hints of figuration. Thus I ascribed a backbone to several of his sculptures.

The thin, spiraling shape in *Steel Watercolor: Purple Arc*, 1986, makes it nearly impossible to discuss this piece without mentioning a corkscrew—not that corkscrews are ultimately the issue. Still, the allusion helps us focus on the distinctively coiled energy of this sculpture. Once the title of *Steel Watercolor: Cube and Ring,* 1990, has directed the attention to these forms, one sees that Benton's interest is not in their self-evident differences. He wants to show that a cube and ring can be put in a relation so precarious that a panoply of other forms, some of them monumental, must come into play if balance is to be achieved. This visual resolution is what matters. The words of the title simply point to several of the forms that posed the original challenge. The *Steel Watercolors* called *Botanicals* (see page 9) key our initial looking to leaves and stems and blossoms. With further looking, these allusions fade and the specifically sculptural logic of each *Botanical* comes into focus.

The *One-Legged Tables* are simply that: square "tabletops" mounted on short pedestals. From these square surfaces all manner of shapes tilt, twist, soar, and fall. Reaching in every direction, these are among Benton's most expansive sculptures—not surprisingly, considering that the series began with a sixty-six-foot sculpture commissioned by the City of Cologne and the Museum Ludwig. In *One-Legged Table: Drop Leaf with Triangle,* 1991, so much is crowded onto the tabletop (a zigzag, the triangle of the title) and off it (a large ring and a tall thin curving line), and so much rises up from it (a complex play of straight and curving lines), that the table—the sculpture's premise—nearly vanishes. With it goes the allusion to furniture and to the figure—the human presence—that furniture implies. The abiding point is the composition.

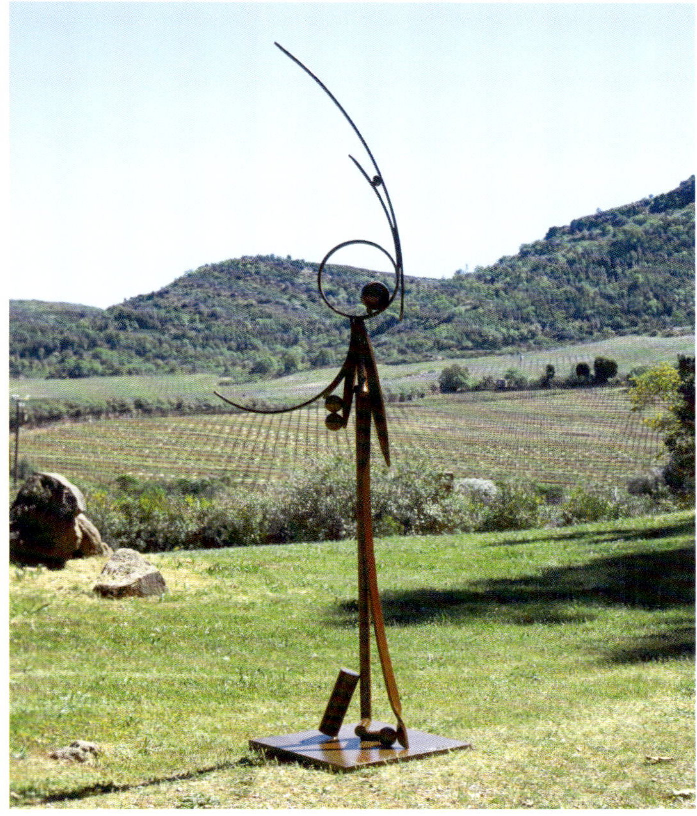

Botanical Rose

1993, steel with patina
96 x 26 x 20 inches
244 x 66 x 51 cm

One-Legged Table: Drop Leaf with Triangle is at once complex and clear. It can be both because its elements, in their variety, all work toward the same end—an ordered unity. In this sculpture, similarities are mostly triangular. There is, first of all, the triangle mentioned in the title. The drop leaf, too, is a triangular form, as are the negative forms generated by the horizontal zigzag. In contrast to this flurry of straight lines and sharp angles is the ring that rests on the ground and leans against the tabletop. Curving forms—portions of much larger rings?—ascend into the upper regions of this very tall sculpture. Intensifying the contrast with angularity, they begin to resolve it. For they share their upward-reaching energies with the triangle of the title, whose acute angle points with such certainty toward the sky. To trace this sculpture's play of contrast and similarity is to see all its curves and angles—even those of horizontal elements—caught up in the vertical surge that culminates in the central pole. Ultimately, contrast and similarity are themselves resolved, and we understand circles and triangles as variations on one another.

Not all the *One-Legged Tables* are as tall as *Drop Leaf with Triangle.* Like other sculptures in the *Steel Watercolor* series, however, the *Tables* are vertical and so we see them as doing what we do when we look at them: they stand. Thus we read them as figurative, no matter how little they may resemble us in any other way. Earlier, with the *Folded* sculptures, Benton expanded flat surfaces into three dimensions with results that feel more architectural than figurative. A panoramic view of his sculpture shows an ongoing contrast between slim and blocky compositions. Then, in 1998, he constructed a piece that resolved even that contrast. Both slim and blocky, *Blocks on Blocks: Three on One, Zig and Balls* (see page 10) suggests a building at one with its sole inhabitant.

Since the late 1970s, that has been Benton's purpose: to build oneness from disparity. But disparity cannot be simply defeated. If it were, there would be no sense of a sculpture's having come into being—no sense of its elements' having

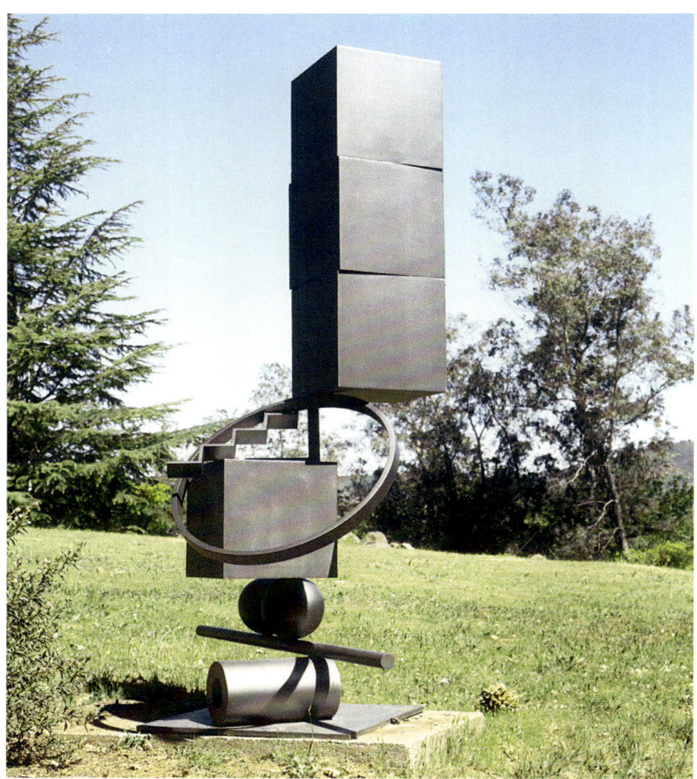

Blocks on Blocks
Three on One, Zig and Balls
1998, painted steel
94 x 72 x 50 inches
239 x 183 x 127 cm

worked through their differences to the point of working together. Of course we can never know precisely how a sculpture developed. Nonetheless, Benton always makes it possible to imagine the conflicts that animated the struggle. From a sense of the whole we intuit what was at stake in the placement of every element. Eventually, we focus on a sculpture as a realized composition. But even then, when the work is immersed in the present created by its harmonies, its history continues to hover around it. And that history gives it an aura—a light and an atmosphere—distinctively its own.

Sculptors make sculptures, yet my discussion of Benton's work has sometimes implied that his sculptures make themselves—as if the elements of a *One-Legged Table* or a *Steel Watercolor* somehow reconcile their differences on their own. This way of speaking would be odd if it weren't standard practice. We find it difficult to talk about works of art without attributing intentions to their parts—saying, for instance, that a curve is responding to a certain angle or that a triangle must stretch out to a sharp point if it is to come to terms with all the thin, upward-reaching forms surrounding it. What is odd, after all, is that we do this so naturally. It is as if we don't really begin to see a work of art until we see it as having evolved by itself from its own basic premises.

Of course, it is only when we place Benton's works against an art-world backdrop, where aesthetic values prevail, that we see them as absolutely self-sufficient. The moment we widen our view, we read their self-sufficiency as an evocation of the very idea of the individual, distinct and independent. And we admire Benton for invoking this ideal with such humane dignity, though our admiration is usually more intuitive than conscious. Face to face with his works, we focus on the interplay of line and curve, plane and angle, not on concepts, however exalted. Yet his art is imbued with the ideas of difference and harmony, multiplicity and individuality, and they insinuate themselves into our looking.

Double Folded Circle (see page 176) could be seen as a challenge to the gridded buildings that define its site, to Los Angeles, and to urban environments everywhere. This view of the sculpture would not be wrong, for *Double Folded Circle* generates its power not only through the monumental harmonies of its curves but also from their contrast to the nearby buildings. Nonetheless, this view would not be entirely right, either, for this work of art shares much with its site. Amid its preponderance of curves, the segmentation of the interior discs creates straight lines and right angles, nor is this the only resemblance between this sculpture and the surrounding architecture. Both are imposing in scale, spare in form, and smoothly finished. And both belong to their era, much as their site belongs to them. Here and throughout his oeuvre, Benton reconciles seeming opposites. The chords struck within *Double Folded Circle*, by the interplay of curves and angles, are repeated by the scale of the site itself, in the juxtaposition of sculpture and buildings. Yet there is one difference that cannot be reconciled. Architecture is utilitarian. Sculpture is not, and that is why we call it autonomous. To paraphrase Immanuel Kant, its purpose is to have no purpose.

Follow this argument in the wrong direction and one ends up with a deceptive dichotomy: such things as buildings and automobiles are useful; works of art are useless. However, being useless is not the same as being purposeless on purpose. To see the difference, it is necessary to sense an irony at work—or possibly just extreme hyperbole. In any case, aesthetic autonomy is comparative, not absolute; and, Kant to the contrary, purposeful purposelessness is not a pure, transcendent state that transports art to art-heaven. It is an ever-shifting quality that works of art acquire in and for their moment, in contrast to whatever varieties of usefulness hem them in.

These days, the contrast between architectural design and sculptural composition seems unbreachable. The former is driven by practical needs; the latter invents its needs out of itself with no concern for practicality. However, in another time and place—in an 18th-century English garden, for example—a building might be intended as an object of aesthetic contemplation, and the contrast between architecture and sculpture would collapse. Art's situation is forever shifting, and that is why the ideal of autonomy must constantly be reinvented. Or—to resort once again to irony—the purposelessness of art is always in need of having its purpose renewed.

Autonomy's purpose is to establish a realm of freedom from whatever mundane purposes drive us daily. I've mentioned the utilitarian ones that, since before Kant's time, writers have routinely called upon when contrasting aesthetic objects with other things. A tool or a piece of furniture may be beautiful, but the object's beauty is a function of—and thus subservient to—its fitness for a practical purpose. This is beauty in chains, to borrow the style of old-fashioned allegory, and the purposes to which it is chained are obvious. The demands of style are subtler, for we often think of style as the product of unfettered invention. As it happens, a style is usually accepted under duress. Pressured by the zeitgeist or the market or both, artists give their art certain looks for the strictly utilitarian purpose of hitching up with the zeitgeist or entering the market. Behind the practicalities of style stands a coercive idea of history, which Benton chose to resist when he stopped making kinetic art and entered the three dimensions of sculpture.

Kinetic art was among the last developments that could be seen as historically necessary. By the 1960s, the failure of utopian modernism had diminished the scale of art history—its future no longer offered glimpses of the perfect metropolis—yet the faith in progress guided by necessity was still intense. Of course, there was little agreement about the ultimate goal. The color-field painters and their critics offered one version of progress, the Minimalists and their critics another. Proponents of Happenings argued that progress in art required a sort of de-definition. In this competition for the future, kineticism was all the more powerful a contender because many in the '60s were infatuated by technology. The lingering authority of the Constructivist avant-garde gave the movement a further boost. This jostling of styles and modes was animated by the notion that some new development must, inevitably, come to dominate the future, and hidden in this faith in historical necessity was a utilitarian purpose: to define the necessity, submit to it, and thereby win the competition. By opting out, Benton won his freedom.

He talks less of freedom than of the responsibility it brings. In his interview with Paul Karlstrom,[3] he said, "I think artist become artists—those who stick it out—because they want to be . . . one hundred percent responsible for their actions . . . responsible from beginning to end for every single decision." Only if one refuses to have any purpose but one's own can one feel this degree of responsibility—and of freedom. Refusing to understand history as a set of demands, Benton found that history is generous: an array of possibilities. Arriving at three dimensions, Benton set about reinventing for himself the tradition of geometric sculpture.

This was his first decision as a sculptor: to work with cubes and circles and the other Euclidean givens. And each sculpture begins with a decision about which givens to employ. Other decisions follow, and when there are no more to be made, the work finds its independence. The sculpture's autonomy stands for that of the artist—and for that of the viewer who has discovered not only the workings of the sculptural composition, in all its harmonious complexity, but also the sense of freedom Benton felt when he was building it. Feeling free, we feel connected to the world on the right terms. Opening the way to that connection, Benton's art realizes what may well be its ultimate purpose.

Notes

1. This remark comes from an interview with the artist conducted by Paul Karlstrom for the Smithsonian Archives of American Art in May 1987.
2. The excerpt from Naum Gabo and Antoine Pevsner's "The Realistic Manifesto," 1920, appears in *The Tradition of Constructivism*, edited by Stephen Bann. New York, NY: Da Capo Press, 1974, p. 9.
3. This remark comes from an interview with the artist conducted by Paul Karlstrom for the Smithsonian Archives of American Art in May 1987.

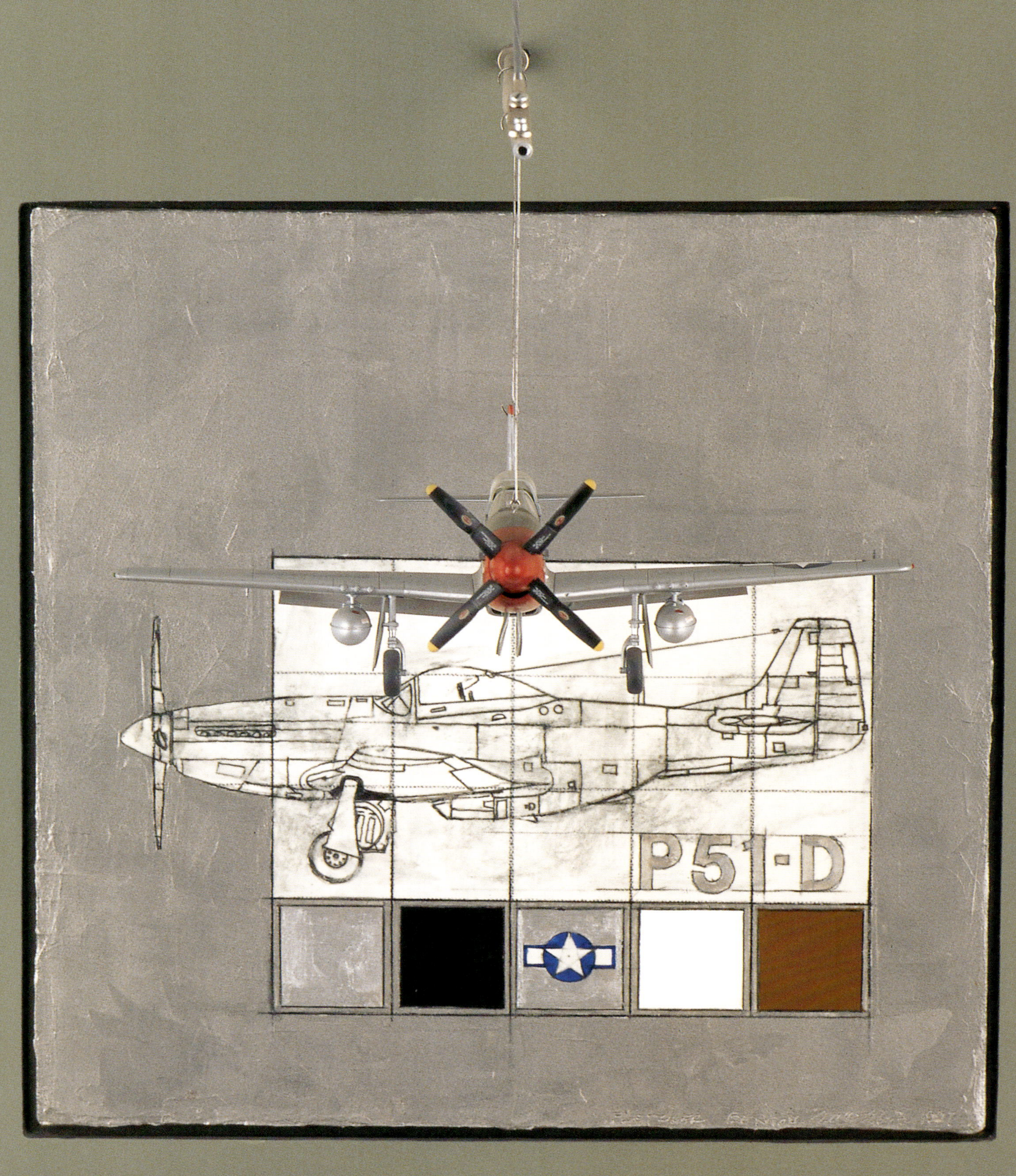

Homage to WW II Aircraft: P51-D

1997, assemblage
22 x 22 inches
56 x 56 cm

The Aircraft and Circus Works

Collette Chattopadhyay

Time-space, conceived as an indivisible entity, rather than two separate coordinates,[1] has been one of the most central elements of Fletcher Benton's artworks since the late 1950s. From his early figurative paintings to his seminal, kinetic works of the 1960s and subsequent monumental sculptures of the last three decades, Benton's exploration of artistic space has always been intricately fused with allusions to time. His most recent *World War II Aircraft* works, *Circus Paintings,* and *Circus Constructions* are built upon this finely tuned awareness. The unique integrity of his recent works emerges in part from their exploration of the artistic implications of modern physics, which argues that "Our world is not Euclidean"; rather "the geometrical nature of our world is shaped by masses and their velocities."[2]

This essay focuses on Benton's three new bodies of work, examining the manner in which they reevaluate artistic allusions to space as geometry, and gravity as an element related to time. Benton's articulation of these areas is imbued with a sense of psychological expansiveness or loss, and with allusions to magnitudes of distance or proximity through elements that tenuously define balance or disequilibrium. Exploring the correlation between the material and immaterial realms, the following discussion investigates the manner in which Benton's manipulation of artistic materials ends up defining important metaphysical realities. For some, this has always been one of the grand conundrums of art: that art can endow paper, canvas, paint, wood, wax, metal, or other physical materials with conceptual meaning. Yet it is this very transformative capability that is one of art's greatest powers, for through these processes, art is able silently to address a broad range of concepts and ideas. Benton's newest works utilize that authority to address contemporary concerns regarding the breadth and ultimate brevity of human existence.

The selected subject matter of both these works, namely World War II aircraft and circus acts, abstractly focuses on precision performances executed in specific arenas of time-space that result in accomplishment or defeat. In this connection, it is intriguing that most, if not all, of the recent *World War II Aircraft* works, *Circus Paintings,* and *Circus Constructions* begin with a square, historically regarded both as a form of perfection and a symbol of the terrestrial sphere, a space historically deemed to be compromised by less-than-perfect realities.

In composition after composition the square becomes, in these works, an arena in which abstract forms parlay—through their precise, and often imperiled, visual placement—the demands, challenges, and even threats that constitute the struggles, defeats, and victories of human existence. Whether the struggle is articulated in works that revisit and champion the battles of ace fighter pilots during World War II, or in works that manifest daring circus feats, Benton utilizes the abstract language of art to discuss the brute realities endemic to the labor of life.

Living and working in the postmodern era, Benton intriguingly invokes from afar the ancient Greco-Roman fascination with ideal, geometric form. His visual references to such concepts are premised in part on the ground breaking developments of the early 20th-century Constructivist artists such as Naum Gabo, Antoine Pevsner, El Lissitzky, and Josef Albers among others, who developed for art an abstract, geometric visual vocabulary that has since permitted artists to speak of reality without visually describing the external appearance of things.

Benton's newest works manifest a wide-ranging knowledge of and respect for such visual histories which appear as structural references within his work. In this manner, each work establishes a breadth of historical references that function as a conceptual *terra firma* for his own visual arguments and conclusions. The ancient Roman writer and architect Marcus Vitruvius, for example, regarded symmetry as critical to the construction of architecture and art, and proposed that certain basic geometric forms, in particular the square, circle, and triangle, were elemental building blocks of the visual world. In the 16th century Italian Renaissance, Leonardo da Vinci drew the *Vitruvian Man* (1513), building upon these inherited artistic ideals. There humanity is conceived in relationship to the Vitruvian ideal at the center of a rationalized geometric space. For the ancients the square was said to be a visual symbol of the finite world, and the circle a symbol of the infinite, cosmic sphere.

It is this ancient artistic thought that Benton uses in his *World War II Aircraft* works, *Circus Paintings*, and *Circus Constructions* to enrich the interpretative scope of his newest works. At the same time, being a consummate postmodernist, his works do not adhere to the boundaries established by such legacies. Rather, such classical precepts serve as a conceptual backdrop to the artist's contemporary investigations, evidencing both a respect for and skepticism of the artistic repertoire.

The WW II Aircraft Works

Returning to a childhood passion with a mature, artistic mind, Benton began a suite of works known as the *Homage to WW II Aircraft* works in the closing years of the 20th century. These assemblage paintings feature museum-quality model airplane replicas as a focal point of their compositions. Usually suspended in front of a painted, square canvas, the model planes exist allusively within space, suggesting both the kinetic act of flying and the flight's relation to the terrestrial sphere of the square. Each work presents a different type of World War II aircraft, and subtly alludes to the daring air maneuvers that historically made these aircraft renowned.

Homage to WW II Aircraft: ME 262 Europe 1945 (see page 137), for example, features as its focal point a Messerschmitt ME 262, which was a German-built bomber capable of flying at 540 miles per hour. At the time, its fierce speed was unsurpassed, beating the most agile plane in the Allied arsenal, the North American P-51 *Mustang* (see page 134), whose top speed was roughly 440 miles per hour. For those flying a P-51, the ME 262 was a potentially lethal aircraft. Thus, the Allies sought and eventually discovered the ME 262's Achilles' heel, namely its long takeoff and landing requirements. In war, as in life, the work suggests, the challenges of winning or losing in any given arena have as much to do with one's material arsenal as with strategic logic, cunning, and innovation.

Another assemblage, *Homage to WW II Aircraft: MK VIII* (see page 120), pays tribute on one level to the British-designed aircraft that began to be produced in July 1936 for the British Royal Air Force. In 1944, the British shipped a tropical version of these aircrafts to India where they flew in combat against the Japanese at the conclusion of the war. As with all aircraft, the identifying colors of each plane were crucial for pilots to determine through symbolic codes whether a plane was friend or foe. As in all the works profiled in the *Homage to WW II Aircraft* series, this work displays the model replica of the MK VIII against a canvas background that denotes the colorations associated with that aircraft. As in war, so in art, selected visual codes make viewers aware of the strategic alliances of any given artist.

These types of cross-linked associations are particularly intriguing when the MK VIII spitfire work is compared with Benton's *Homage to WW II Aircraft: P-38J* assemblage (see page 121). Both the MK VIII and the P-38J assemblages evidence a strong cognizance of centralized, geometric order: the replica aircraft are situated above the center point of the square canvases that thematically define each plane's flying space. On one level these works build conceptual links between the artist's visual interest in kinetics suggesting the link between matter and space–time that has always been one of his central concerns. On another level, the *Aircraft* works function as a metaphor of the creative process, which entails comparable daring, perseverance, agility, and shrewdness in order to survive.

Folding together geometric classicism with moorings in American Beat and neo-Dada art, Benton's works reconsider and converse with Robert Rauschenberg's combines, George Herms's assemblages, and Jasper Johns's mid-20th century paintings of *Targets*, *Alphabets*, or *Maps*. Intriguingly, both Johns's *Flag* paintings and Benton's *Aircraft* works carry public and private innuendos that are subtle and complex. While Johns's *Flag* paintings champion, on one hand, a symbol of American patriotism, they also harbor a subtle critique by suggesting that national allegiance in the postmodern age is a commodity that is bought and sold in terms of small, medium, and large-size flags. Such sublimated allusions complicate and challenge the more overt reading that can be associated with these works.

Likewise Benton's *Aircraft* works are on one level honorific in tone, paying homage to the valor of World War II pilots, celebrating their strategies, skills, and risks. At the same time, these works contain more generalized references to individual challenges of survival, which are determined as much by skill, knowledge, and visual cognizance as by fate. These works further redress traditional concepts of artistic genius, suggesting that success in life or art has as much to do with finding a way to exist in time–space, given the reality and possibility of free fall.

The Circus Paintings

The recent *Circus* paintings explore similar terrains, deploying elemental geometric forms to define various scenarios. Often infused with an ironic unbalanced balance, these works describe the tentativeness of existence in ways that profoundly resonate with postmodern uncertainties. In the early 20th century the Russia artist Kasimir Malevich proposed a visual riddle related to the square in his *White on White* (1918) painting, proposing the square's fall from grace as a moniker of balance and symmetry. At least from the time of the High Renaissance in 16th-century Italy, the square had borne allusions to the terrestrial affairs of the world, while the circle had been classically associated with the celestial, metaphysical realms. By invoking the square, Benton abstractly alludes to the struggles of existence, in particular the struggles for a sense of equilibrium in a world replete with physical and psychological challenges that threaten to derail ideals of individual and even collective well-being.

Circus Painting No. 3 invokes Malevich's conundrum by presenting the illusion of a gray square falling within a white ground. Its form is echoed by a smaller square that bears the traces of its journey, fractured as it is, along diagonals that convert its form into an assembly of interconnected triangles. The forces that threaten to imperil the square include an array of skewered lines, one near the bottom of the composition that sets the middle-size, gray square metaphorically sliding down a gentle hill while holding in its midst an array of precariously balanced forms.

Circus Painting No. 7 complements *Circus Painting No. 3* by presenting a related, abstract cast of characters in reverse. While *Circus Painting No. 3* focuses attention predominantly on the right half of the canvas plane, *Circus Painting No. 7* presents an imperiled square on the left side of the painting. This is the earliest work in this series to invoke the circus through the introduction of a ladder and step motifs, suggesting through such allusions the tightropes drawn horizontally across the picture plane. With its array of multiple focus areas, *Circus Painting No. 7* invokes in abstract form Benton's first *Circus* installation, which was exhibited as a room-size installation at Gump's Gallery, San Francisco, in 1964.[3] There, high-wire circus acts were profiled with wires strung across the gallery space. The ten major and minor horizontal lines in *Circus Painting No. 7* invoke this legacy, addressing the challenges of performance in space, be it that of a circus performer, an artist, or individuals from other walks of life.

That Benton invokes the *Circus* as a metaphor in these paintings suggests that for the artist, as for Shakespeare, "All life's a stage and all men and women merely actors."[4] It is, Benton seems to suggest, the performance that counts for all, and in its execution, there is always both the prospect of imperilment or failure, as well as the utopian dream of balance and success. In Benton's *Circus Painting No. 7* the two most balanced shapes are the outlined canvas upon which everything occurs and a thin, linear steel "L" shape—flipped backward as though having survived a windstorm—that balances and defines the rectangular space of action. The dream of rising above harrowing odds is presented in the shape of a steel ladder that extends past the frame of the painting, hinting of the dream of transcendence. But ironically, even that vision is compromised by a strong diagonal that runs nearly through the center of the composition, extending into the space beyond its frame.

Circus Painting No. 13 (see page 197) presents a world spinning out of balance. There is only one small perpendicular line and one small horizontal wedge within the work. By virtue of their diminutive size, neither can hold nor balance the surrounding, cascading forms and related gravitational forces. The whole composition suggests an avalanche of forms that cannot be held by the three major anchor points that attempt to stay the sagging world witnessed within the image. The right-hand structures of the work invoke the annual rite of spring that occurs along the California Big Sur coast when rain-soaked cliffs that rise hundreds of feet above the ocean begin to crumble and slip onto a thin ribbon of road that winds along the continent's edge connecting Southern and Northern California. Battling to equilibrate the tensions that exist between travelers enjoying breathtaking views of the Pacific, and nature's forces of entropy, construction crews annually buttress the cliffs with cables and steel nets, managing to build stopgap measures of control in a geologically unstable region. This painting sets up similar checks in a realm that promises never to be fully balanced.

Circus Painting No. 15 presents among its visual scenarios a little train engine that has fallen backward, as though into a ditch. Nothing promises to rescue the train. Yet, while jammed, it balances on its front hood an array of small complex forms and indeed ironically comes to serve as the central balancing force within the painting. It is in many ways an incredibly tragic composition that plays against the simplistic narratives of television movies, suggesting that there are no perfect realities; rather, that broken contexts, situations, and individuals paradoxically come to construct a semblance of balance out of almost impossible situations of imperilment and chaos.

Circus Painting No. 17 (see page 199), by contrast, is anchored by two circles that evoke a pendulum, suggesting the marking of time by a grandfather clock. The painting visually studies duality, presenting sequences of juxtapositions of forms that are visually echoed by counterpart, shadow, or cousin forms. These structures yield complex allusions that query the relation between reality and illusion, sculpture and painting, or—perhaps most poignantly—reality and art, the physical and the metaphysical.

If any work in Benton's oeuvre exemplifies his own musings and fascinations with art's essence and its relationship to reality, it is works such as this that articulate the complexity of interrelationships between sculpture and painting. The work also probes the reality of bas-relief sculpture, by presenting forms that cast real shadows while also presenting painted illusions of cast shadows. "Sculpture is real, in space," Benton told Paul Karlstrom. "There's nothing illusionary about it."[5] Ironically, the created world of this painting appears like an old-fashioned film in the colors of black, steel gray, and white. A few lively colorful exceptions of orange red, ocher, and yellow create engaging accents that lead the eye through this landscape of balancing acts in which abstract forms rather than people enact scenarios of trials and tribulations. It is as though we find ourselves reading the Biblical stories of Job.

The Circus Constructions

The *Circus Constructs* by contrast, are fully three–dimensional and feature such elements as performing platforms, ladders, trapeze swings, and the fire circle through which animals traditionally leap. These works also raise the disturbing question of the continued relevance of art in a media age that is more obsessed with news reports of wars, serial killers, and natural disasters than with the imagery of contemporary painters or sculptors. Such doubts first began to surface in the late 19th century when artists including Georges Seurat and Henri Toulouse-Lautrec created works that variously studied Parisian society's demimonde, locales, and protagonists.

Seurat's renowned painting *The Side Show* (1888), for example, presents a centralized, yet abstracted figure leading a small, musical band in a performance that is tolerated by a motley assortment of bystanders who wait for the major circus show. That Seurat makes the sideshow the subject of his painting suggests he views such performances as akin to the increasingly imperiled status of the artist in late 19th–century society. That Benton chooses to return to the circus as a theme, knowing full well that it reflects a retro social entertainment whose heydays have predominantly passed, suggests an extension of the theme of the fine arts' imperilment in modern times. Indeed, in Benton's *Circus Constructions*, the contemporary era's fixation on spectacles of daunting and life-threatening proportions is underscored by the harrowing types of spaces and acts that are intimated.

Circus Construct 9 (see page 196), for example, is simultaneously a litany of the accoutrements of a circus, child's swing set, or a hangman's gallows. The work is simultaneously innocent and knowing. The danger of the impending, implied circus act is presented in the spatial placement of circus objects, rather than being literally depicted with figures. The entire space of the piece rises, ironically, from a square platform but then expands thematically with the swing into a space beyond that defined by the base.

This kinetic potential, even promise, in Benton's *Circus Constructs* is pushed further by *Circus Construct 12* (see page 185) where a steel "circus ball" rolls beyond the defined square base of the work, creating a forceful counter-focus to the tightrope act that is the major focus of the work. Though no photographs of the 1963 Benton *Circus* tightrope performers remain, the artist describing those works mentioned a nude female performer riding a bike while balancing a long thin rod.[6] The reality of that complex balancing act is here both remembered and recast, this time without the literal presence of a human figure.

Trapeze performances are evoked in the *Circus Constructs 14*, *16*, and *18* (see pages 190, 191), always in ways that articulate the harrowing daring that is implicit in the spectacle. *Construct 14* features a steel, T-shaped structure fitted with a swing that is occupied by a rectangular shape that balances circles at each end of a pole. *Construct 16*, by contrast, invokes the swinging trapeze performer, who prepares to catch or be caught by another, unseen performer. The work forms an interesting analogy to art generally, where artists ubiquitously evolve the visual works of others, constructing dynamic conversations across time-space.

In Benton's case, the invocation is manifest in silent evocations and references to Calder and Giacometti, particularly to their respective sculptural explorations of balance and imperilment. Calder inverted sculpture's traditional mooring and placement on the ground, creating mobiles that dangled in space. That material transposition was interpreted as daring and liberating by subsequent artists, particularly as it also invoked the element of time. At the same time, Benton's late *Circus Constructs* reverberate against the memory of Giacometti's *Suspended Ball* (1930–31), which also whispered of imperilment through abstract means, foreshadowing the themes and concerns that remain current in the present age.

Conclusion

As a continuum of works, the *Aircraft* bas-reliefs, *Circus Paintings,* and *Circus Constructions* configure the dilemmas, conundrums, and challenges endemic to the struggle to survive. In their own ways, these three bodies of work suggest the manner in which the world of abstract art contemplates reality, configuring matter to reconsider the tenuousness of life that continuously teeters between endurance and extinction. Manifesting a classically derived respect for the placement of forms within space, while exploring tensions between perceived unity and disunity within compositional structures based upon elemental, geometric shapes, Benton's works unfold secrets of existence with assured visual clarity, character, and candor.

Notes

1. It was the young German physicist Albert Einstein who argued that time and space were not two separate coordinates, but rather an indivisible entity. For a brief summary of Einstein's impact on early 20th-century thought, see Gloria K. Fiero, *The Humanistic Tradition, Book 6: Modernism, Globalism, and the Information Age*. New York: McGraw-Hill, 2002, p. 3.
2. Einstein quoted by Leonard Shlain, *Art and Physics: Parallel Visions in Space, Time, and Light* (1991), listed in the Documents section of Francoise Balibar's *Einstein: Decoding the Universe*. New York: Discoveries: Harry N. Abrams, Inc., 2001, p. 134.
3. See this author's analysis of Benton's early *Circus Works* in the Hudson Hills Press publication *Fletcher Benton: The Kinetic Years*.
4. From Shakespeare's play *As You Like It*.
5. This remark comes from an interview with the artist conducted by Paul Karlstrom for the Smithsonian Archives of American Art, May 1987.
6. This remark comes from an interview with the artist conducted by the author in San Francisco on August 16, 2006. See also this author's remarks on Benton's early *Circus Works* in the Hudson Hills Press publication *Fletcher Benton: The Kinetic Years*.

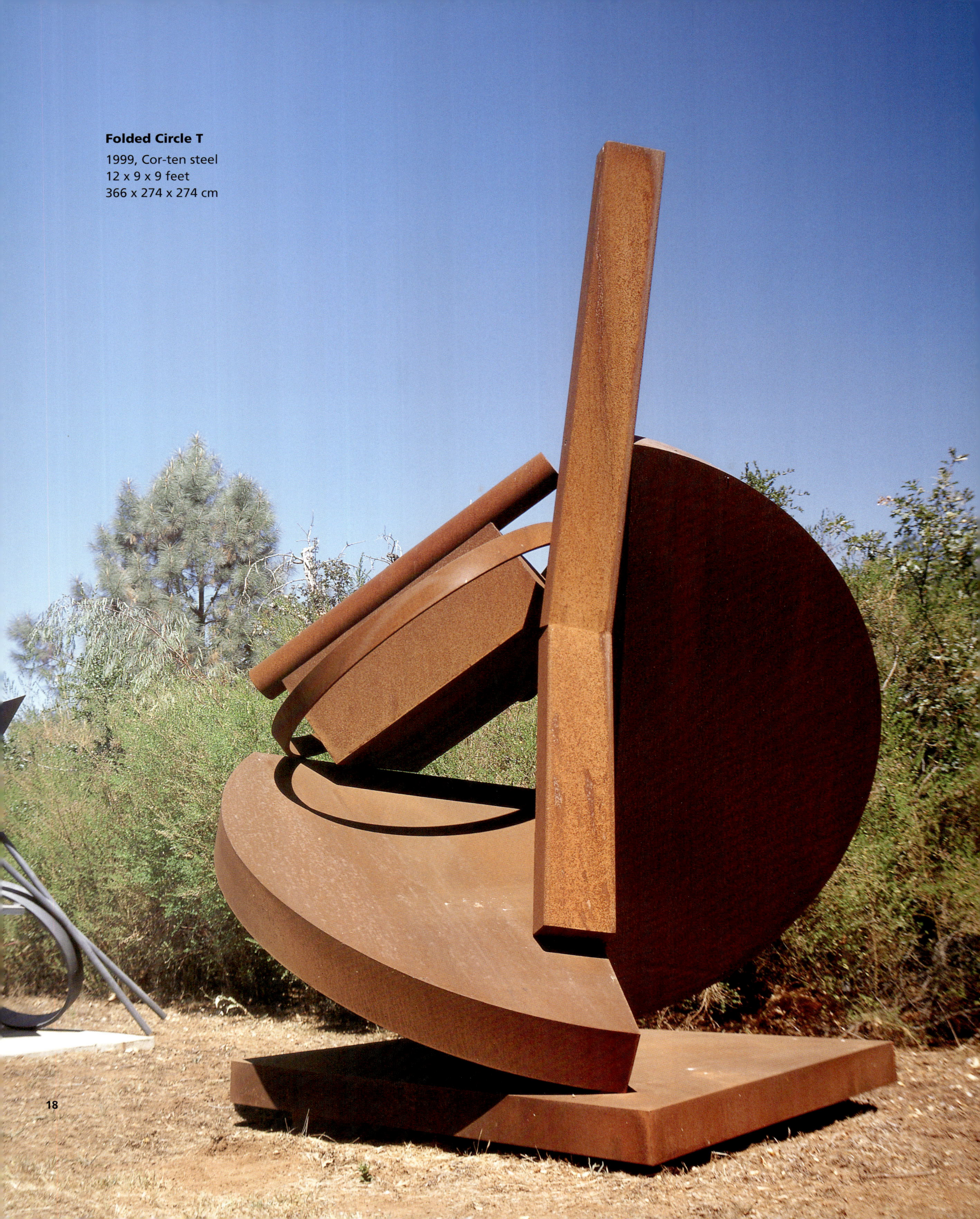

Folded Circle T
1999, Cor-ten steel
12 x 9 x 9 feet
366 x 274 x 274 cm

Creating the Truth

Jolei Leisegang

"And the peculiar thing is," Goethe said [to Eckermann], "that only those born with talent actually know what matters and all the rest more or less are astray."

Introduction

At the beginning of 1979, the German broadcasting service in Frankfurt (Hessischer Rundfunk) sent me to San Francisco for a few months to conduct interviews and reports on the city's art scene. Judy Chicago was busy with the installation of the "Dinner Party" at the San Francisco Museum of Modern Art and despite her tight schedule, she granted me an interview. Speaking with Chicago gave me real insight into the women's movement of that time. Painters Wayne Thiebaud, Mel Ramos, Richard Diebenkorn, and the sculptor Arnaldo Pomodoro, who was then teaching at Mills College, the writer Kay Boyle and her colleague Herbert Gold had all previously spoken into my microphone as I, on the first of March, a Thursday afternoon, met with Fletcher Benton in his studio on Bryant Street.

It was an impressive first encounter, which grew into a long-standing friendship, and my esteem for the artist and his work has flourished significantly throughout the years. Fletcher Benton is one of the most important and authentic contemporary American artists. He has provided me with a profound insight into his artistic process.

The world of cognition is a timeless analogy. While analogy pertains to the similarity of ideas, it can also include relating to the mental thought process. The shadows of that which we perceive leave traces that become images. It all begins with the senses and ends in reason—the active mind is a spontaneous agent of potential creativity. In the art world, not only new and contemporary ideas are appreciated; but old artistic convictions also continue to be valued. If, however, everything is mere illusion—not even the reality of the exterior world presenting itself as a proven fact—then would not the liveliness of our imagination that normally signals true perception of the real world be thrown into doubt? Indeed, Descartes' conclusion that "about doubt there is no doubt" holds the case of false perception true, and his "I think therefore I am" secures truth.

These external influences are bound to Fletcher Benton's work, and consequently there exists an understandable developing tension between what is objectively real and subjectively personal in his art. These oppositions fuse together, forming a harmonious balance that marks the sculptor's "vital center." The sculptor's objects, formed by facts, are admittedly connected to the nature of the real. However, everything real and historical in his work surfaces only insofar as it plays into his understanding of value, and when it stands to open artistic possibilities bearing the sculptor's signature. By this, traditional understanding of form is not shattered. If and when the need arises, it is transformed according to its attributed significance and on the basis of an exemplary past. Expression is, after all, the means of making objects real.

Creating the Truth

One can examine the sculptor's or painter's skills to establish whatever significance there may be; however, this in itself is worthless. Learning artistic methods is only in one respect interesting: if it serves freedom, the fundamental principle of art. For one cannot learn art; one practices art.

For the Bauhaus and other similar movements, method was essential because there was a designed technical purpose. However, art, at its original conception, moves toward individual authorship, which does not exclude a gentle sensibility—one needs only to think about the careful vigor in countless works by Picasso, which are masterfully powerful, or of Paul Klee, who presented a powerful gentleness in his works. What the artist intends with his work is important if it is to be an actual truth. But for this very reason, the artist wishes to see the bare essentials perfected. And, therewith, the question as to what then is true art continues to be suppressed.

Real art and true venture, which leaves ideal art untouched, shape the center of Fletcher Benton's work. Benton is an artist, who thinks and feels beautifully. In him there exists a world that outside of the mind is difficult to conceive. His works—both paintings and sculptures—express truth without a trace of reality. Nevertheless, Benton knows every detail of the real world. He employs it only as a means to express the true ideal of art, which utilizes real means ultimately to make truth simulate reality: creating the truth.

Thereby, his eye searches for cause and effect while his hand gives form to method and intent. Intent is a fact; the connection between cause and effect, however, is a truth. Under the influence of deliberate and free singular acts, Fletcher Benton leaves behind all artistic endeavors in one monotonous mass-formed image, and fashions his artificial world. In all of the artistic genres and techniques that Benton utilizes, one observes, with more than just a little amazement, his achievements.

Benton's work as always reflects the conditions of intent and feeling: stylistic movements take place as the material is still waiting to be shaped. These works, when in the process of being formed, move beyond the intellectual center and the indispensable means. The artist does not suppress anything; he, instead, transforms and condenses essence. He accepts the achievements of the past and explores them anew with his own possibilities, thus allowing himself to make fundamental decisions that either tie him down or set him free. However, he can only return what he has received from his time.

Benton's invaluable works possess a third dimension that requires them to be staged in the exhibition space. I first took notice of this in 1980 when I had the opportunity to place a selection of his work on exhibit with drawings by the Swiss artist Claire-Lise Holy at the Suermond–Ludwig–Museum in Aachen.[1] In the years that followed, several installations of Benton's work in Germany have confirmed my initial impression.

The way in which Benton transforms the inner experience into an external space without which the artistic act would be senseless is of some importance. To reach this goal requires genuine effort comparable to that of the experienced climber striving to reach the summit. Benton's is a difficult path on which the promised destination always demands one to reach higher.

That which is universally understood as "normal" perception is generally called reality. There appears, however, to exist a second reality—aside from space and time—a reality art is capable of creating for the individual and which stands aloof from so-called "normal" perception. Purely aestheticized images displace perception that a priori is oriented toward normal understanding. The "painted fish"—even if it is intended to be three days old—does not stink.

Creative activity manifests itself always in dialogue with others. It is not the production of something new that characterizes genuinely original contemporary artists. Instead, genuinely original artists possess the skill to create as if nobody before them had created in this same manner. Fletcher Benton, indeed, has this rare gift at his disposal. The focus of his art is the gracefulness of immediate expression, which he achieves by liquefying the past and injecting it into his creations.

Formal possibilities are infinite, and every novel intellect brings forth new forms. It is exciting to experience how in a masterfully installed exhibit the artist's work—be they sculptures, drawings, or paintings—communicate with one another. One easily has the impression that one is witnessing an event on stage. The ideal distance of sculptures amongst and in opposition to the viewing public is a determining factor in the presentation of the artist's oeuvre.

Great minds discover their own artistic language and extend it. It is a totality that these artists present to the public. The viewer is involved in the process, being transported from the so-called exterior to the interior. The physicality of the sculpture has no object. It is simply itself as well as reminiscent of the object. An event of this kind consumes audiences without depersonalizing them. It points to an outward expansion of an acquired inner strength that culminates in "creating the truth." And that means: to seize something and not let it go, to realize it according to its artistic aptitude and intellectual meaning without posing any other questions. It takes intention, which precedes art, courage, and patience.

Notes

1. Claire-Lise Holy: Zeichnungen aus New York-Suermond–Ludwig–Museum, Aachen, 1980, Germany. In later works by Holy, Benton's sculptures appear frequently as motifs.

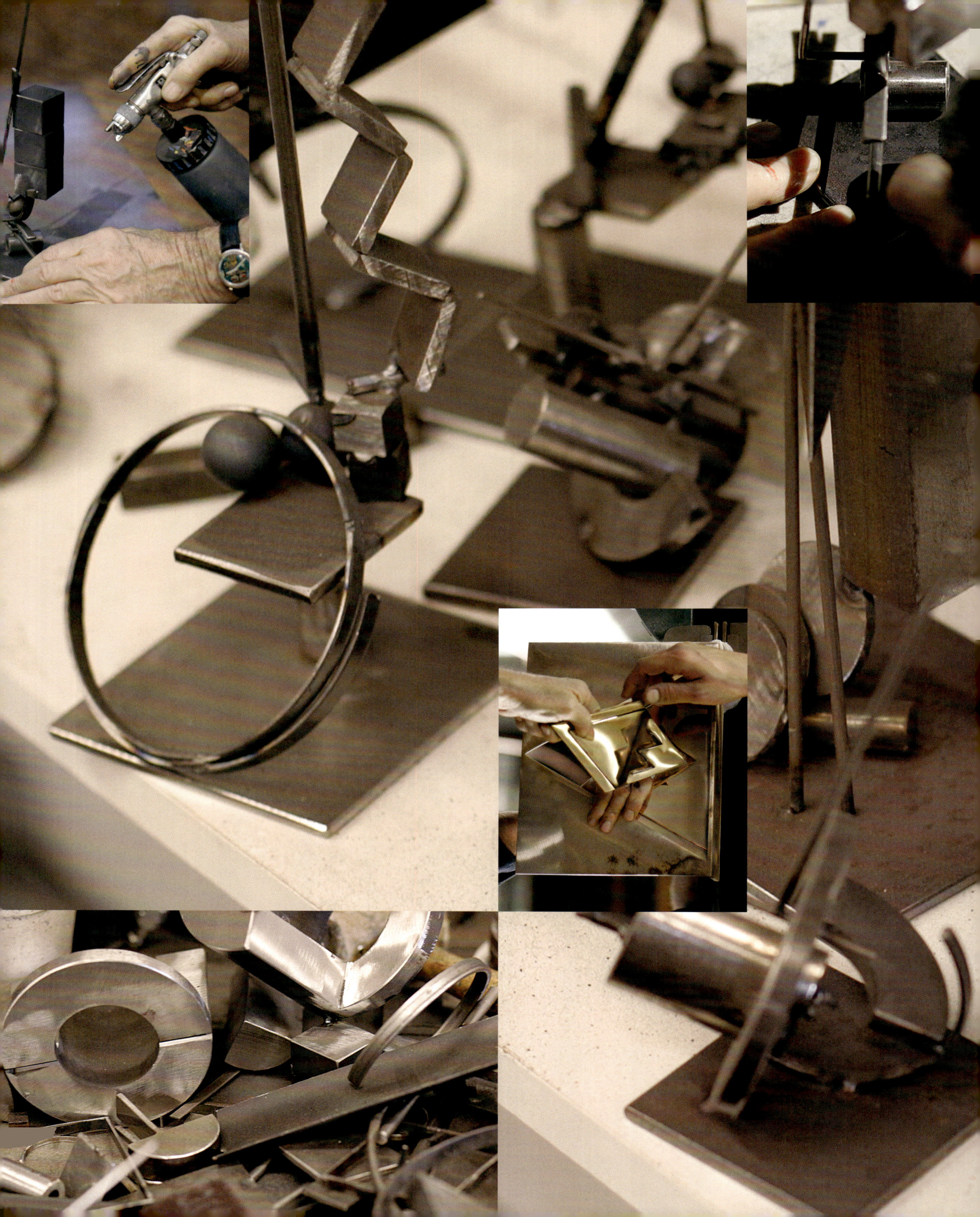

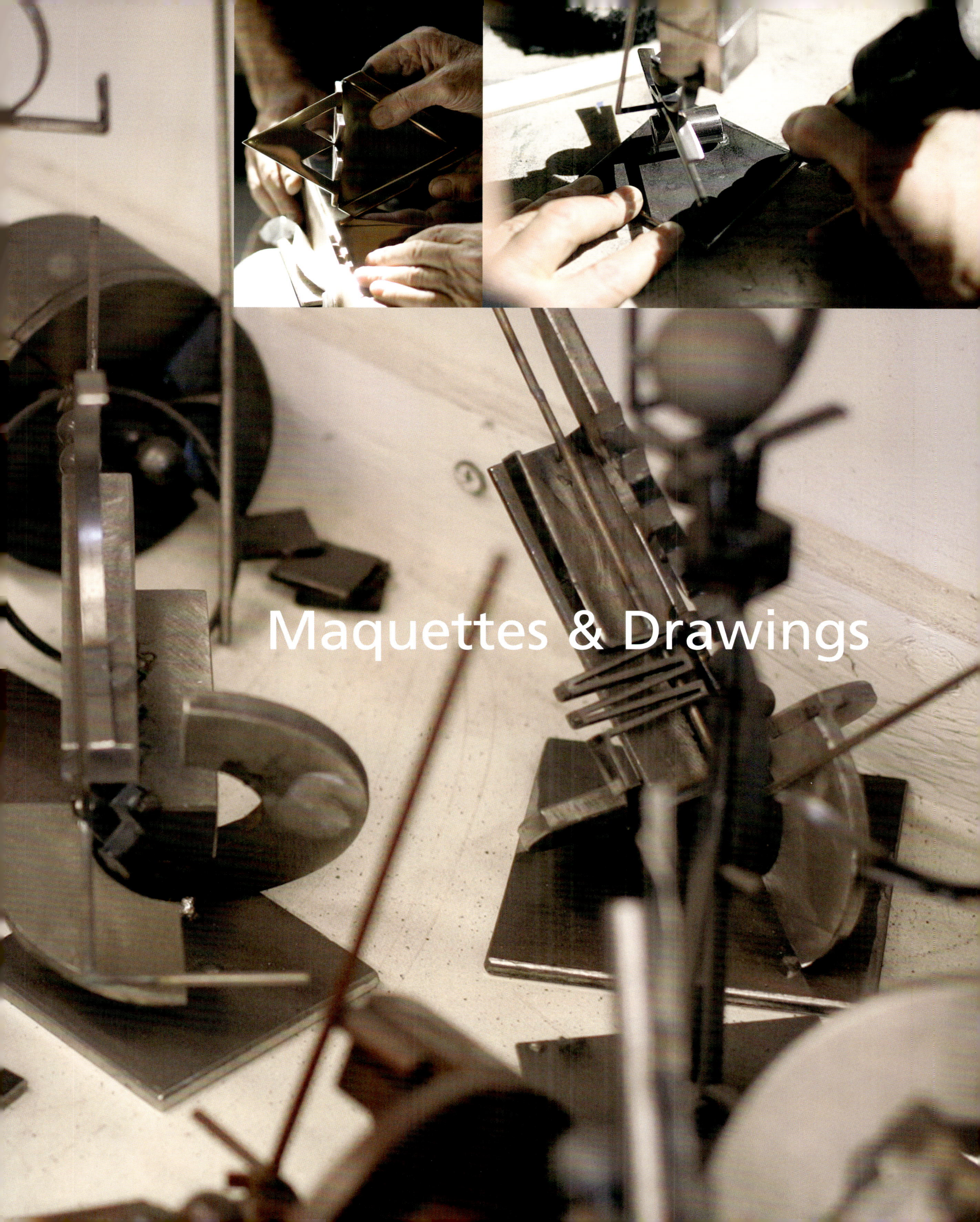

Maquettes & Drawings

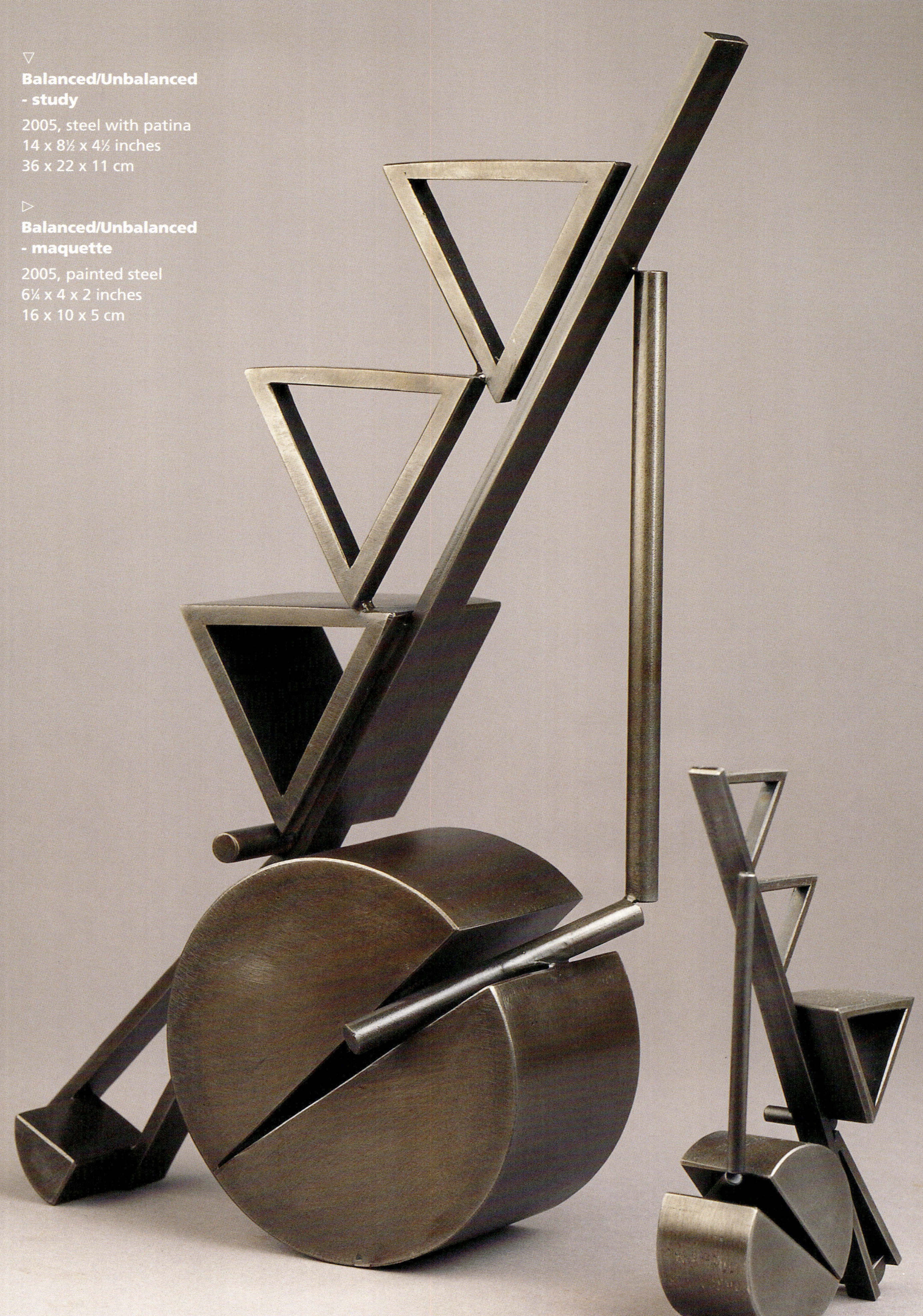

▽
Balanced/Unbalanced - study

2005, steel with patina
14 x 8½ x 4½ inches
36 x 22 x 11 cm

▷
Balanced/Unbalanced - maquette

2005, painted steel
6¼ x 4 x 2 inches
16 x 10 x 5 cm

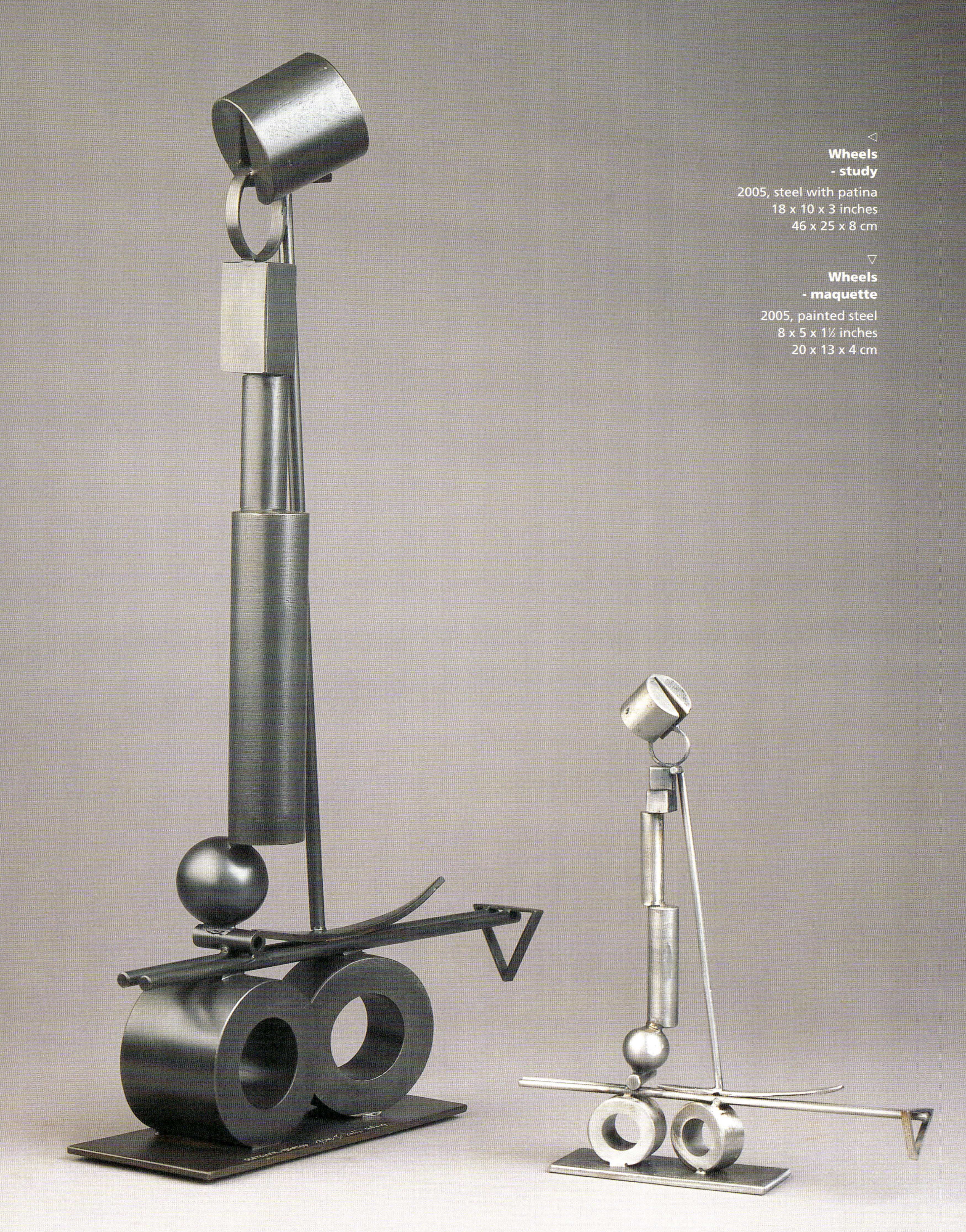

◁
Wheels
- study
2005, steel with patina
18 x 10 x 3 inches
46 x 25 x 8 cm

▽
Wheels
- maquette
2005, painted steel
8 x 5 x 1½ inches
20 x 13 x 4 cm

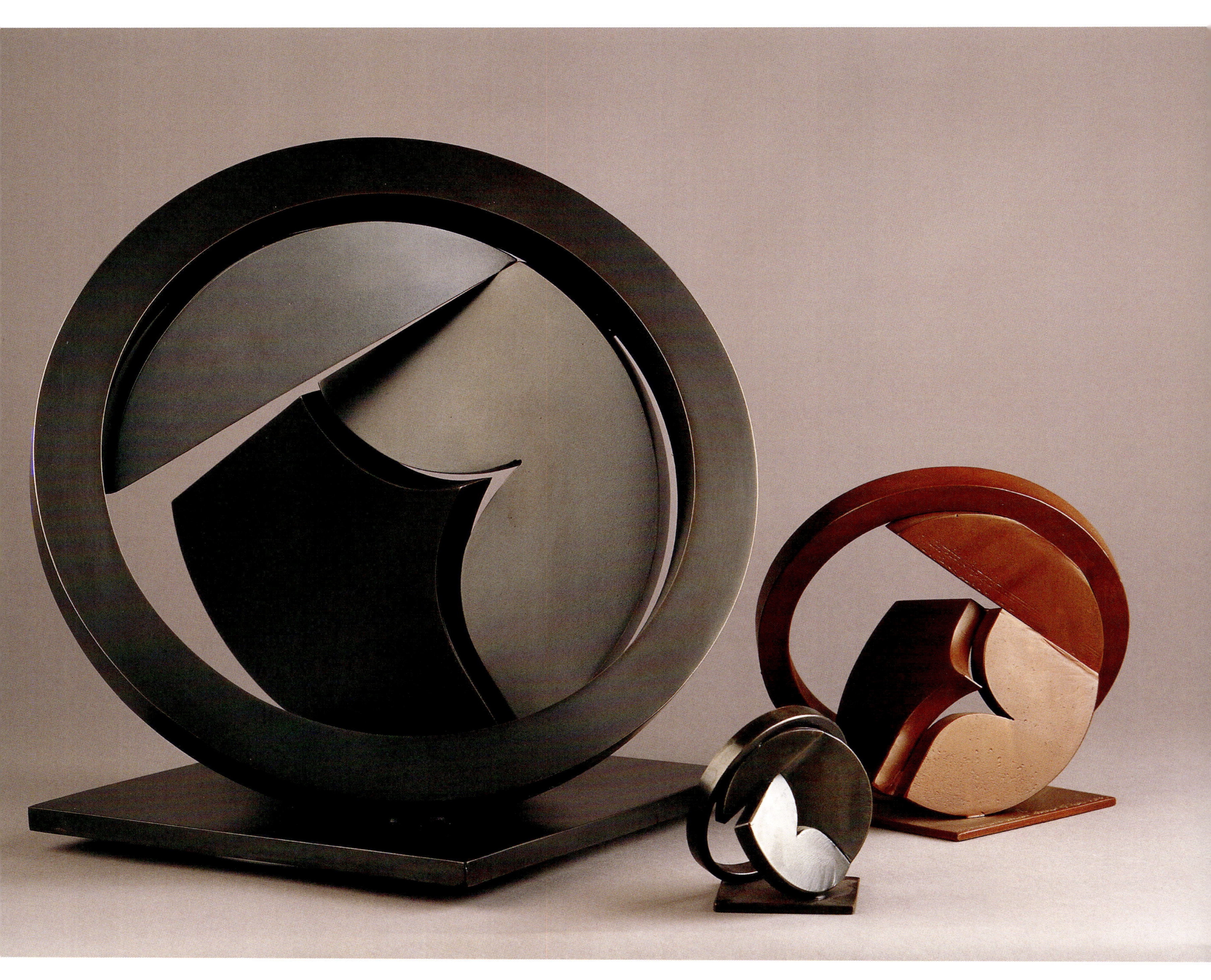

Folded Circle Ring Bezel, Phase II

2002, steel with patina
14 x 14 x 12 inches
36 x 36 x 30 cm

Folded Circle Ring - maquette

2005, painted steel
4 x 3½ x 3½ inches
10 x 9 x 9 cm

Folded Circle Ring - study

2005, steel with patina
7½ x 5½ x 6½ inches
19 x 14 x 17 cm

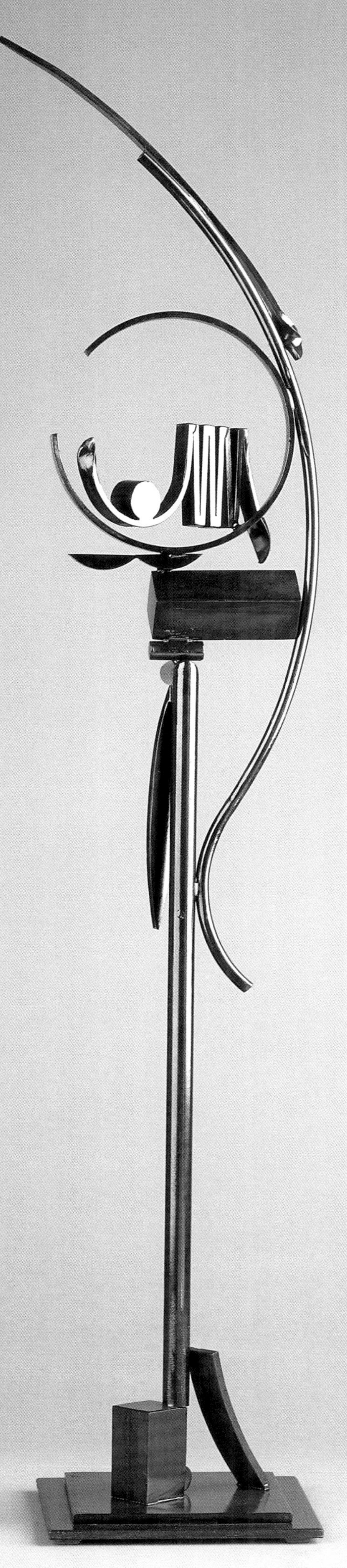

Steel Watercolor Indian - maquette

2005, painted steel
10 x 2½ x 3 inches
25 x 6 x 8 cm

Steel Watercolor Indian - maquette

2005, steel with patina
11 x 2½ x 2½ inches
28 x 6 x 6 cm

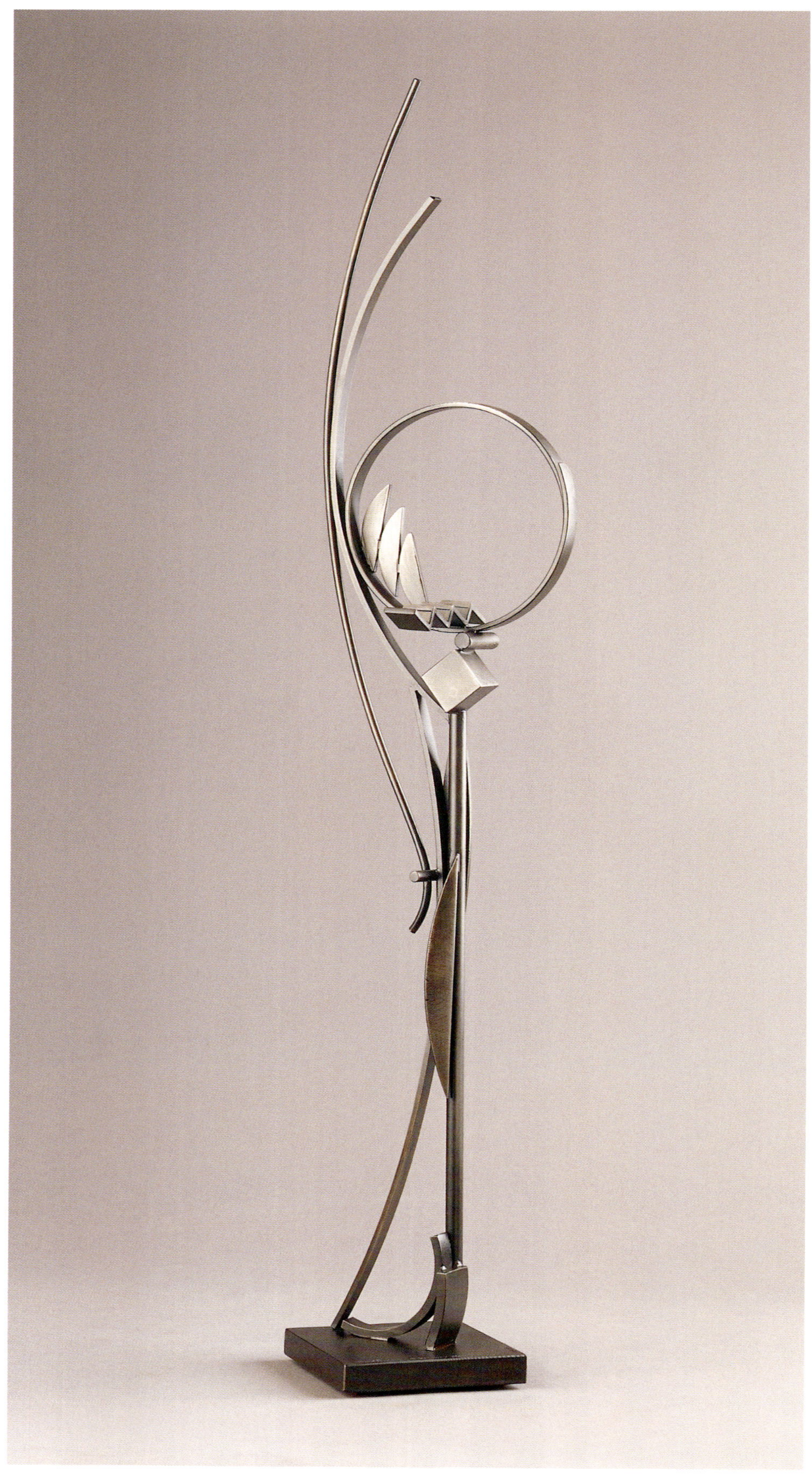

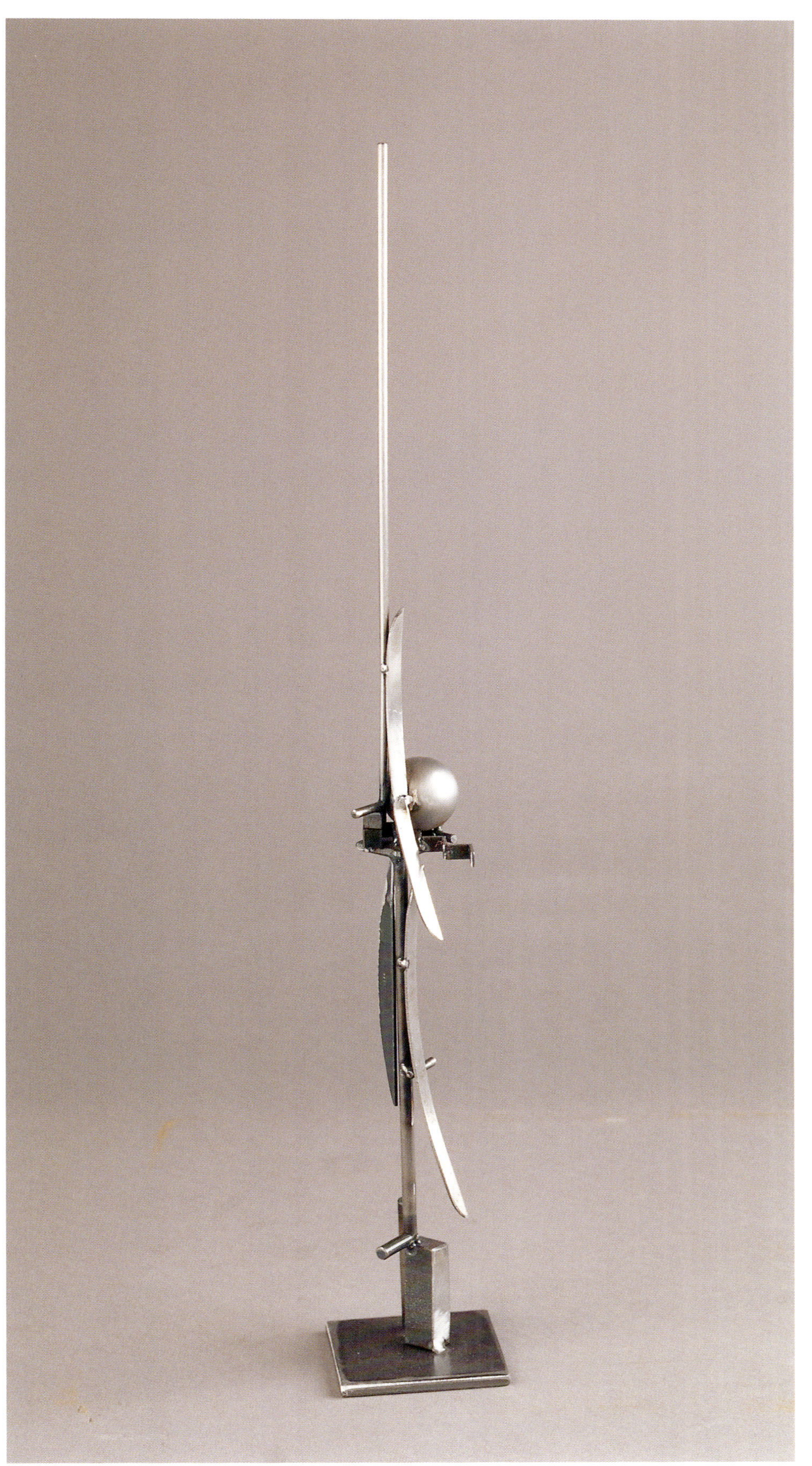

Straight-Up with Ball - maquette

2003, steel
14 x 2 x 2 inches
36 x 5 x 5 cm

▷
Steel Watercolor - study
2005, steel
27 x 4½ x 4 inches
69 x 11 x 10 cm

▷ ▷
Steel Watercolor - maquette
2005, steel
9½ x 1½ x 1½ inches
24 x 4 x 4 cm

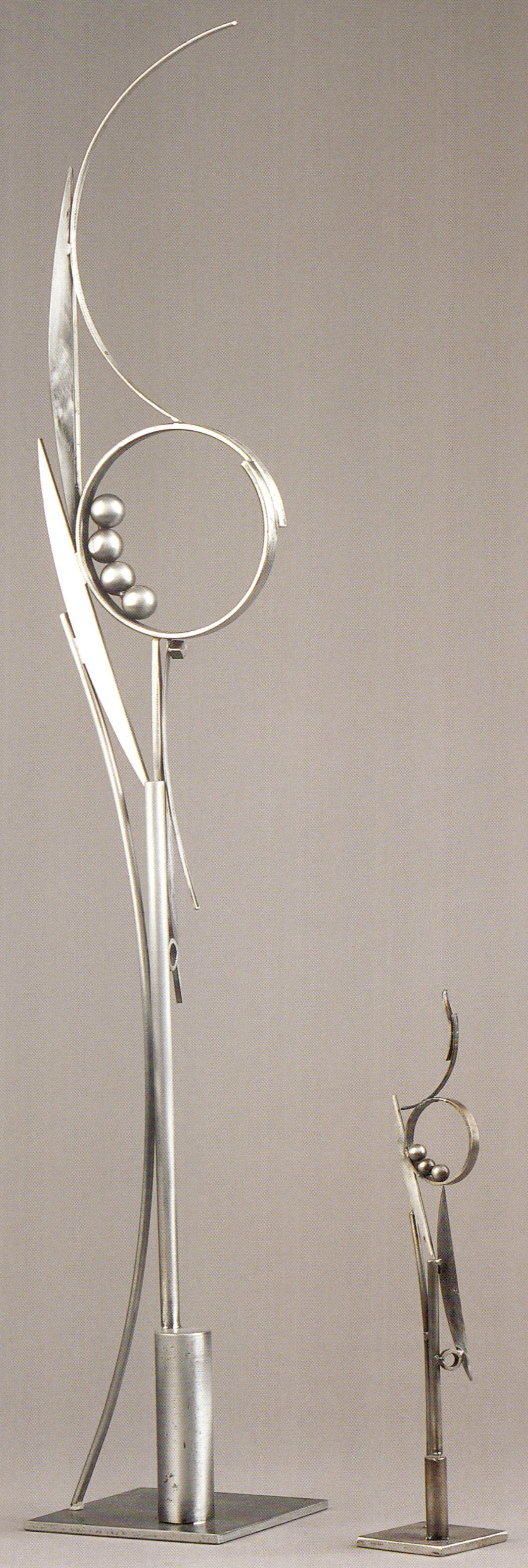

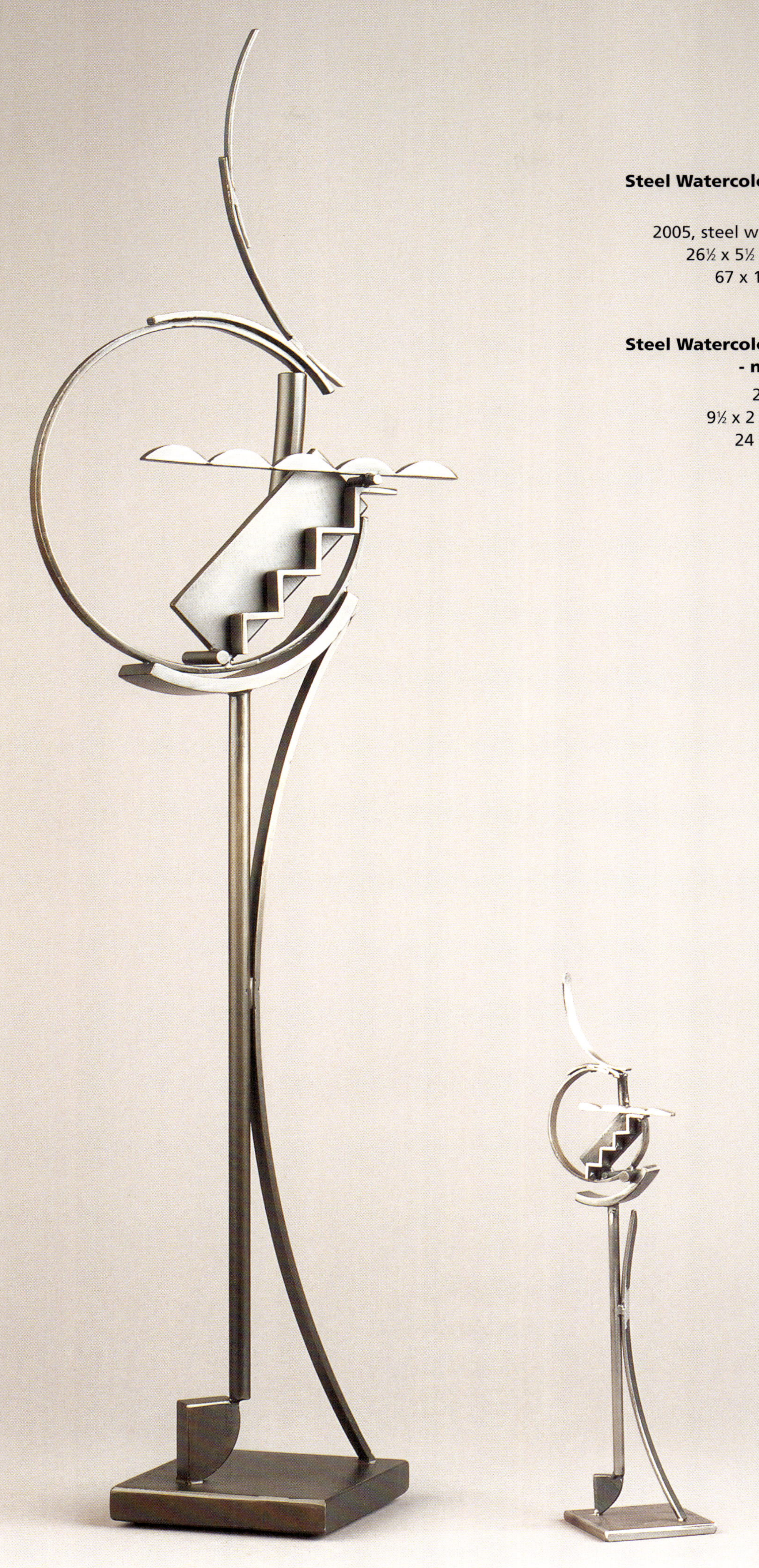

◁
Steel Watercolor Indian - study

2005, steel with patina
26½ x 5½ x 5 inches
67 x 14 x 13 cm

▽
Steel Watercolor Indian - maquette

2005, steel
9½ x 2 x 2 inches
24 x 5 x 5 cm

▽
Balanced/Unbalanced - study

2005, steel with patina
13½ x 9½ x 8 inches
34 x 24 x 20 cm

▷
Balanced/Unbalanced - maquette

2005, steel with patina
5½ x 2½ x 2 inches
14 x 6 x 5 cm

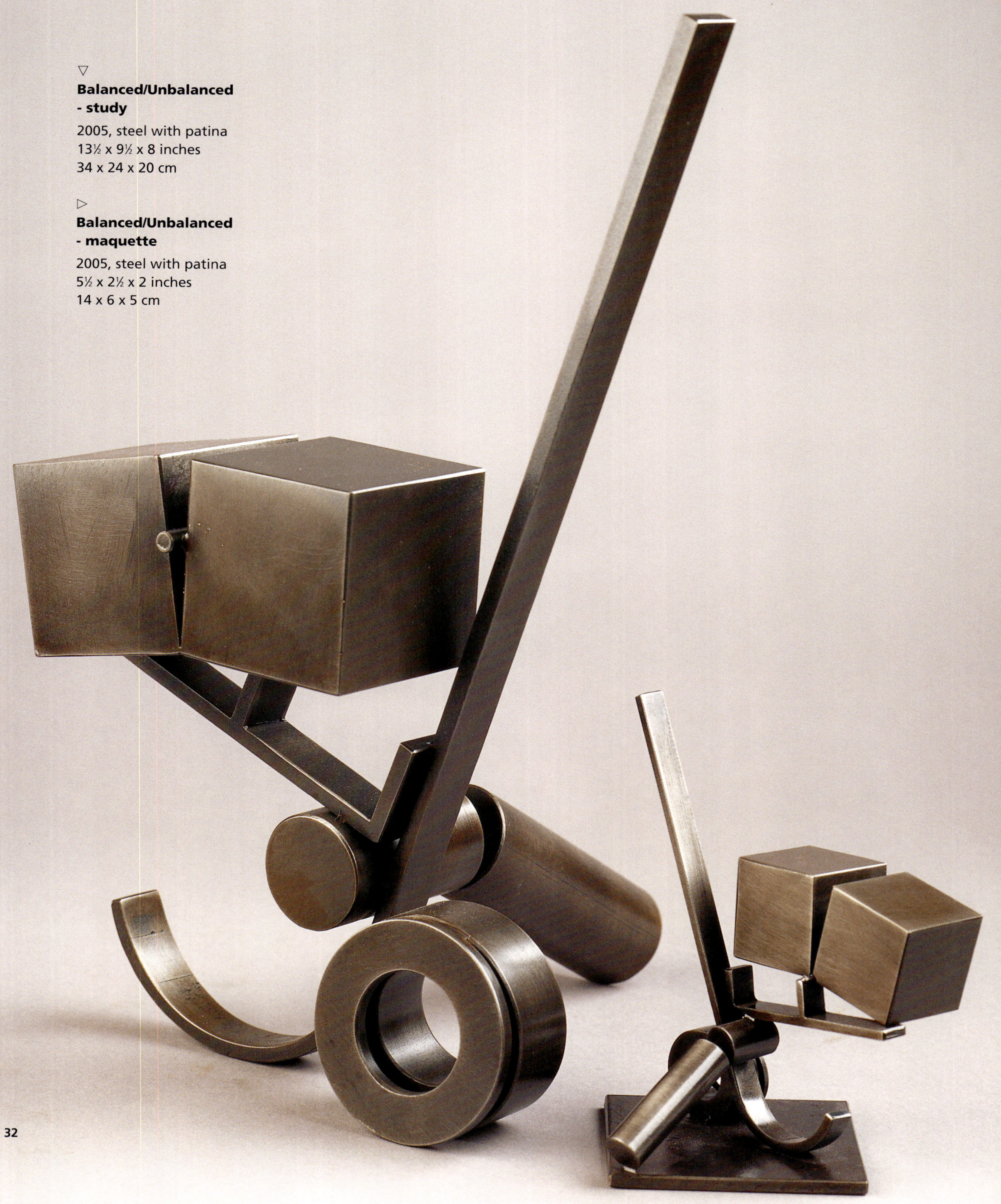

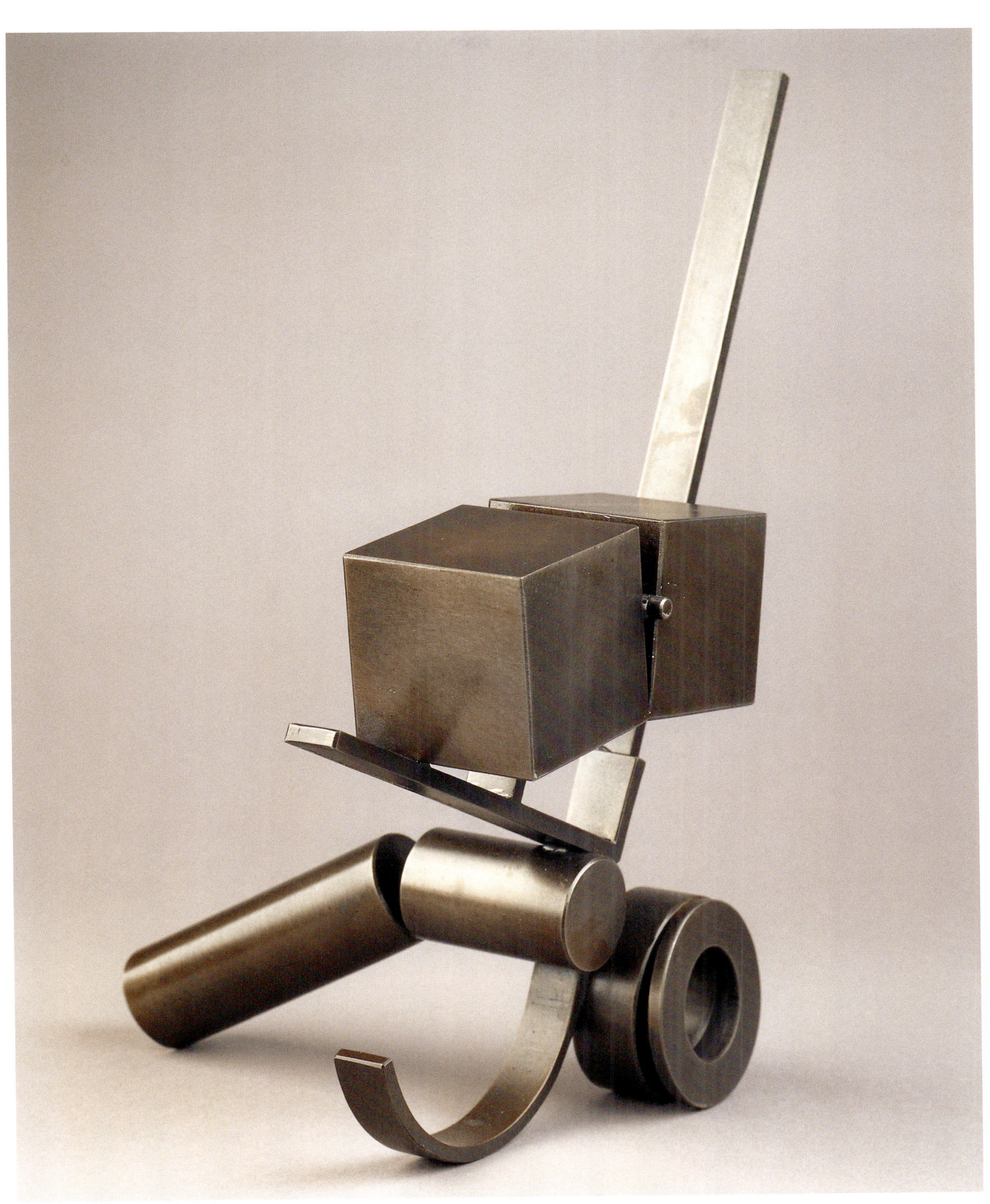

Balanced/Unbalanced - study

2005, steel with patina
13½ x 9½ x 8 inches
34 x 24 x 20 cm

Double Folded Circle Ring - maquette

2005, steel with patina
6½ x 3½ x 3 inches
17 x 9 x 8 cm

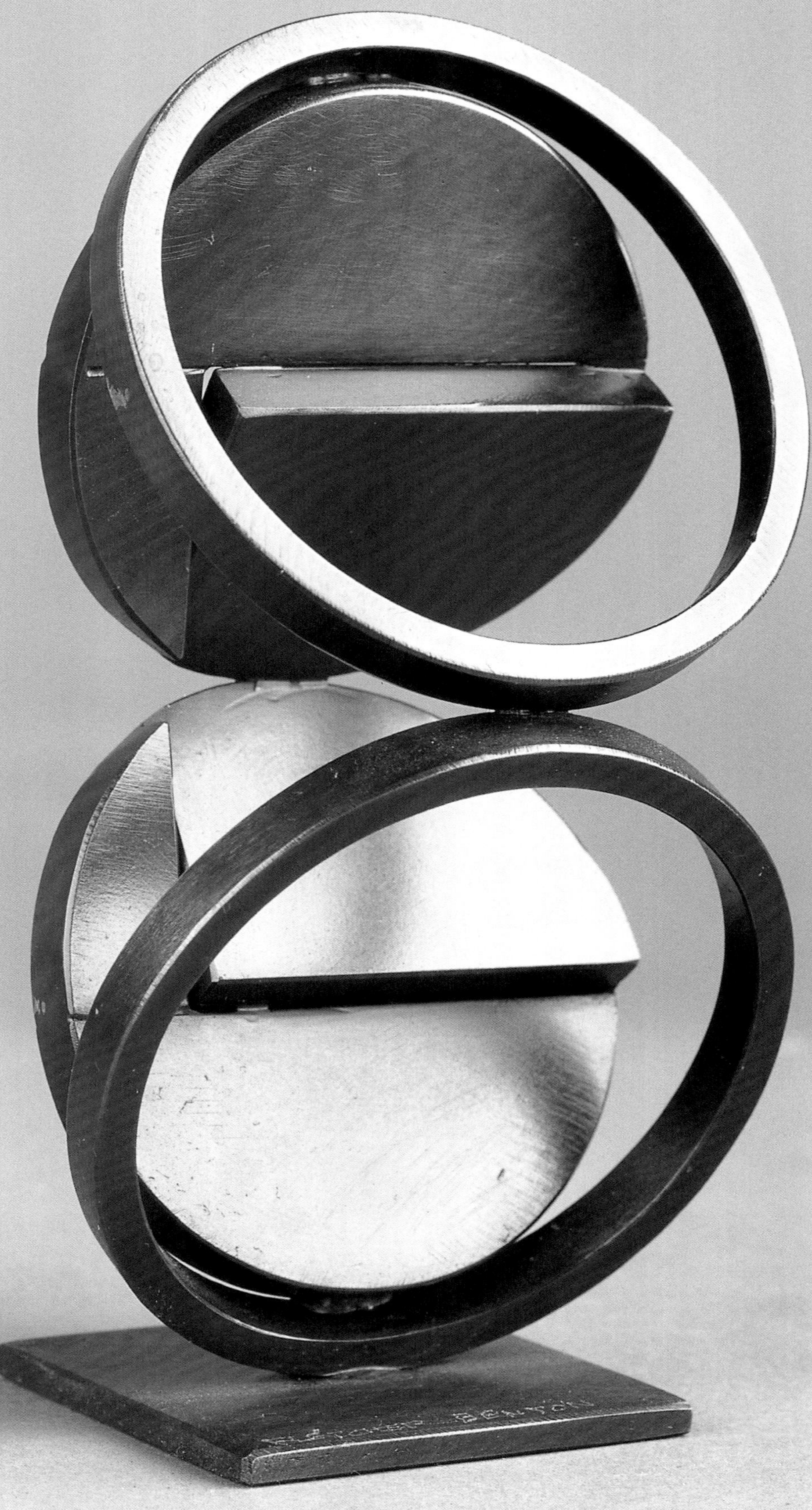

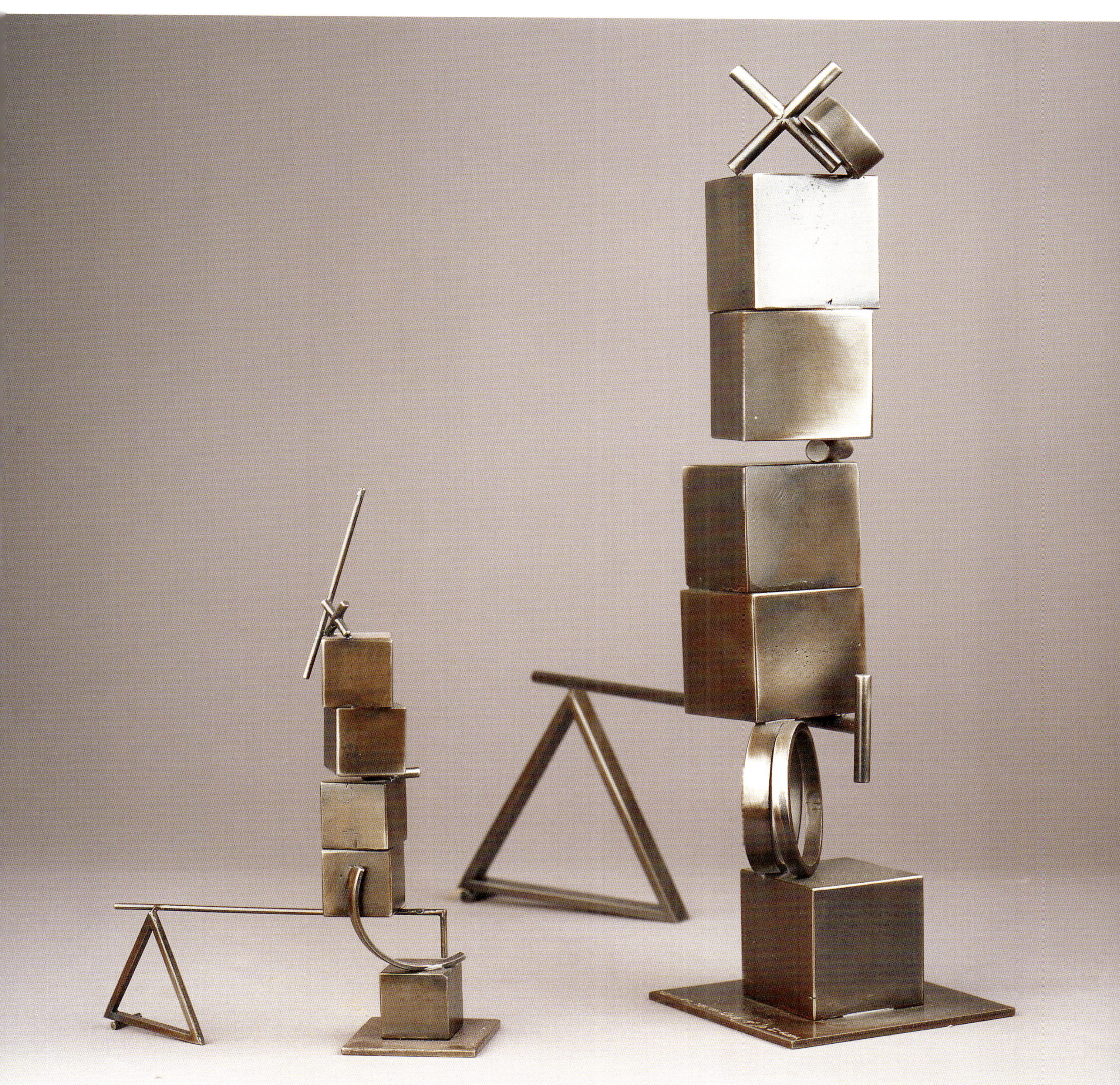

Balanced/Unbalanced - maquette

2005, steel with patina
8¼ x 7 x 2½ inches
21 x 18 x 6 cm

Balanced/Unbalanced - study

2005, steel with patina
14¾ x 13 x 4 inches
37 x 33 x 10 cm

Double Folded Circle Ring - study

2005, painted steel
14¾ x 7 x 7 inches
37 x 18 x 18 cm

▽

Double Folded Circle Ring - maquette

2005, steel
6¾ x 3 x 3 inches
17 x 8 x 8 cm

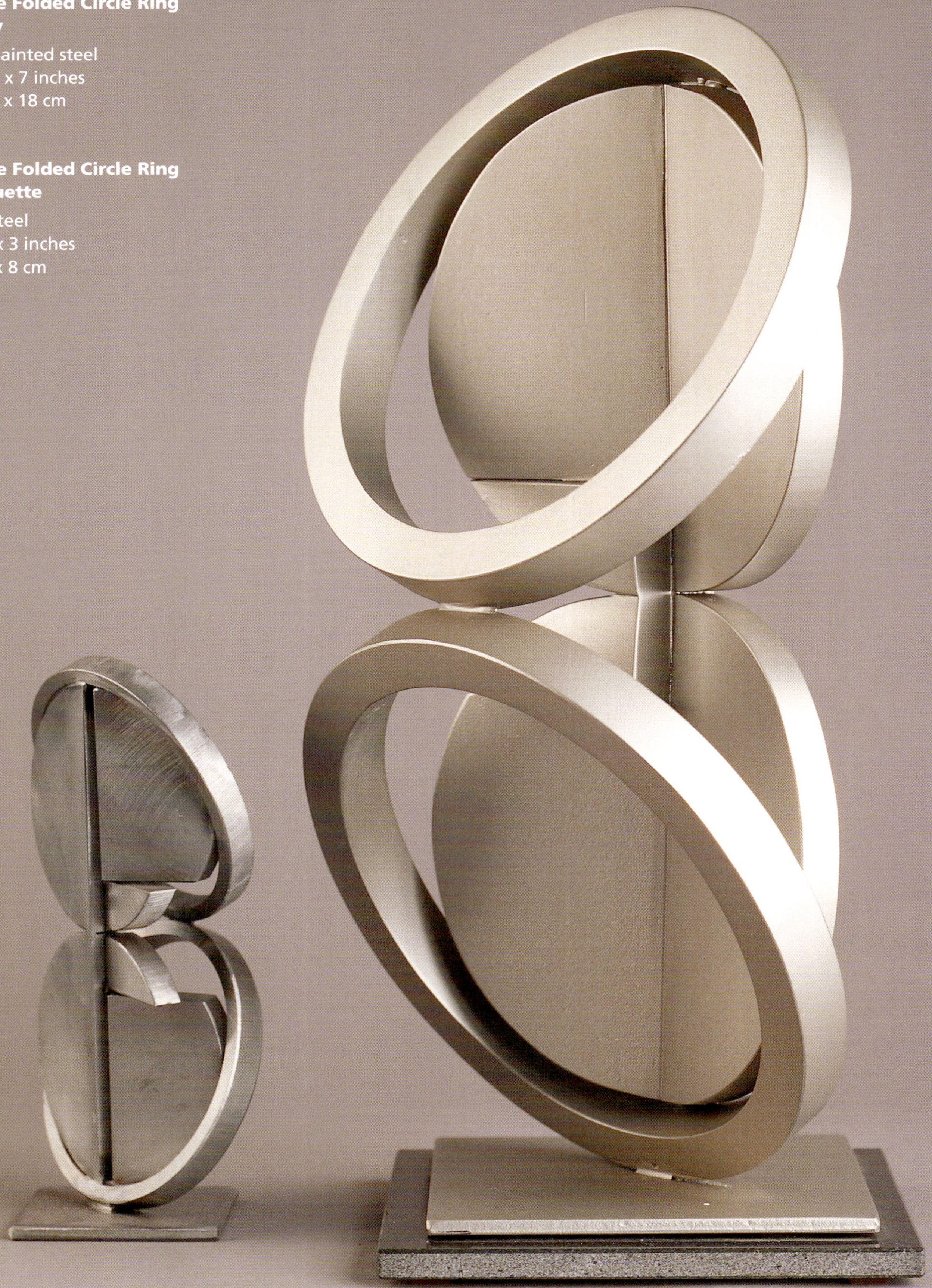

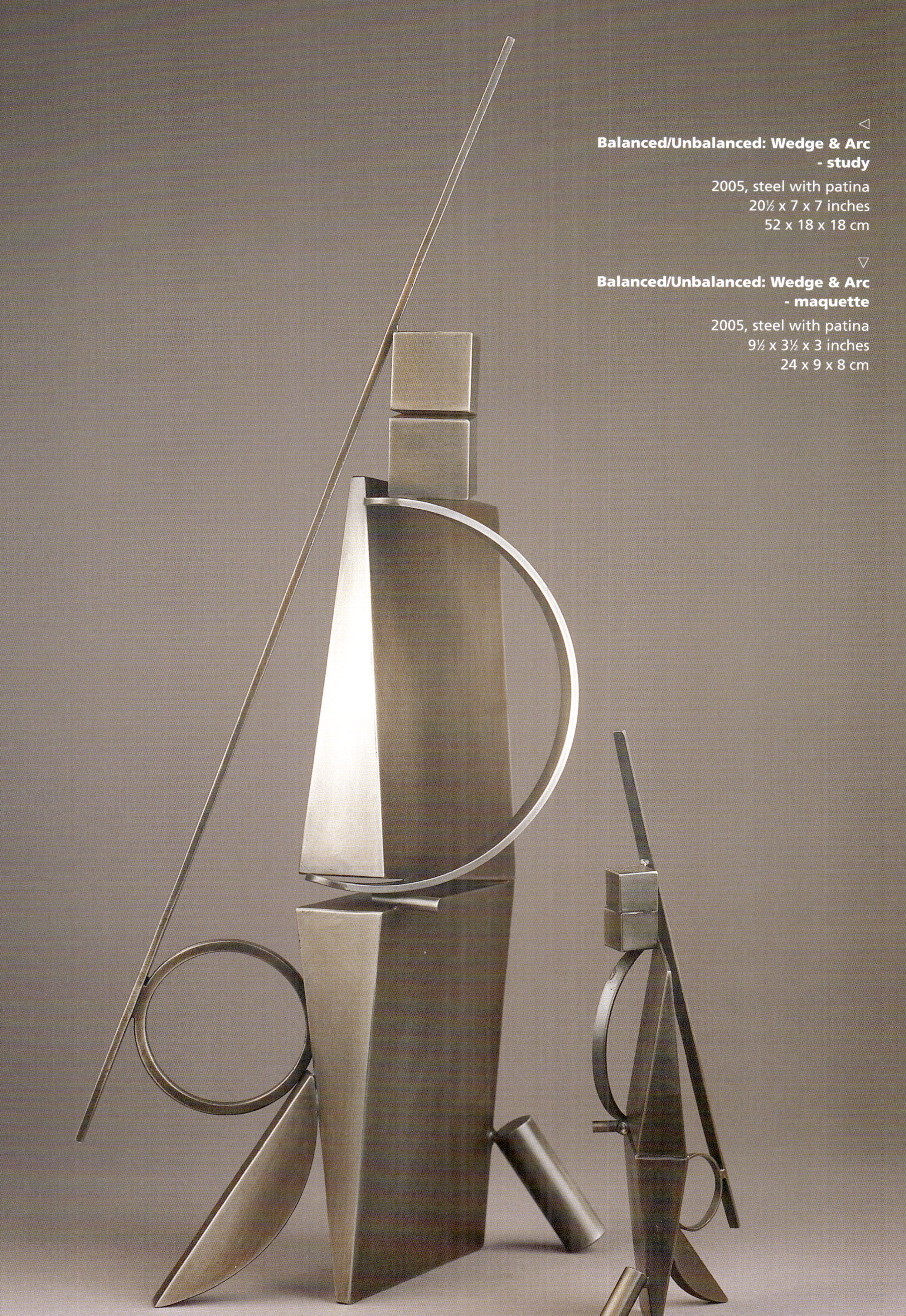

◁
Balanced/Unbalanced: Wedge & Arc - study

2005, steel with patina
20½ x 7 x 7 inches
52 x 18 x 18 cm

▽
Balanced/Unbalanced: Wedge & Arc - maquette

2005, steel with patina
9½ x 3½ x 3 inches
24 x 9 x 8 cm

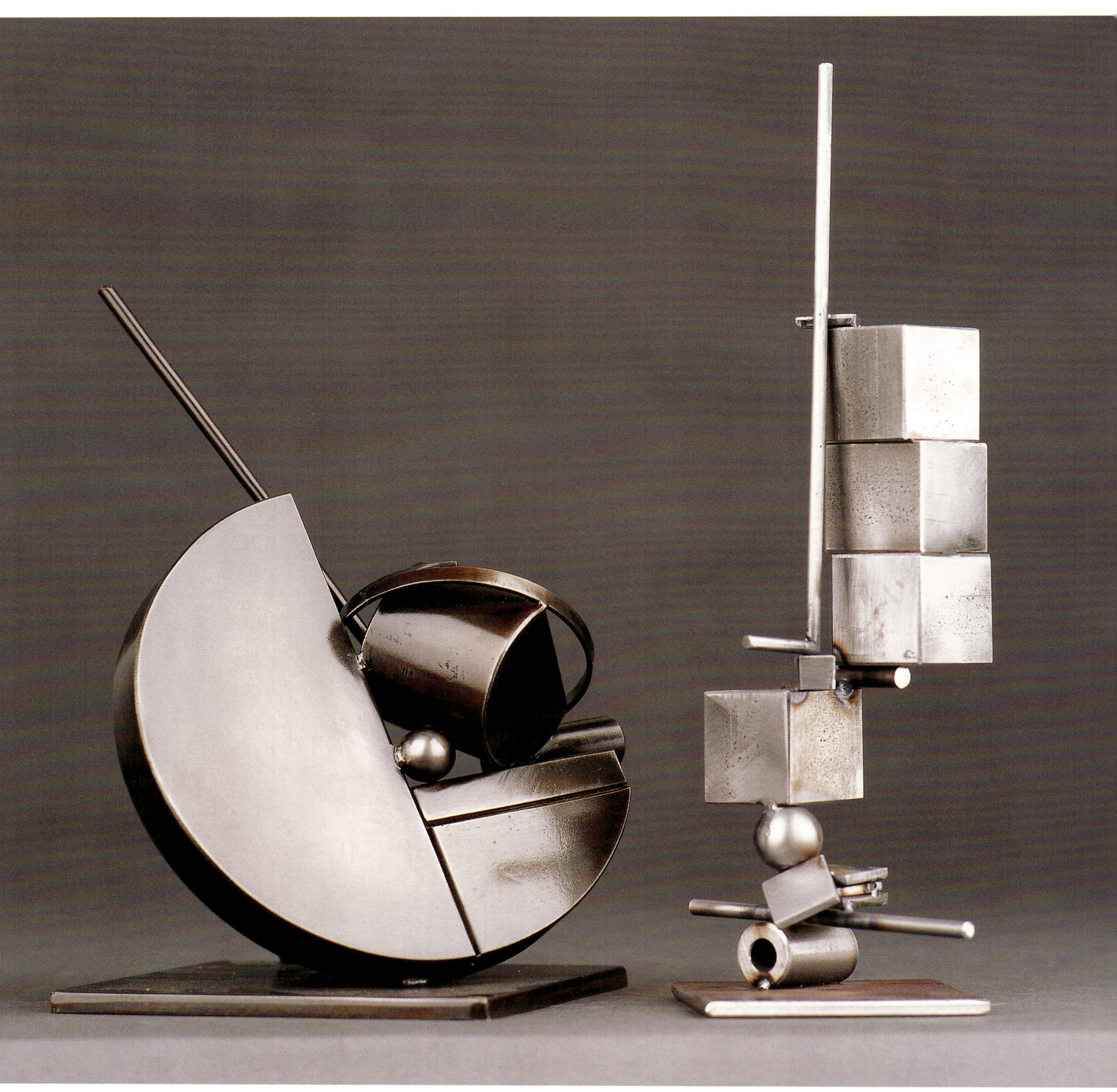

Folded Circle - maquette

2004, steel with patina
8¼ x 6 x 6 inches
21 x 15 x 15 cm

Blocks on Blocks - maquette

2004, steel with patina
11 x 3 x 3½ inches
28 x 8 x 9 cm

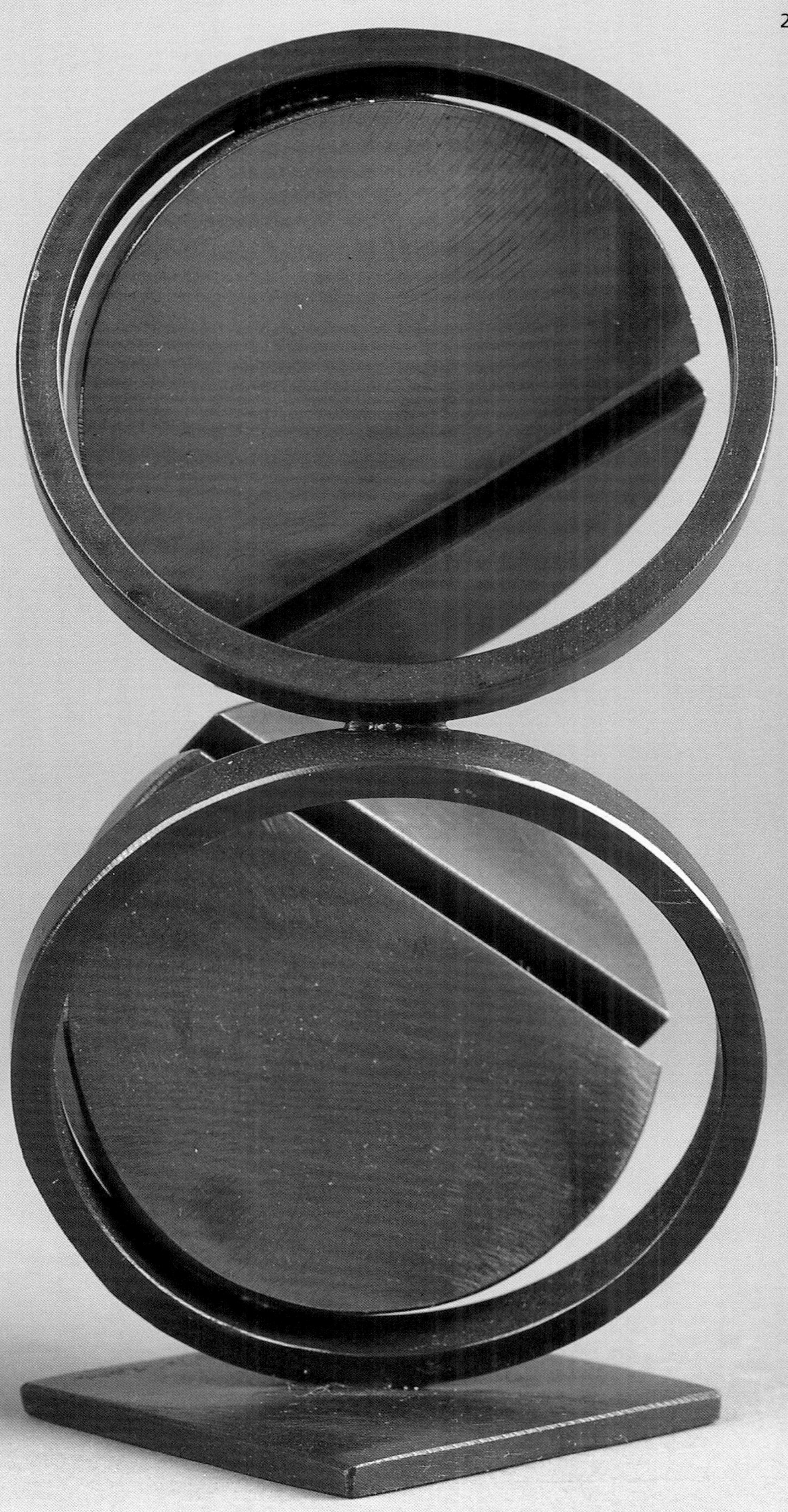

Double Folded Circle Ring - maquette

2005, steel with patina
6¾ x 3½ x 3 inches
17 x 9 x 8 cm

Double Folded Circle Ring - study

2001, steel with patina
14½ x 7½ x 7½ inches
37 x 19 x 19 cm

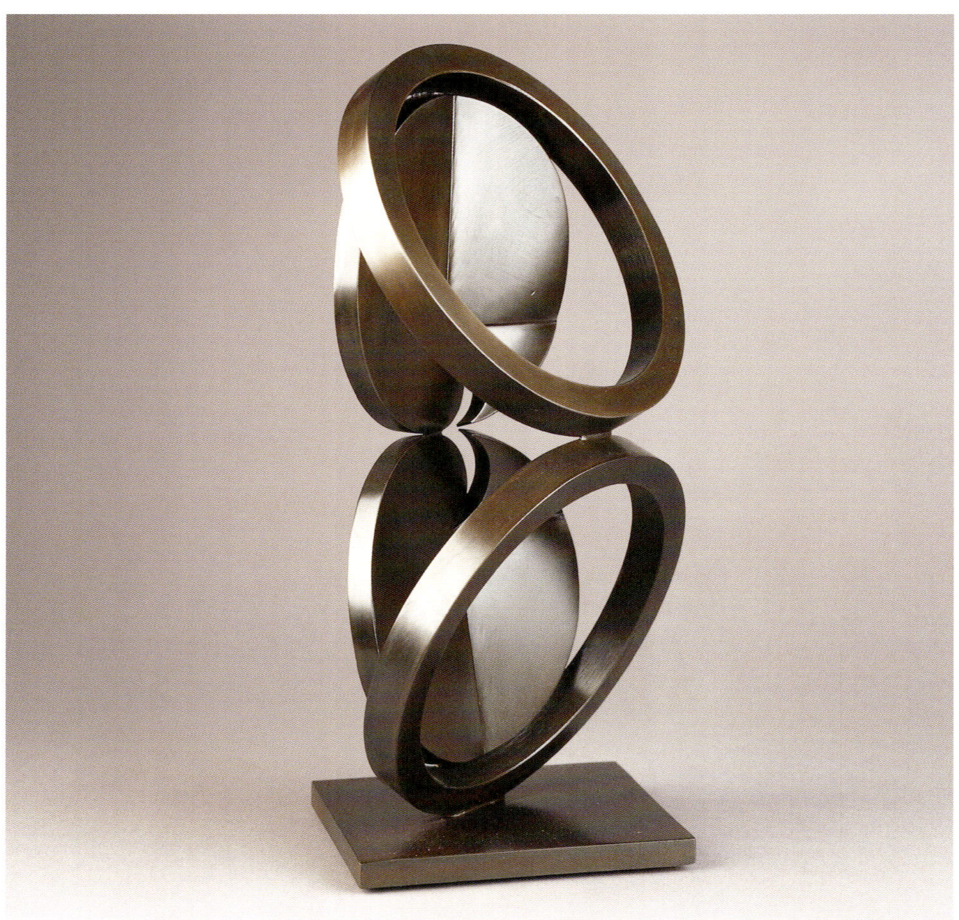

Double Folded Circle Ring – study

2001, steel with patina
14½ x 7½ x 7½ inches
37 x 19 x 19 cm

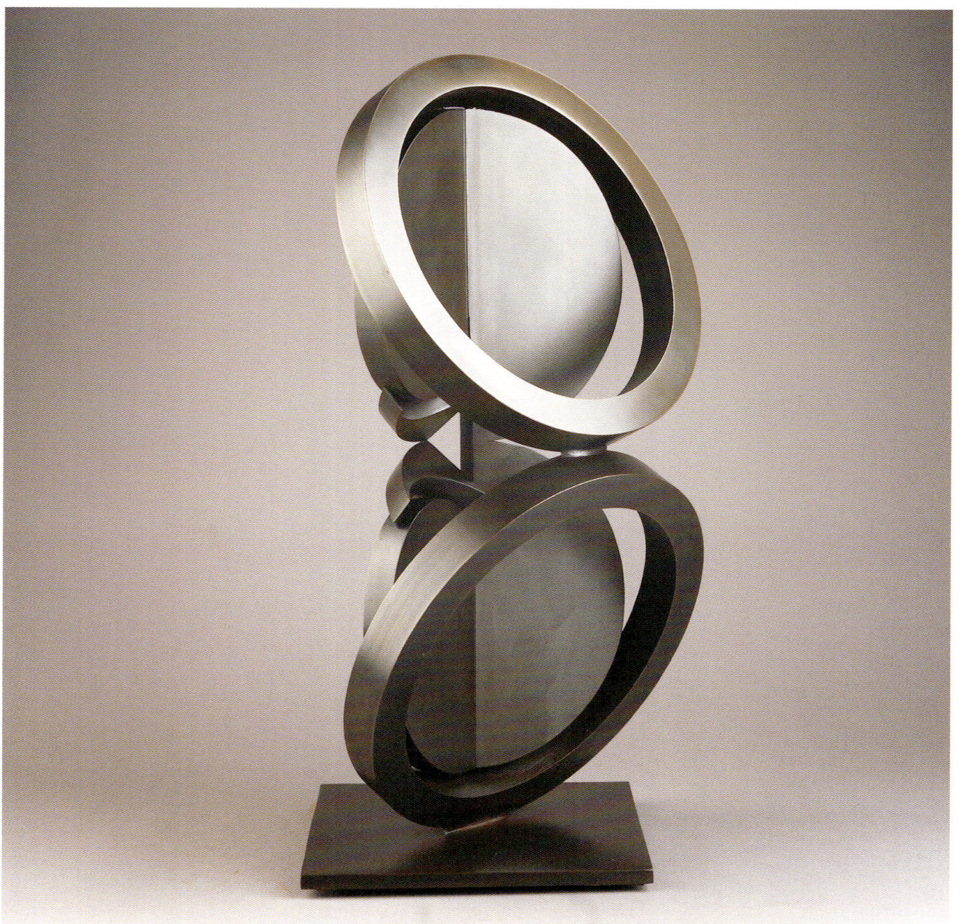

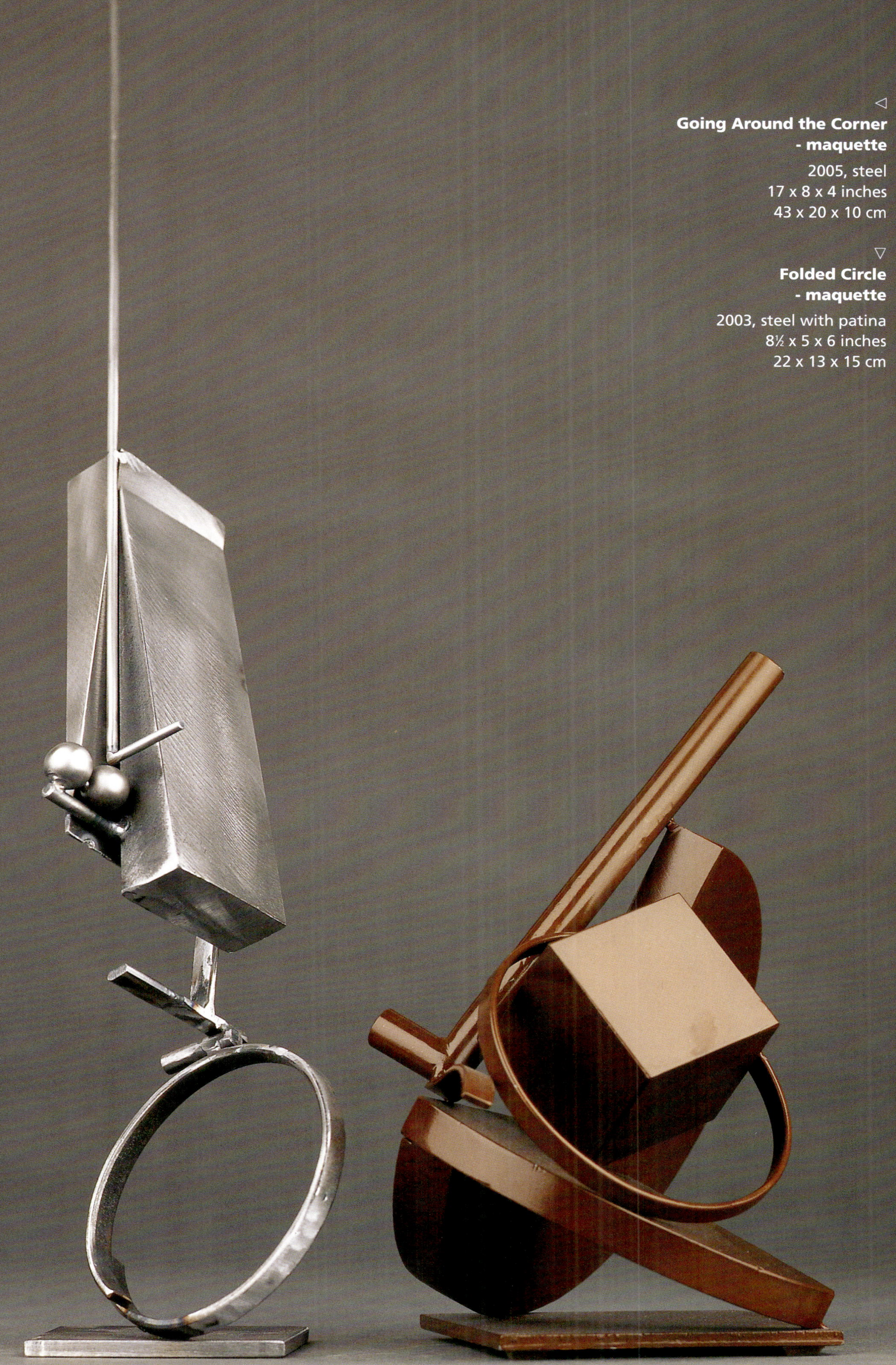

◁
Going Around the Corner - maquette
2005, steel
17 x 8 x 4 inches
43 x 20 x 10 cm

▽
Folded Circle - maquette
2003, steel with patina
8½ x 5 x 6 inches
22 x 13 x 15 cm

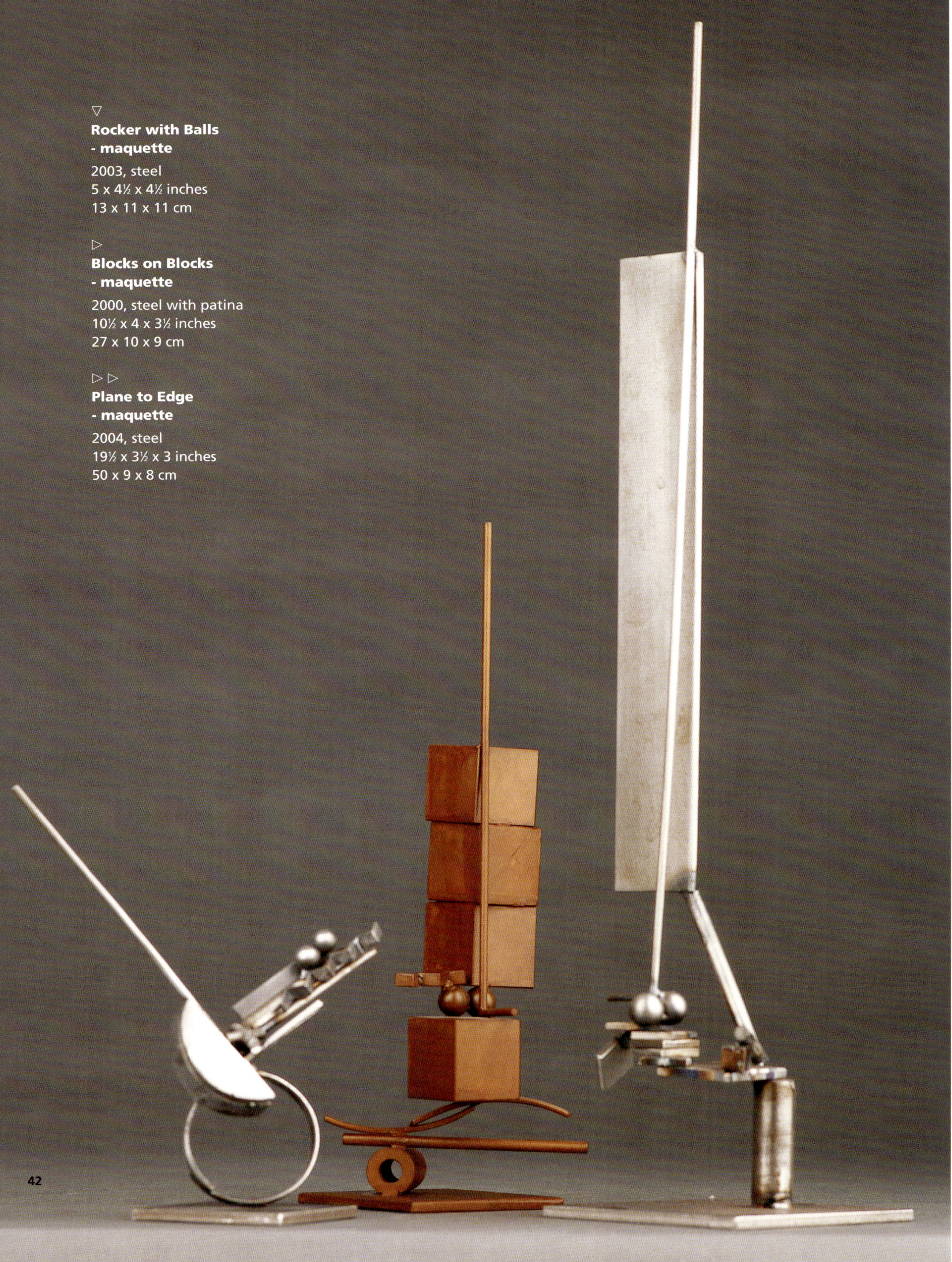

▽
Rocker with Balls - maquette
2003, steel
5 x 4½ x 4½ inches
13 x 11 x 11 cm

▷
Blocks on Blocks - maquette
2000, steel with patina
10½ x 4 x 3½ inches
27 x 10 x 9 cm

▷ ▷
Plane to Edge - maquette
2004, steel
19½ x 3½ x 3 inches
50 x 9 x 8 cm

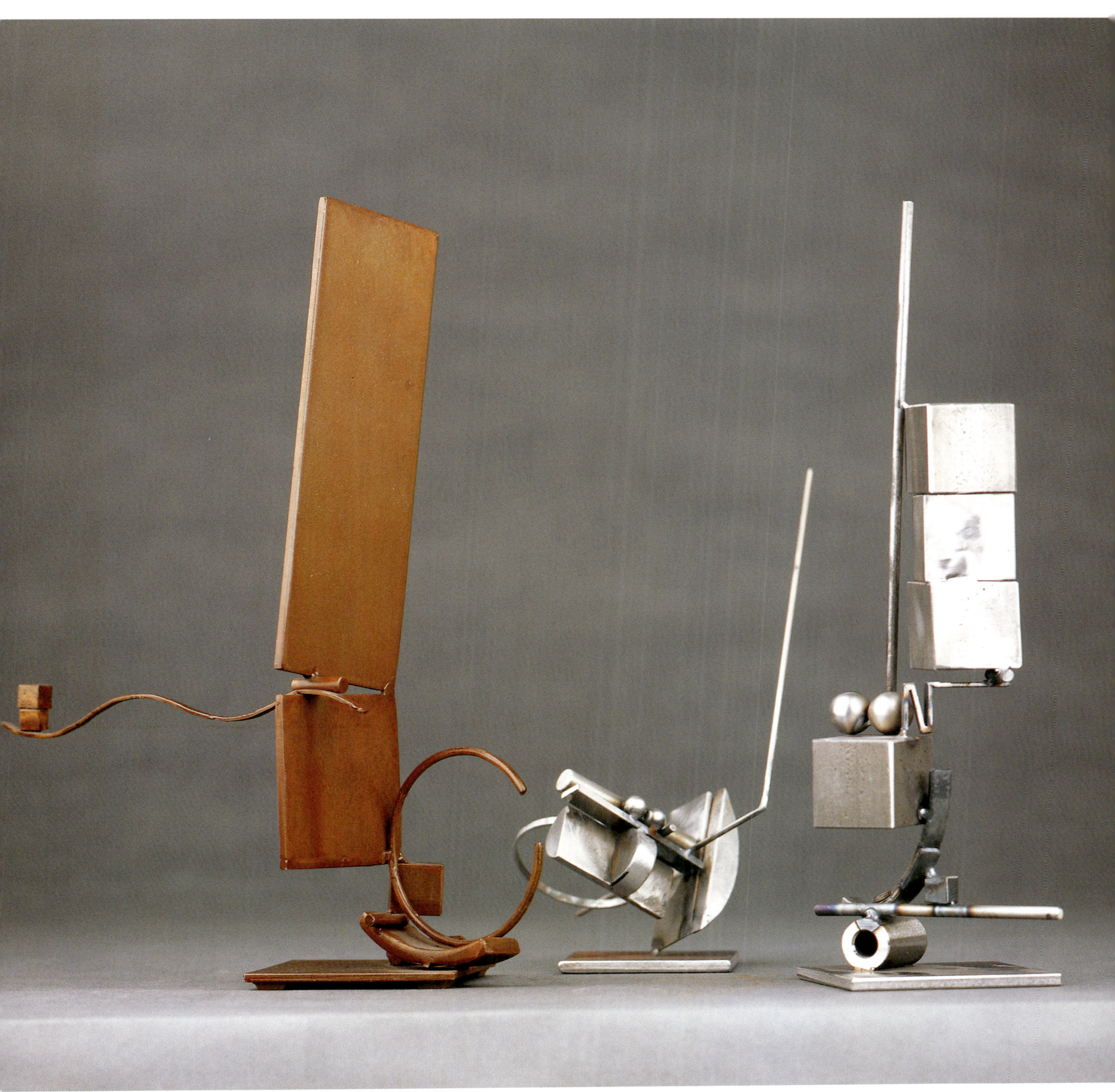

Wedge - maquette
2003, steel with patina
14 x 8 x 4 inches
36 x 20 x 10 cm

Rocker with Balls - maquette
2005, steel with patina
8 x 4 x 3 inches
20 x 10 x 8 cm

Blocks on Blocks - maquette
2005, steel
12 x 3½ x 3 inches
30 x 9 x 8 cm

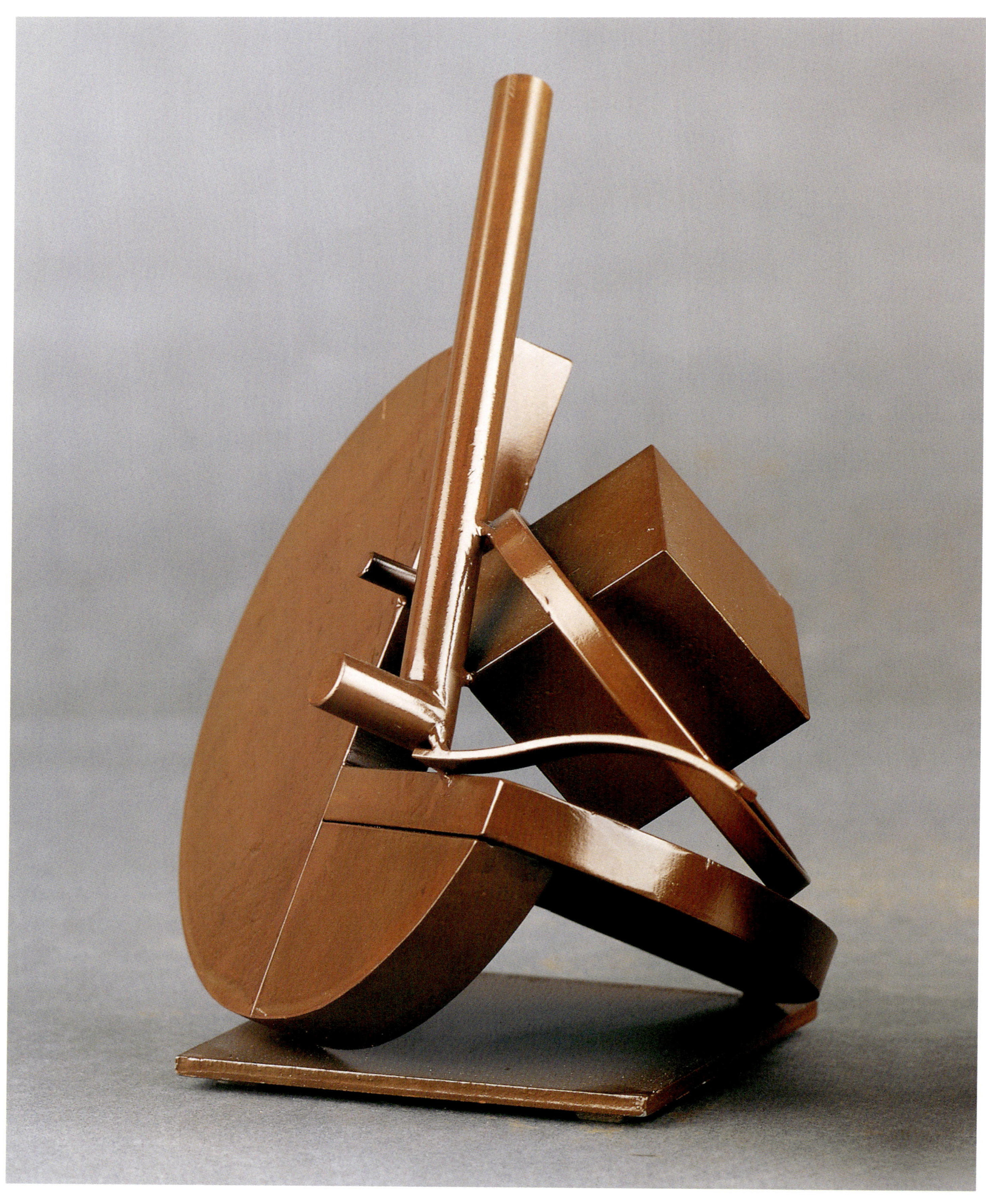

Folded Circle - maquette

2003, steel with patina
8½ x 5 x 6 inches
22 x 13 x 15 cm

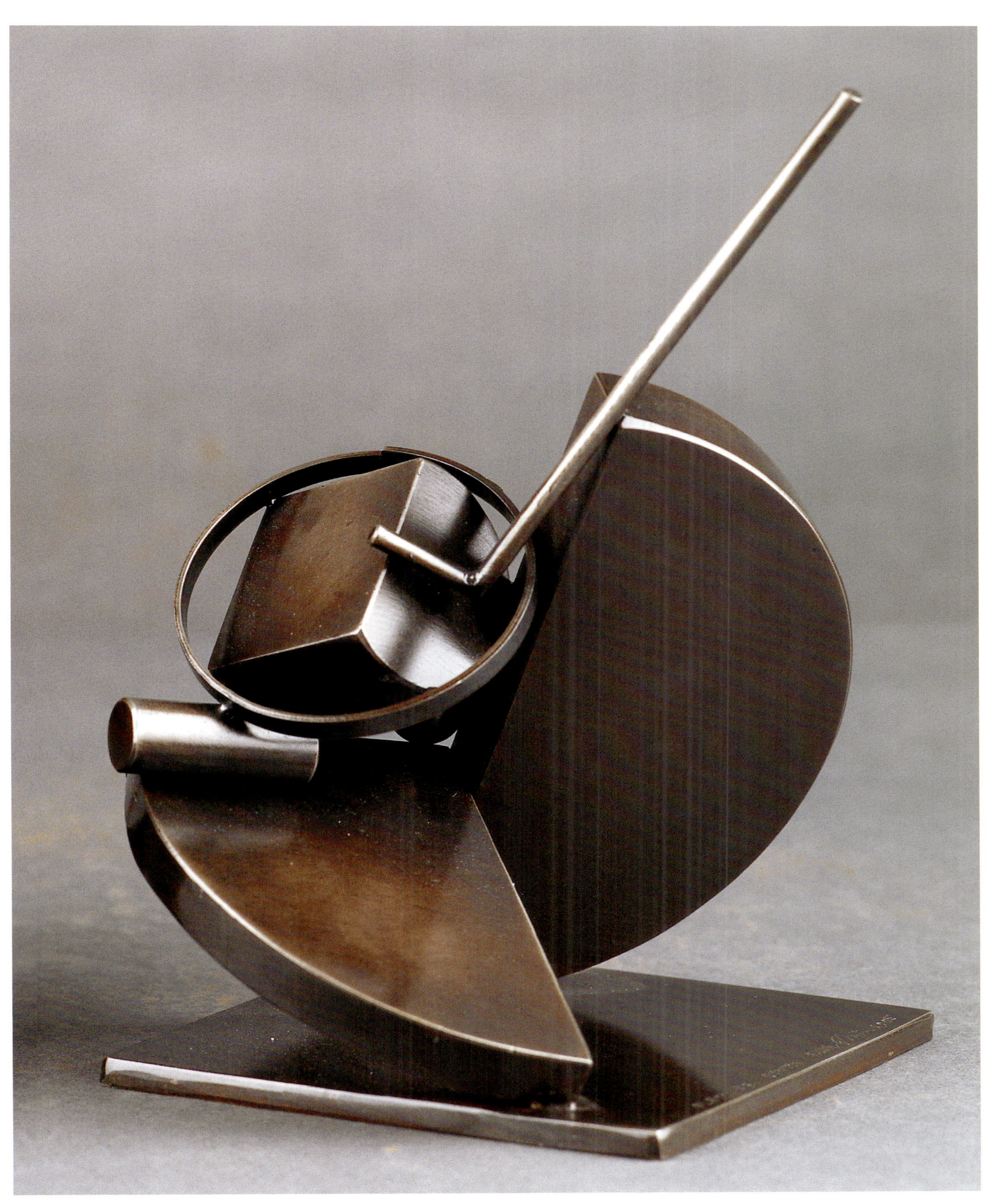

Folded Circle - maquette

2004, steel with patina
8¼ x 6 x 6 inches
21 x 15 x 15 cm

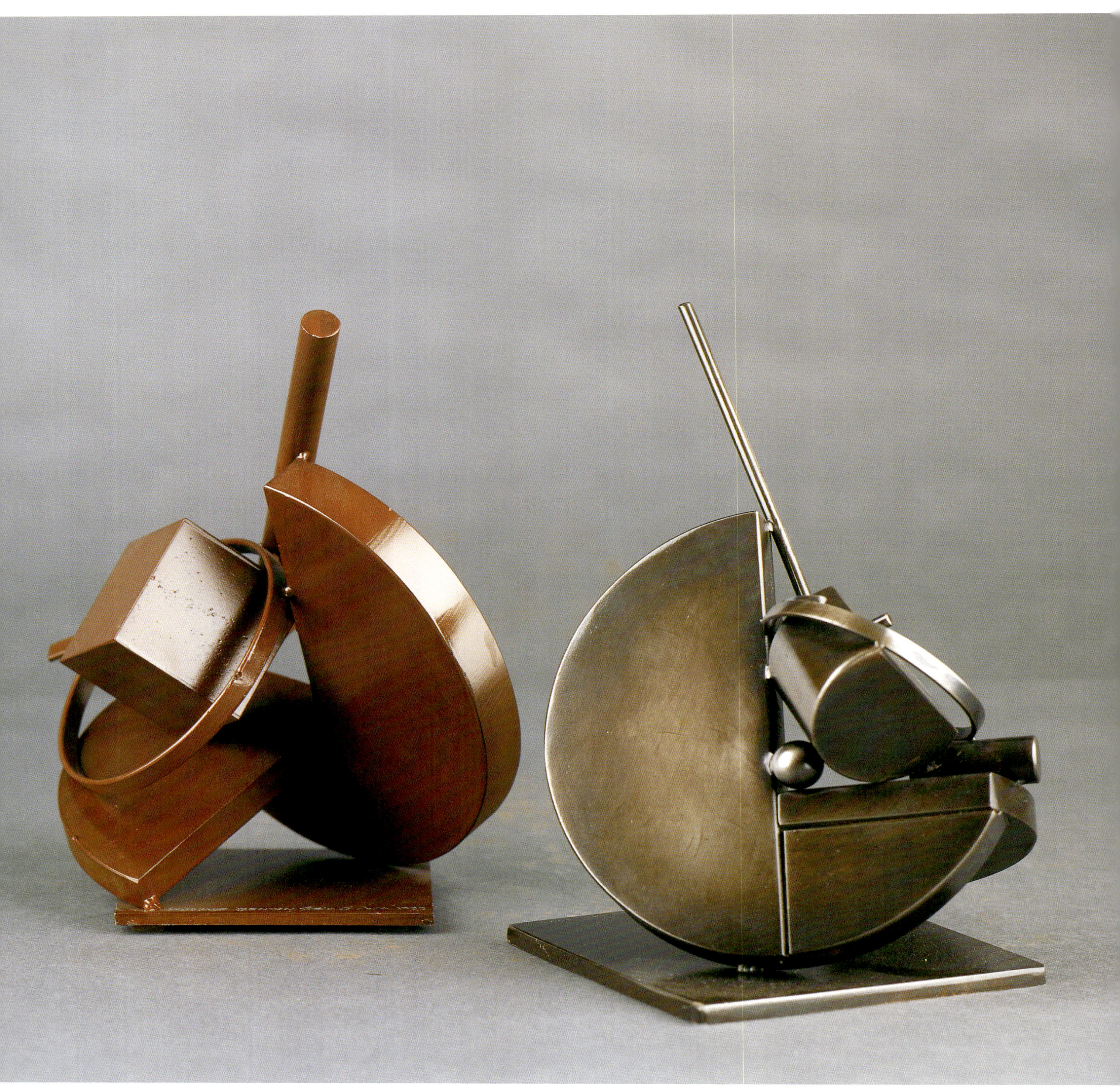

Folded Circle - maquette

2003, steel with patina
8½ x 5 x 6 inches
22 x 13 x 15 cm

Folded Circle - maquette

2004, steel with patina
8¼ x 6 x 6 inches
21x 15 x 15 cm

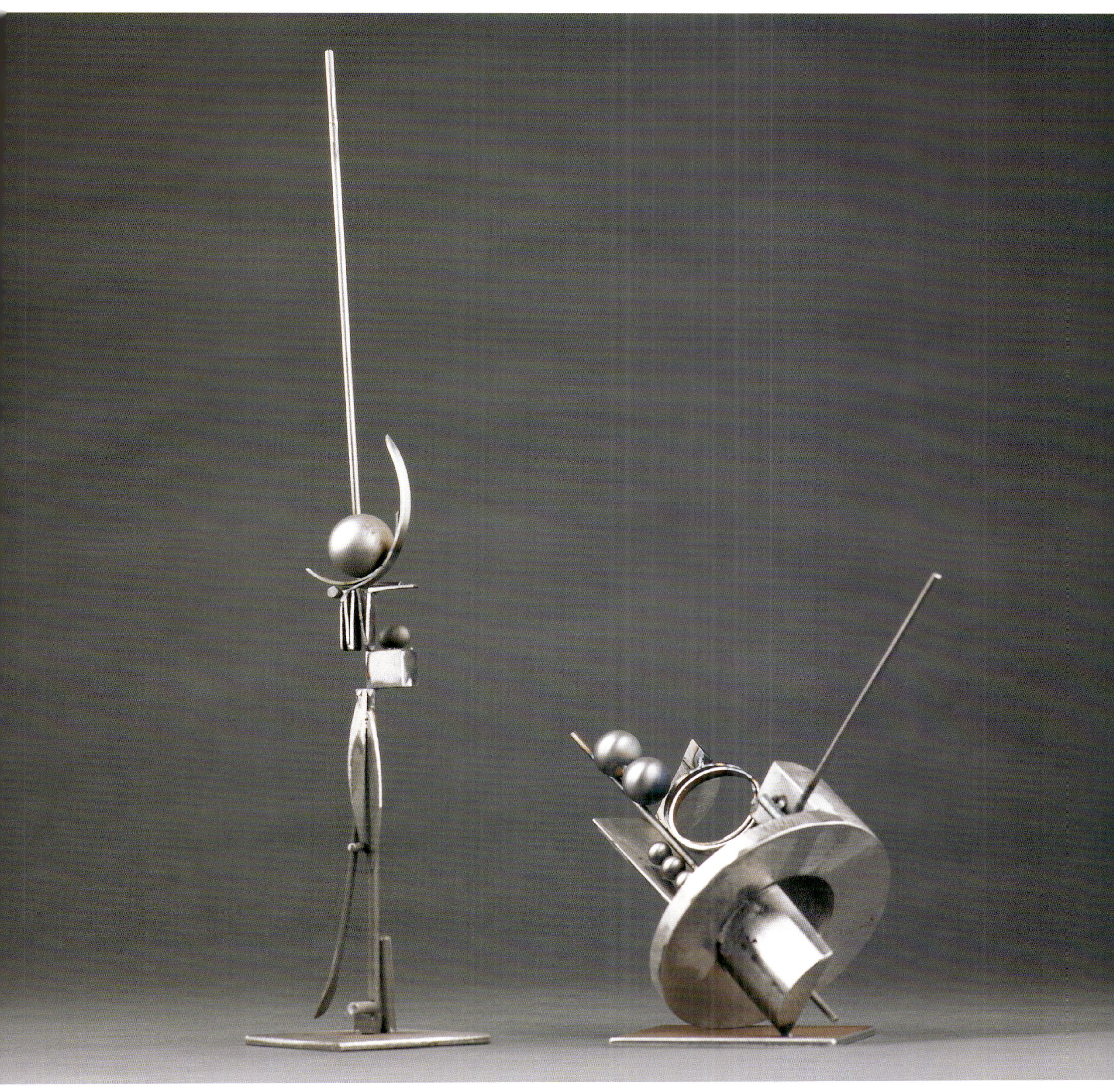

Straight-Up with Ball - maquette

2005, steel
17 x 3 x 3 inches
43 x 8 x 8 cm

Tilted Donut - maquette

2003, steel with patina
8½ x 6 x 6½ inches
22 x 15 x 17 cm

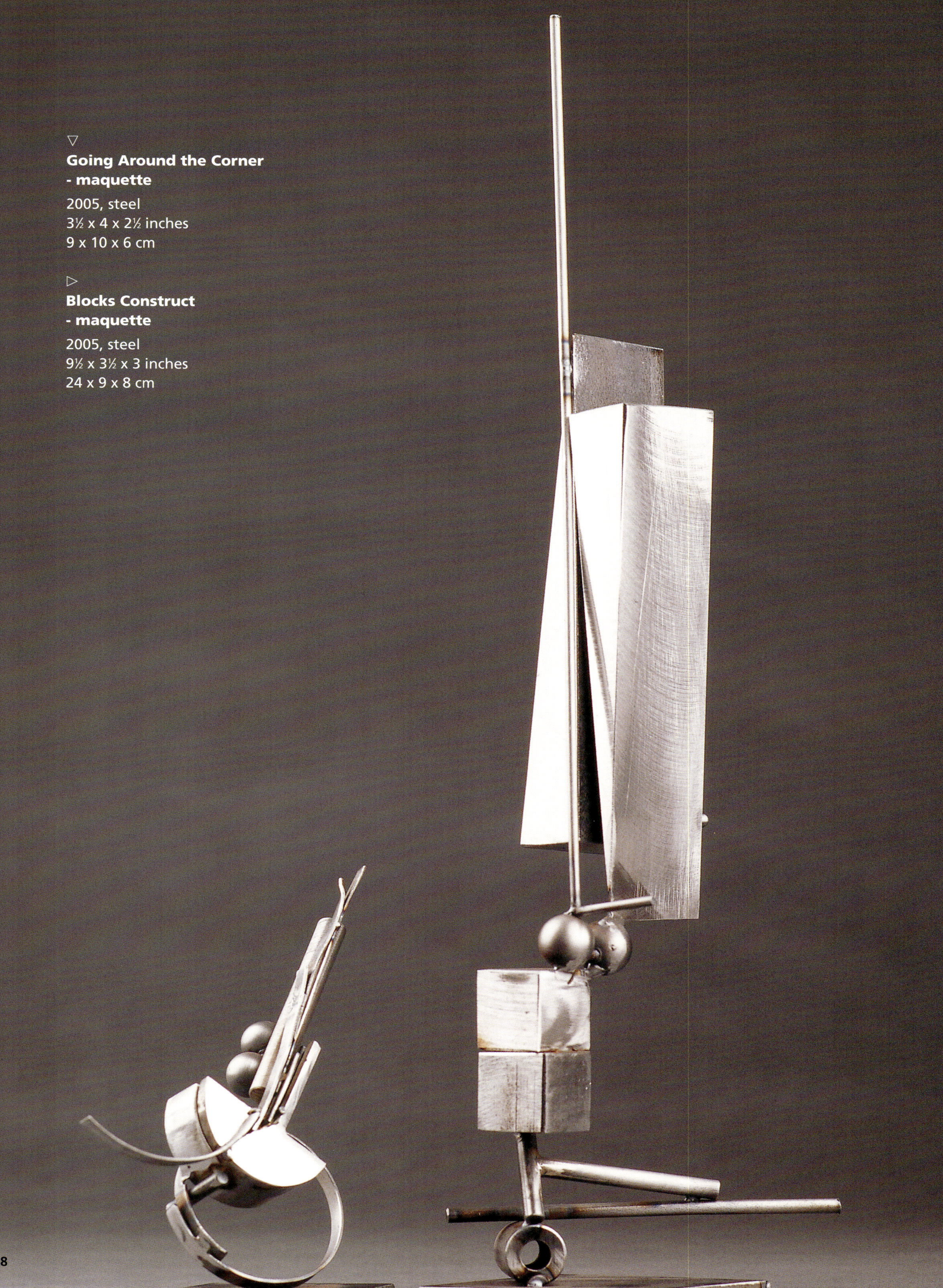

▽
Going Around the Corner - maquette
2005, steel
3½ x 4 x 2½ inches
9 x 10 x 6 cm

▷
Blocks Construct - maquette
2005, steel
9½ x 3½ x 3 inches
24 x 9 x 8 cm

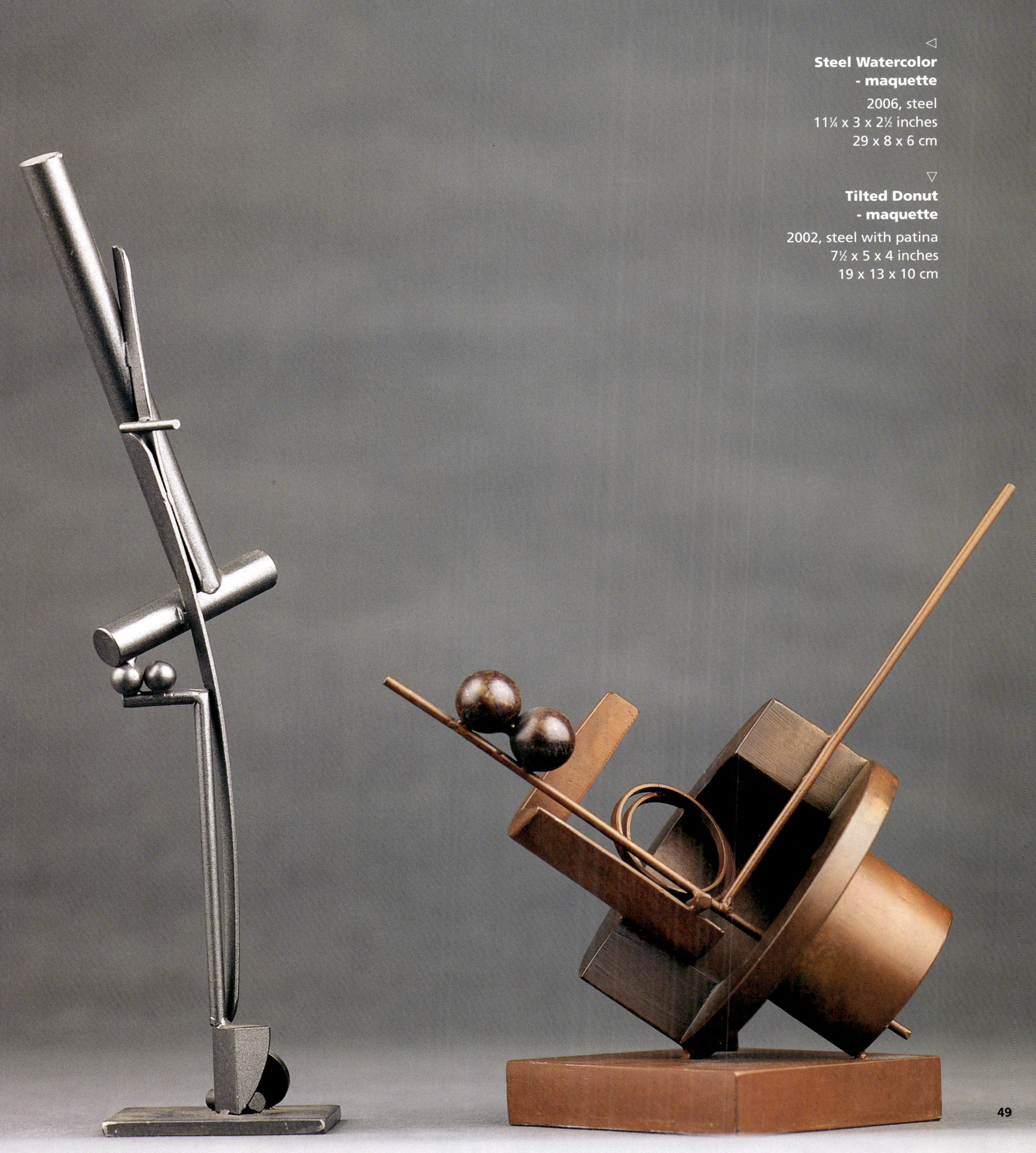

◁
Steel Watercolor - maquette
2006, steel
11¼ x 3 x 2½ inches
29 x 8 x 6 cm

▽
Tilted Donut - maquette
2002, steel with patina
7½ x 5 x 4 inches
19 x 13 x 10 cm

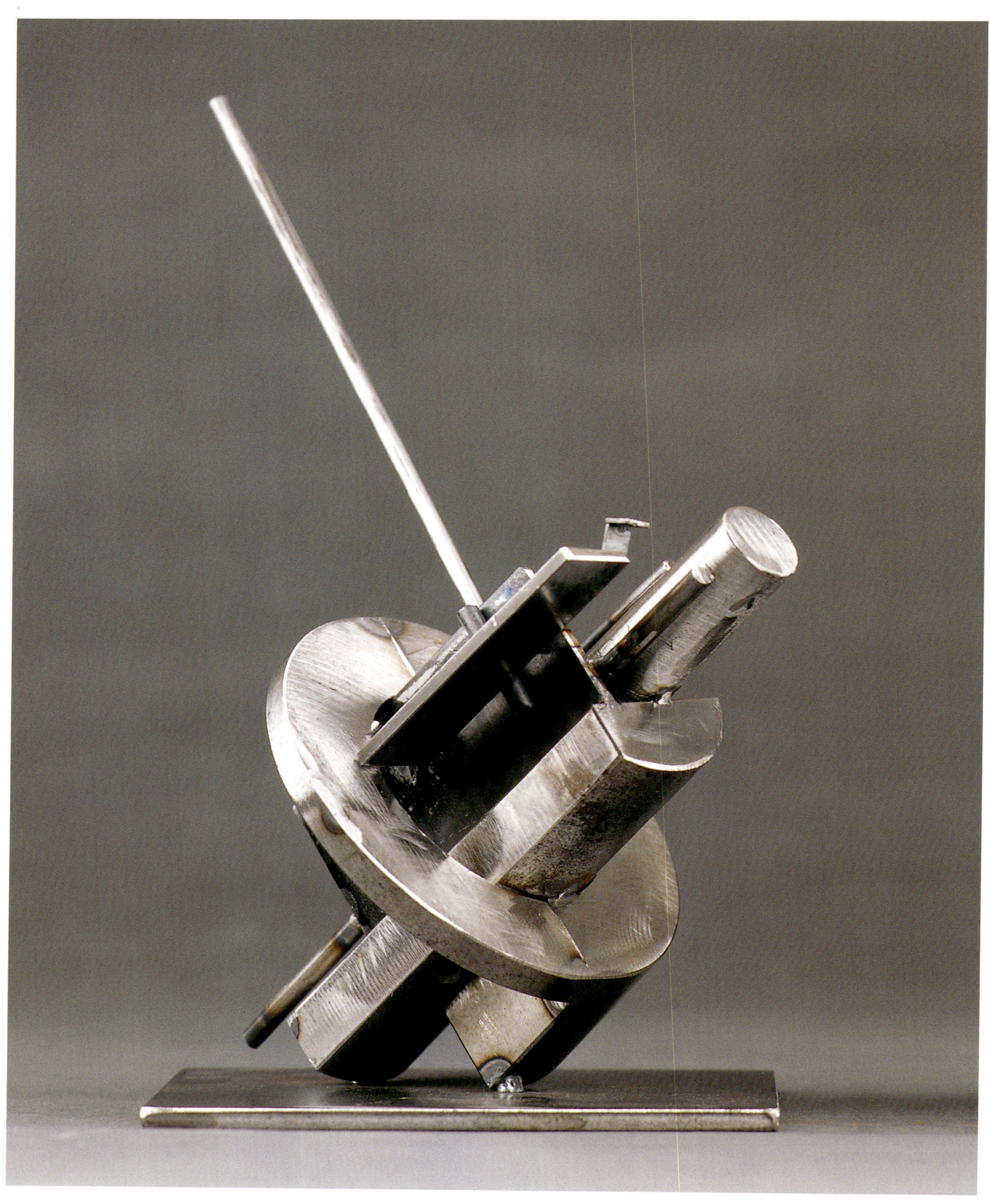

Tilted Donut - maquette

2005, steel
9 x 6 x 6 inches
23 x 15 x 15 cm

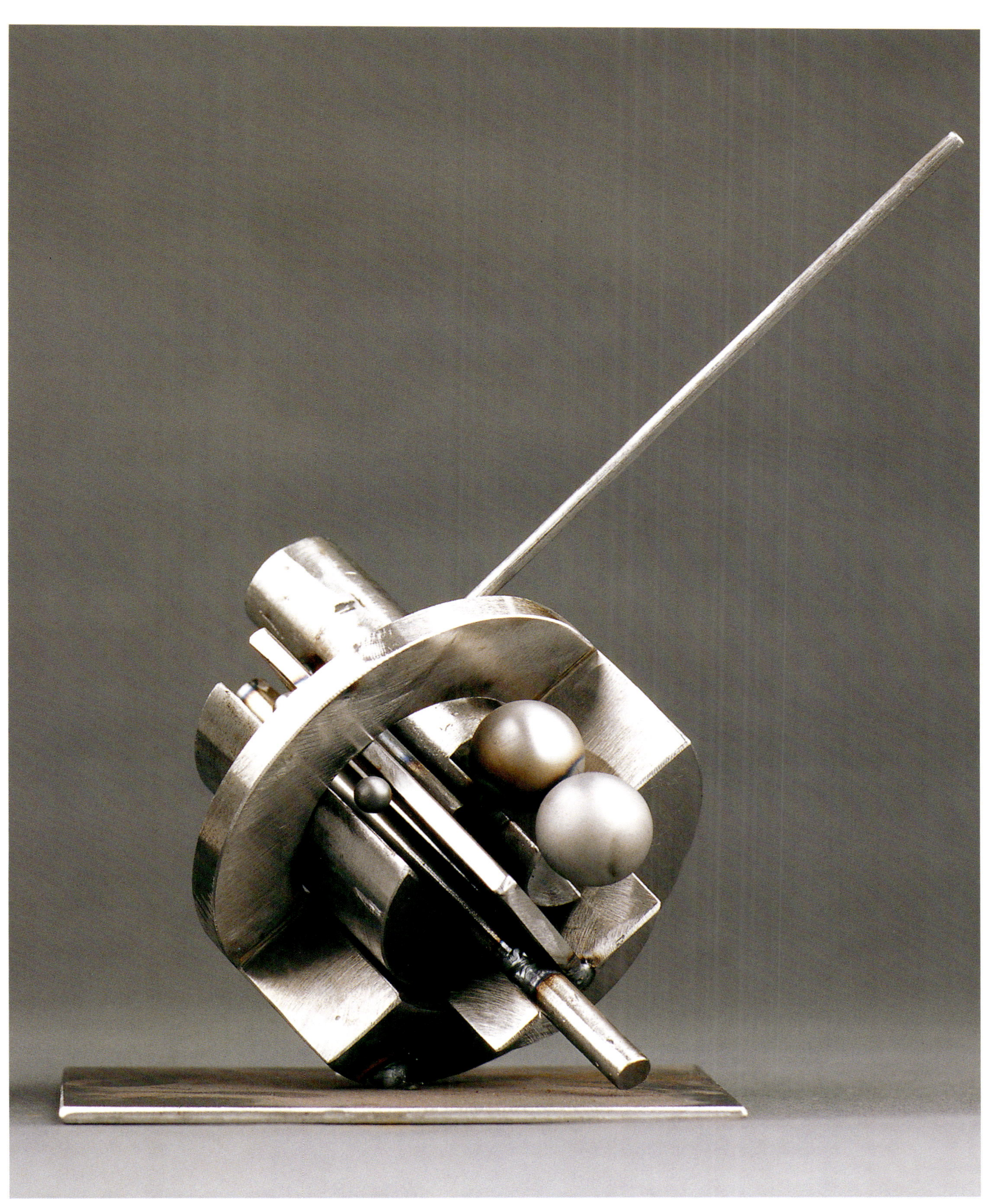

Tilted Donut - maquette

2005, steel
8½ x 8 x 6 inches
22 x 20 x 15 cm

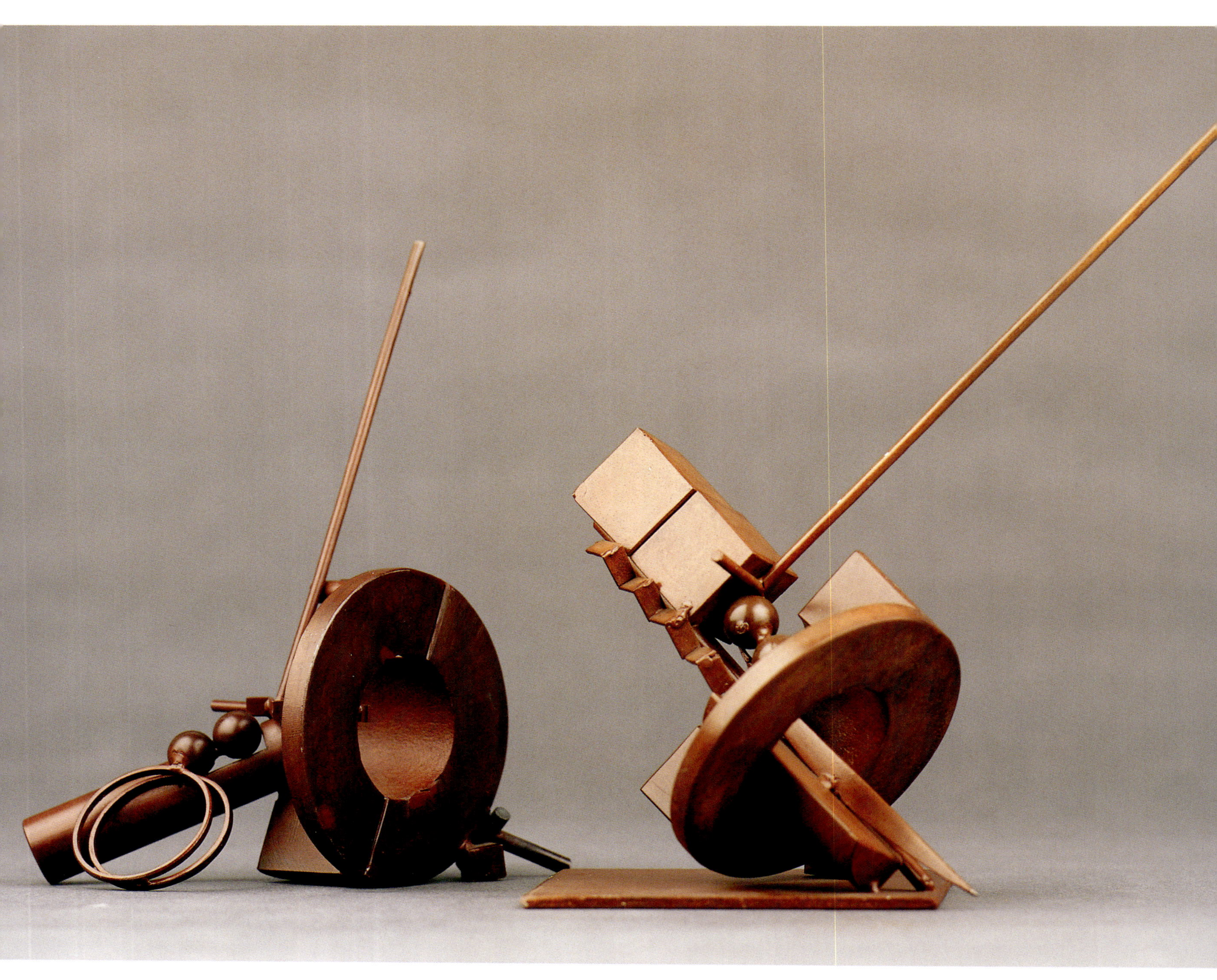

Donut - maquette

2001, steel with patina
7 x 5 x 4 inches
18 x 13 x 10 cm

Tilted Donut - maquette

2002, steel with patina
8½ x 6 x 4 inches
22 x 15 x 10 cm

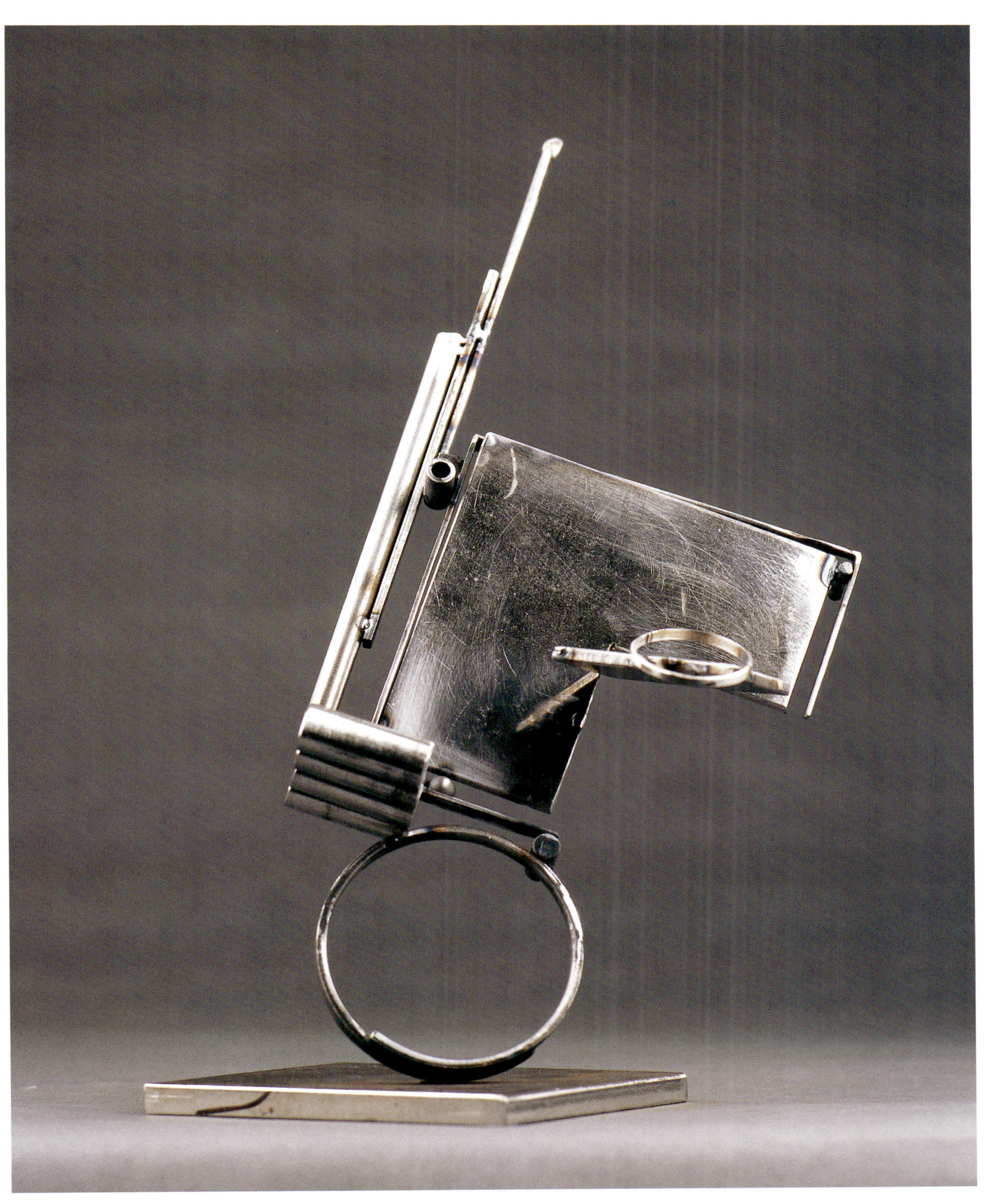

Going Around the Corner - maquette

2005, steel
13 x 6 x 6½ inches
33 x 15 x 17 cm

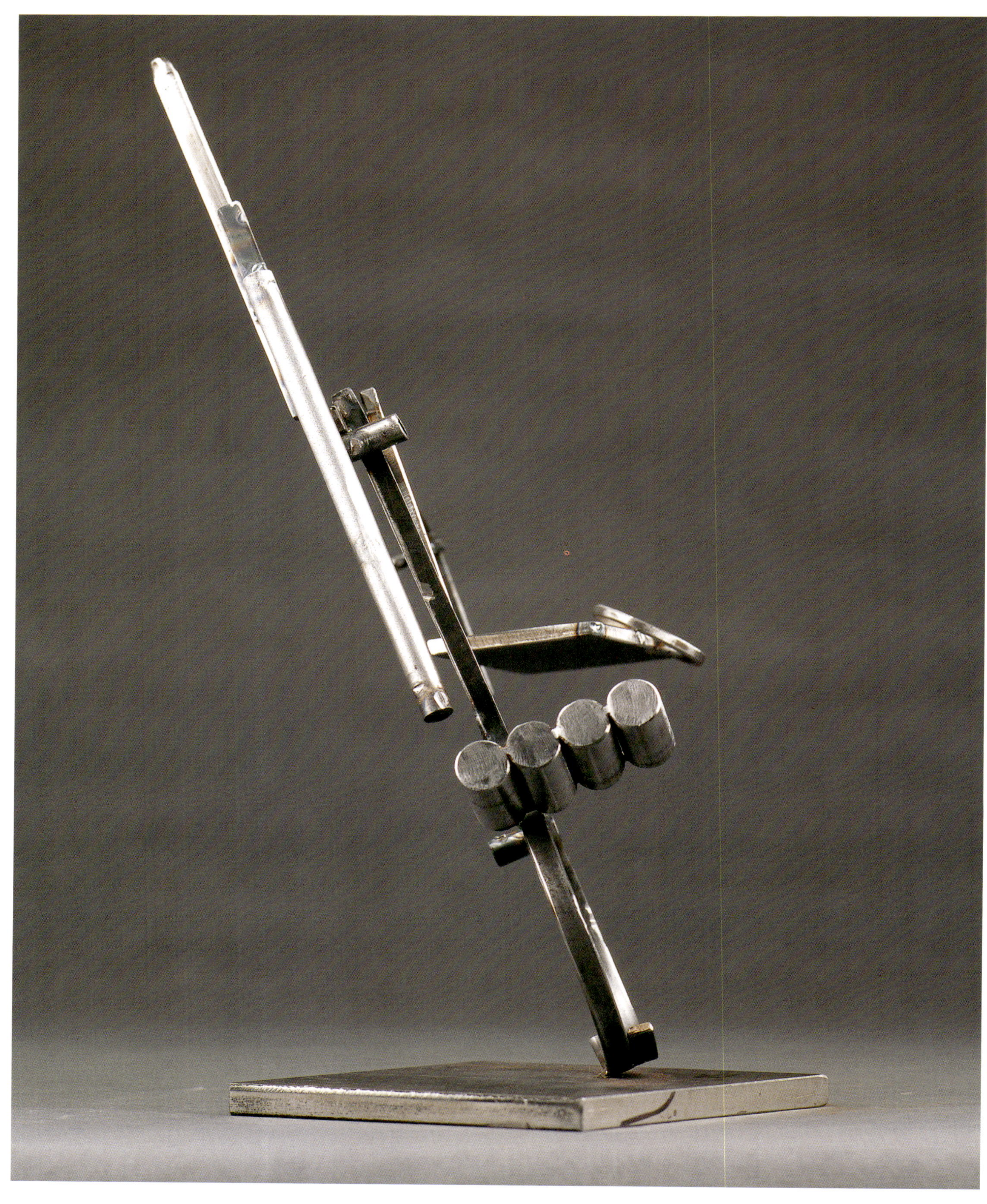

Going Around the Corner - maquette

2005, steel
13 x 6 x 6½ inches
33 x 15 x 17 cm

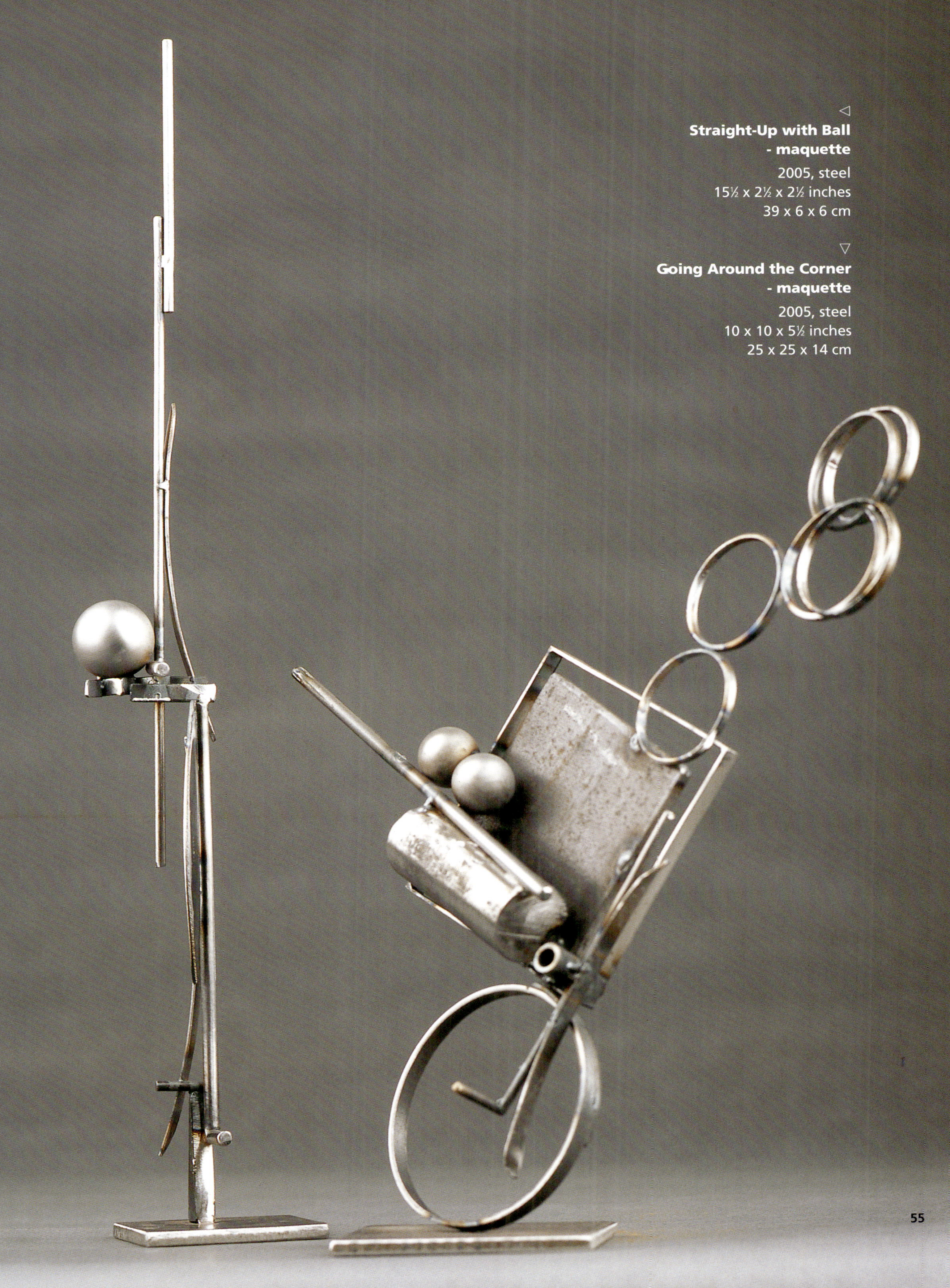

◁
Straight-Up with Ball - maquette
2005, steel
15½ x 2½ x 2½ inches
39 x 6 x 6 cm

▽
Going Around the Corner - maquette
2005, steel
10 x 10 x 5½ inches
25 x 25 x 14 cm

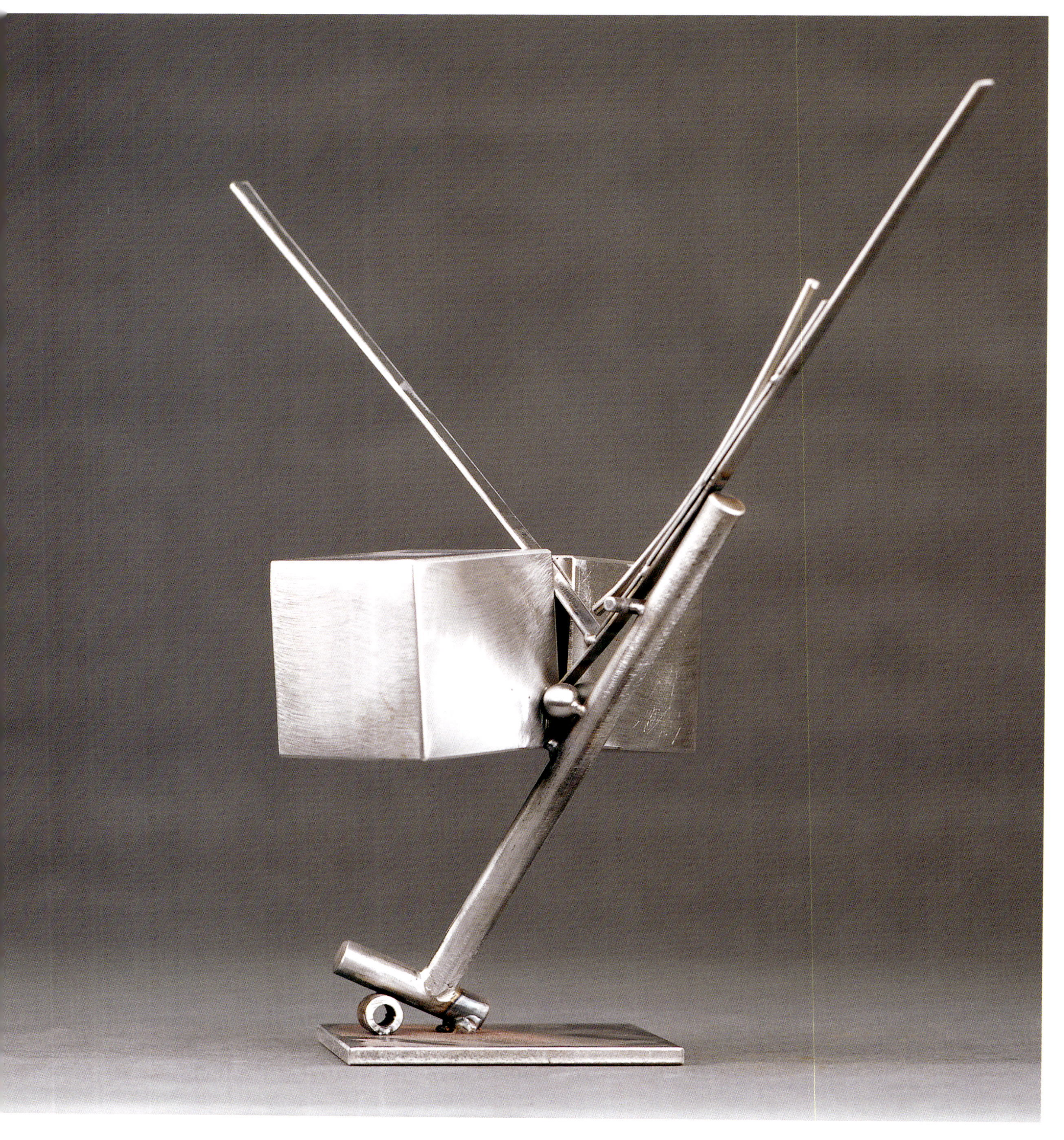

It Is Harder To Do with Balls, T - maquette

2006, steel
22 x 13 x 13 inches
56 x 33 x 33 cm

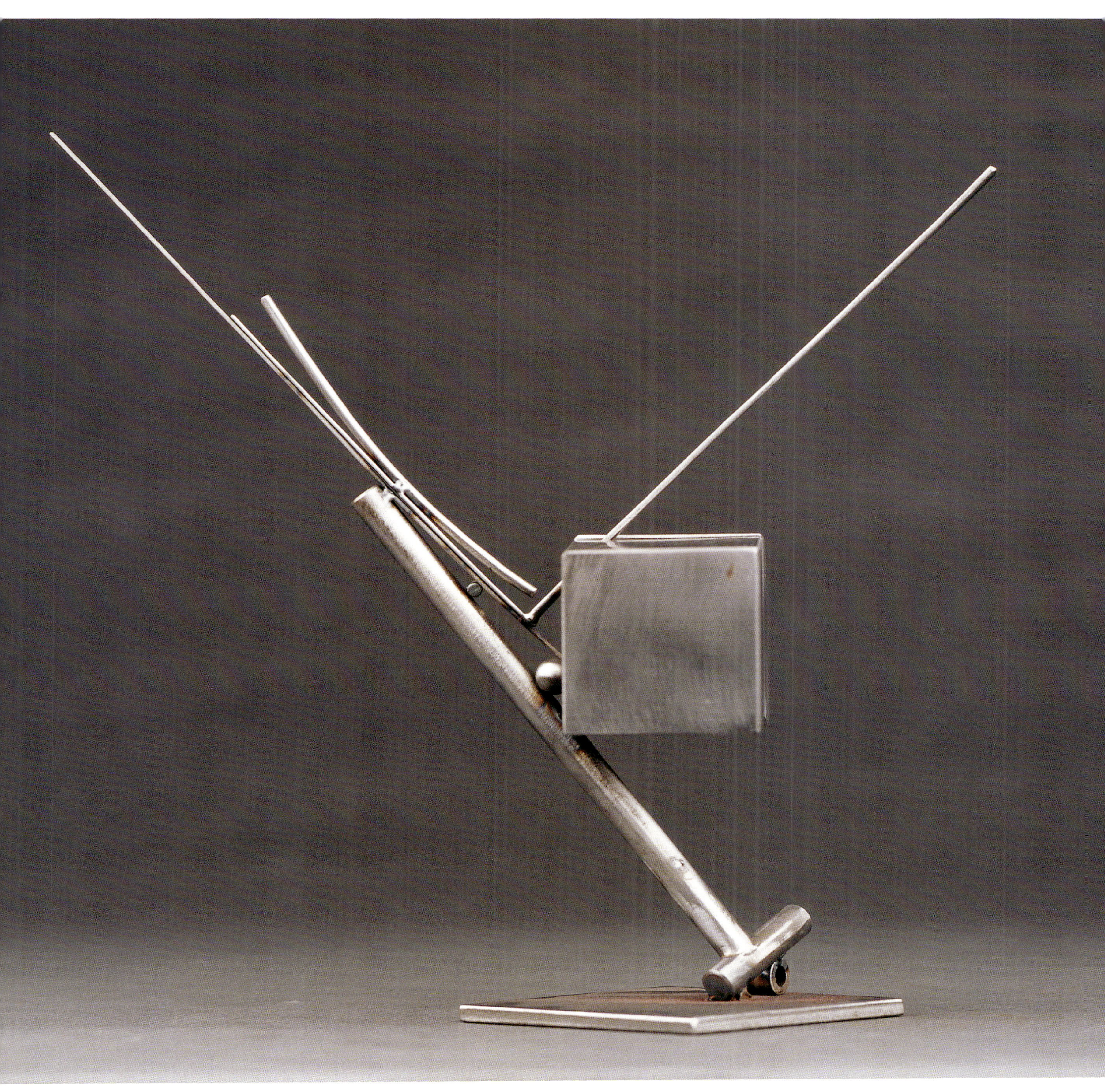

It Is Harder To Do with Balls, T - maquette

2006, steel
22 x 13 x 13 inches
56 x 33 x 33 cm

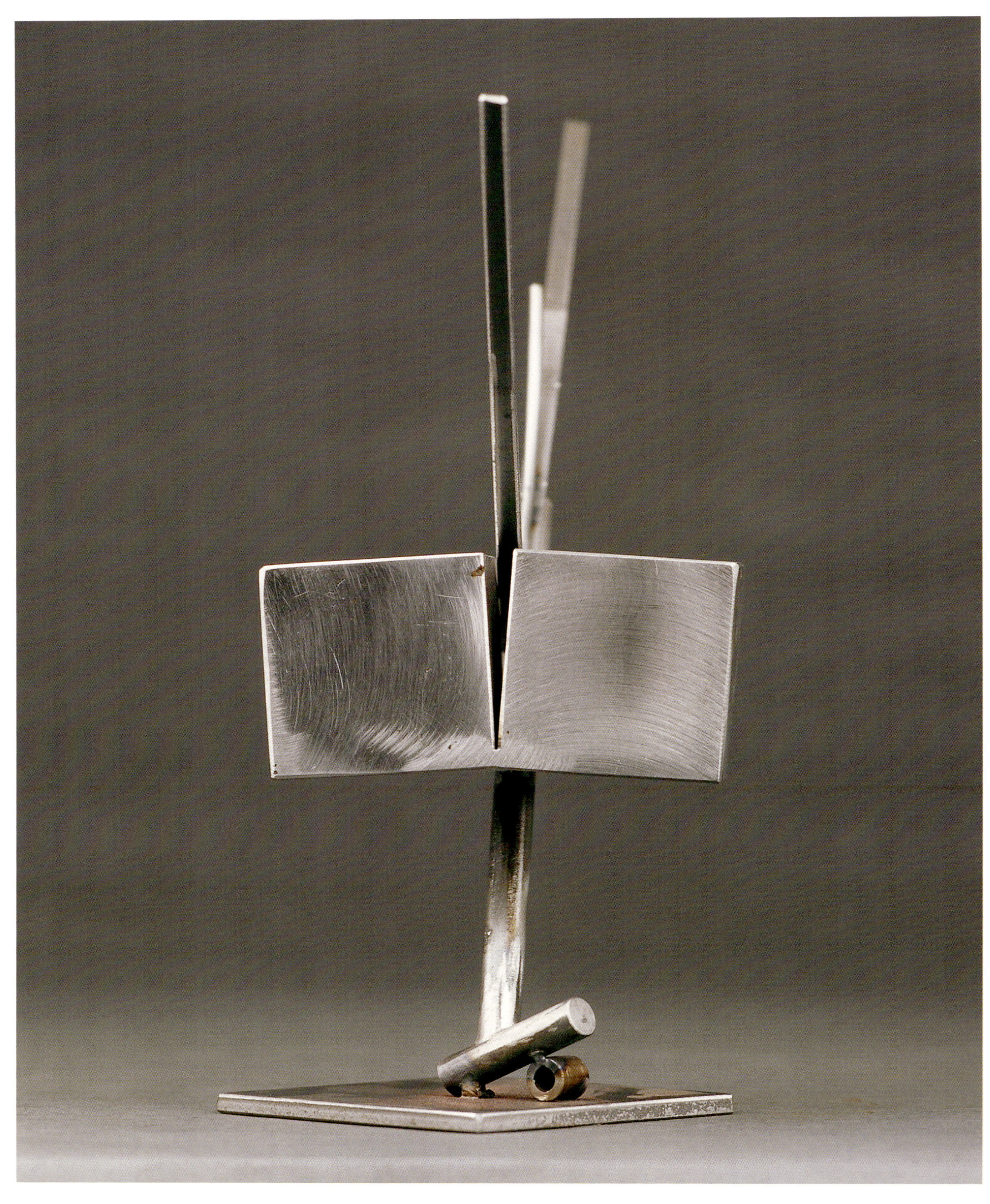

It Is Harder To Do with Balls, T - maquette

2006, steel
22 x 13 x 13 inches
56 x 33 x 33 cm

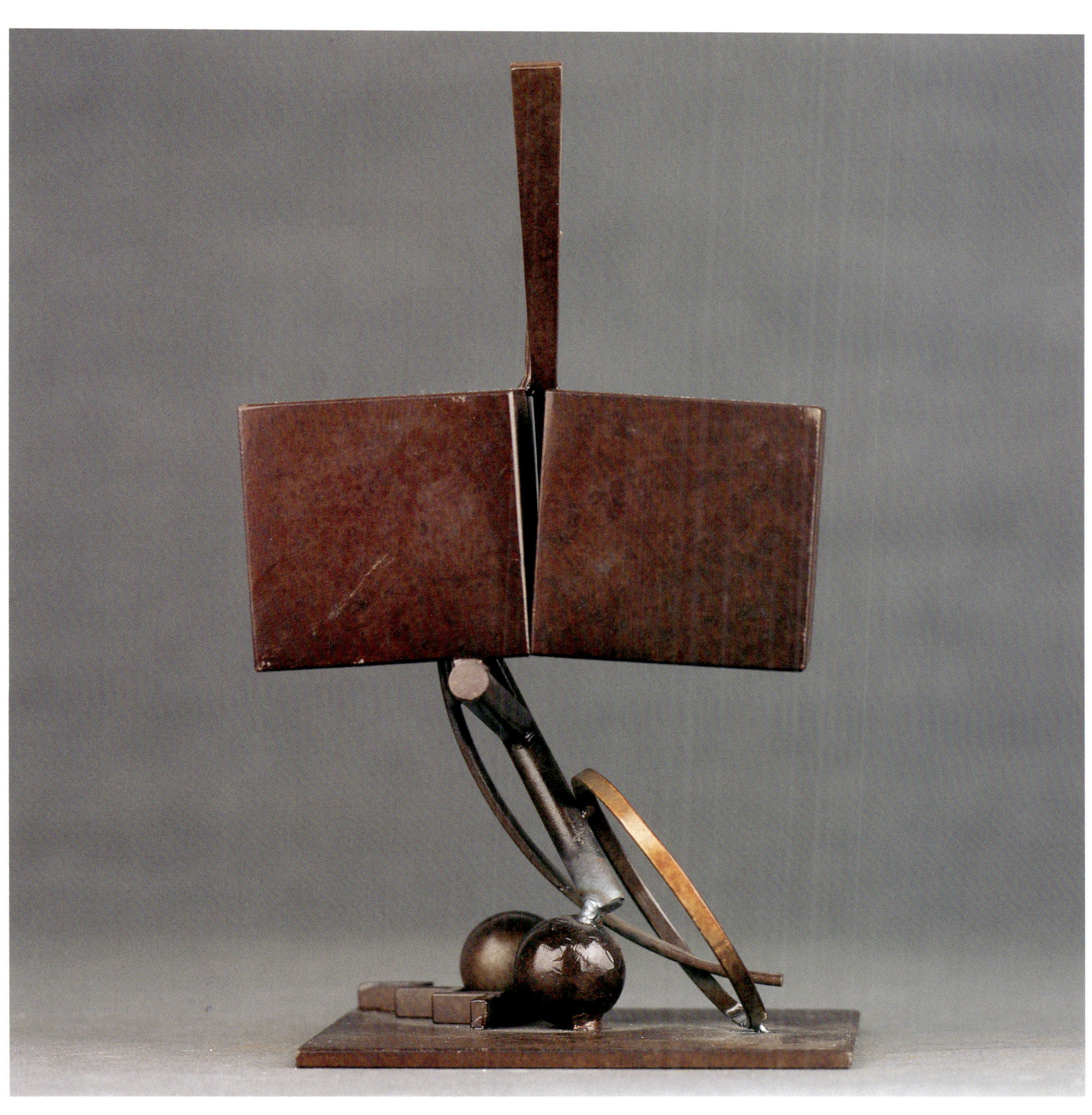

It Is Harder To Do with Balls - maquette

1999, steel with patina
9½ x 5 x 5 inches
24 x 13 x 13 cm

Dynamic Rhythms Orange, Phase III

2004, graphite on watercolor paper
7 x 7 inches
18 x 18 cm

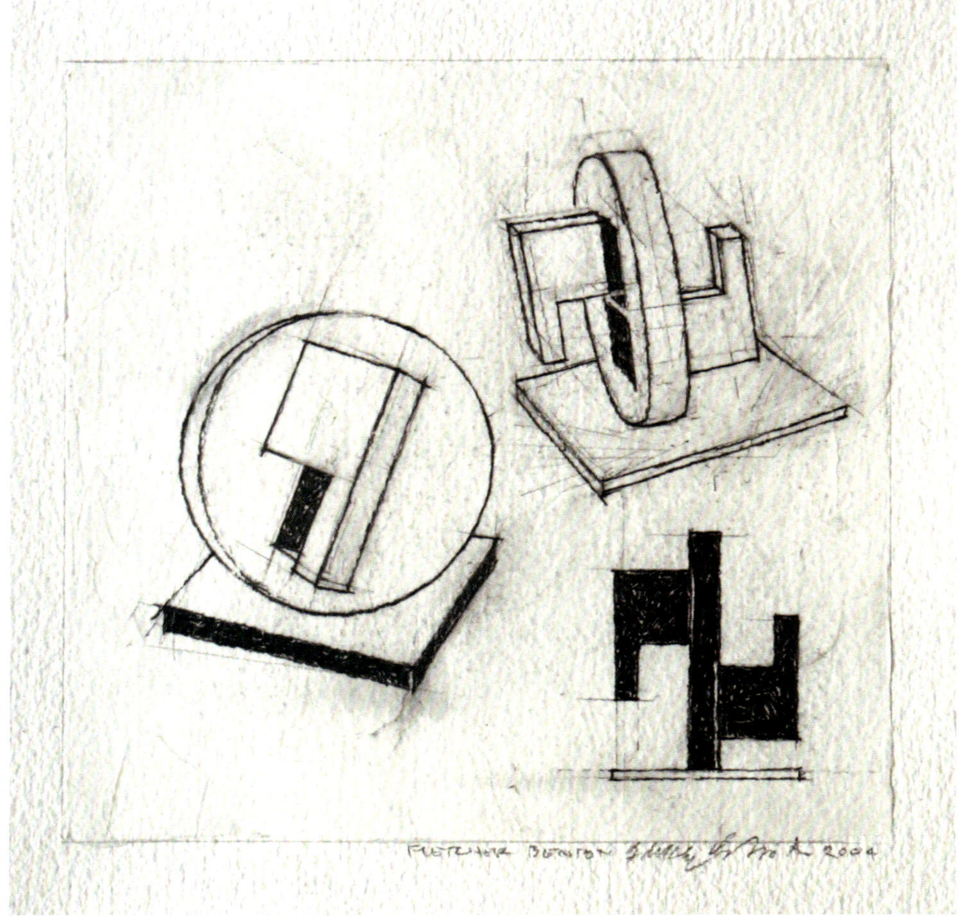

Balanced/Unbalanced: Four Squares

2004, graphite on watercolor paper
7 x 7 inches
18 x 18 cm

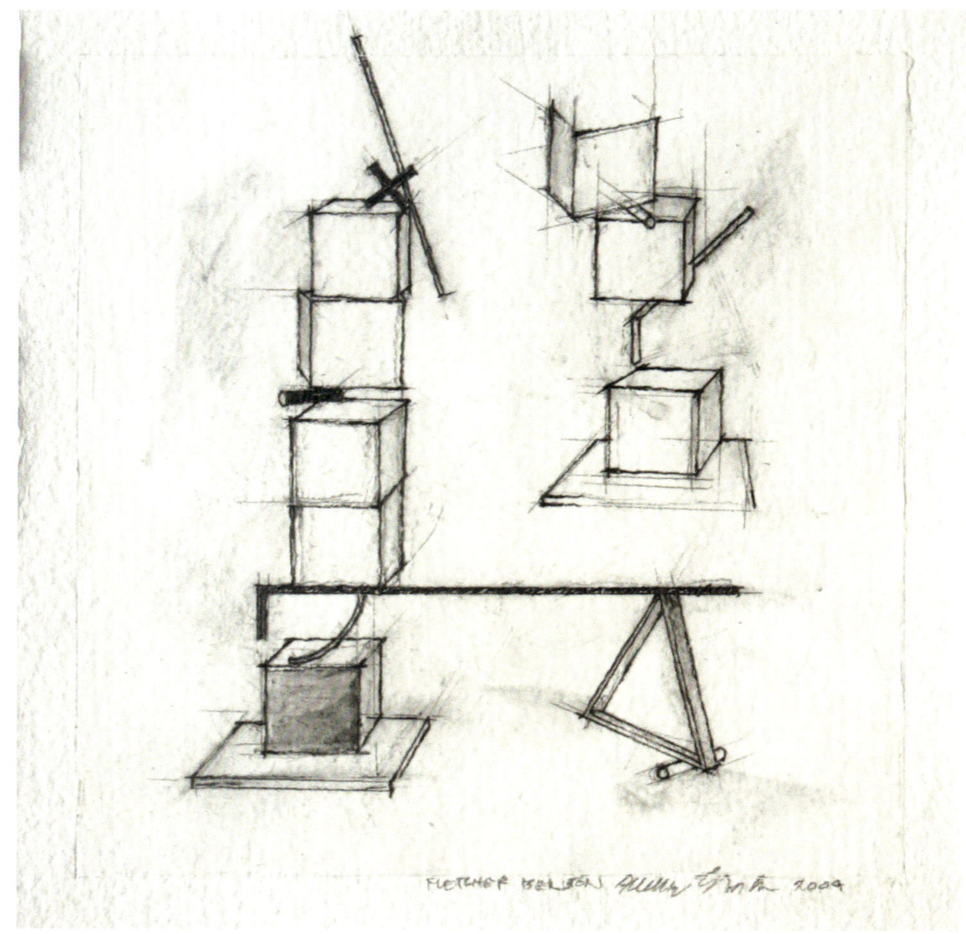

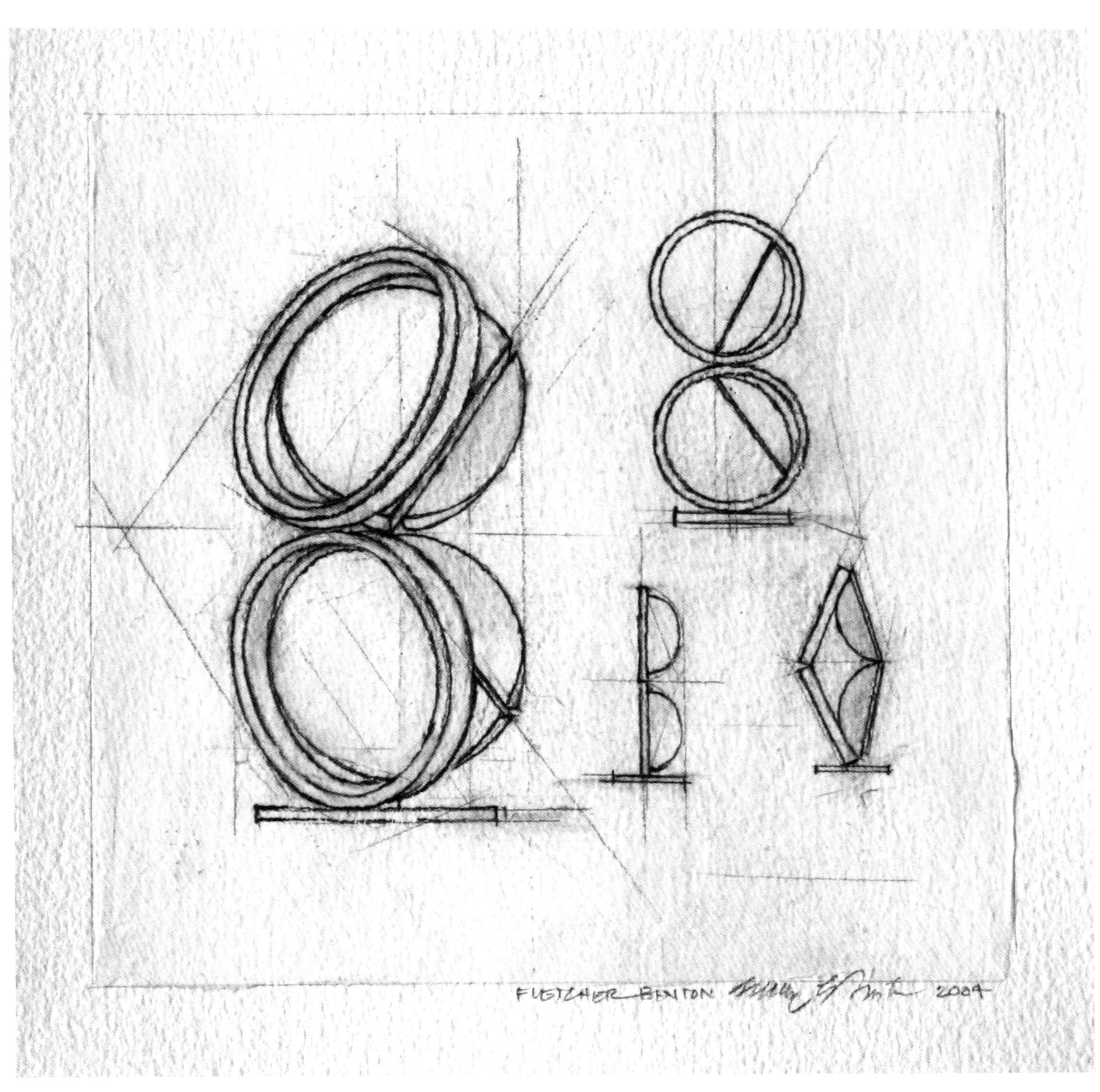

Double Folded Circle Ring 5

2004, graphite on watercolor paper
7 x 7 inches
18 x 18 cm

Wheels I

2004, graphite on watercolor paper
7 x 7 inches
18 x 18 cm

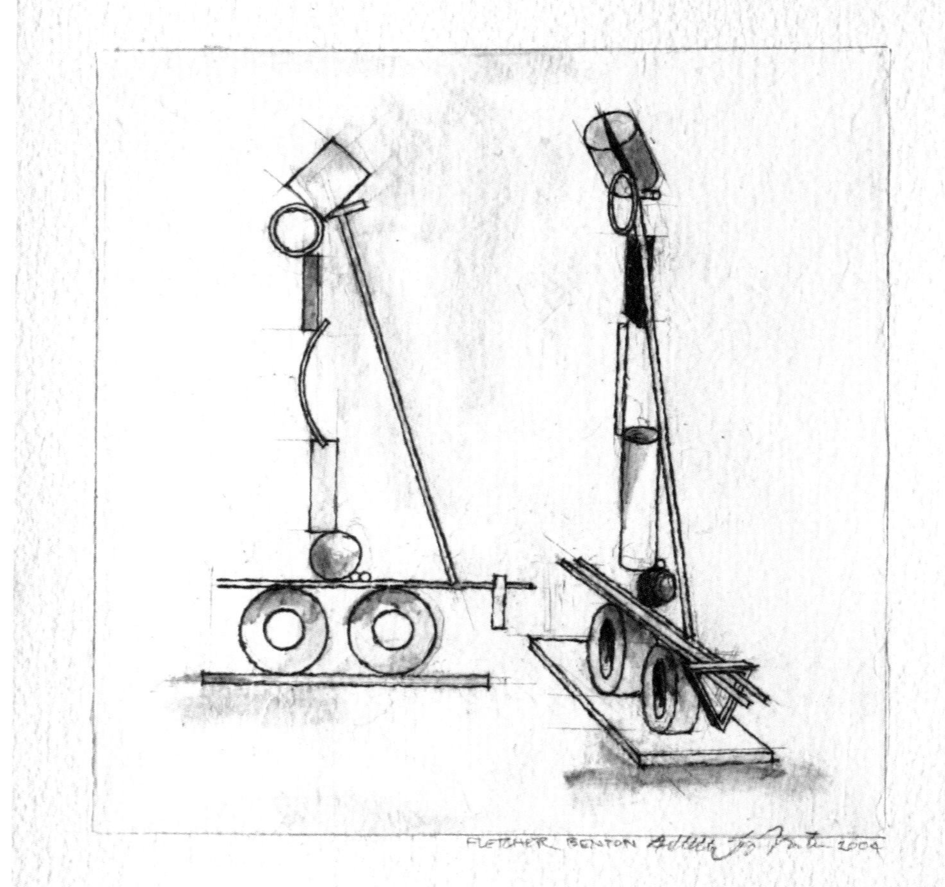

Balanced/Unbalanced: Wedge/Arc

2004, graphite on watercolor paper
7 x 7 inches
18 x 18 cm

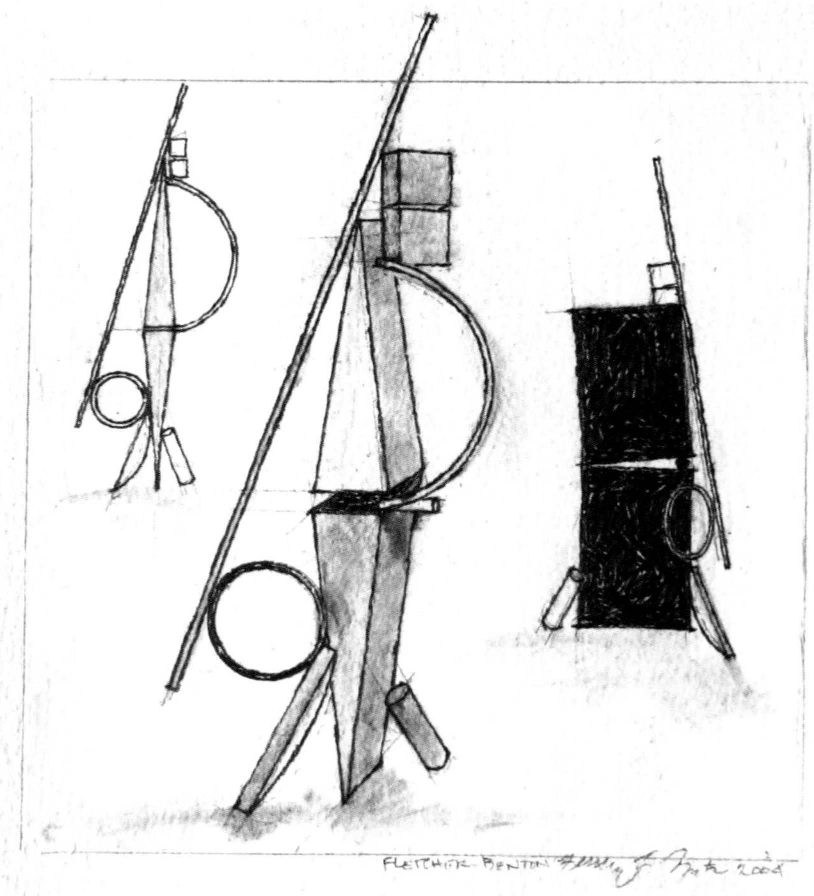

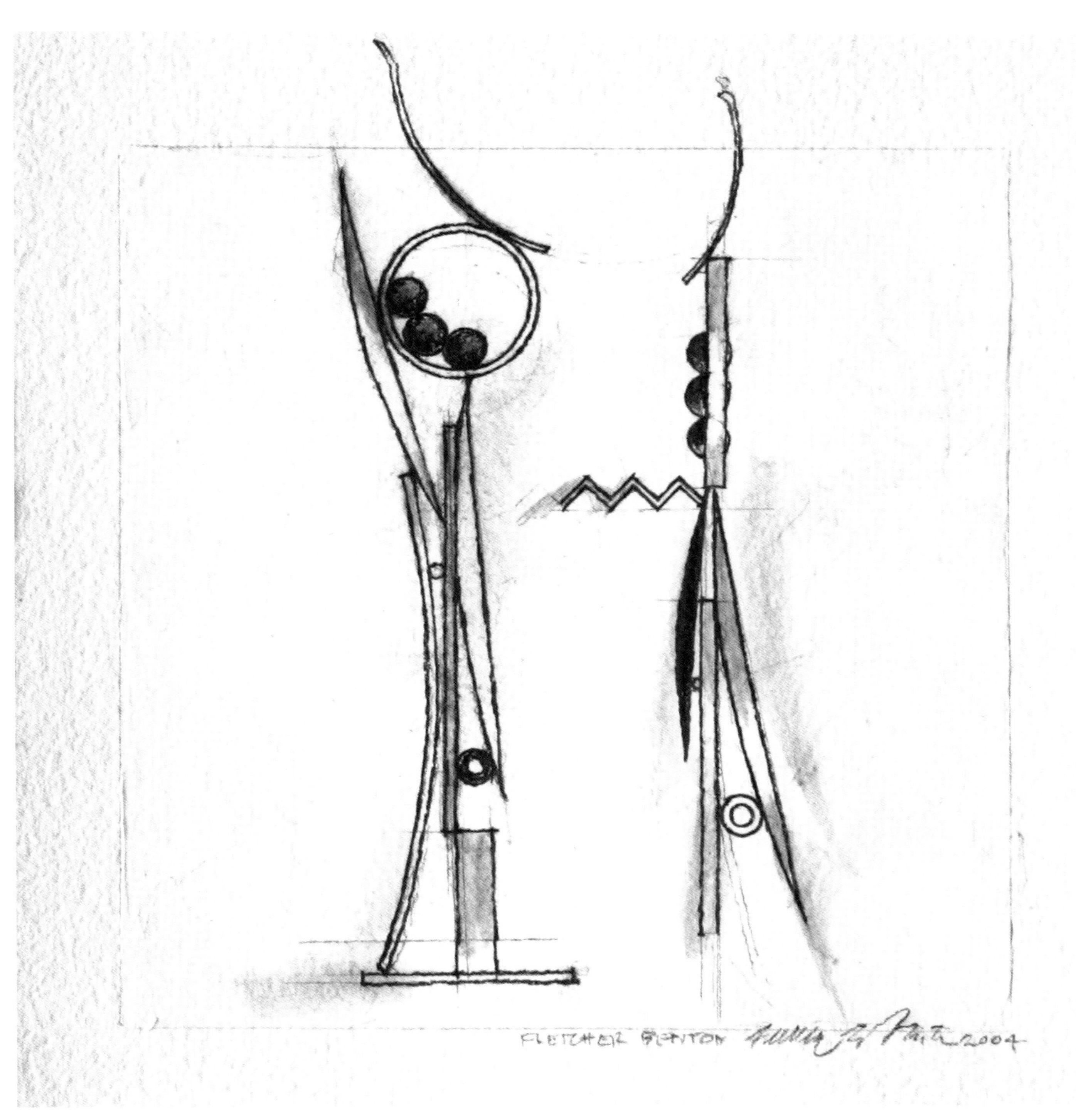

Steel Watercolor 77

2004, graphite on watercolor paper
7 x 7 inches
18 x 18 cm

Balanced/Unbalanced: F

2004, graphite on watercolor paper
7 x 7 inches
18 x 18 cm

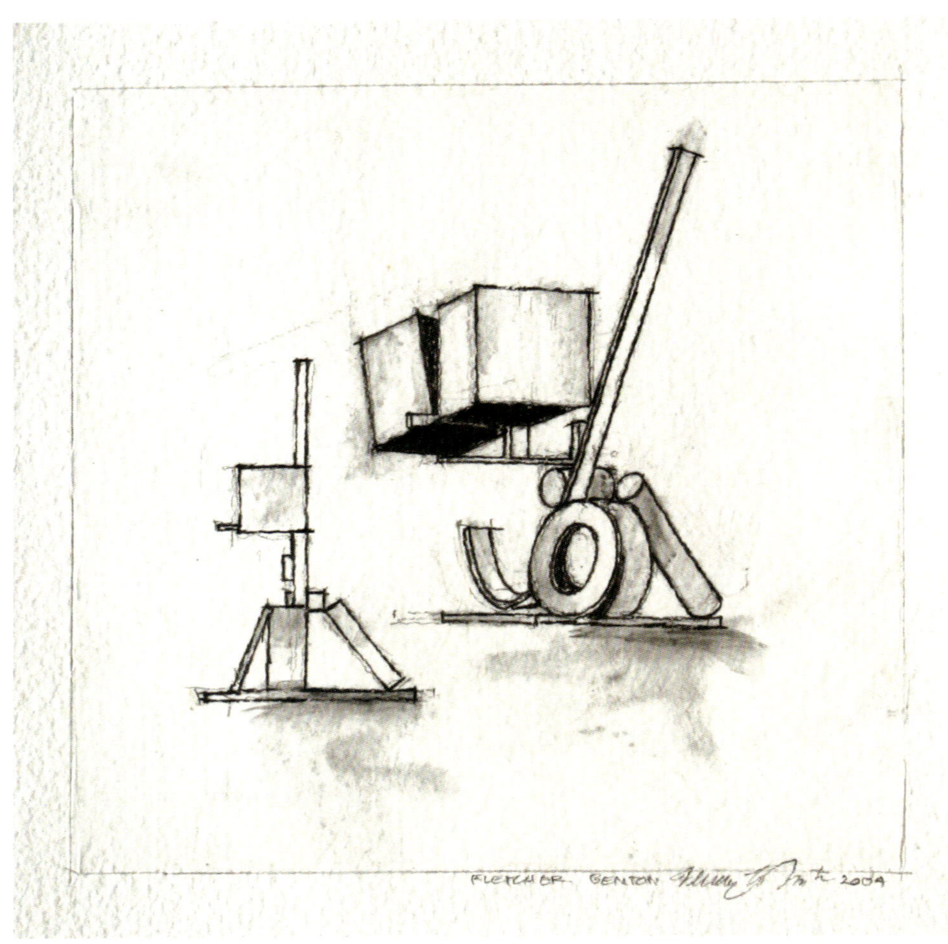

Folded Circle Ring Column

2004, graphite on watercolor paper
7 x 7 inches
18 x 18 cm

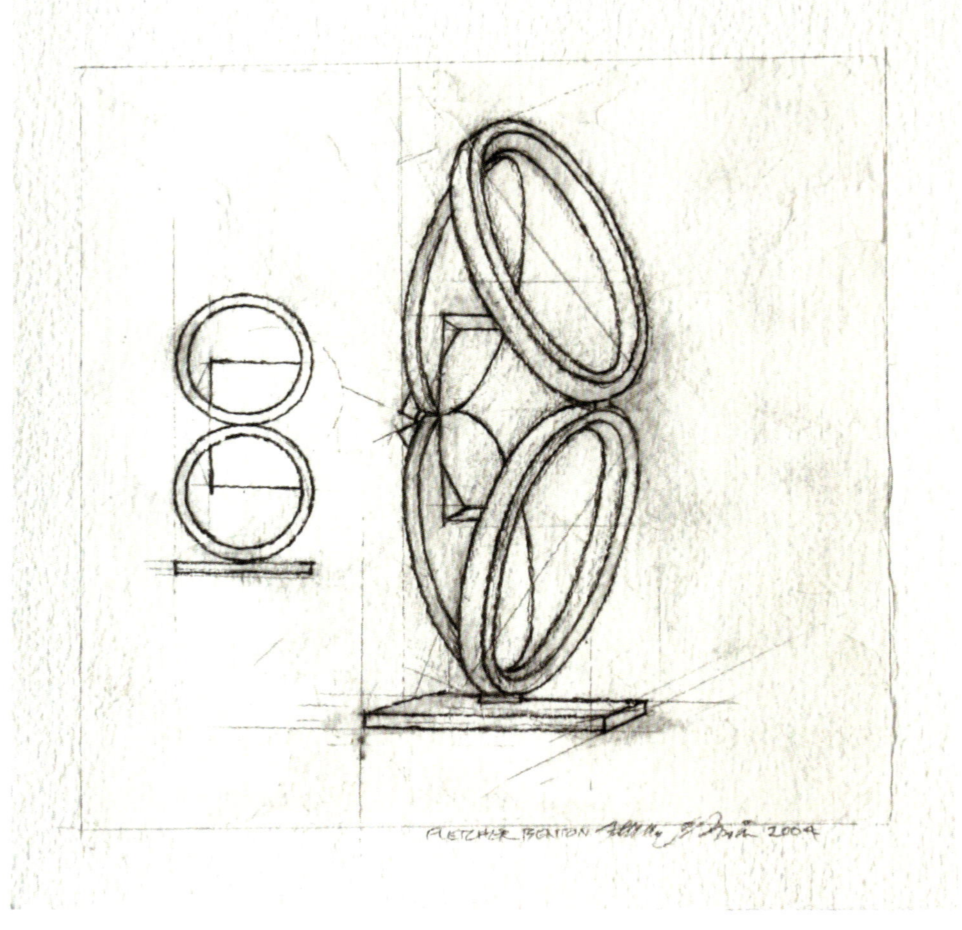

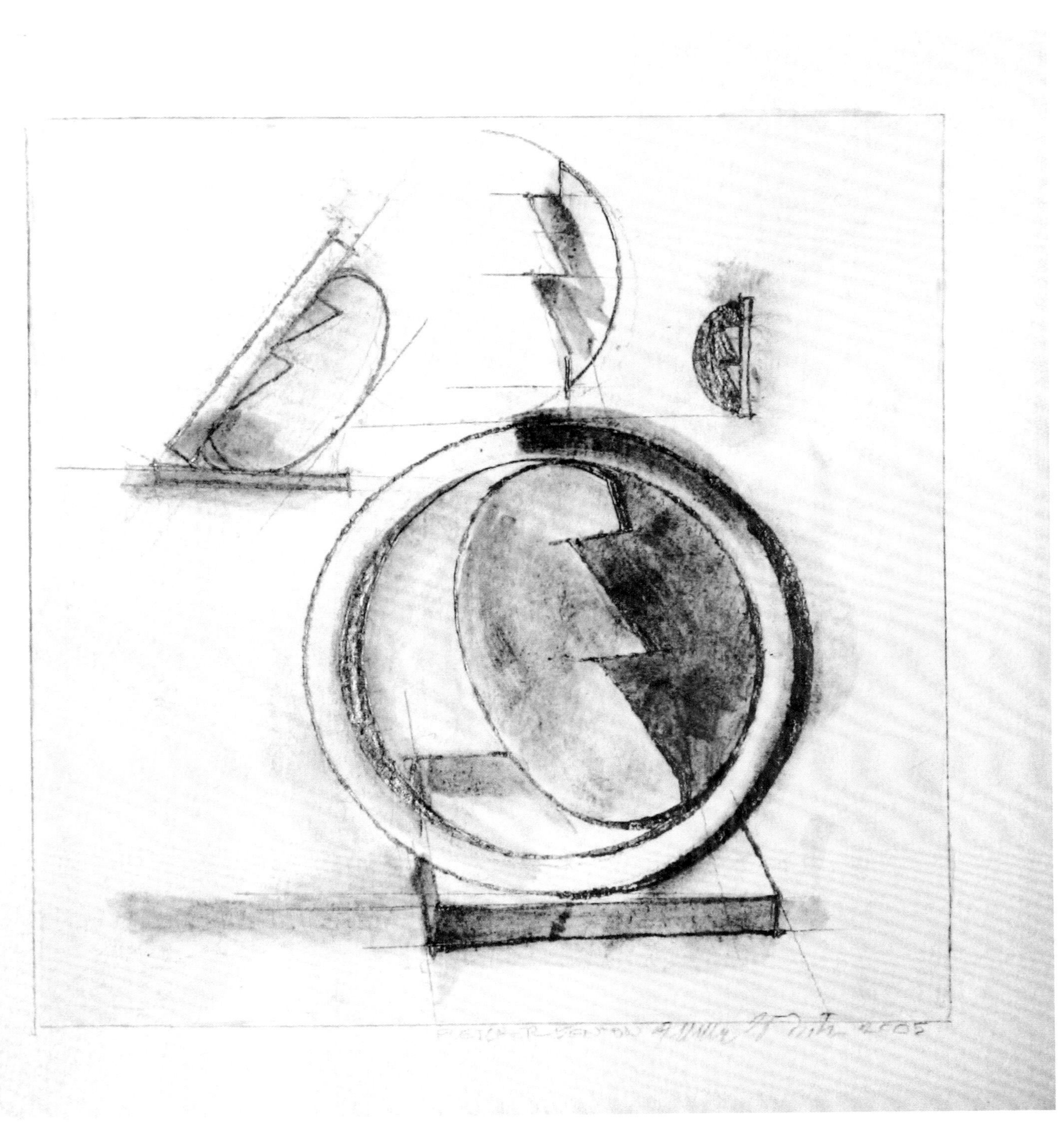

Folded Circle Ring 5

2005, graphite on watercolor paper
7 x 7 inches
18 x 18 cm

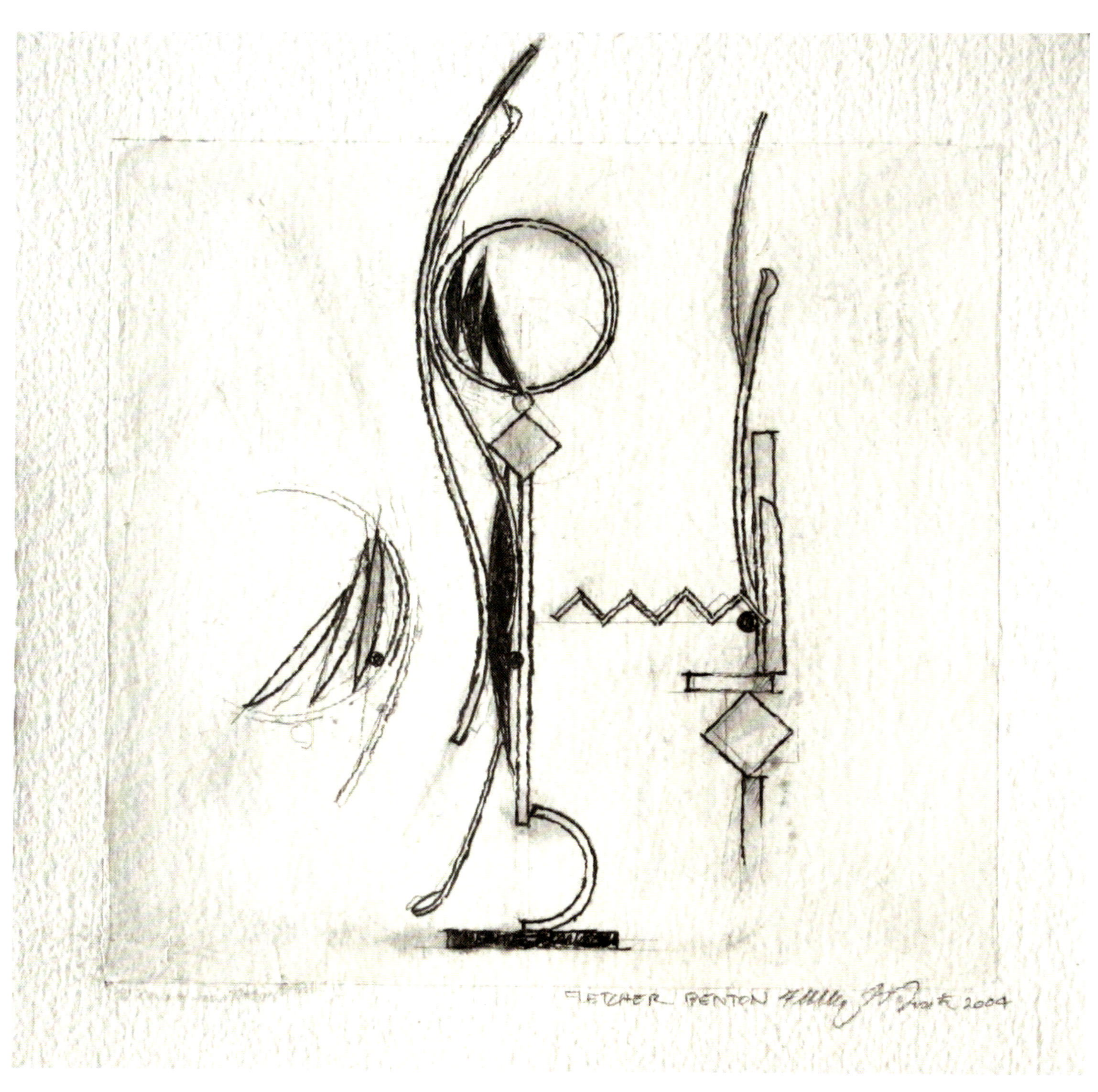

Steel Watercolor: Yellow Lilly

2004, graphite on watercolor paper
7 x 7 inches
18 x 18 cm

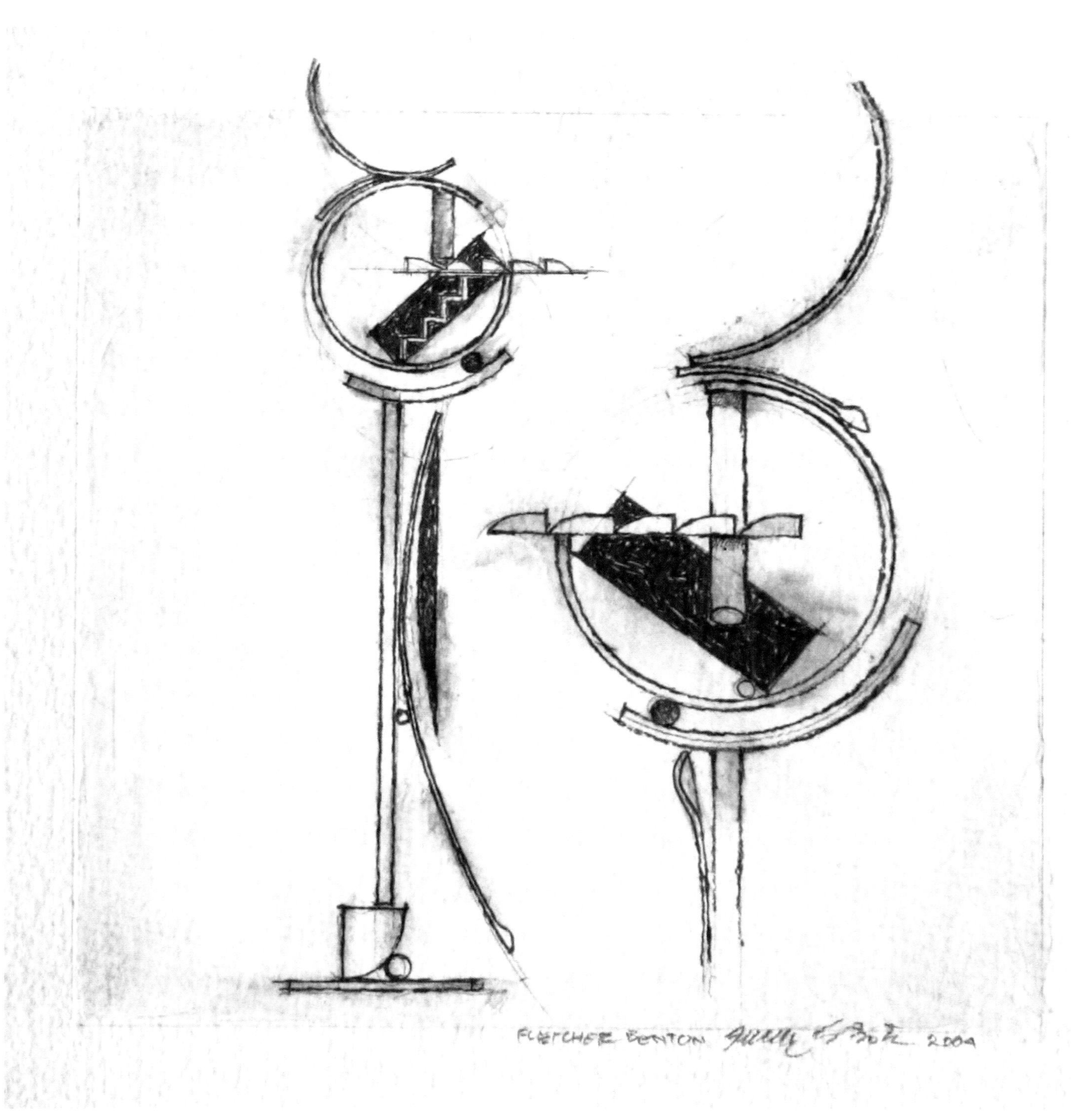

Steel Watercolor: Indian 15

2004, graphite on watercolor paper
7 x 7 inches
18 x 18 cm

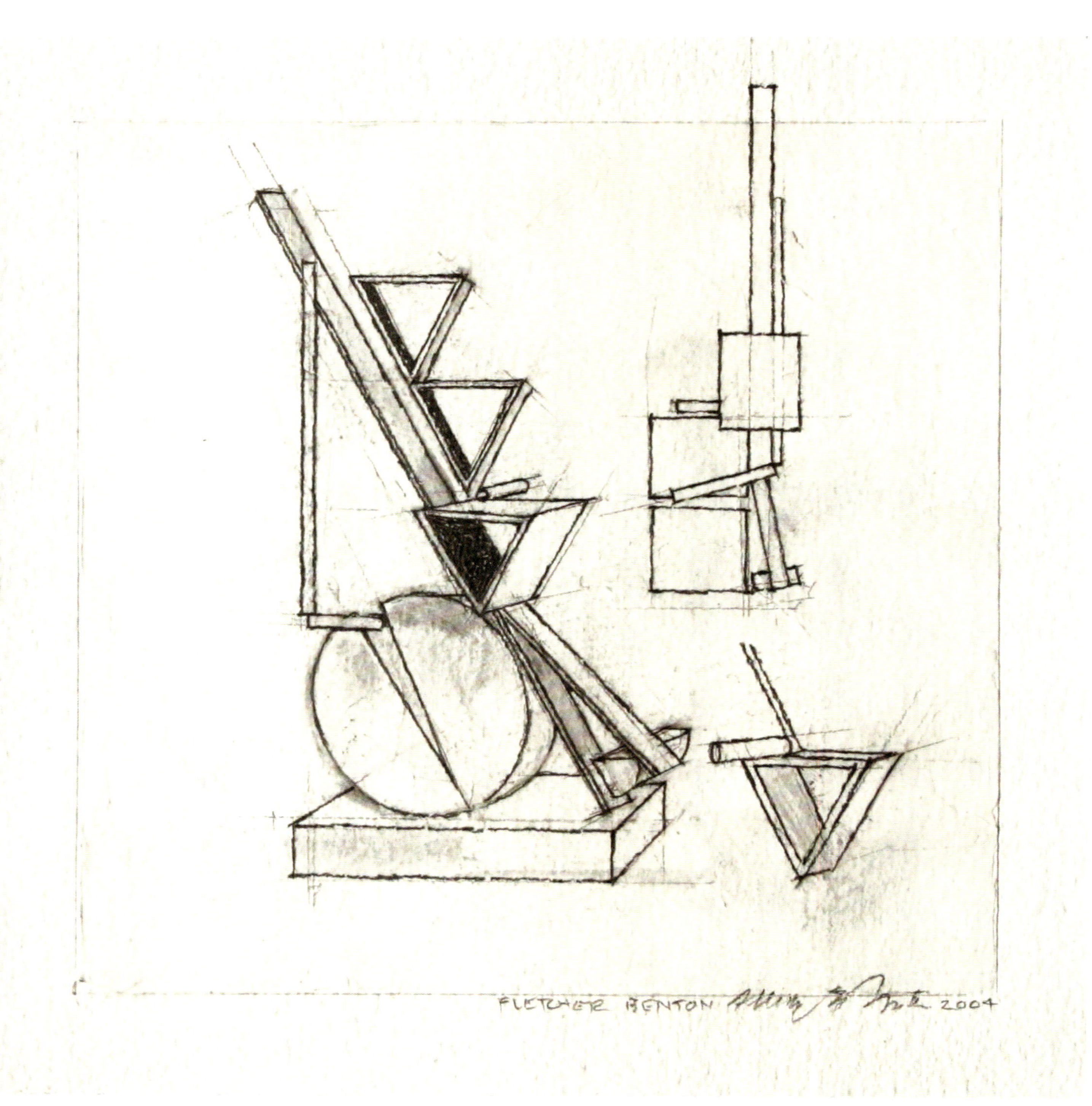

Balanced/Unbalanced: Three Triangles

2004, graphite on watercolor paper
7 x 7 inches
18 x 18 cm

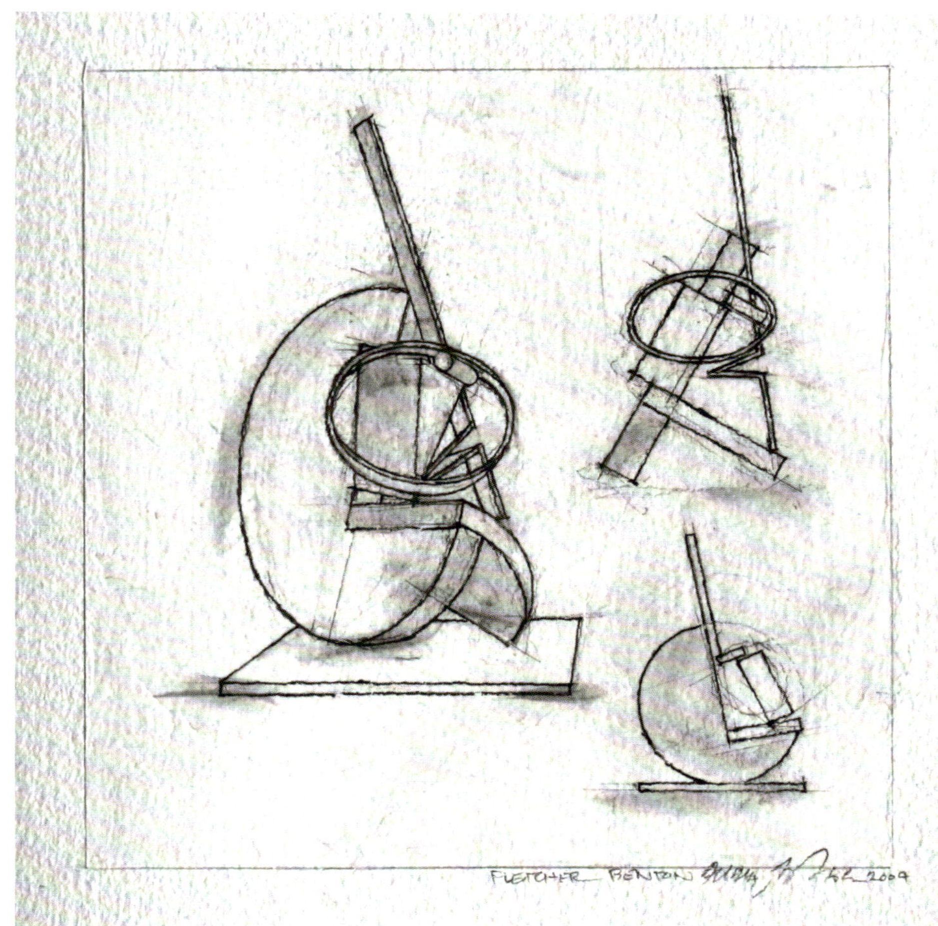

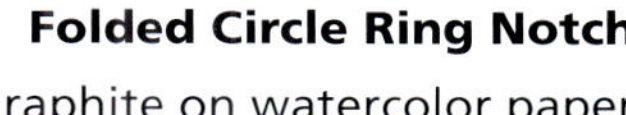

Folded Circle Ring Notch

2004, graphite on watercolor paper
7 x 7 inches
18 x 18 cm

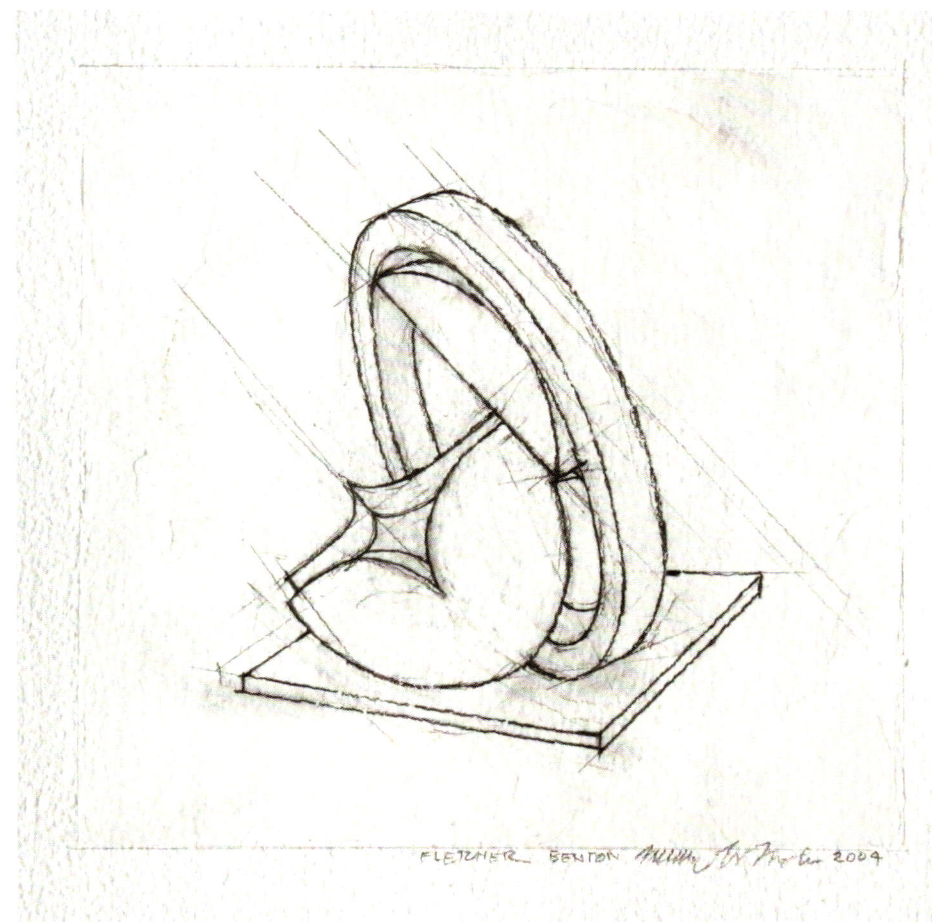

Folded Circle Ring Bezel

2004, graphite on watercolor paper
7 x 7 inches
18 x 18 cm

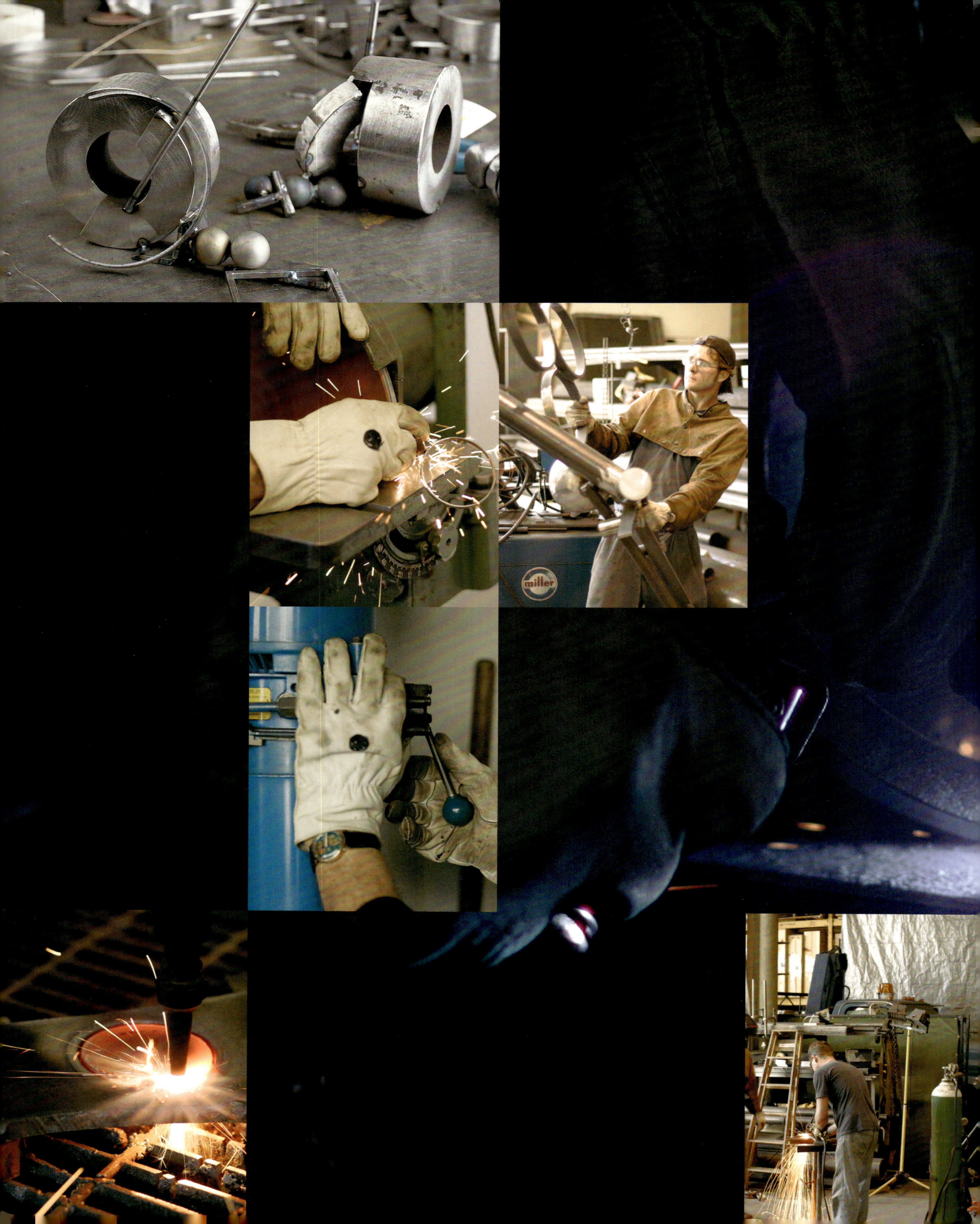
miller

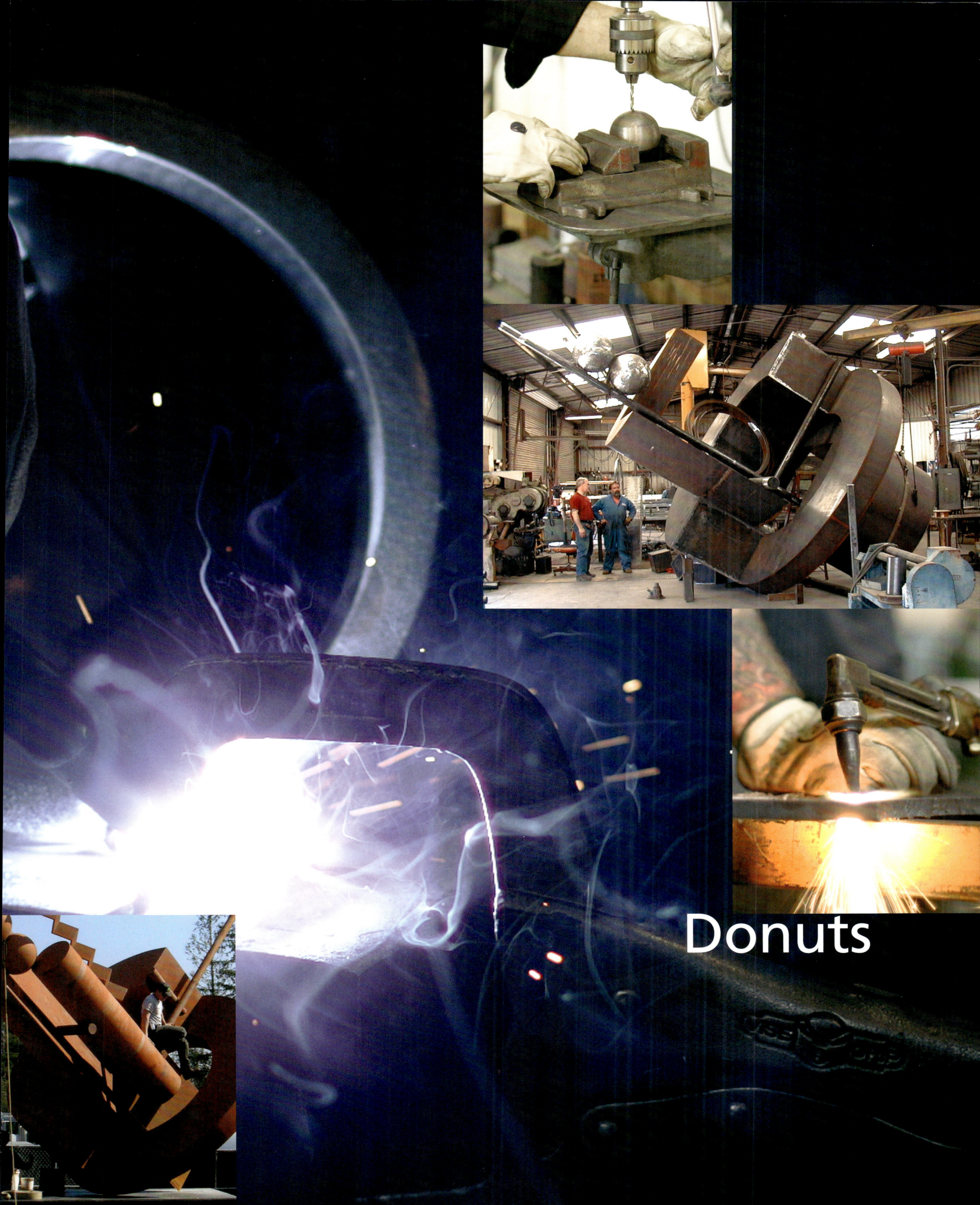

Donuts

Donut with 3 Balls

2001, Cor-ten steel
10 feet diameter, H: 22 feet
305 cm diameter, H: 671 cm

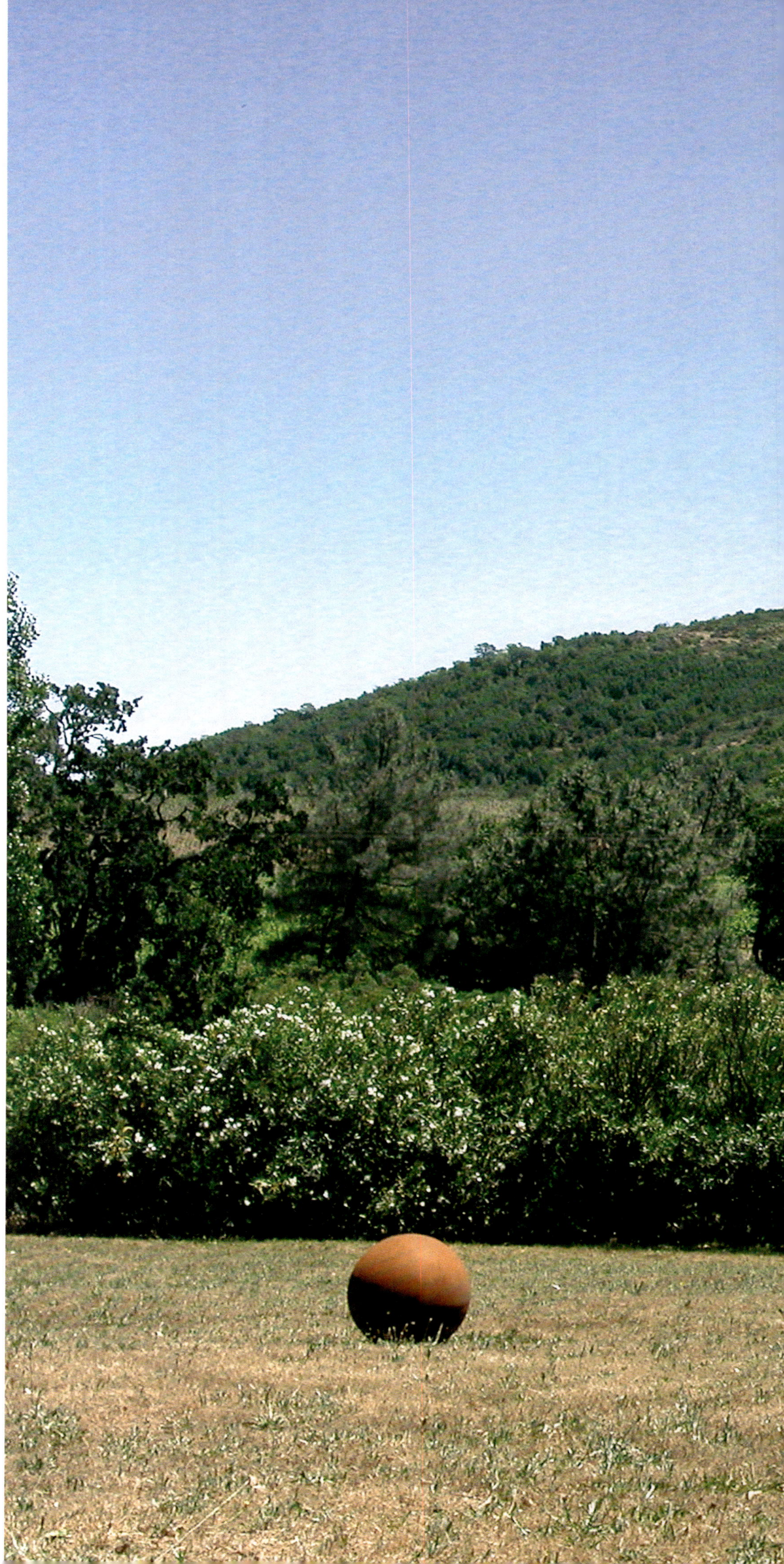

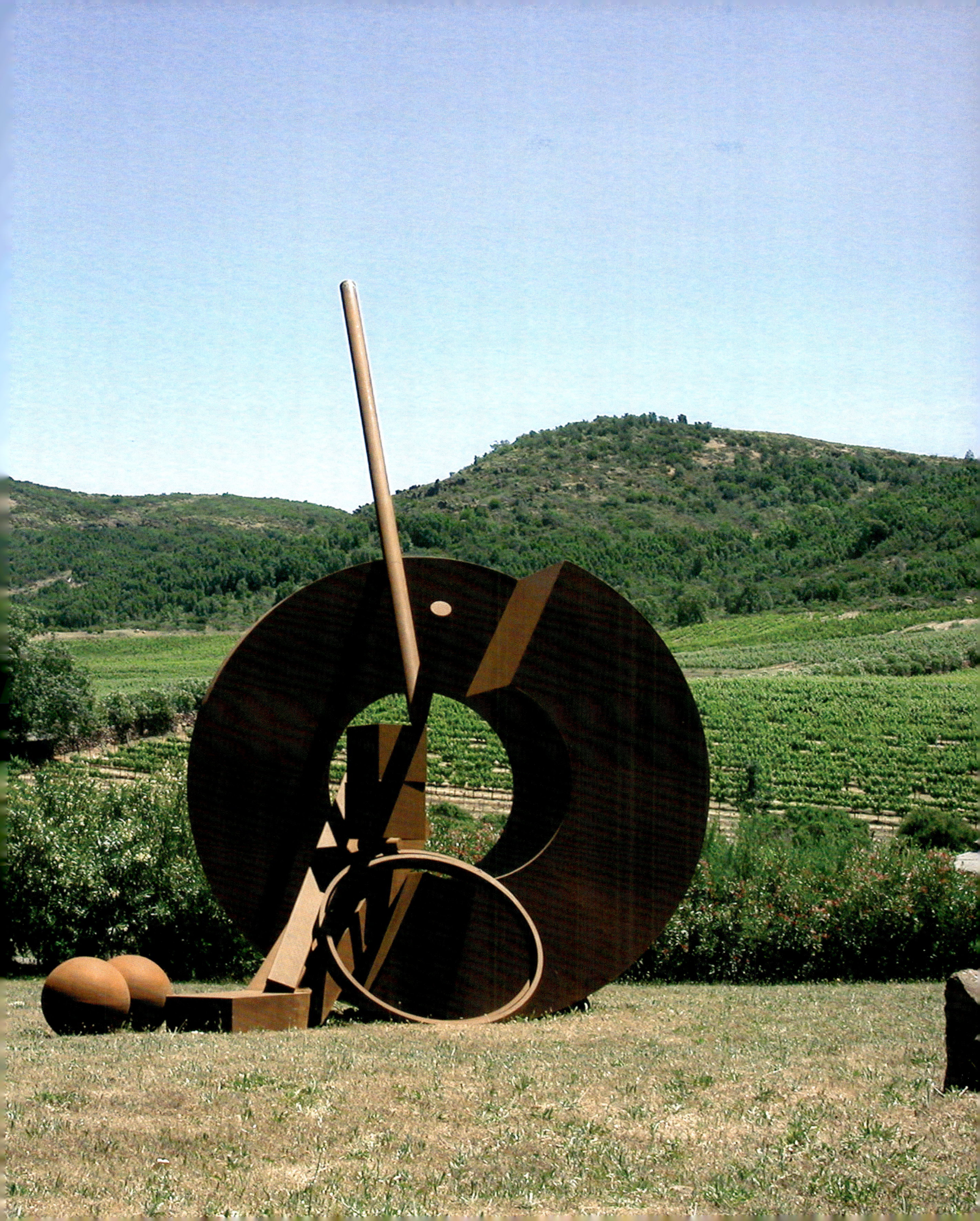

Tilted Donut No. 3

2003, Cor-ten steel
12 feet diameter, H: 22 feet
366 cm diameter, H: 671 cm

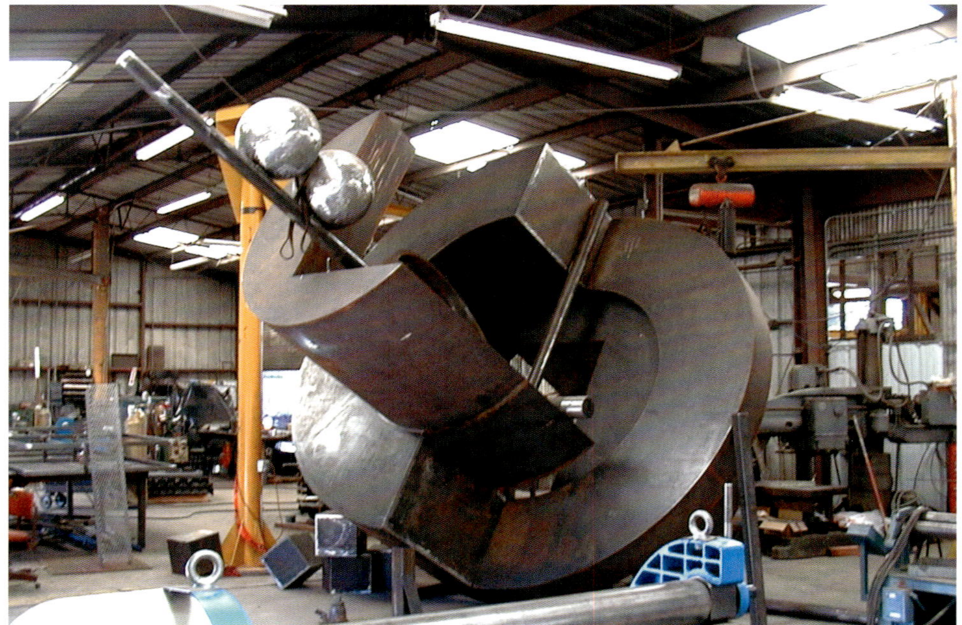

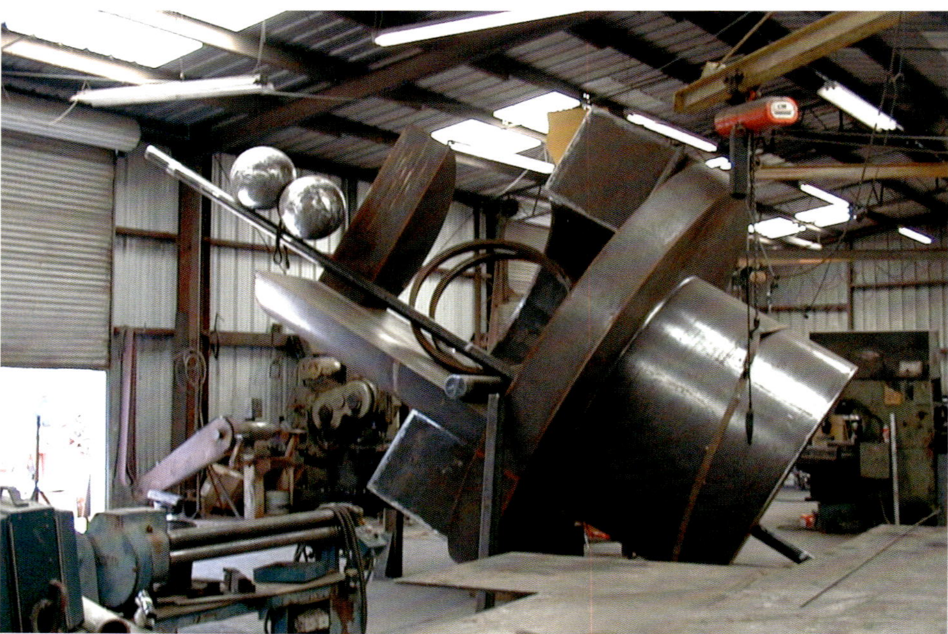

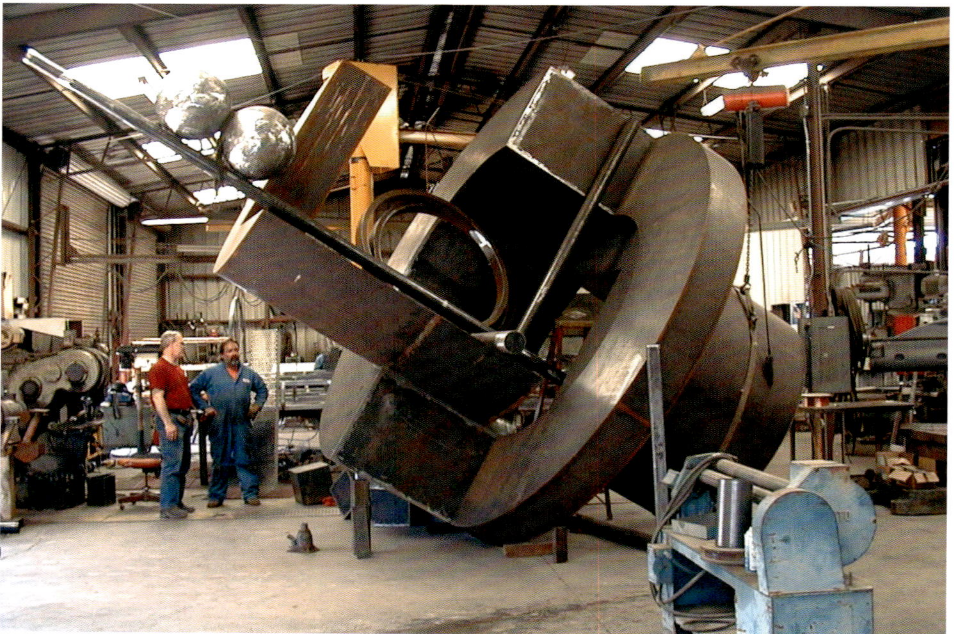

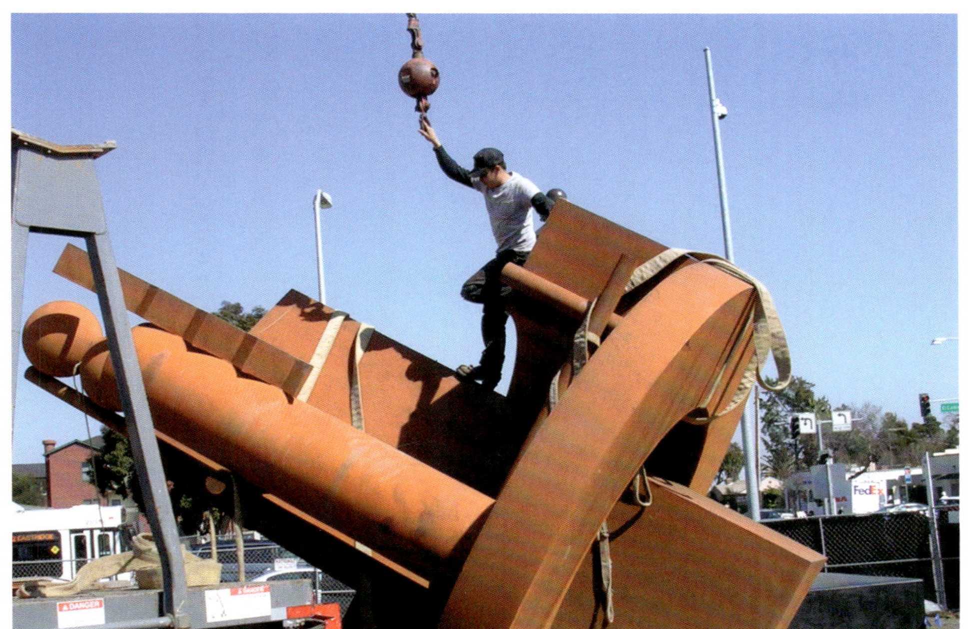

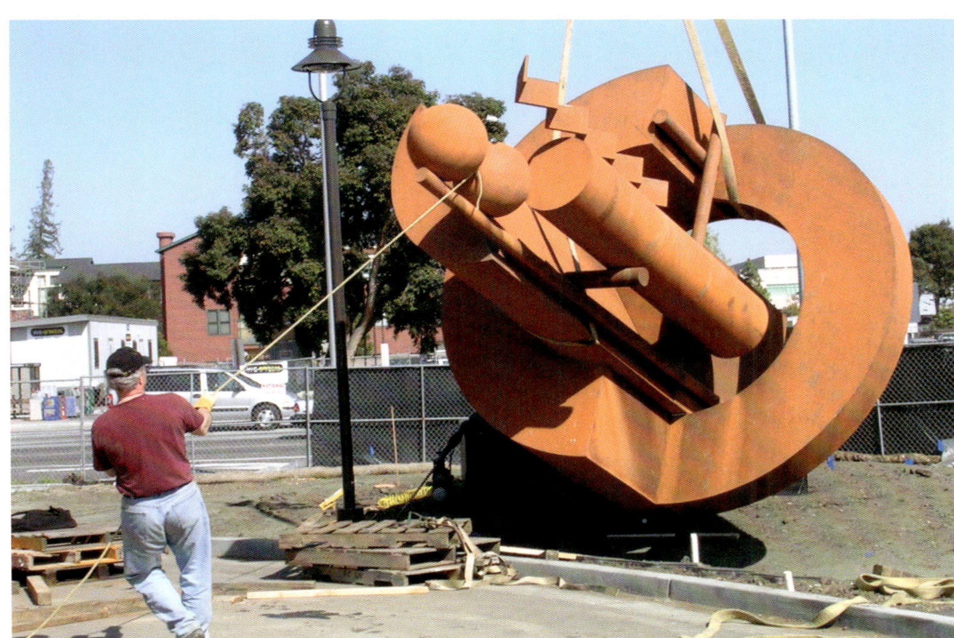

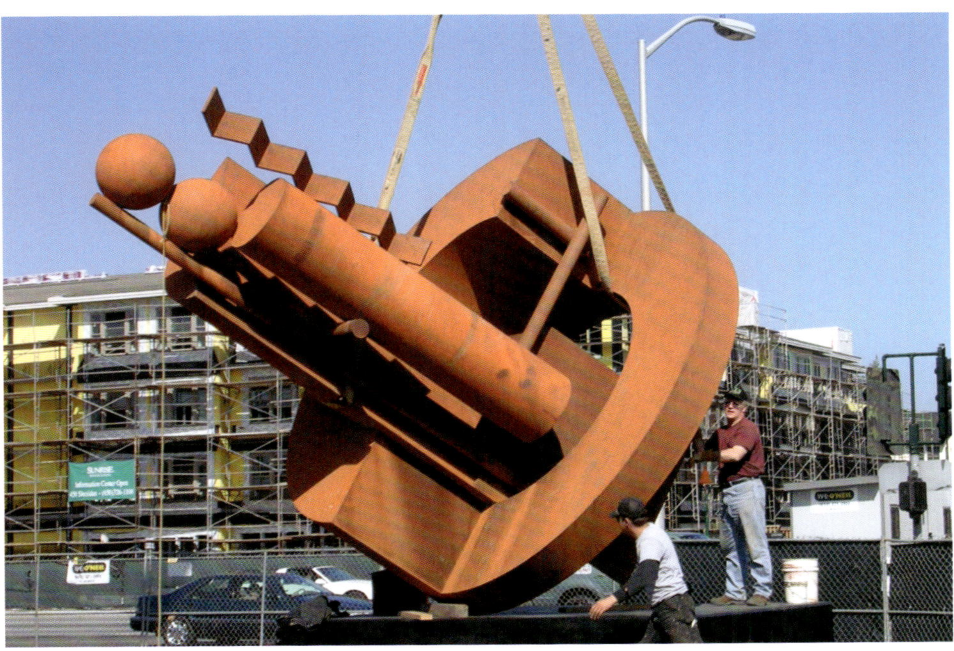

Tilted Donut No. 5

2005, Cor-ten steel
21 x 24 x 12 feet
640 x 732 x 366 cm

Installation at Stanford University,
Property of The Palo Alto Arts
Commission. California, 2006

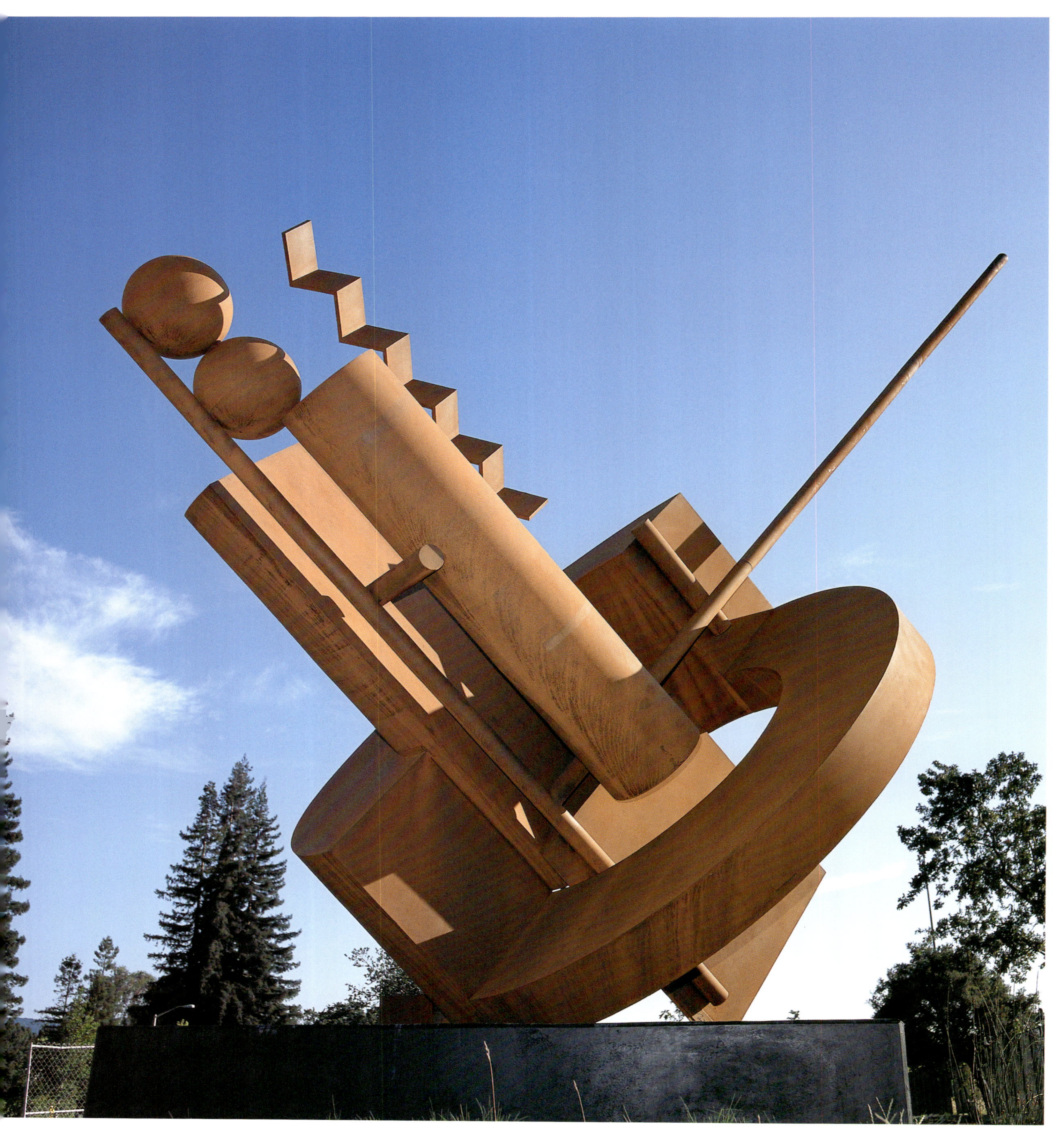

Tilted Donut No. 5

2005, Cor-ten steel
21 x 24 x 12 feet
640 x 732 x 366 cm

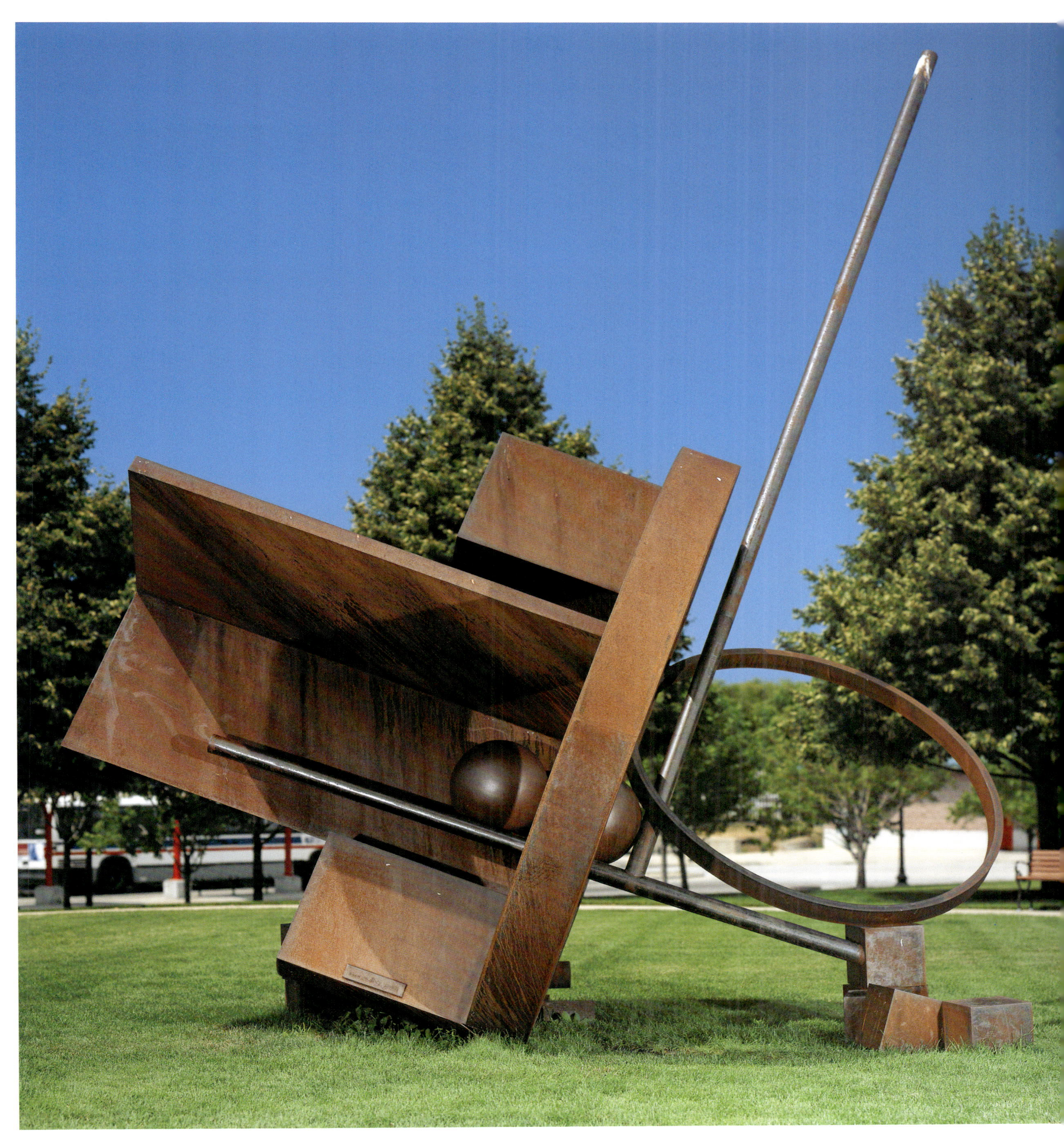

Tilted Donut No. 4

2003, Cor-ten steel
12 feet diameter, H: 20 feet
366 cm diameter, H: 610 cm

Tilted Donut No. 4

2003, Cor-ten steel
12 feet diameter, H: 20 feet
366 cm diameter, H: 610 cm
Chicago

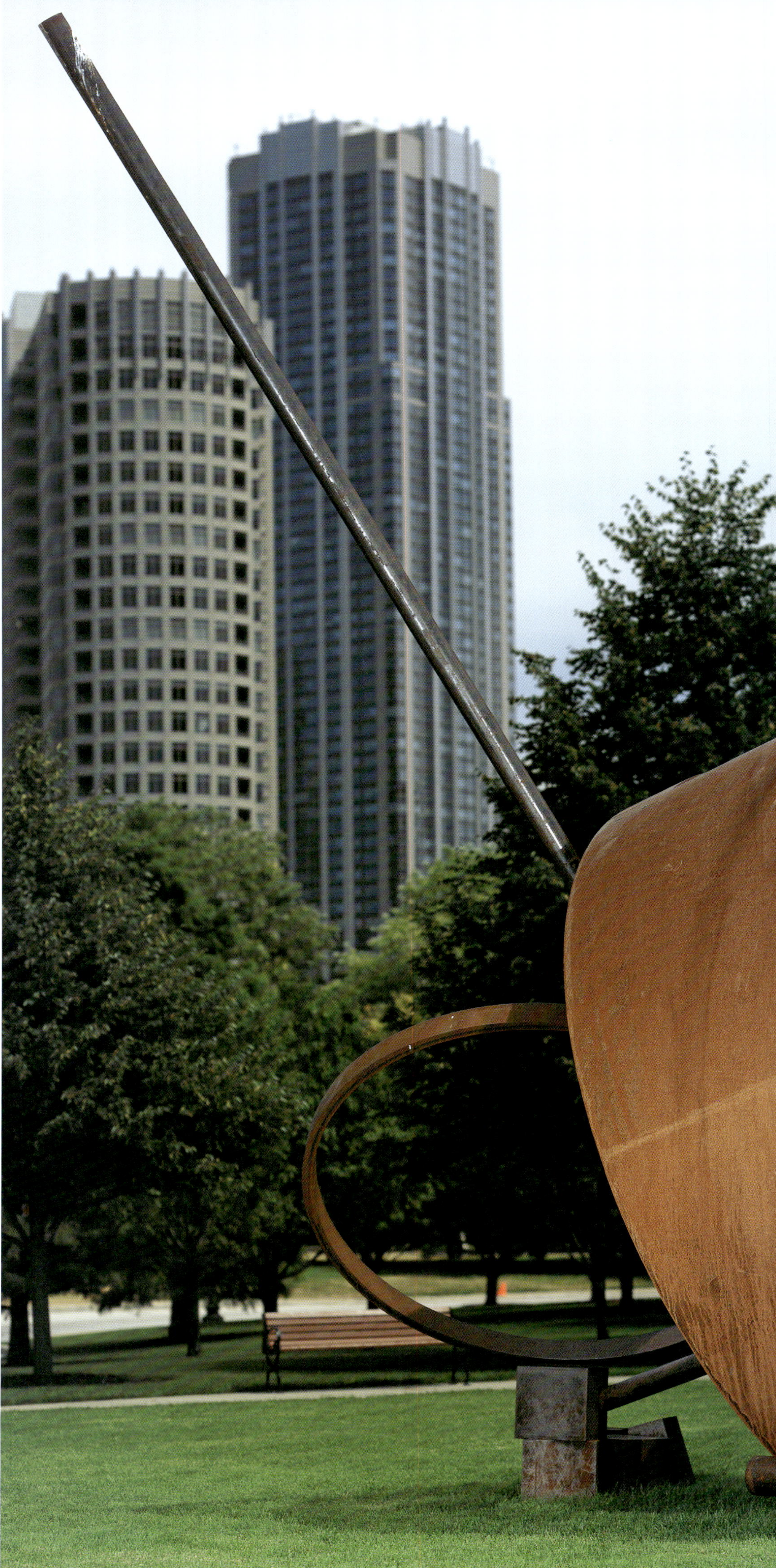

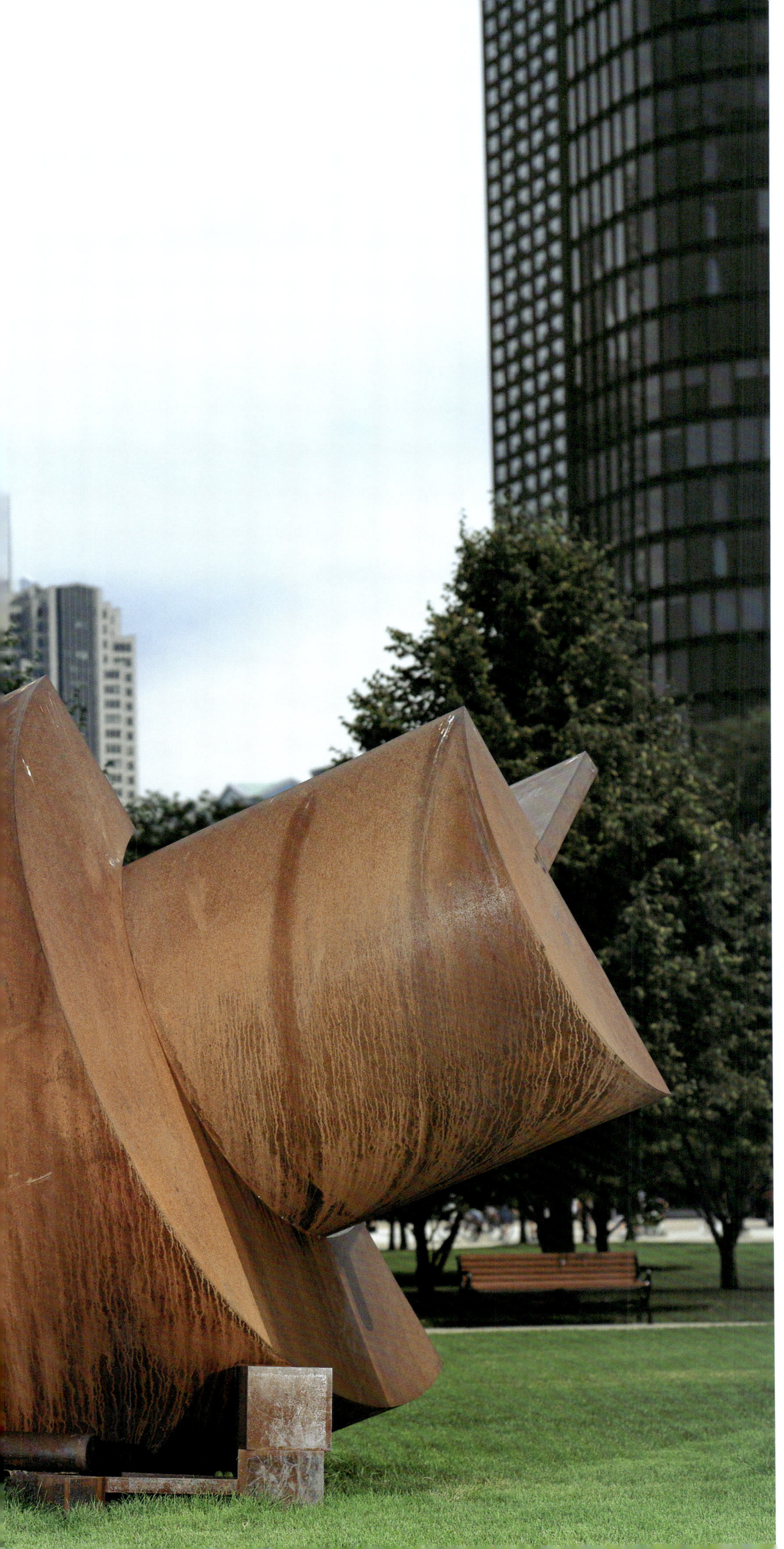

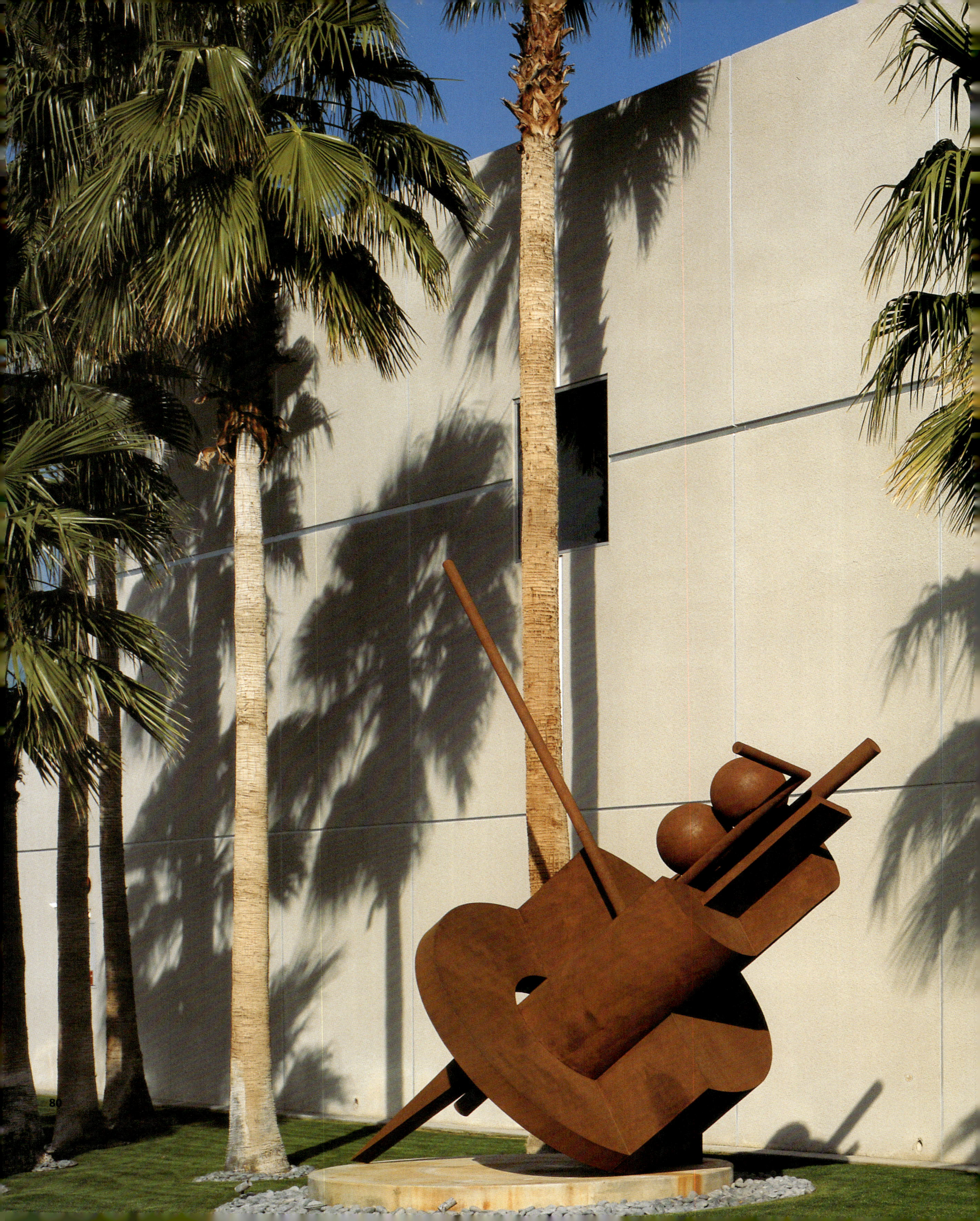

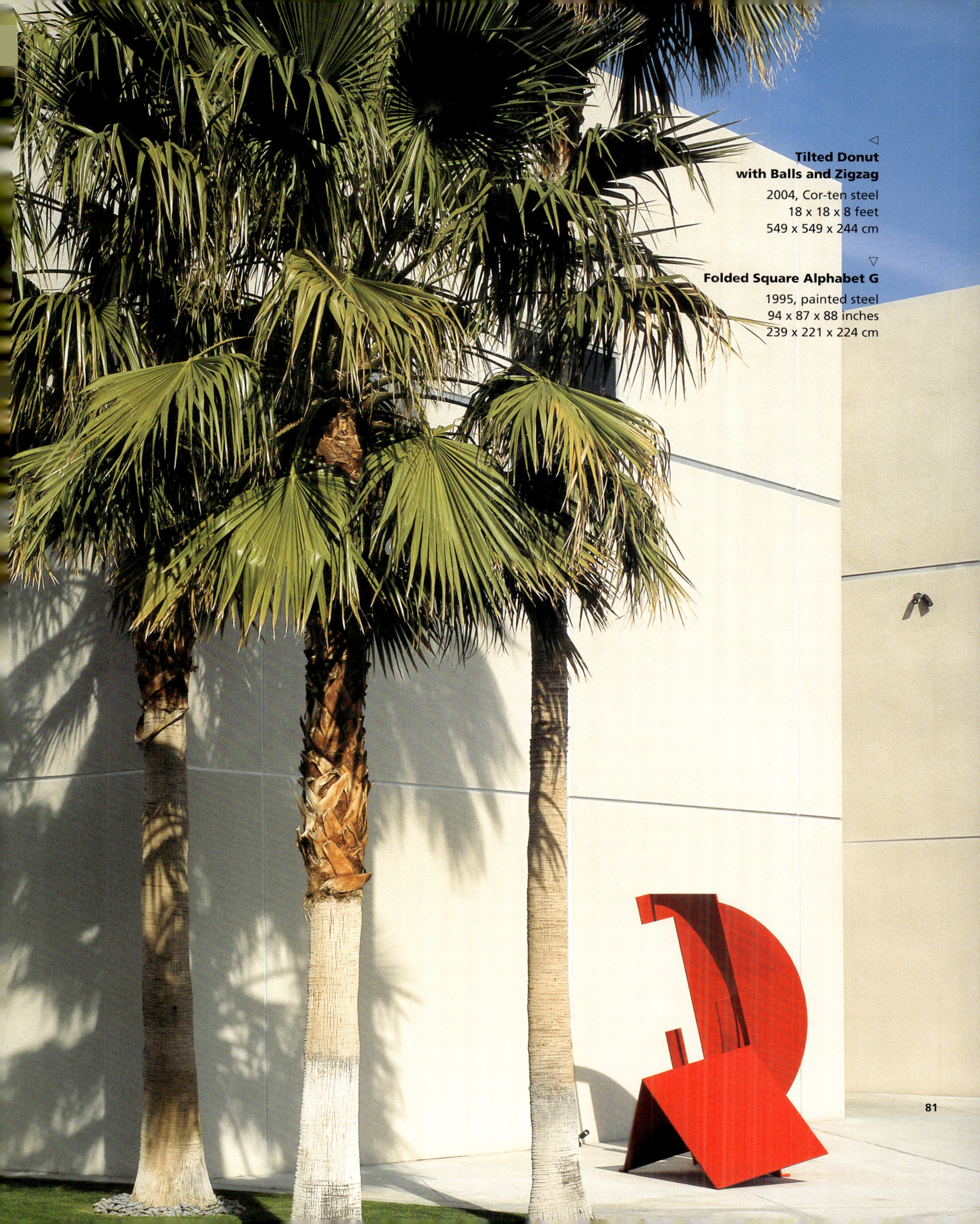

◁
Tilted Donut with Balls and Zigzag

2004, Cor-ten steel
18 x 18 x 8 feet
549 x 549 x 244 cm

▽
Folded Square Alphabet G

1995, painted steel
94 x 87 x 88 inches
239 x 221 x 224 cm

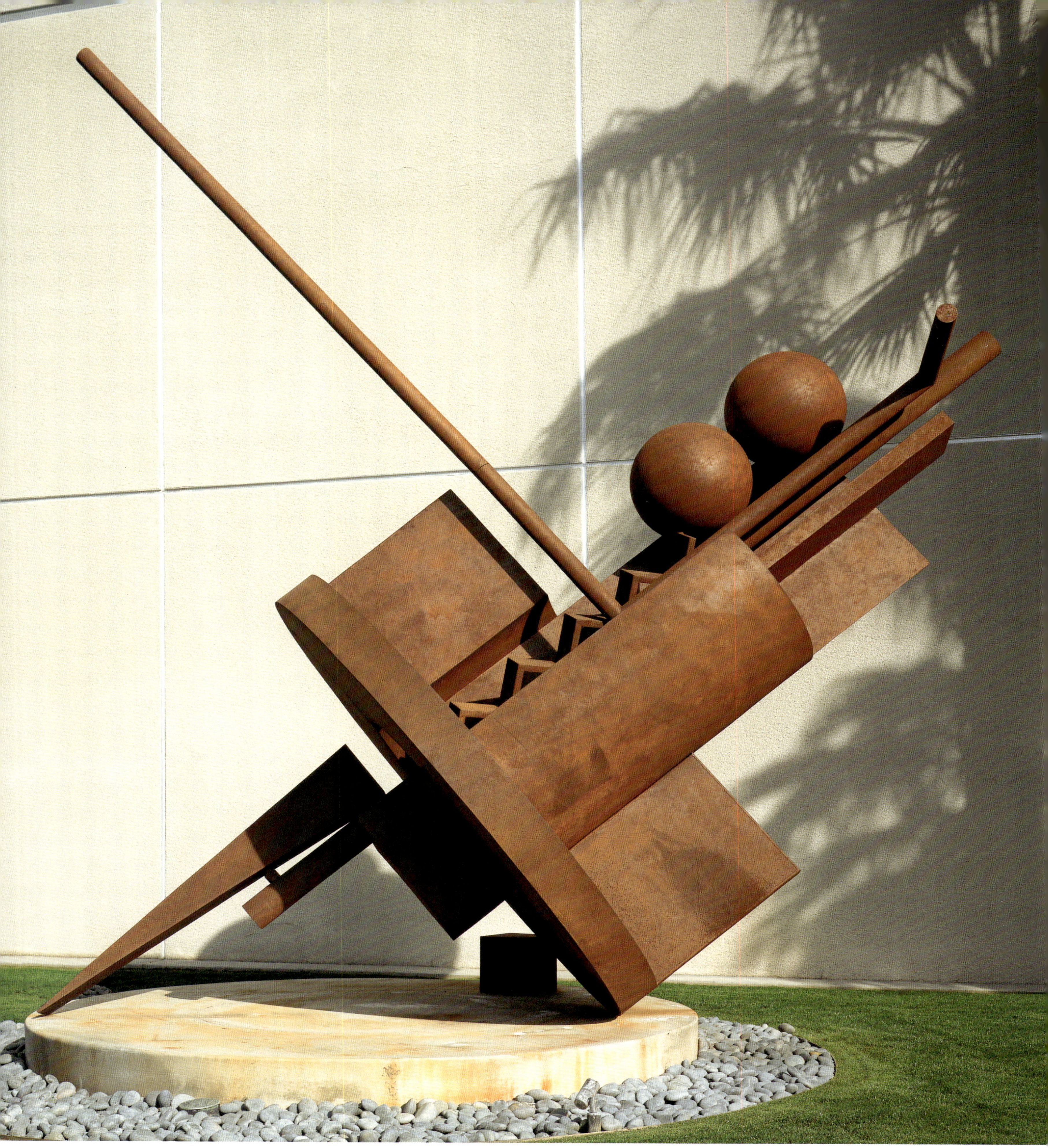

Tilted Donut with Balls and Zigzag

2004, Cor-ten steel
18 x 18 x 8 feet
549 x 549 x 244 cm

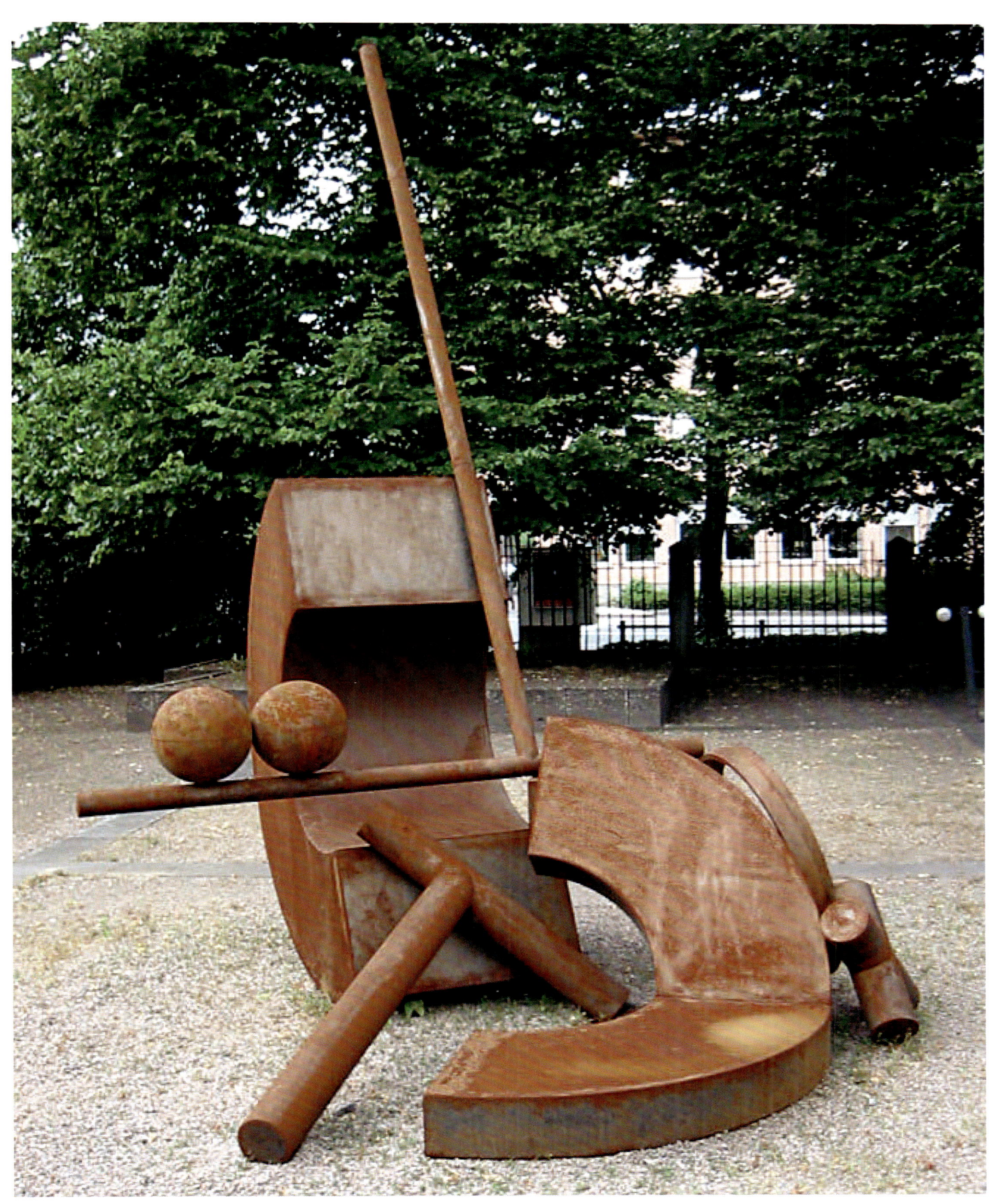

Donut with Balls No. 23

2001, Cor-ten steel
141¾ x 92½ x 92½ inches
360 x 235 x 235 cm

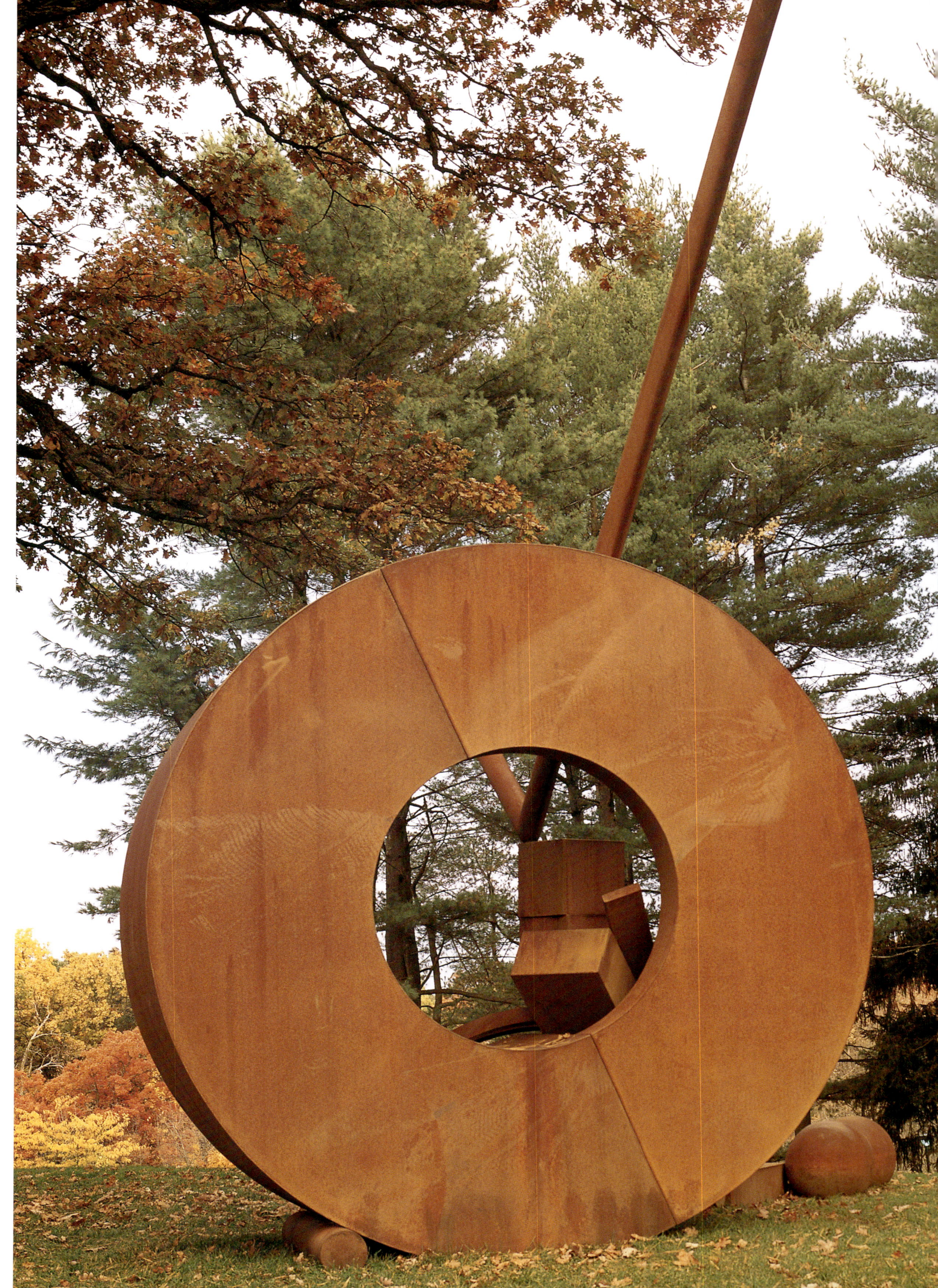

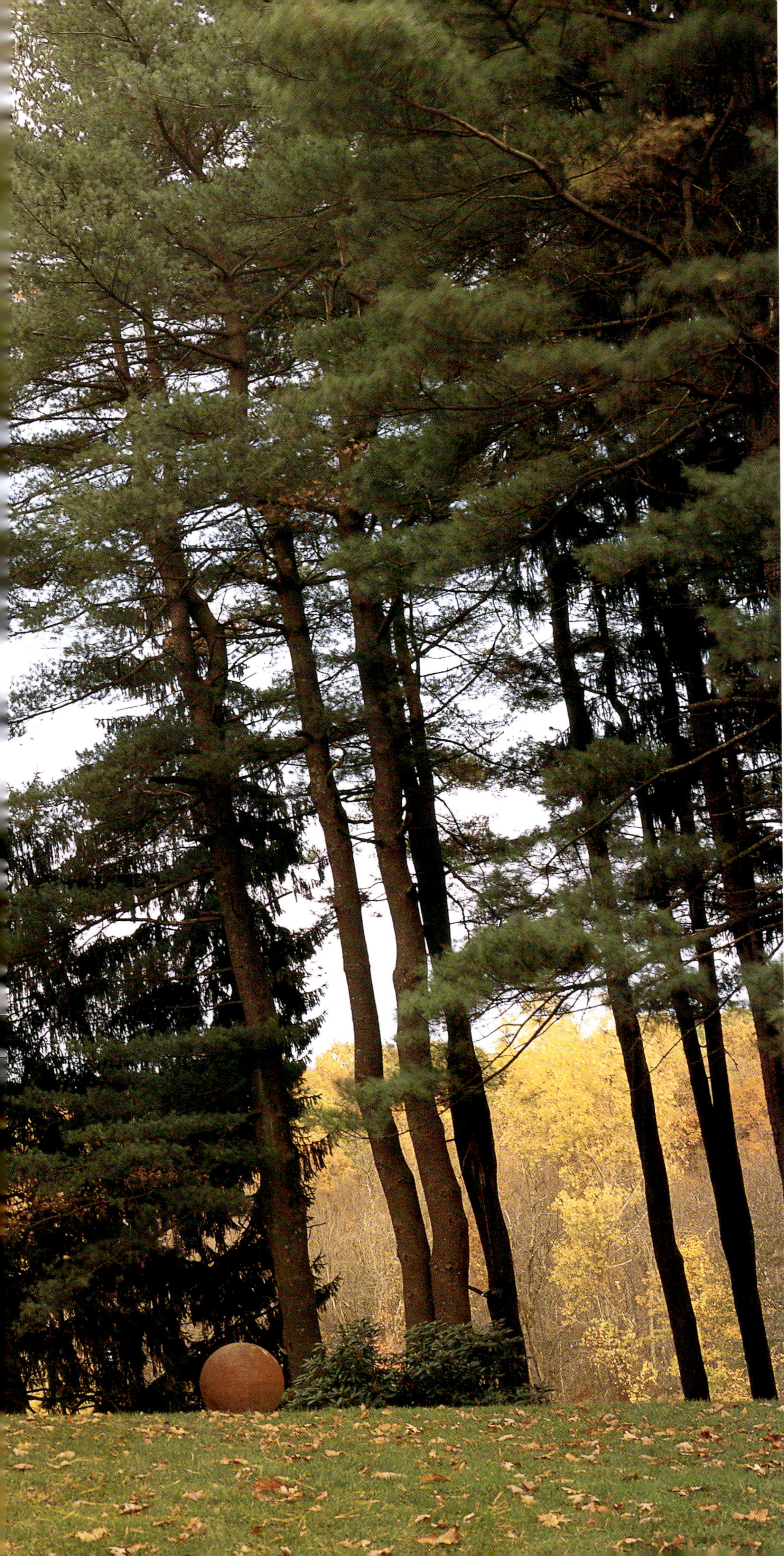

Donut with 3 Balls

2001, Cor-ten steel
10 feet diameter, H: 22 feet
305 cm diameter, H: 671cm
DeCordova Museum and
Sculpture Park, Lincoln, Massachusetts

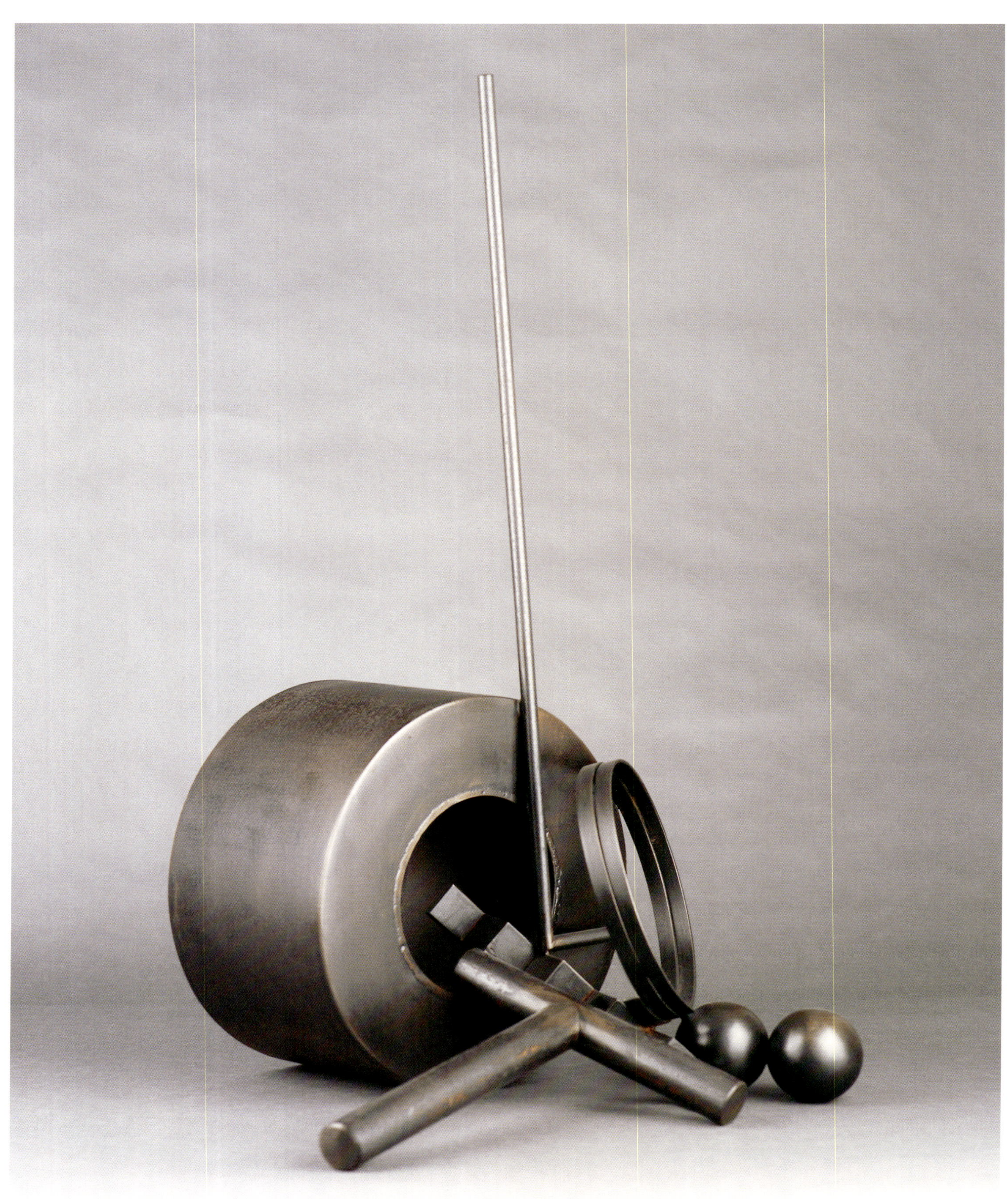

Donut with Balls and T

2000, steel with patina
33 x 19 x 19 inches
84 x 48 x 48 cm

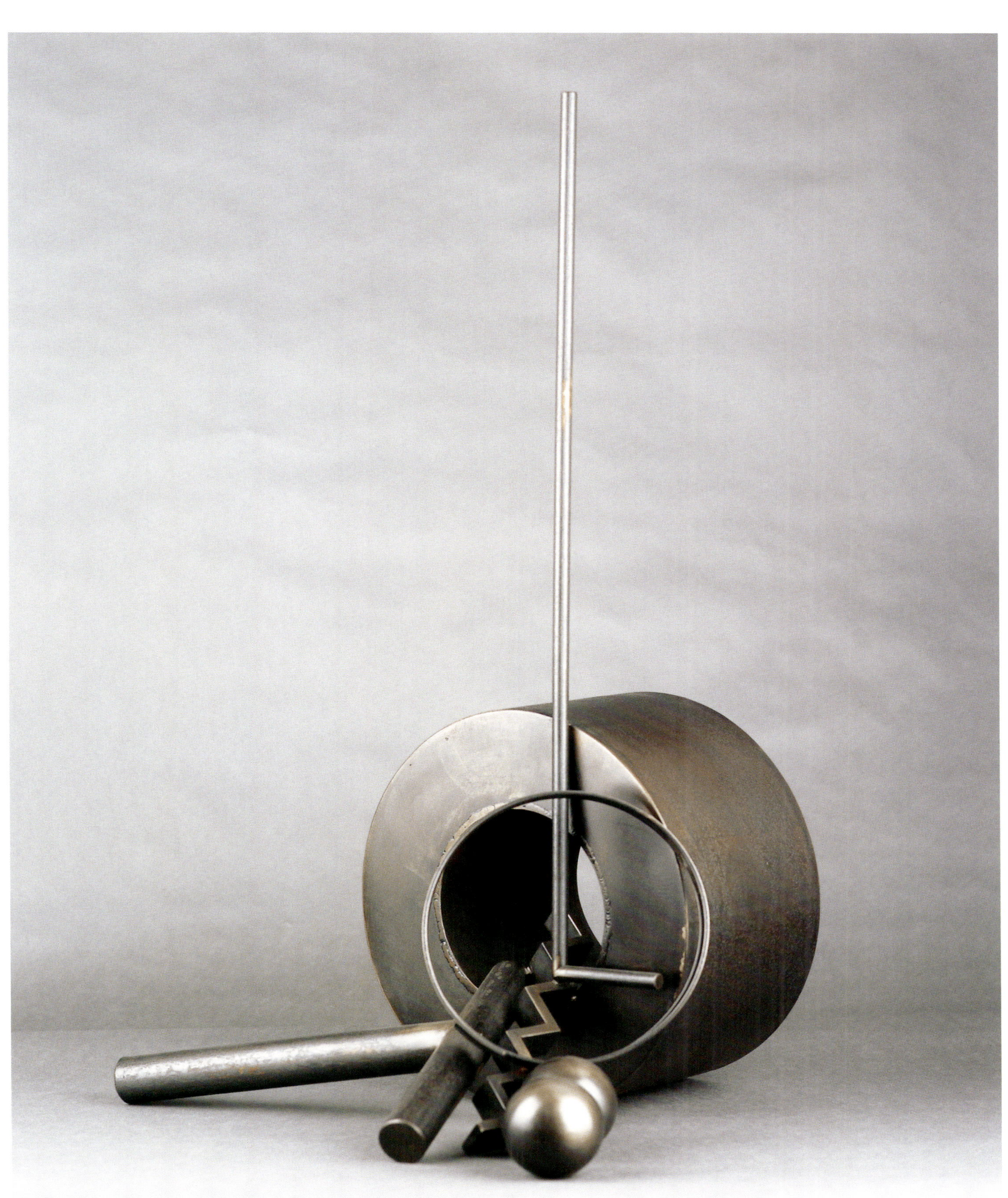

Donut with Balls and T

2000, steel with patina
33 x 19 x 19 inches
84 x 48 x 48 cm

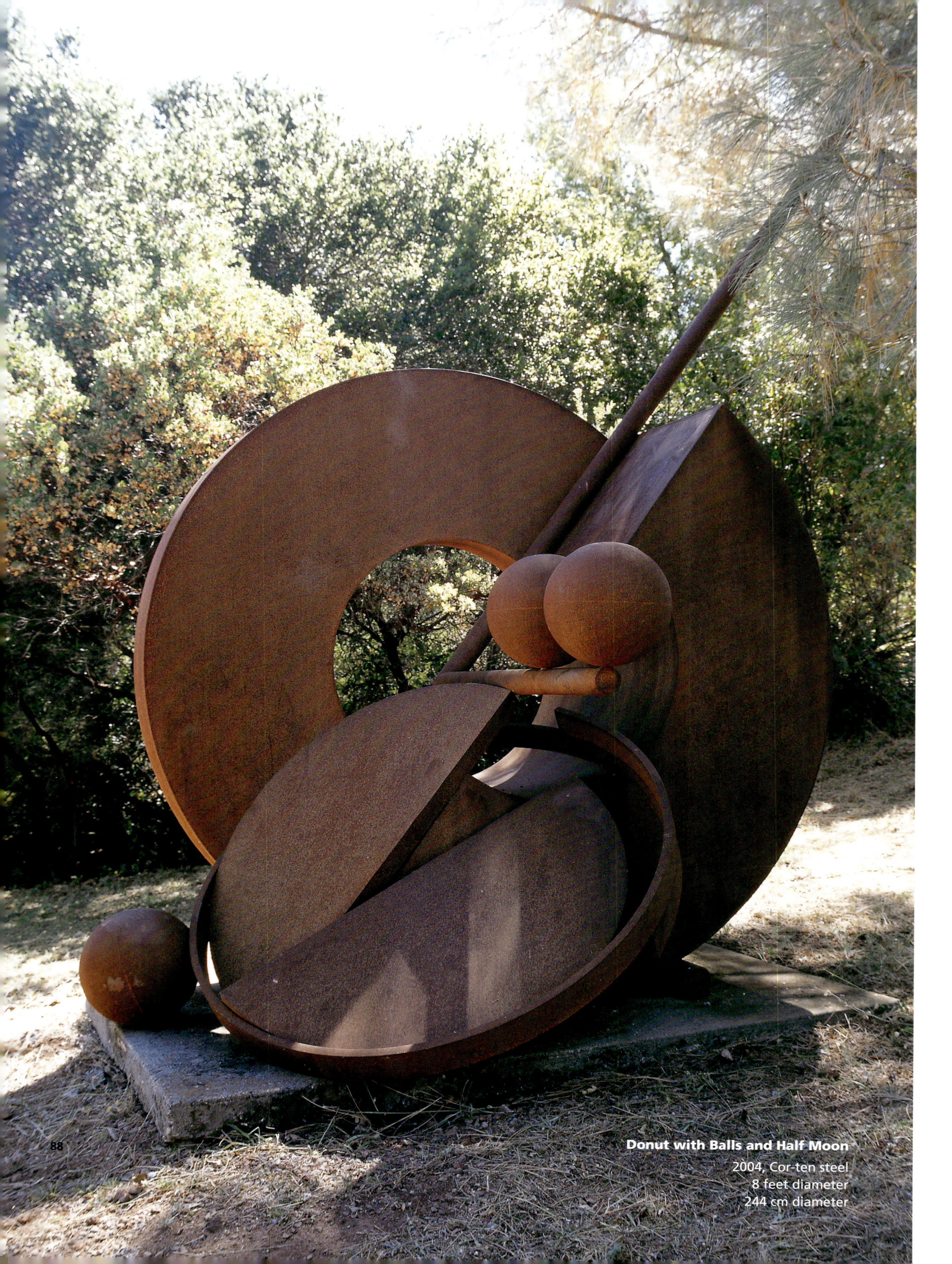

Donut with Balls and Half Moon

2004, Cor-ten steel
8 feet diameter
244 cm diameter

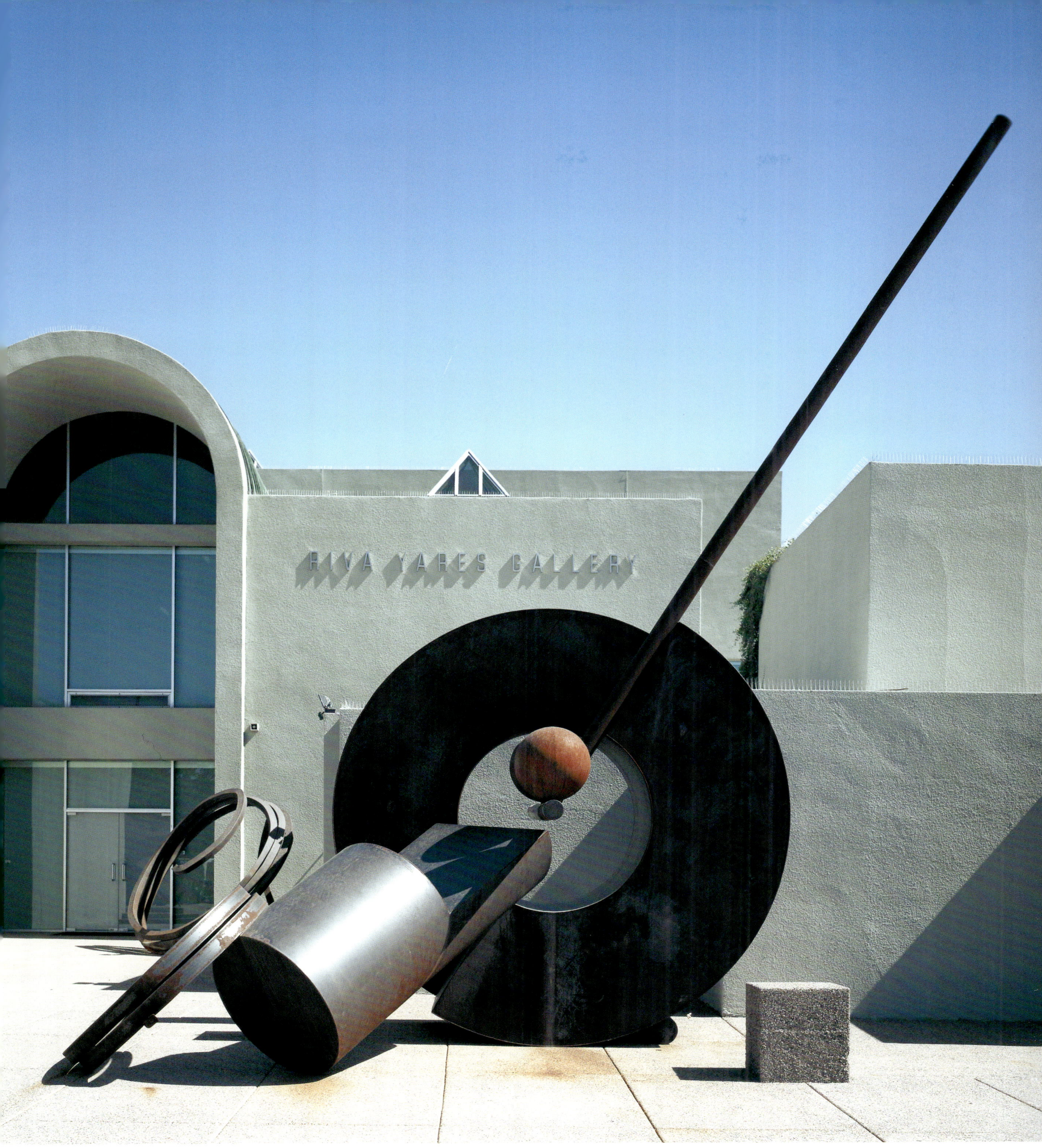

Donut with Balls and Rings

2002, Cor-ten steel
12 feet diameter, H: 20 feet
366 cm diameter, H: 610 cm

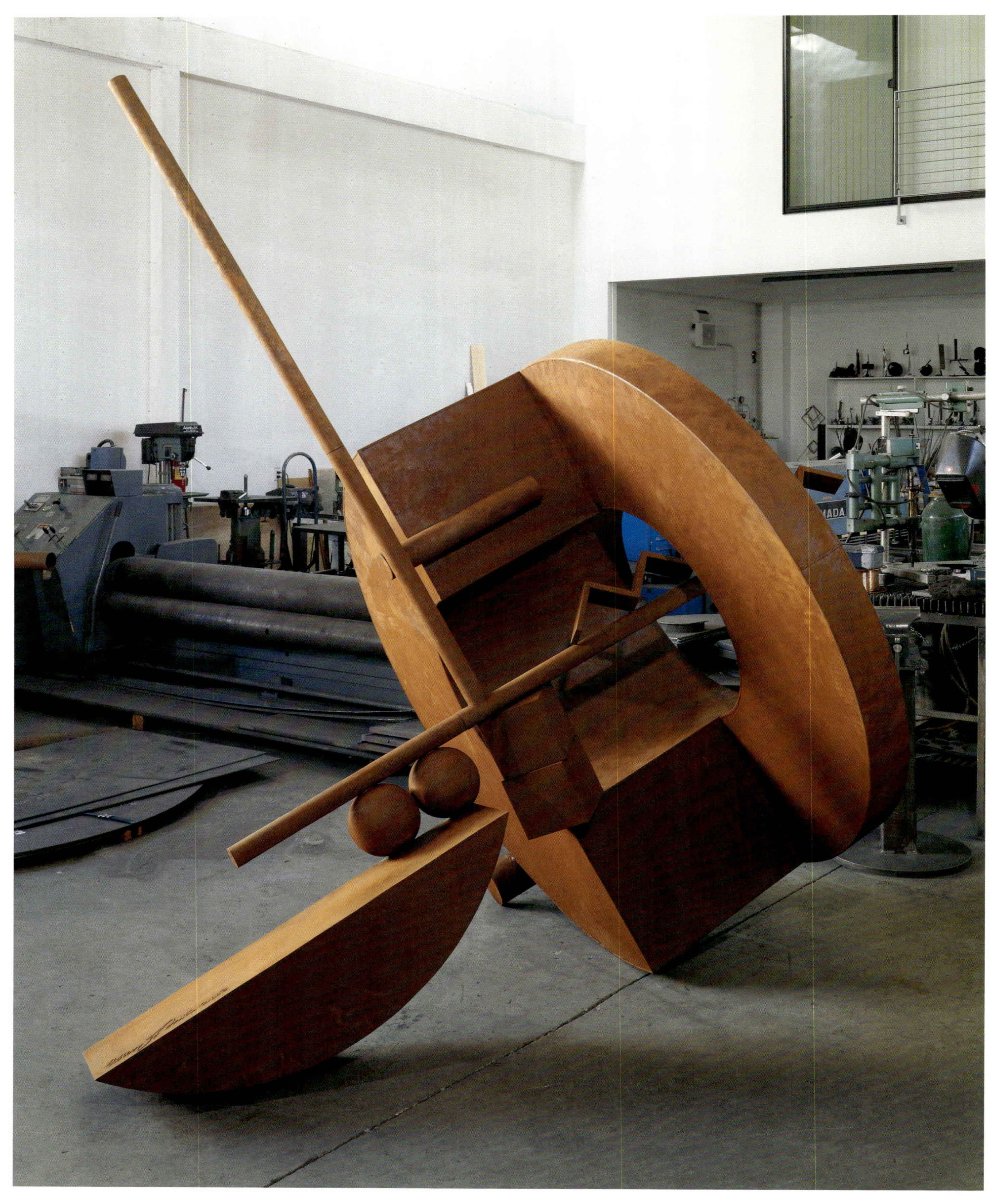

Tilted Donut with Zigzag and Balls

2003, Cor-ten steel
6 feet diameter
183 cm diameter

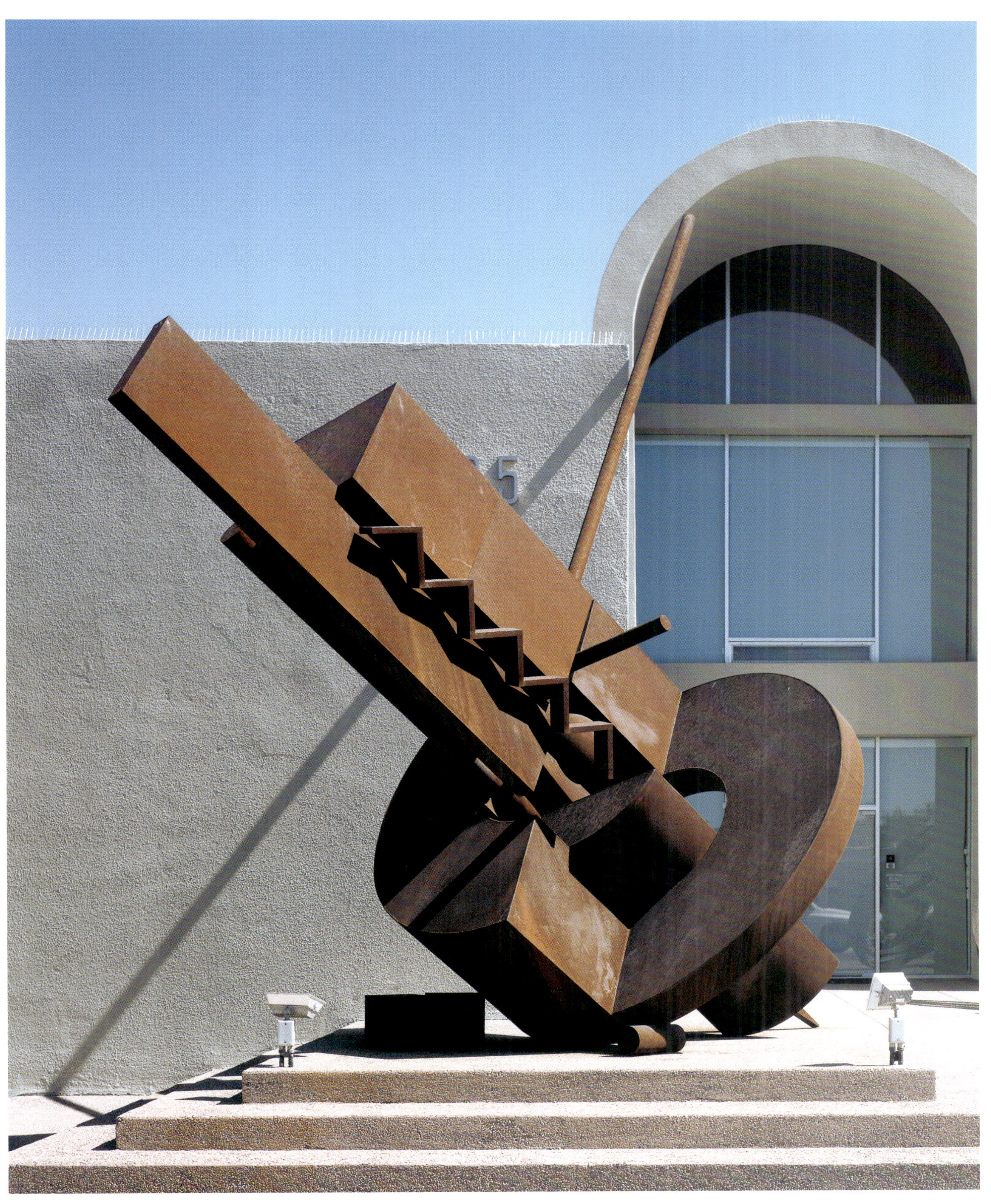

Tilted Donut with 2 Squares

2003, Cor-ten steel
10 x 7 x 8½ feet
305 x 213 x 259 cm

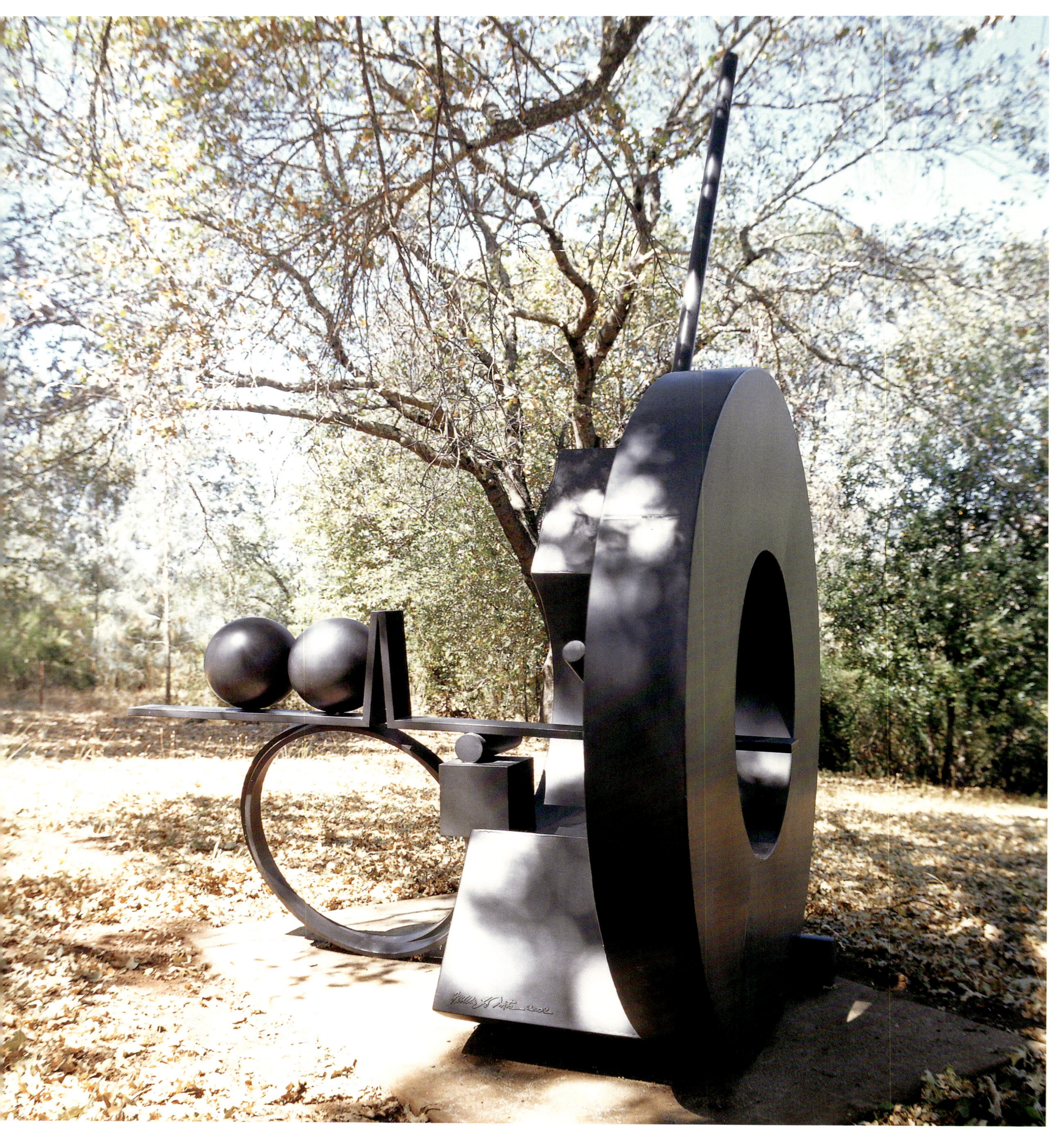

Donut with Balls and L

2002, painted steel
10 x 7 x 8½ feet
305 x 213 x 259 cm

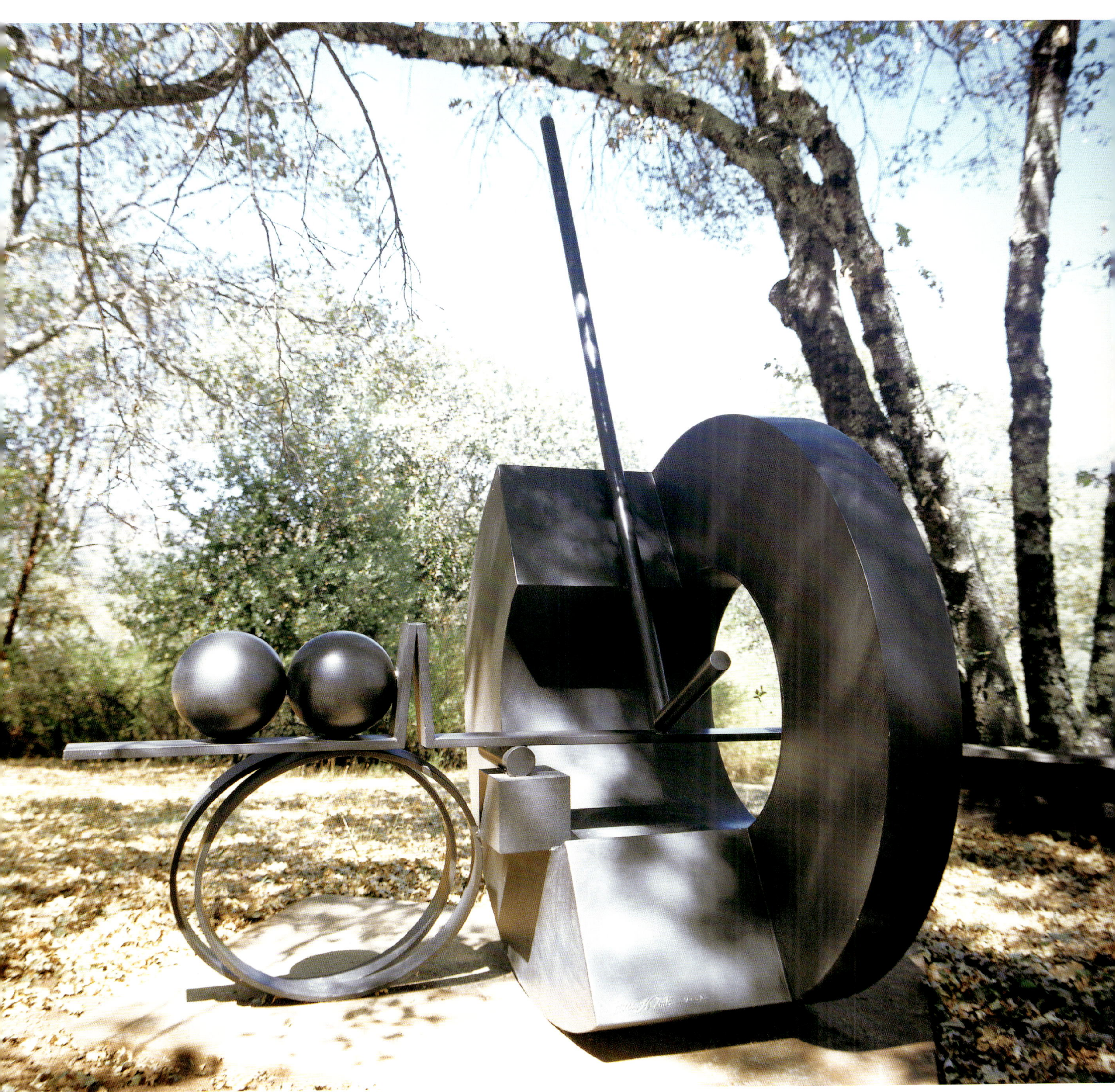

Donut with Balls and L

2002, painted steel
10 x 7 x 8½ feet
305 x 213 x 259 cm

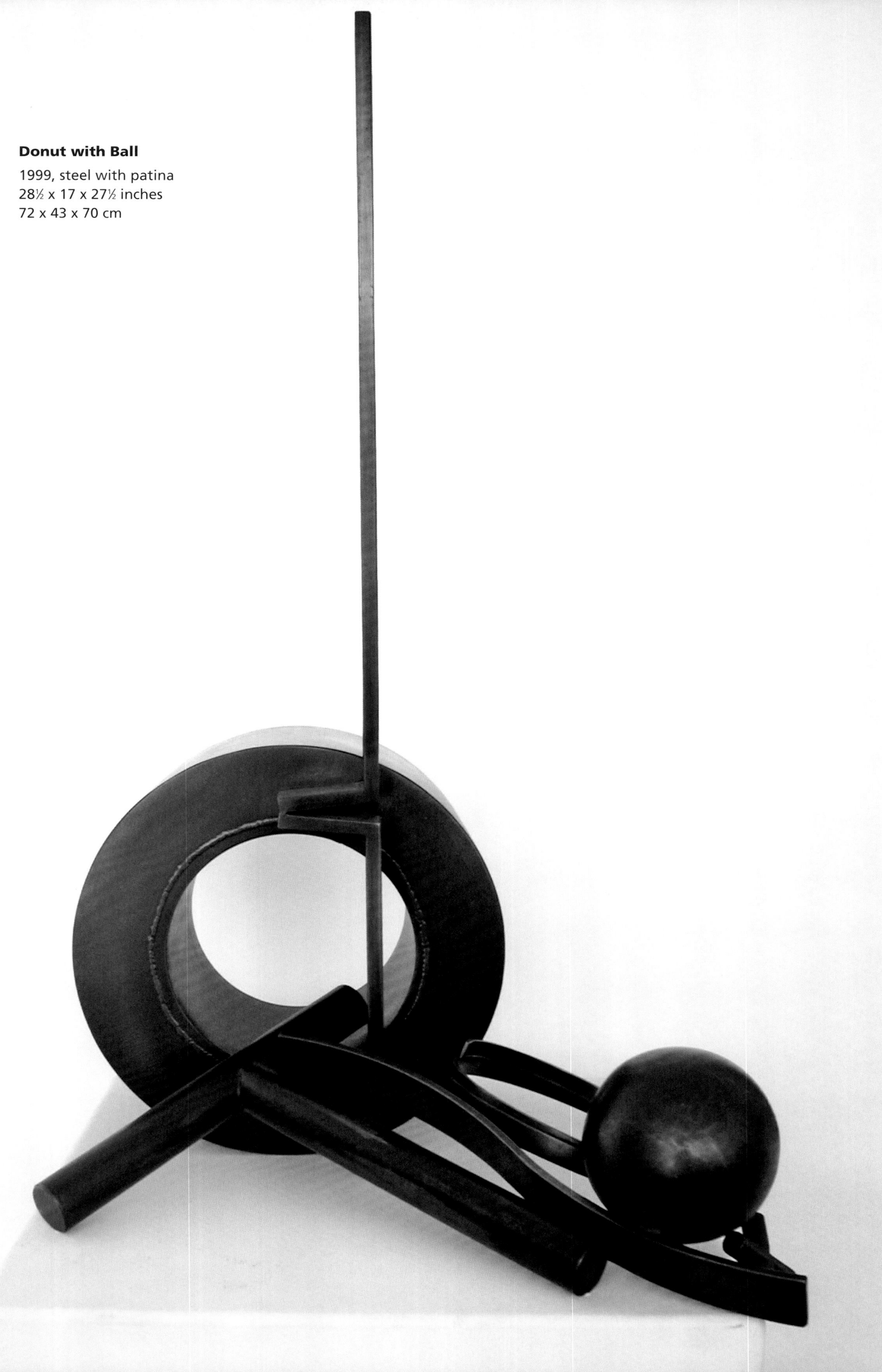

Donut with Ball

1999, steel with patina
28½ x 17 x 27½ inches
72 x 43 x 70 cm

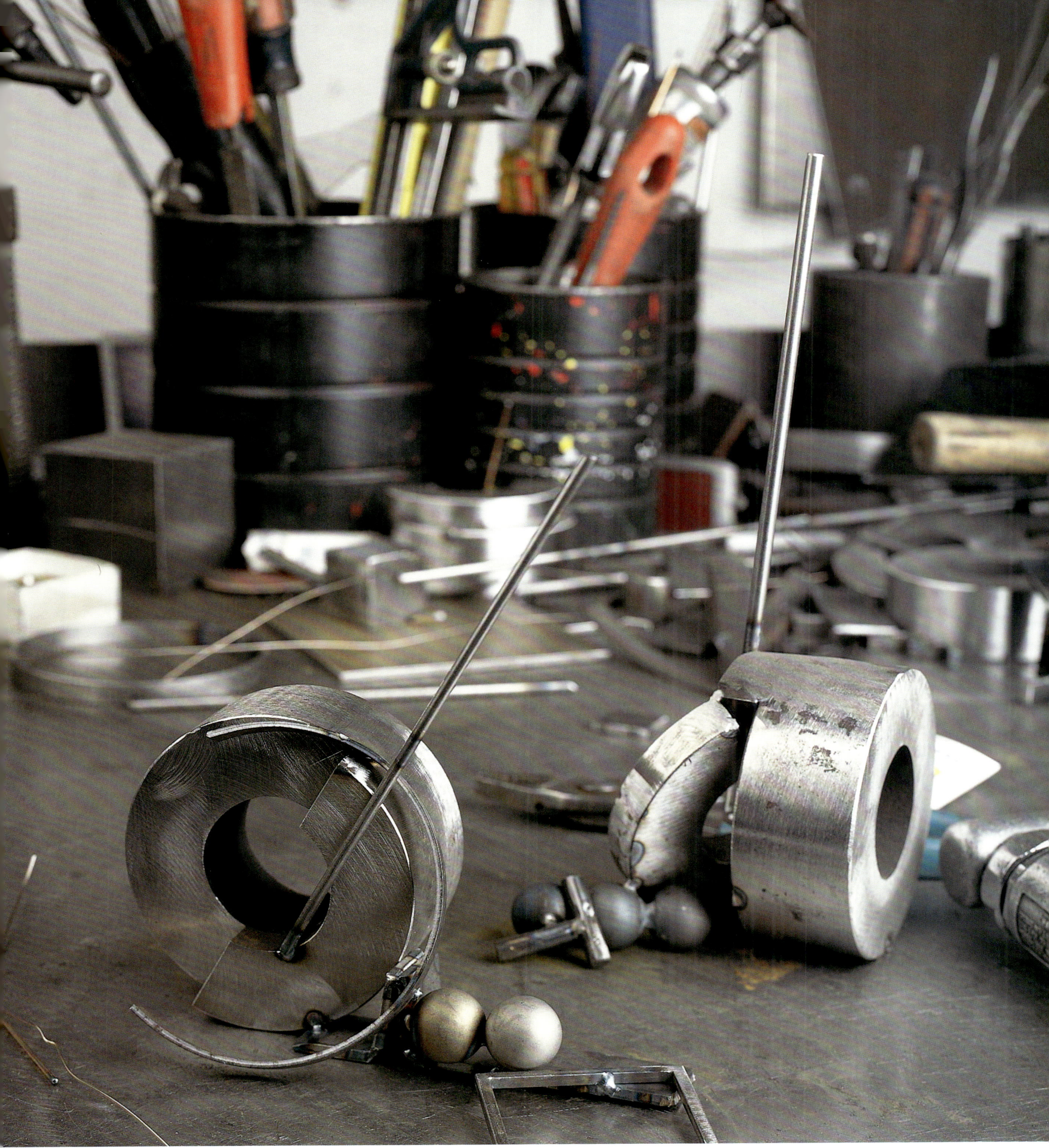

Donut maquettes
Dore Street Studio, 1999

Donut with Balls No. 5 - Maquette

2000, steel with patina
7½ x 5 x 6 inches
19 x 13 x 15 cm

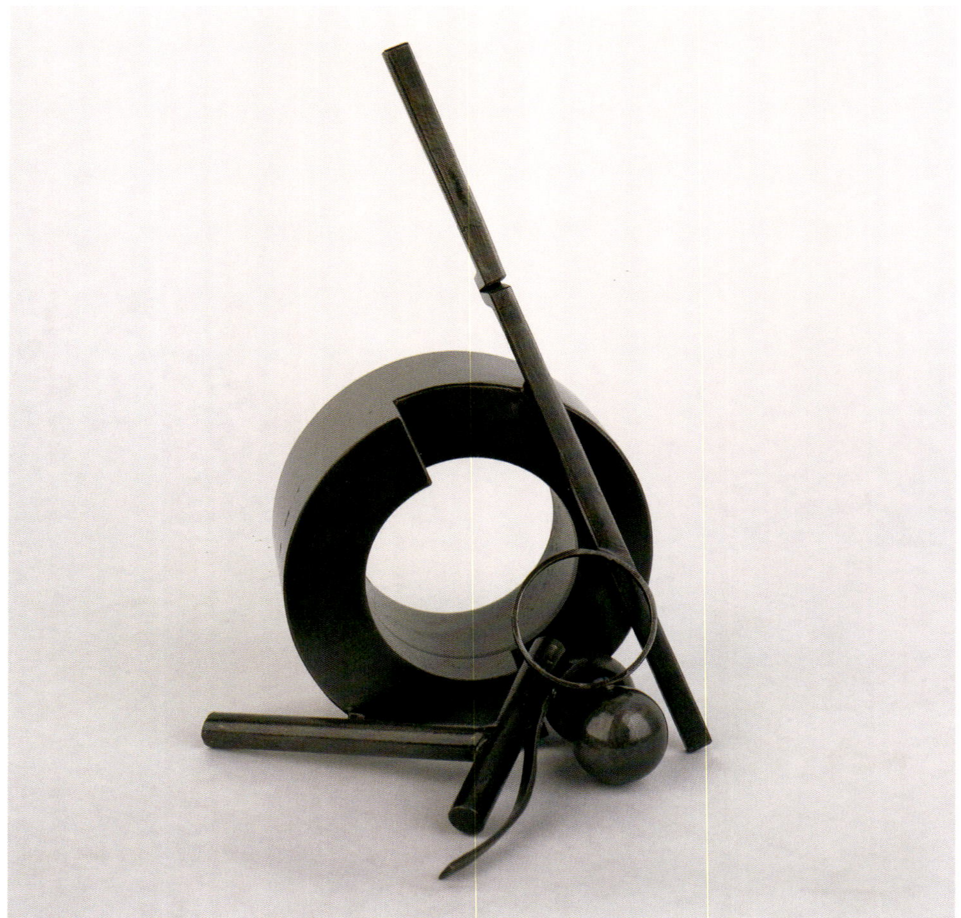

▷
Donut with Balls No. 10 - Maquette

2000, steel
5½ x 4½ x 4 inches
14 x 11 x 10 cm

▷▷
Donut with Balls No. 9 - Maquette

2000, steel with patina
7 x 5 x 4½ inches
18 x 13 x 11 cm

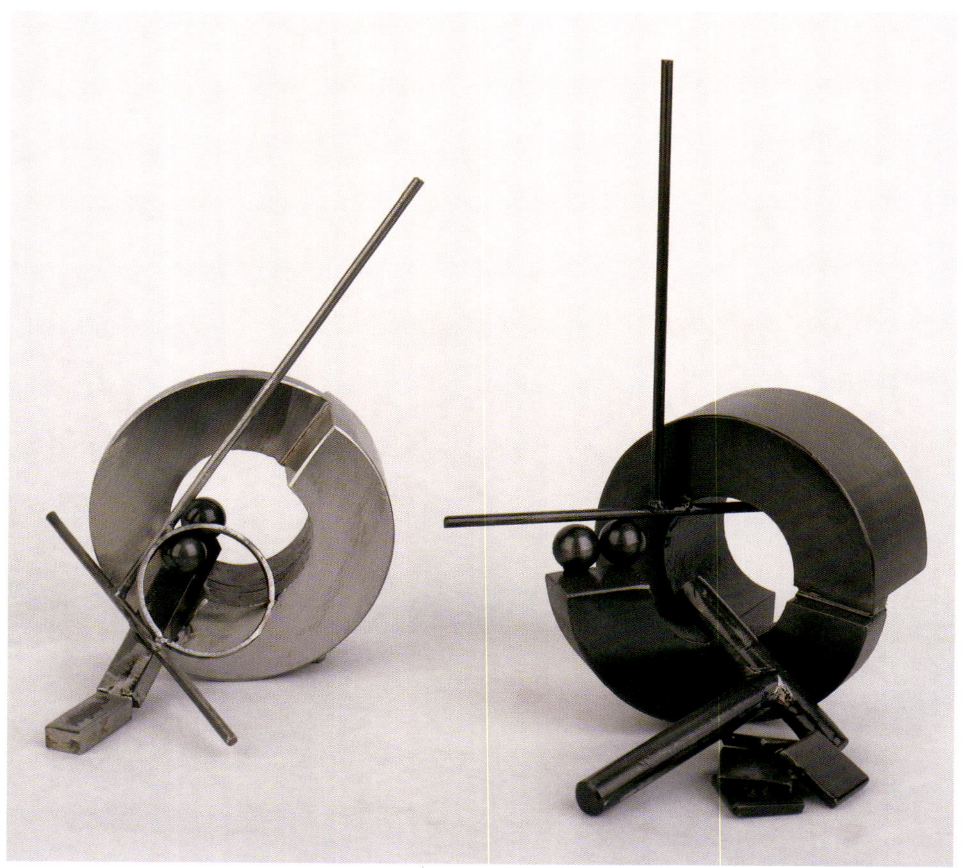

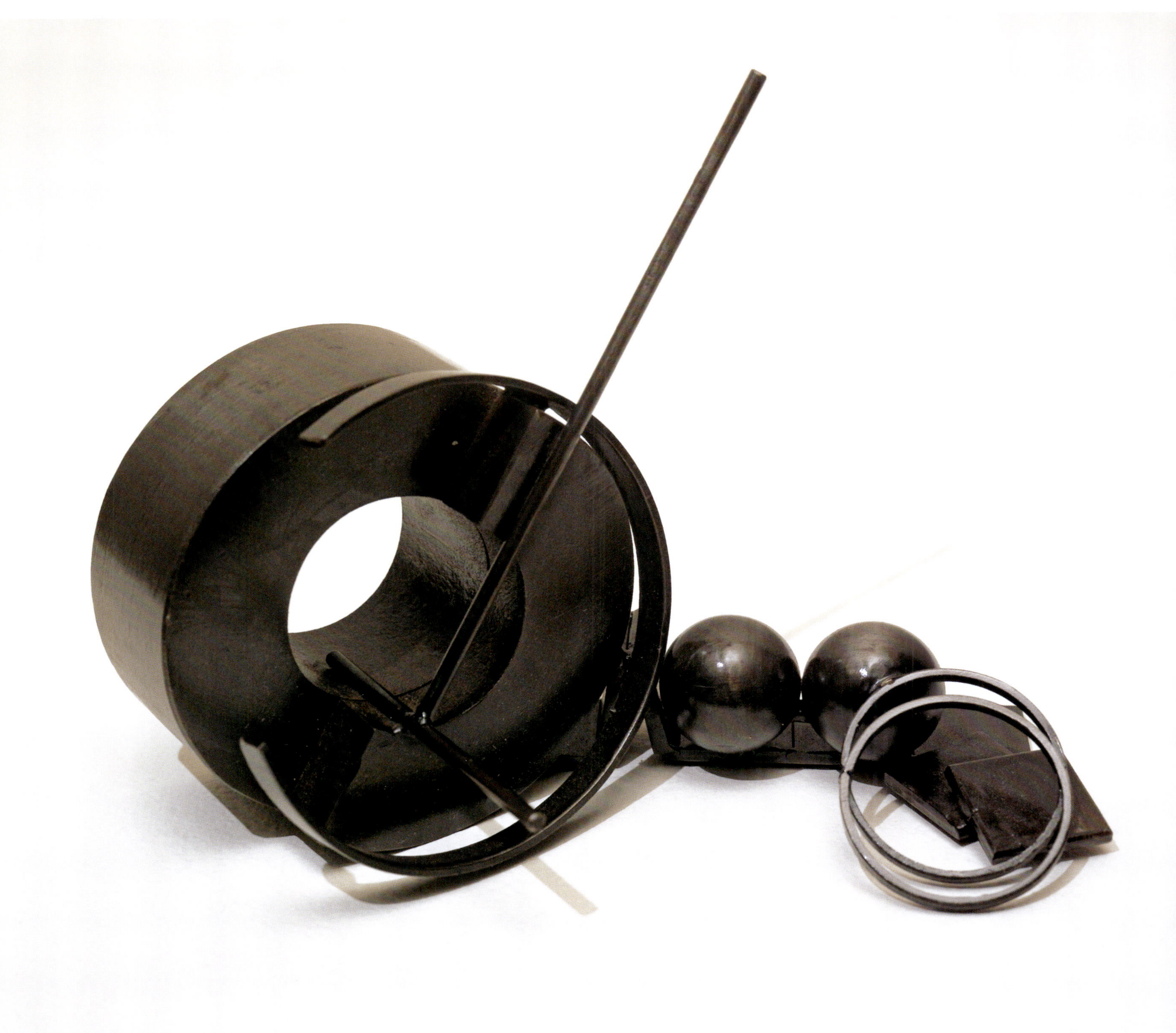

Donut with Balls No. 8 - Maquette

2000, painted steel
5½ x 5 x 6 inches
14 x 13 x 15 cm

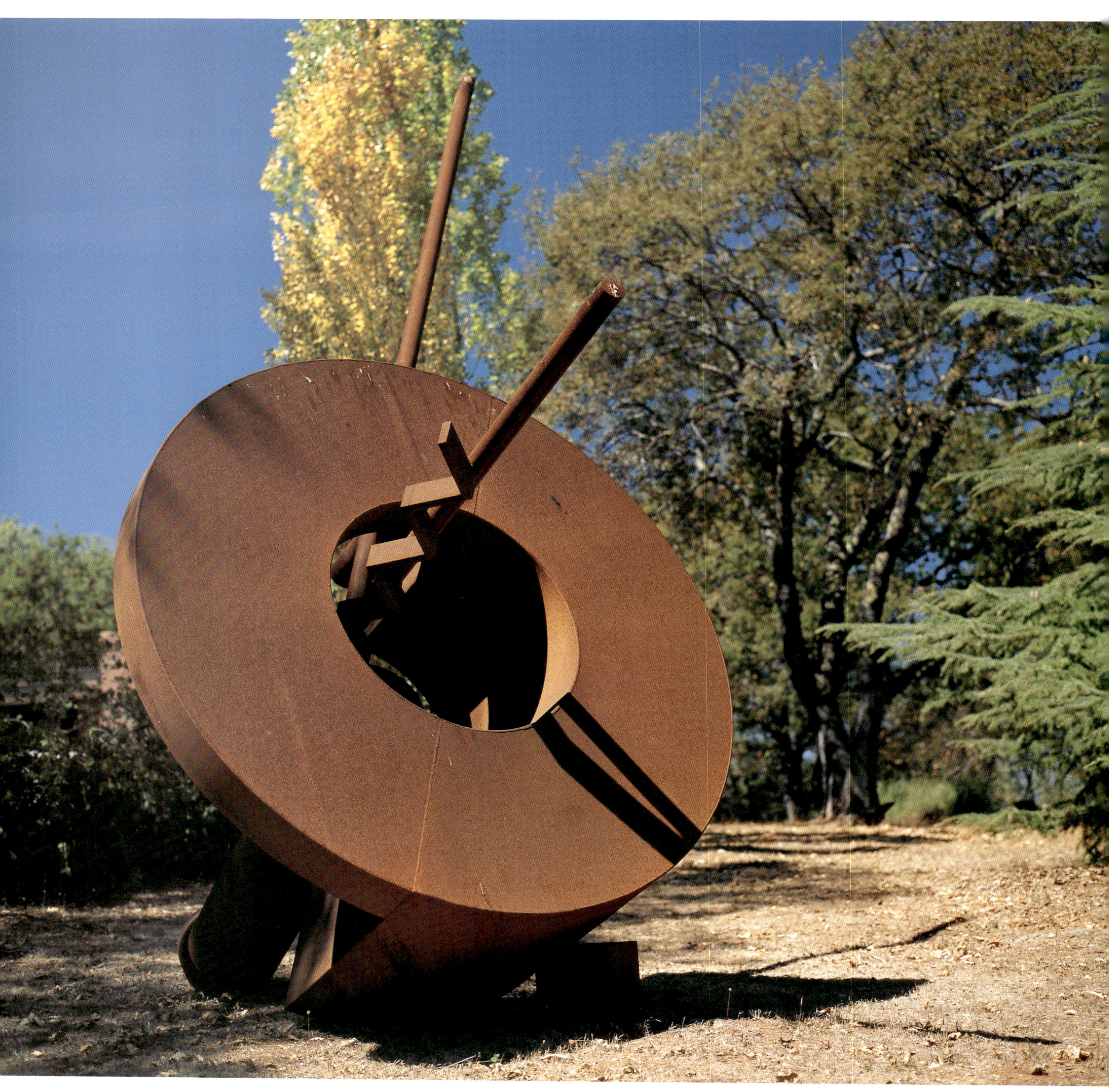

Tilted Donut No. 2

2003, Cor-ten steel
16 x 13 x 8 feet
488 x 396 x 244 cm

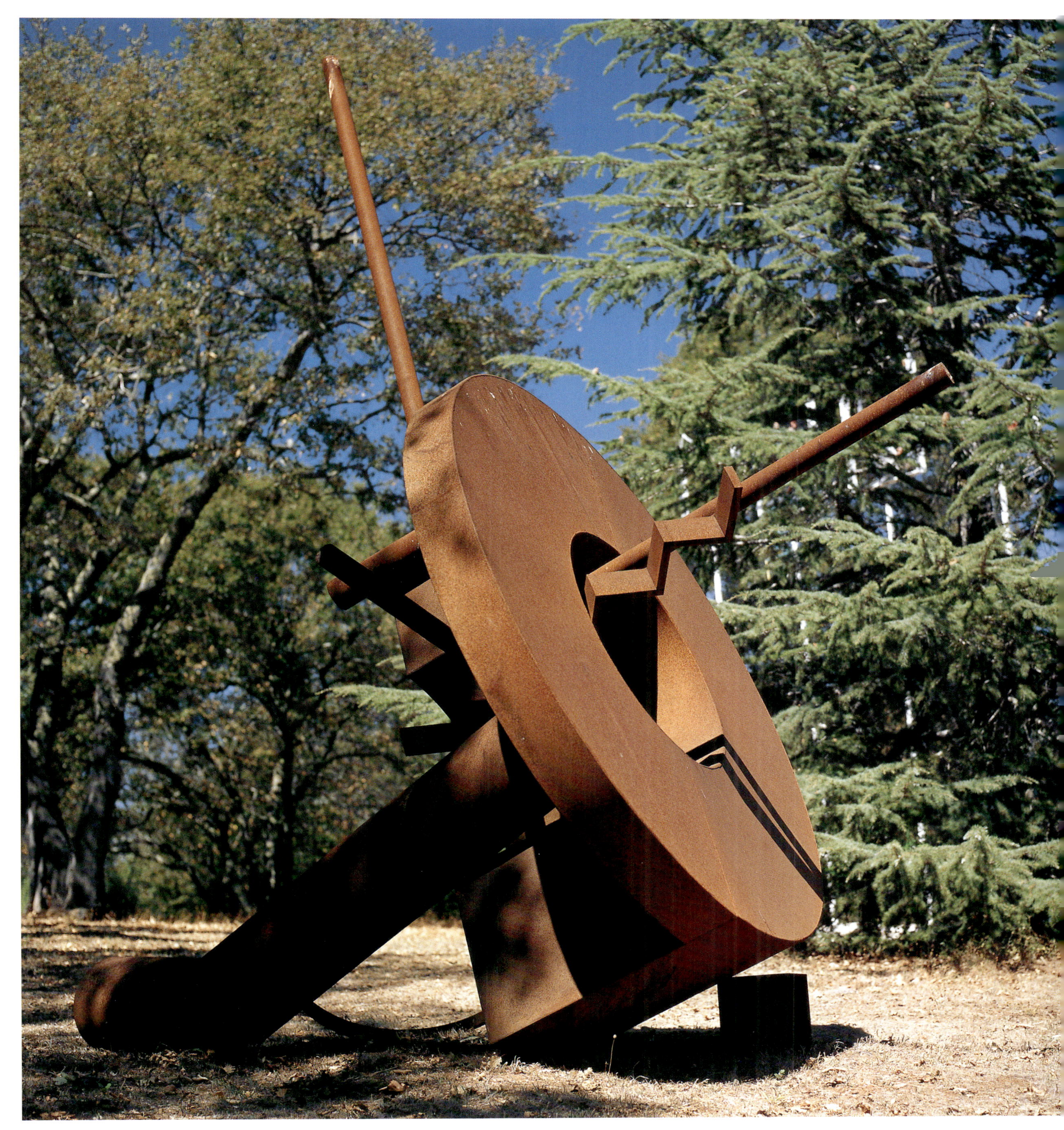

Tilted Donut No. 2

2003, Cor-ten steel
16 x 13 x 8 feet
488 x 396 x 244 cm

Installation view of Benton solo exhibition at Imago Galleries
Palm Desert, California 2004

▷
Folded Circle Split Rectangle

2001, Cor-ten steel
9 feet diameter
274 cm diameter

▷▷
Donut with Balls and L

2002, painted steel
10 x 7 x 8½ feet
305 x 213 x 259 cm

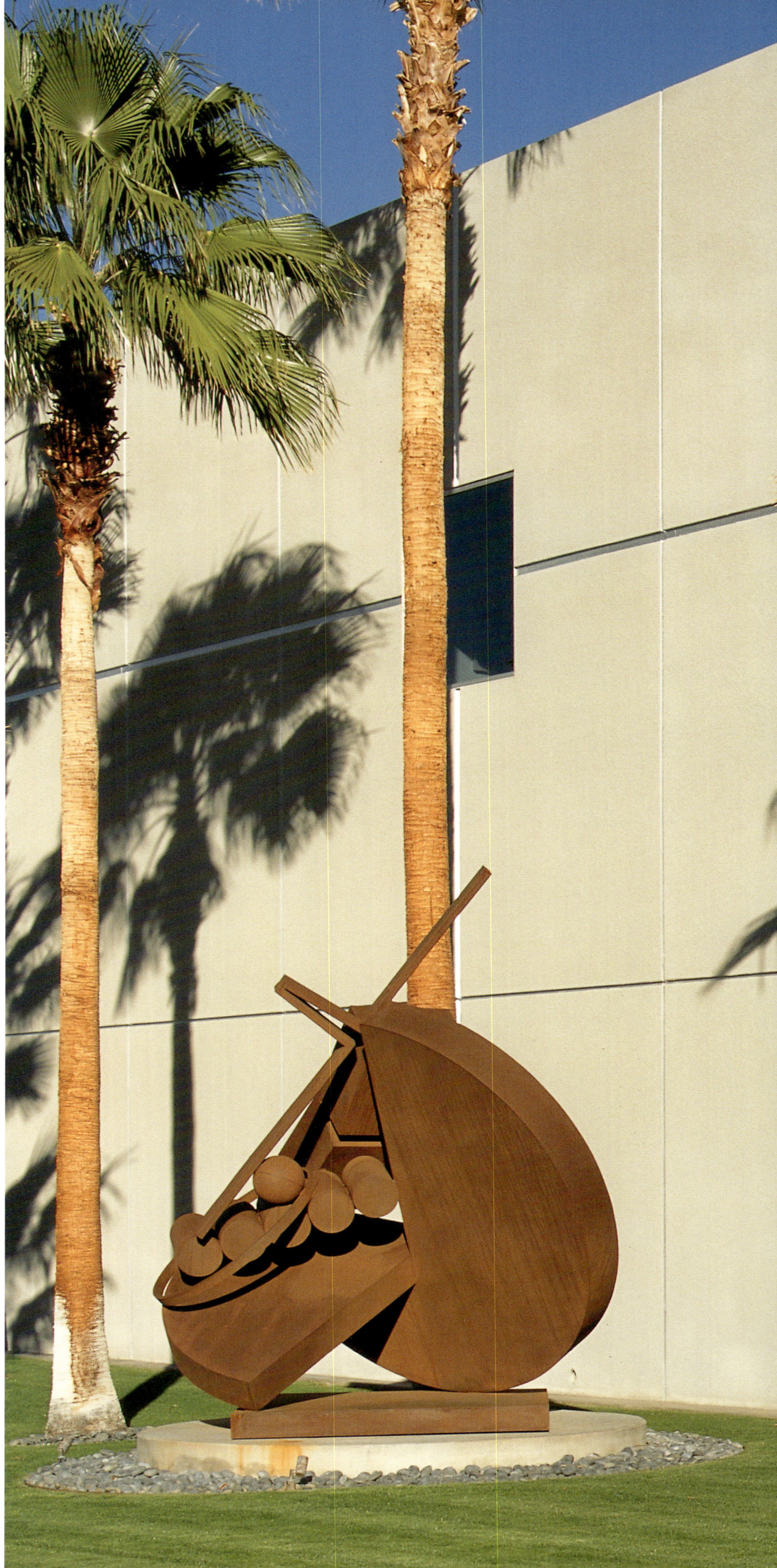

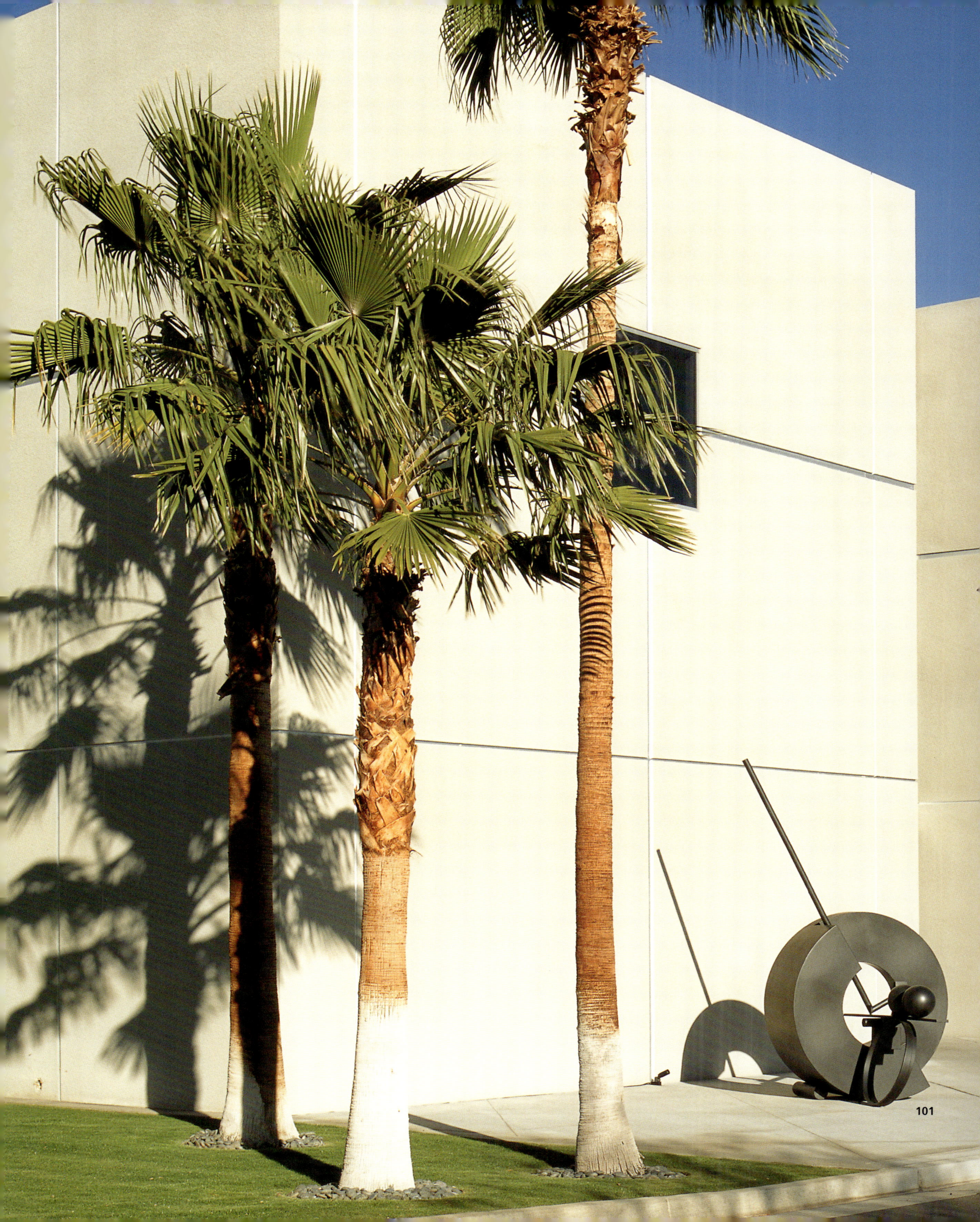

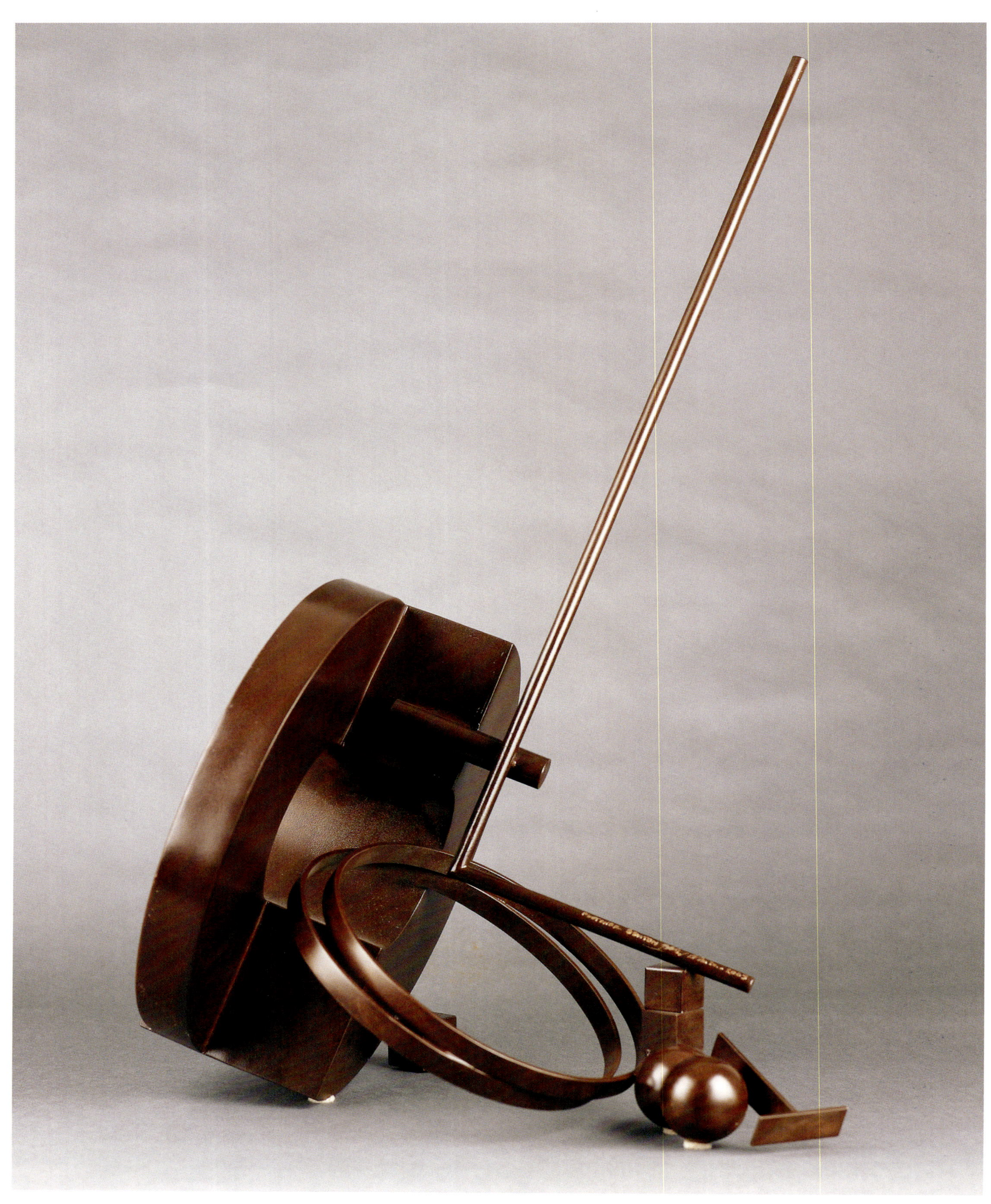

Tilted Donut with Balls and Cubes

2003, steel with patina
31½ x 21½ x 15 inches
80 x 55 x 38 cm

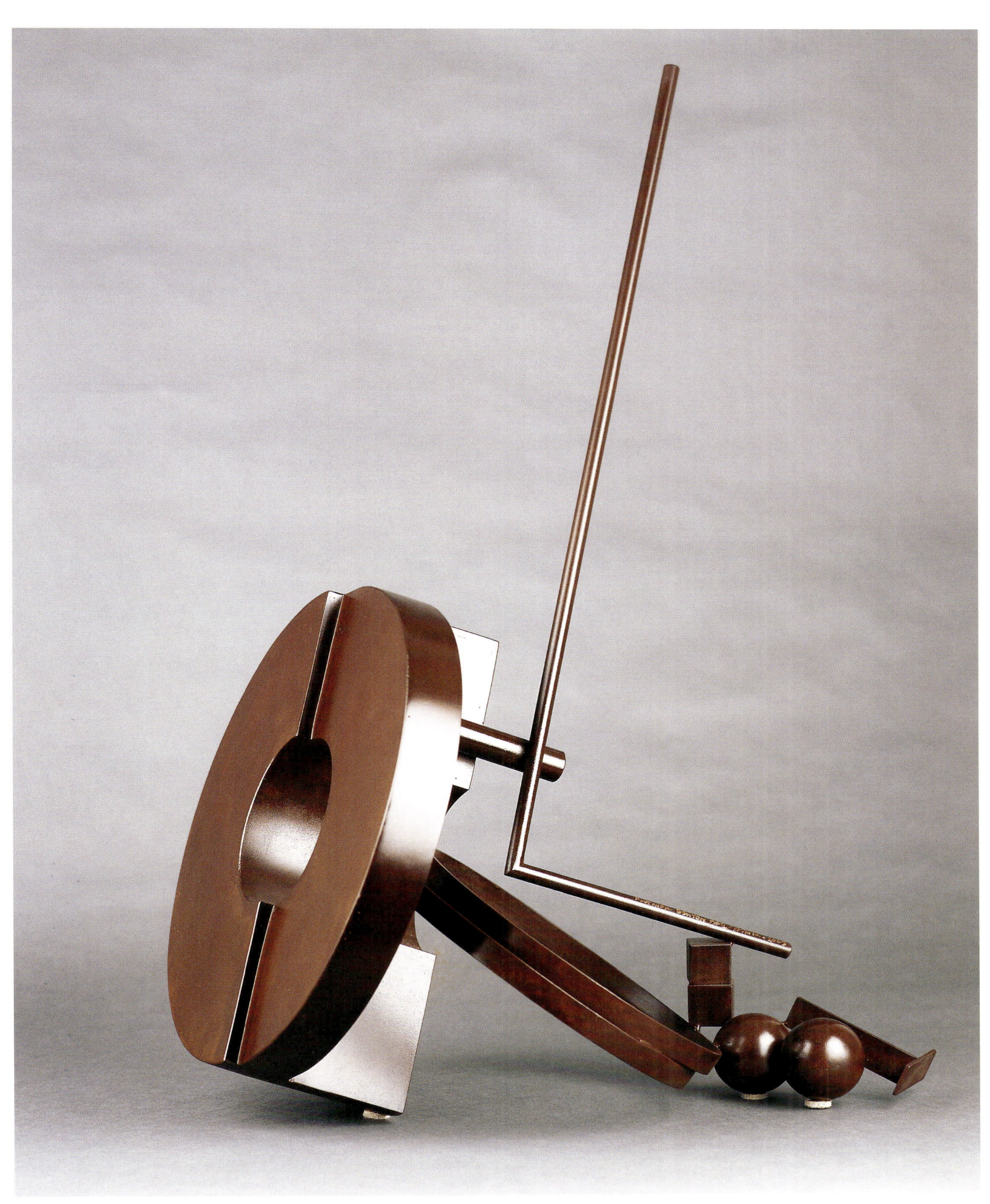

Tilted Donut with Balls and Cubes

2003, steel with patina
31½ x 21½ x 15 inches
80 x 55 x 38 cm

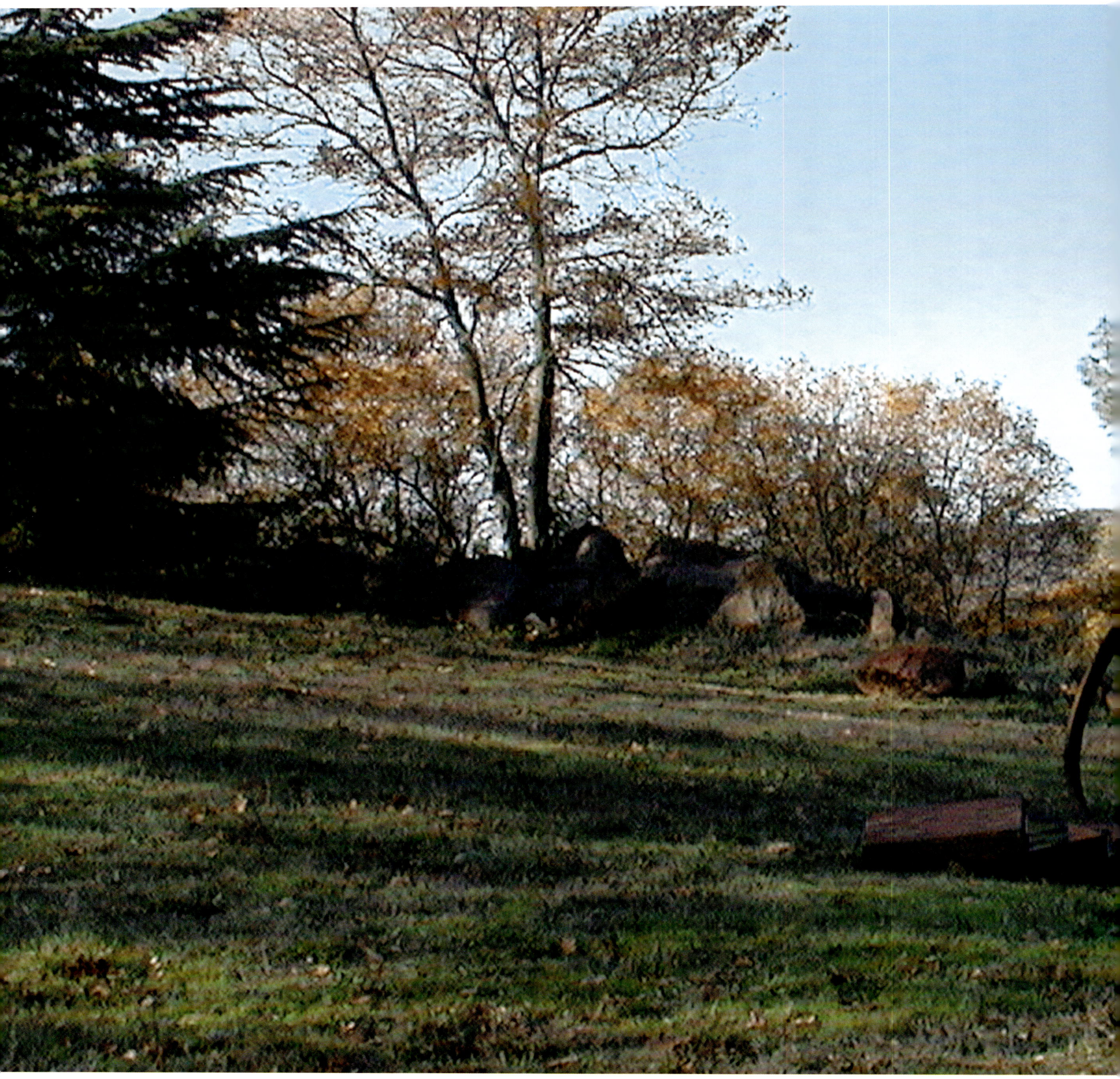

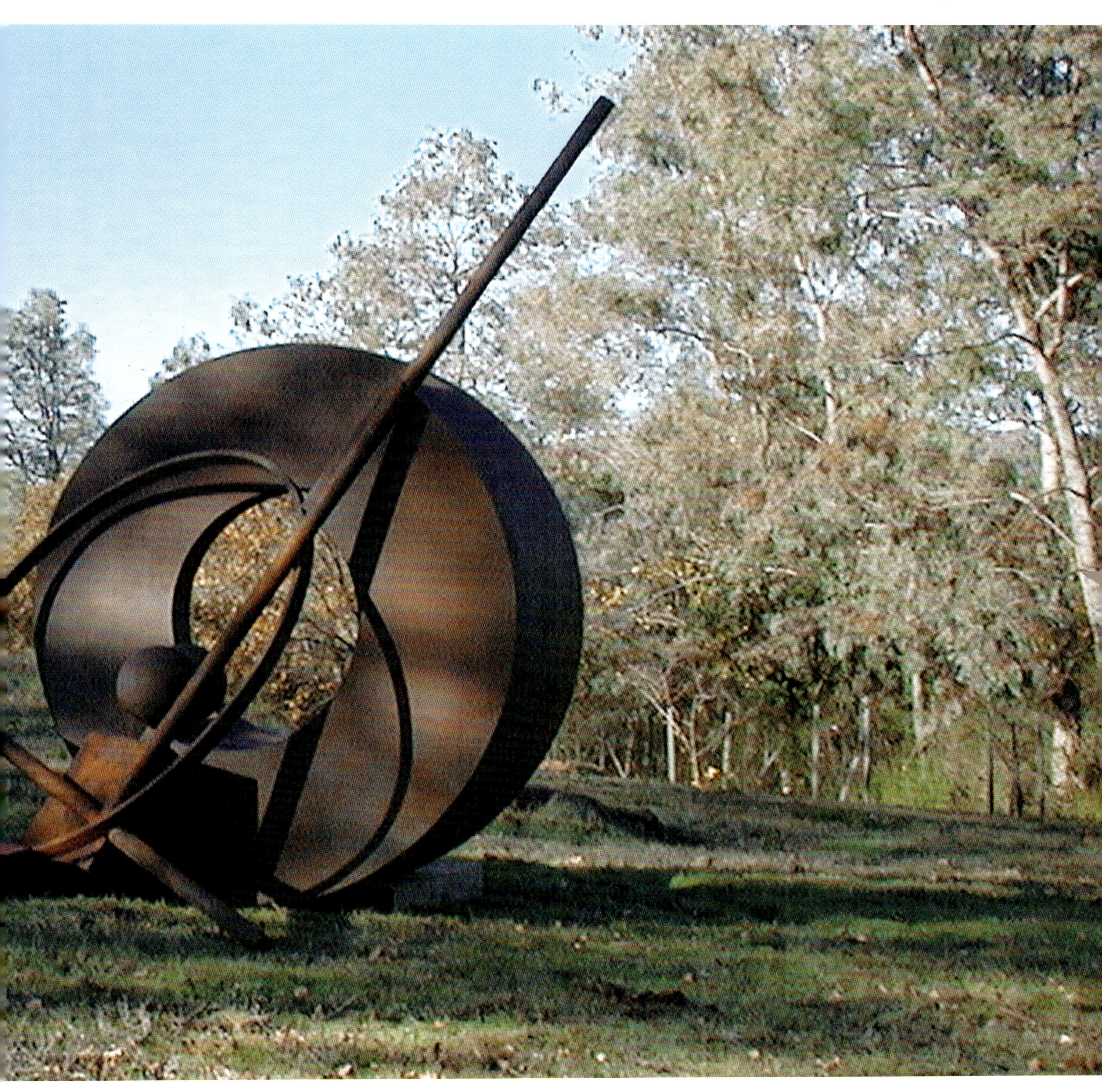

Donut with Balls and Ring

2000, Cor-ten steel
7 feet diameter
213 cm diameter

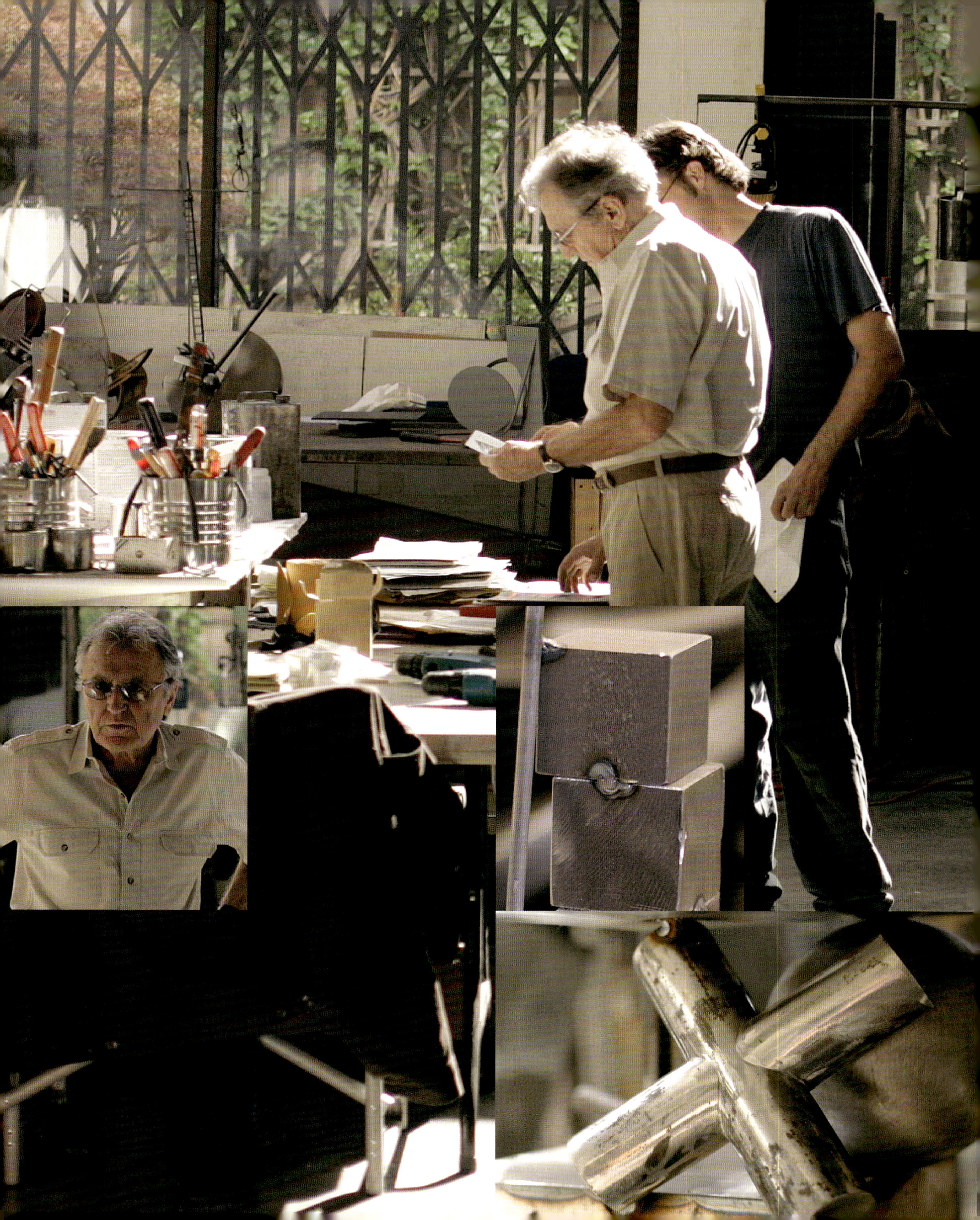

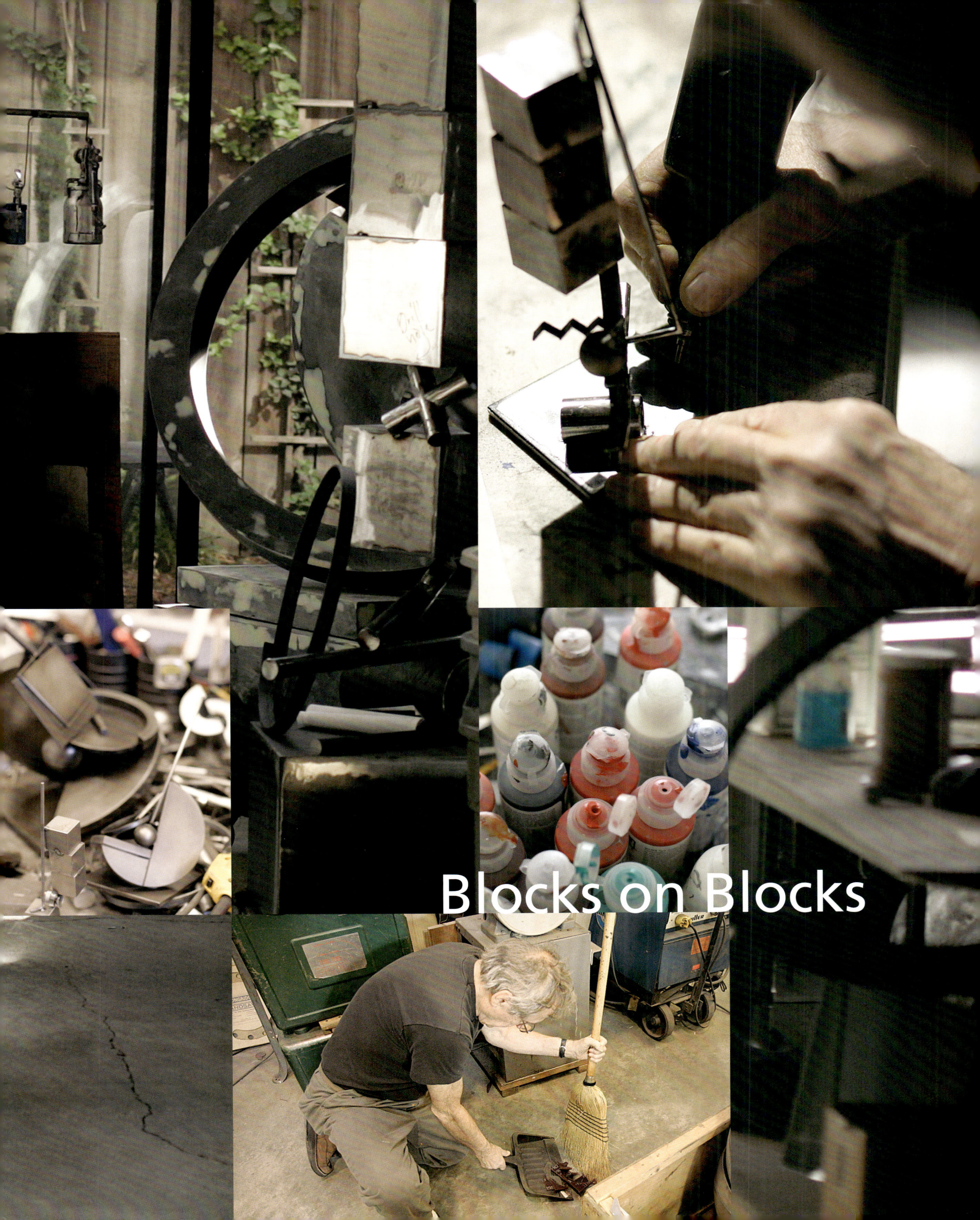

Blocks on Blocks

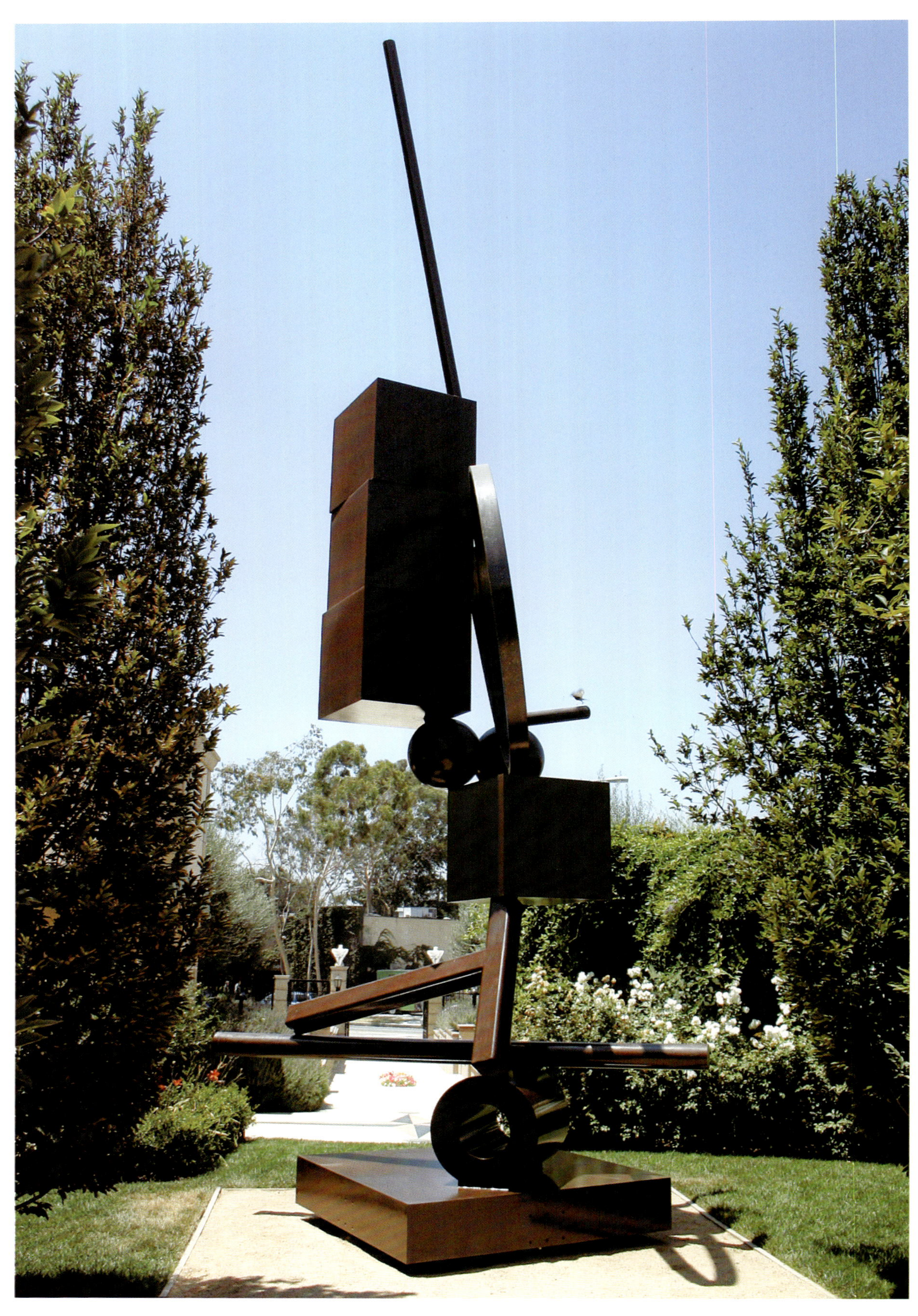

△ ▷

Blocks on Blocks, Putter and Two Balls

2002, varnished Cor-ten steel
H: 27 feet
H: 823 cm
The Pinnacle, Los Angeles

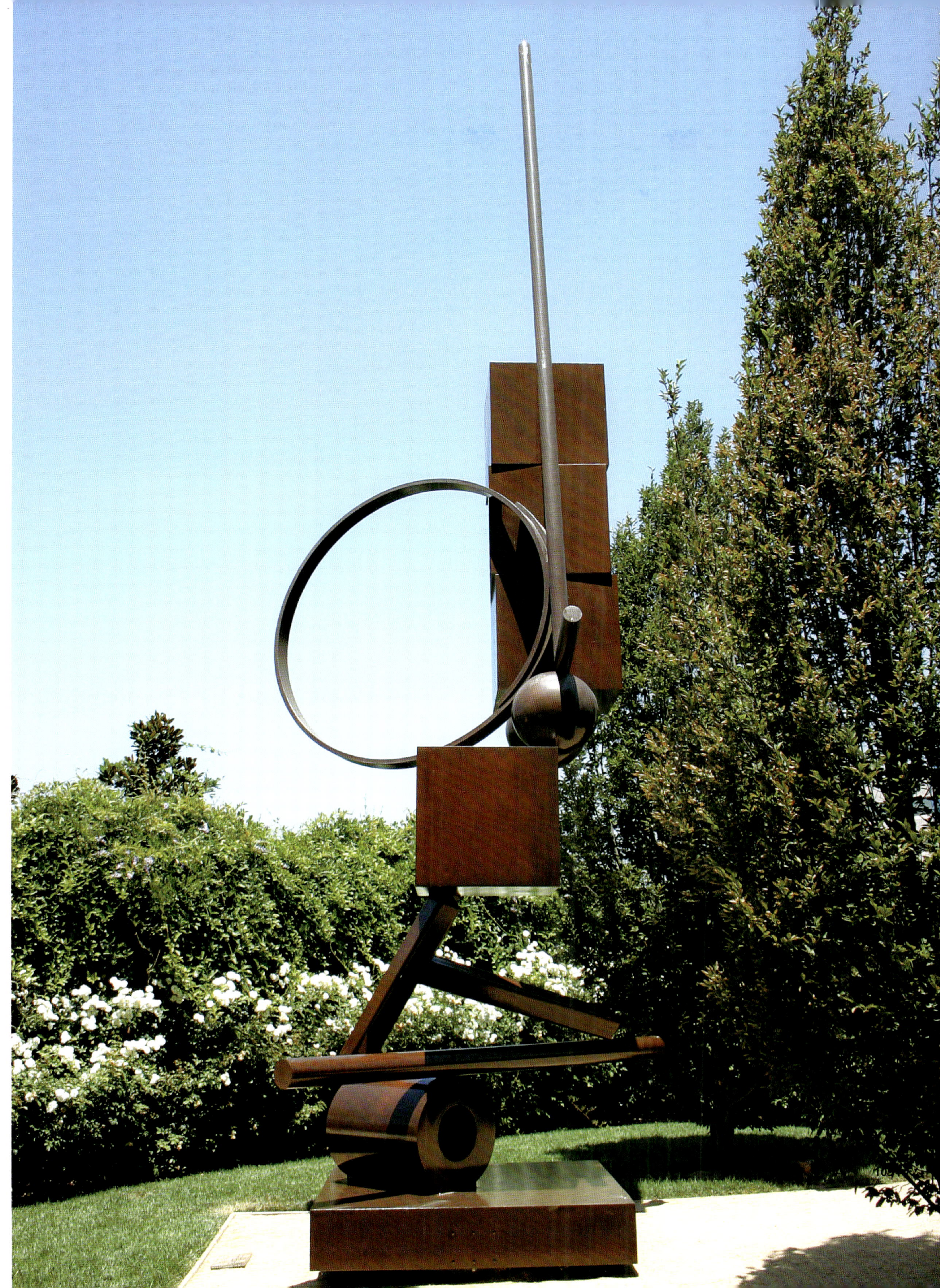

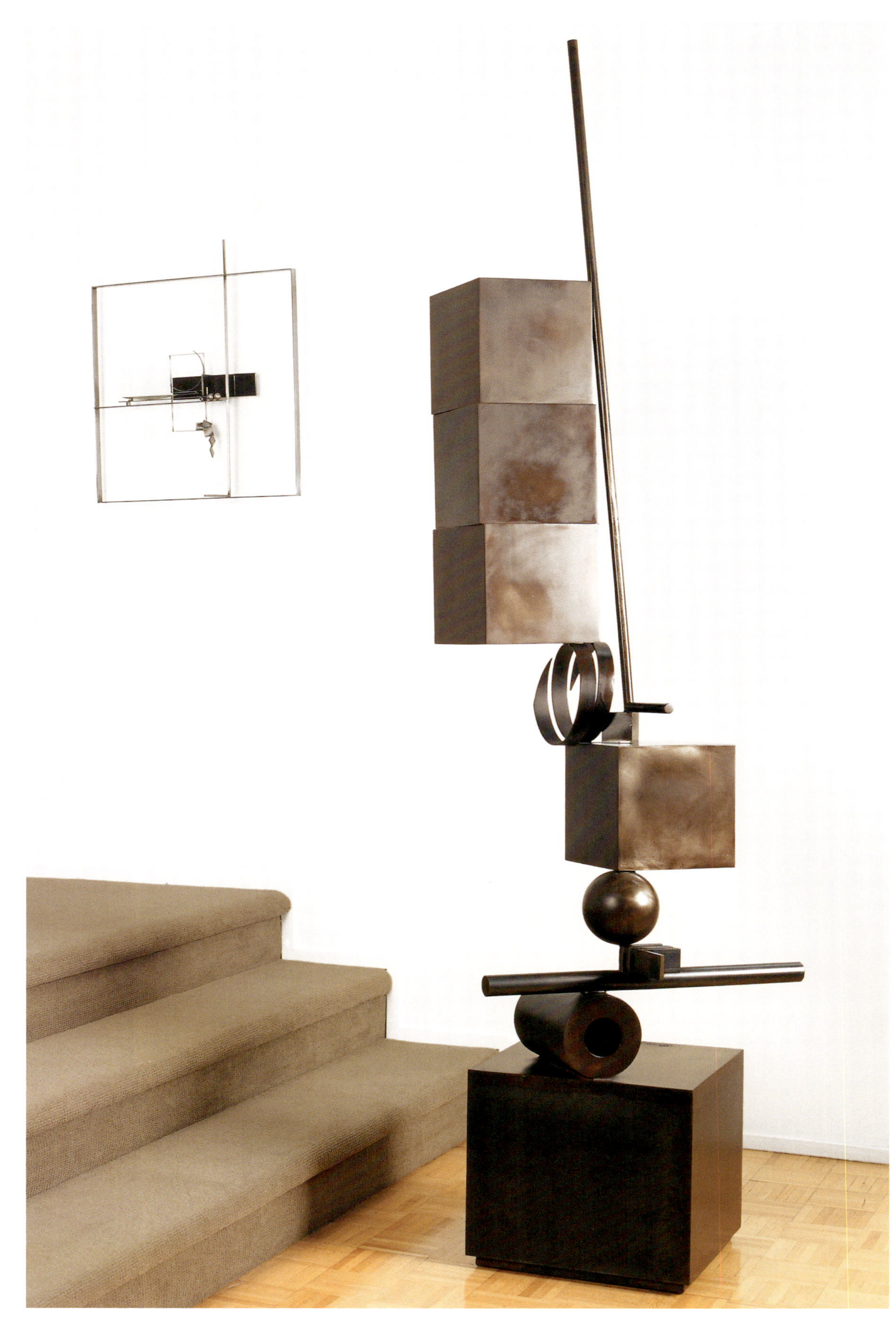

Blocks on Blocks: Three on One, Spring

2005, steel with patina
101 x 27 x 24 inches
257 x 69 x 61 cm

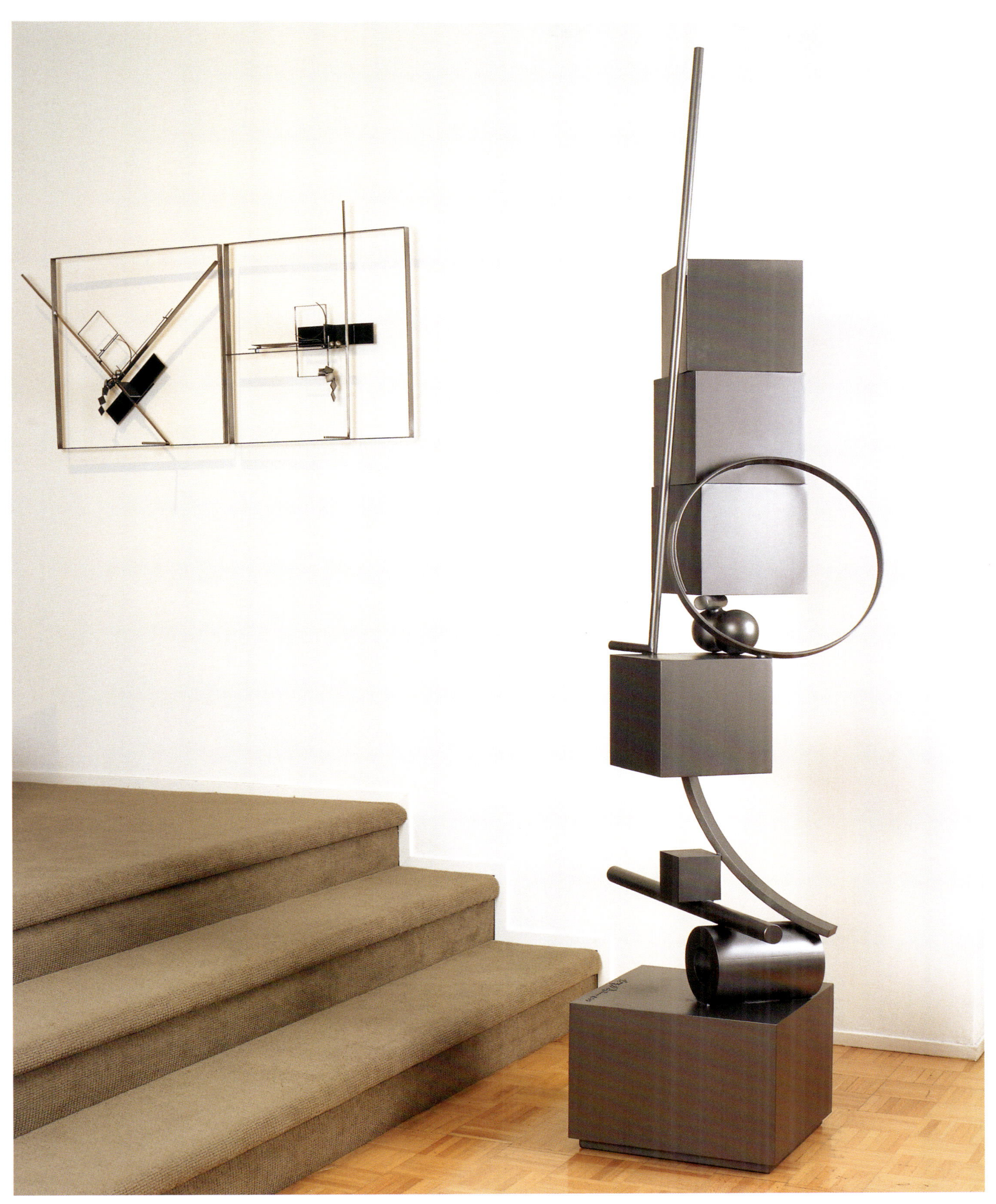

Blocks on Blocks: Three on One, Cube

2005, painted steel
98 x 29 x 26 inches
249 x 74 x 66 cm

Blocks on Blocks: Three on One, Falling Squares

2005, steel with patina
36½ x 11 x 11 inches
93 x 28 x 28 cm

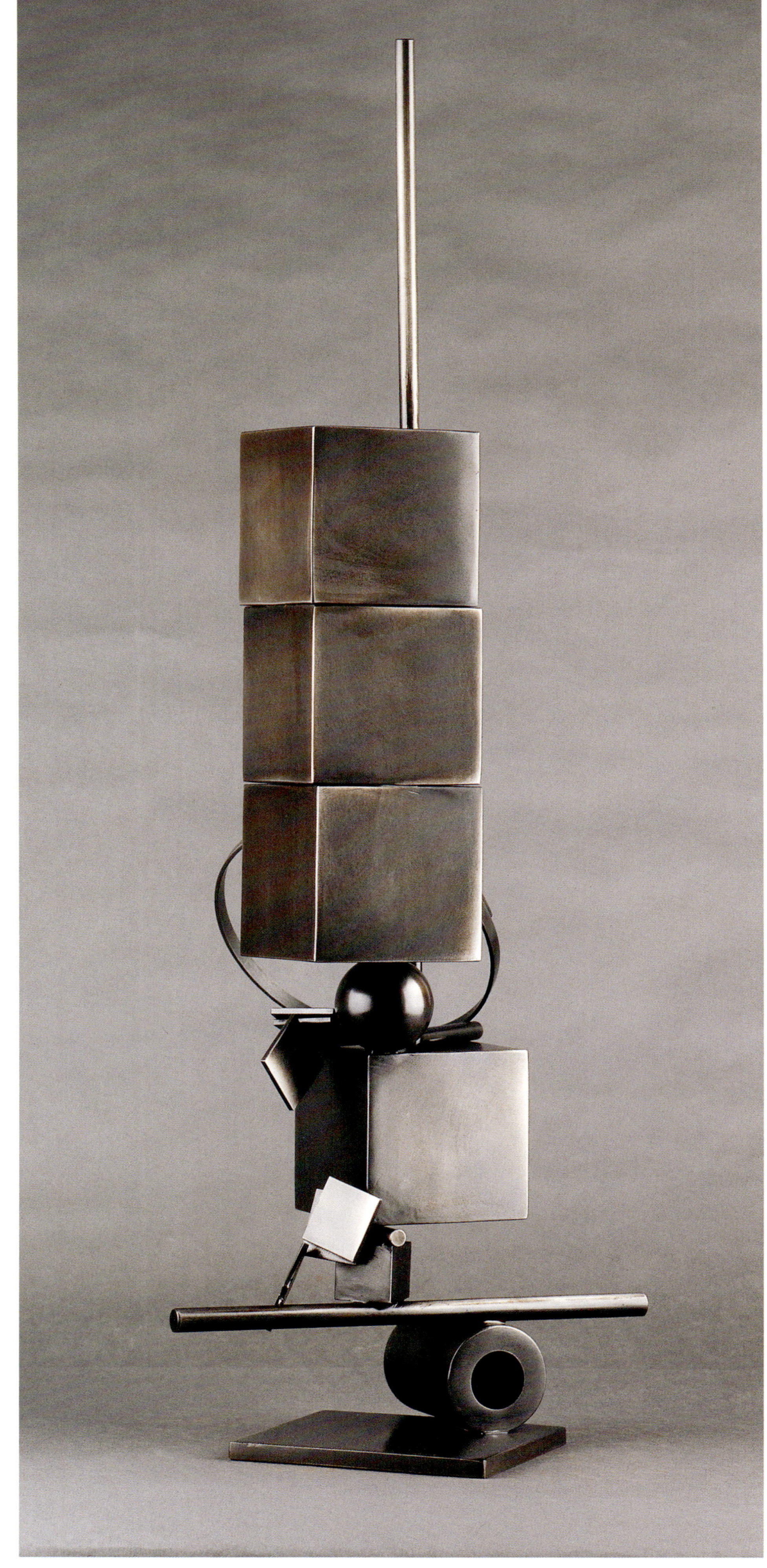

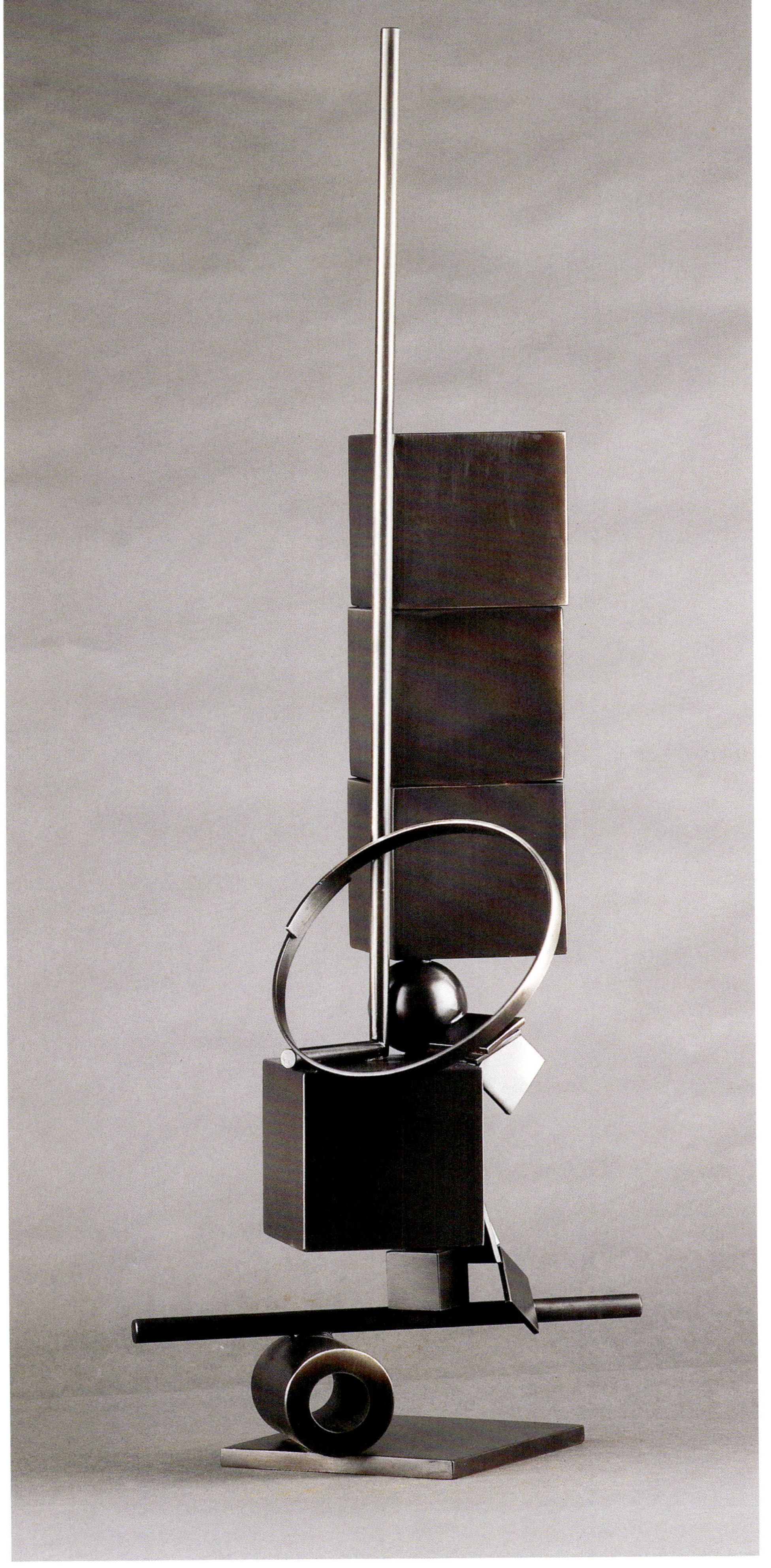

Blocks on Blocks: Three on One, Falling Squares

2005, steel with patina
36½ x 11 x 11 inches
93 x 28 x 28 cm

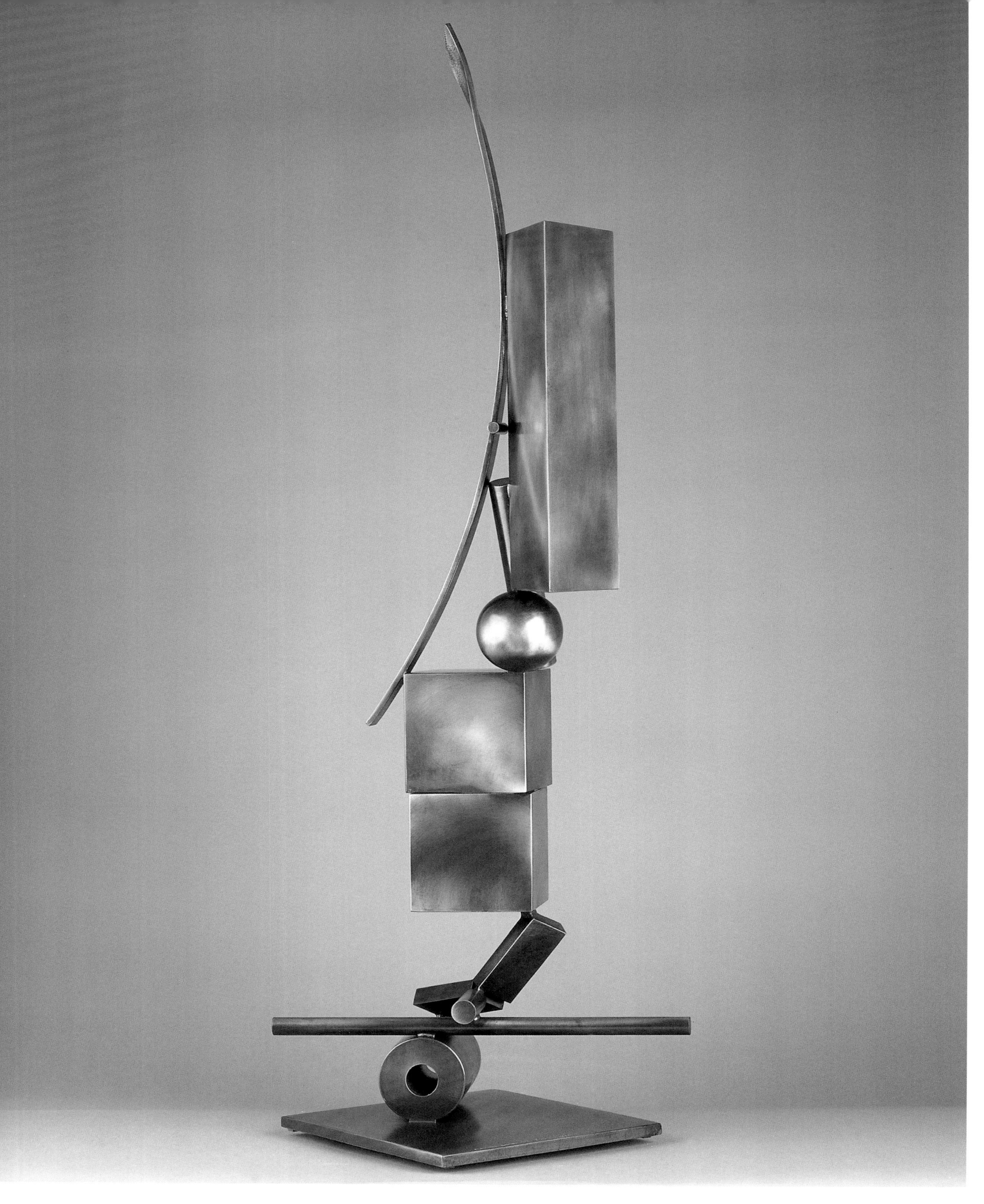

Blocks on Blocks: 1 on 1, Ball

2005, steel with patina
46 x 13½ x 11½ inches
117 x 34 x 29 cm

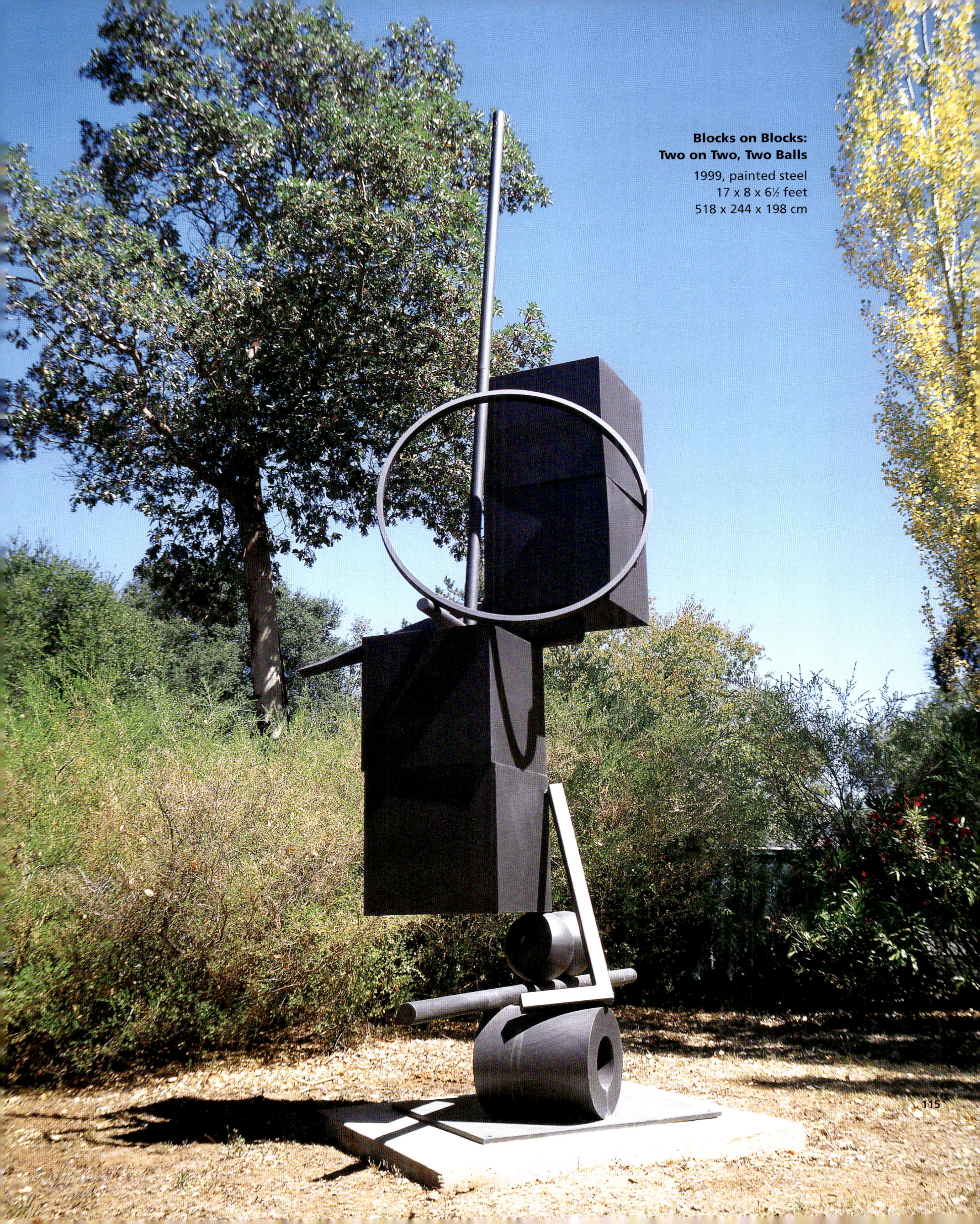

Blocks on Blocks:
Two on Two, Two Balls
1999, painted steel
17 x 8 x 6½ feet
518 x 244 x 198 cm

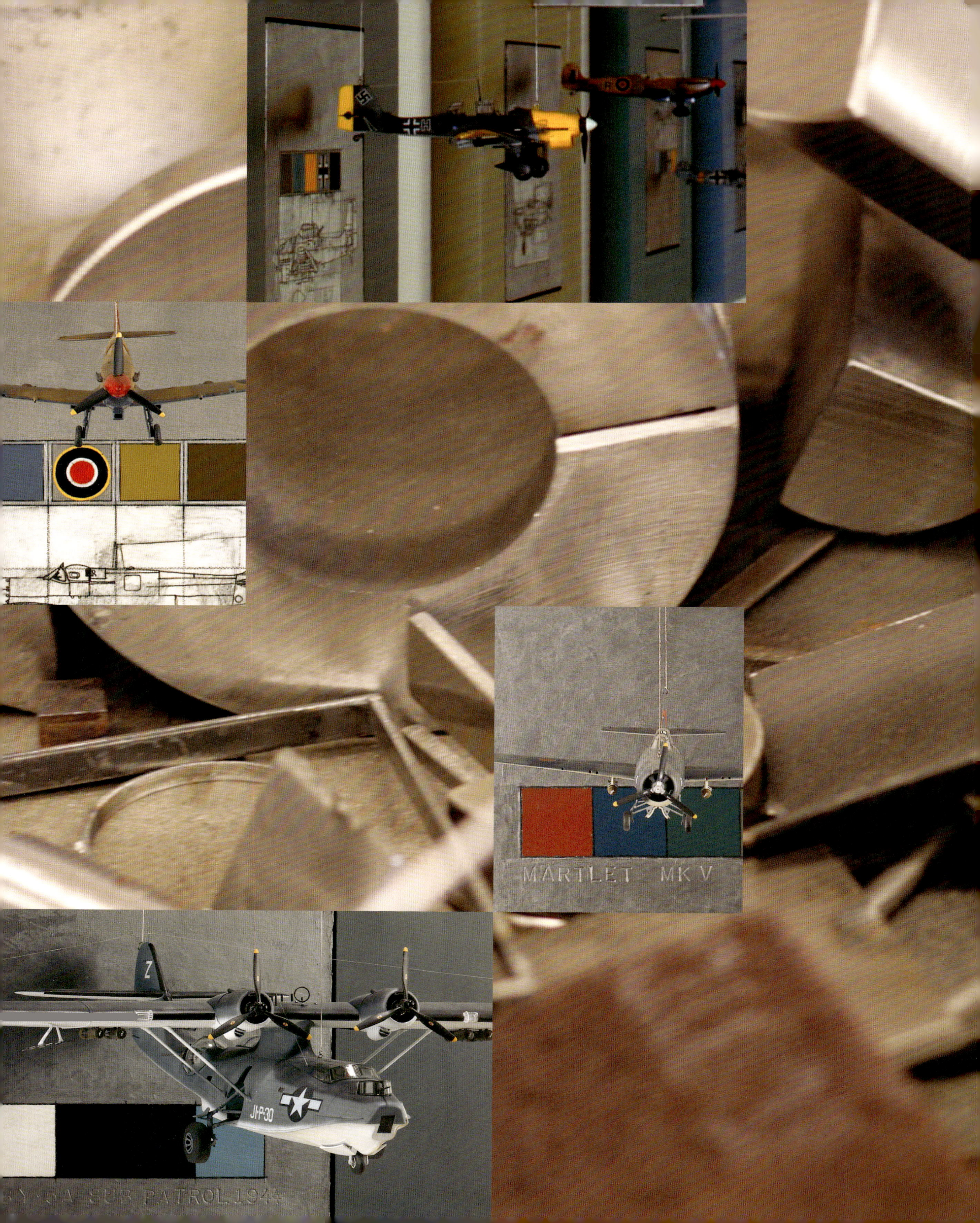
MARTLET MK V
SUB PATROL 1944

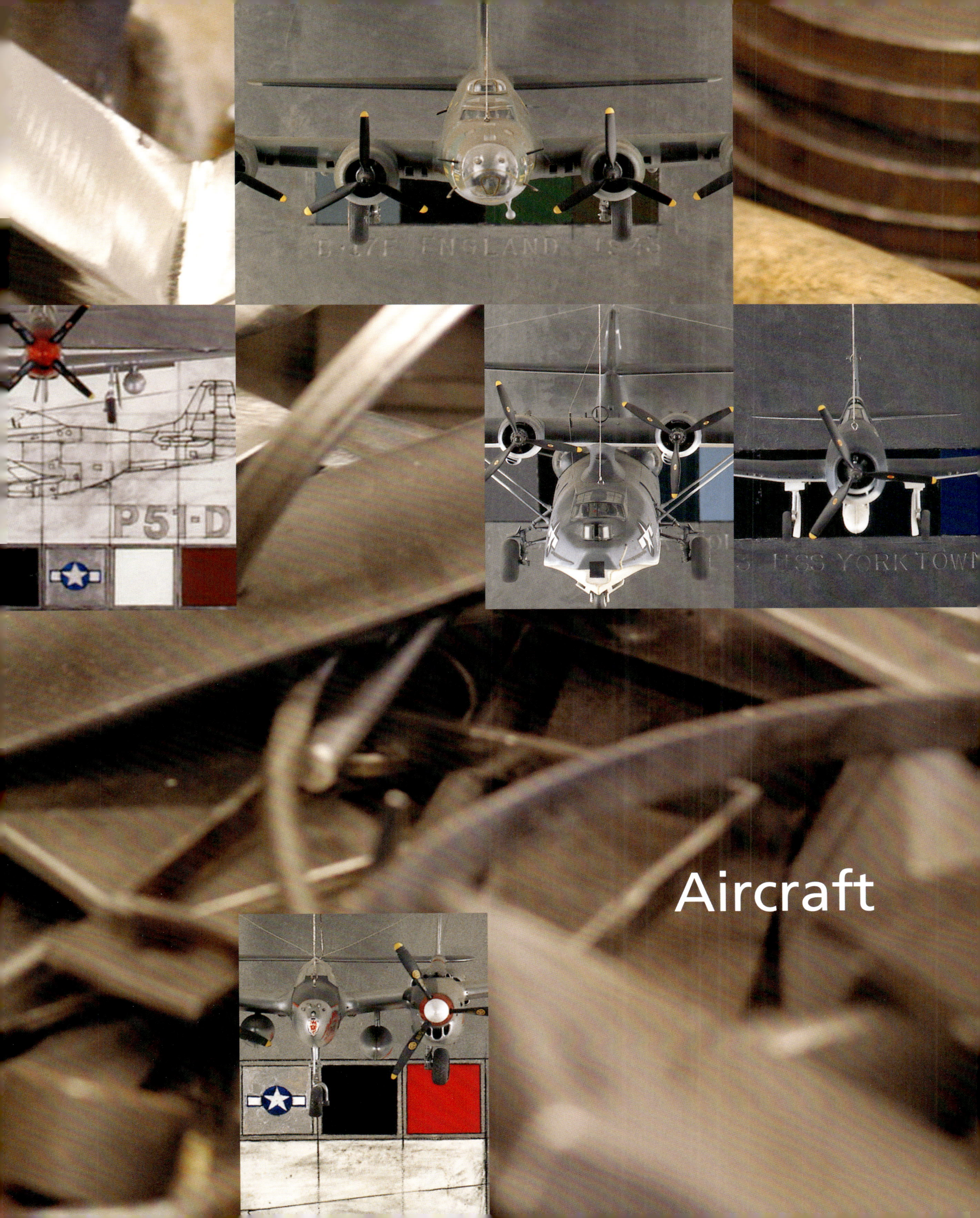

Aircraft

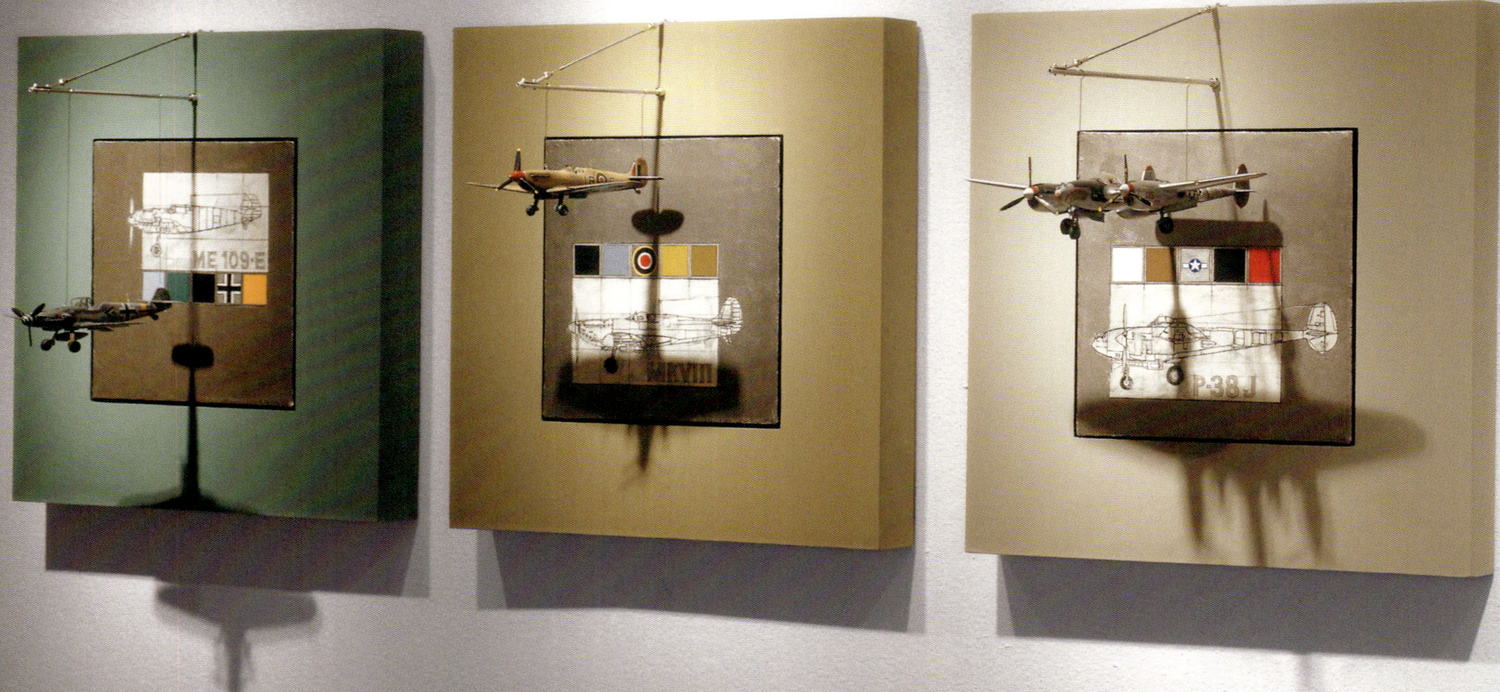

Homage to WW II Aircraft
Installation view at Riva Yares Gallery,
Scottsdale, Arizona 1998

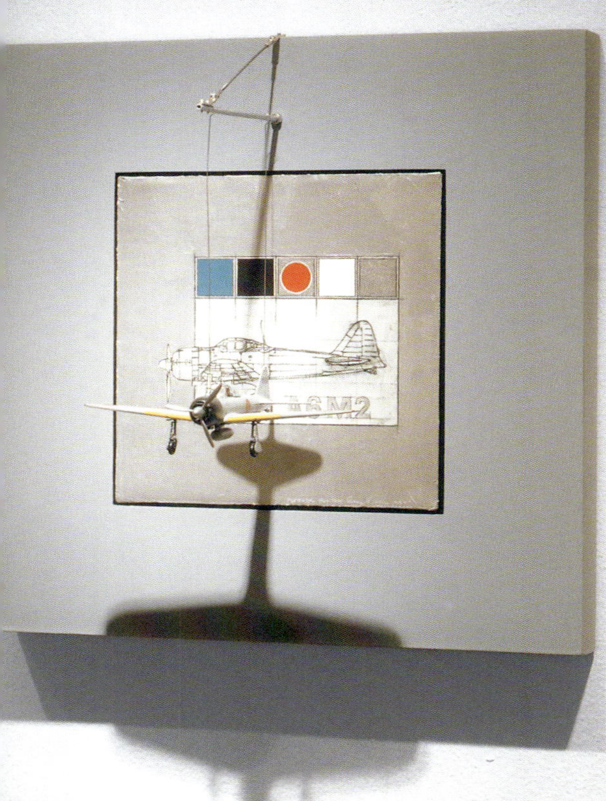

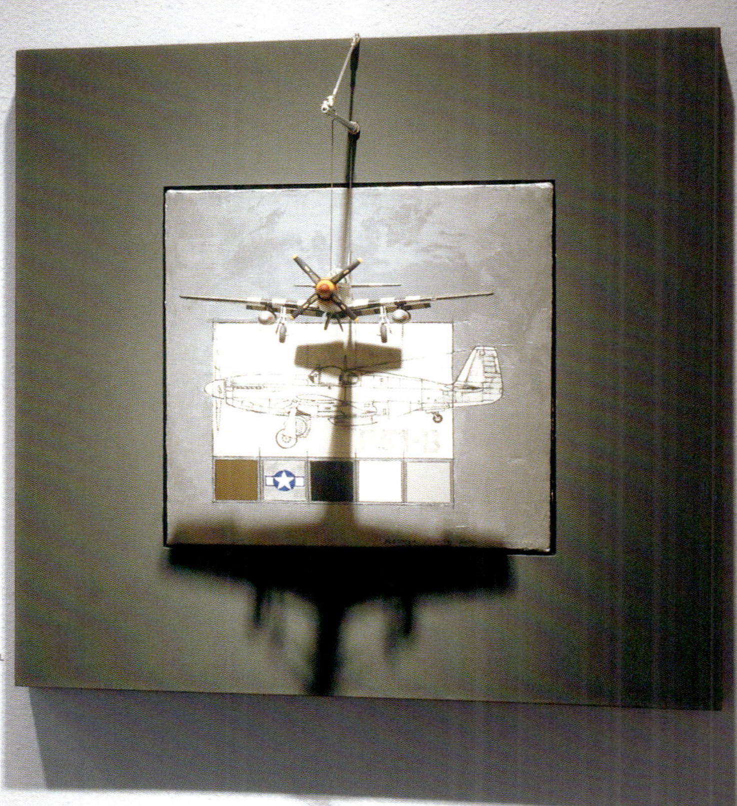

Homage to WW II Aircraft: TBF.10.U.S.N 8/2 1944

1997, assemblage
22 x 22 inches
56 x 56 cm

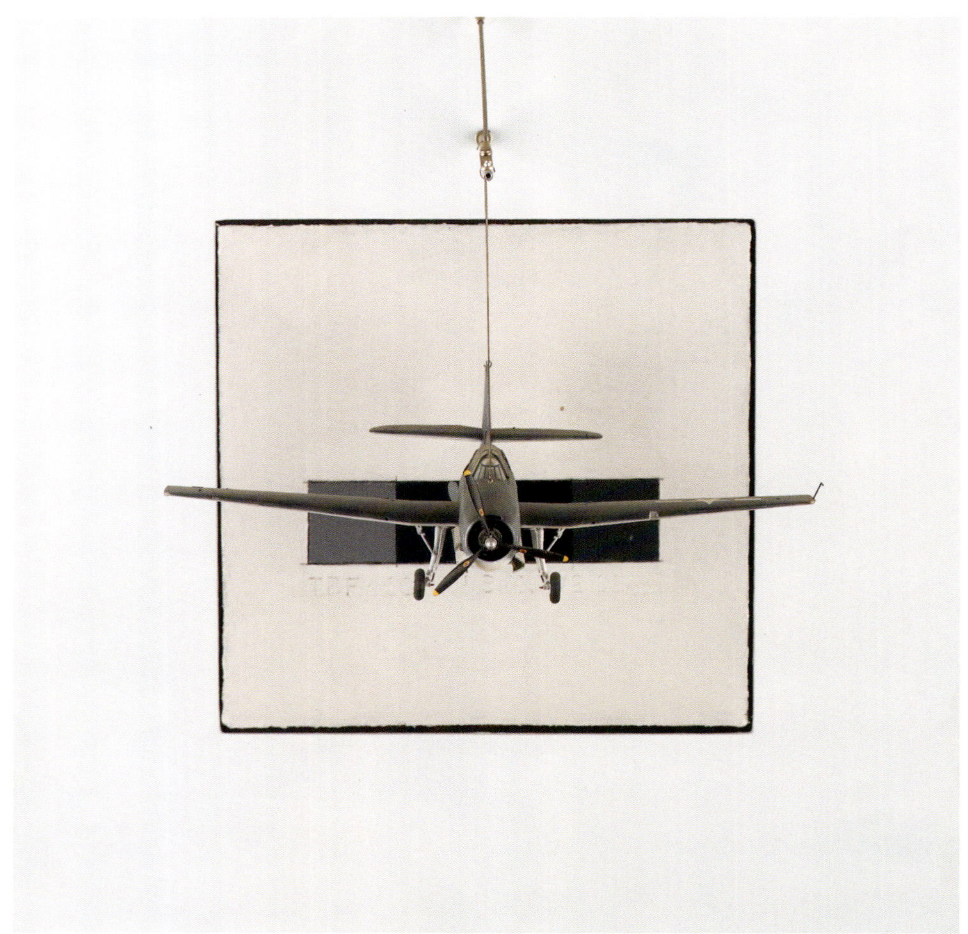

Homage to WW II Aircraft: MKVIII

1997, assemblage
22 x 22 inches
56 x 56 cm

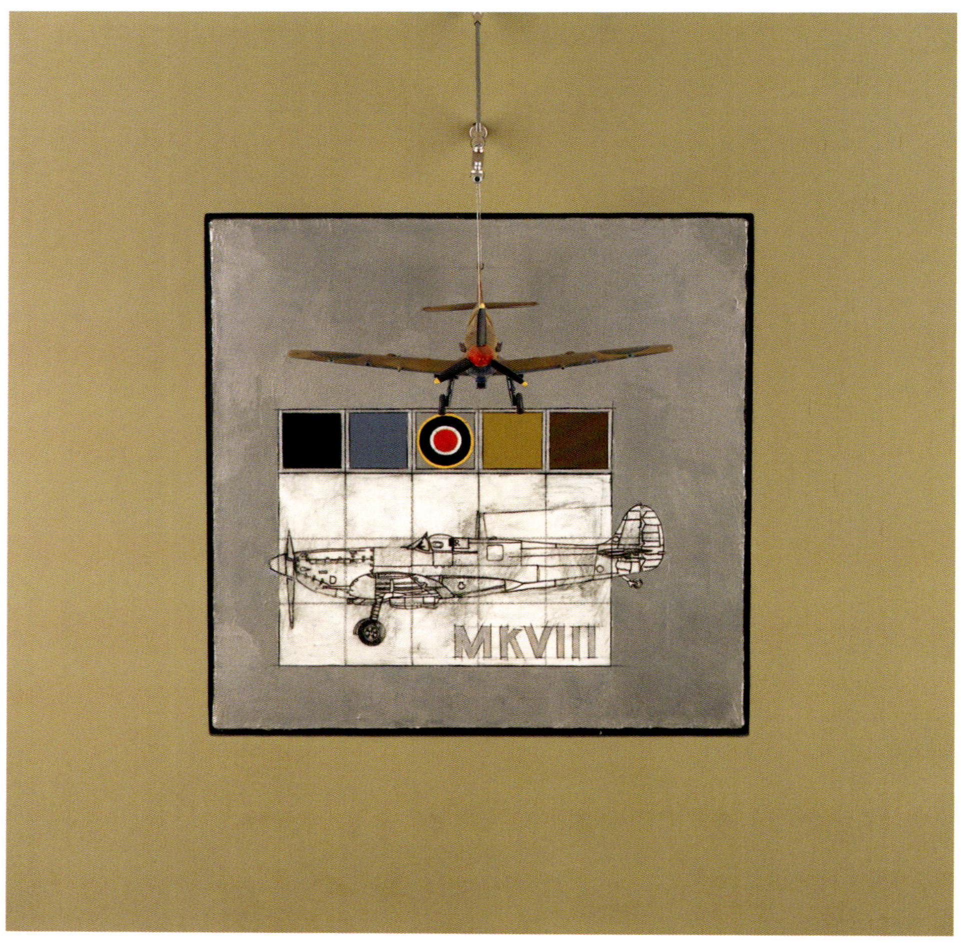

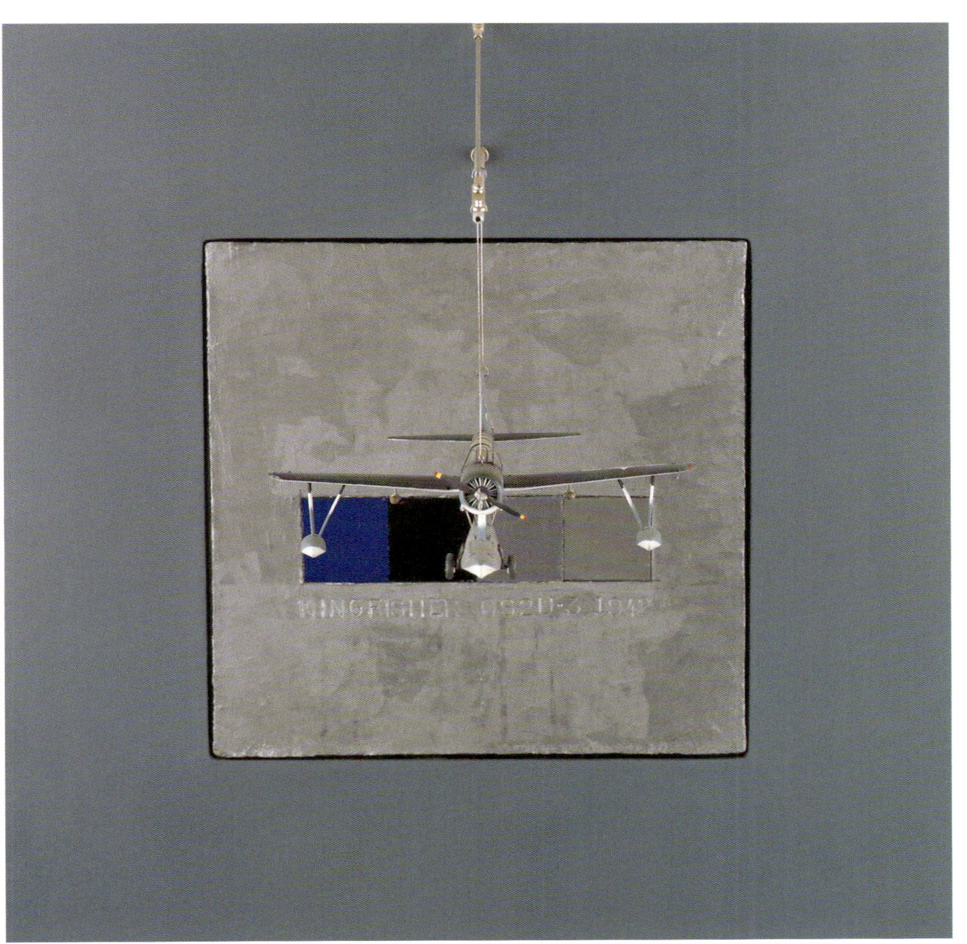

Homage to WW II Aircraft: Kingfischer, OS2U3

1996, assemblage
22 x 22 inches
56 x 56 cm

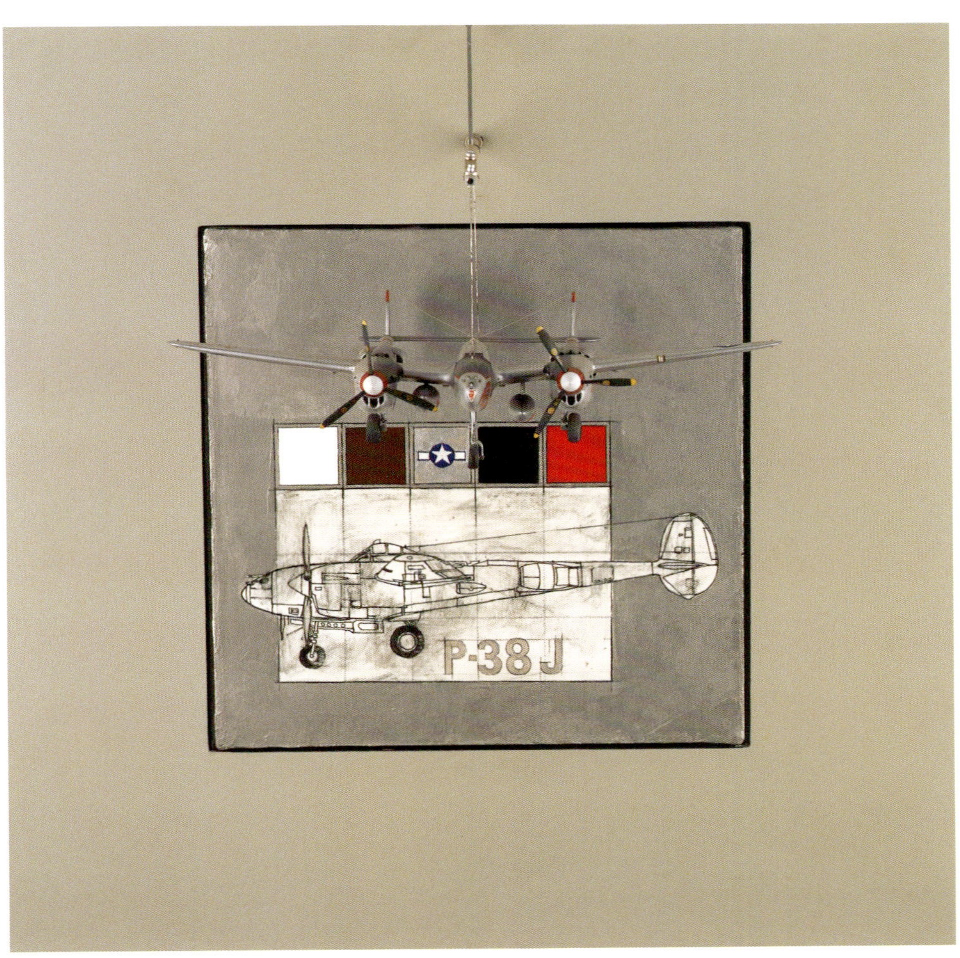

Homage to WW II Aircraft: P-38J

1997, assemblage
22 x 22 inches
56 x 56 cm

Homage to WW II Aircraft: B.17 F

1997, assemblage
22 x 25 inches
56 x 64 cm

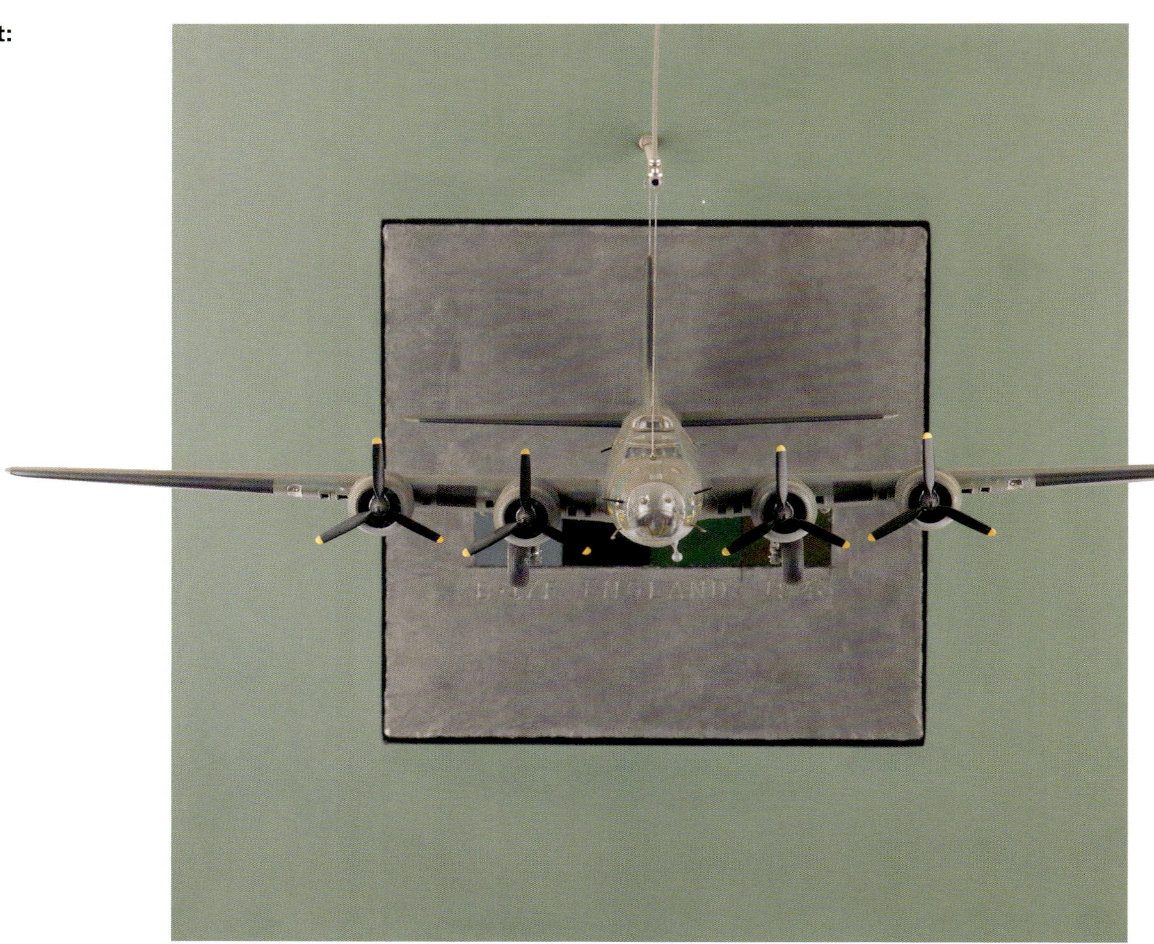

Homage to WW II Aircraft: PBY-5A

1997, assemblage
22 x 25 inches
56 x 64 cm

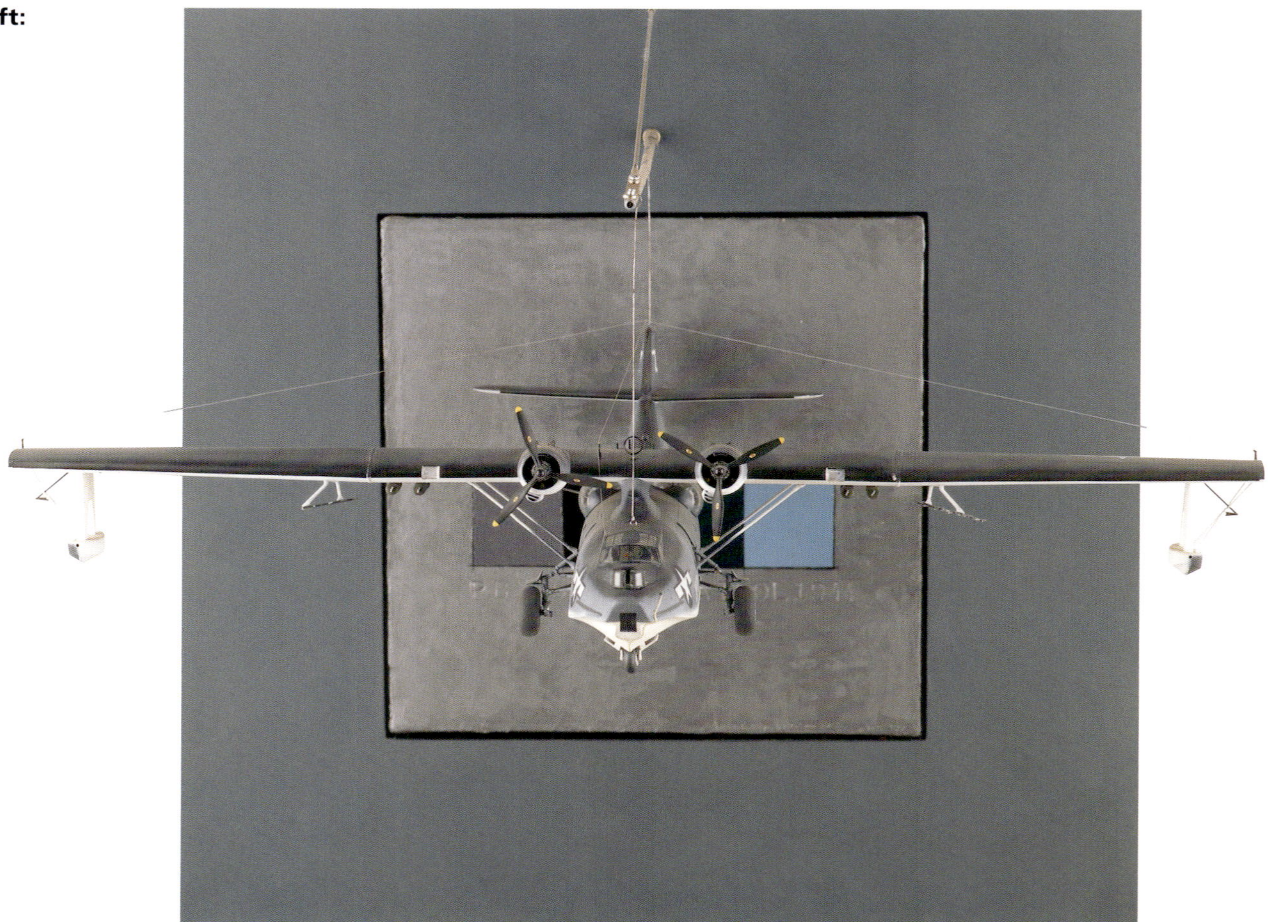

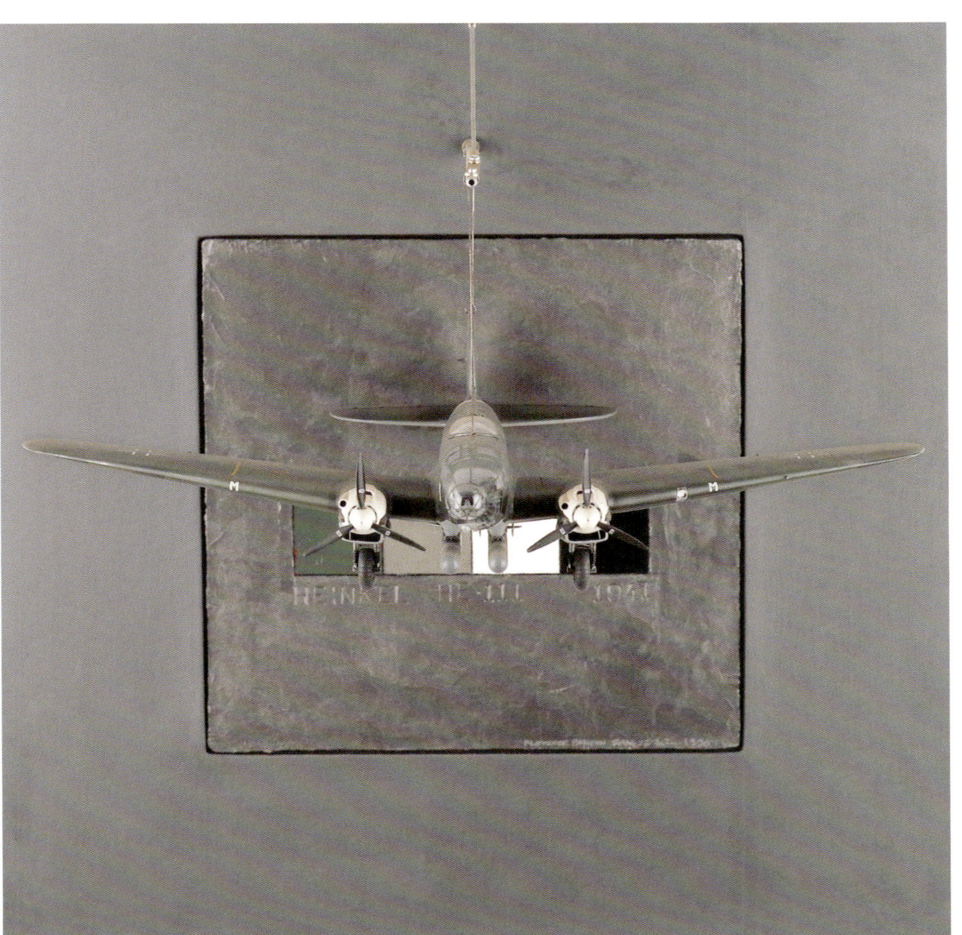

Homage to WW II Aircraft: Heinkel, HE-111 1941

1996, assemblage
22 x 22 inches
56 x 56 cm

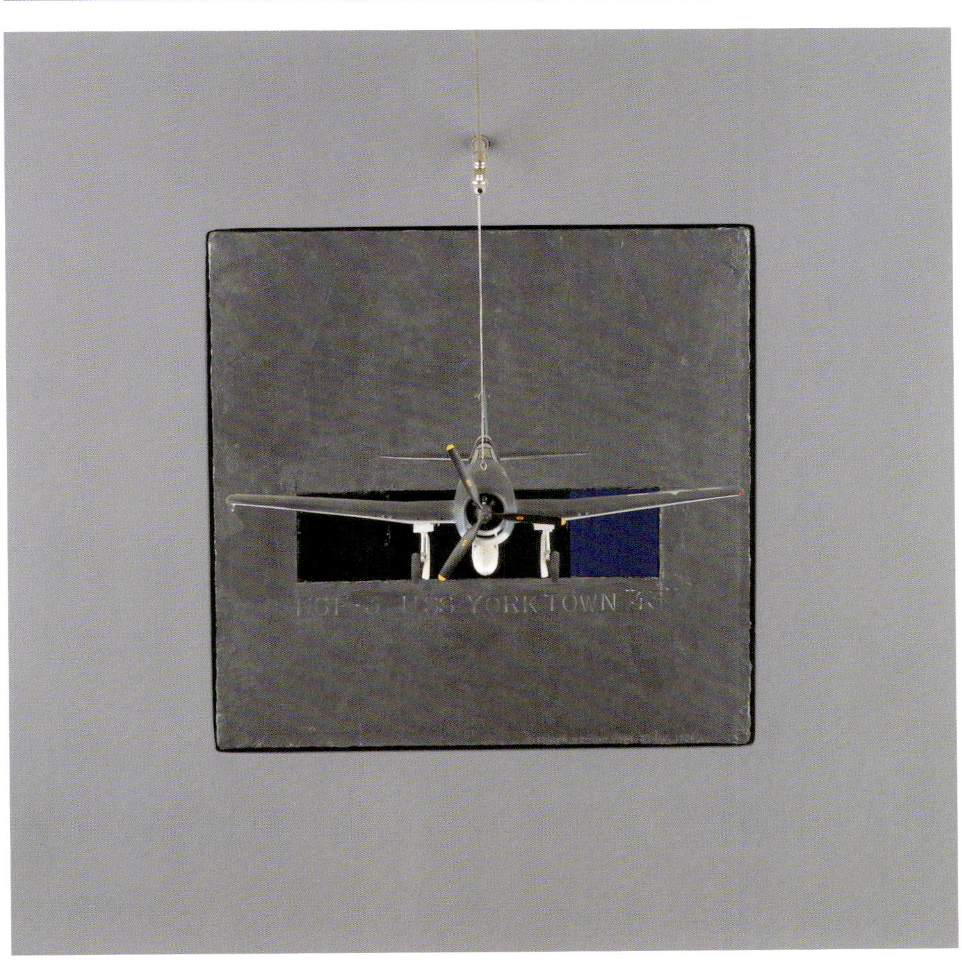

Homage to WW II Aircraft: F6F-3, USS Yorktown

1996, assemblage
22 x 22 inches
56 x 56 cm

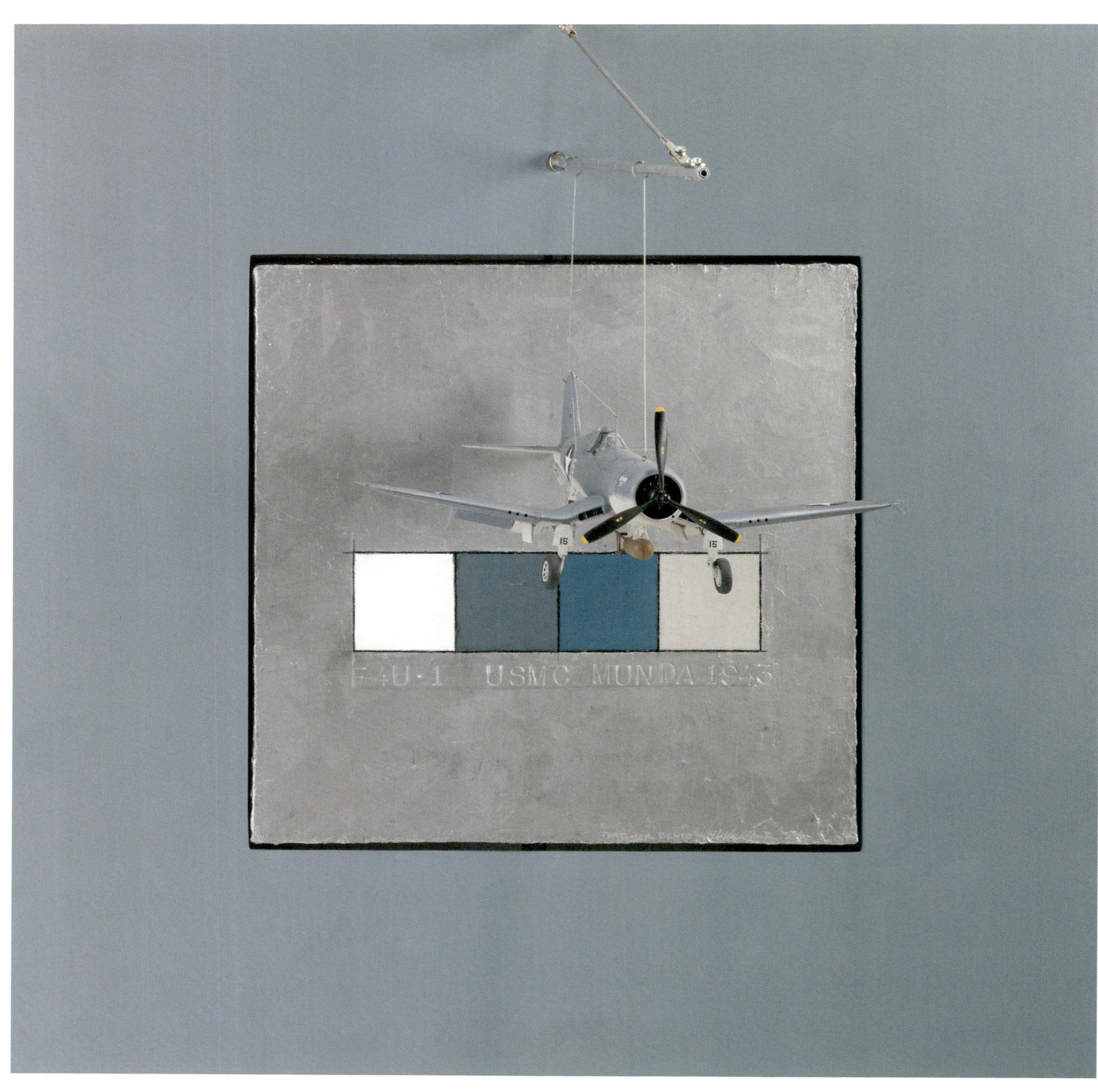

Homage to WW II Aircraft: F4U-1 USMC Munda 1943

1997, assemblage
22 x 22 inches
56 x 56 cm

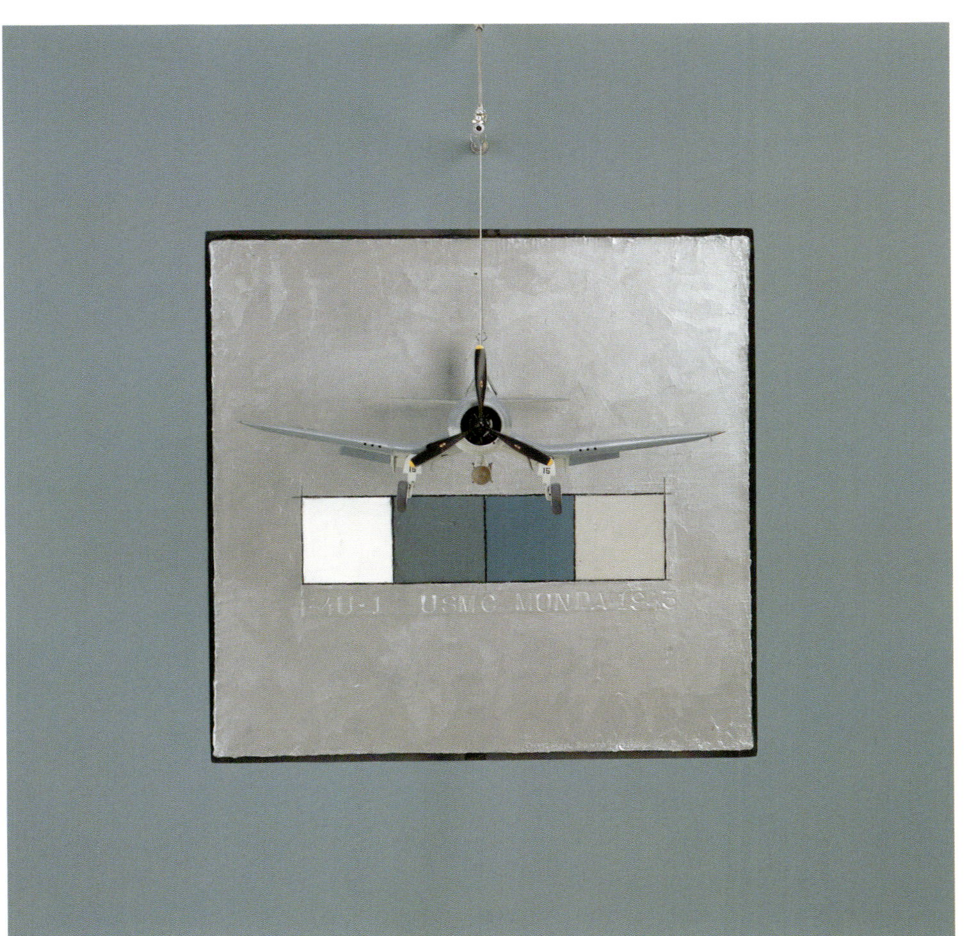

Homage to WW II Aircraft: F4U-1 USMC Munda 1943

1997, assemblage
22 x 22 inches
56 x 56 cm

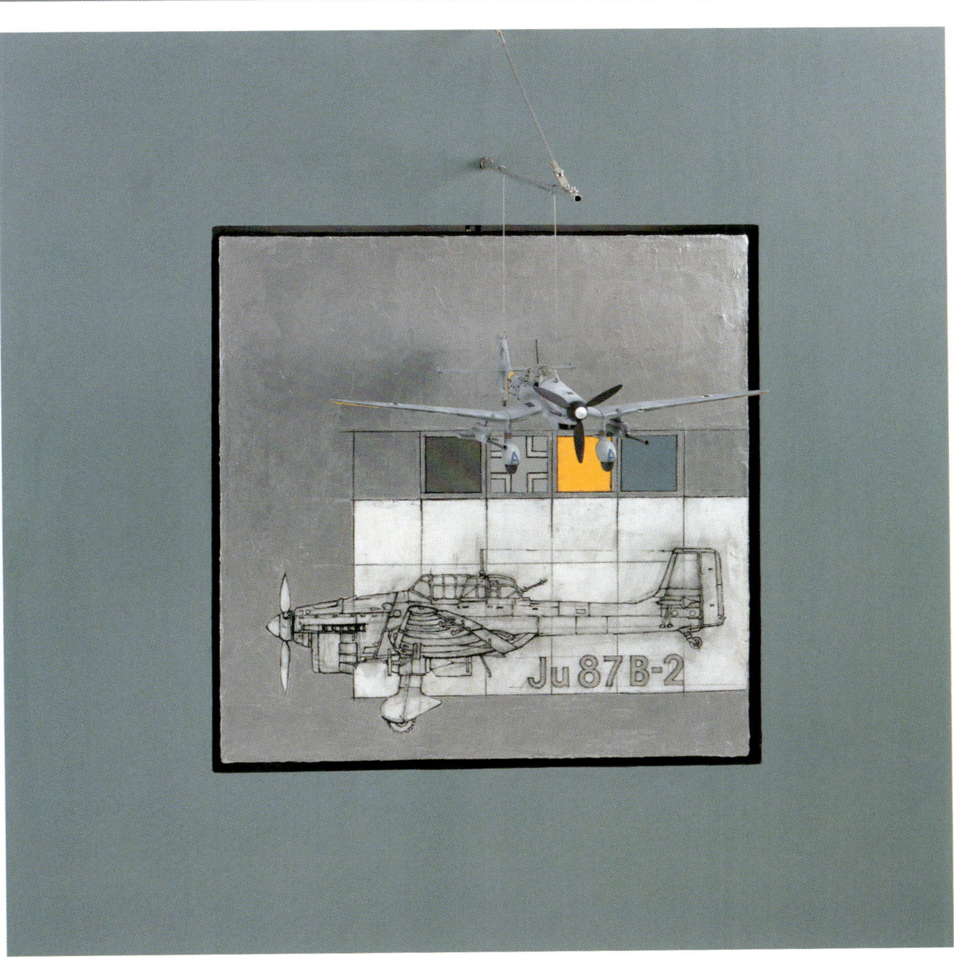

Homage to WW II Aircraft: JU 87 B-2

1997, assemblage
22 x 22 inches
56 x 56 cm

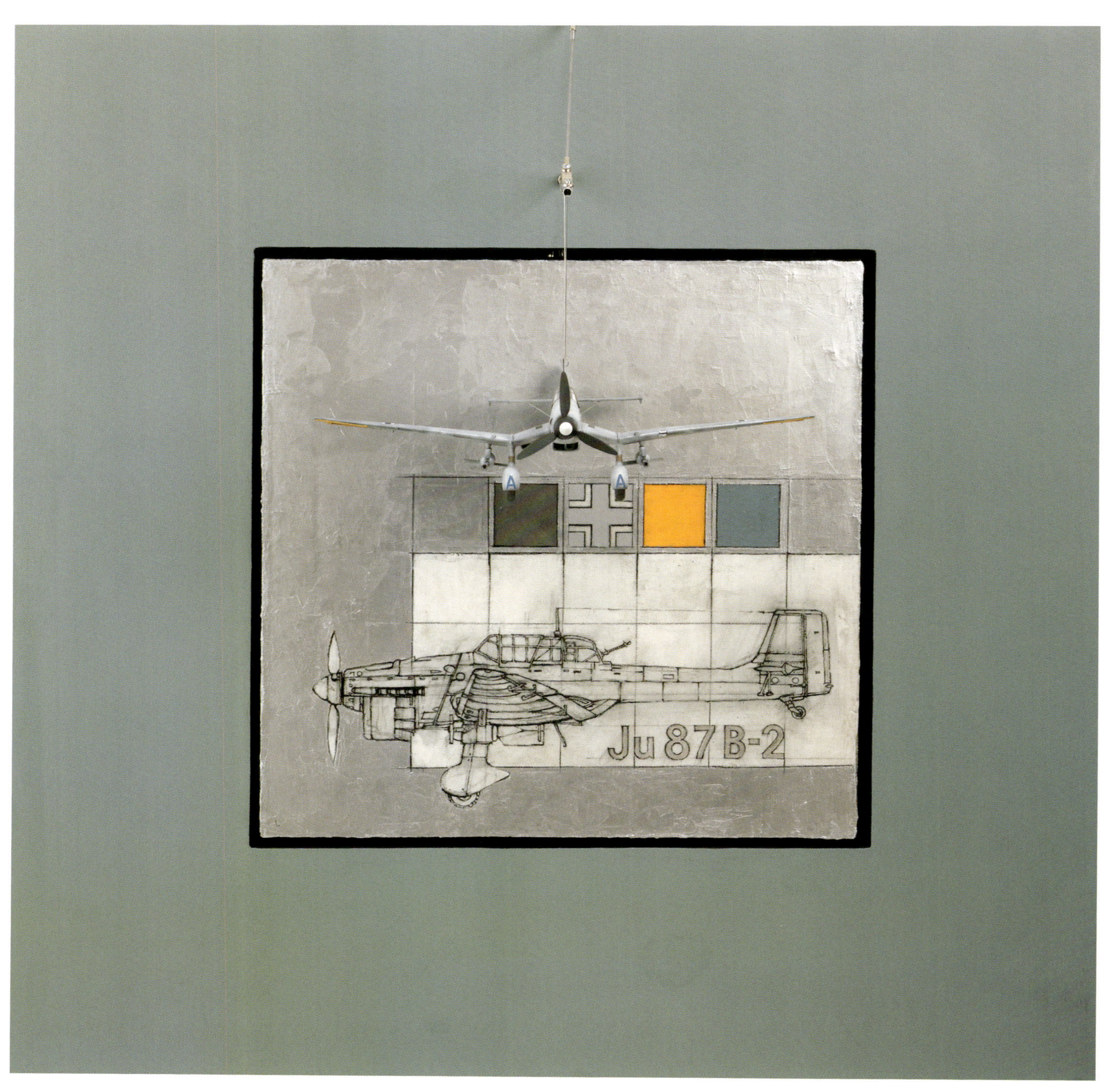

Homage to WW II Aircraft: JU 87 B-2

1997, assemblage
22 x 22 inches
56 x 56 cm

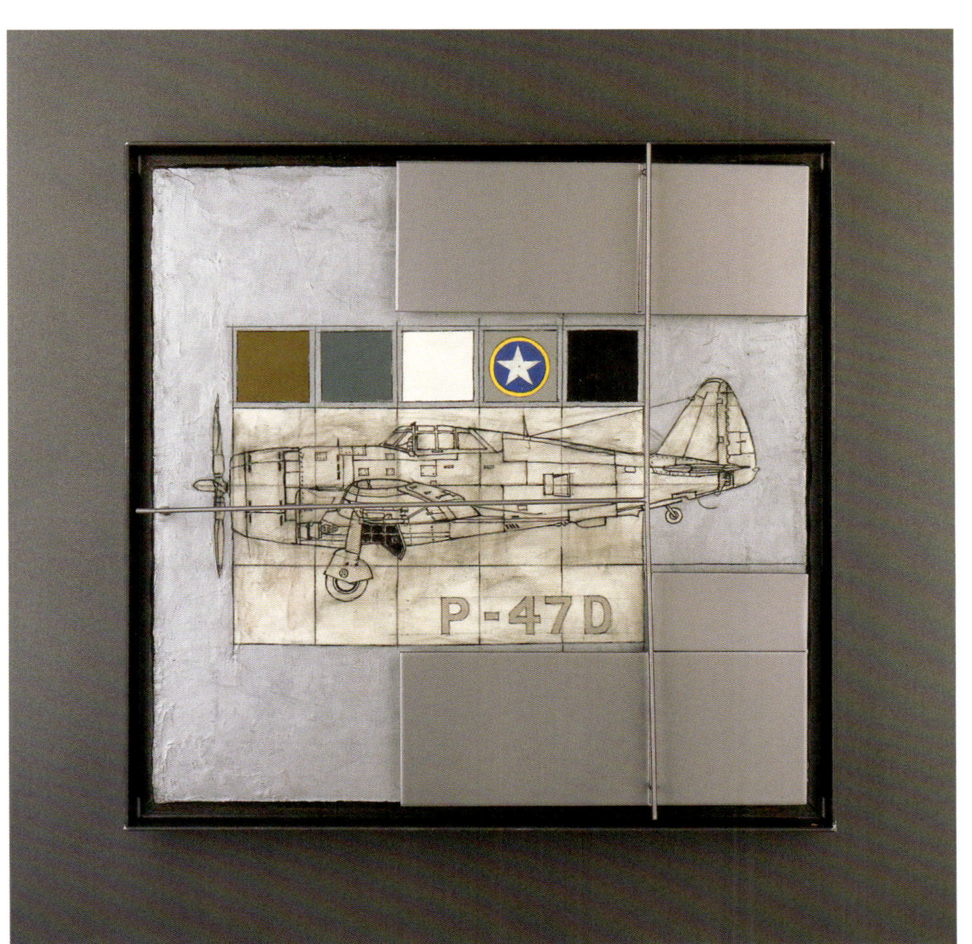

Homage to WW II Aircraft: P-47 D, Composition 2

2003, steel and acrylic on canvas
17¼ x 17¼ inches
44 x 44 cm

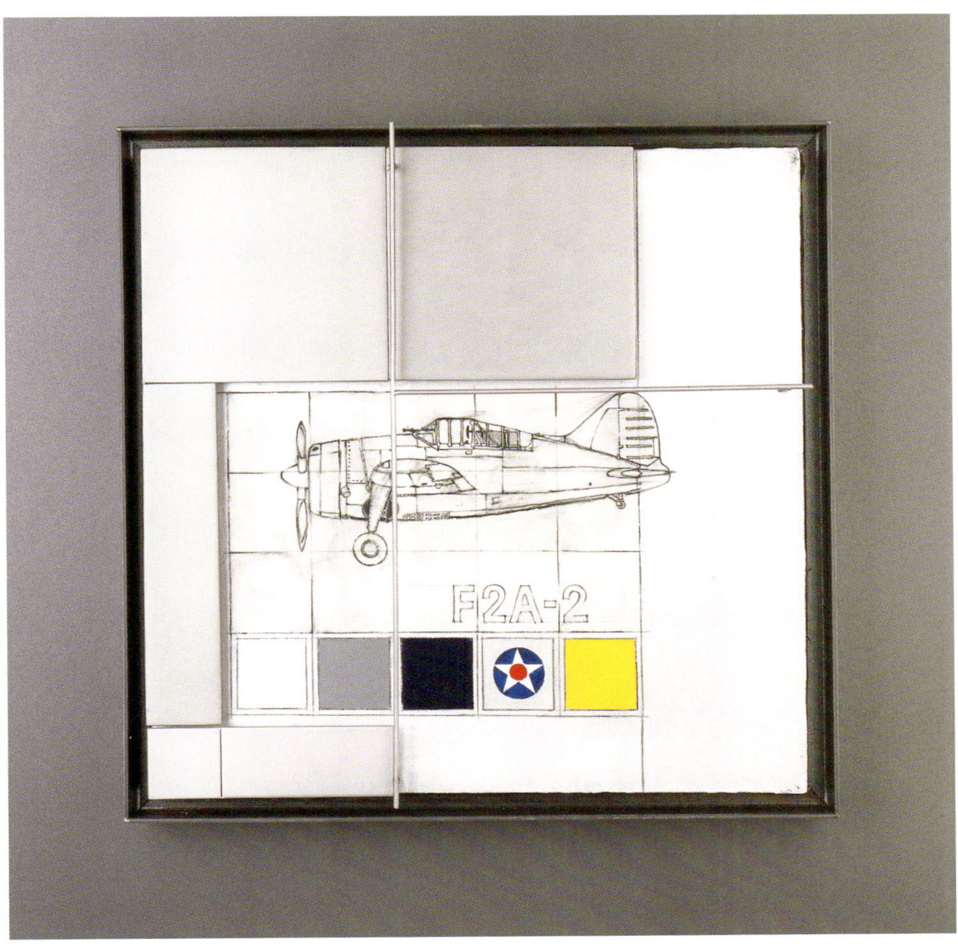

Homage to WW II Aircraft: F2A-2, Composition 2

2003, steel and acrylic on canvas
17¼ x 17¼ inches
44 x 44 cm

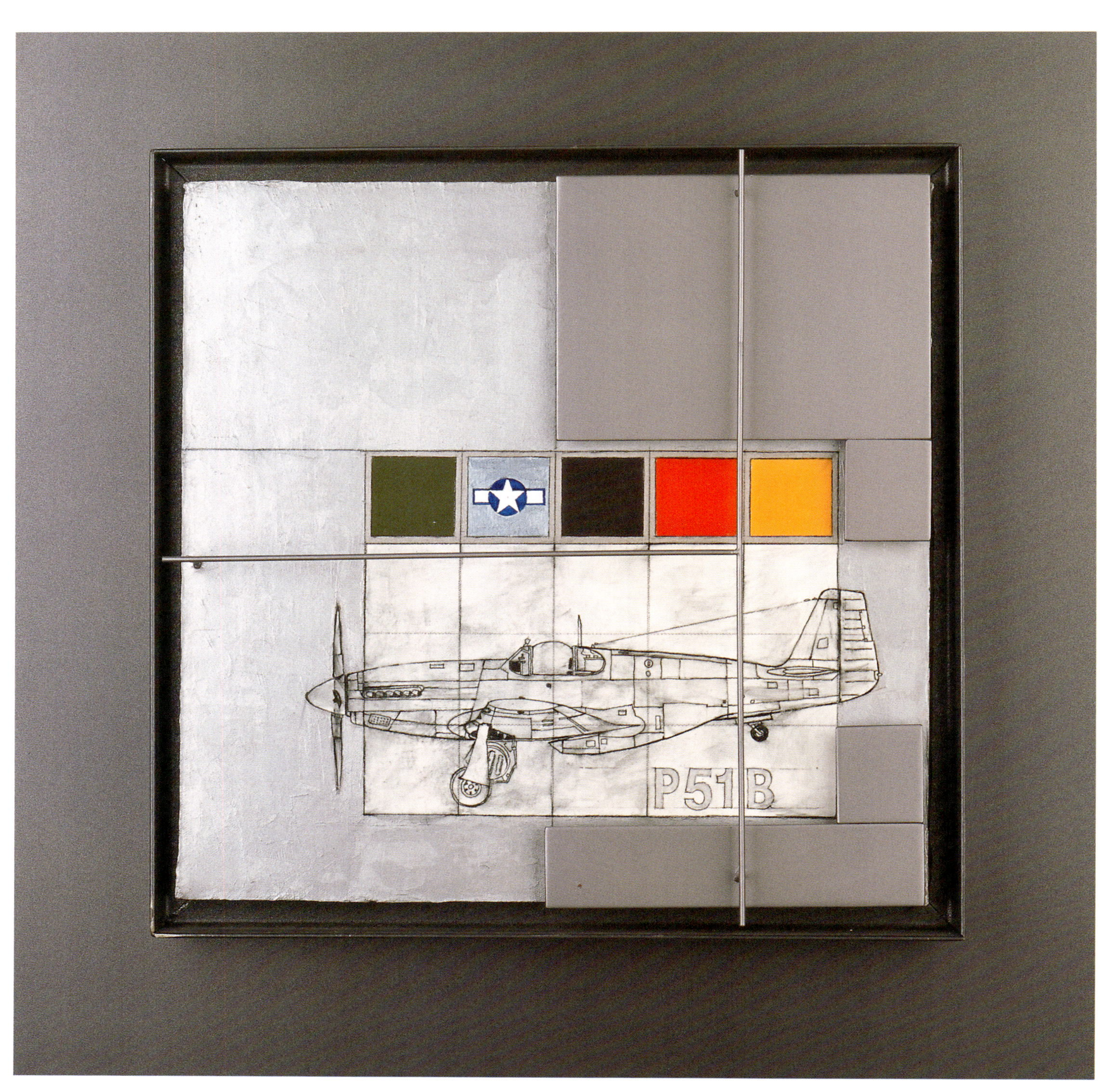

Homage to WW II Aircraft: P51-B, Composition 2

2003, steel and acrylic on canvas
17¼ x 17¼ inches
44 x 44 cm

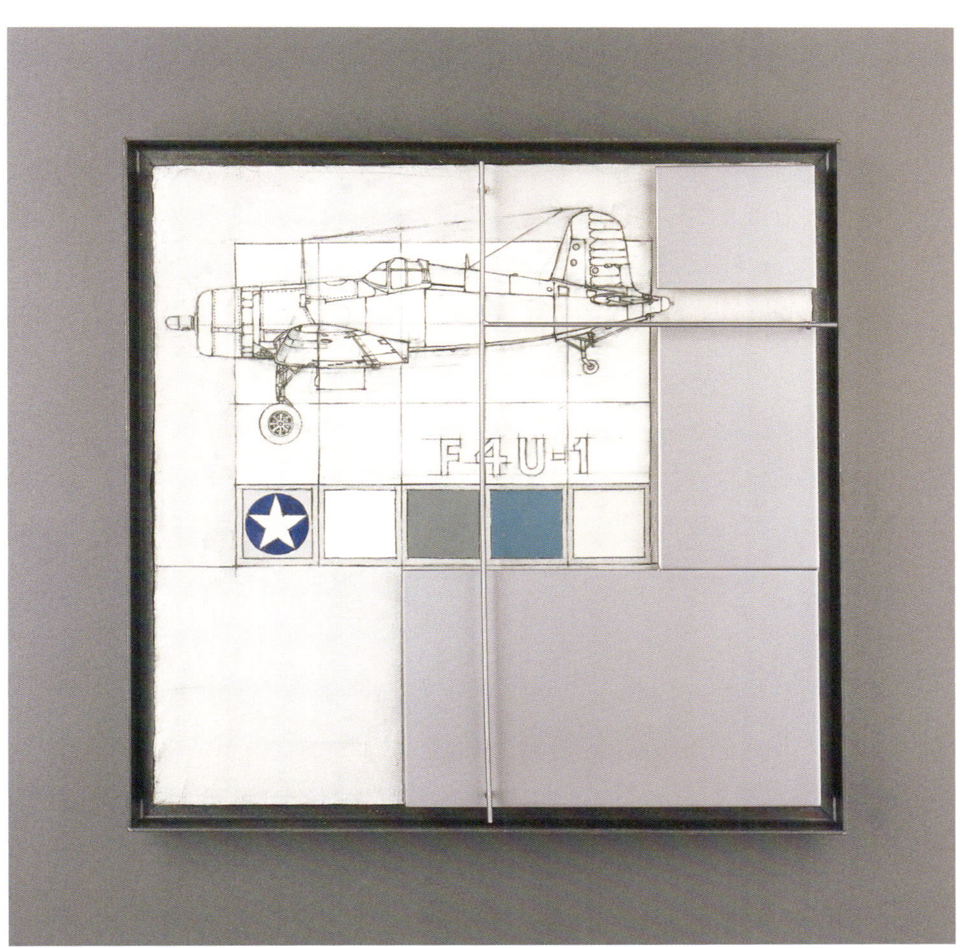

Homage to WW II Aircraft: F4U-1, Composition 2

2003, steel and acrylic on canvas
17¼ x 17¼ inches
44 x 44 cm

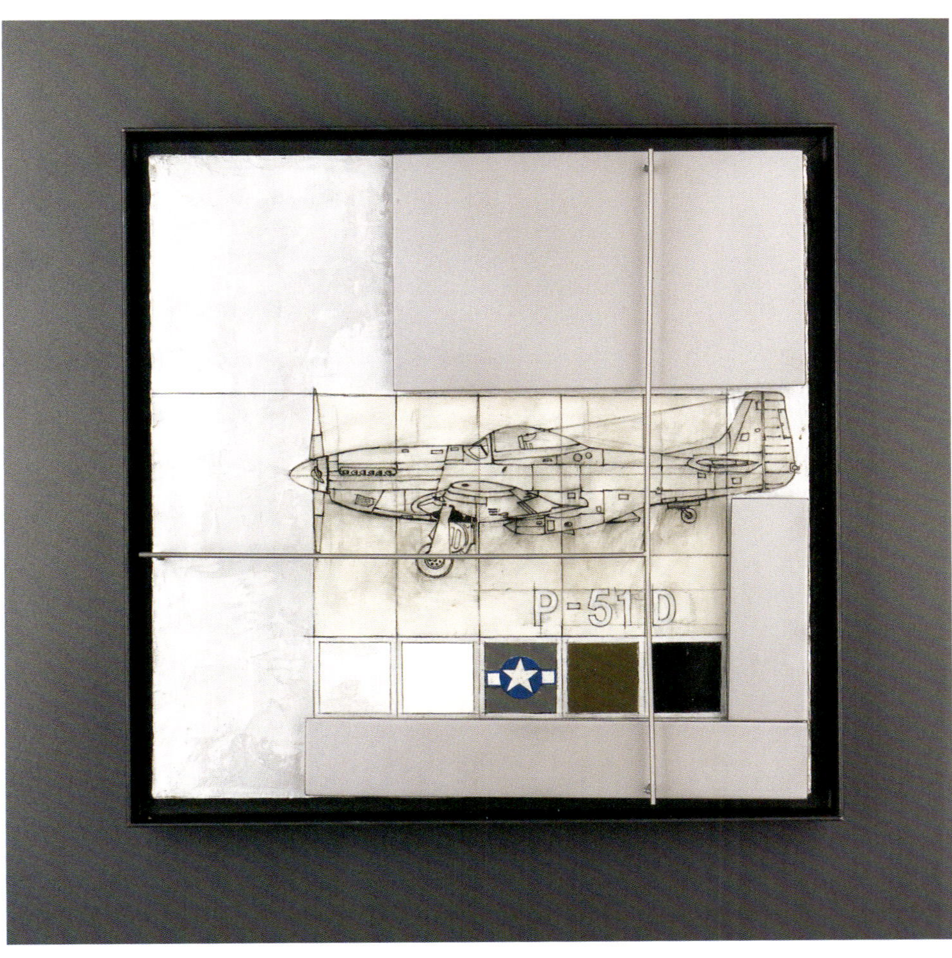

Homage to WW II Aircraft: P 51-D, Composition 2

2003, steel and acrylic on canvas
17¼ x 17¼ inches
44 x 44 cm

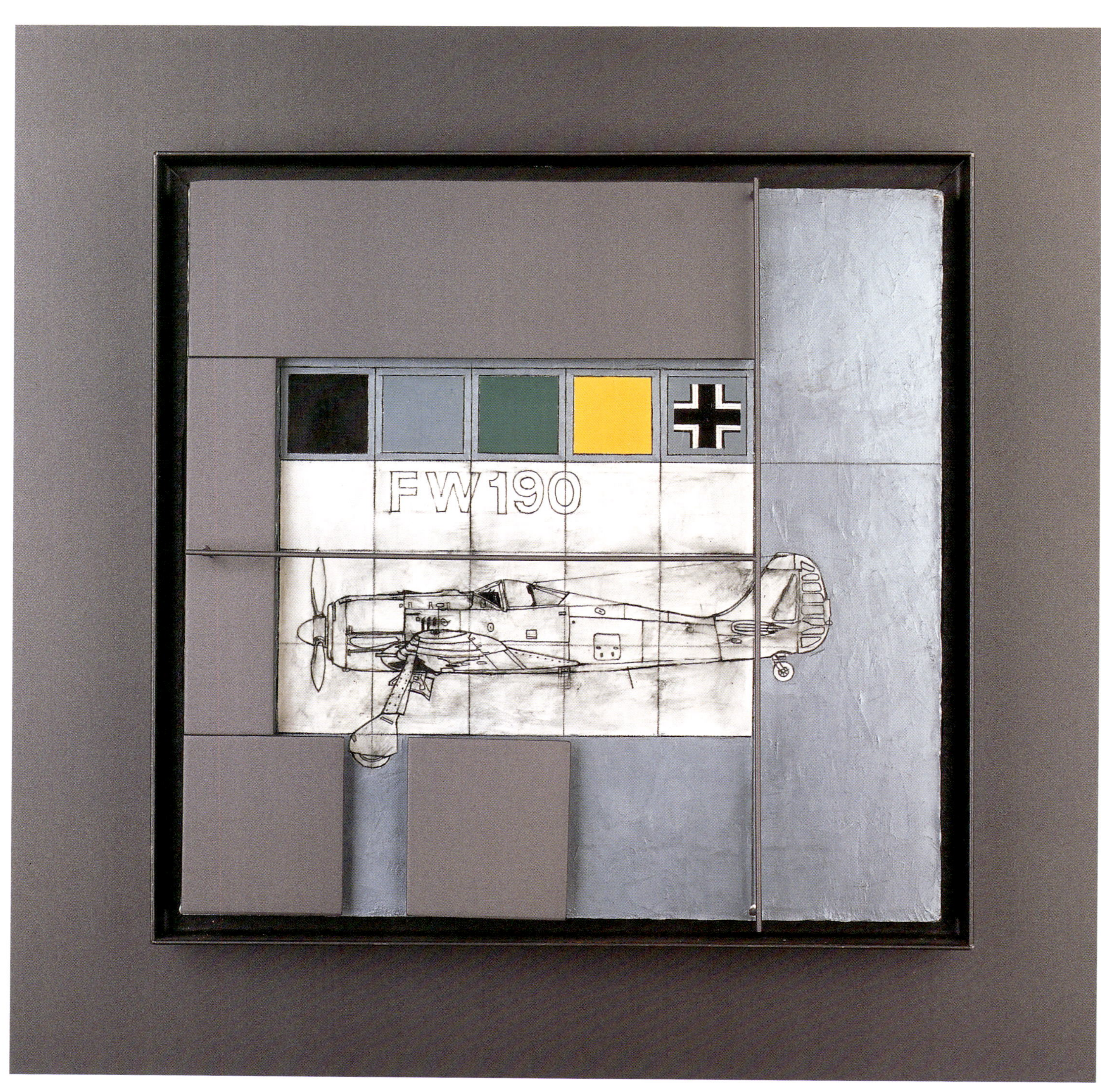

Homage to WW II Aircraft: FW 190, Composition 2

2003, steel and acrylic on canvas
17¼ x 17¼ inches
44 x 44 cm

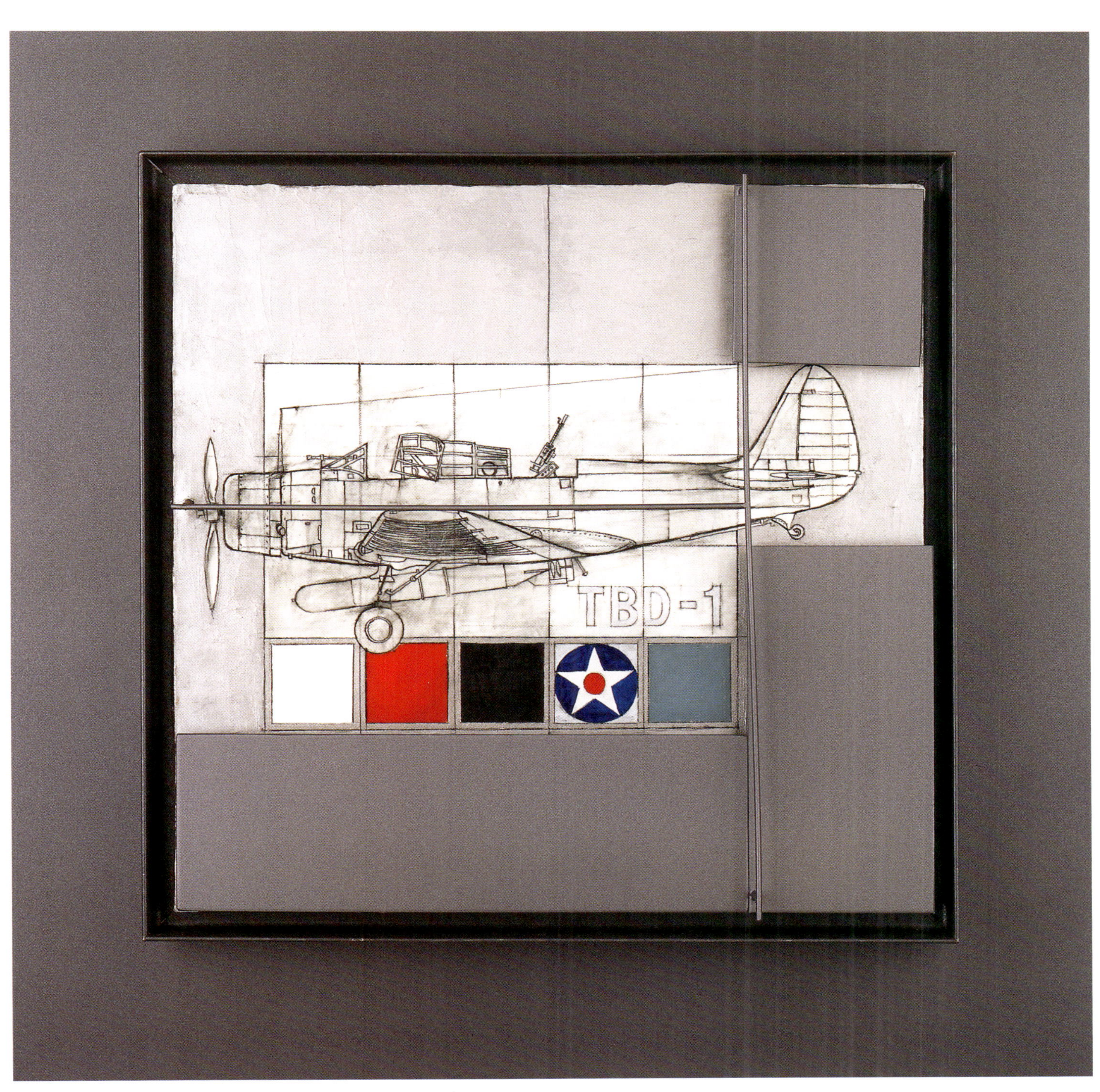

Homage to WW II Aircraft: TBD-1, Composition 2

2003, steel and acrylic on canvas
17¼ x 17¼ inches
44 x 44 cm

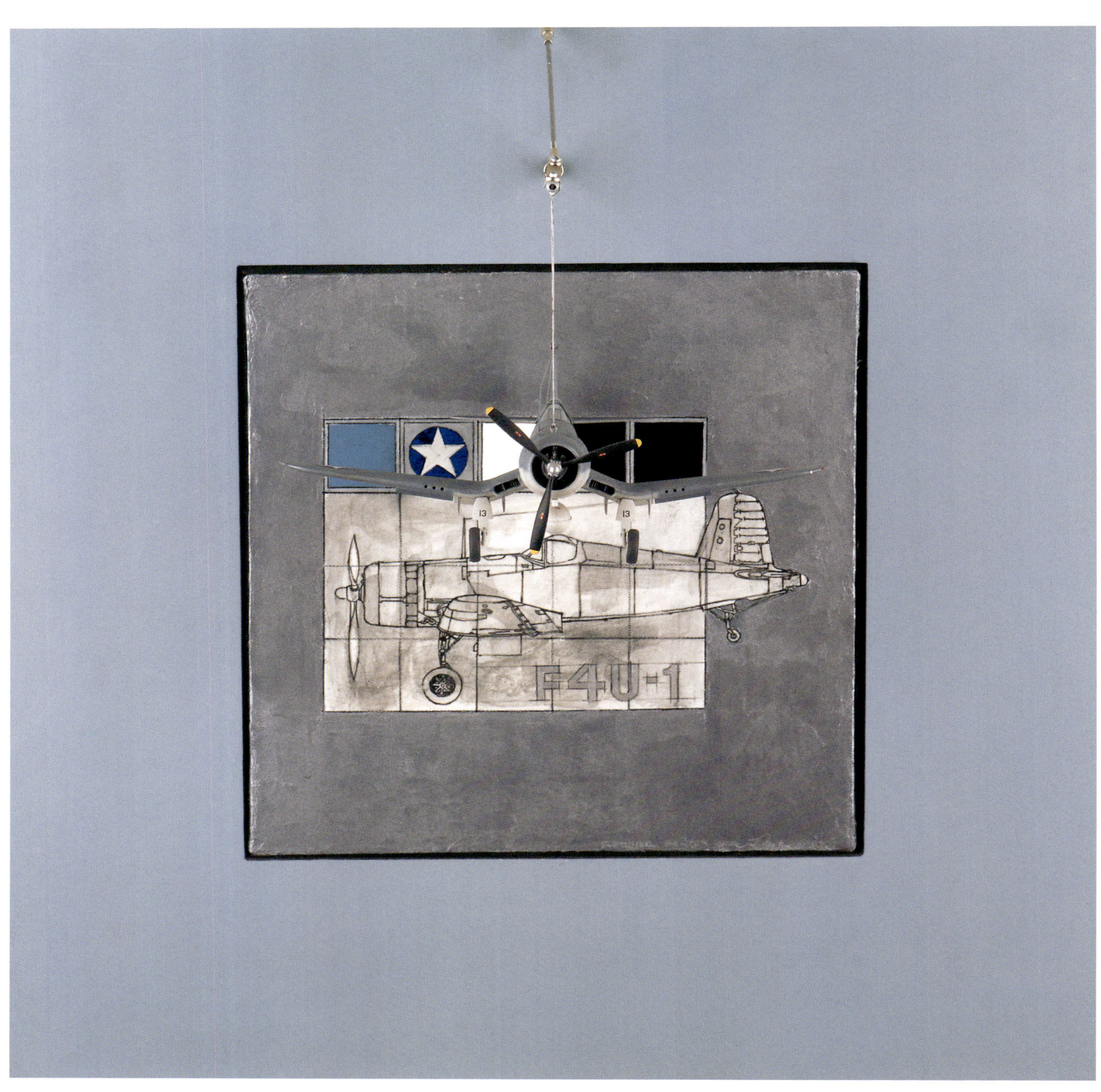

Homage to WW II Aircraft: F4U-1

1997, assemblage
22 x 22 inches
56 x 56 cm

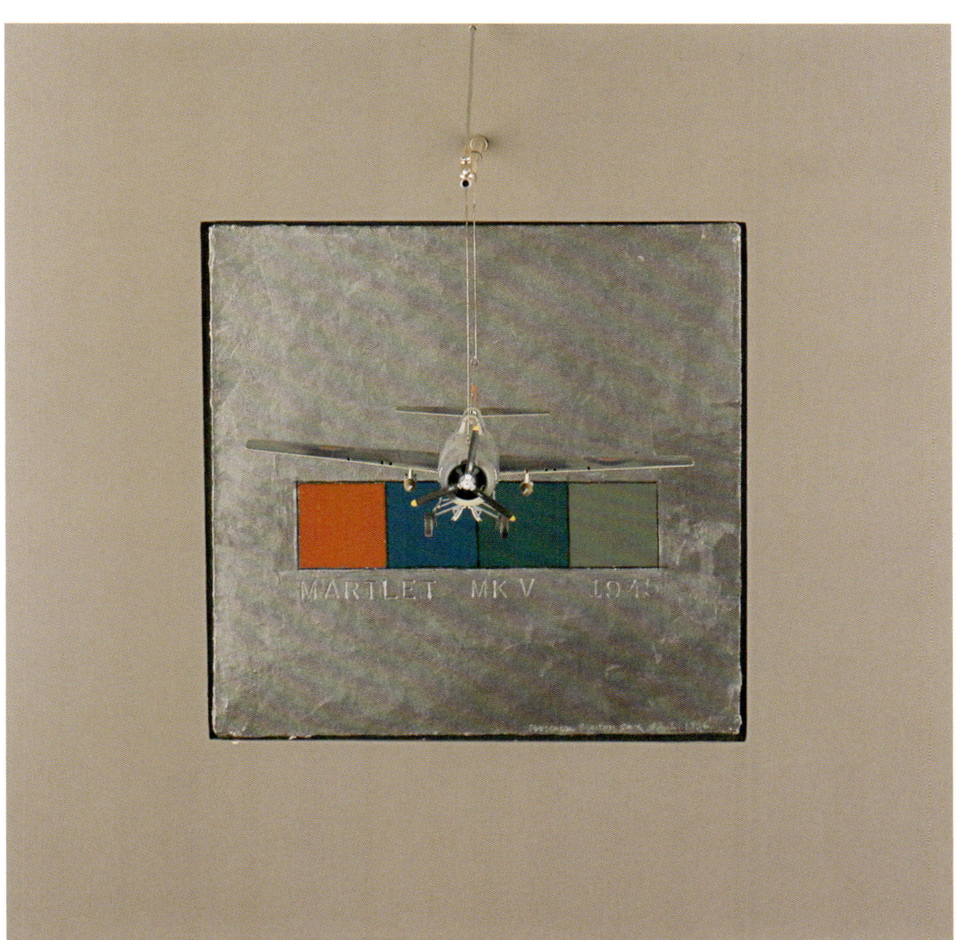

Homage to WW II Aircraft: Martlet, MKV

1996, assemblage
22 x 22 inches
56 x 56 cm

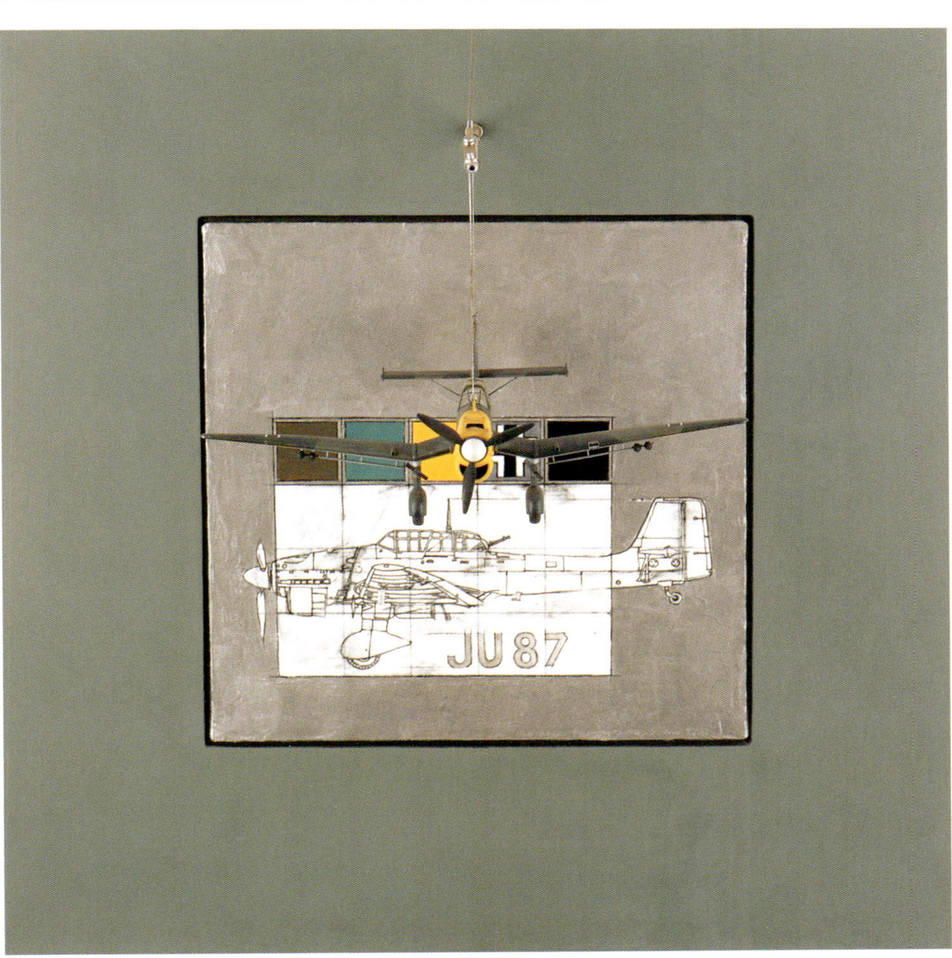

Homage to WW II Aircraft: JU 87

1997, assemblage
22 x 22 inches
56 x 56 cm

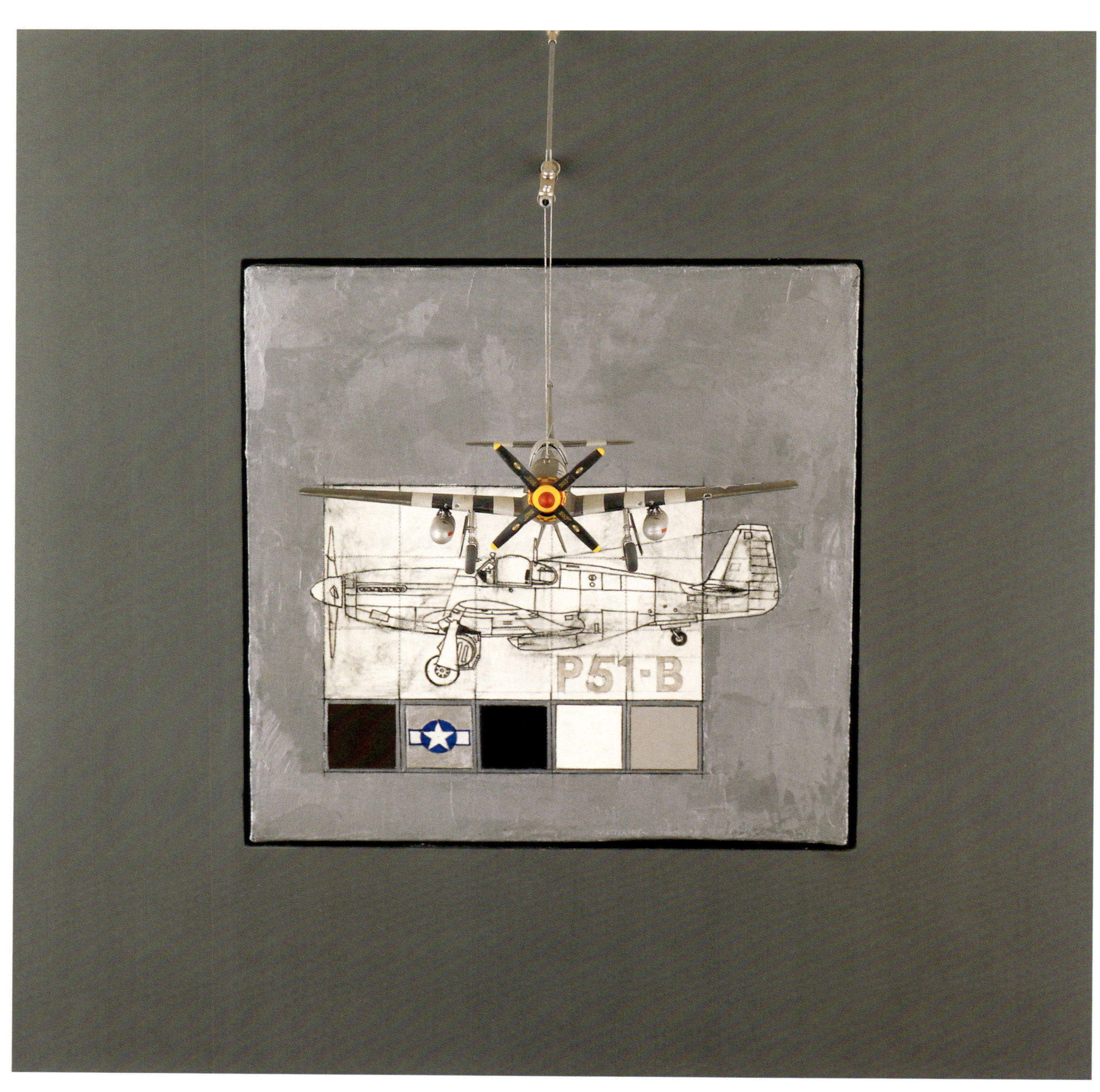

Homage to WW II Aircraft: P51- B

1997, assemblage
22 x 22 inches
56 x 56 cm

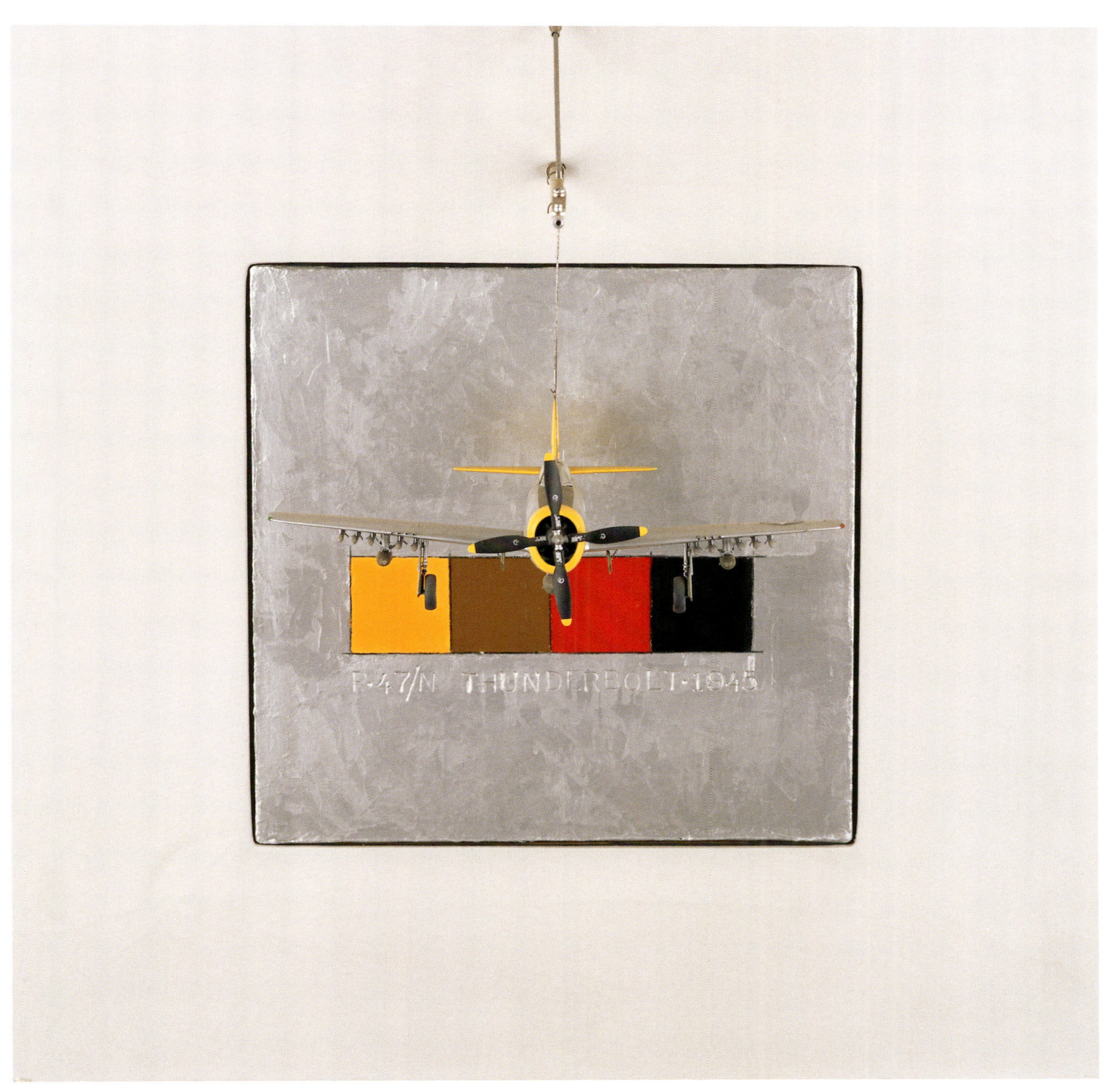

Homage to WW II Aircraft: Thunderbolt, P.47 N

1996, assemblage
22 x 22 inches
56 x 56 cm

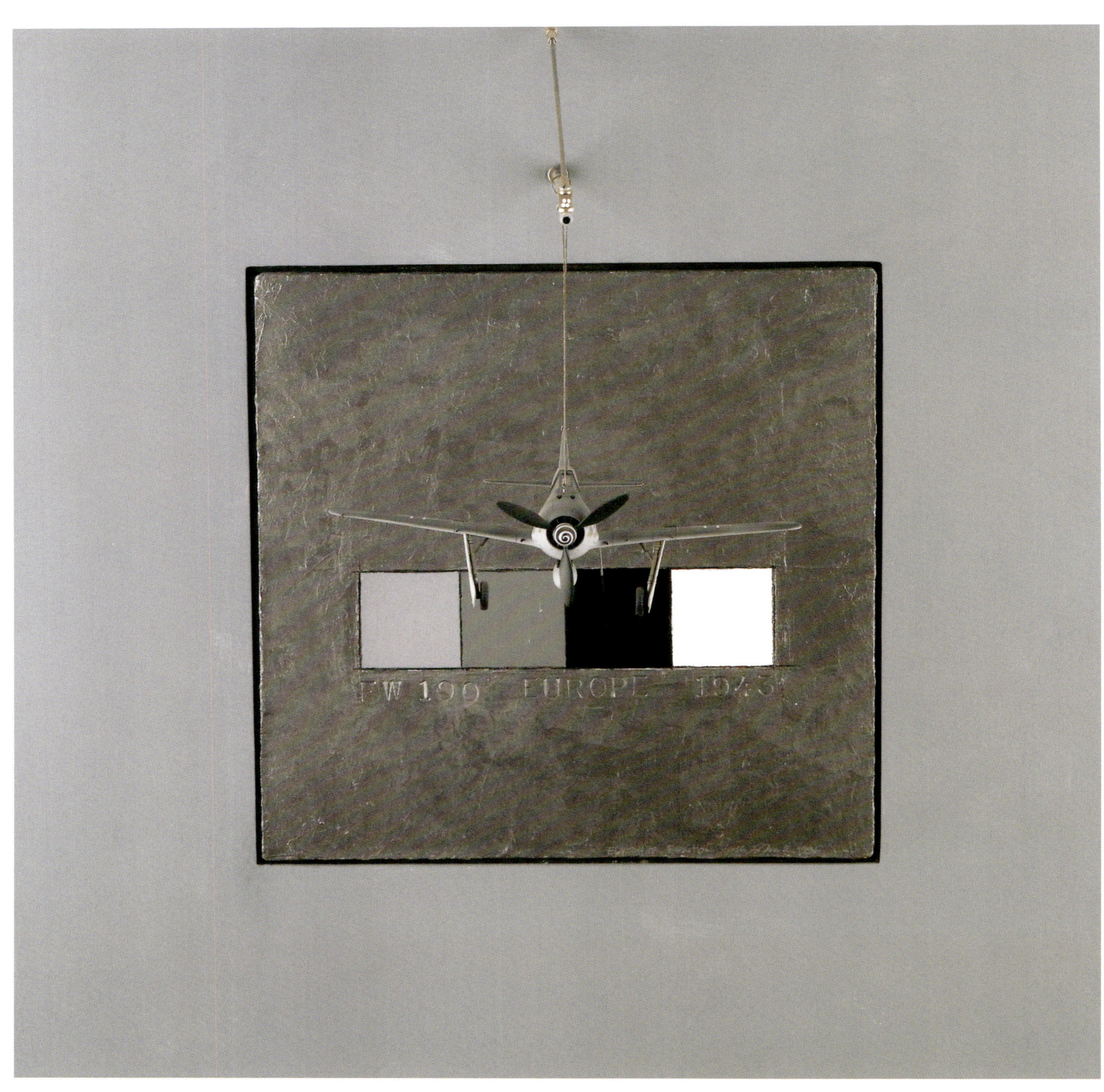

Homage to WW II Aircraft: FW 190, Europe 1943

1996, assemblage
22 x 22 inches
56 x 56 cm

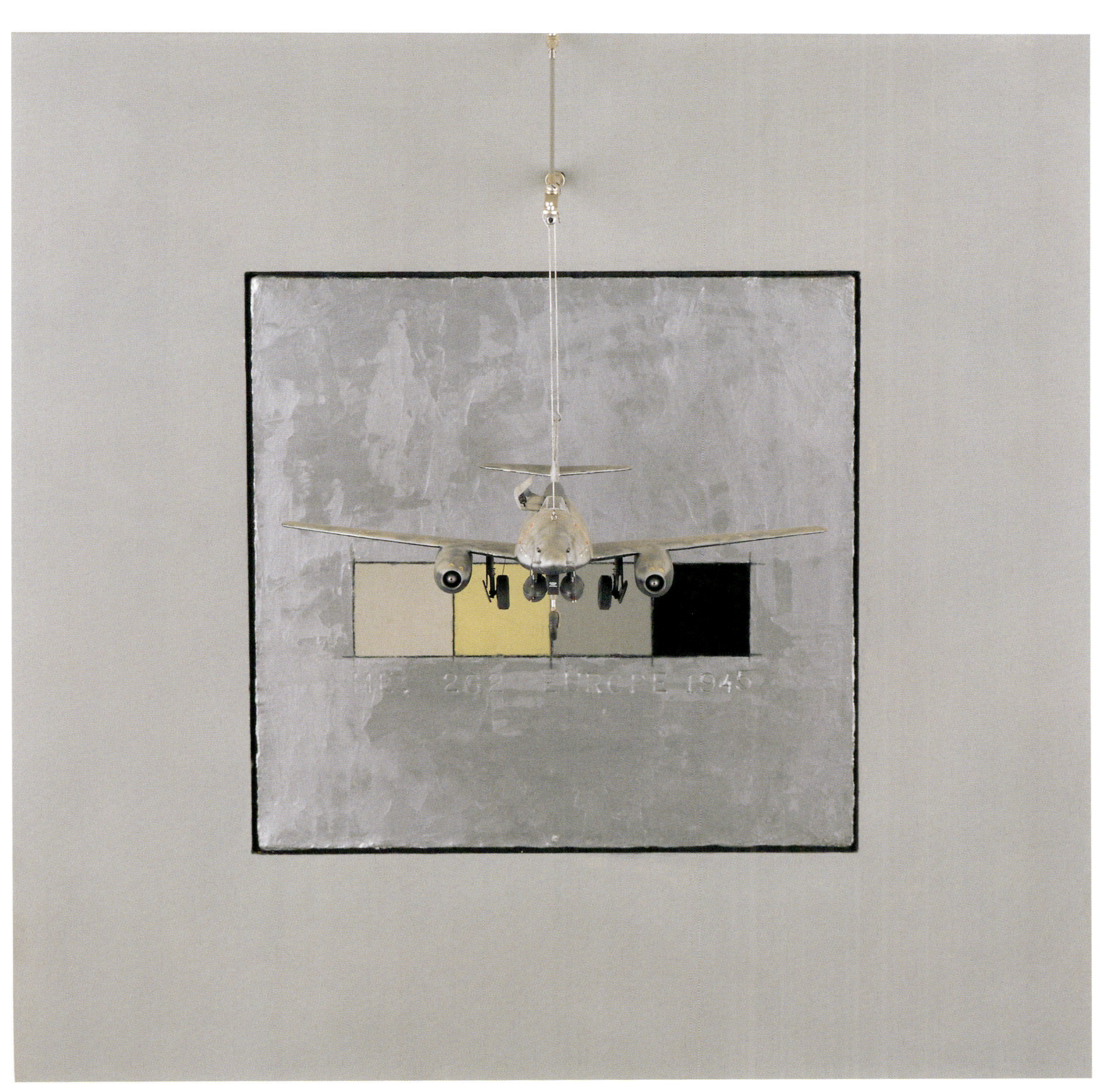

Homage to WW II Aircraft: ME 262, Europe 1945

1997, assemblage
22 x 22 inches
56 x 56 cm

Homage to WW II Aircraft: PBY-5A Sub Patrol 1944

1997, assemblage
22 x 25 inches
56 x 64 cm

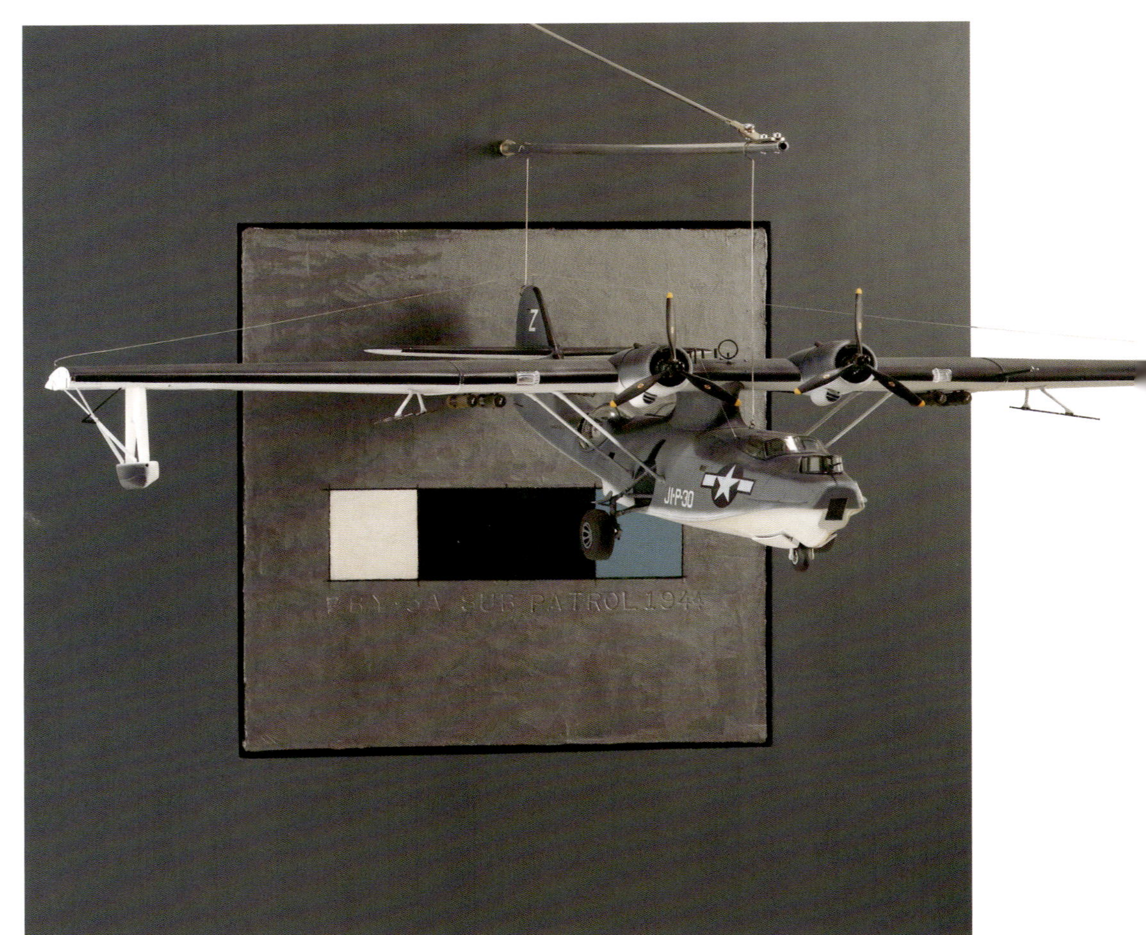

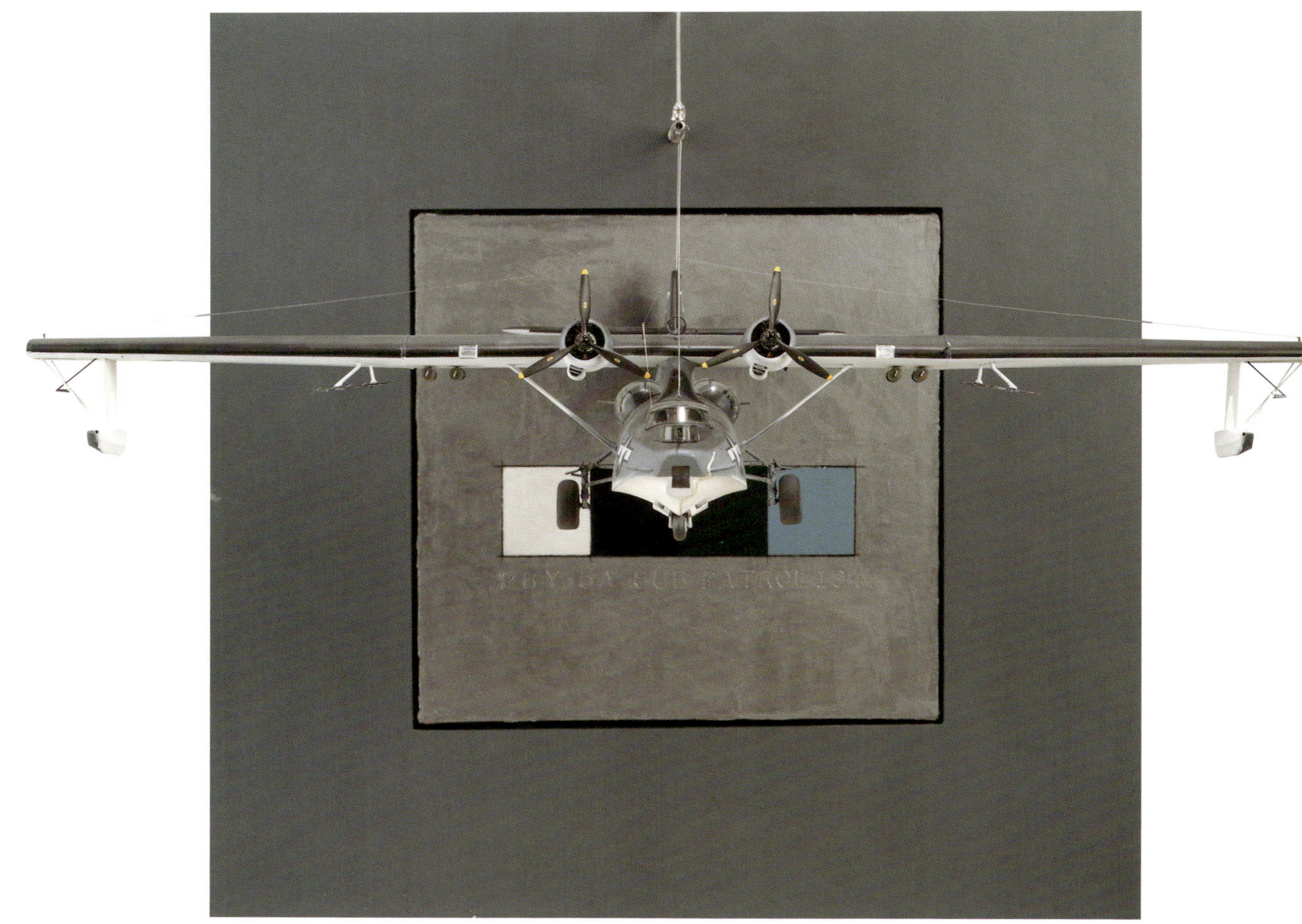

Homage to WW II Aircraft: P51-B Europe 1944

1996, assemblage
22 x 22 inches
56 x 56 cm

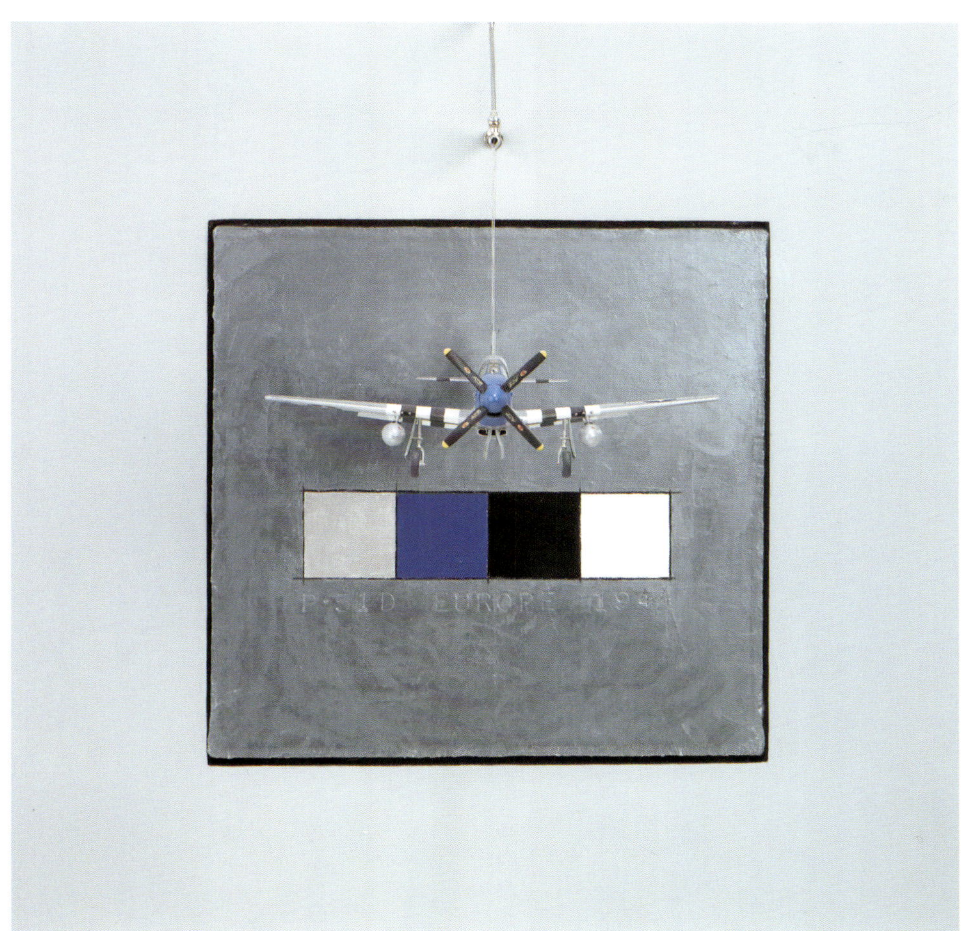

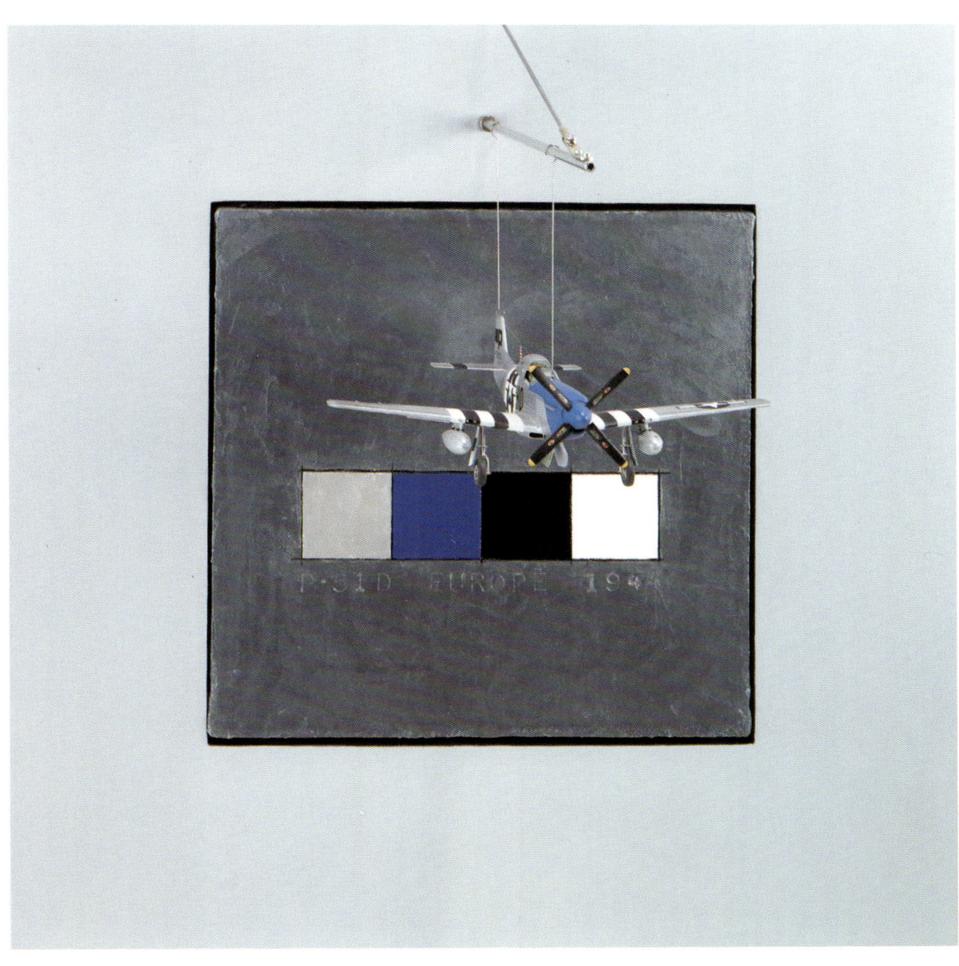

Homage to WW II Aircraft
Installation view at Riva Yares Gallery
Scottsdale, Arizona 1998

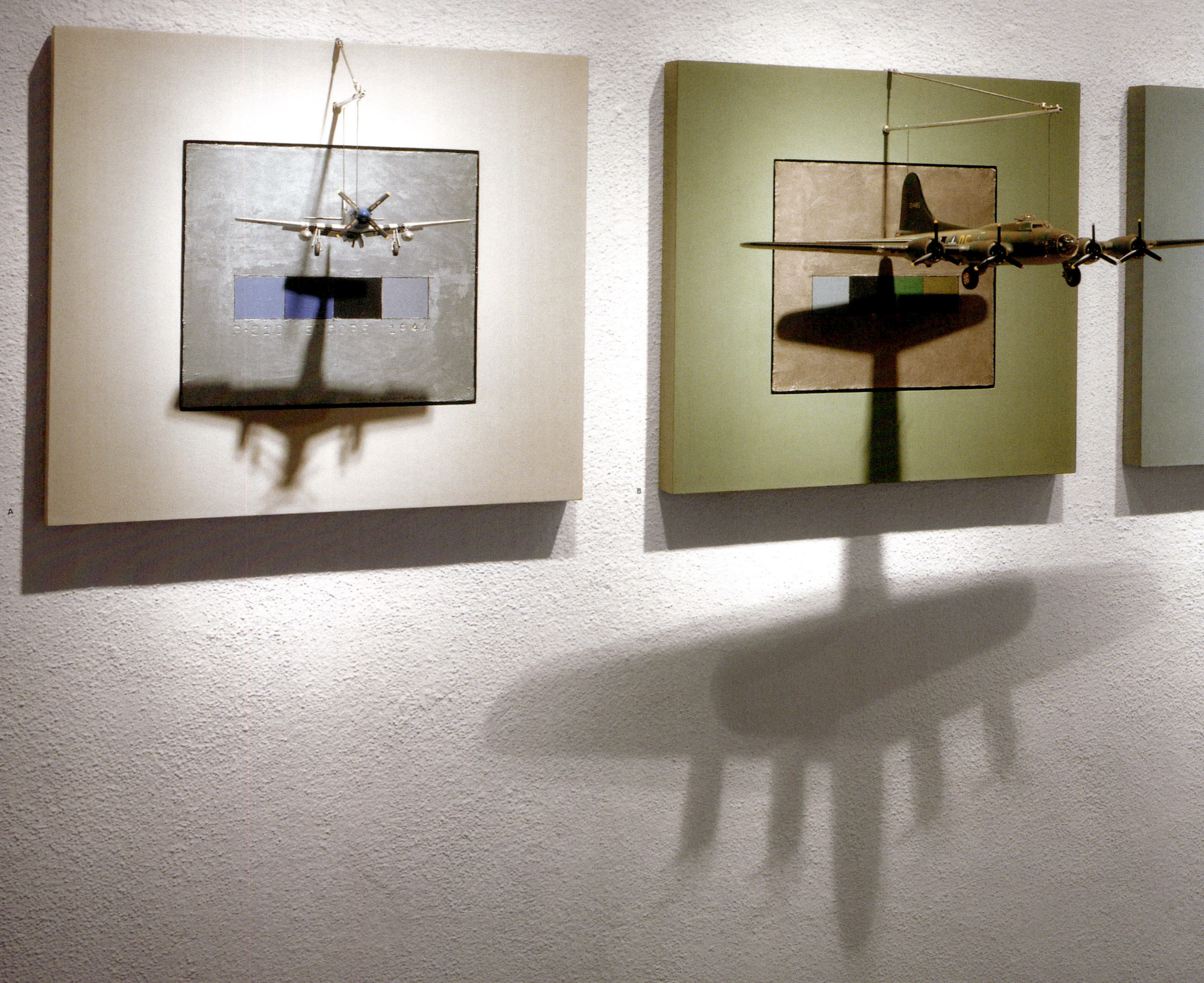

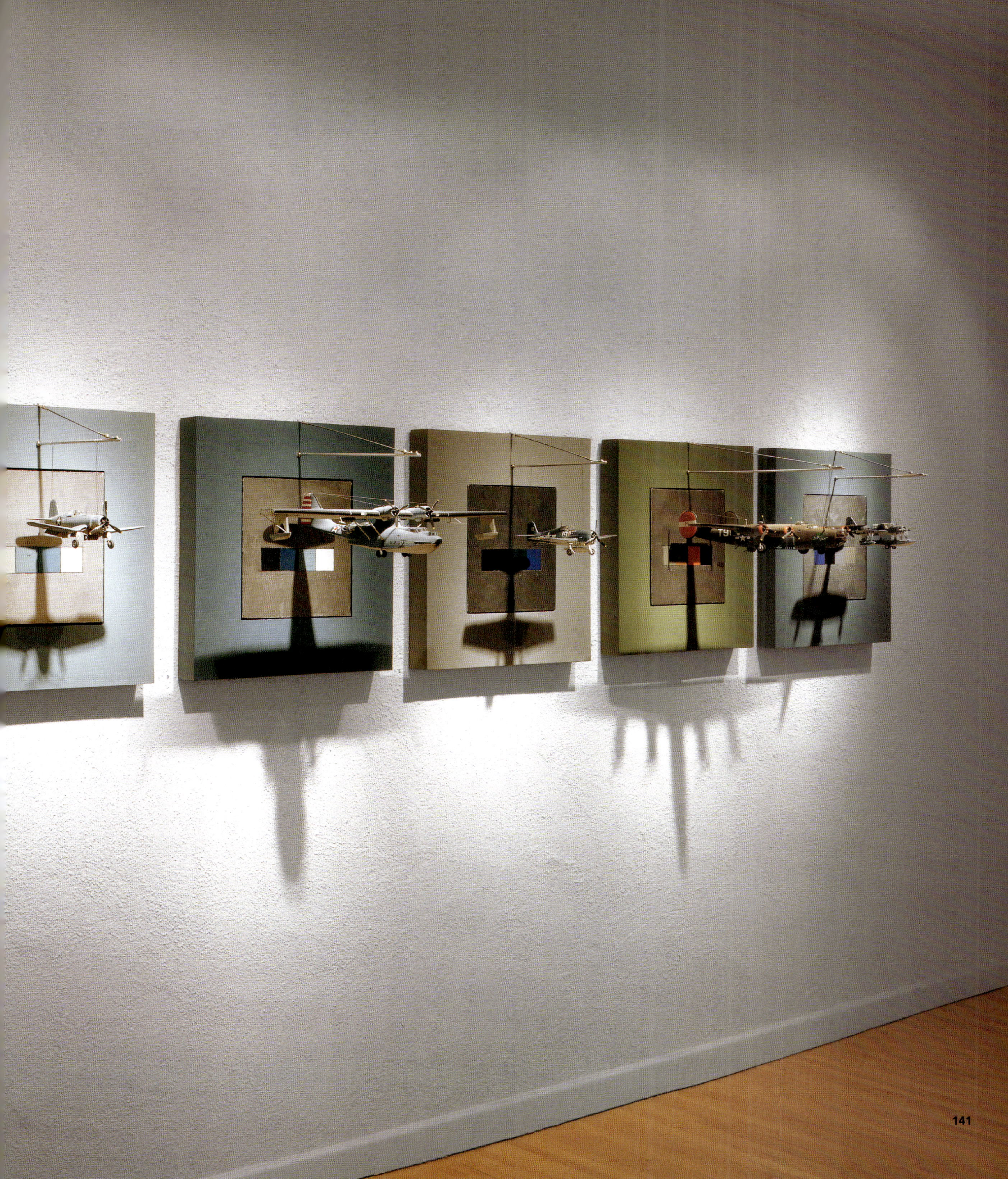

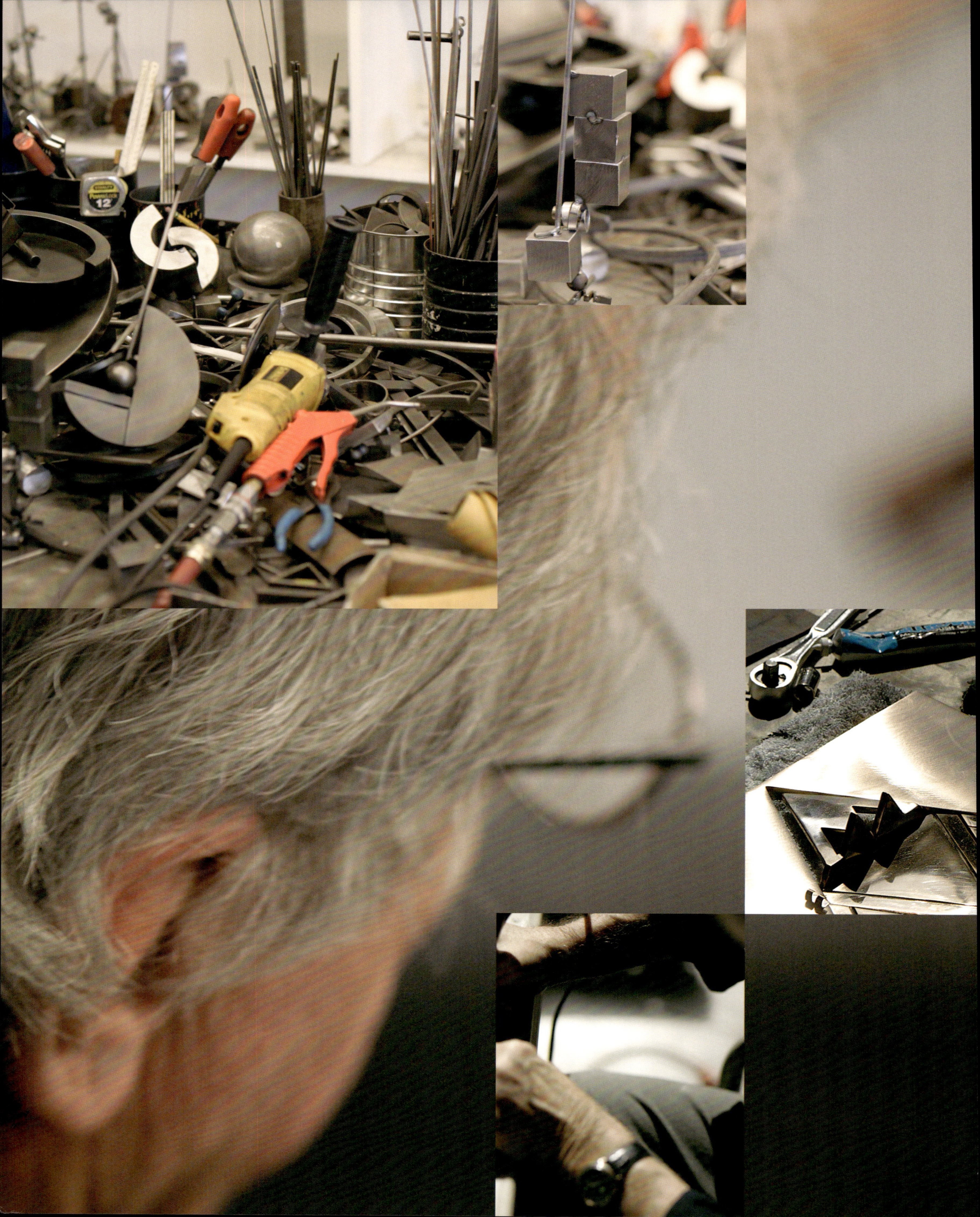
12

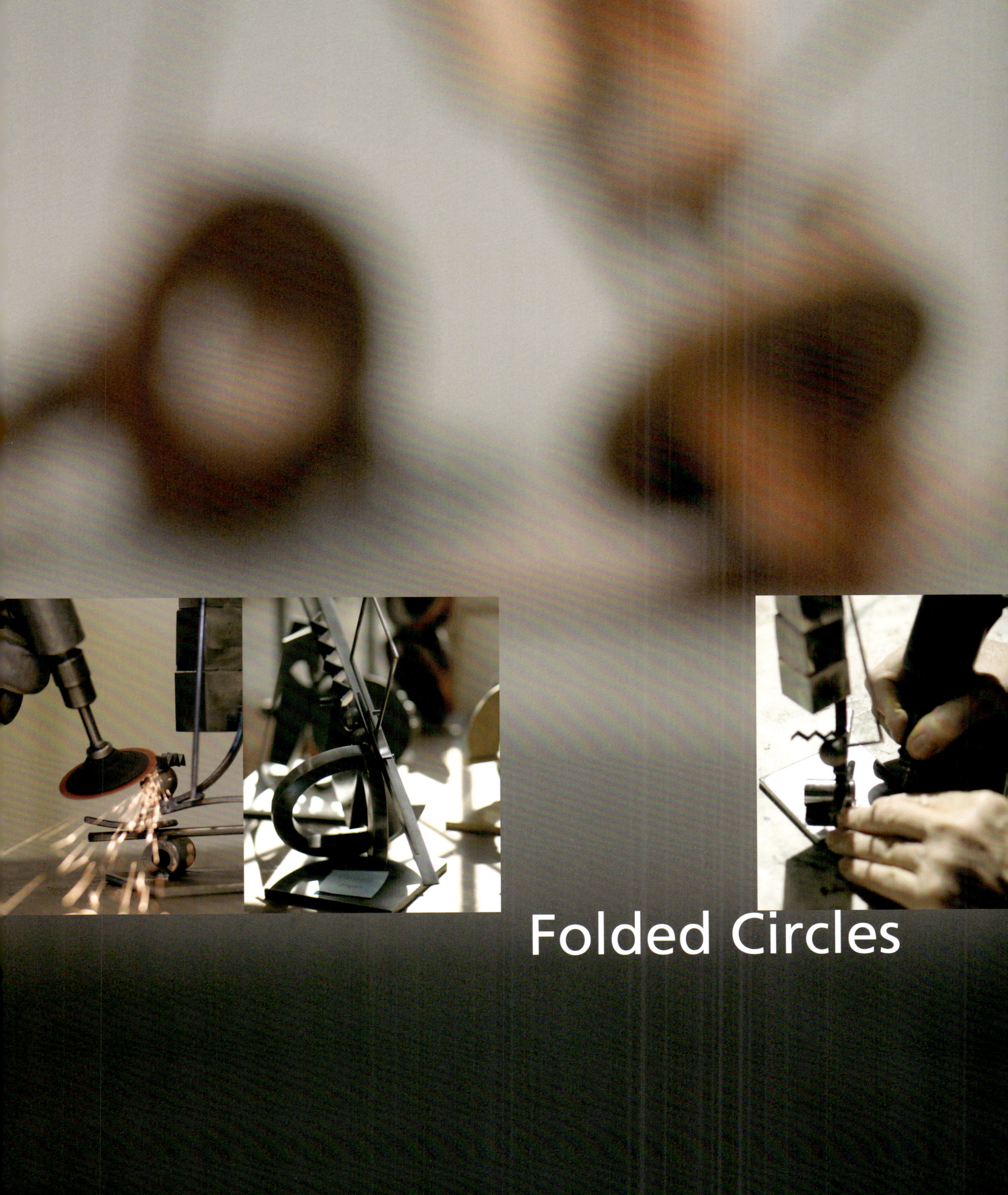

Folded Circles

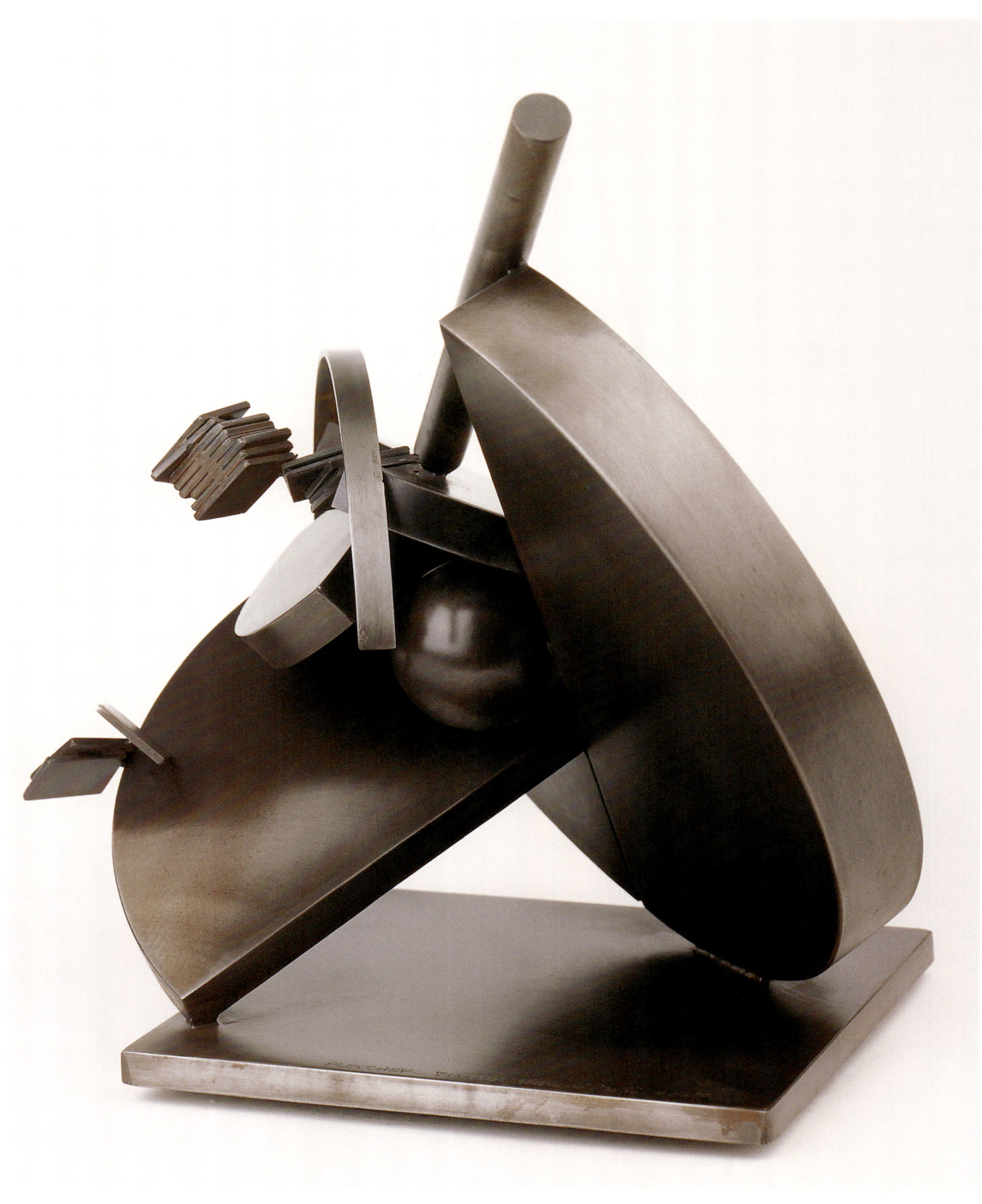

Folded Circle Study with Squares and Ring

2005, steel with patina
14 x 14 x 11 inches
36 x 36 x 28 cm

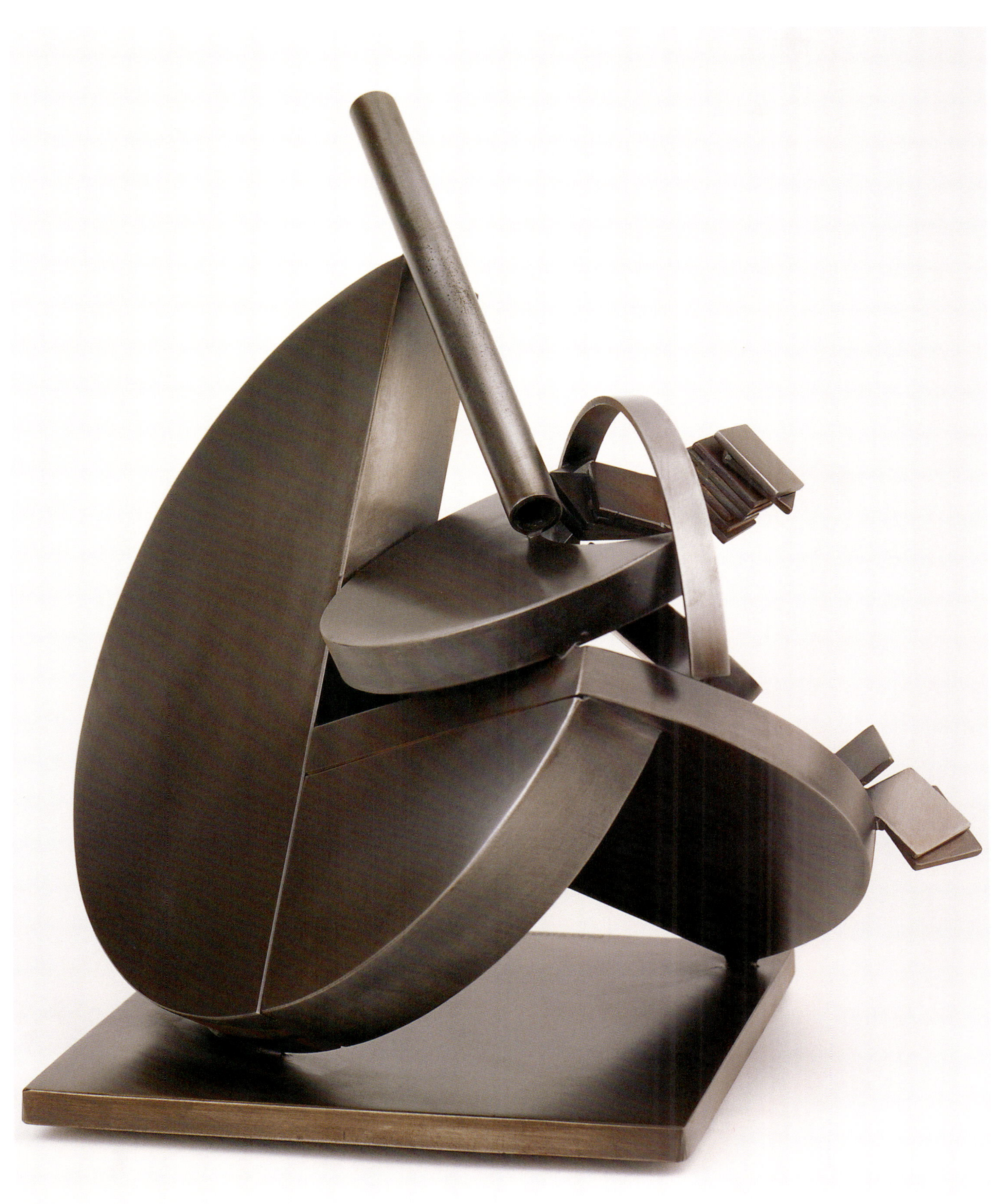

Folded Circle Study with Squares and Ring

2005, steel with patina
14 x 14 x 11 inches
36 x 36 x 28 cm

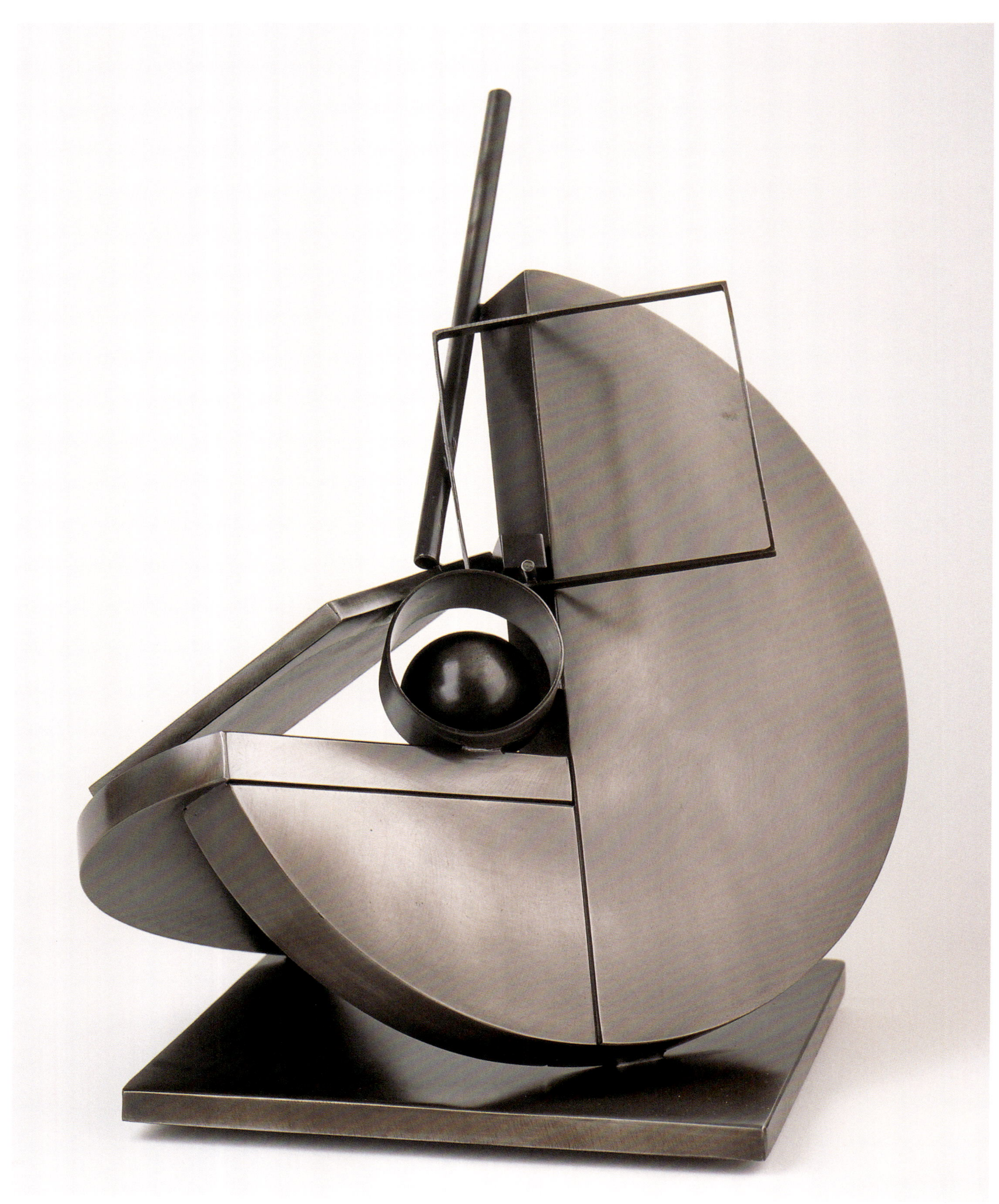

Folded Circle Study with Cylinder

2005, steel with patina
14½ x 10 x 12 inches
37 x 25 x 30 cm

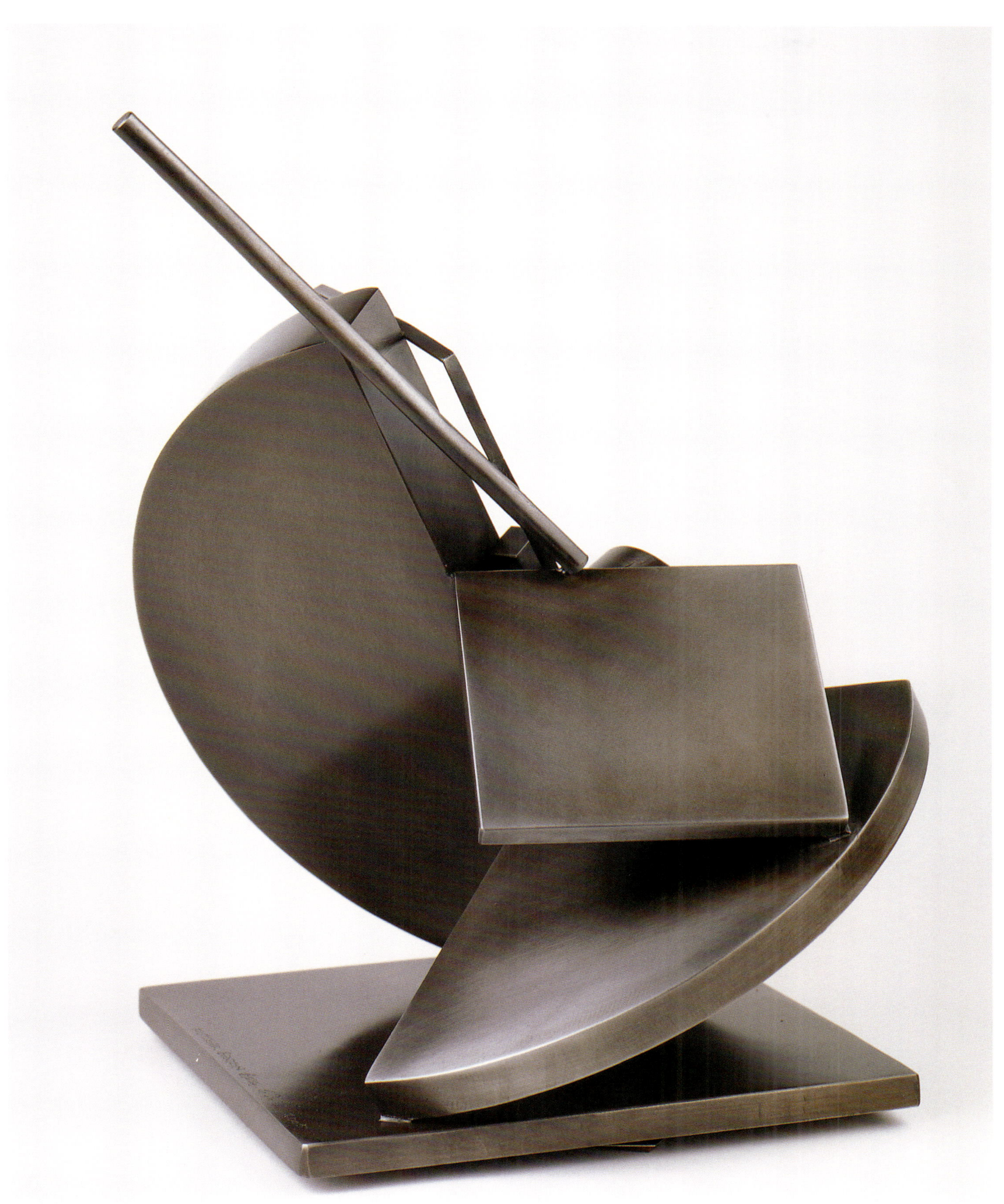

Folded Circle Study with Cylinder

2005, steel with patina
14½ x 10 x 12 inches
37 x 25 x 30 cm

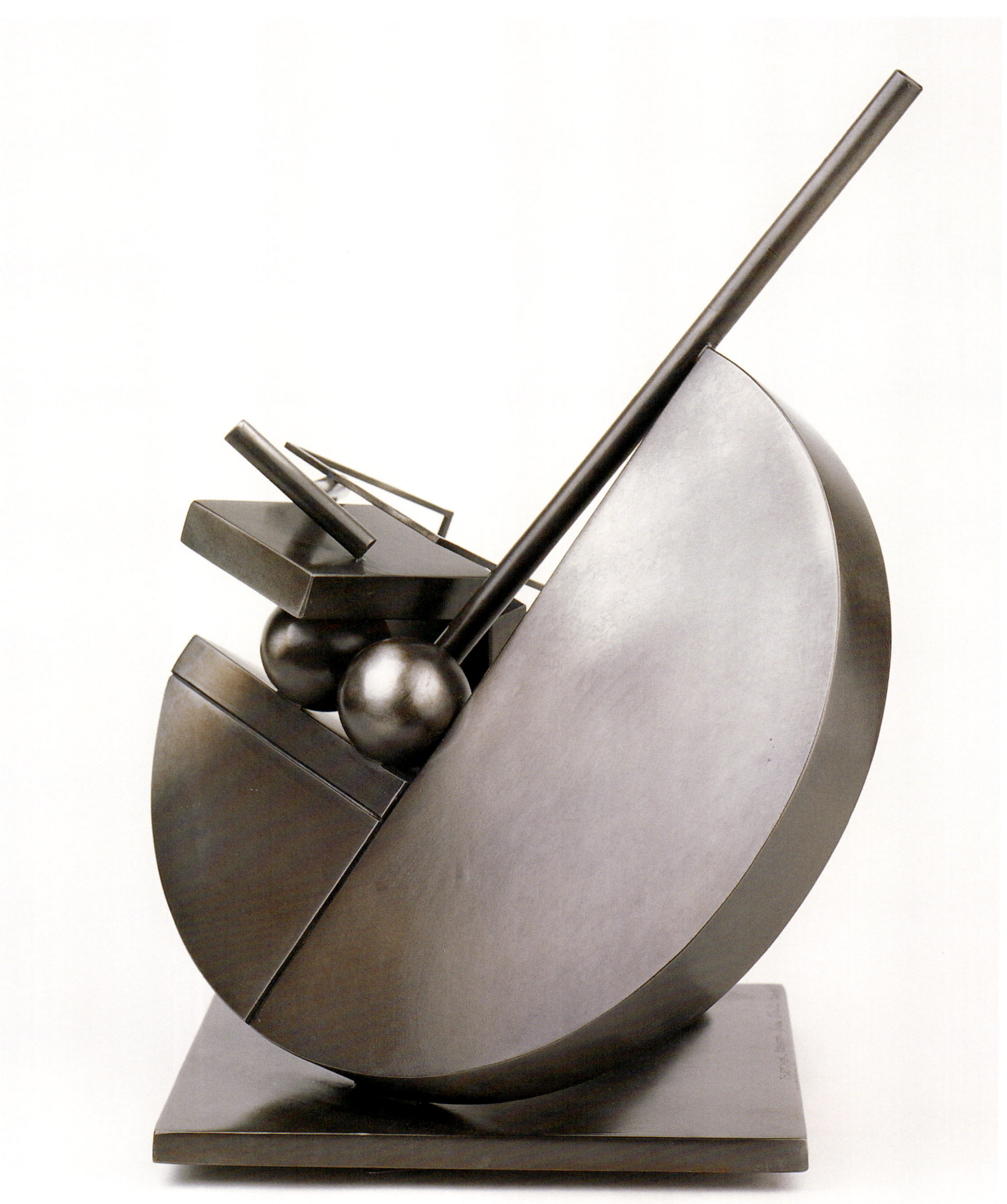

Folded Circle Study with Open L

2005, steel with patina
16 x 11 x 11 inches
41 x 28 x 28 cm

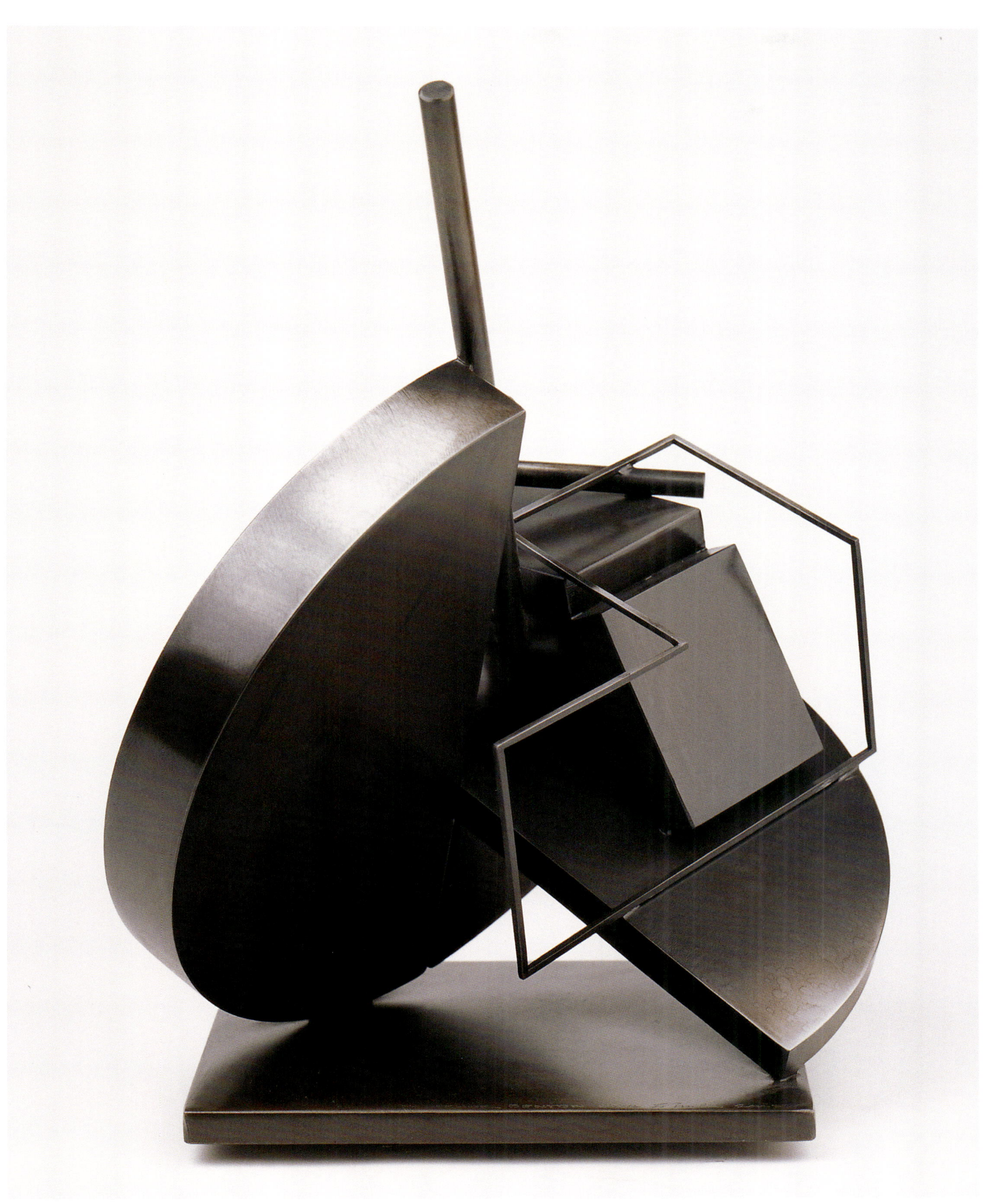

Folded Circle Study with Open L

2005, steel with patina
16 x 11 x 11 inches
41 x 28 x 28 cm

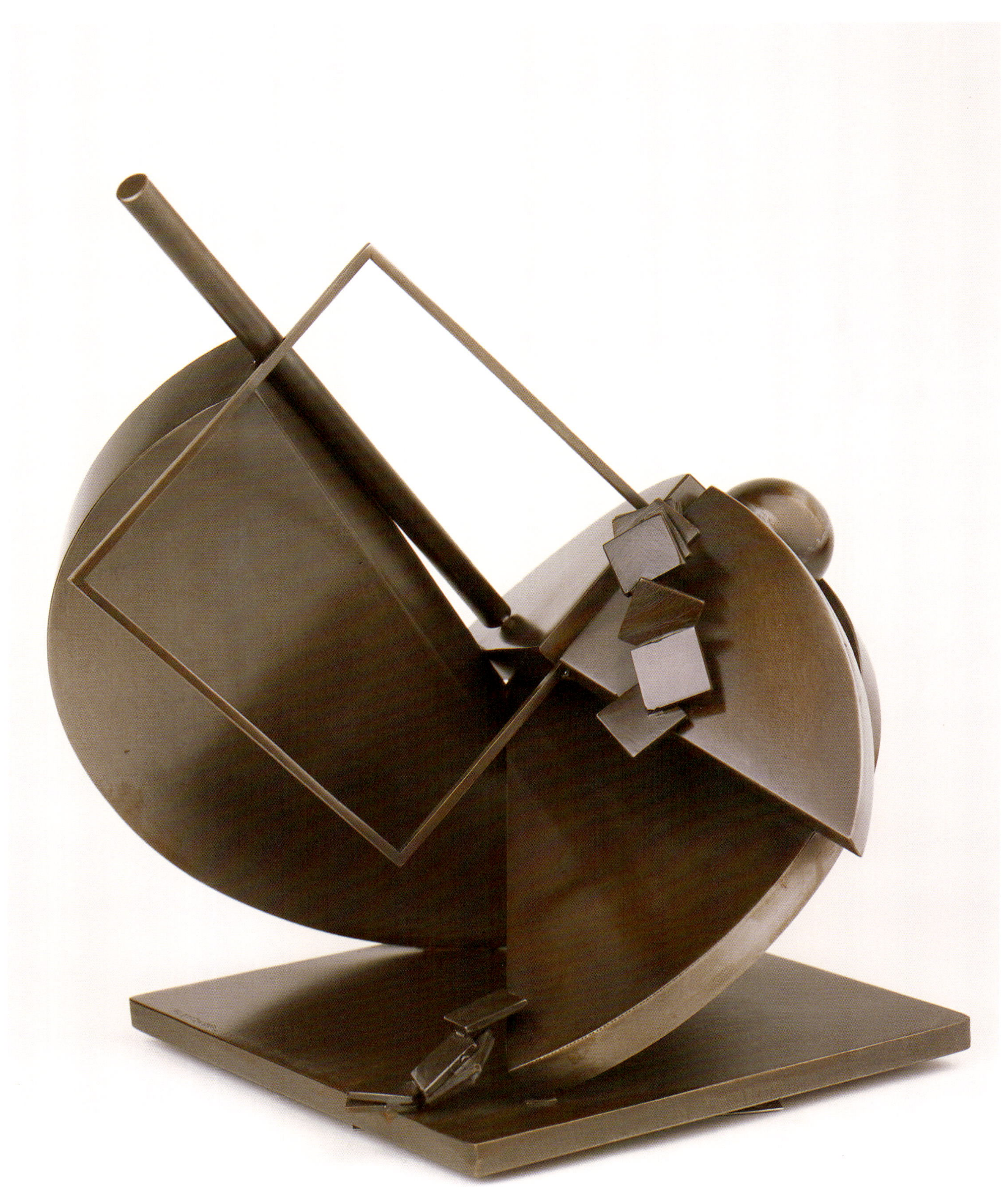

Folded Circle Study with Open Square

2005, steel with patina
14 x 13 x 14 inches
36 x 33 x 36 cm

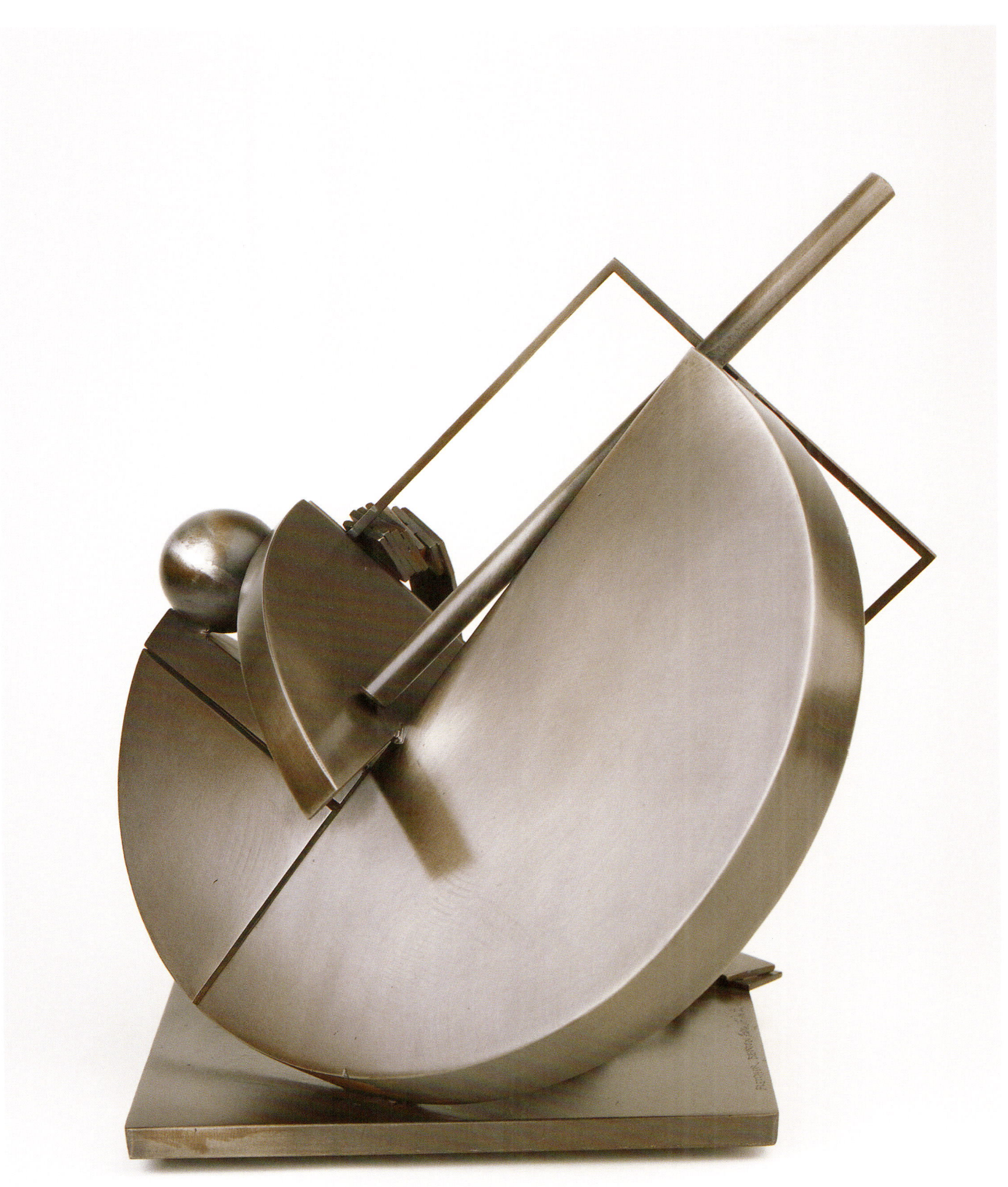

Folded Circle Study with Open Square

2005, steel with patina
14 x 13 x 14 inches
36 x 33 x 36 cm

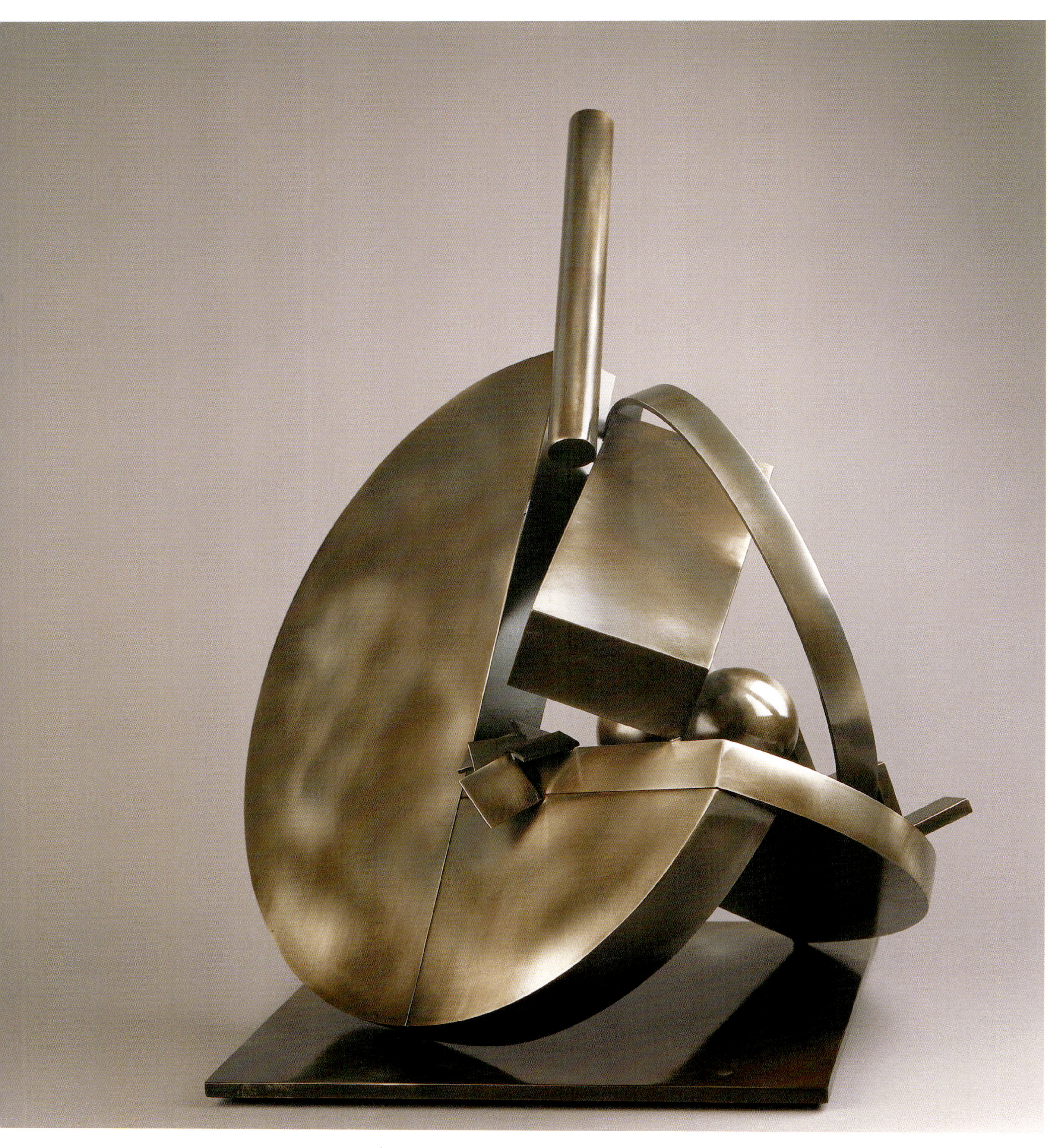

Folded Circle with Rectangle and Balls

2003, steel with patina
29 x 24 x 24 inches
74 x 61 x 61 cm

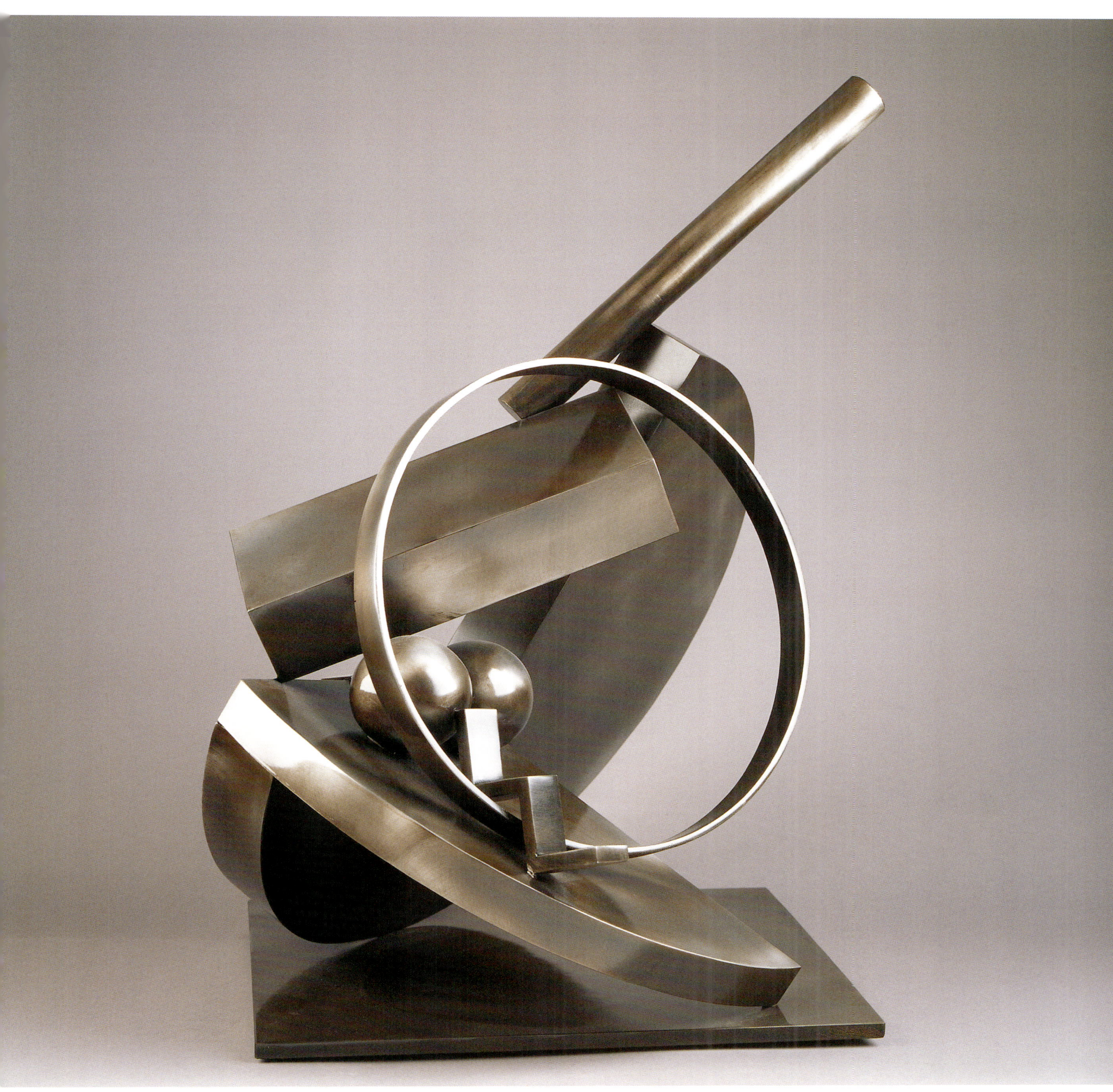

Folded Circle with Rectangle and Balls

2003, steel with patina
29 x 24 x 24 inches
74 x 61 x 61 cm

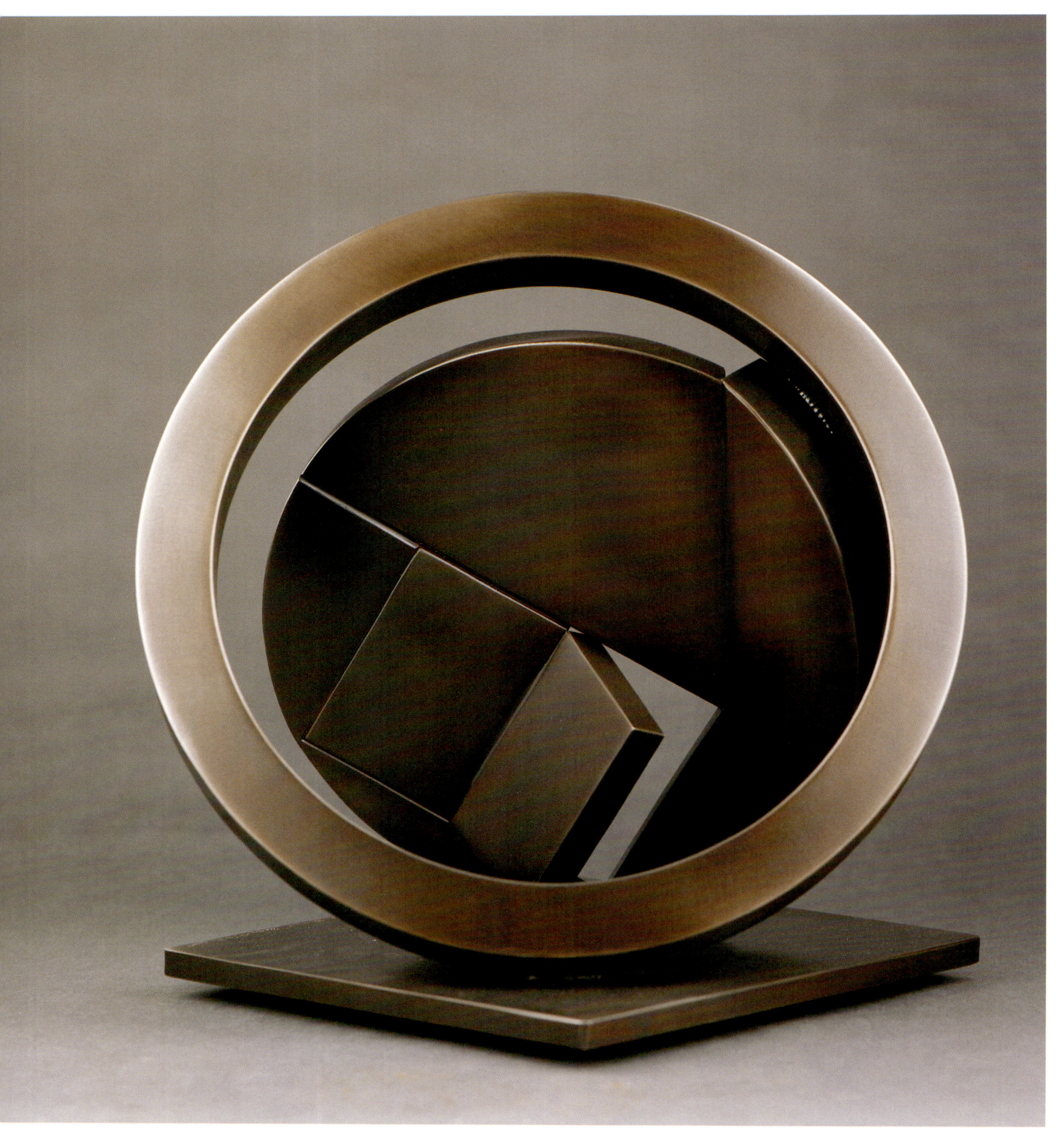

Folded Circle Ring: Three Rectangles

2005, steel with patina
14 x 14 x 12 inches
36 x 36 x 30 cm

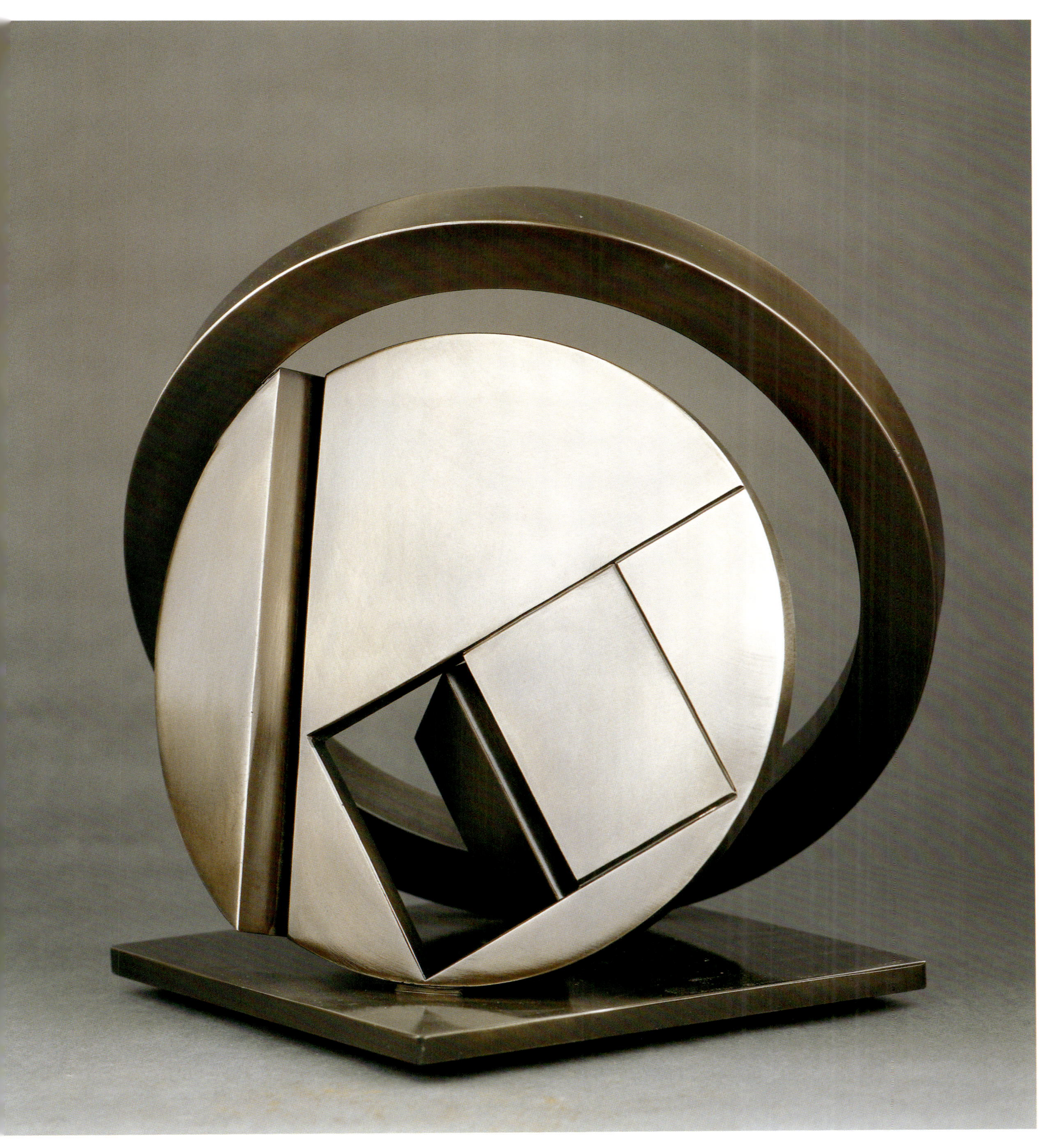

Folded Circle Ring: Three Rectangles

2005, steel with patina
14 x 14 x 12 inches
36 x 36 x 30 cm

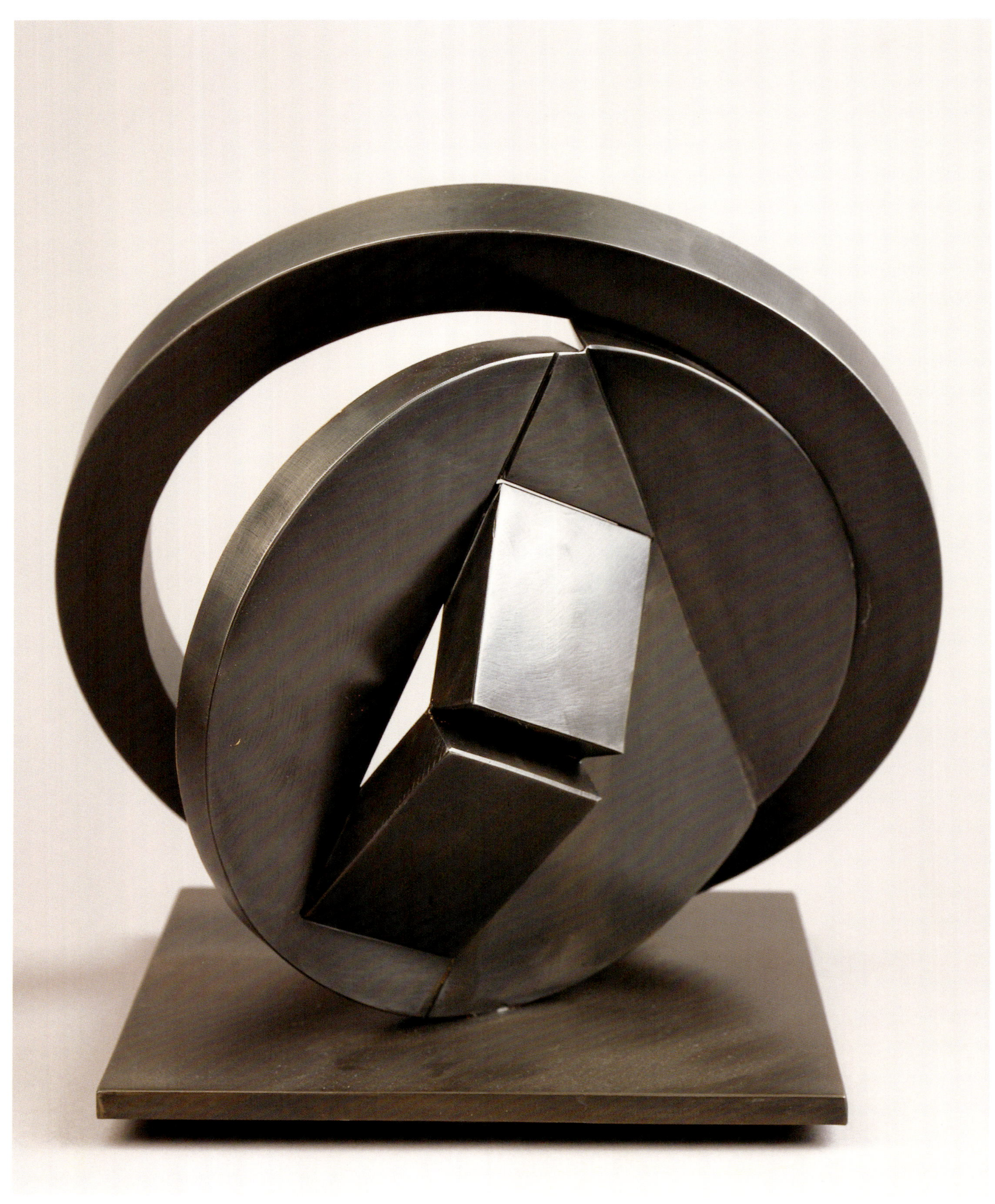

Folded Circle Ring: Broken Rectangle

2005, steel with patina
14 x 14 x 11 inches
36 x 36 x 28 cm

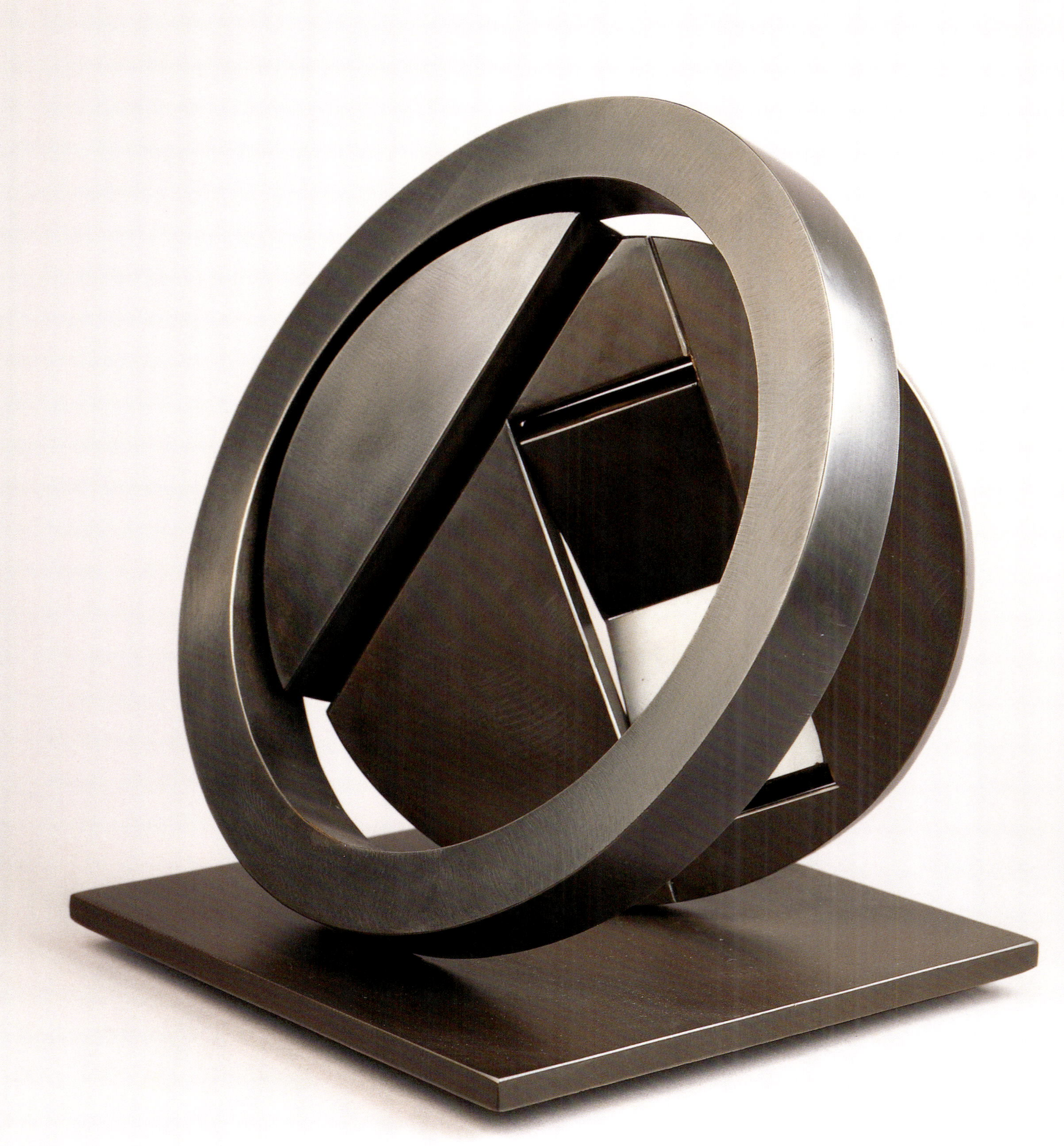

Folded Circle Ring: Broken Rectangle

2005, steel with patina
14 x 14 x 11 inches
36 x 36 x 28 cm

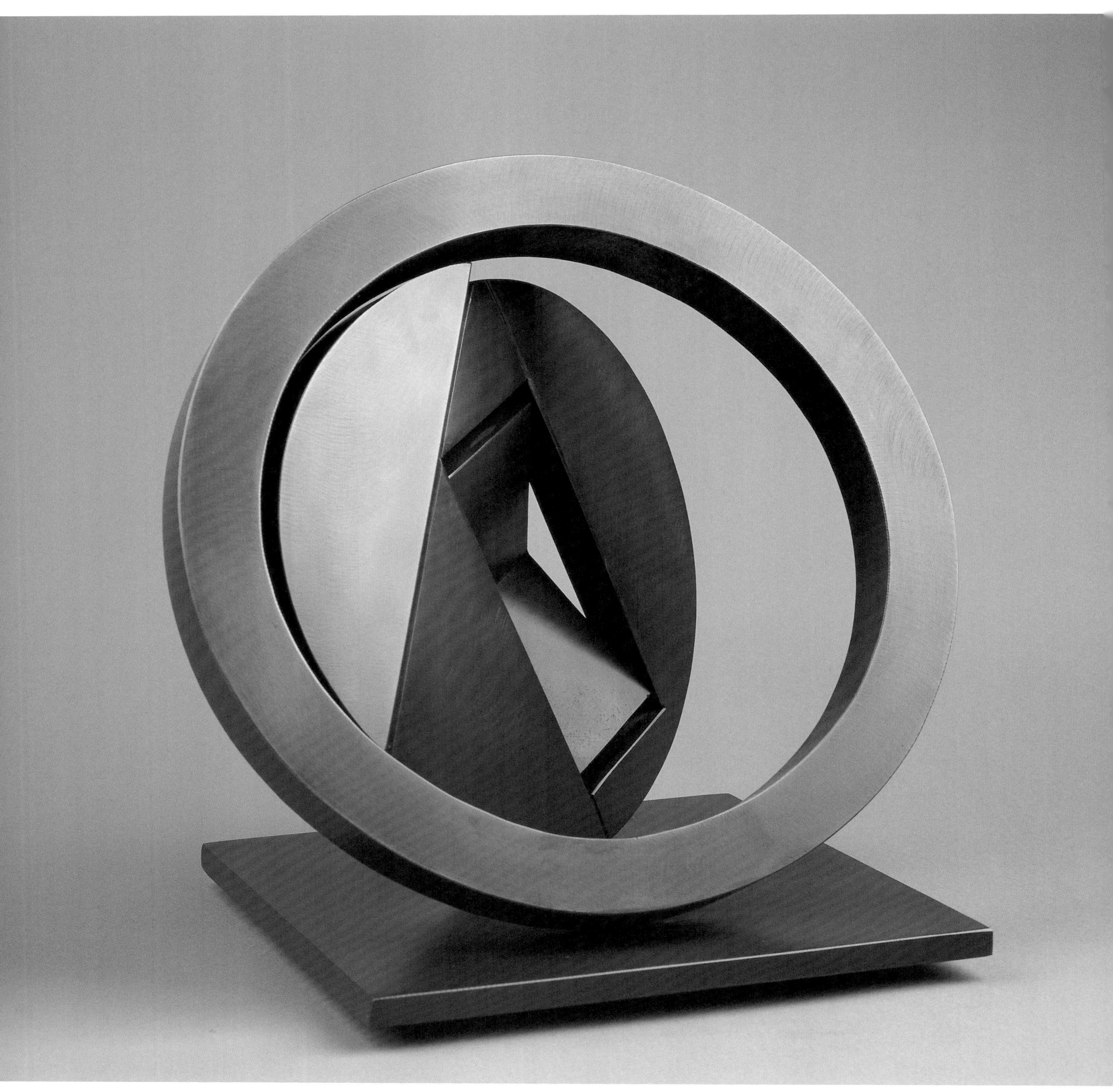

Folded Circle Ring: Broken Rectangle

2005, steel with patina
14 x 14 x 11 inches
36 x 36 x 28 cm

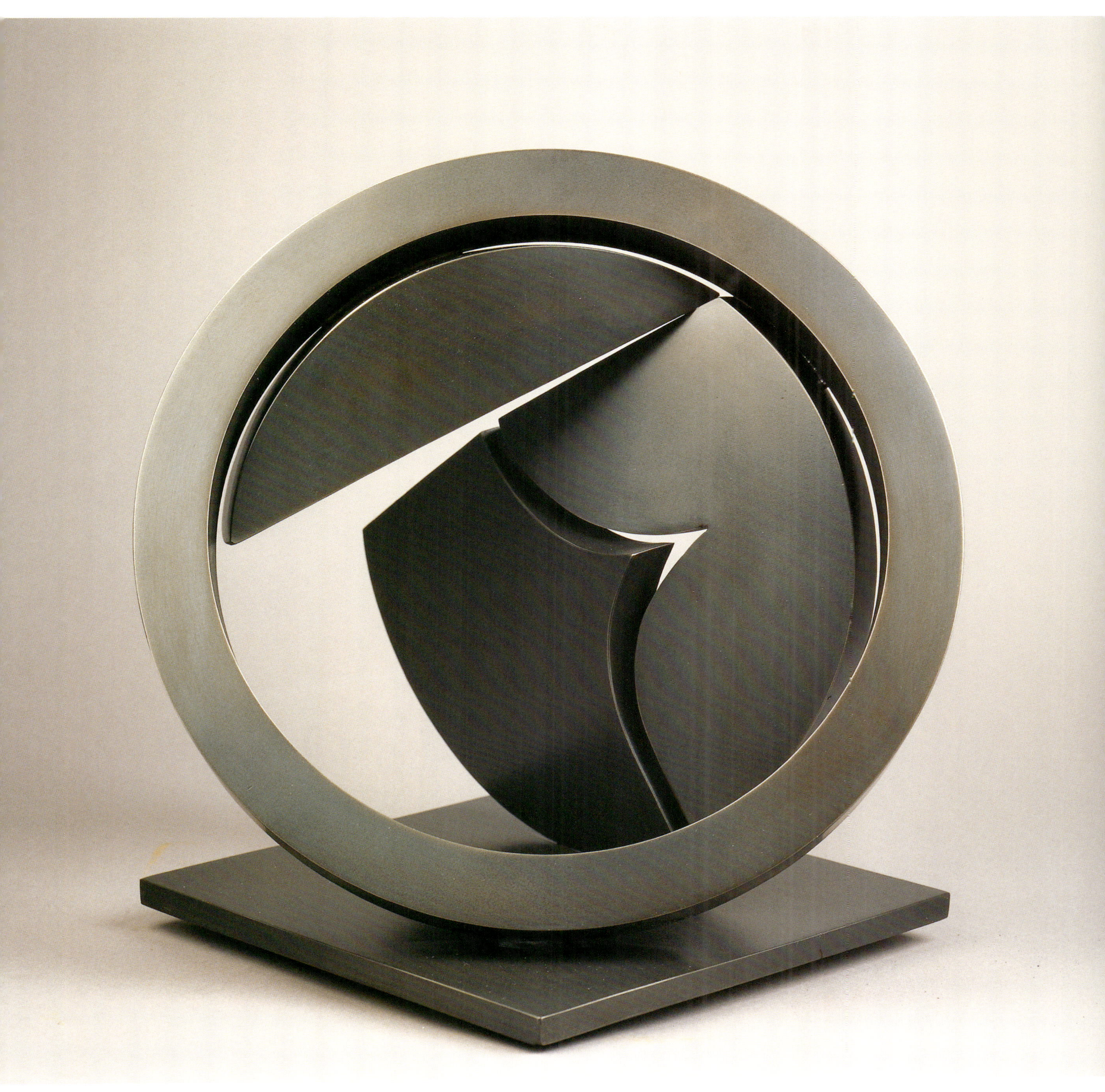

Folded Circle Ring Bezel, Phase II

2005, steel with patina
14 x 14 x 12 inches
36 x 36 x 30 cm

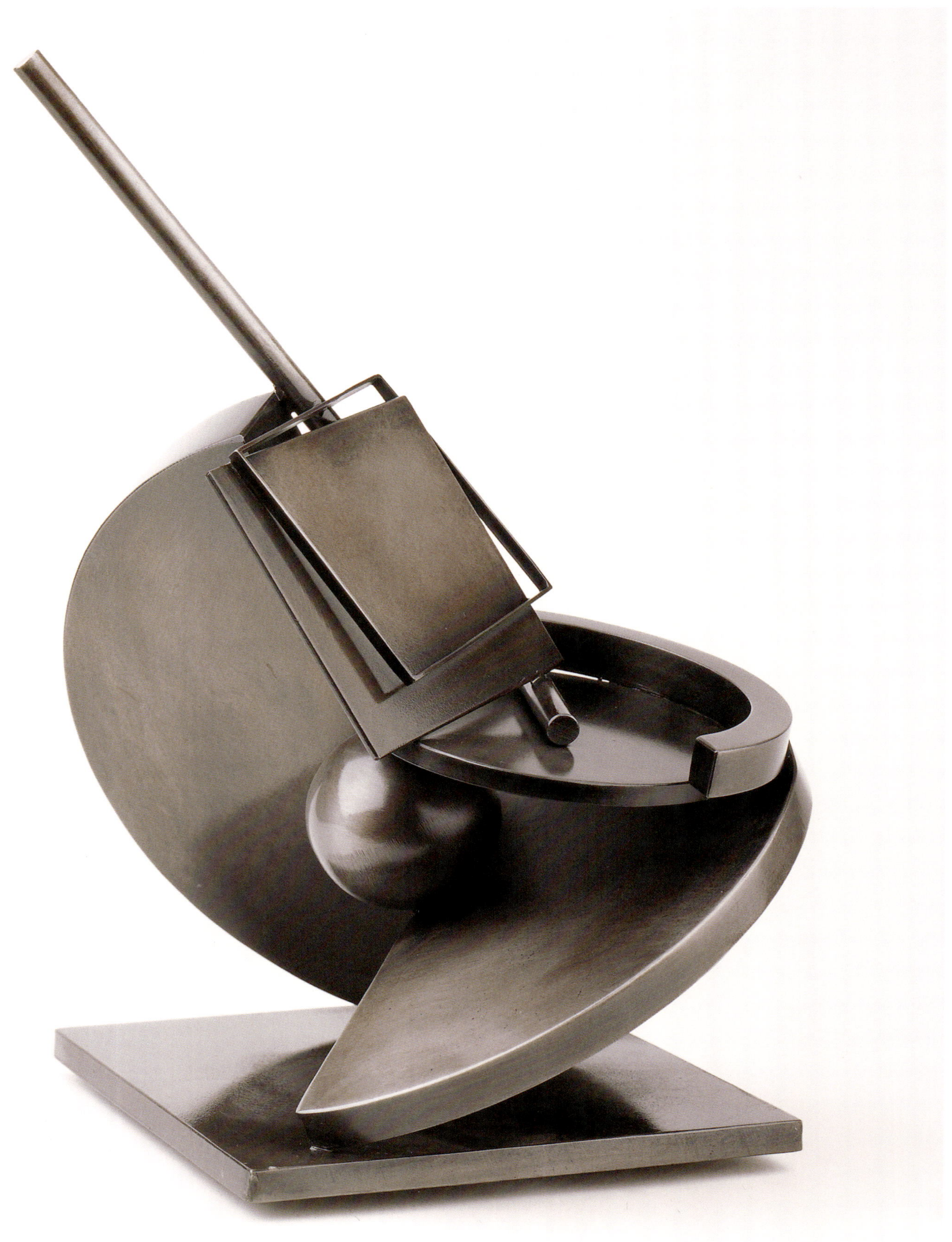

Folded Circle Study with Ball

2005, steel with patina
16 x 11 x 11 inches
41 x 28 x 28 cm

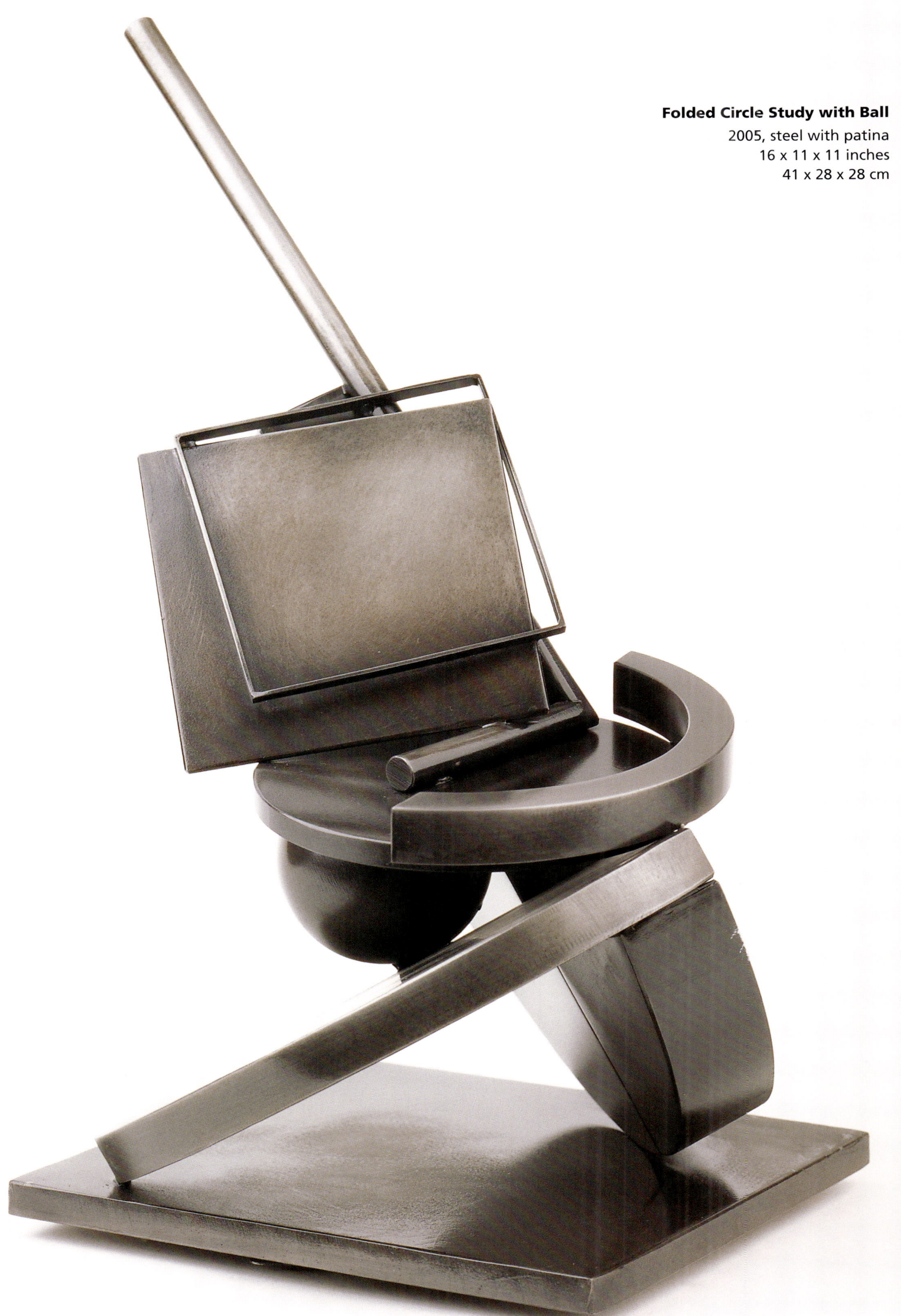

Folded Circle Study with Ball
2005, steel with patina
16 x 11 x 11 inches
41 x 28 x 28 cm

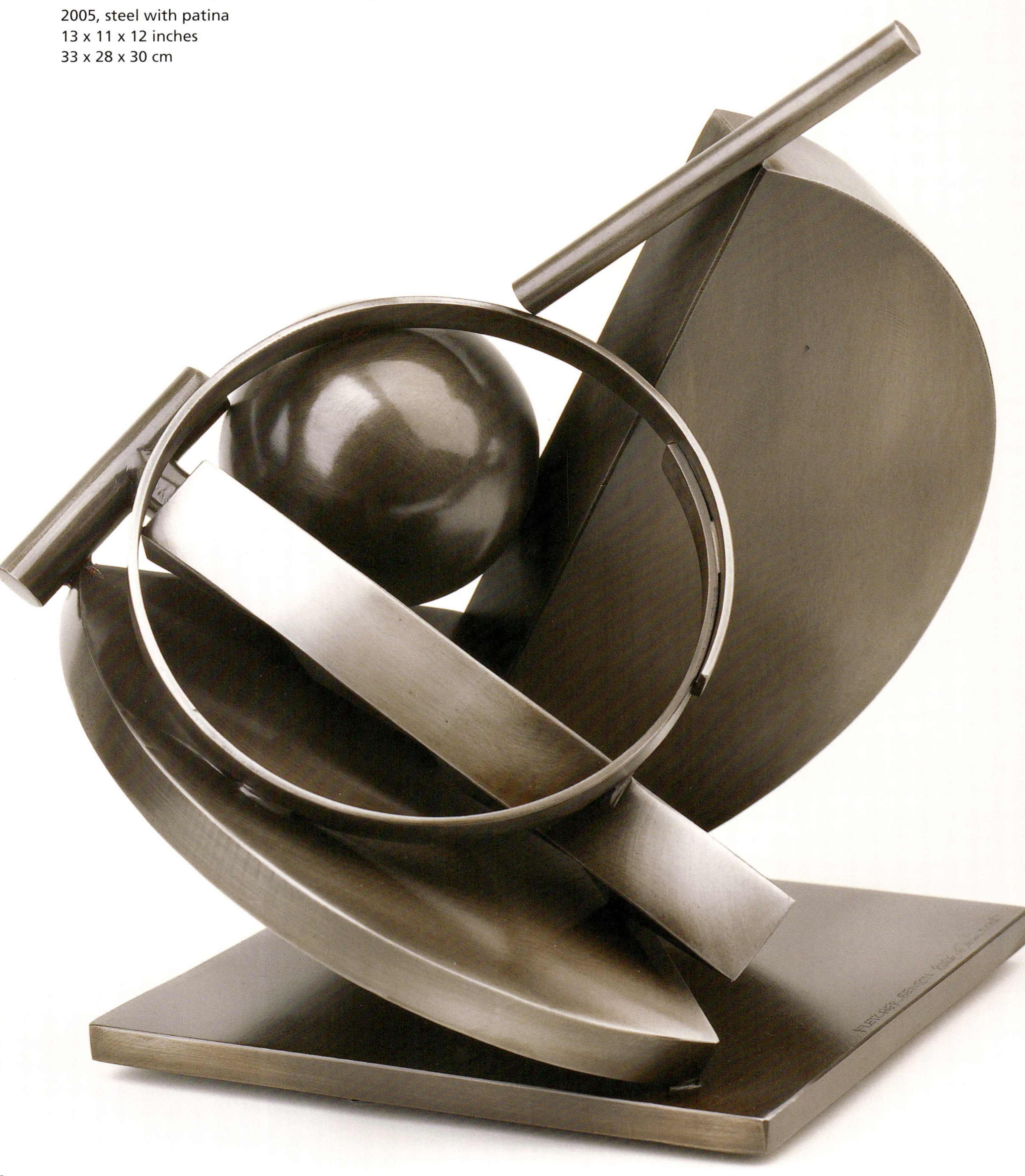

Folded Circle Study with Ball and Ring
2005, steel with patina
13 x 11 x 12 inches
33 x 28 x 30 cm

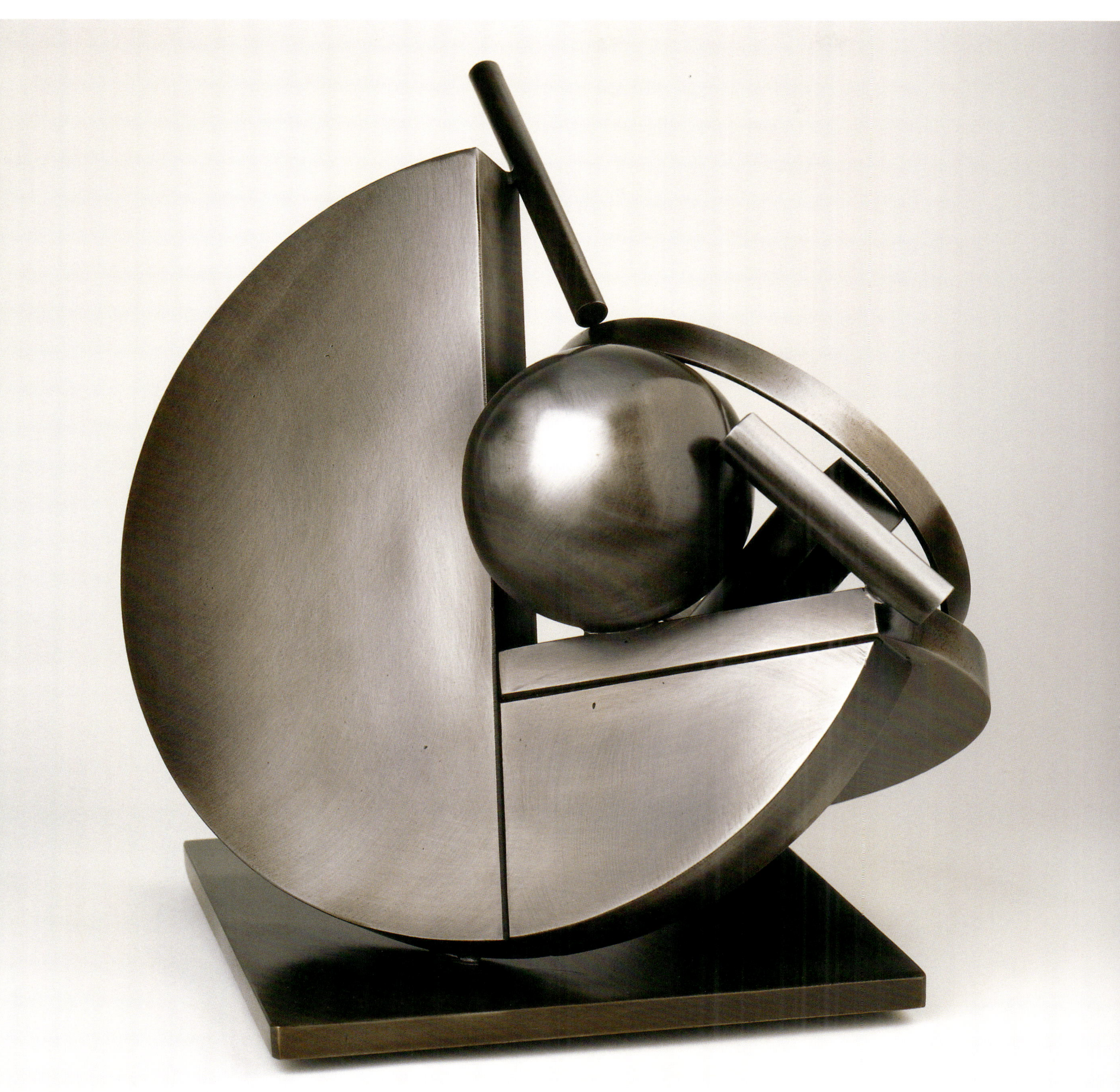

Folded Circle Study with Ball and Ring

2005, steel with patina
13 x 11 x 12 inches
33 x 28 x 30 cm

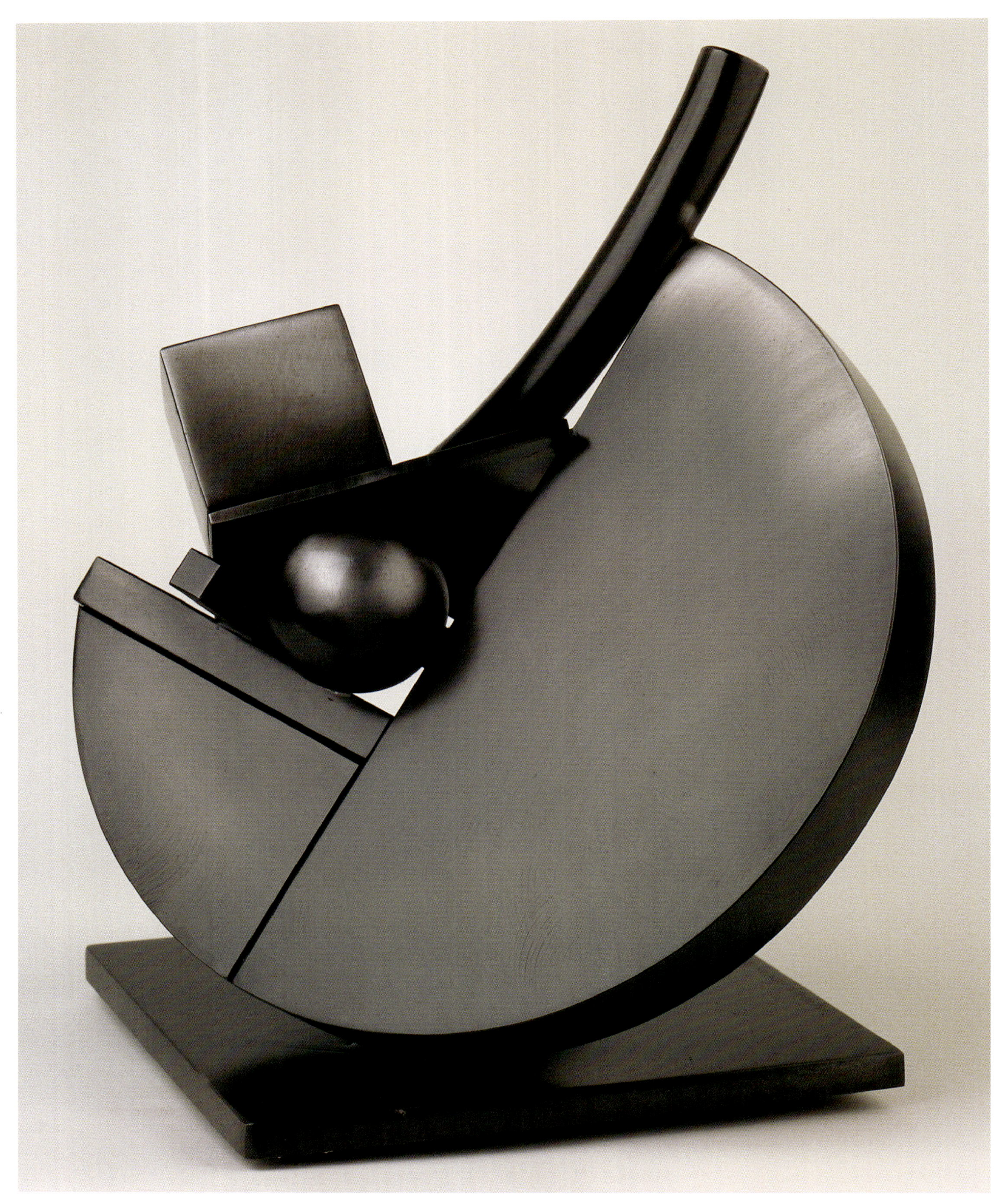

Folded Circle Study with Ball and Square

2005, steel with patina
15 x 13 x 12 inches
38 x 33 x 30 cm

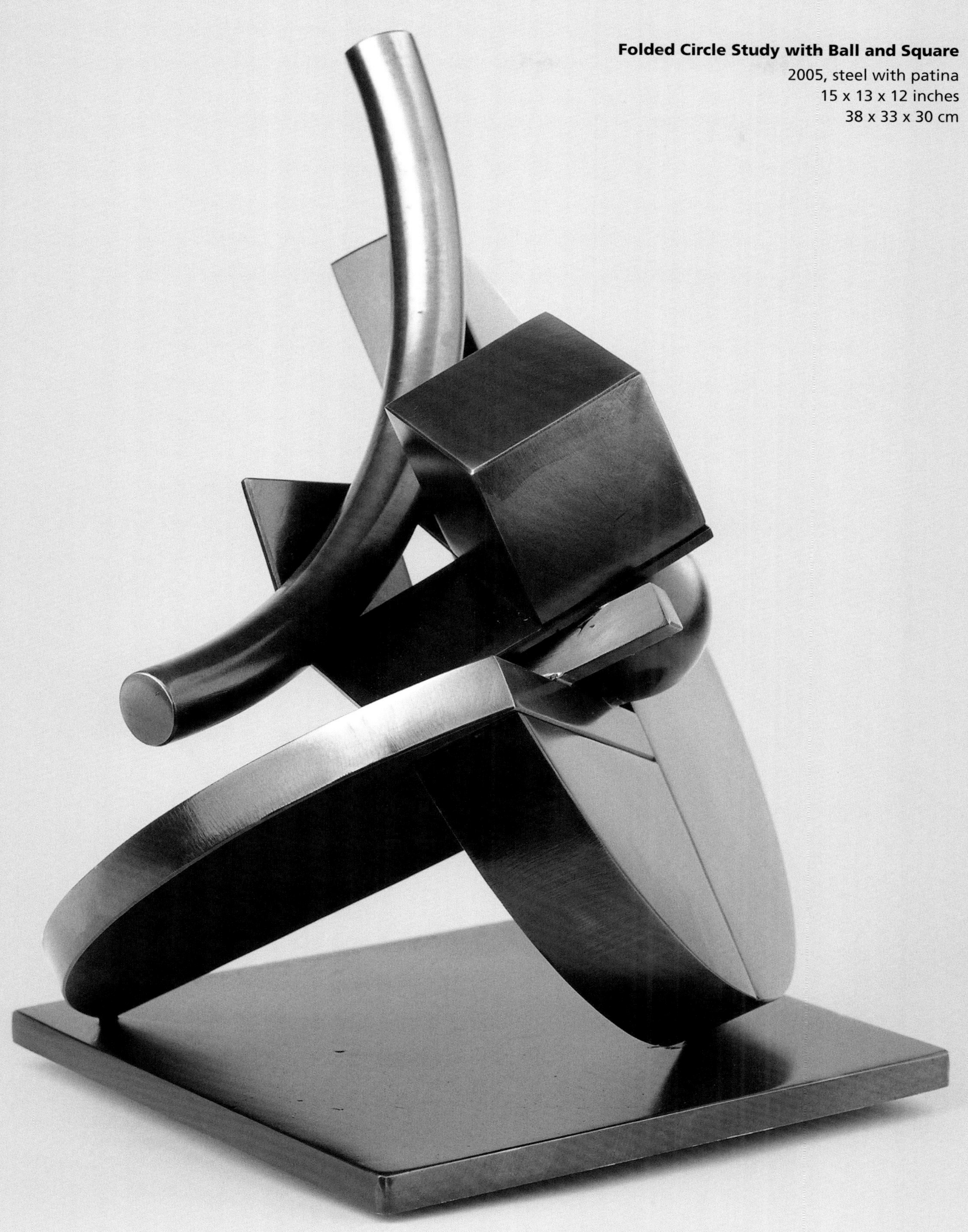

Folded Circle Study with Ball and Square
2005, steel with patina
15 x 13 x 12 inches
38 x 33 x 30 cm

Folded Circle Study with Leaf

2005, steel with patina
14 x 11 x 13 inches
36 x 28 x 33 cm

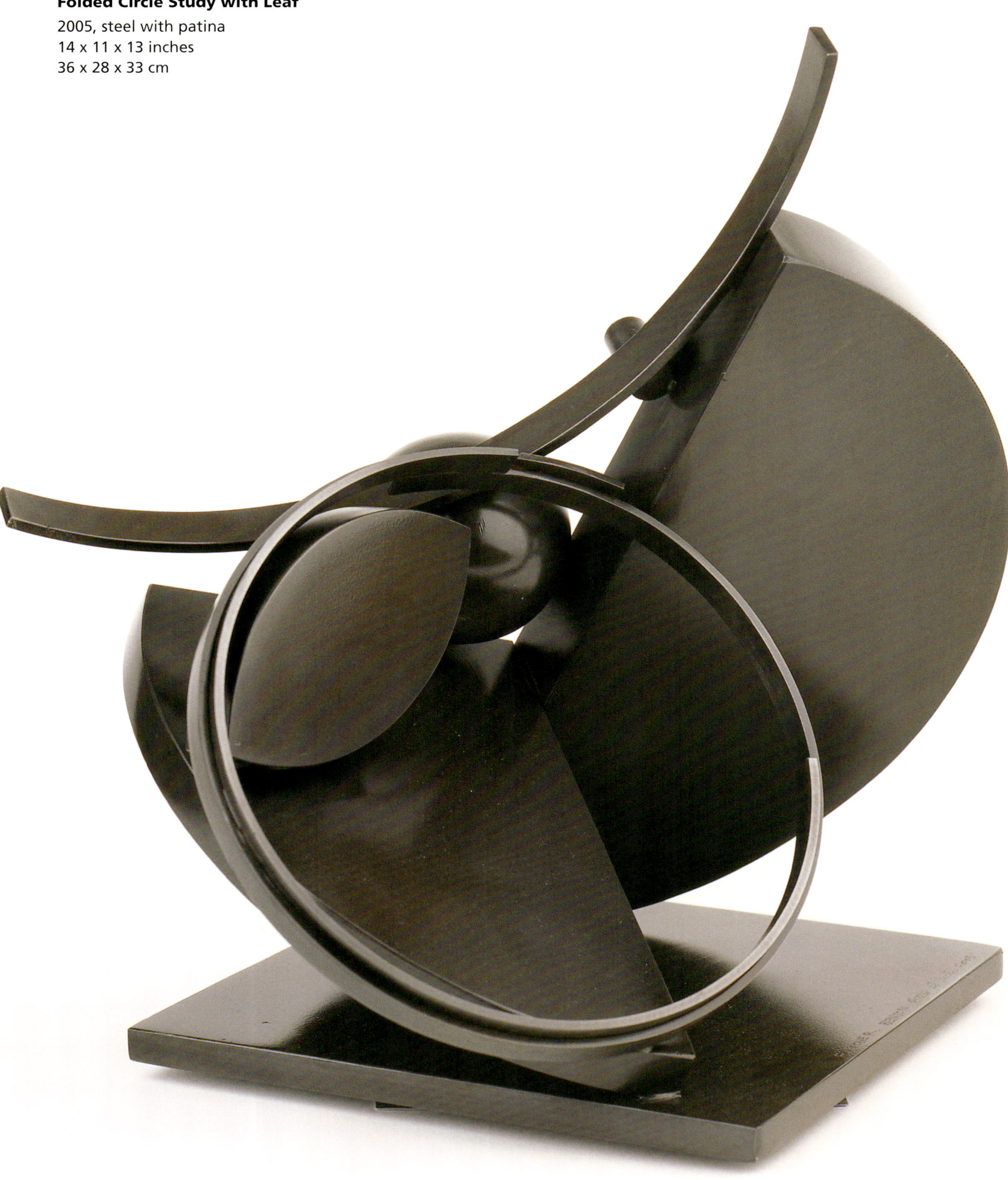

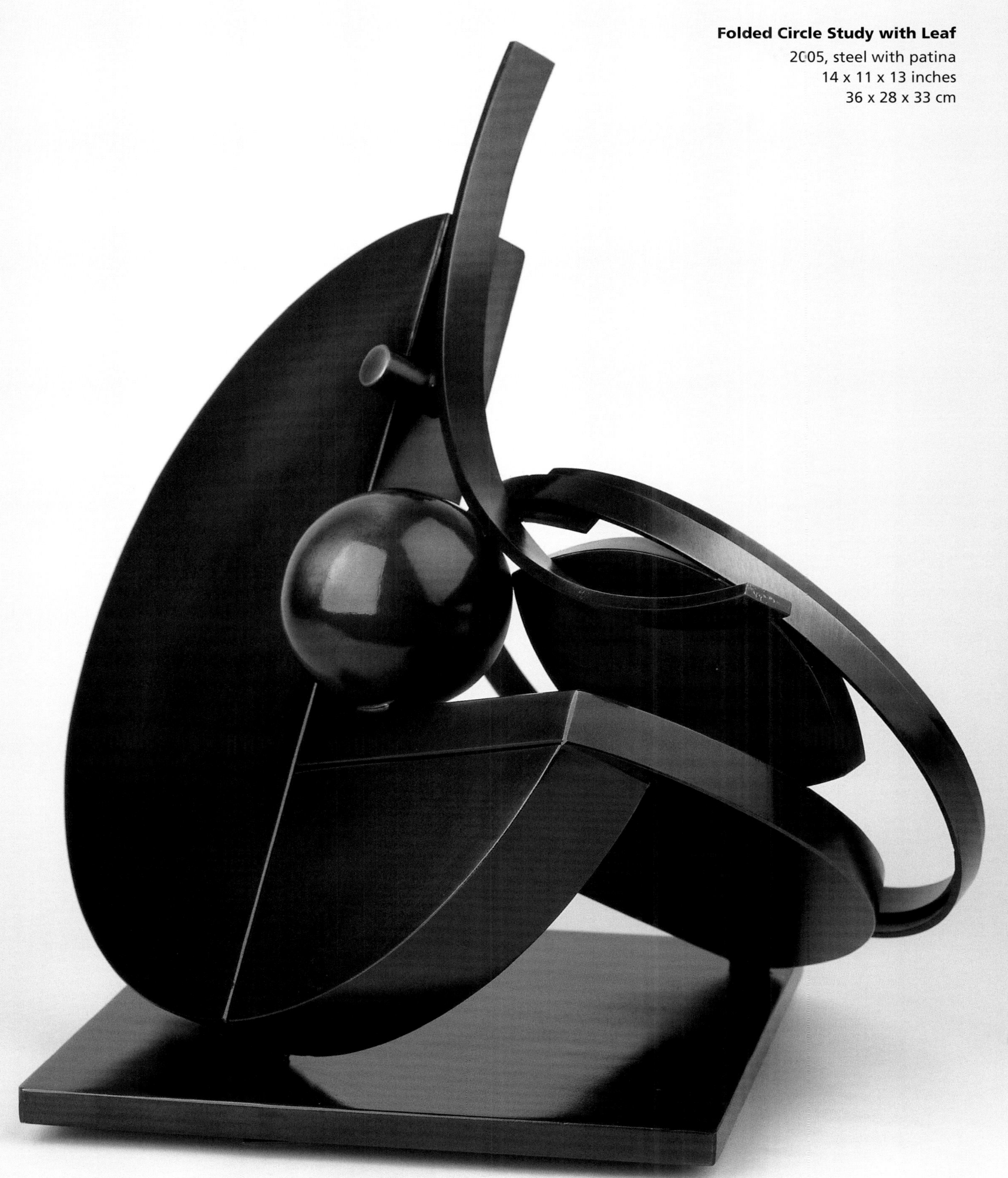

Folded Circle Study with Leaf
2005, steel with patina
14 x 11 x 13 inches
36 x 28 x 33 cm

Folded Circle Study with Square
2005, steel with patina
18 x 13 x 13 inches
46 x 33 x 33 cm

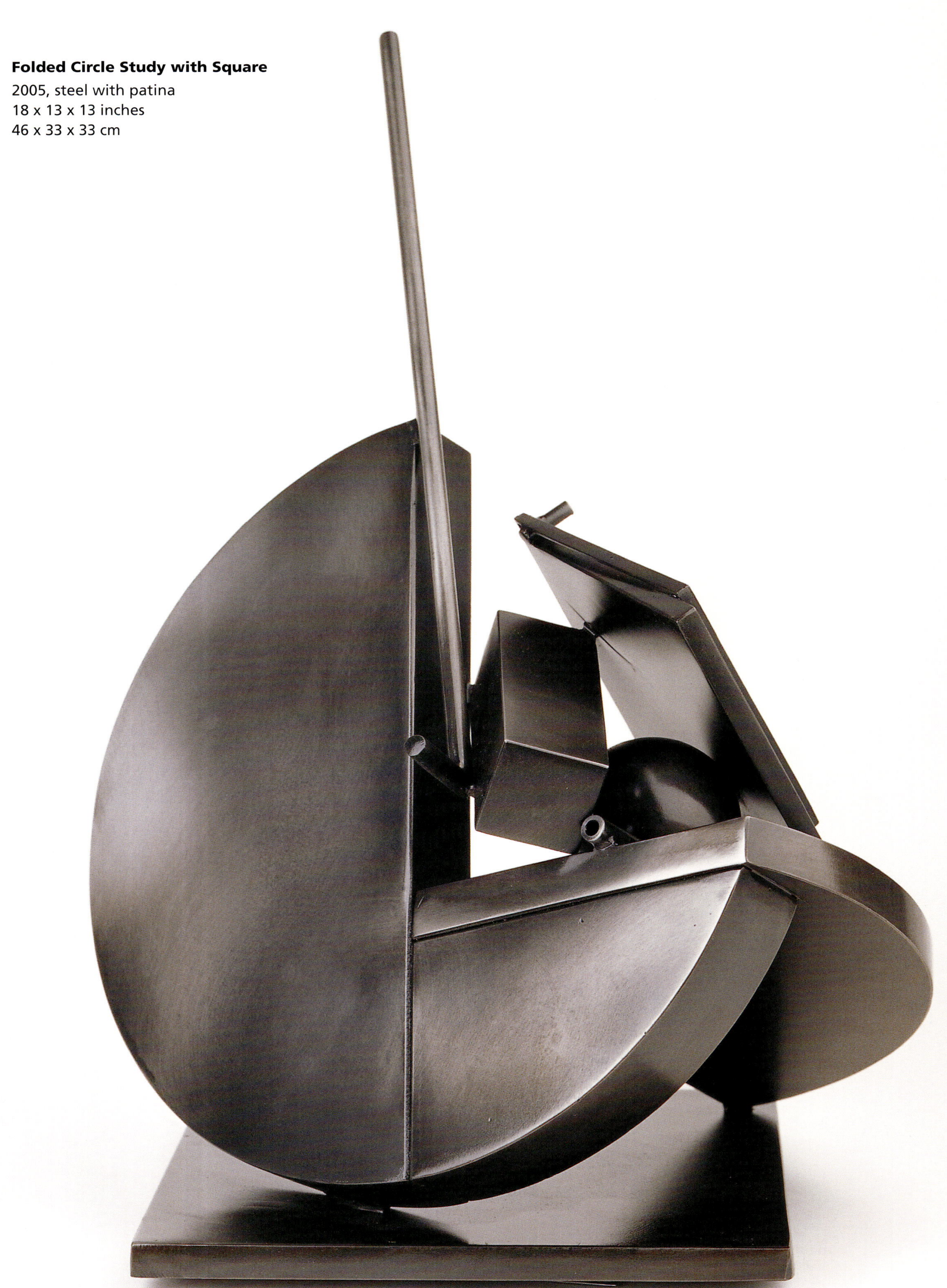

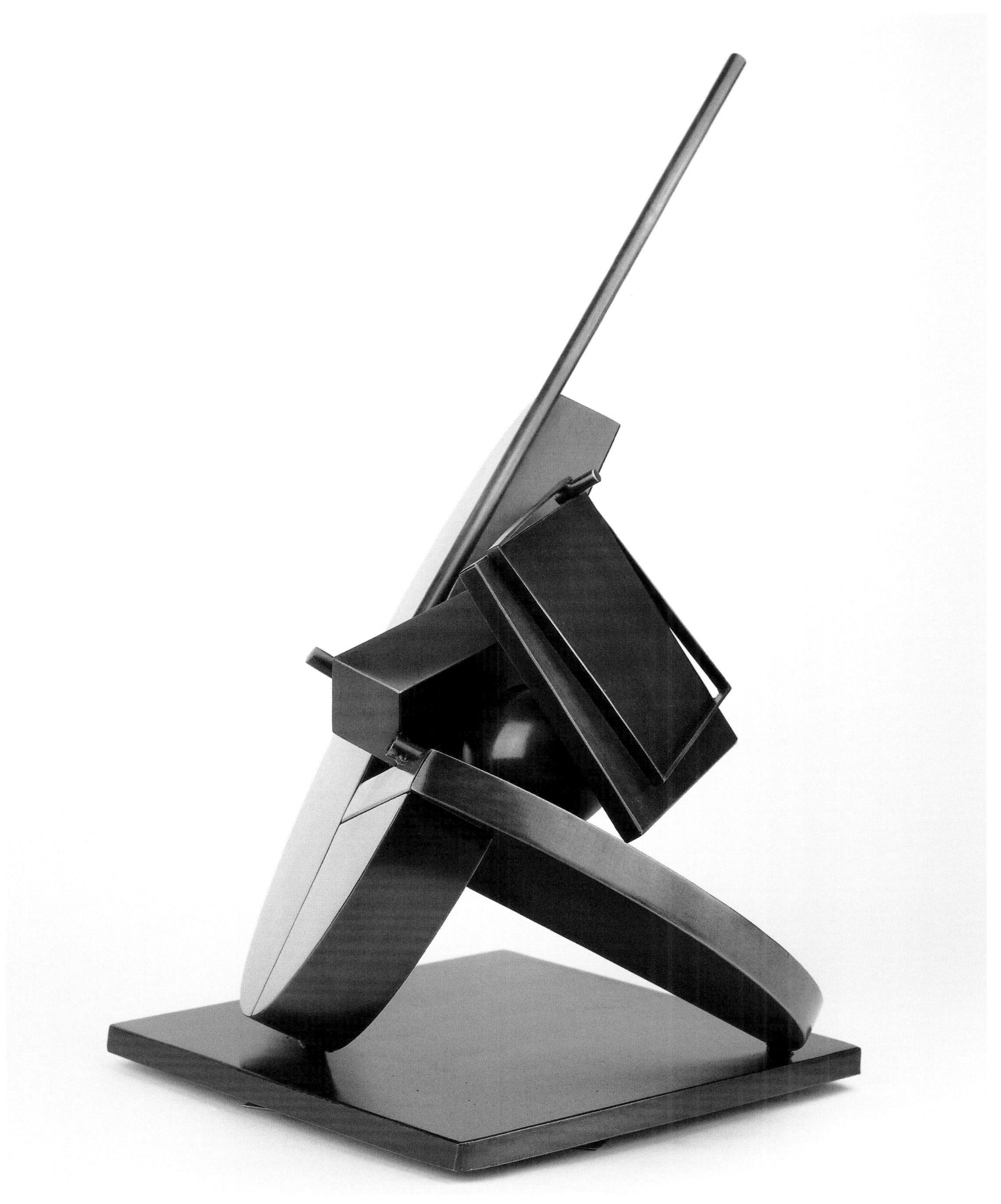

Folded Circle Study with Square

2005, steel with patina
18 x 13 x 13 inches
46 x 33 x 33 cm

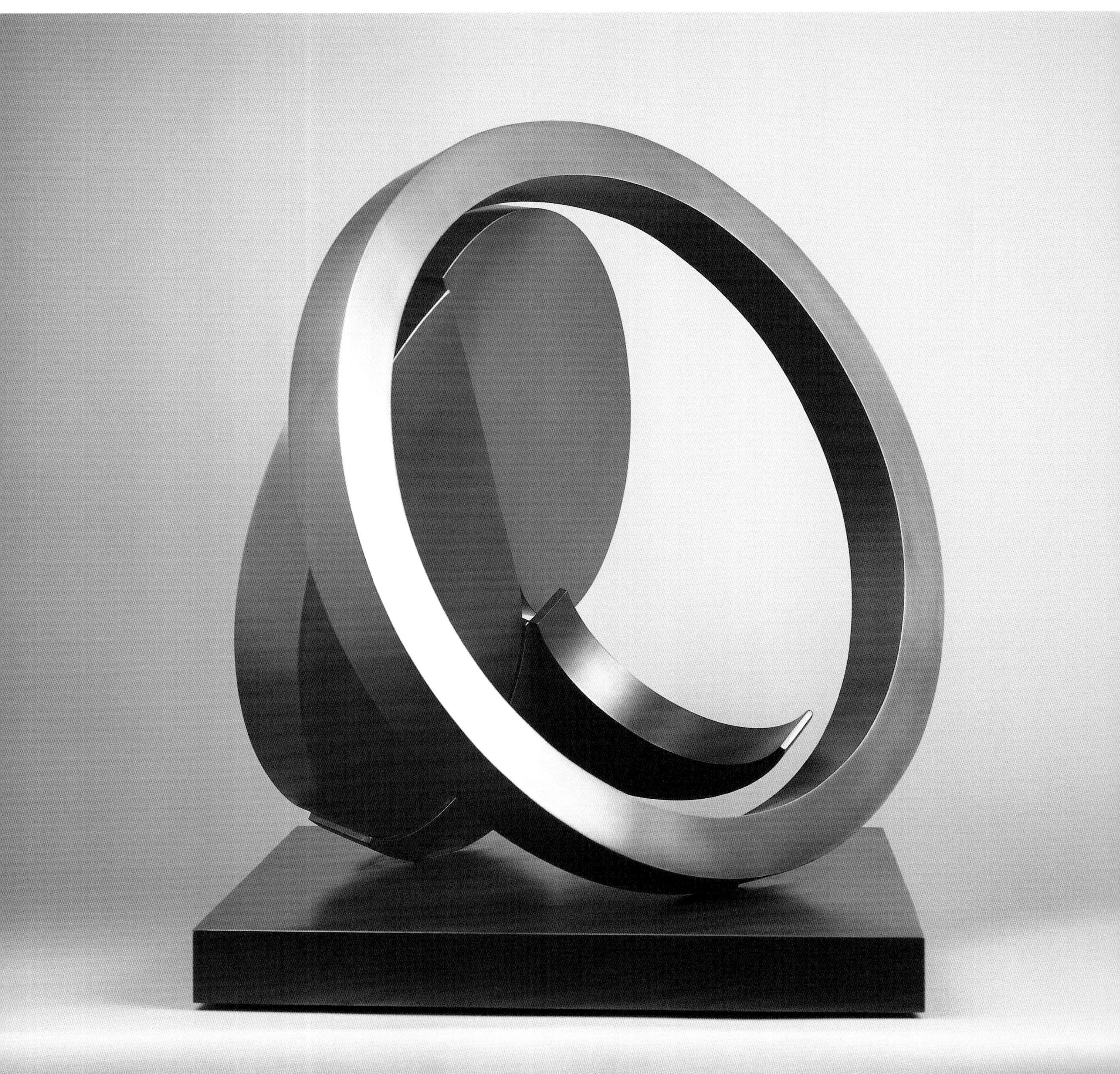

Folded Circle Ring Marilyn

2005, steel with patina
28 x 25 x 21 inches
71 x 64 x 53 cm

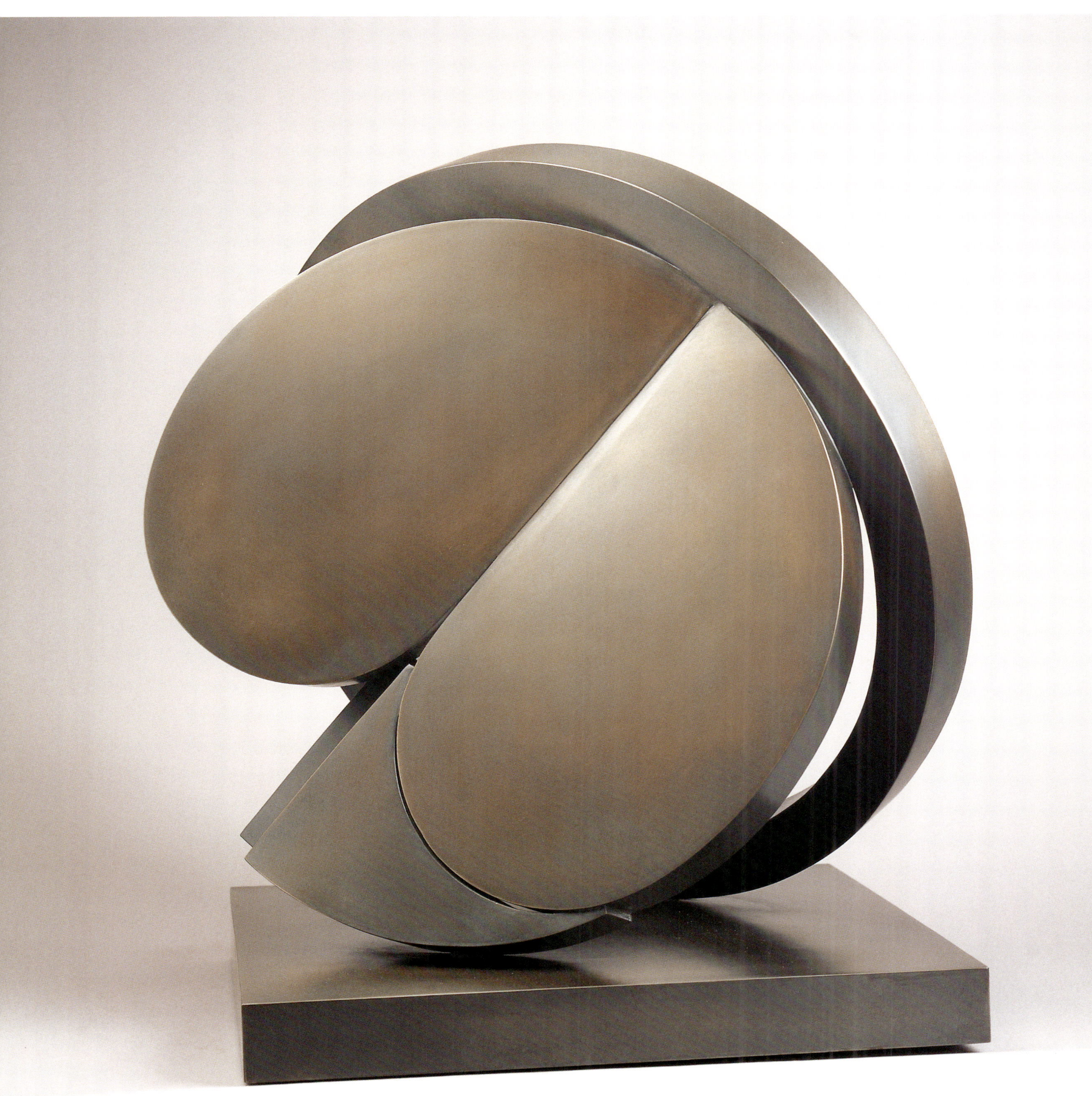

Folded Circle Ring Marilyn

2005, steel with patina
28 x 25 x 21 inches
71 x 64 x 53 cm

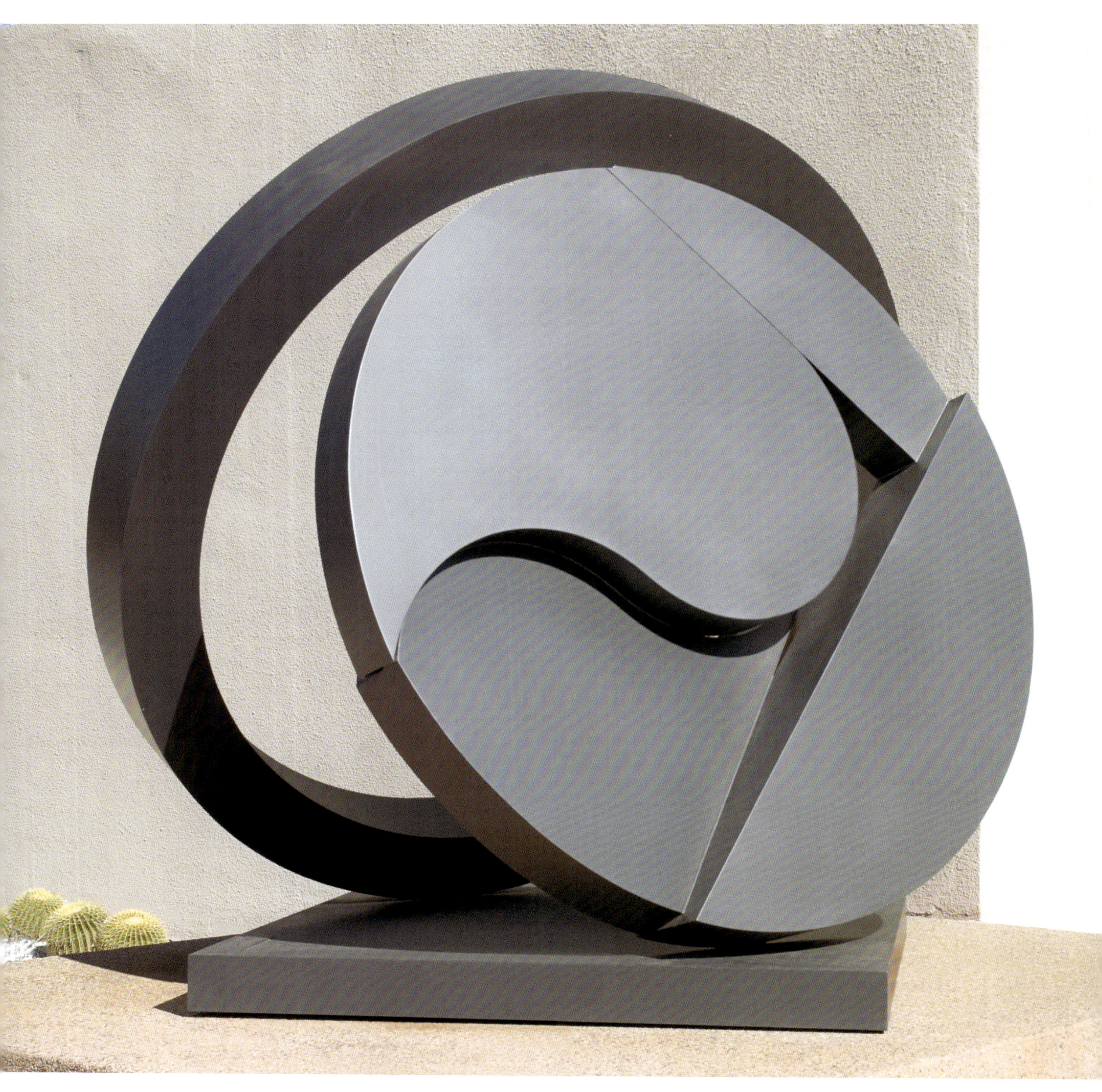

Folded Circle Ring S Composition No. 3

2008, painted steel
108 x 108 x 108 inches
274 x 274 x 274 cm

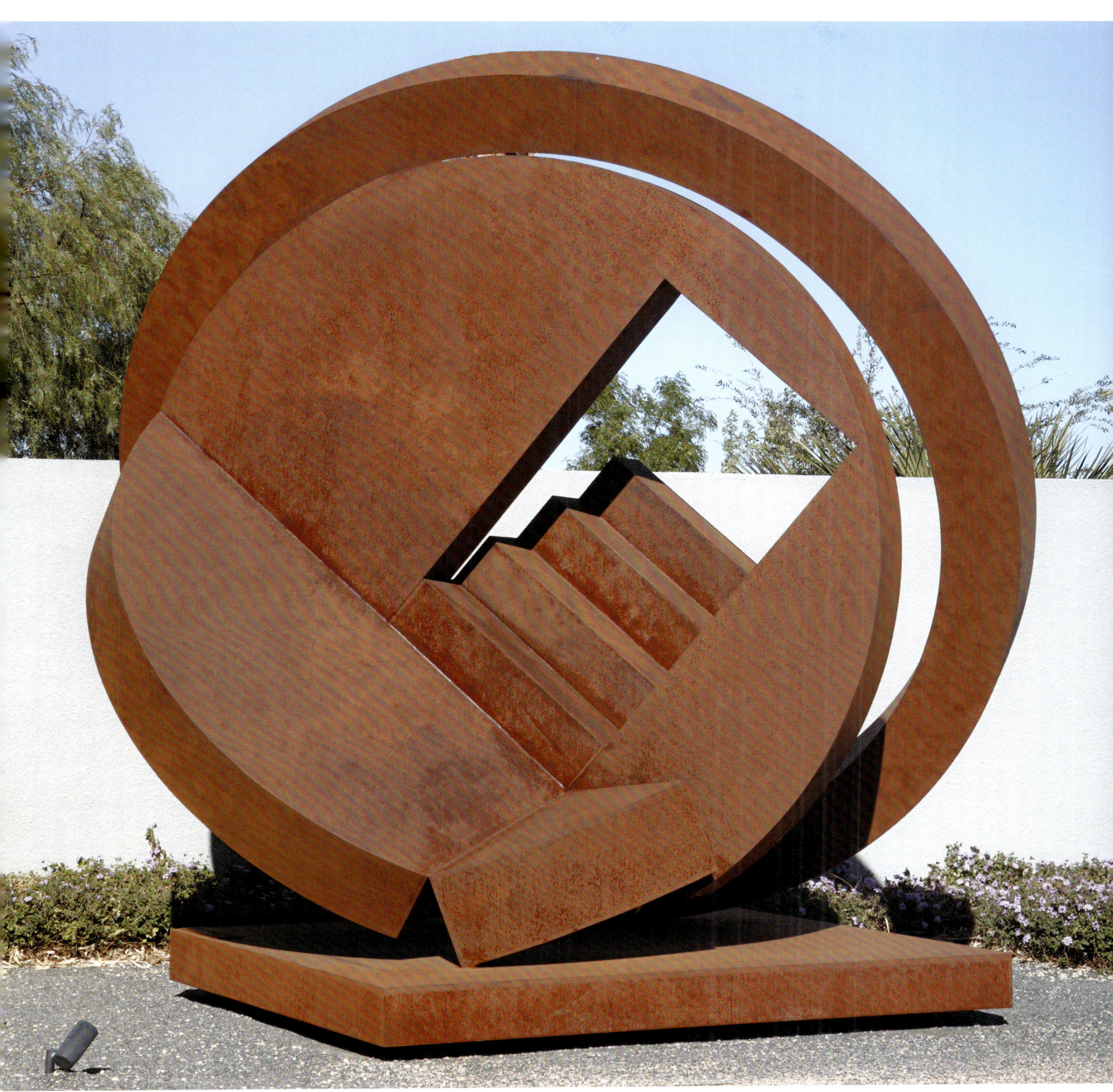

Folded Circle Ring Steps

2008, Cor-ten steel
108 x 108 x 108 inches
274 x 274 x 274 cm

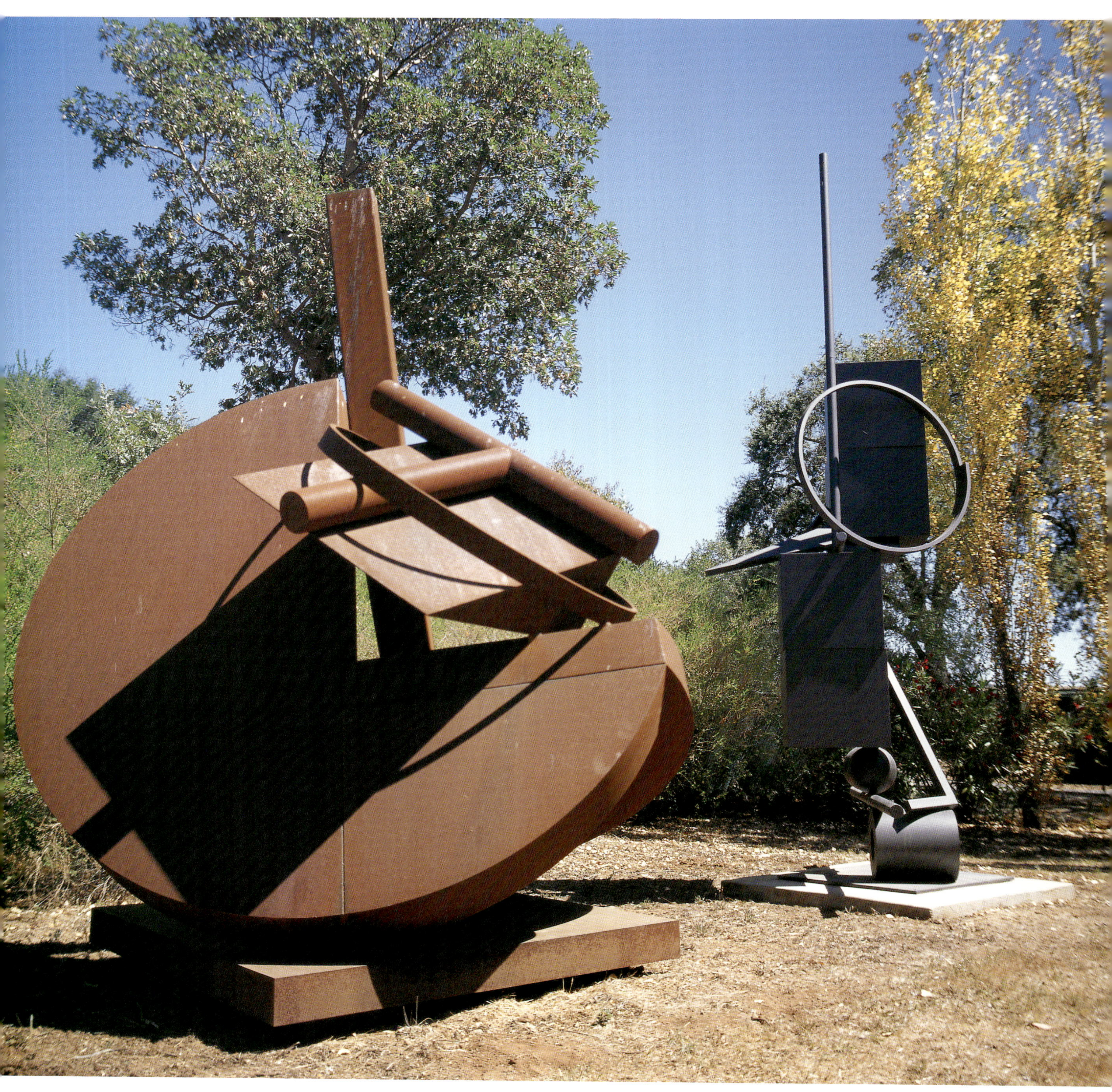

Folded Circle T

1999, Cor-ten steel
12 x 9 x 9 feet
366 x 274 x 274 cm

Blocks on Blocks: Two on Two, Two Balls

1997, painted steel
17 x 8 x 6½ feet
518 x 244 x 198 cm

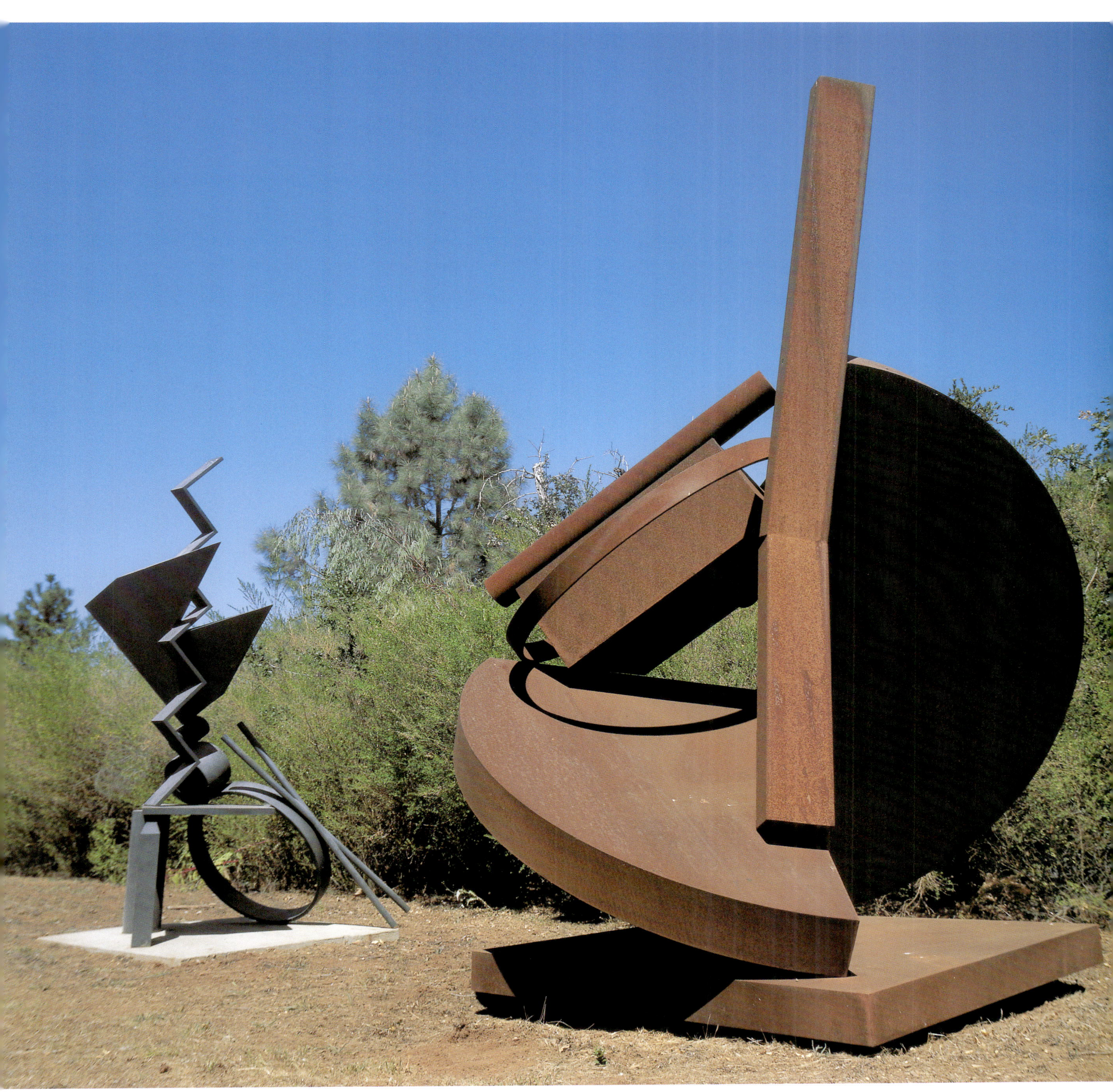

One-Legged Table 3

1989, painted steel
120 x 48 x 46 inches
305 x 122 x 117 cm

Folded Circle T

1999, Cor-ten steel
12 x 9 x 9 feet
366 x 274 x 274 cm

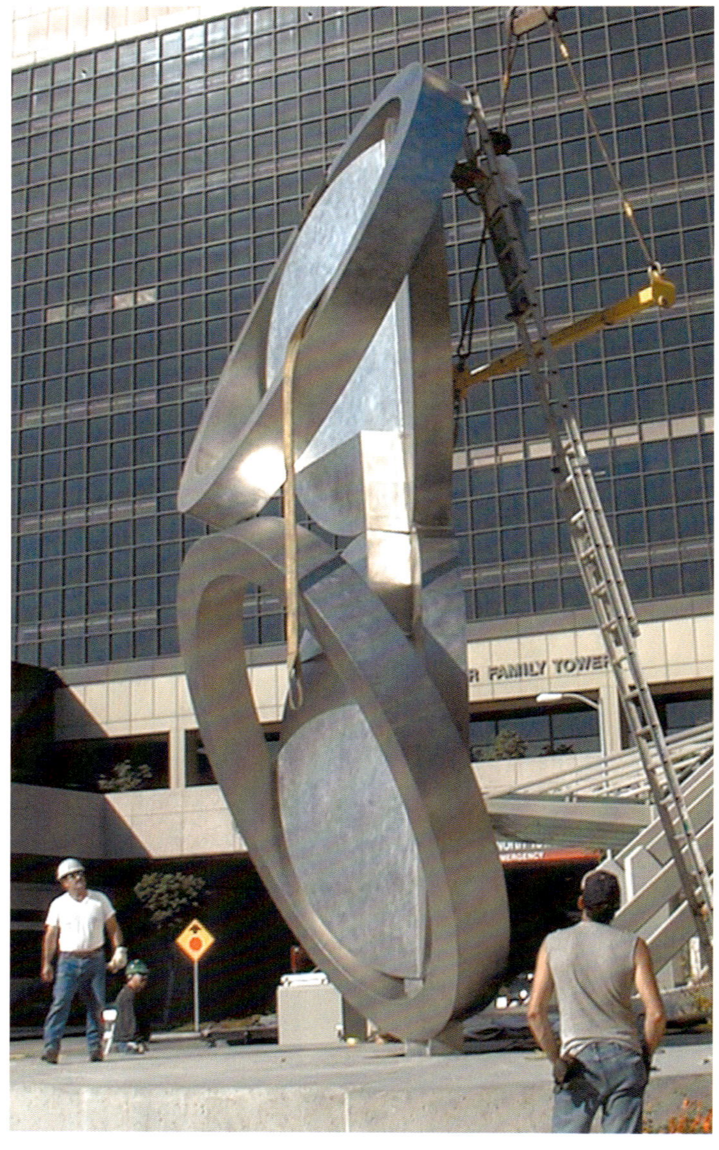

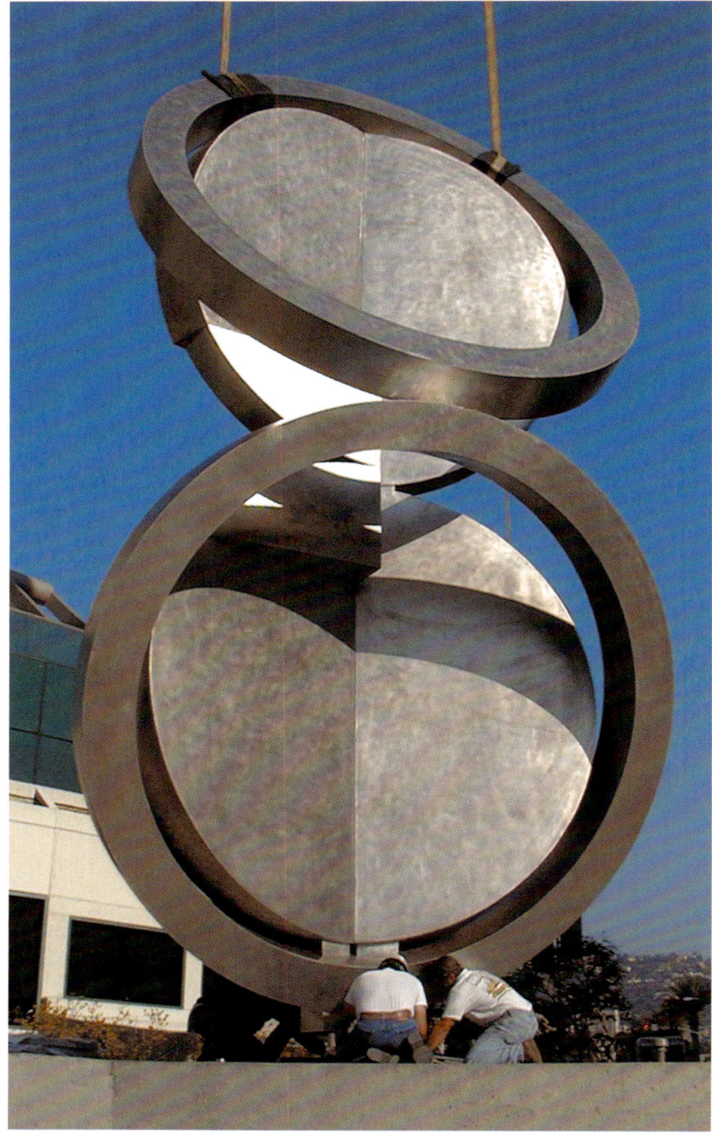

Double Folded Circle

2002, 316-L stainless steel
H: 30 feet
H: 914 cm
Cedars-Sinai Medical Center, Los Angeles

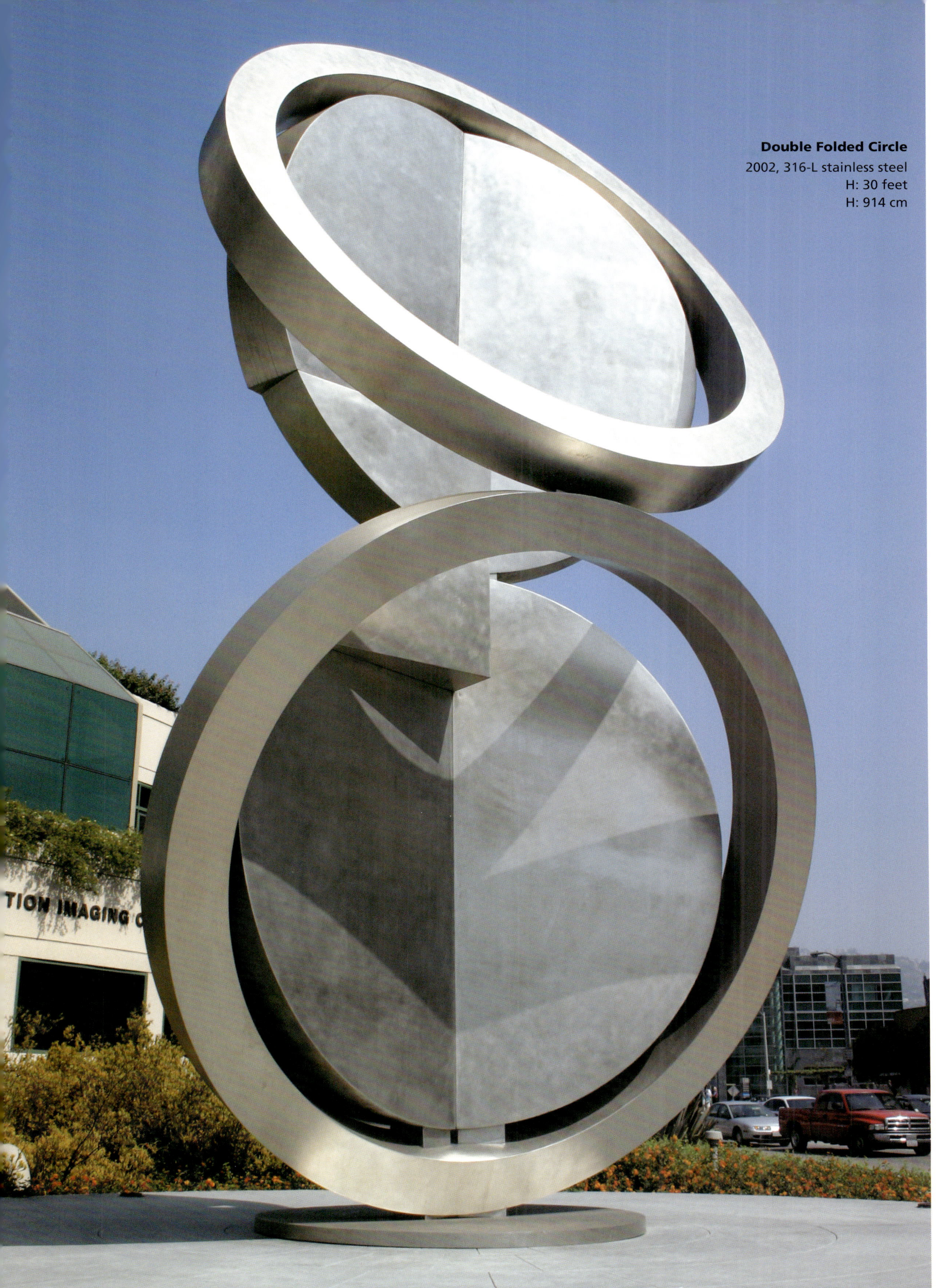

Double Folded Circle
2002, 316-L stainless steel
H: 30 feet
H: 914 cm

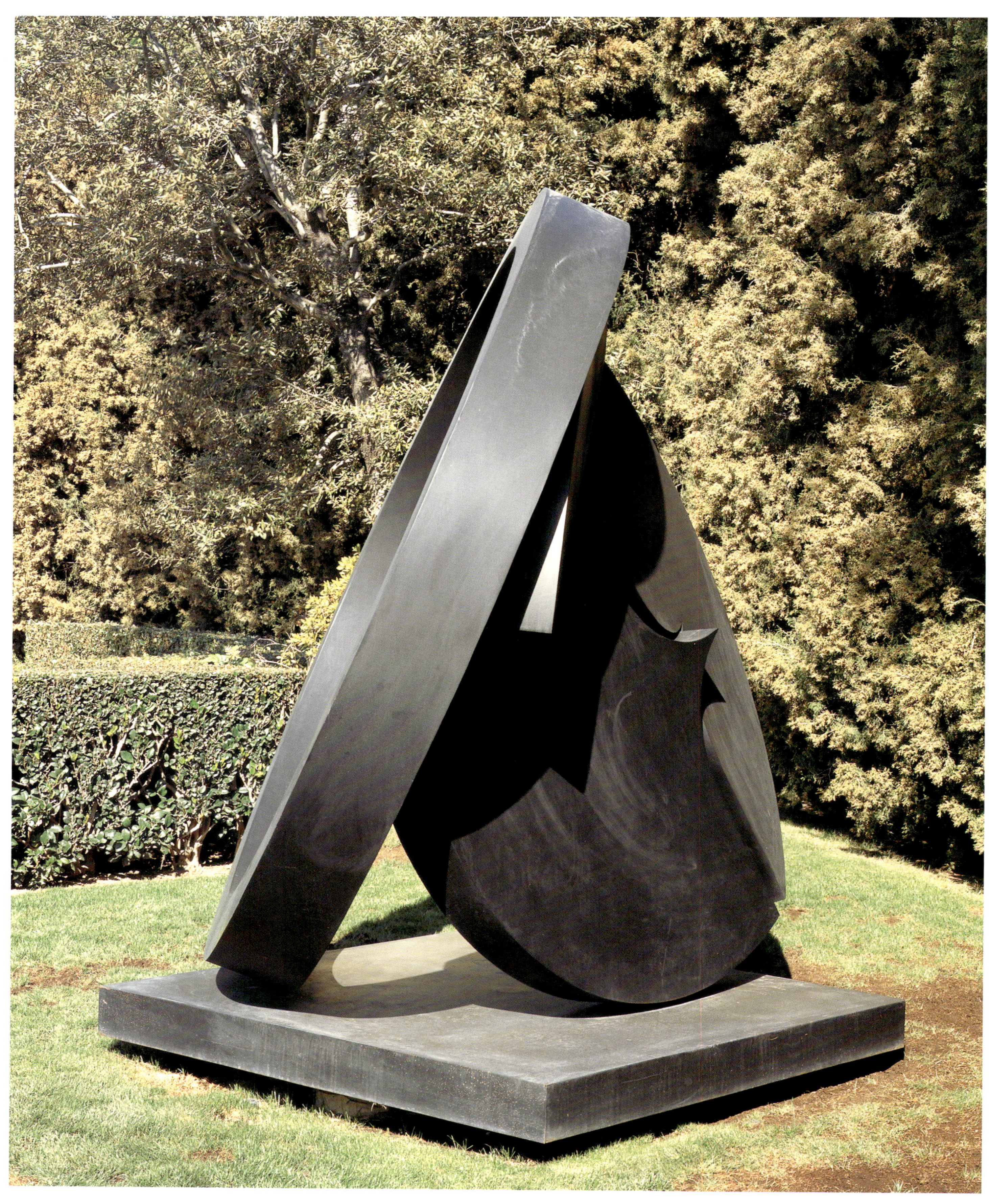

Folded Circle Ring Point

1993, painted steel
108 x 108 x 108 inches
274 x 274 x 274 cm

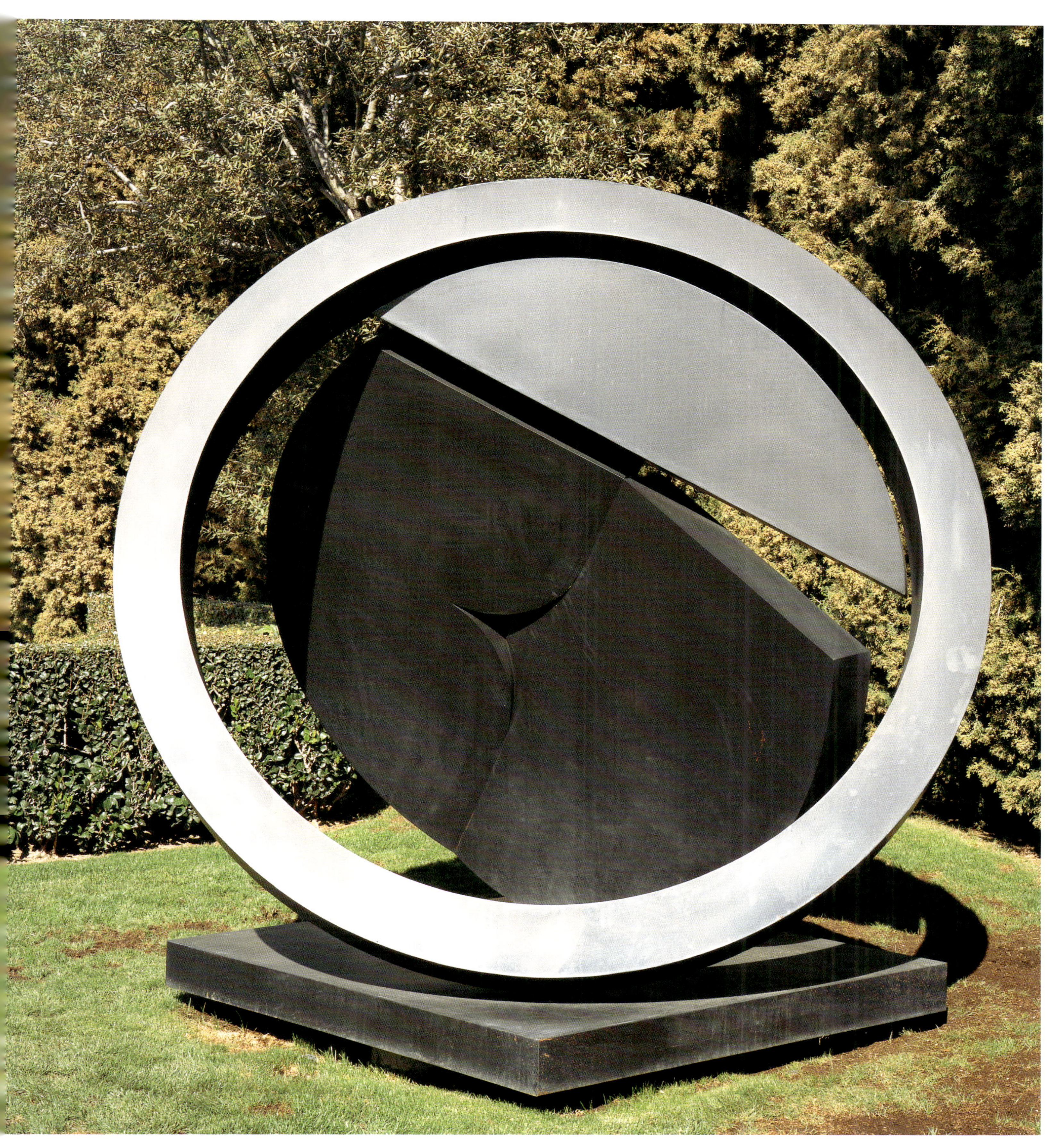

Folded Circle Ring Point

1993, painted steel
108 x 108 x 108 inches
274 x 274 x 274 cm

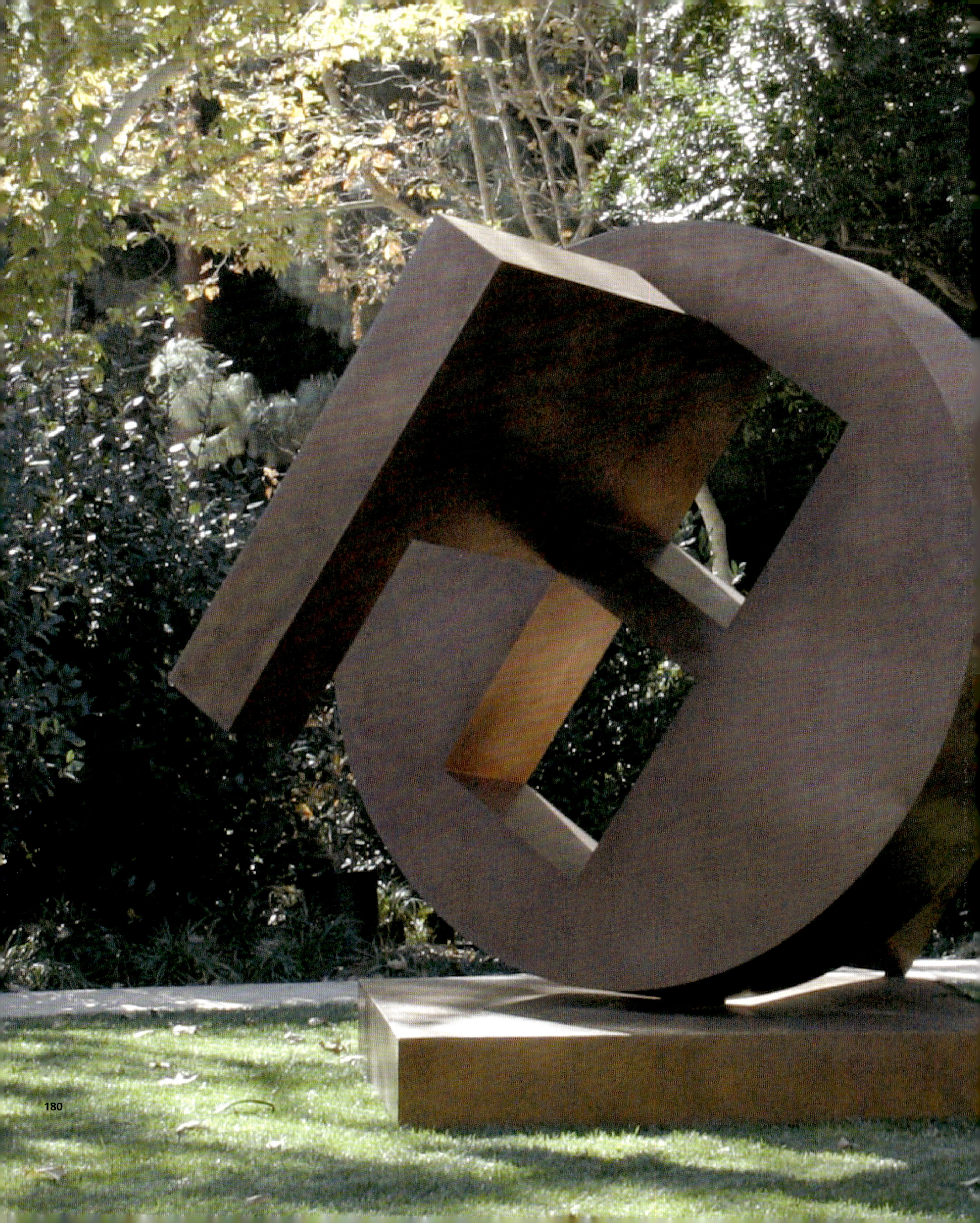

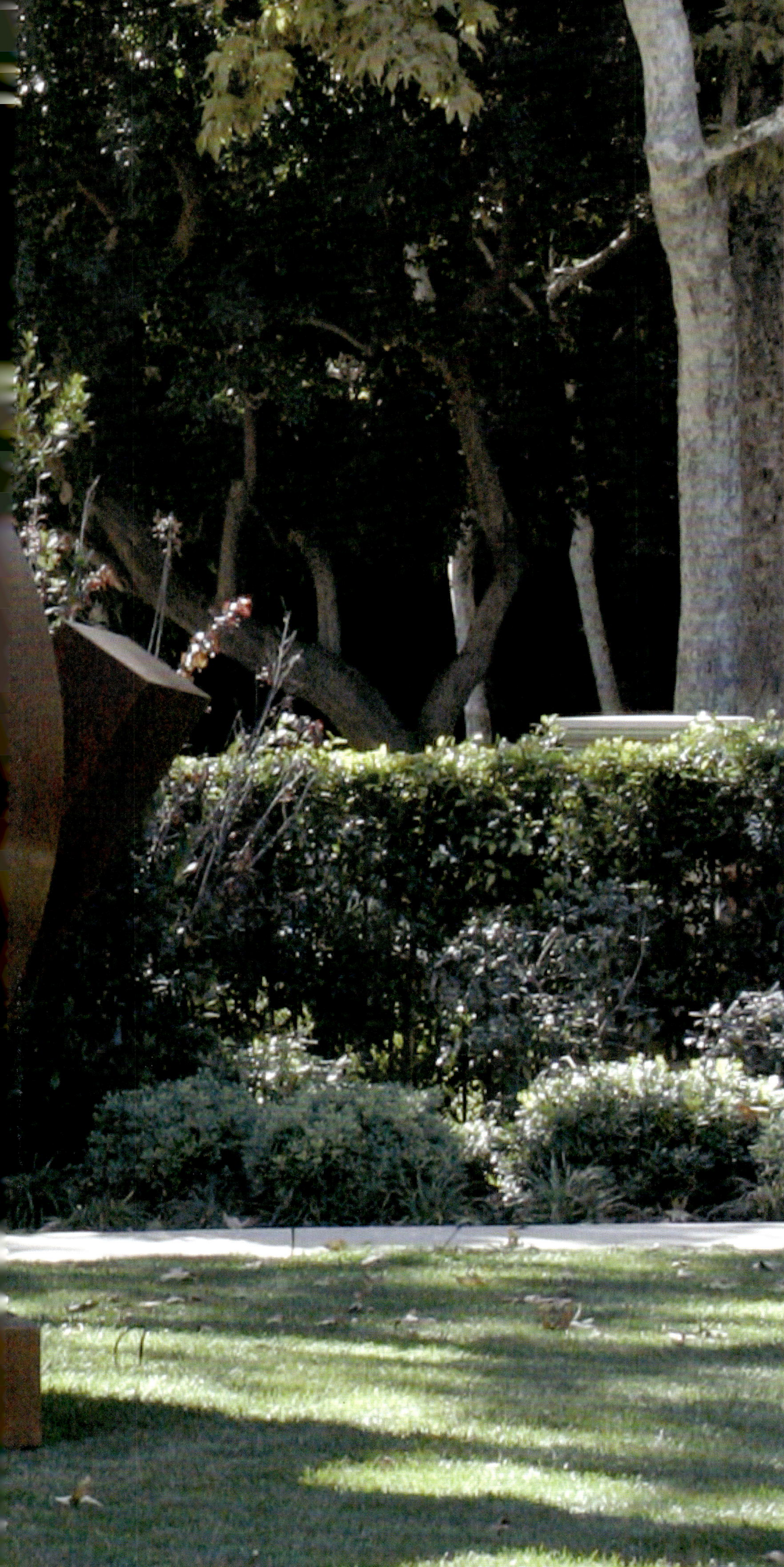

Dynamic Rhythms Orange, Phase IV
2003, bronze
9 x 9½ x 8½ feet
274 x 290 x 259 cm

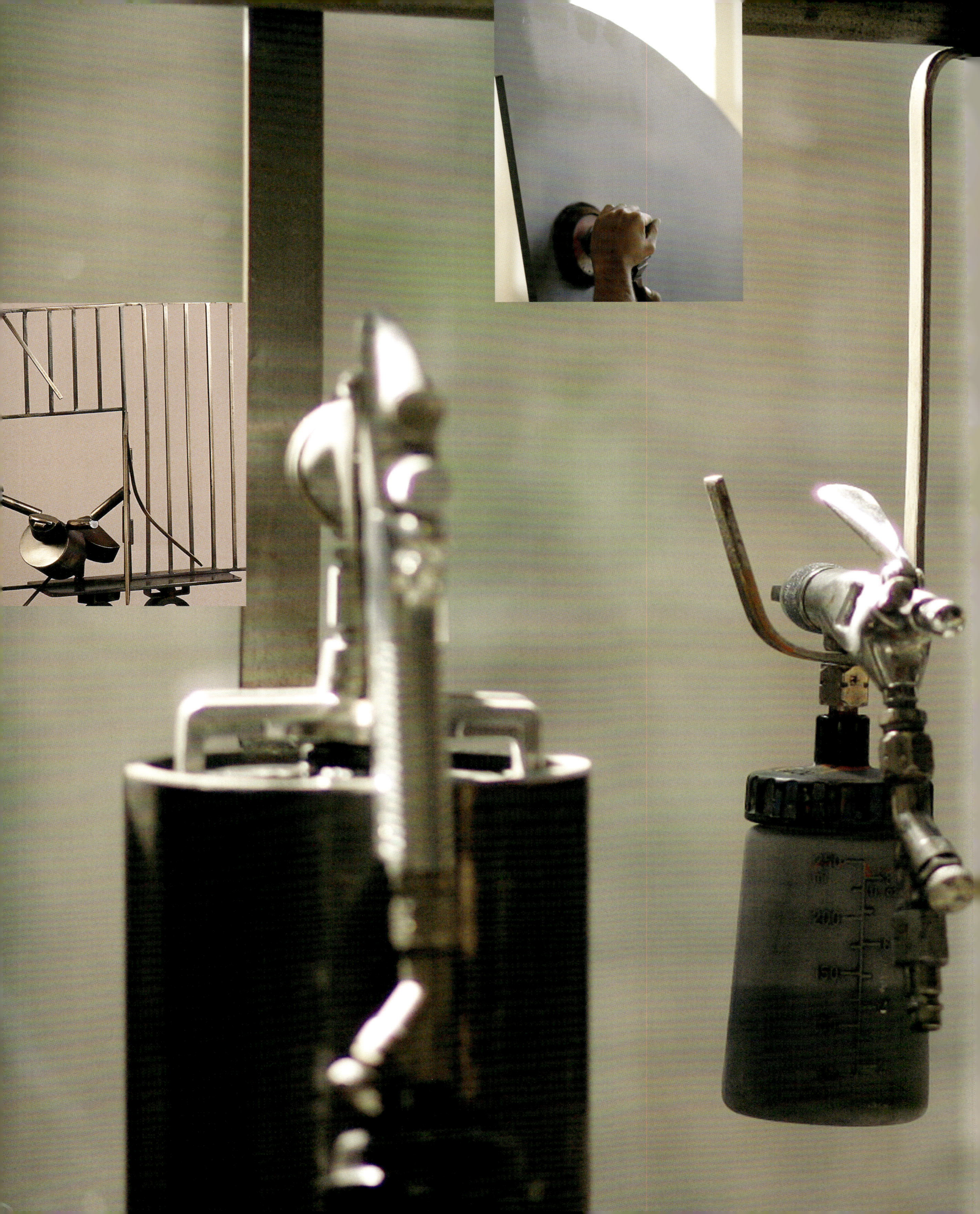
200
50

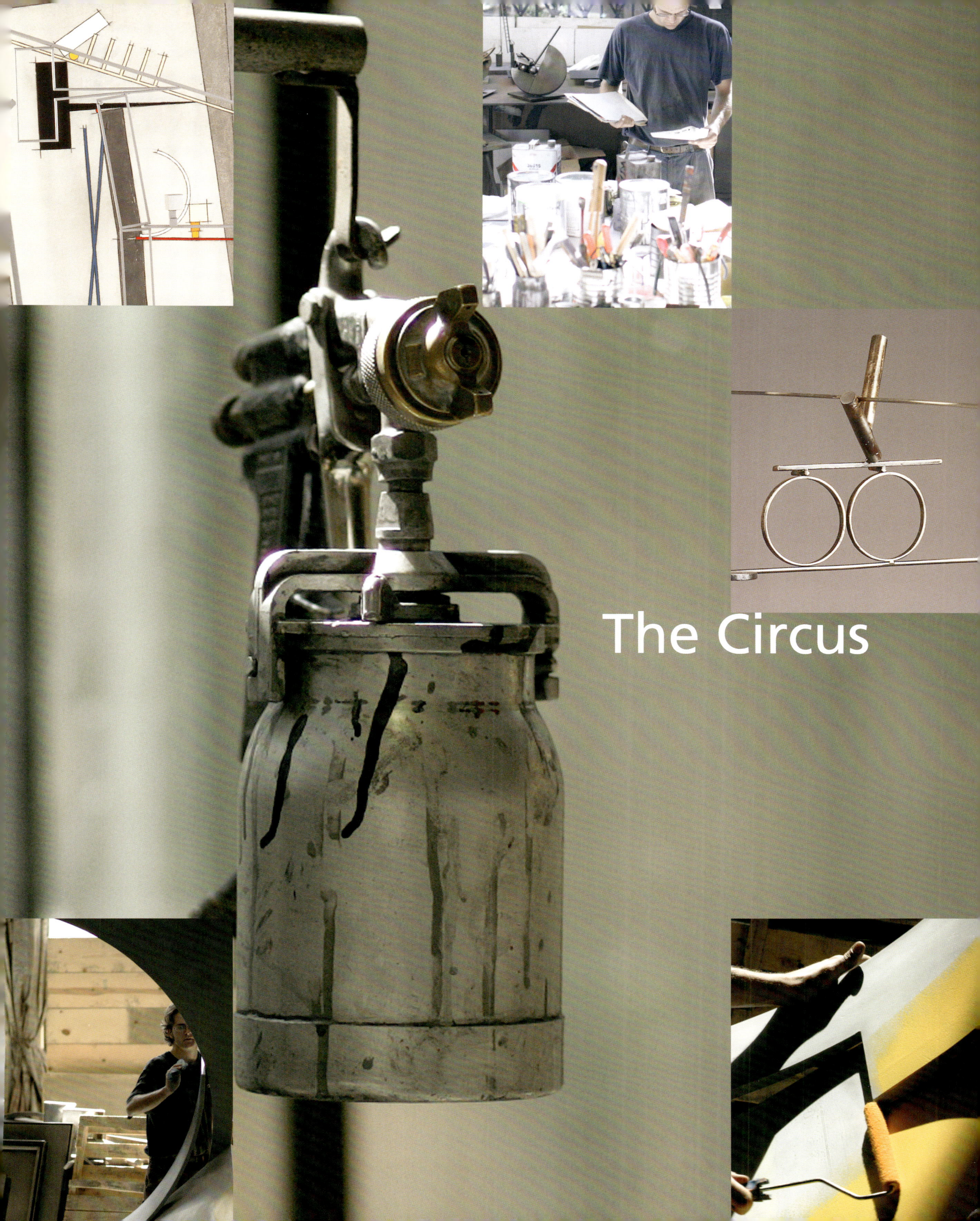

The Circus

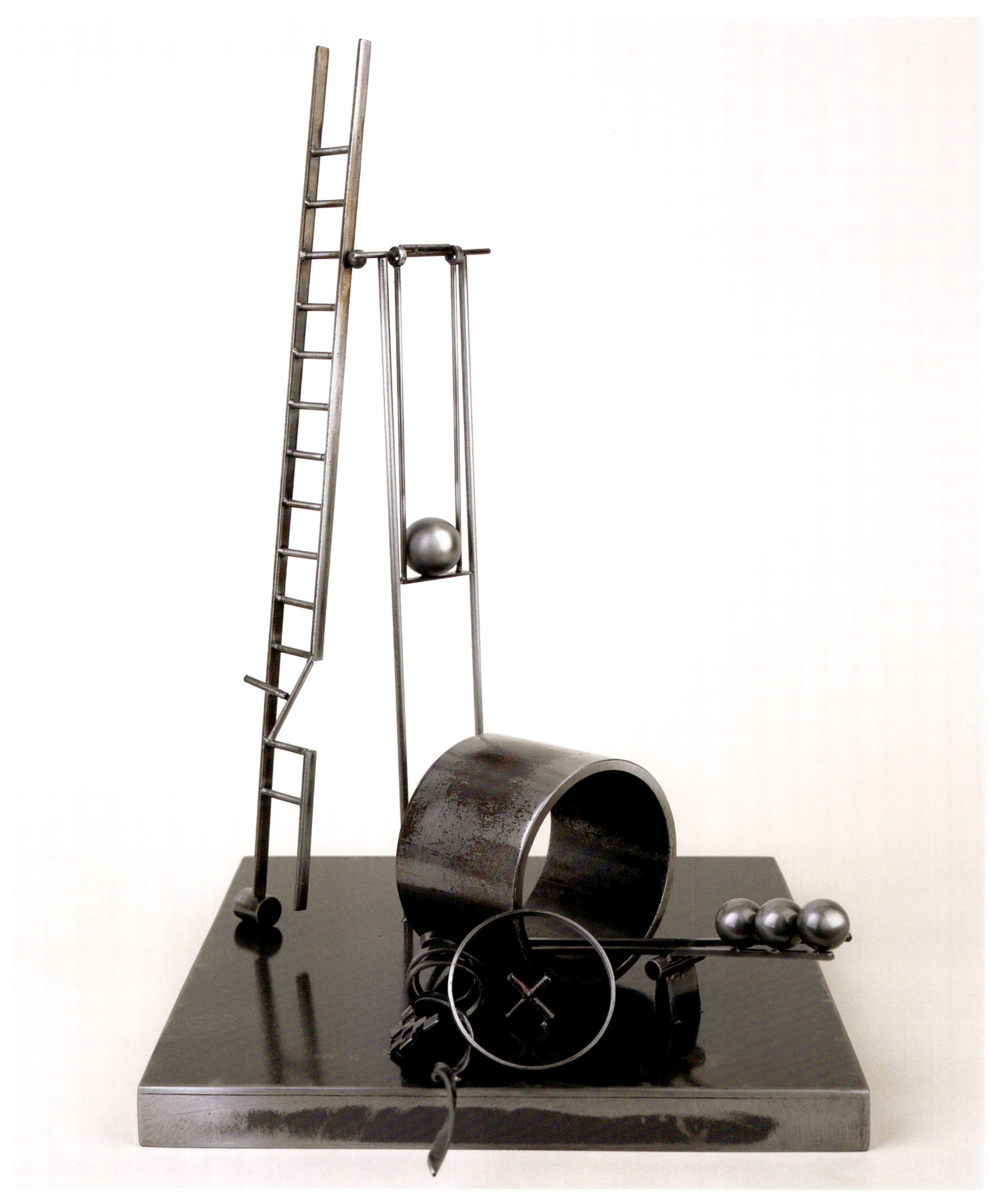

Ode to Calder: Circus Construct 10

2000, steel with patina
19¼ x 15 x 12 inches
49 x 38 x 30 cm

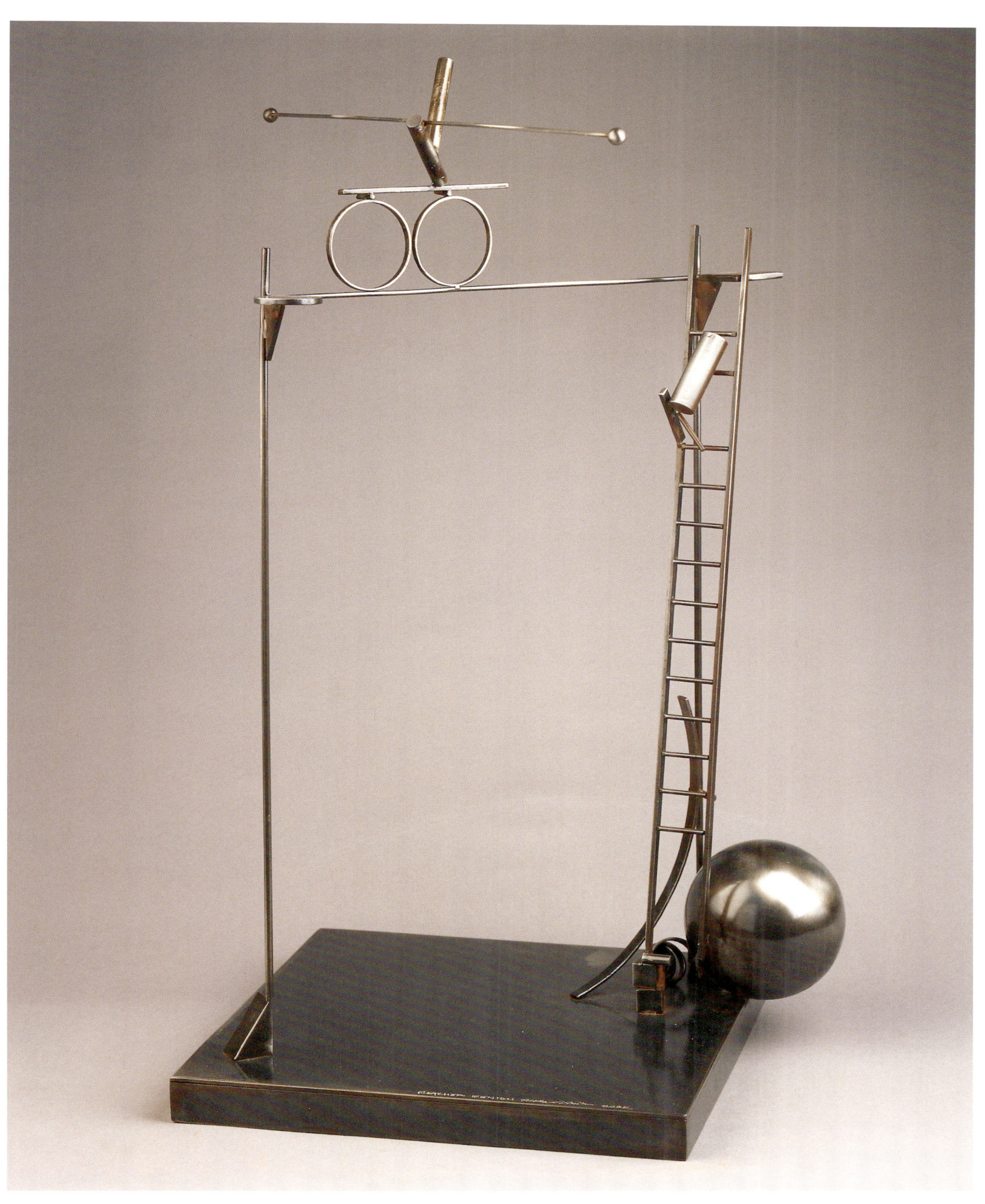

Ode to Calder: Circus Construct 12

2002, steel with patina
25 x 14 x 17 inches
64 x 36 x 43 cm

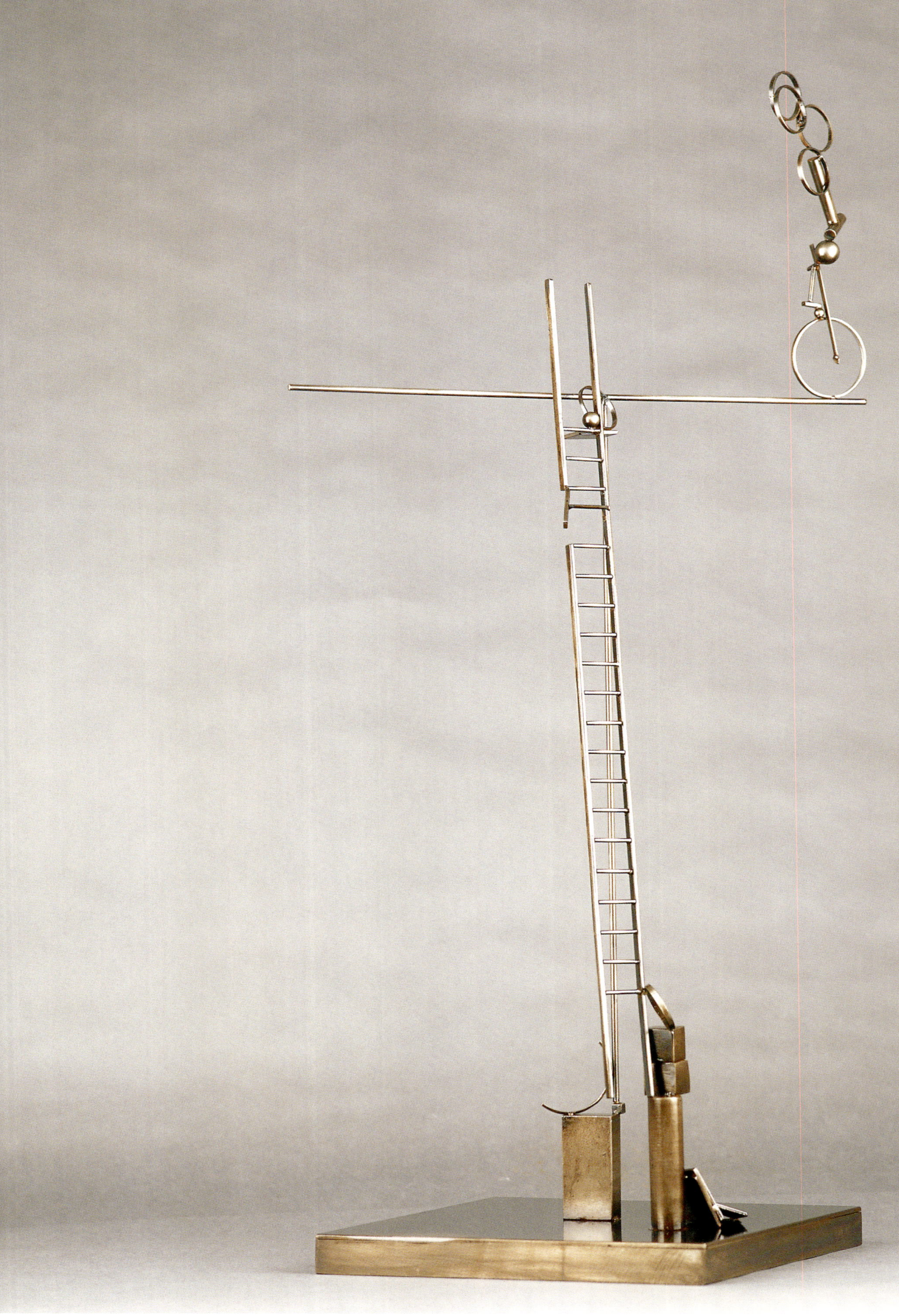

Ode to Calder: Circus Construct 4

2000, steel with patina
33 x 13½ x 12 inches
84 x 34 x 30 cm

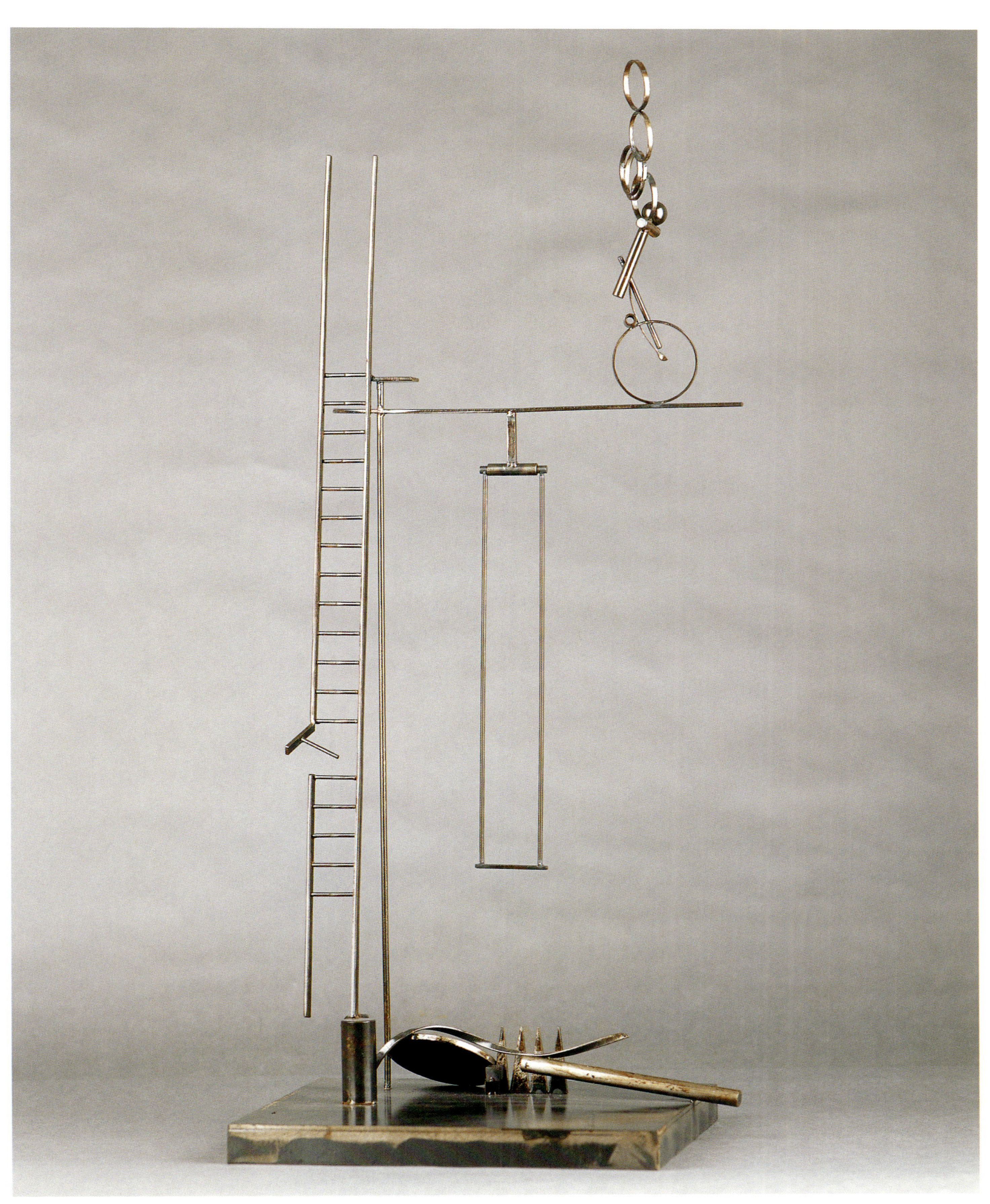

Ode to Calder: Circus Construct 11

2000, steel with patina
33 x 13½ x 12 inches
84 x 34 x 30 cm

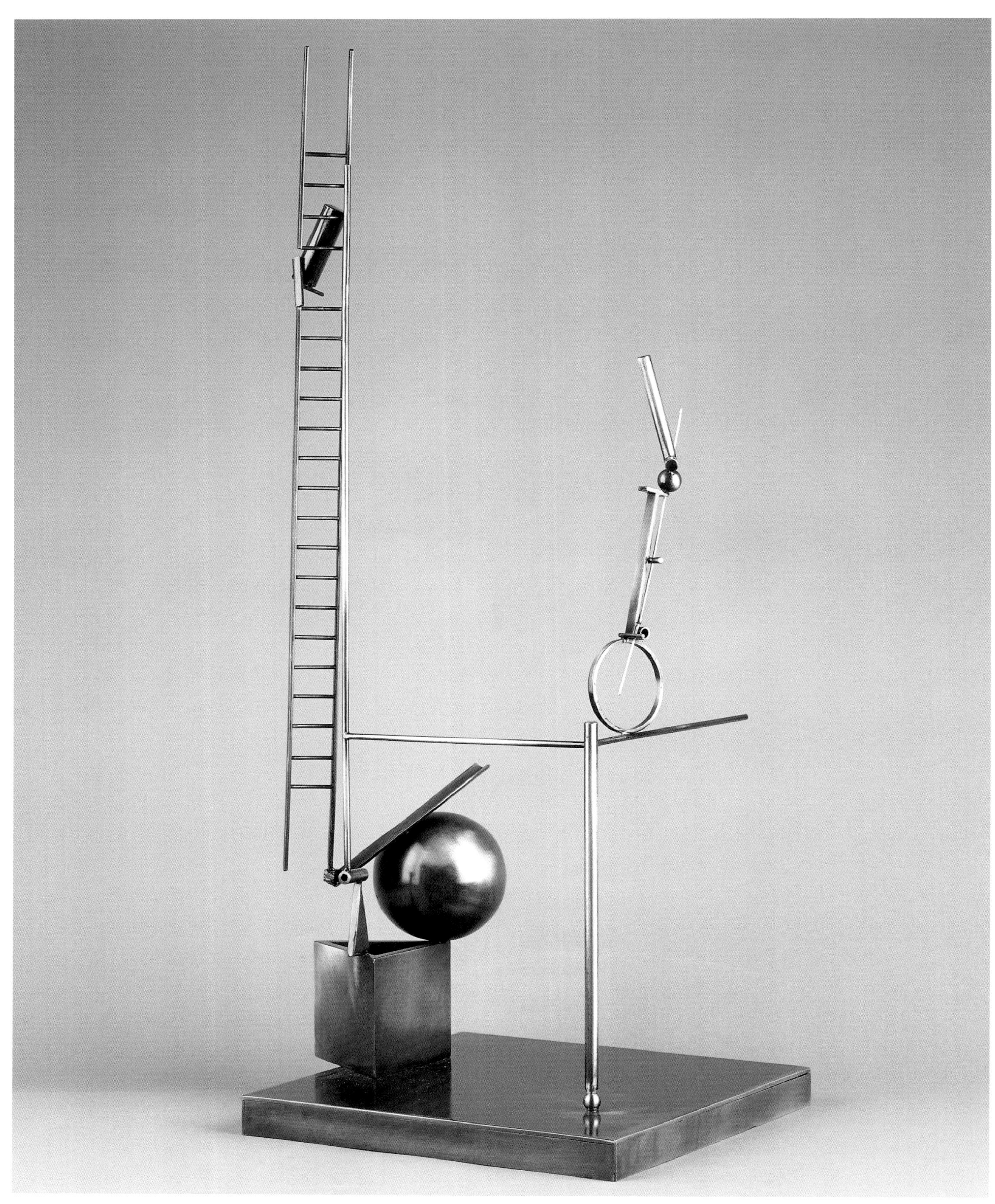

Ode to Calder: Circus Construct 15

2002, steel with patina
31¾ x 13½ x 14 inches
81 x 34 x 36 cm

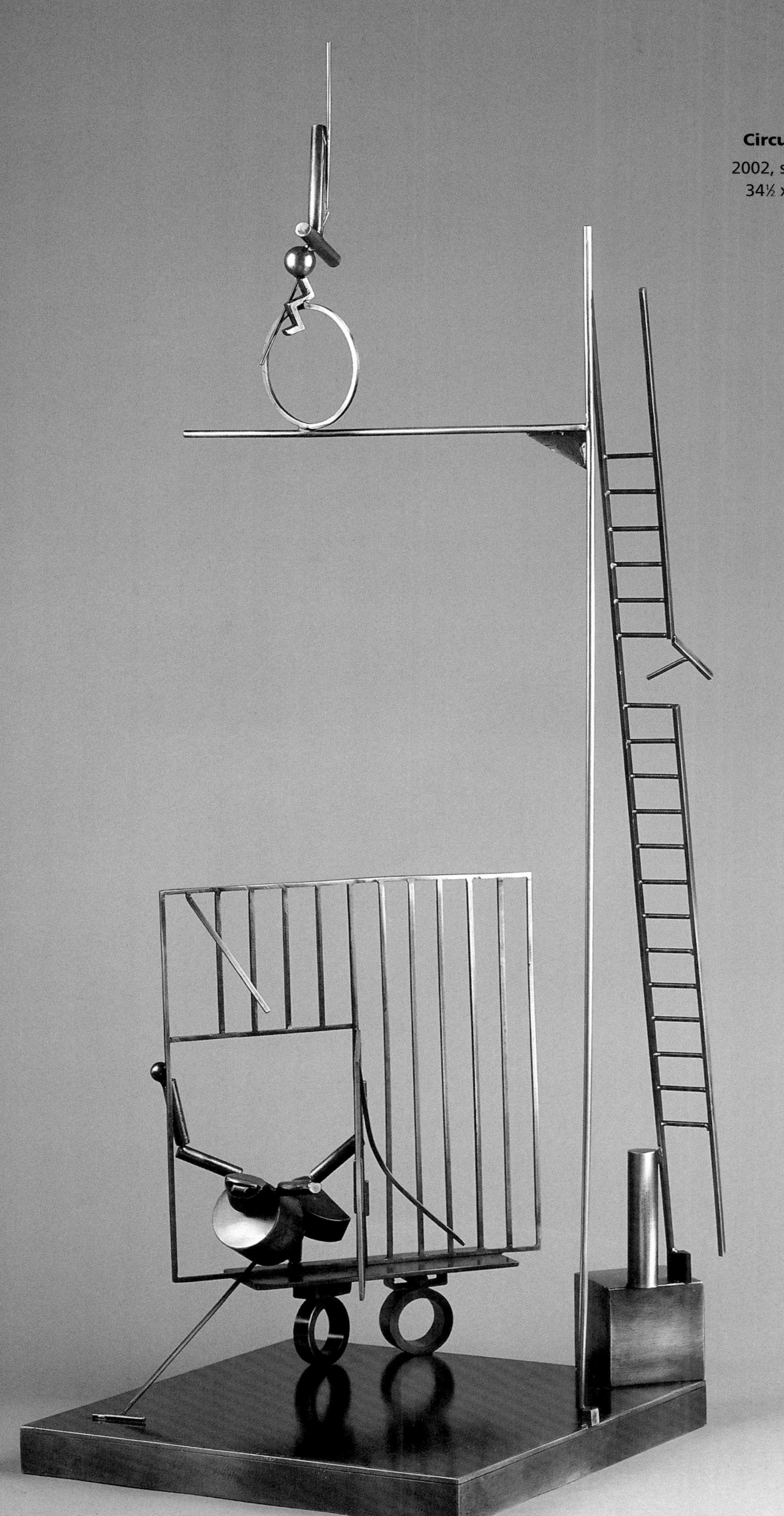

Ode to Calder: Circus Construct 17

2002, steel with patina
34½ x 14½ x 14 inches
88 x 37 x 36 cm

Ode to Calder:
Circus Construct 18

2002, steel with patina
33 x 14 x 13 inches
84 x 36 x 33 cm

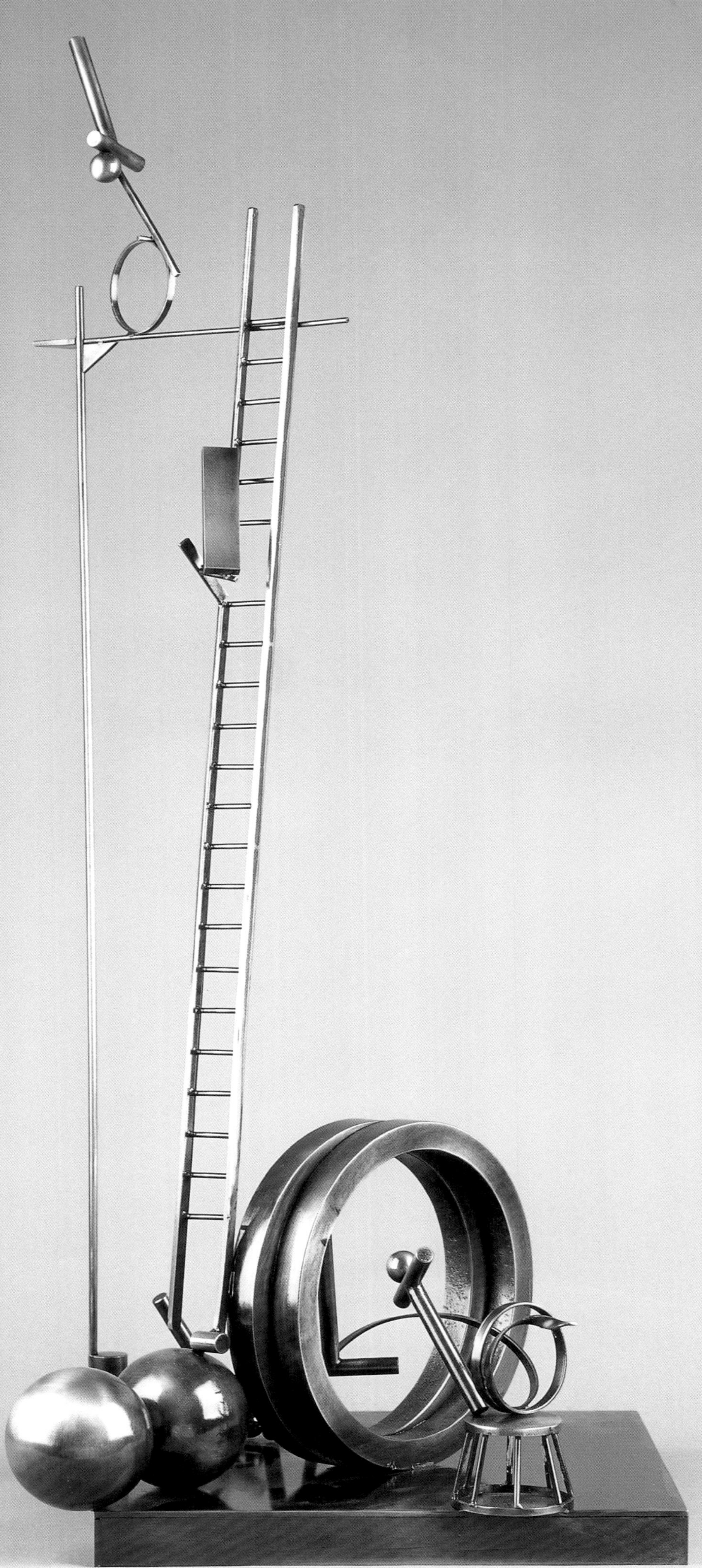

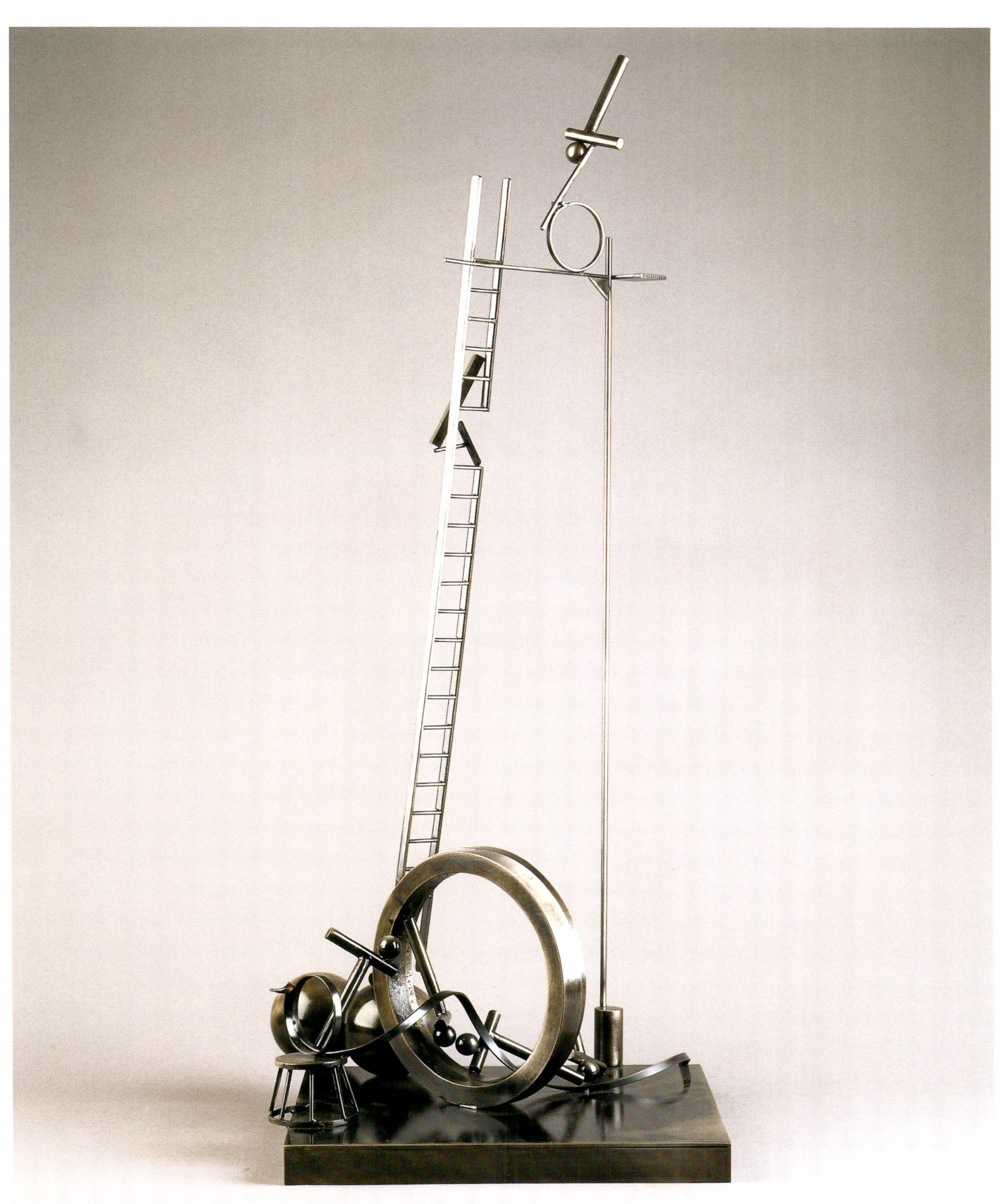

Ode to Calder: Circus Construct 18

2002, steel with patina
33 x 14 x 13 inches
84 x 36 x 33 cm

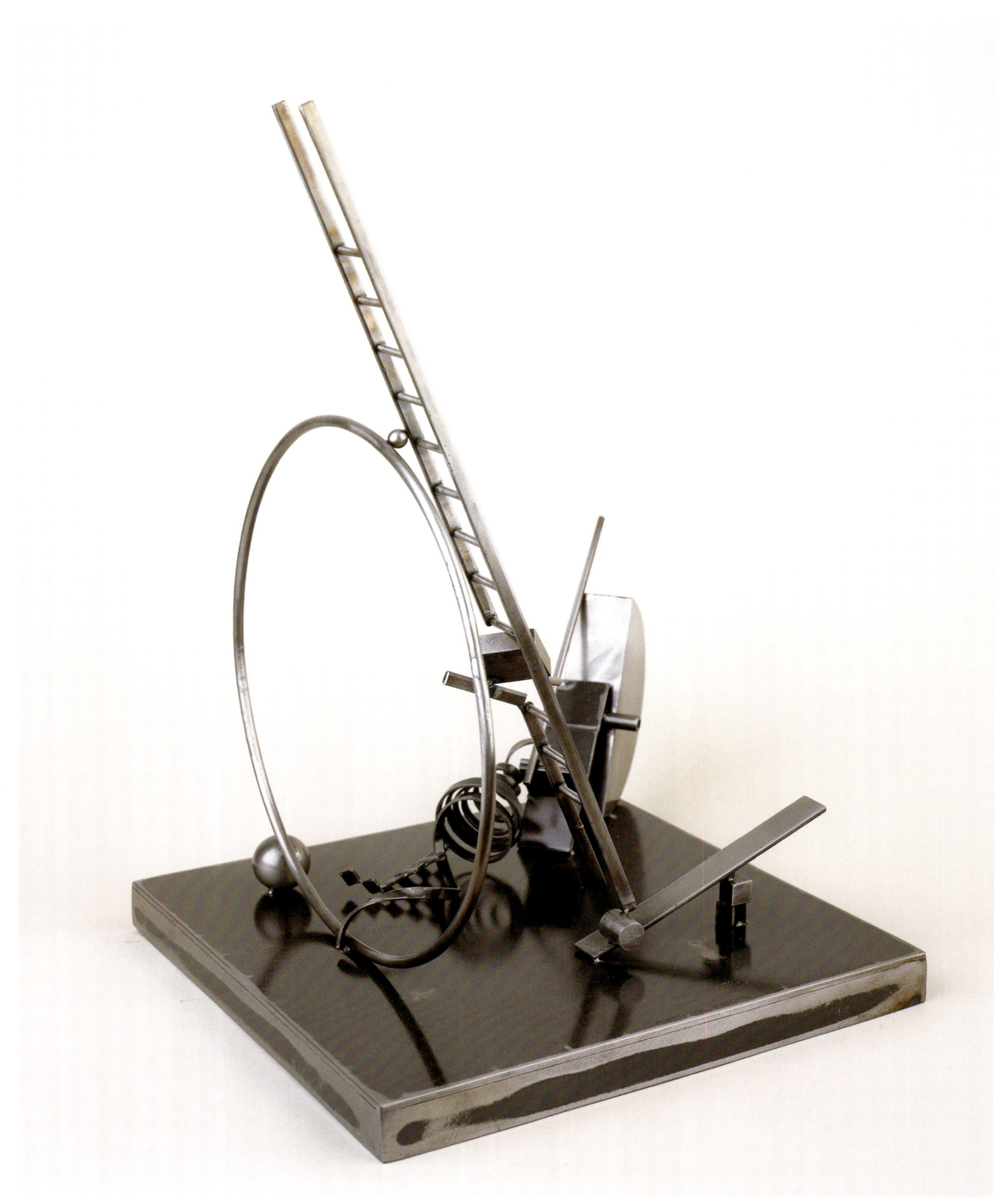

Ode to Calder: Circus Construct 5

2000, steel with patina
18 x 13 x 12½ inches
46 x 33 x 32 cm

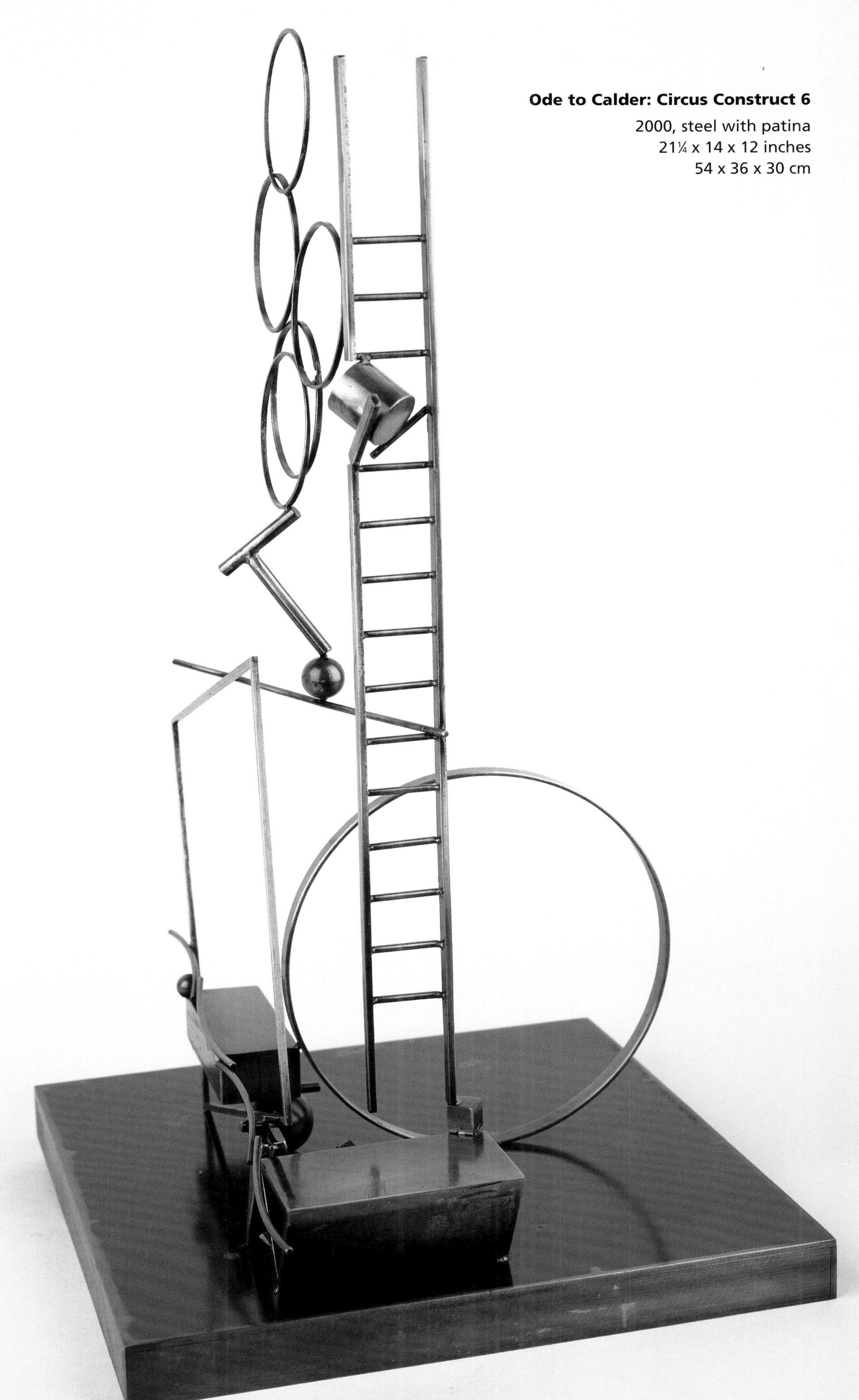

Ode to Calder: Circus Construct 6

2000, steel with patina
21¼ x 14 x 12 inches
54 x 36 x 30 cm

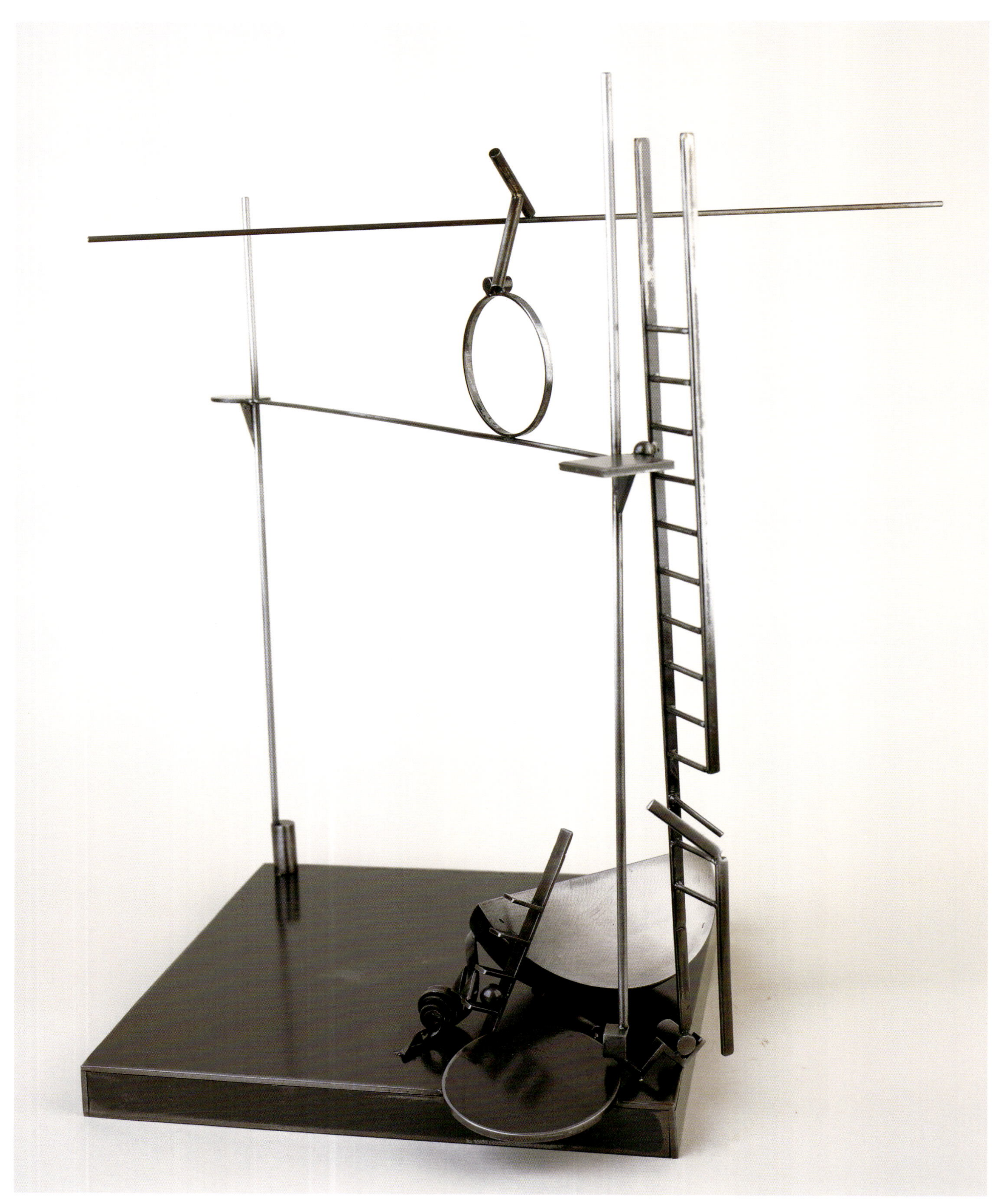

Ode to Calder: Circus Construct 7

2000, steel with patina
20½ x 14½ x 16½ inches
52 x 37 x 42 cm

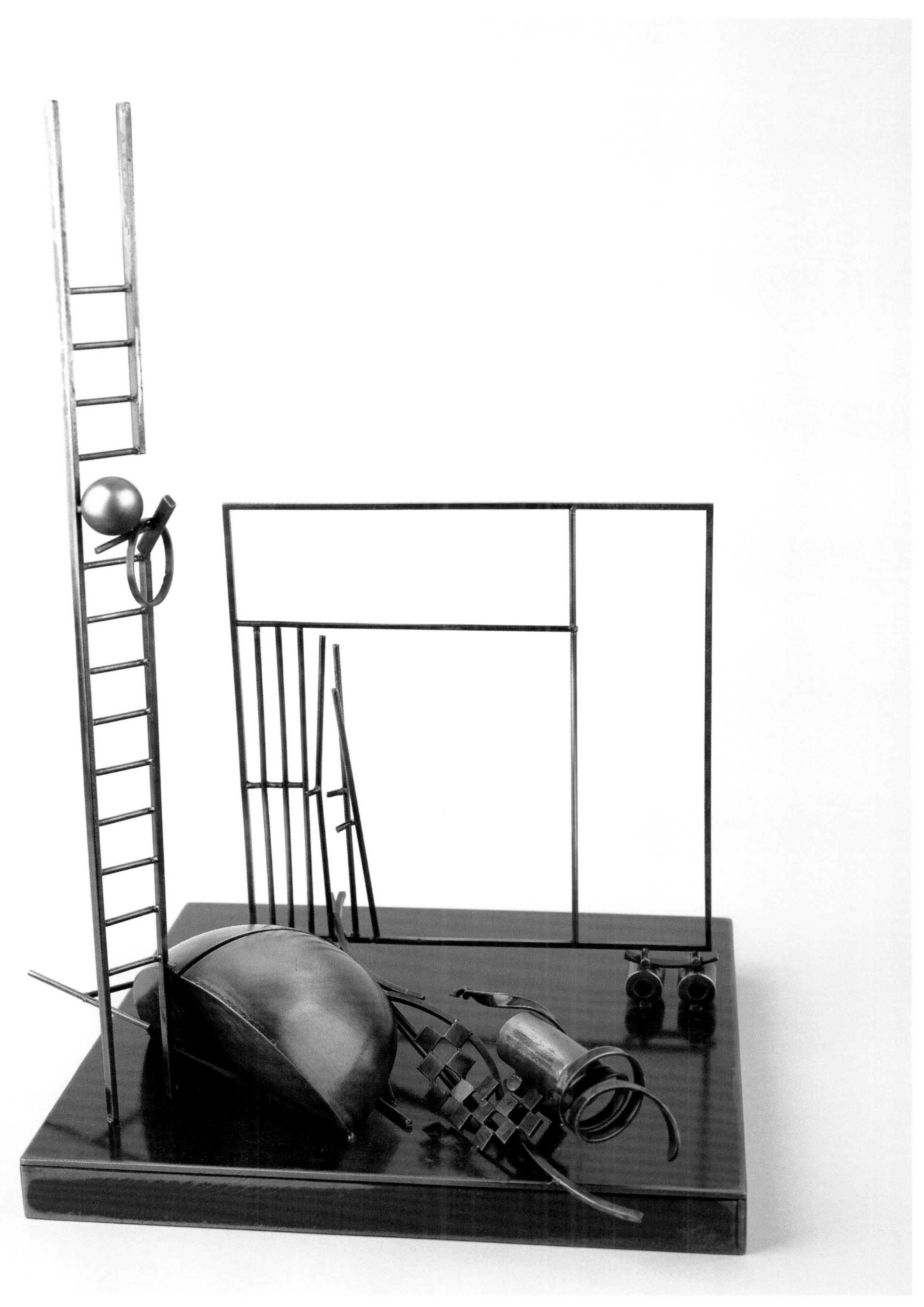

Ode to Calder: Circus Construct 8

2000, steel with patina
28¾ x 13 x 13 inches
73 x 33 x 33 cm

Ode to Calder: Circus Construct 9

2000, steel with patina
19 x 13 x 12 inches
48 x 33 x 30 cm

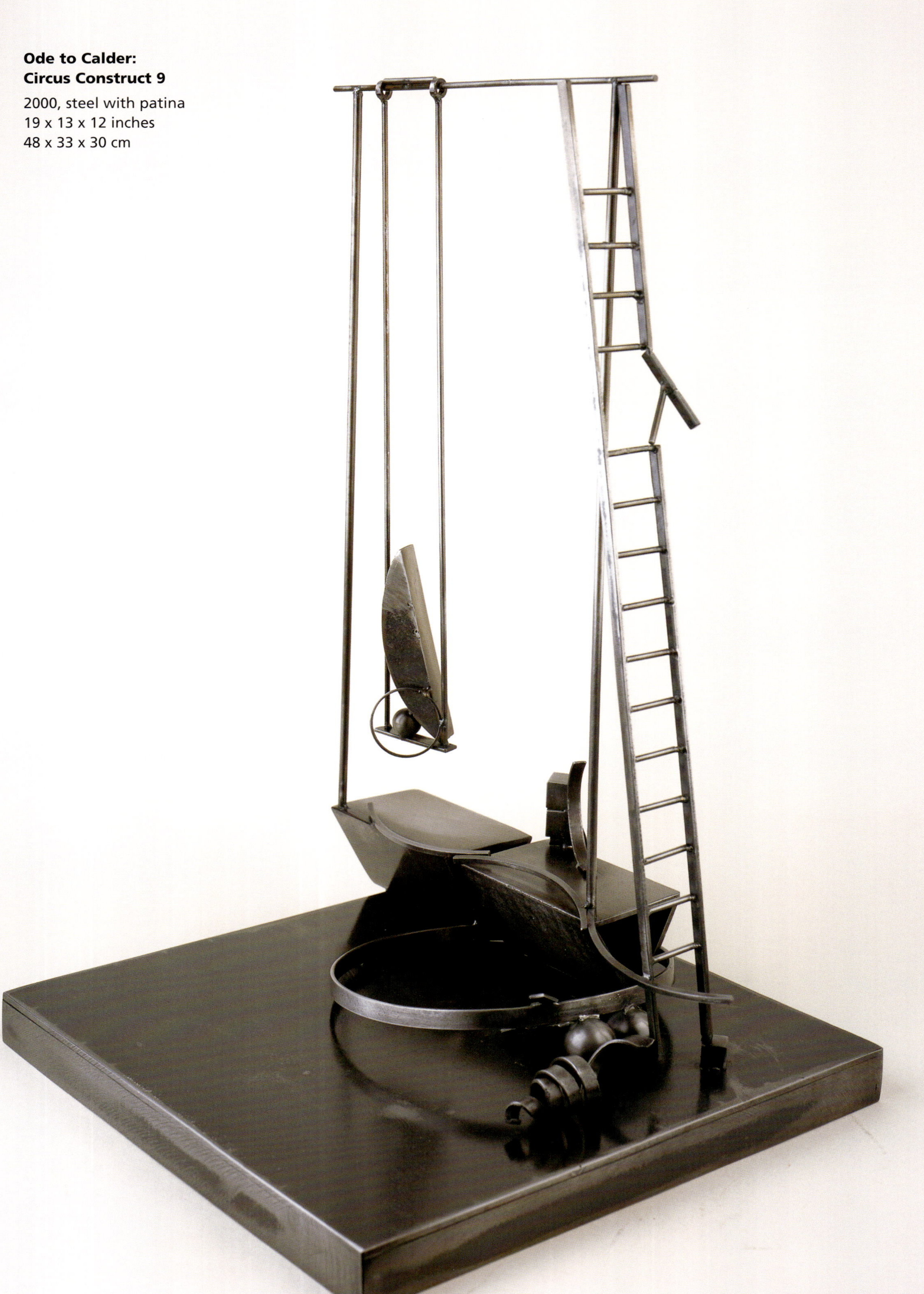

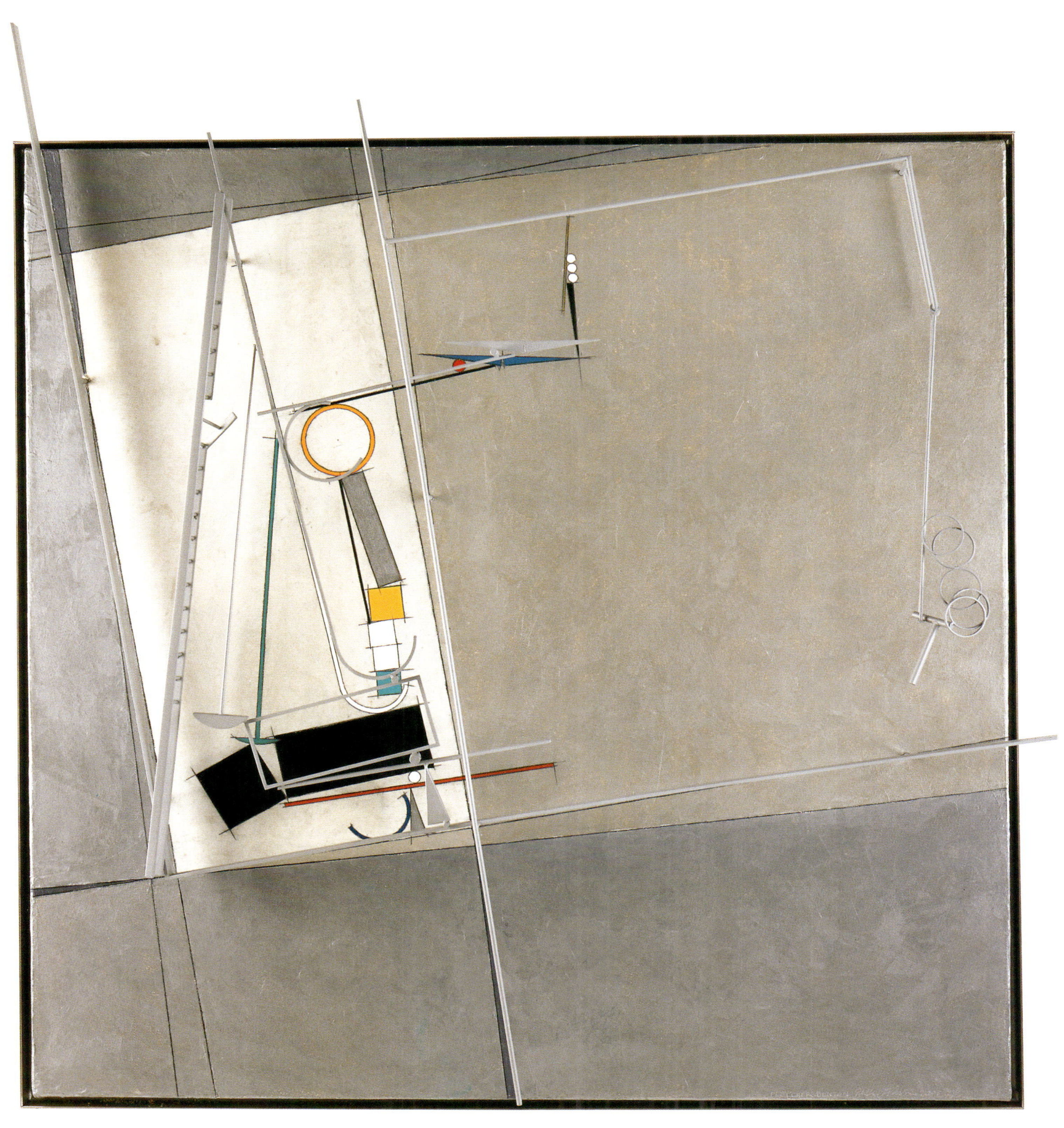

Circus Painting No. 13

2002, steel and acrylic on canvas
40 x 37 inches
102 x 94 cm

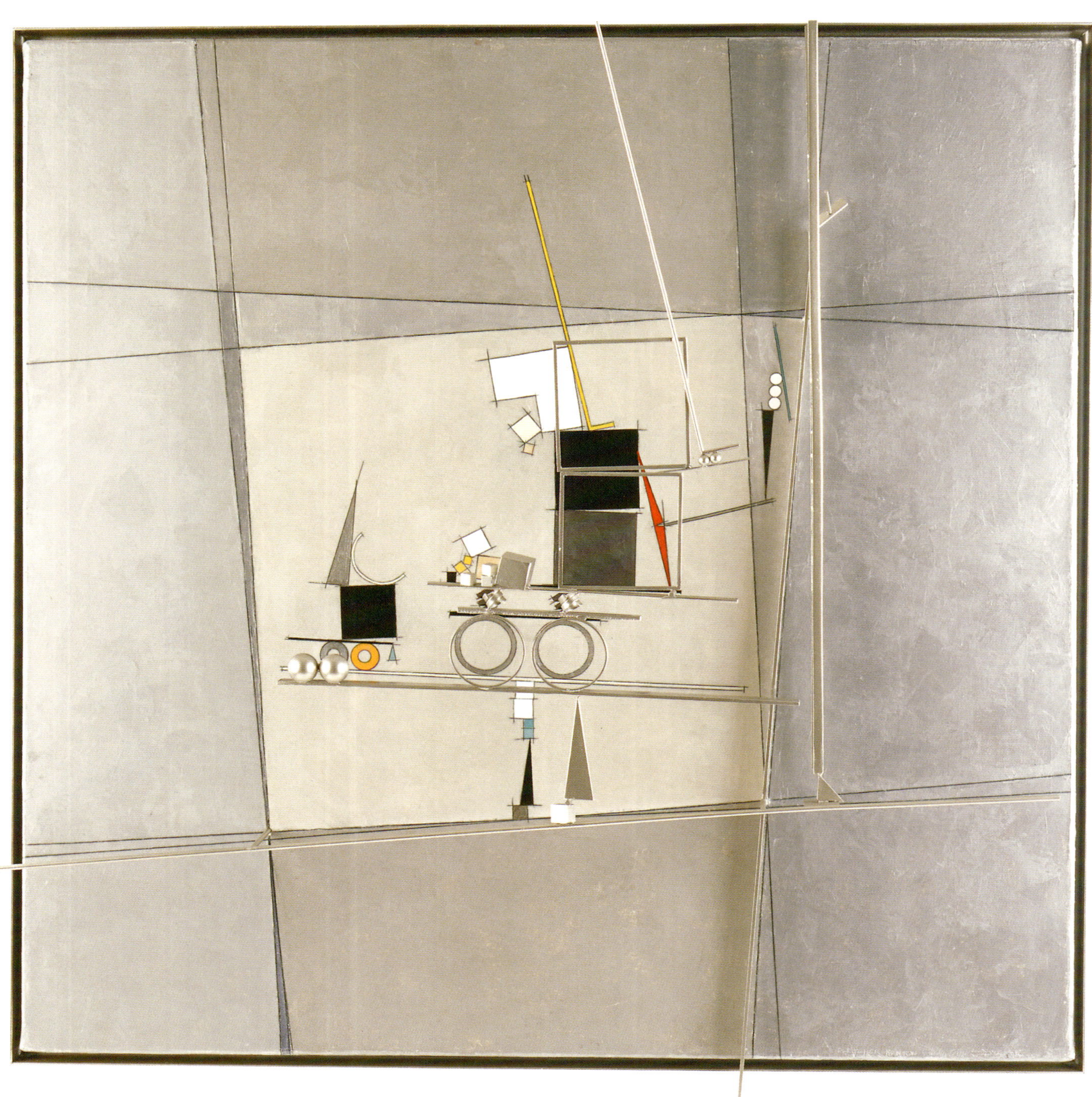

Circus Painting No. 12

2002, steel and acrylic on canvas
37 x 41 inches
94 x 104 cm

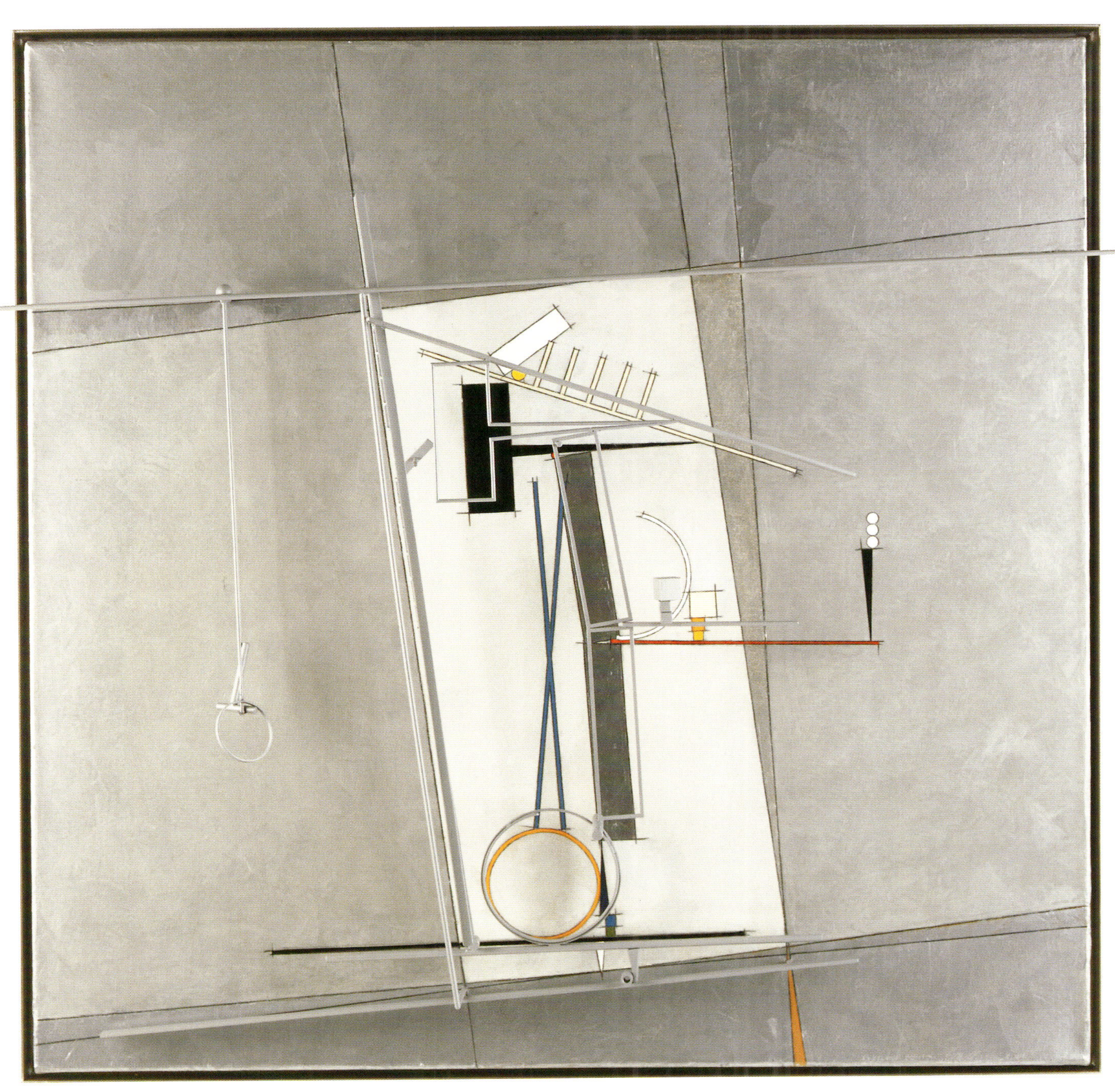

Circus Painting No. 17

2002, steel and acrylic on canvas
36 x 40 inches
91 x 102 cm

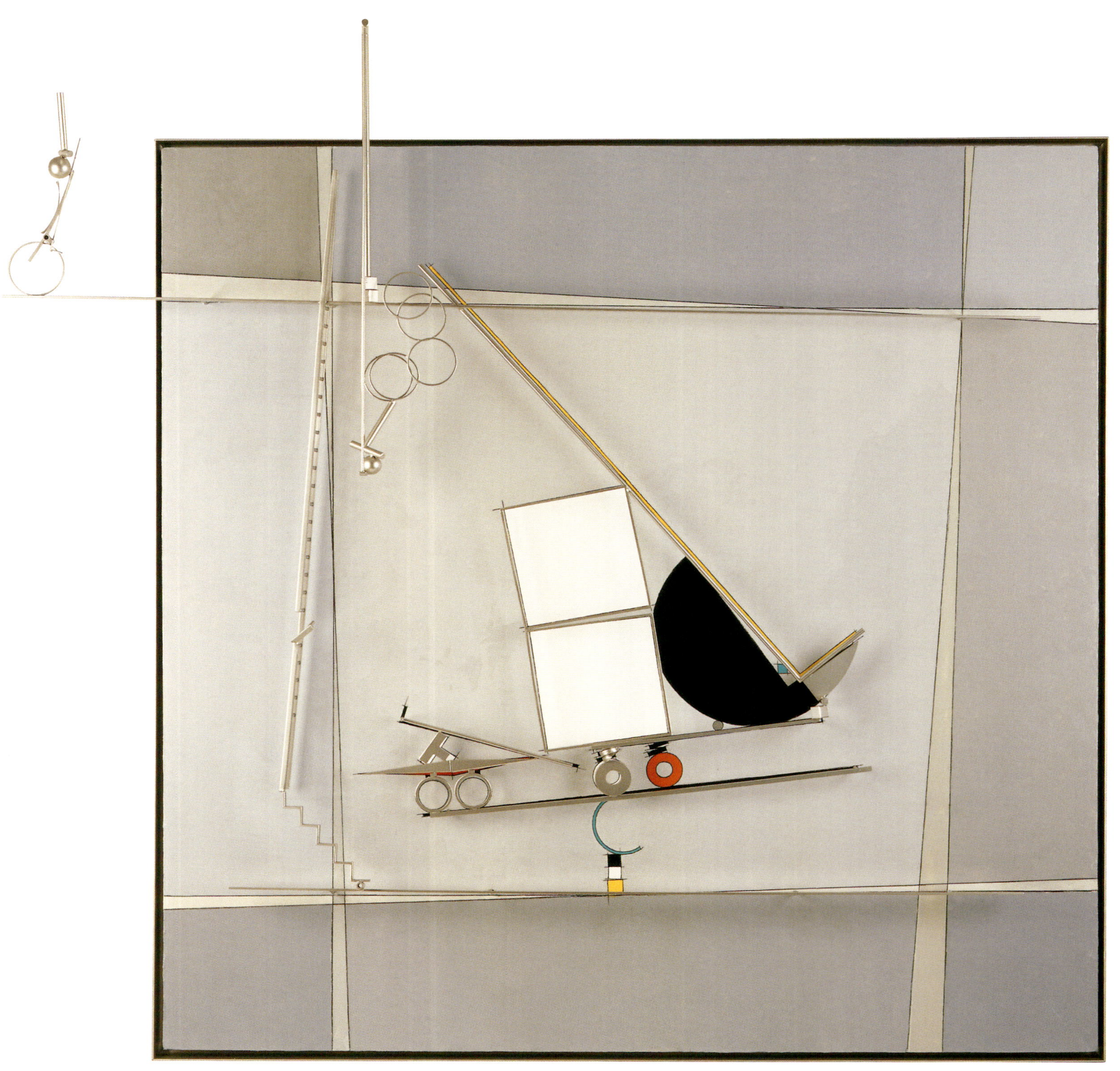

Circus Painting No. 24

2005, steel and acrylic on canvas
39 x 43 inches
99 x 109 cm

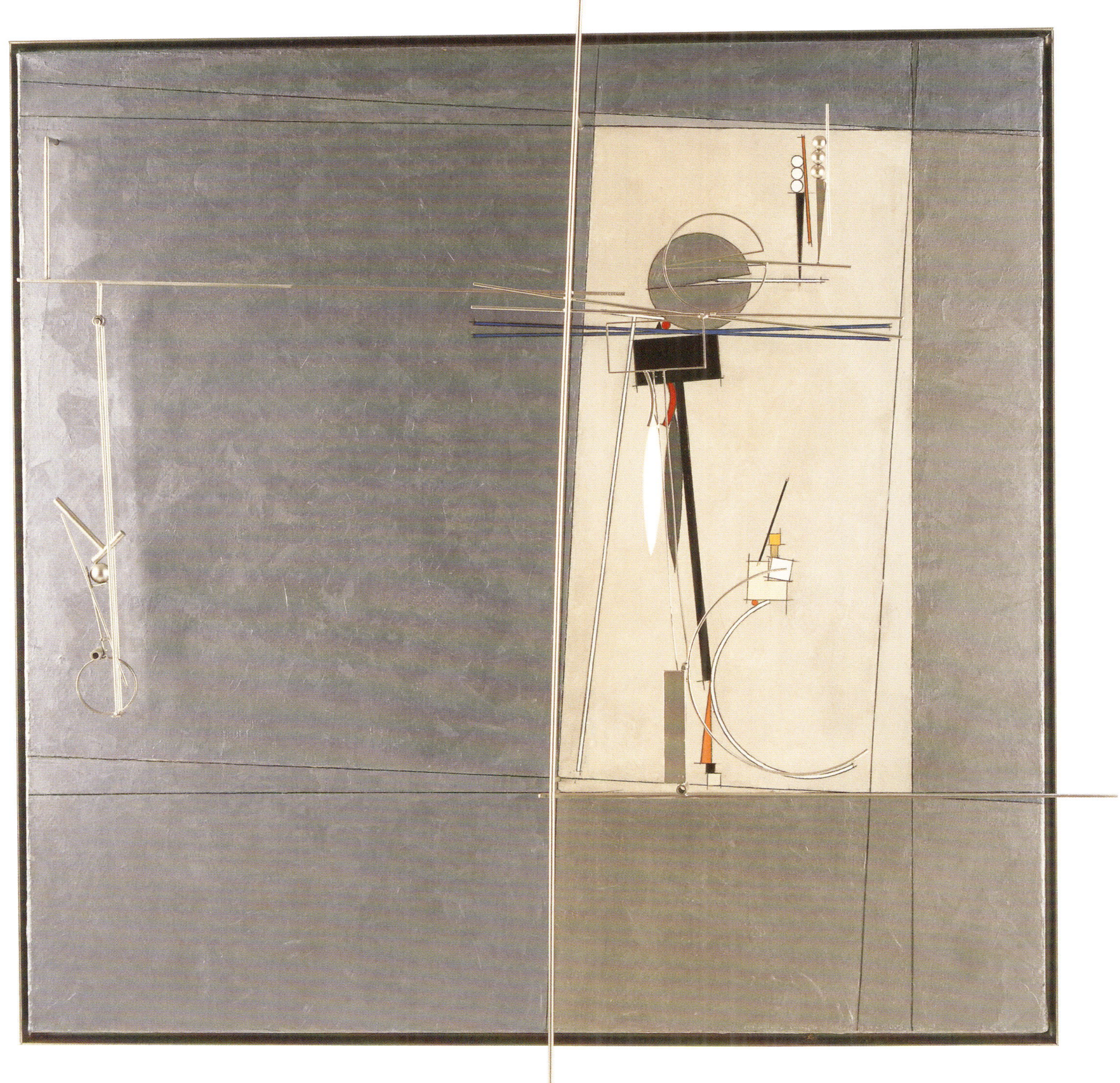

Circus Painting No. 19

2002, steel and acrylic on canvas
40 x 38 inches
102 x 97 cm

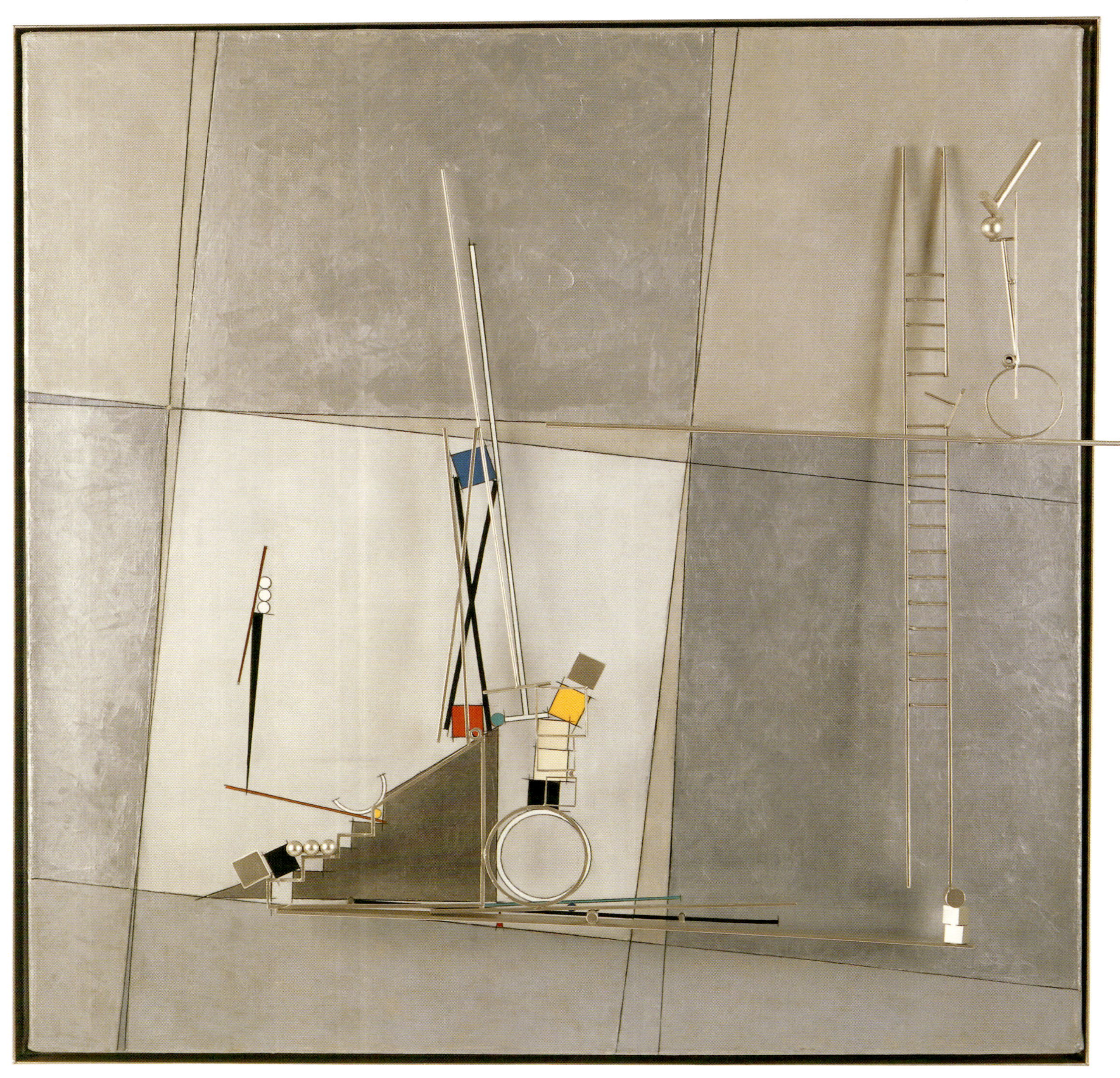

Circus Painting No. 20

2002, steel and acrylic on canvas
36 x 37 inches
91 x 94 cm

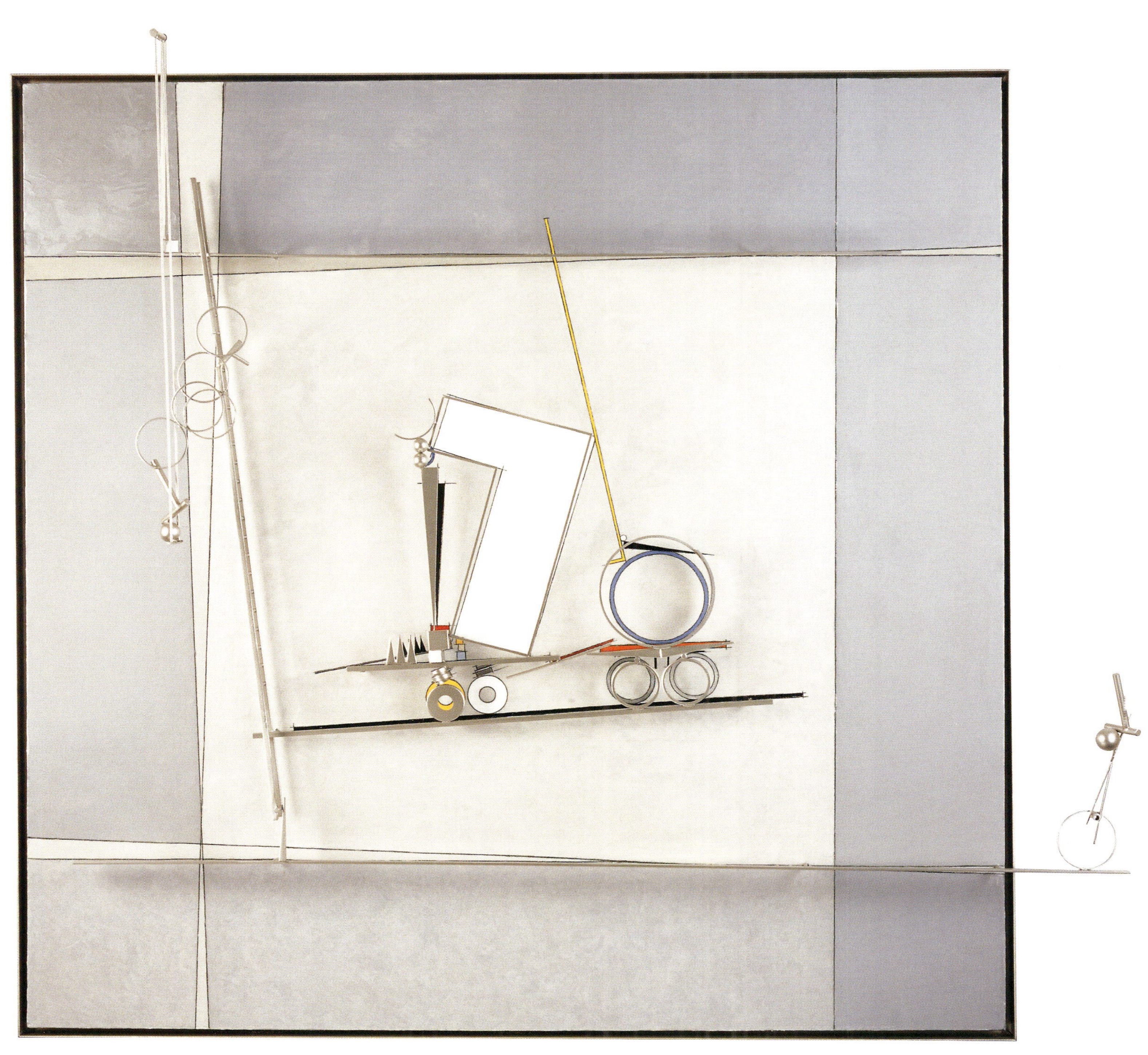

Circus Painting No. 25

2005, steel and acrylic on canvas
43 x 44 inches
109 x 112 cm

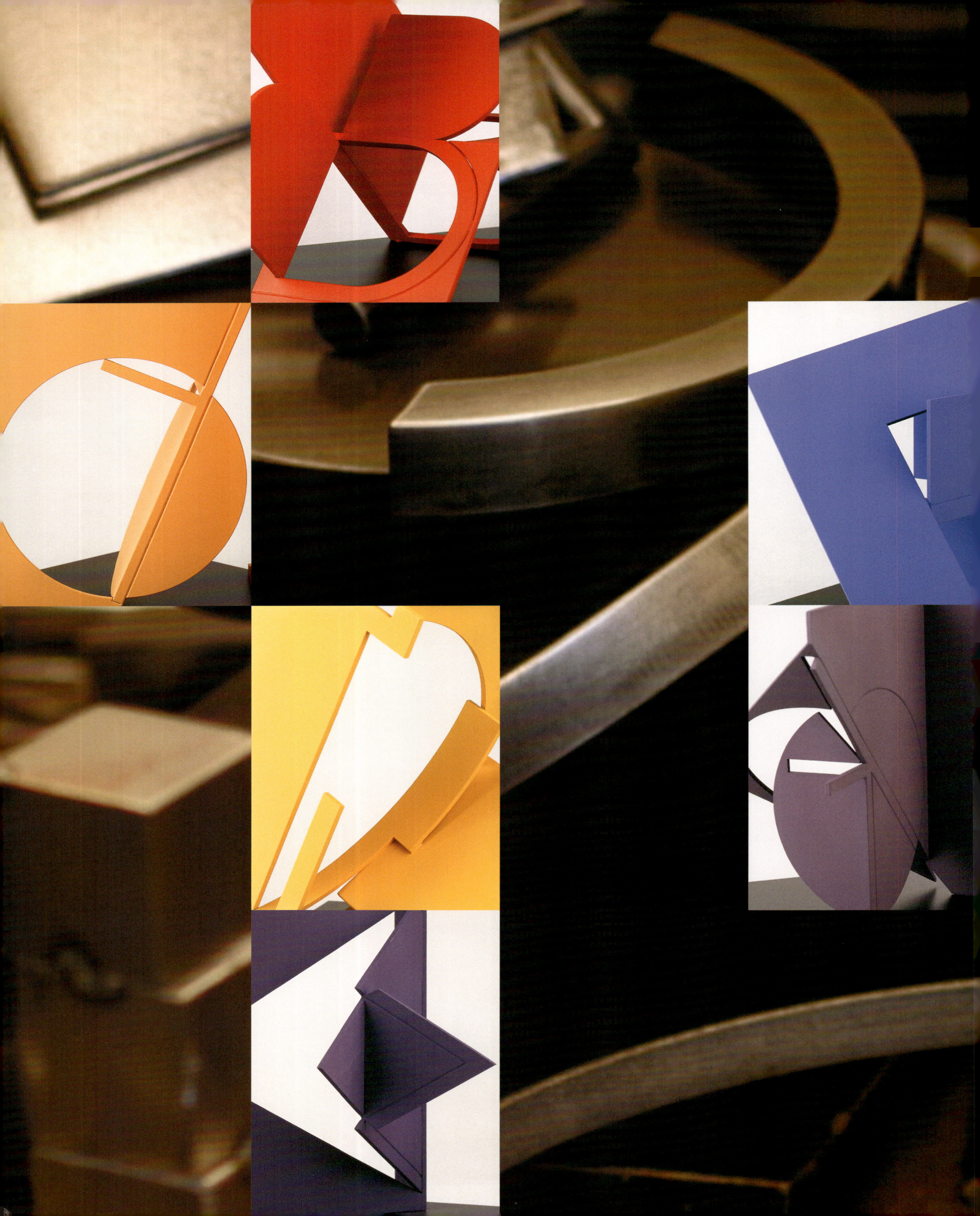

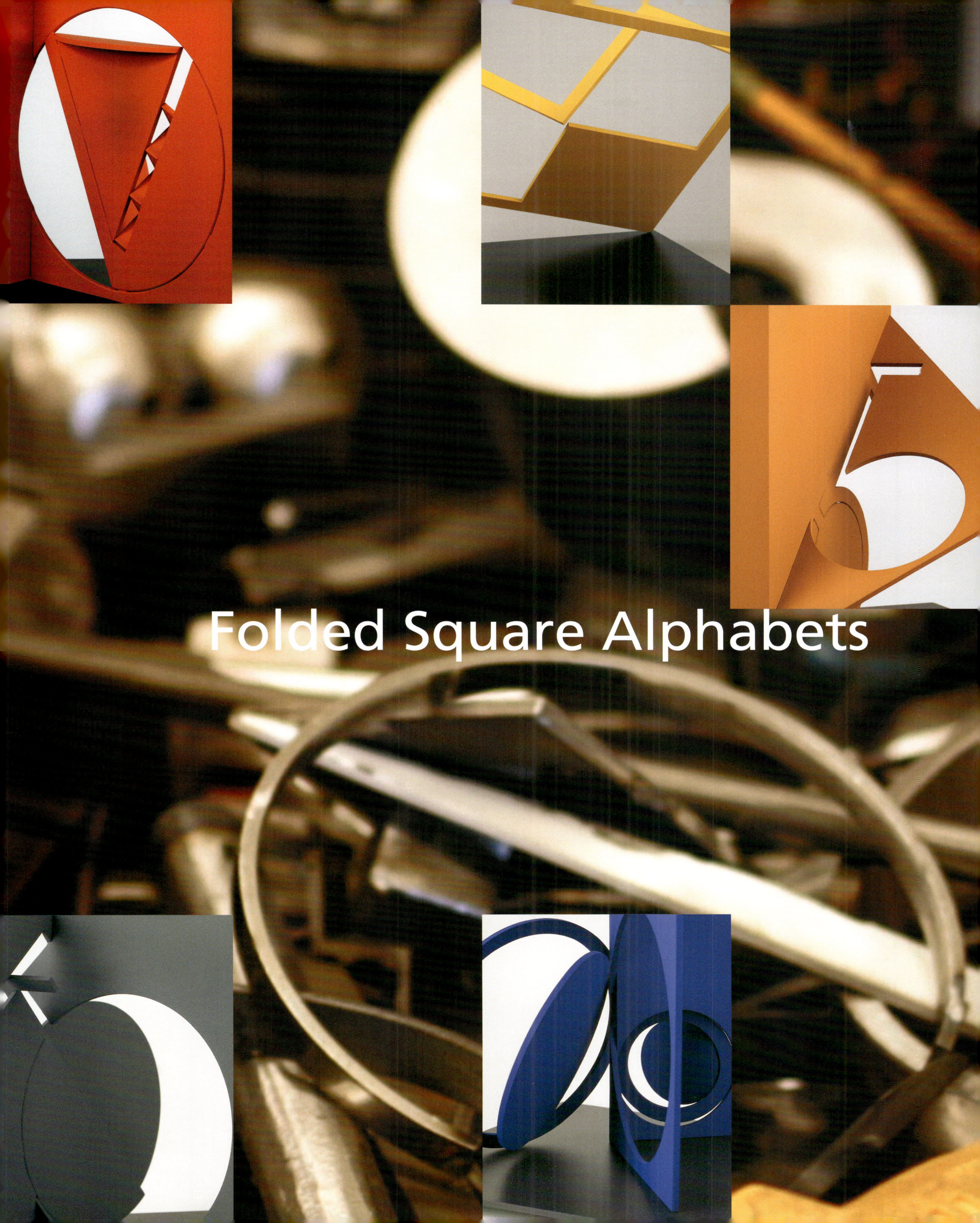

Folded Square Alphabets

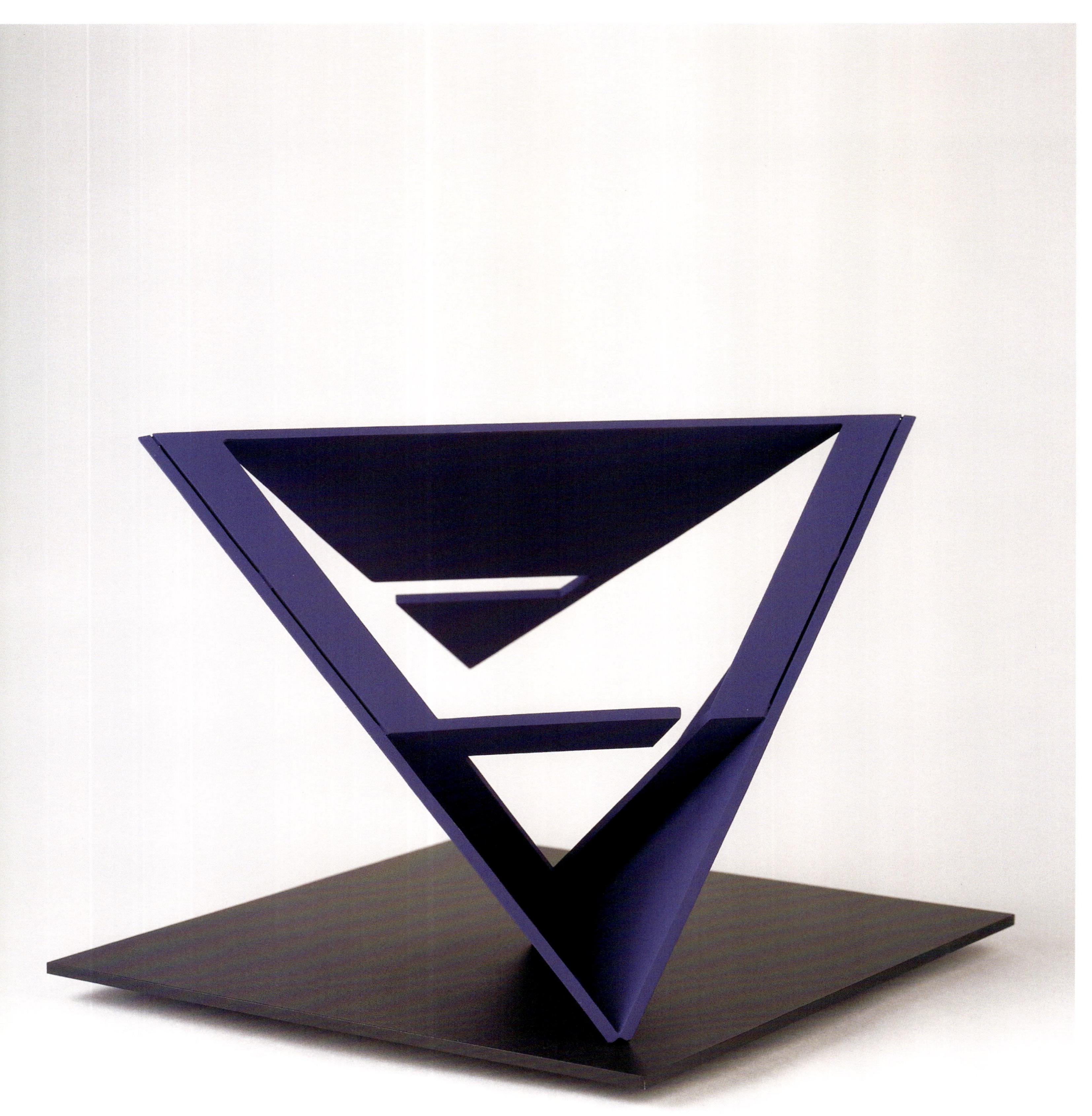

Folded Square Alphabet A

2004, painted steel
12 x 12 x 12 inches
30 x 30 x 30 cm

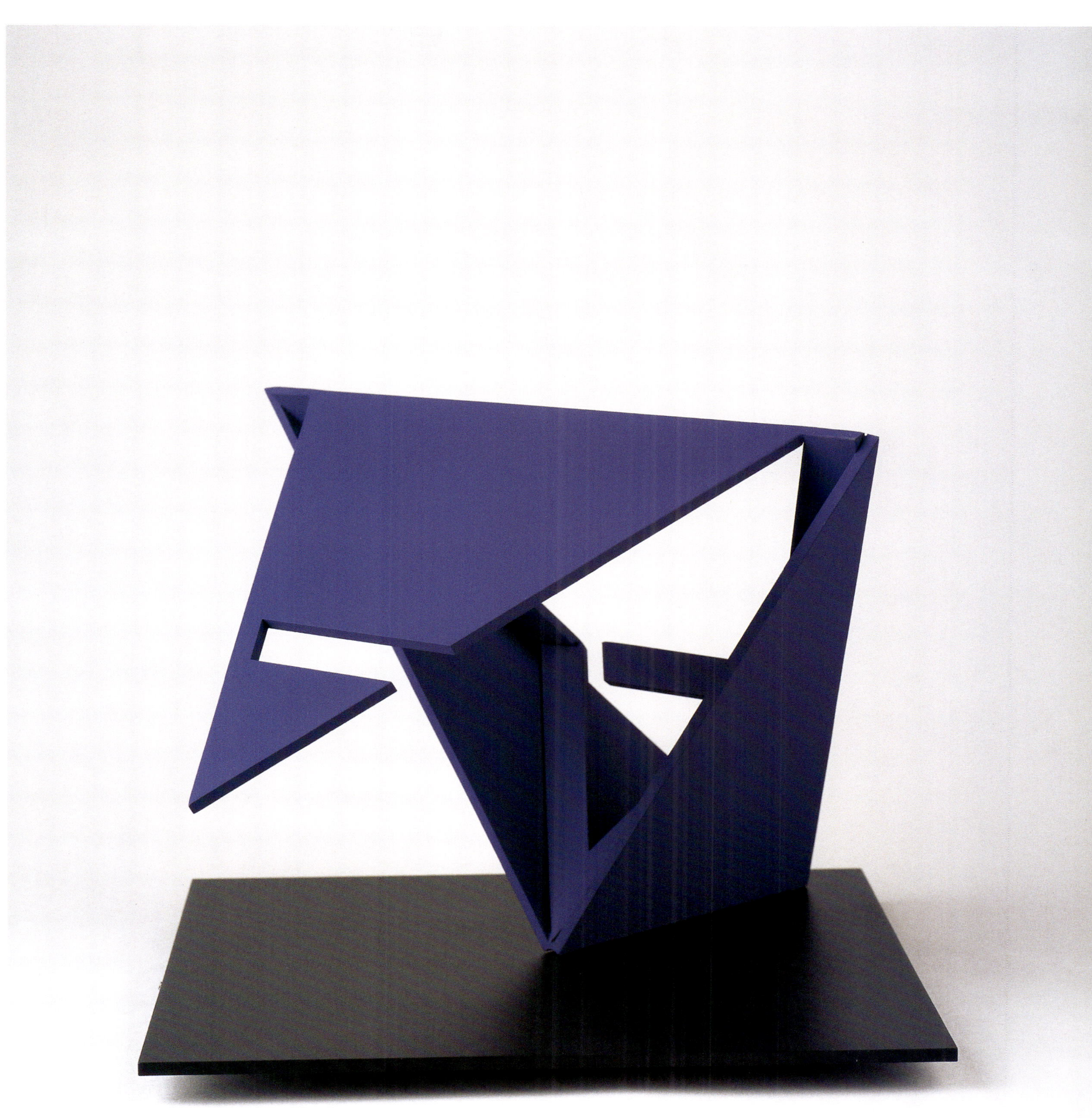

Folded Square Alphabet A

2004, painted steel
12 x 12 x 12 inches
30 x 30 x 30 cm

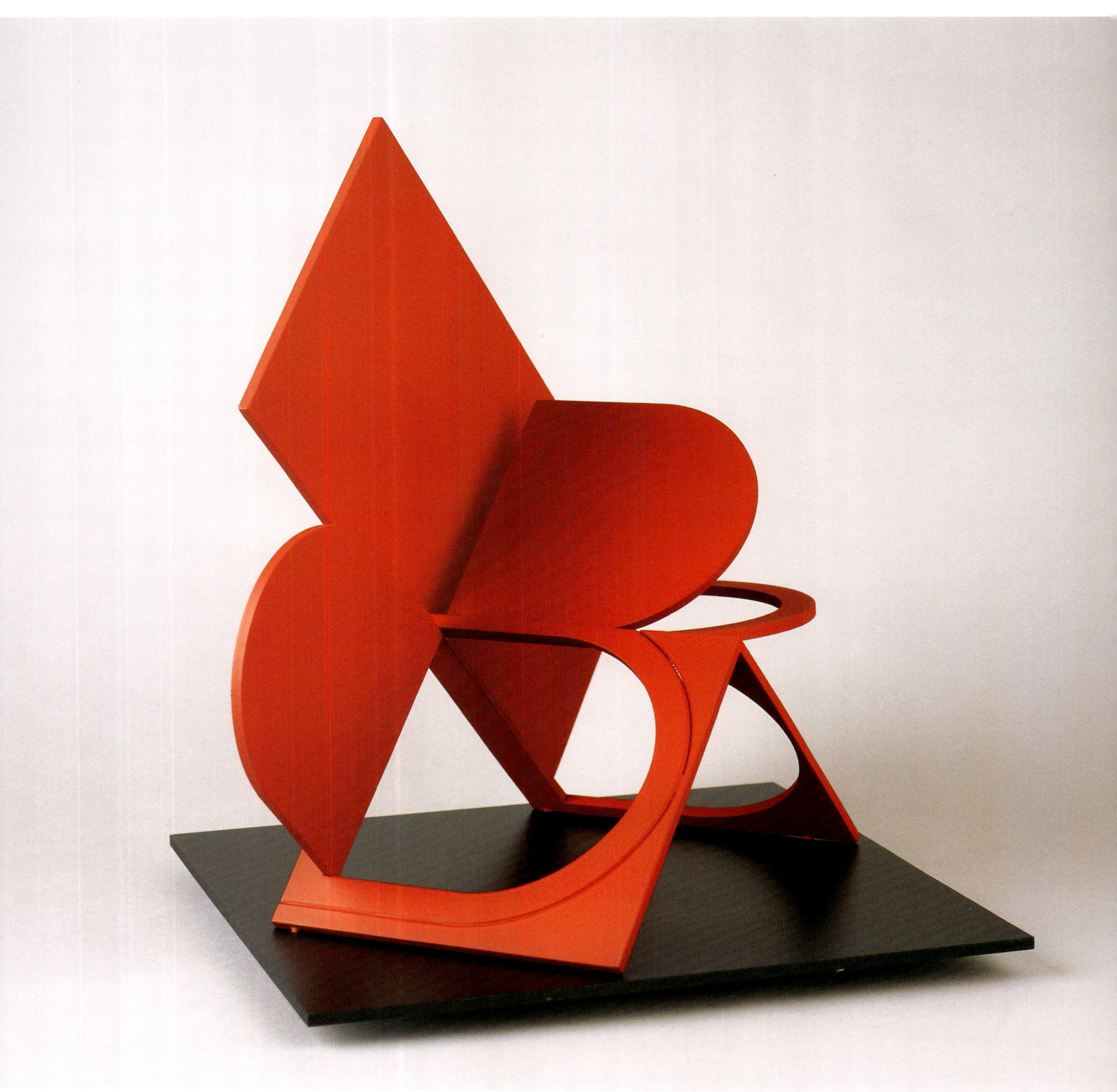

Folded Square Alphabet B

2004, painted steel
12 x 12 x 12 inches
30 x 30 x 30 cm

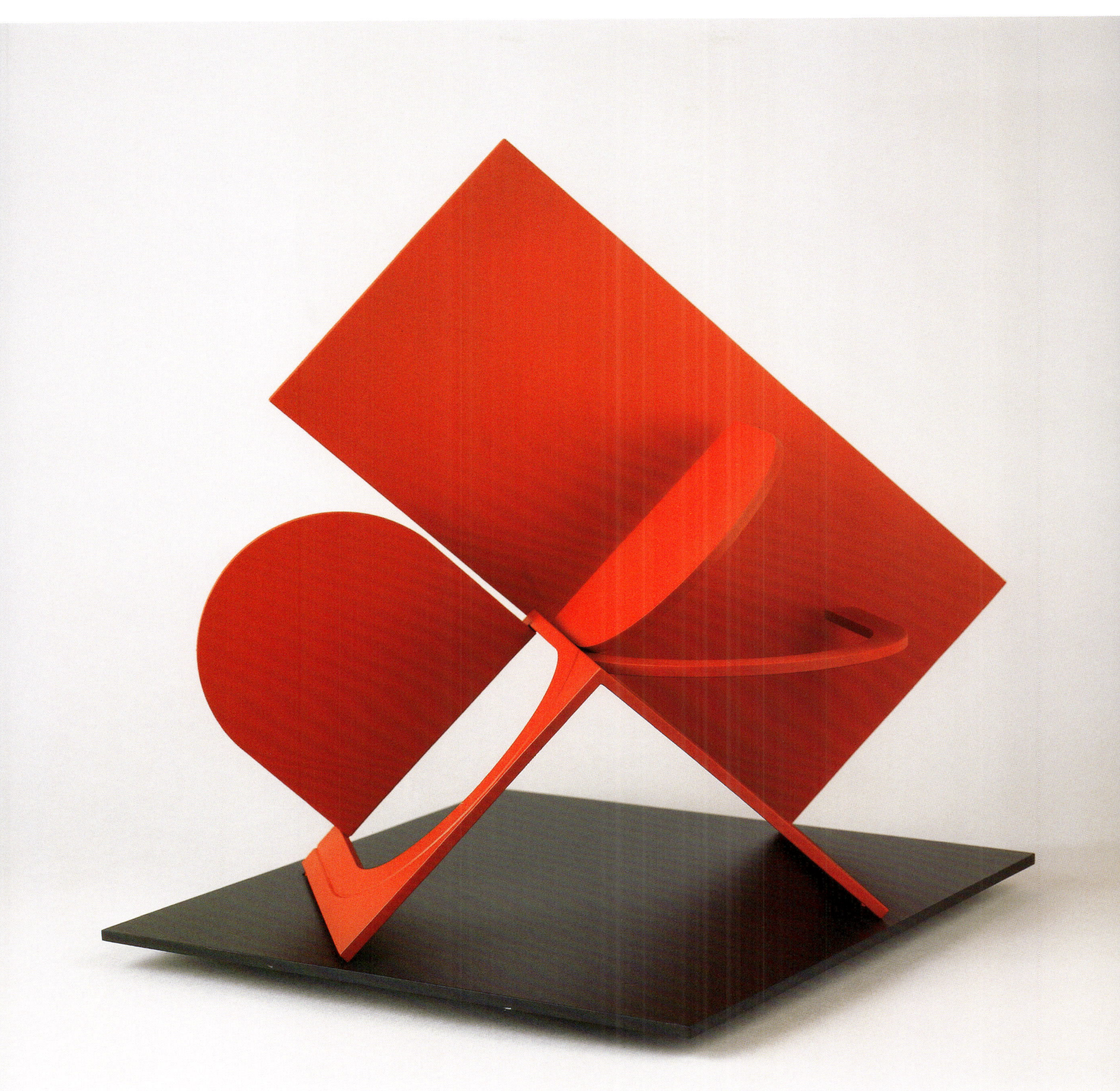

Folded Square Alphabet B

2004, painted steel
12 x 12 x 12 inches
30 x 30 x 30 cm

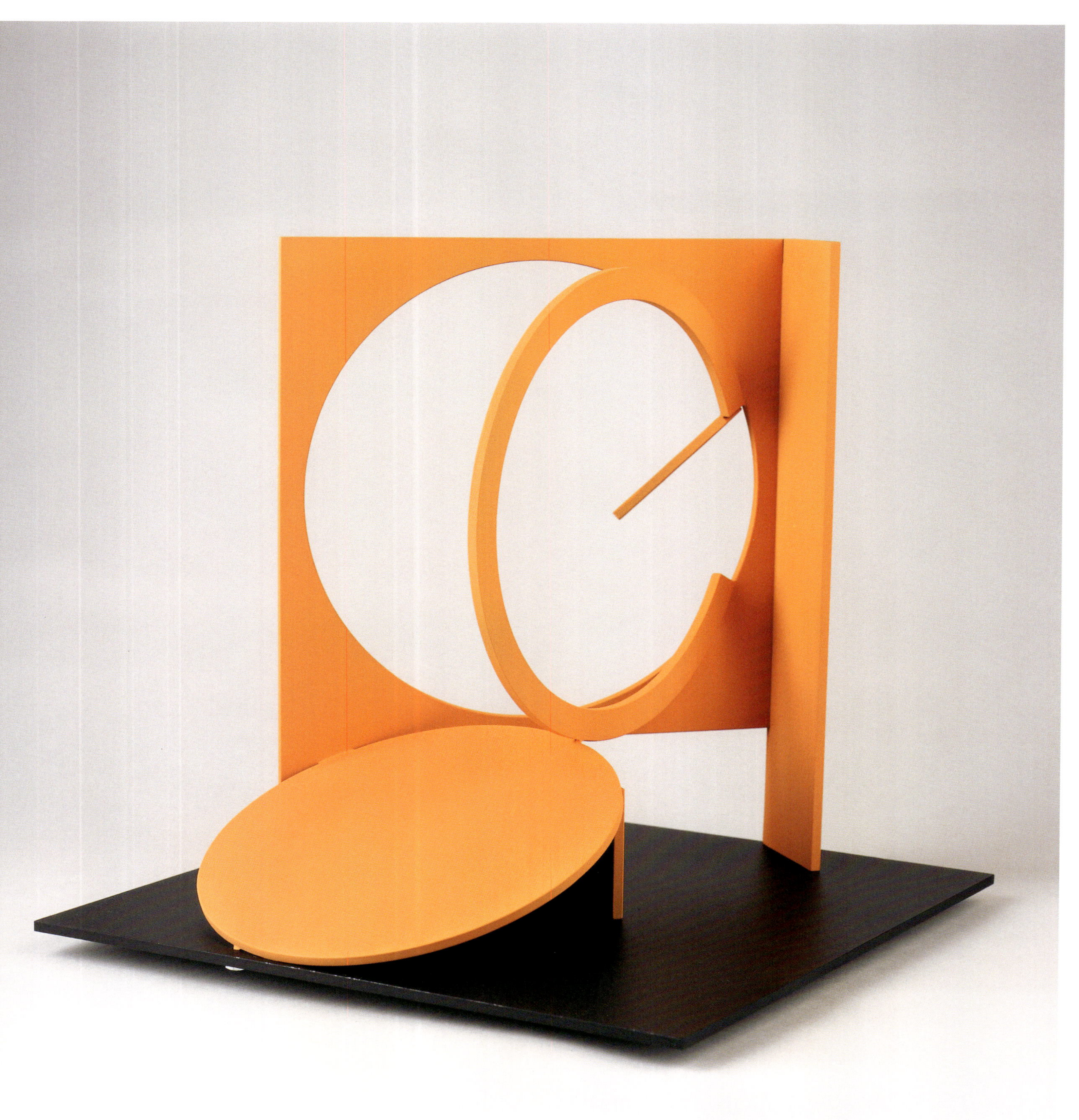

Folded Square Alphabet C

2004, painted steel
12 x 12 x 12 inches
30 x 30 x 30 cm

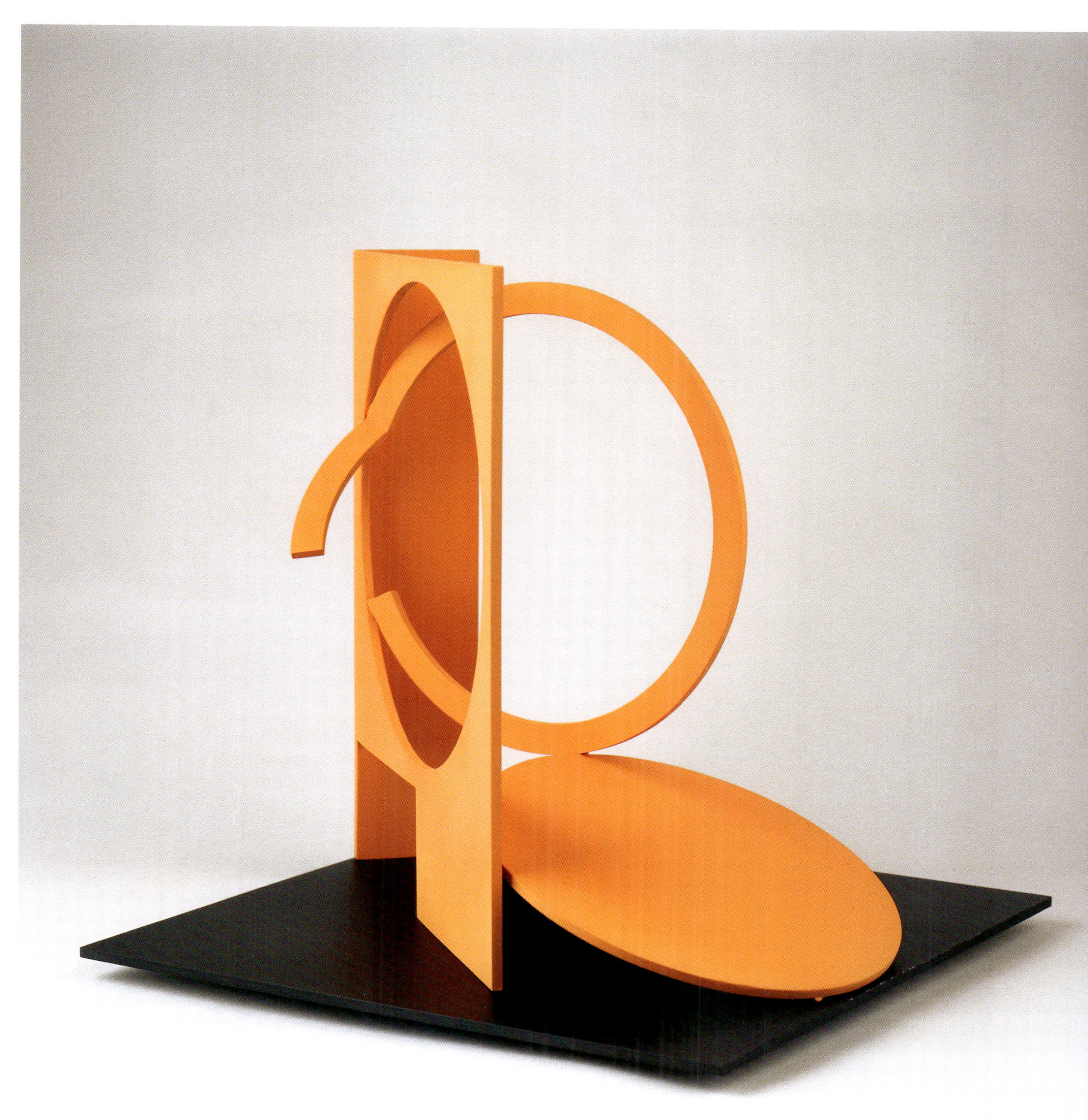

Folded Square Alphabet C

2004, painted steel
12 x 12 x 12 inches
30 x 30 x 30 cm

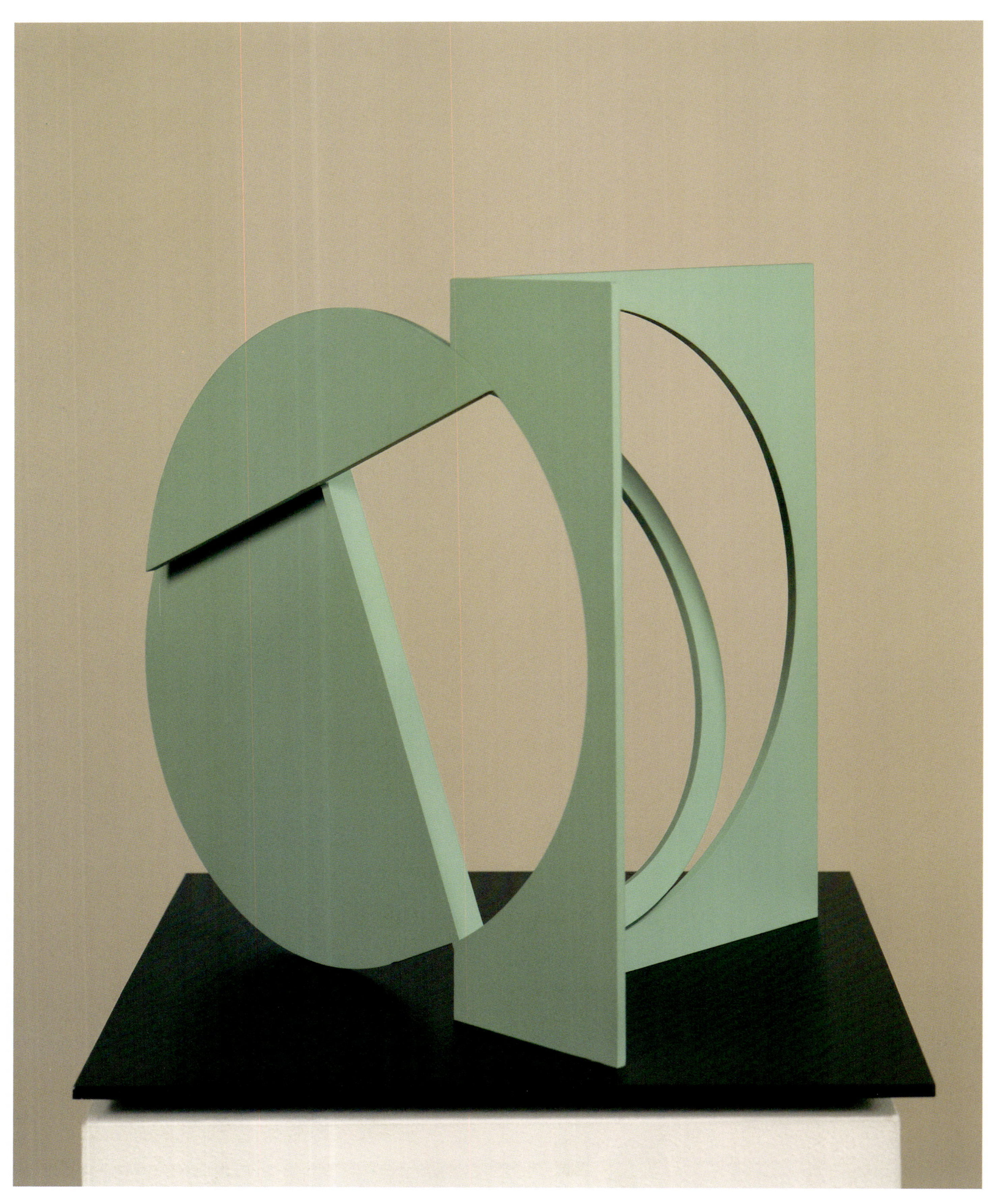

Folded Square Alphabet D

2004, painted steel
12 x 12 x 12 inches
30 x 30 x 30 cm

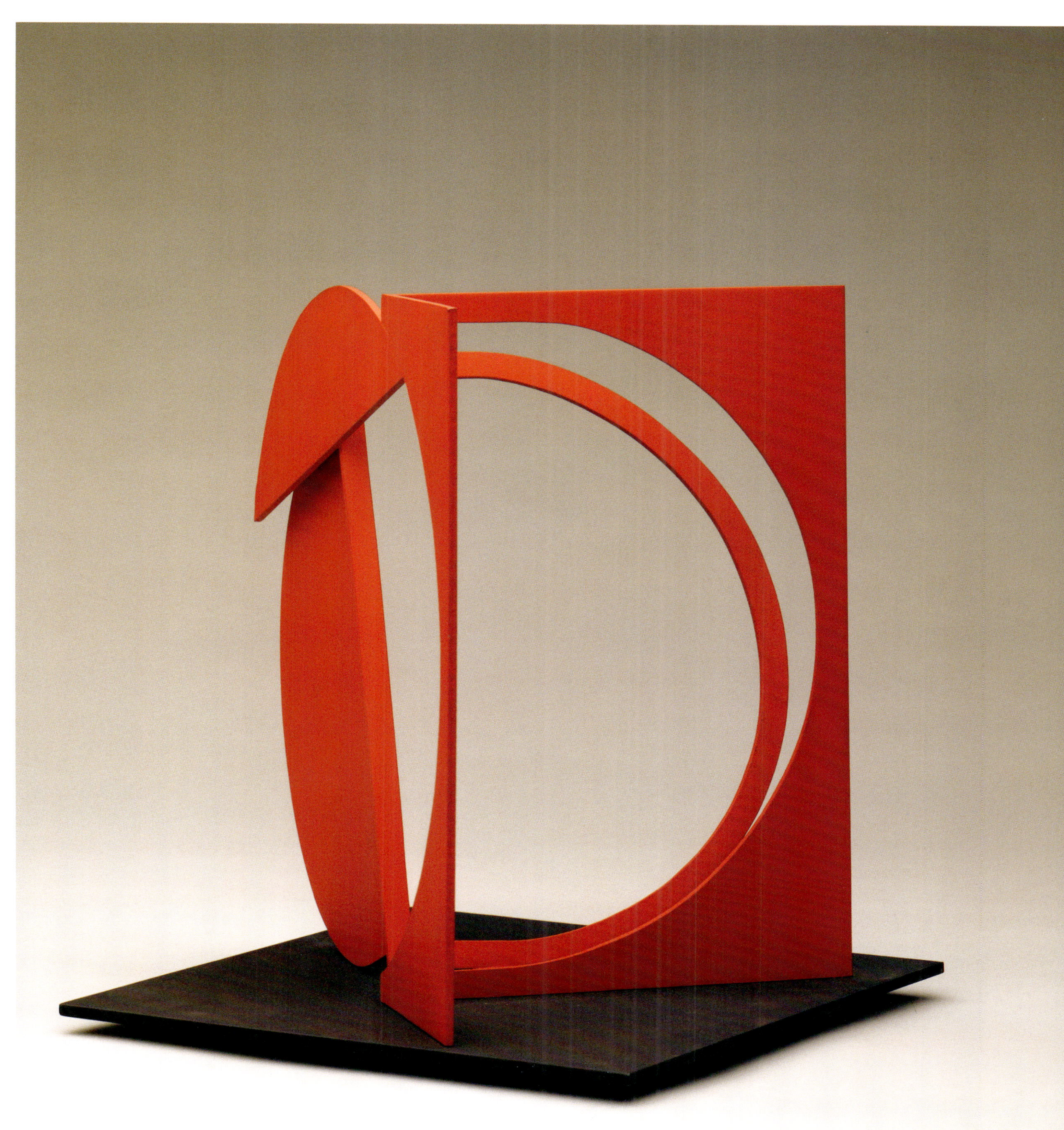

Folded Square Alphabet D

1981, painted steel
10 x 10 x 10 inches
25 x 25 x 25 cm

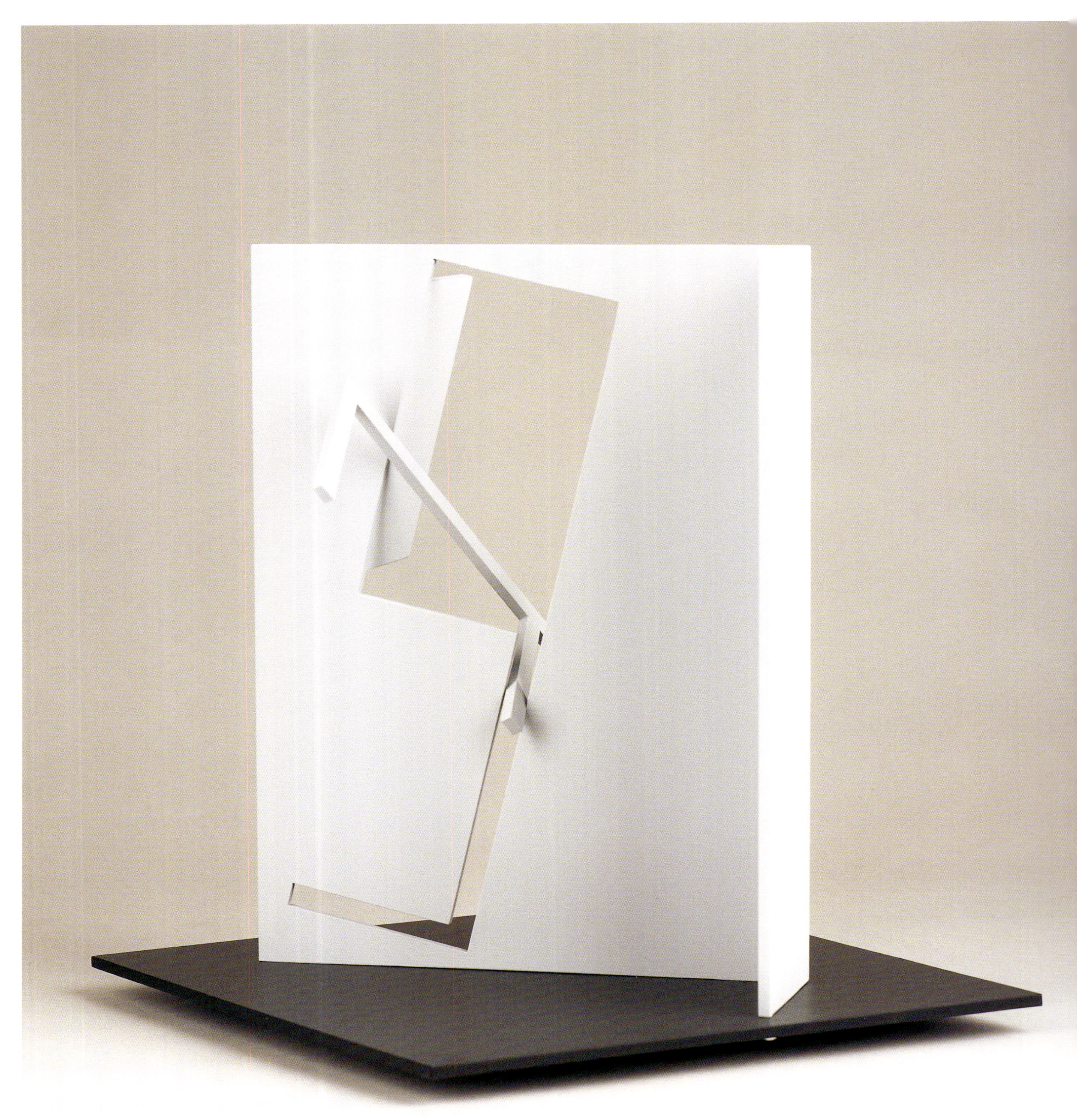

Folded Square Alphabet E

2004, painted steel
12 x 12 x 12 inches
30 x 30 x 30 cm

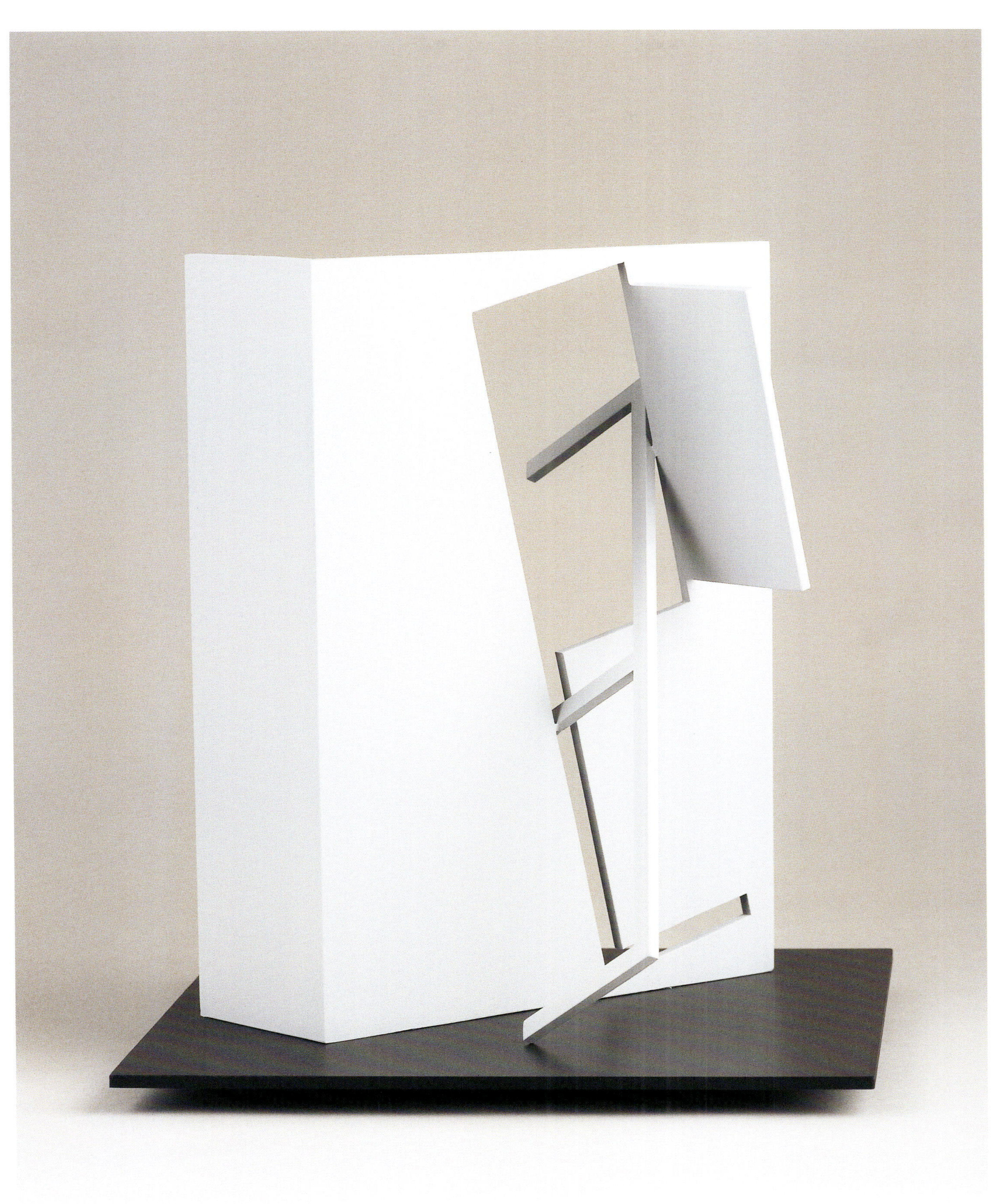

Folded Square Alphabet E

2004, painted steel
12 x 12 x 12 inches
30 x 30 x 30 cm

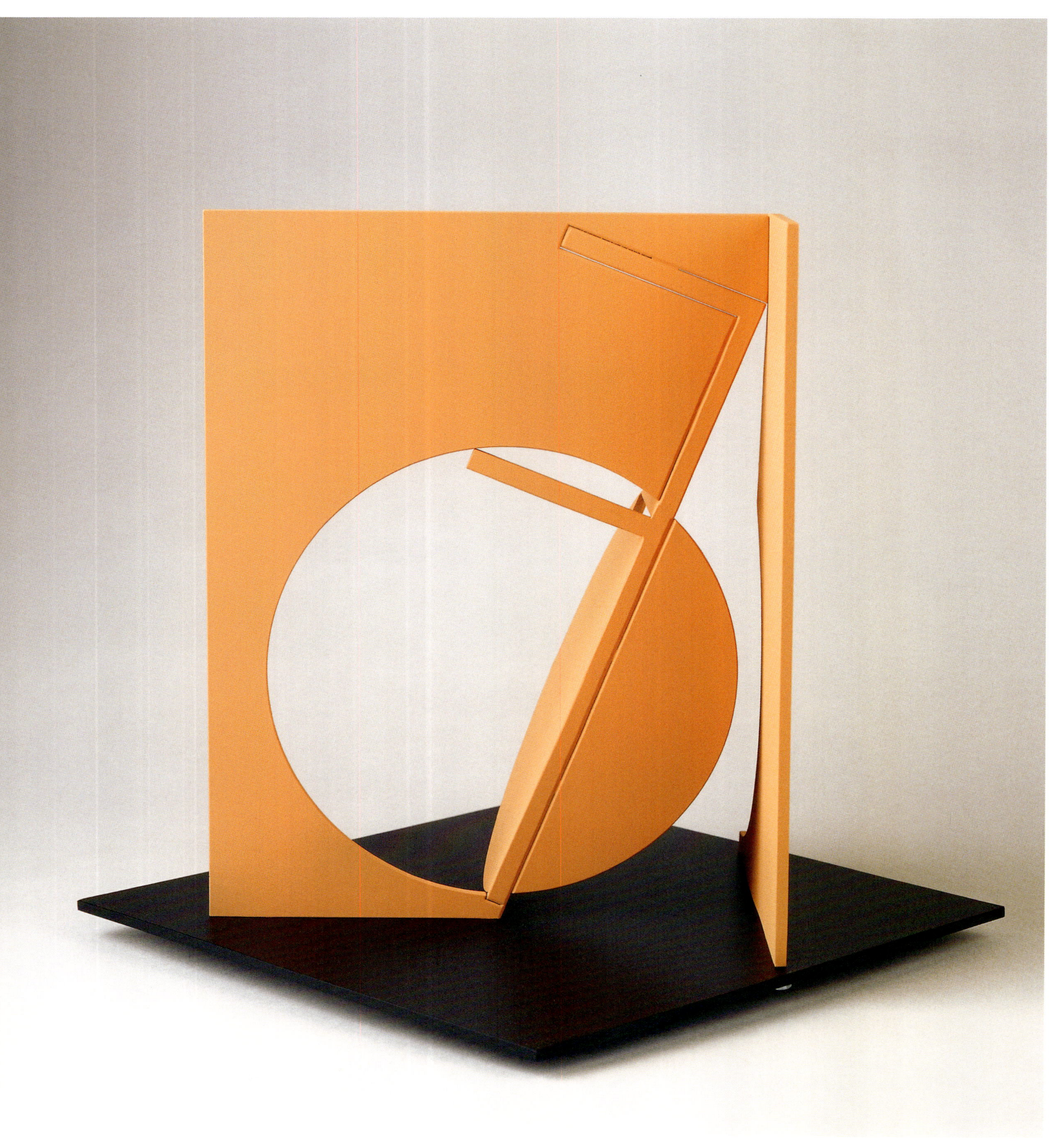

Folded Square Alphabet F

2004, painted steel
12 x 12 x 12 inches
30 x 30 x 30 cm

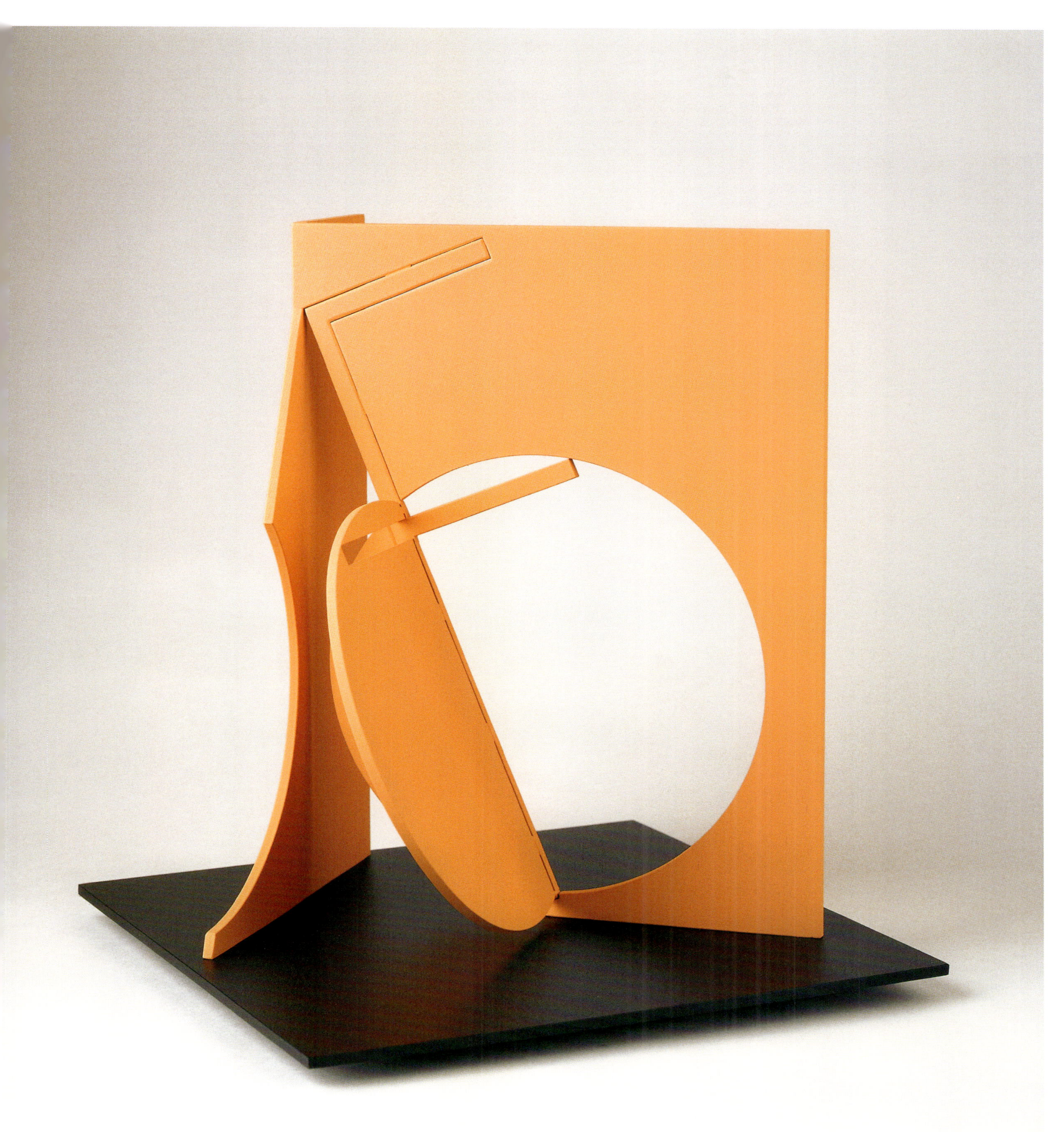

Folded Square Alphabet F

2004, painted steel
12 x 12 x 12 inches
30 x 30 x 30 cm

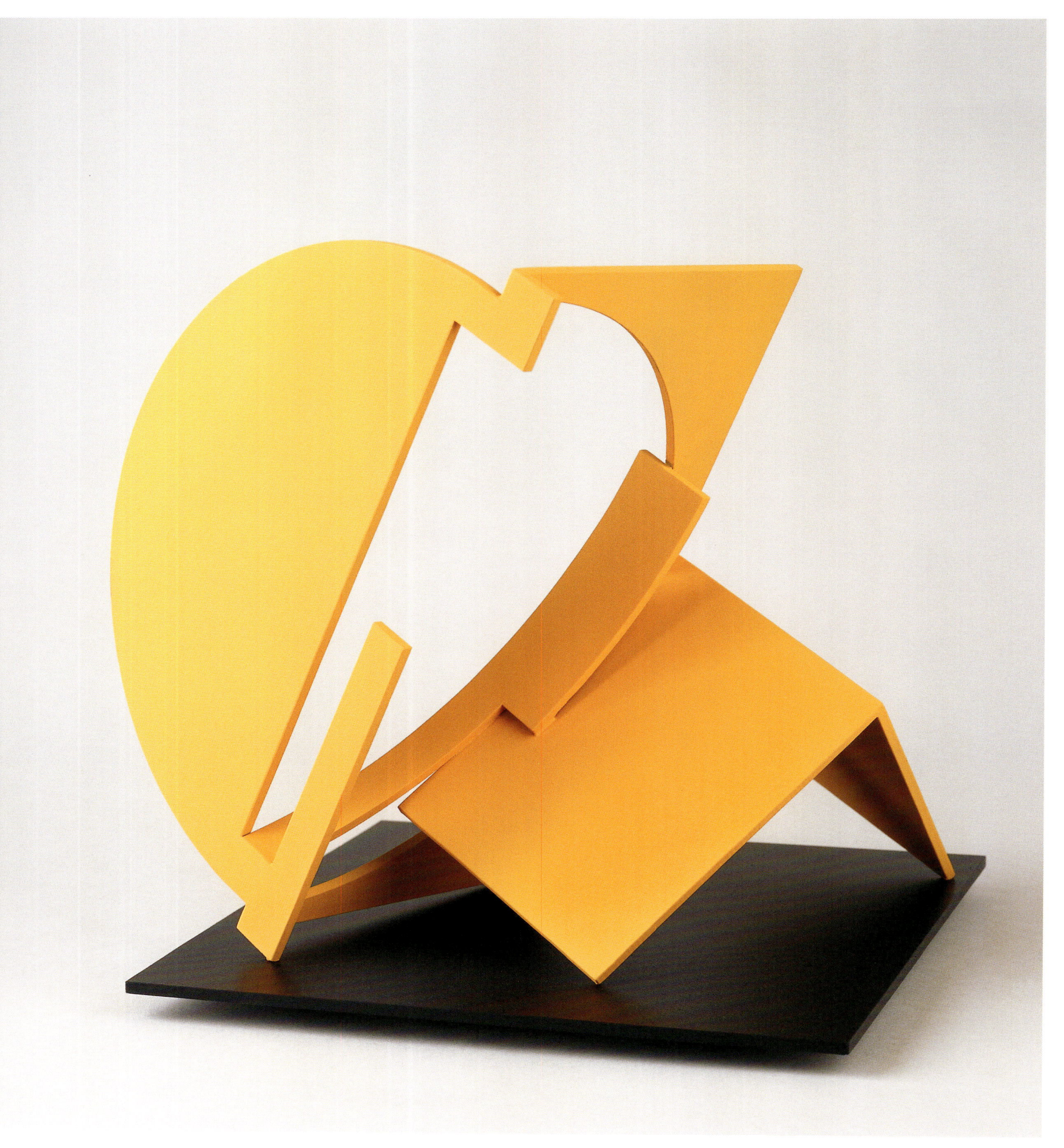

Folded Square Alphabet G

2004, painted steel
12 x 12 x 12 inches
30 x 30 x 30 cm

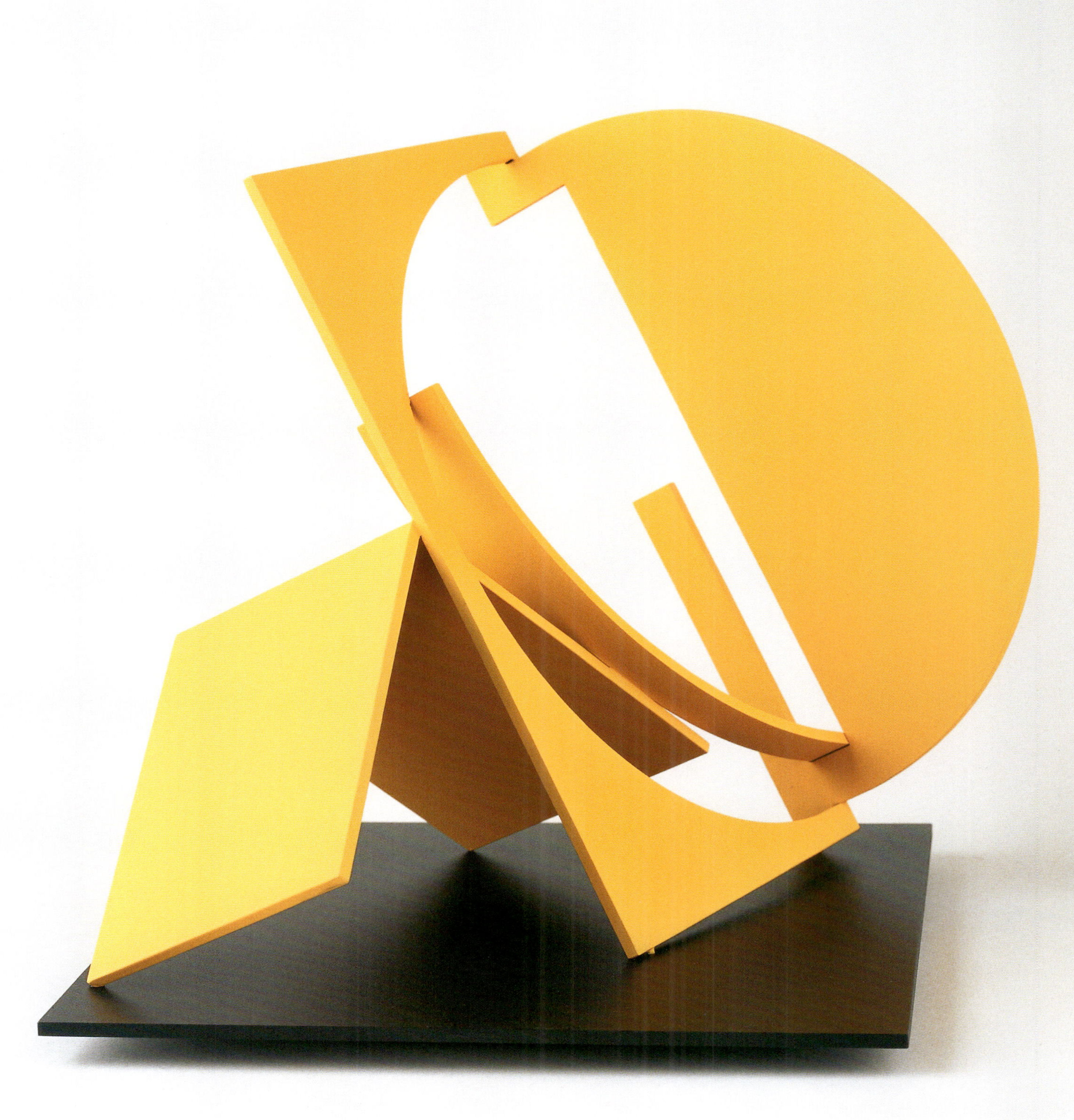

Folded Square Alphabet G

2004, painted steel
12 x 12 x 12 inches
30 x 30 x 30 cm

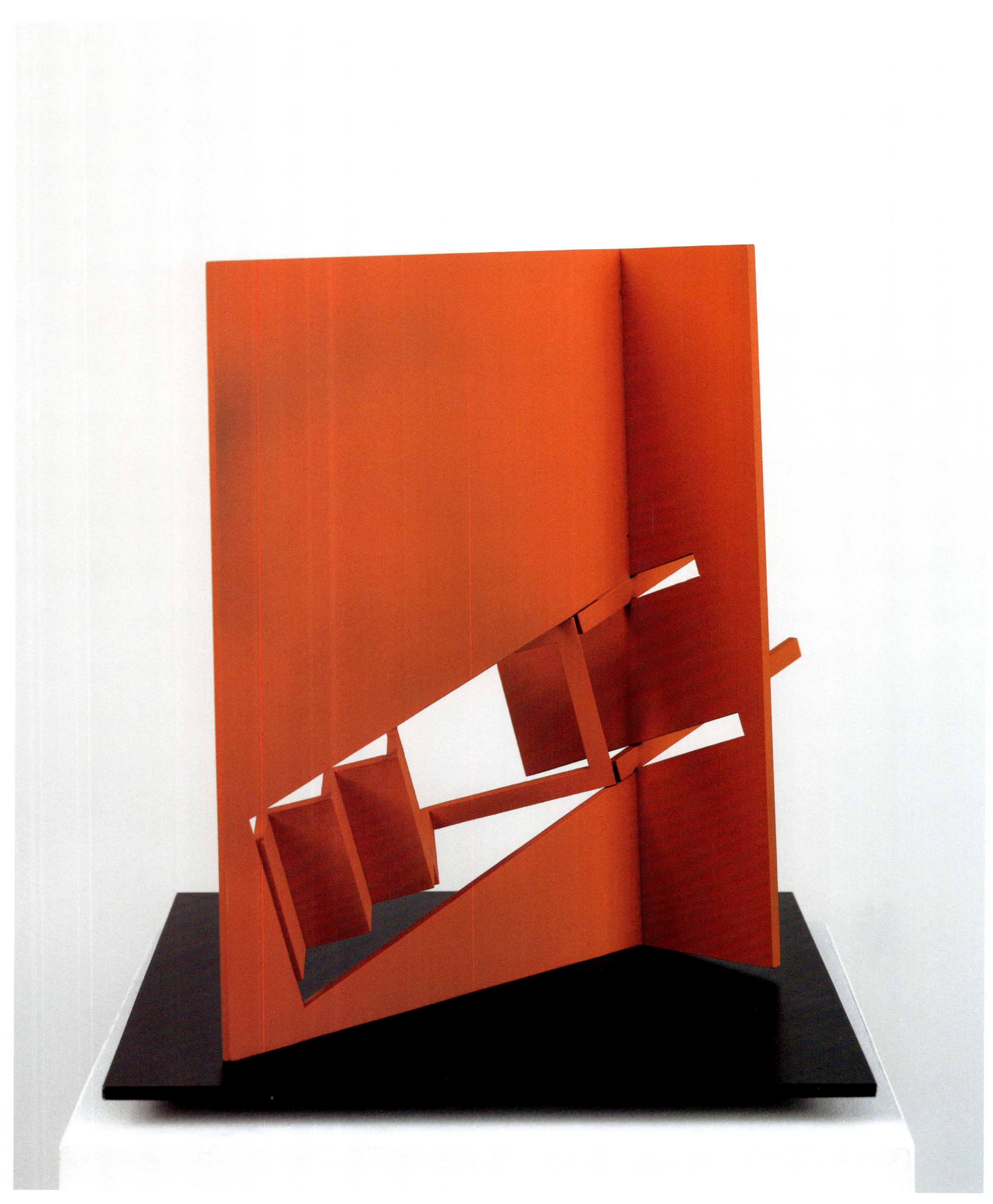

Folded Square Alphabet H

2004, painted steel
12 x 12 x 12 inches
30 x 30 x 30 cm

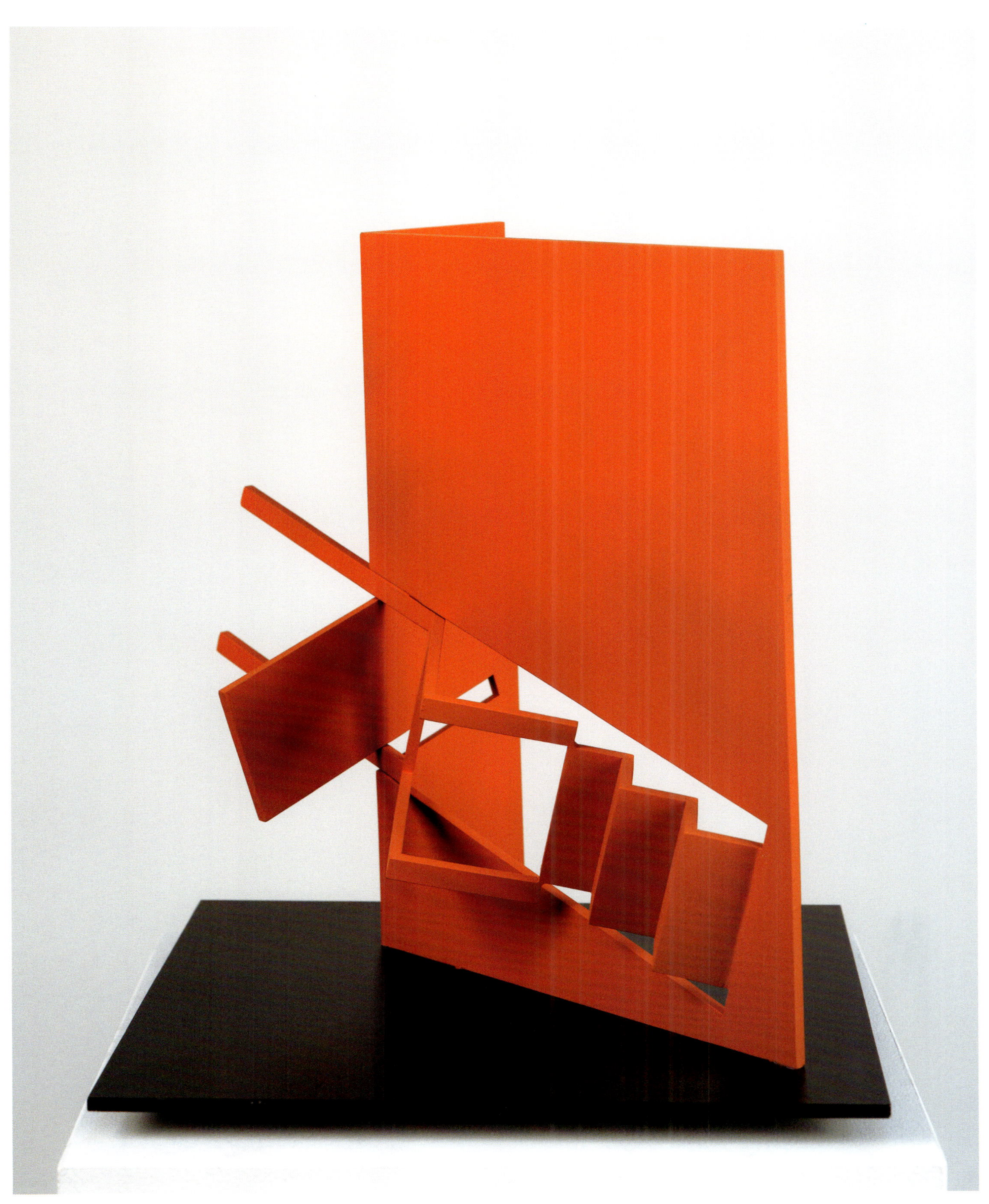

Folded Square Alphabet H

2004, painted steel
12 x 12 x 12 inches
30 x 30 x 30 cm

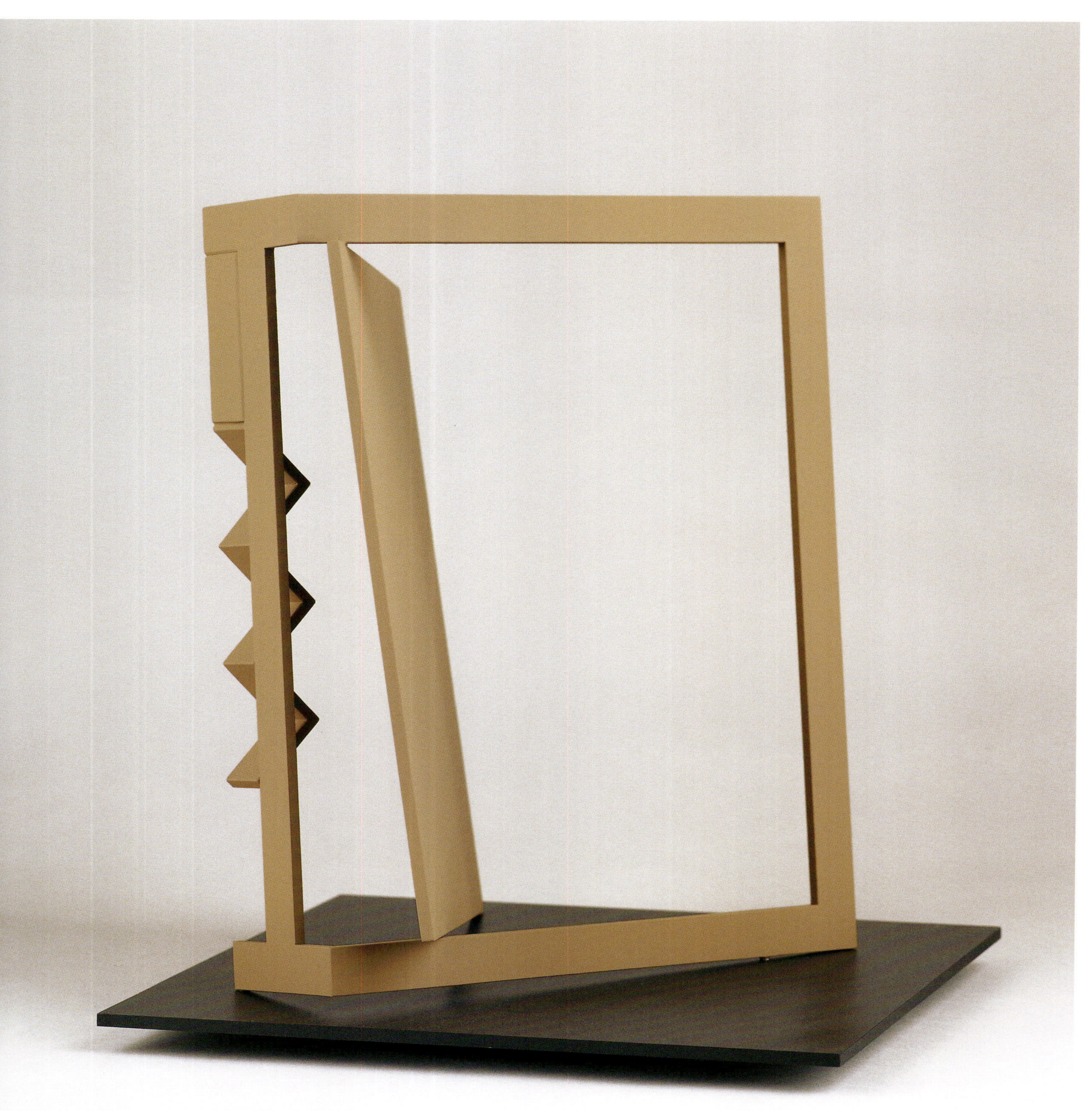

Folded Square Alphabet I

2004, painted steel
12 x 12 x 12 inches
30 x 30 x 30 cm

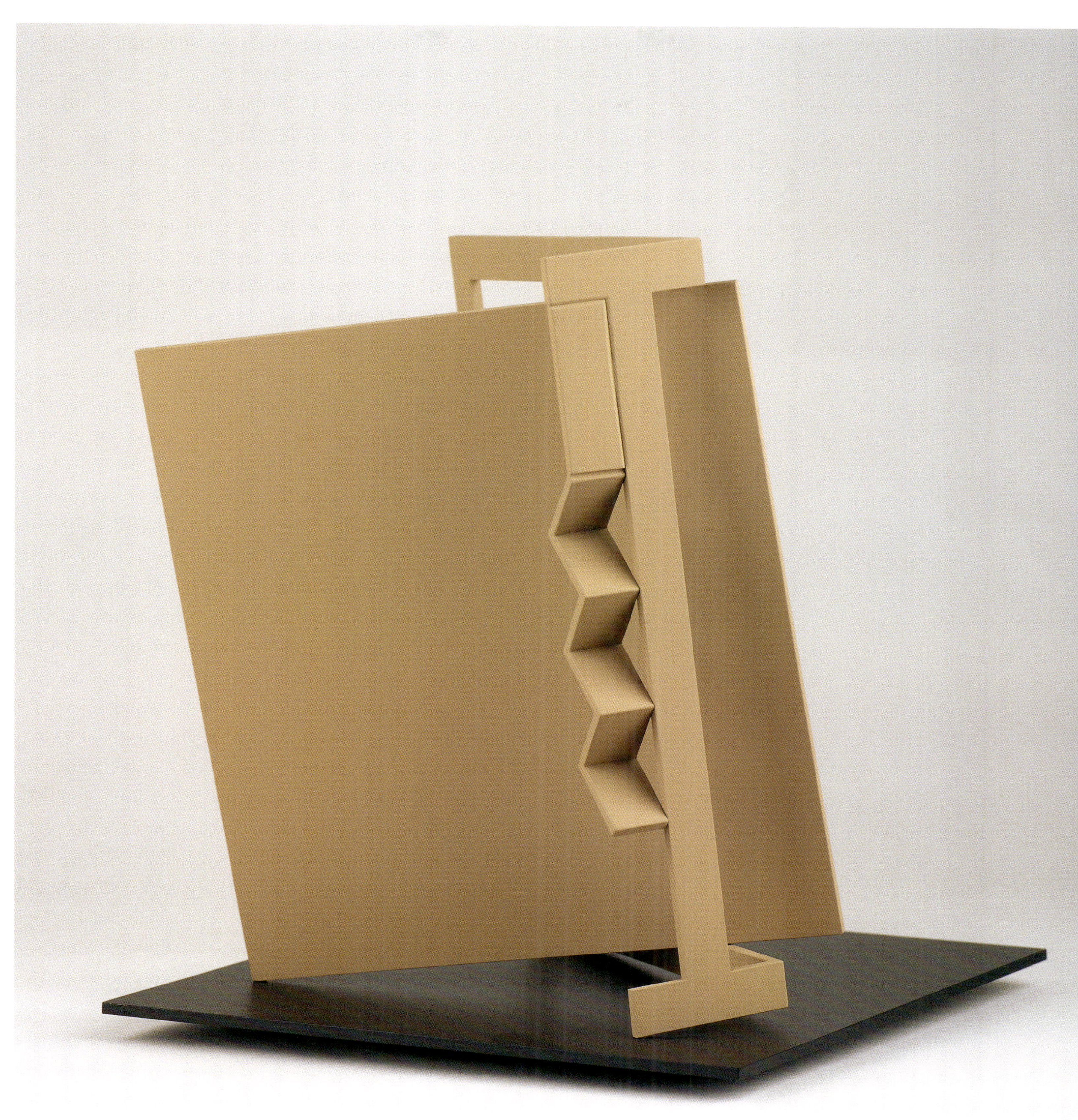

Folded Square Alphabet I

2004, painted steel
12 x 12 x 12 inches
30 x 30 x 30 cm

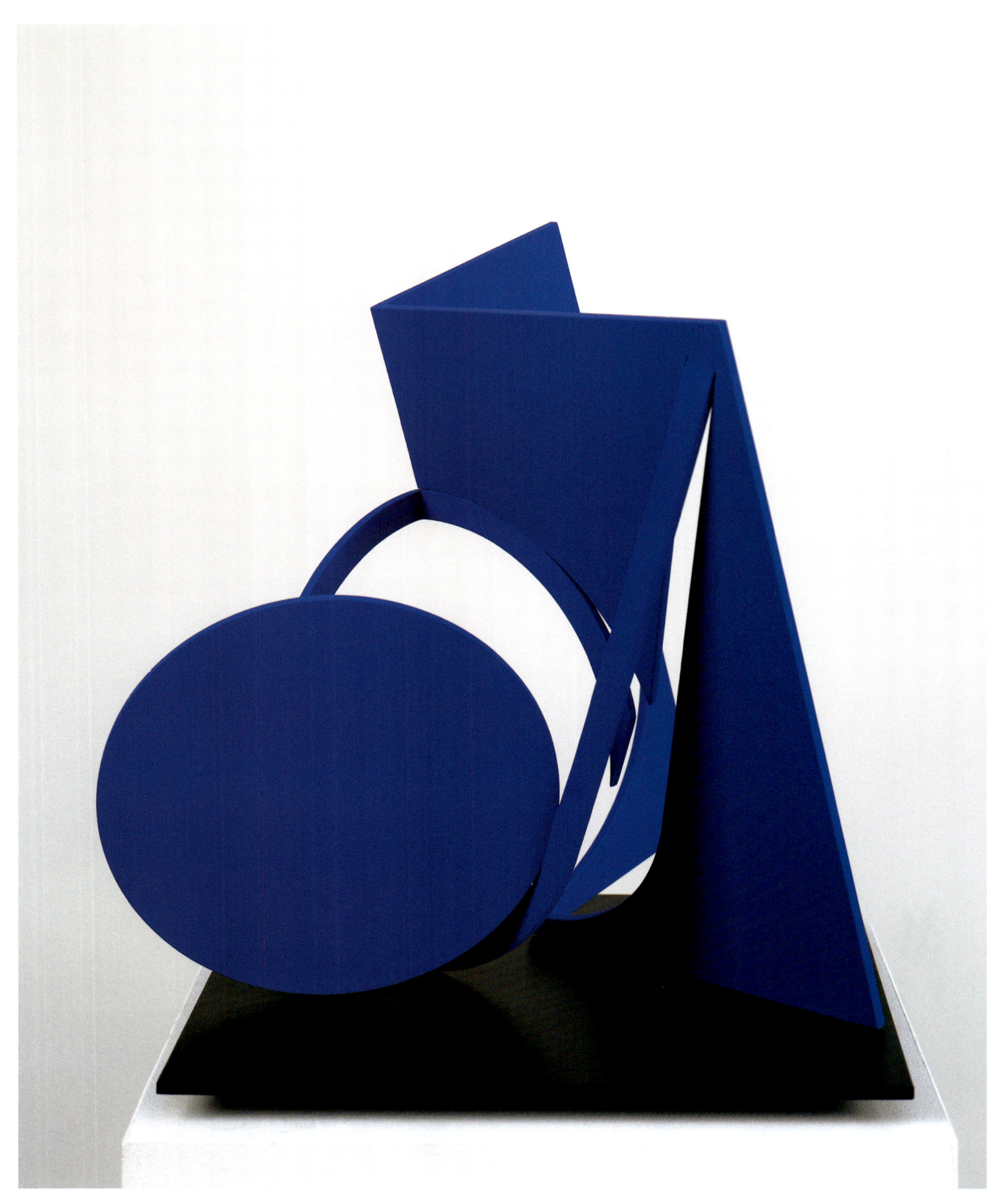

Folded Square Alphabet J

2004, painted steel
12 x 12 x 12 inches
30 x 30 x 30 cm

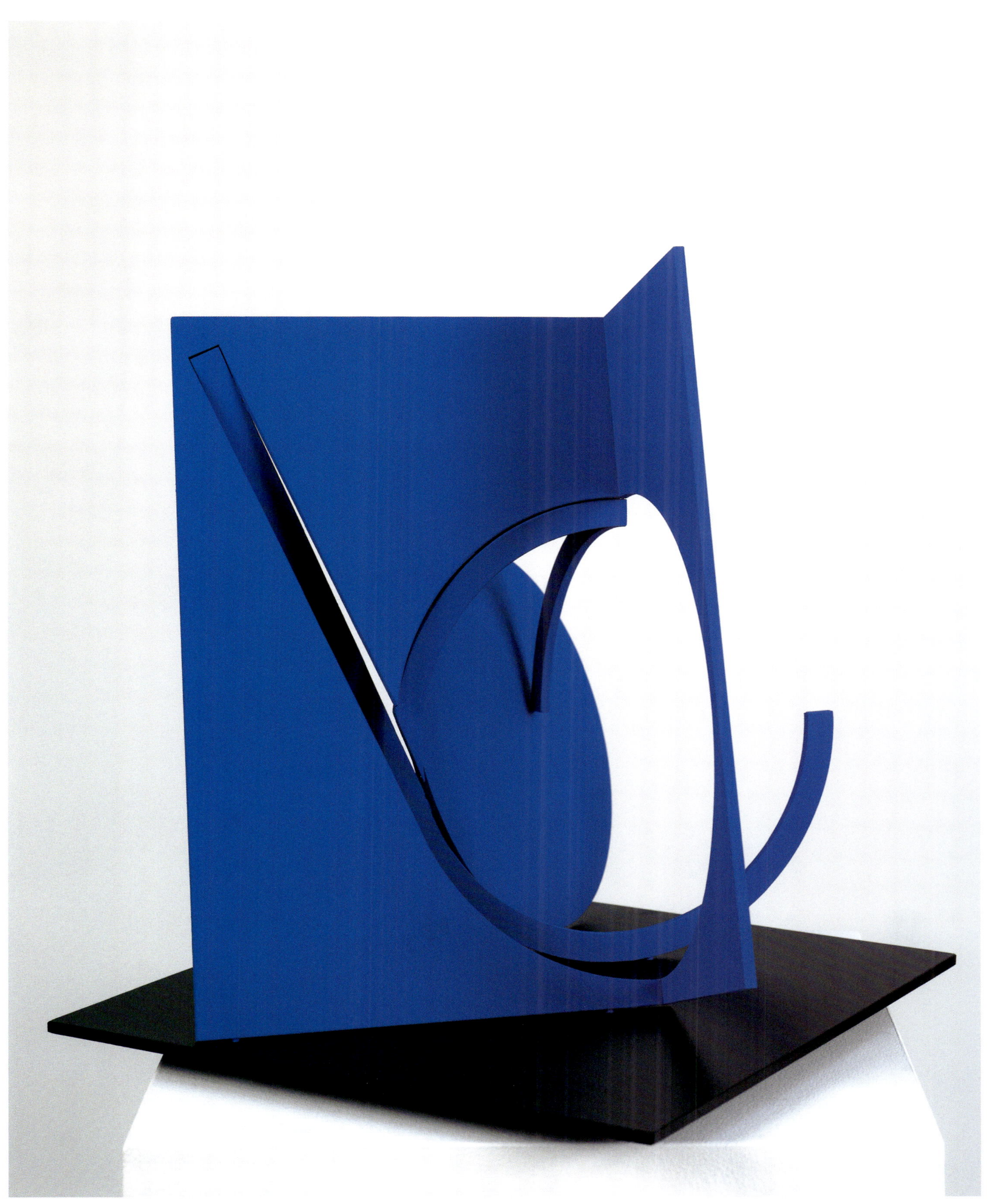

Folded Square Alphabet J

2004, painted steel
12 x 12 x 12 inches
30 x 30 x 30 cm

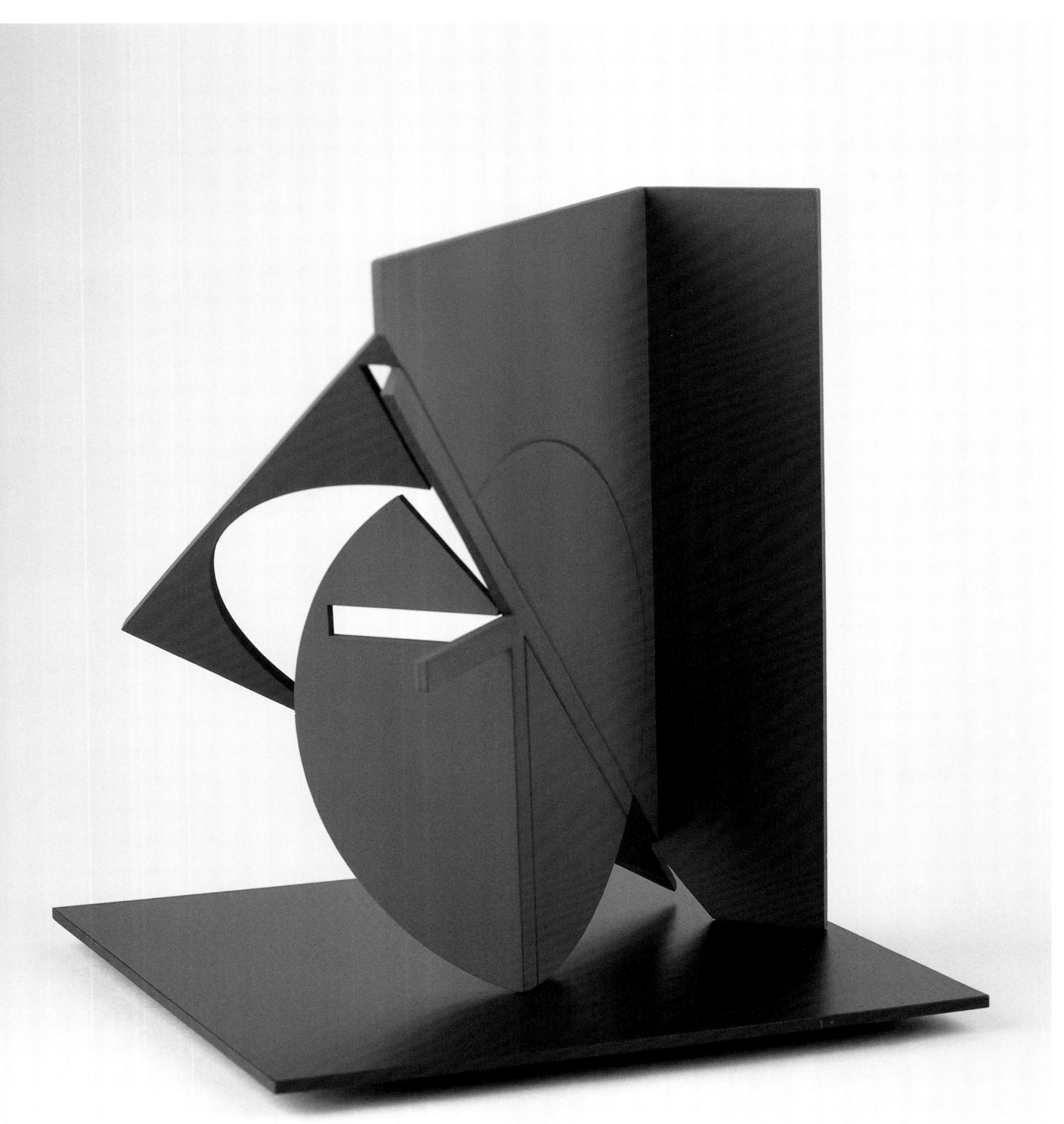

Folded Square Alphabet K

2004, painted steel
12 x 12 x 12 inches
30 x 30 x 30 cm

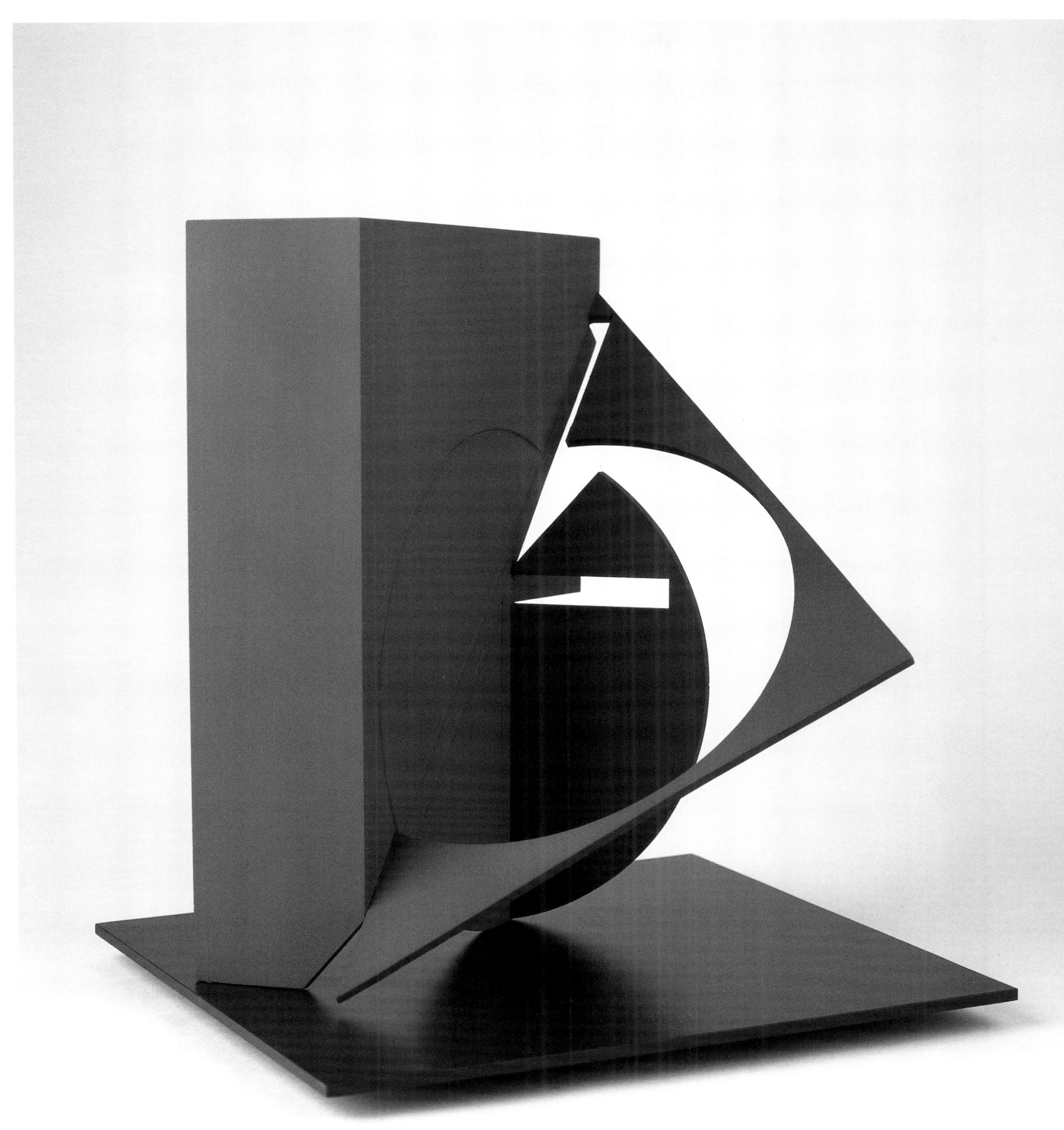

Folded Square Alphabet K

2004, painted steel
12 x 12 x 12 inches
30 x 30 x 30 cm

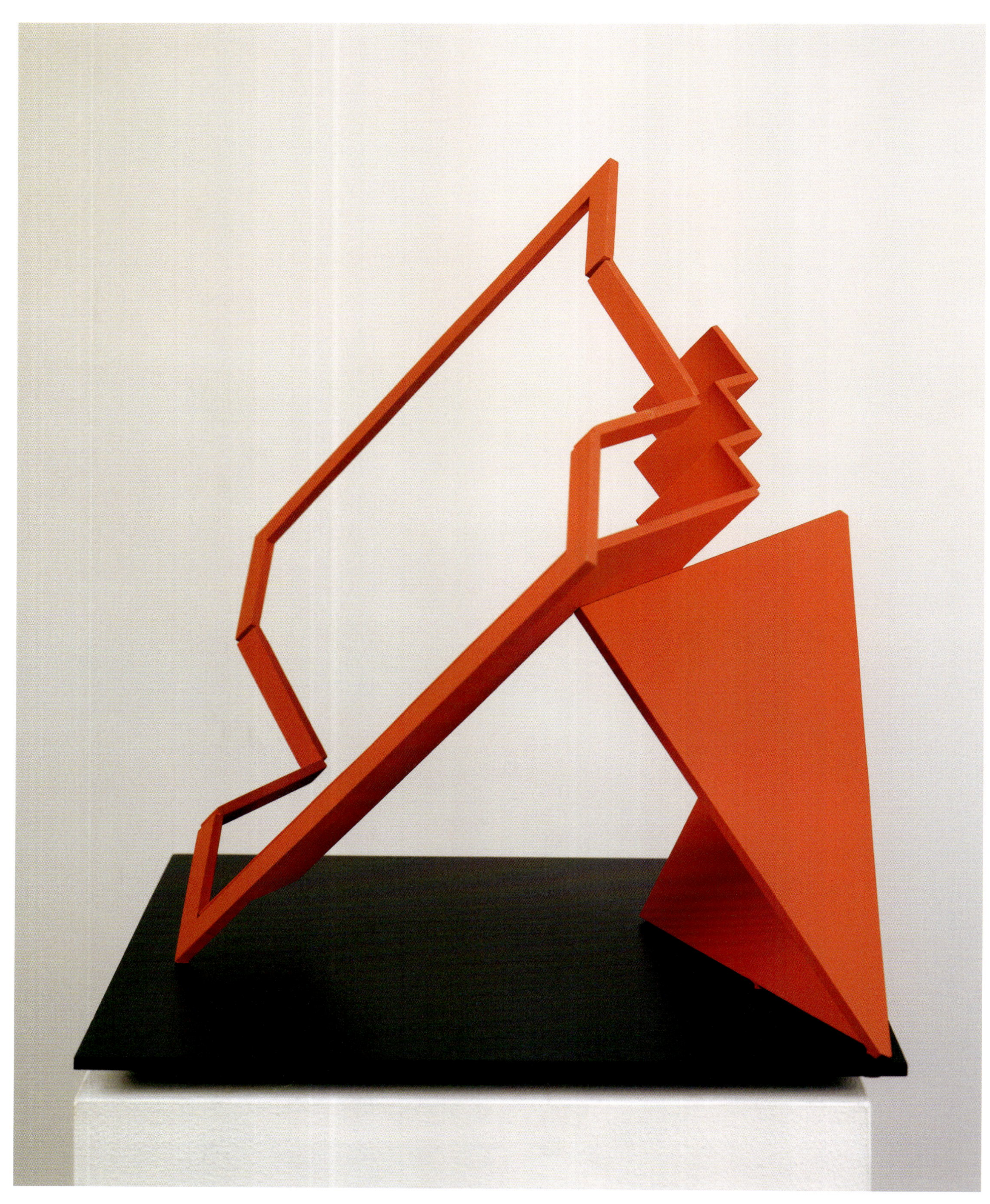

Folded Square Alphabet L

2004, painted steel
12 x 12 x 12 inches
30 x 30 x 30 cm

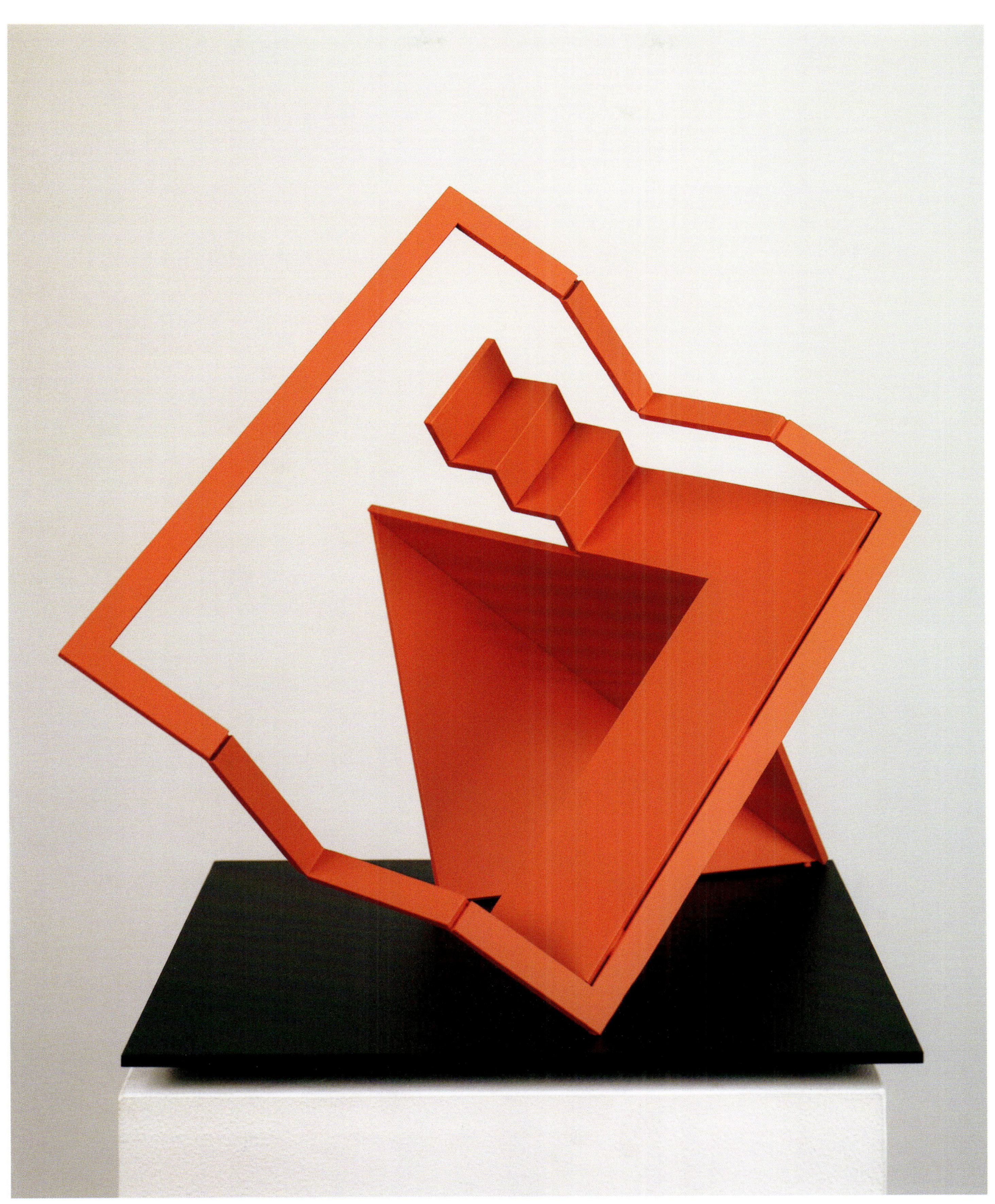

Folded Square Alphabet L

2004, painted steel
12 x 12 x 12 inches
30 x 30 x 30 cm

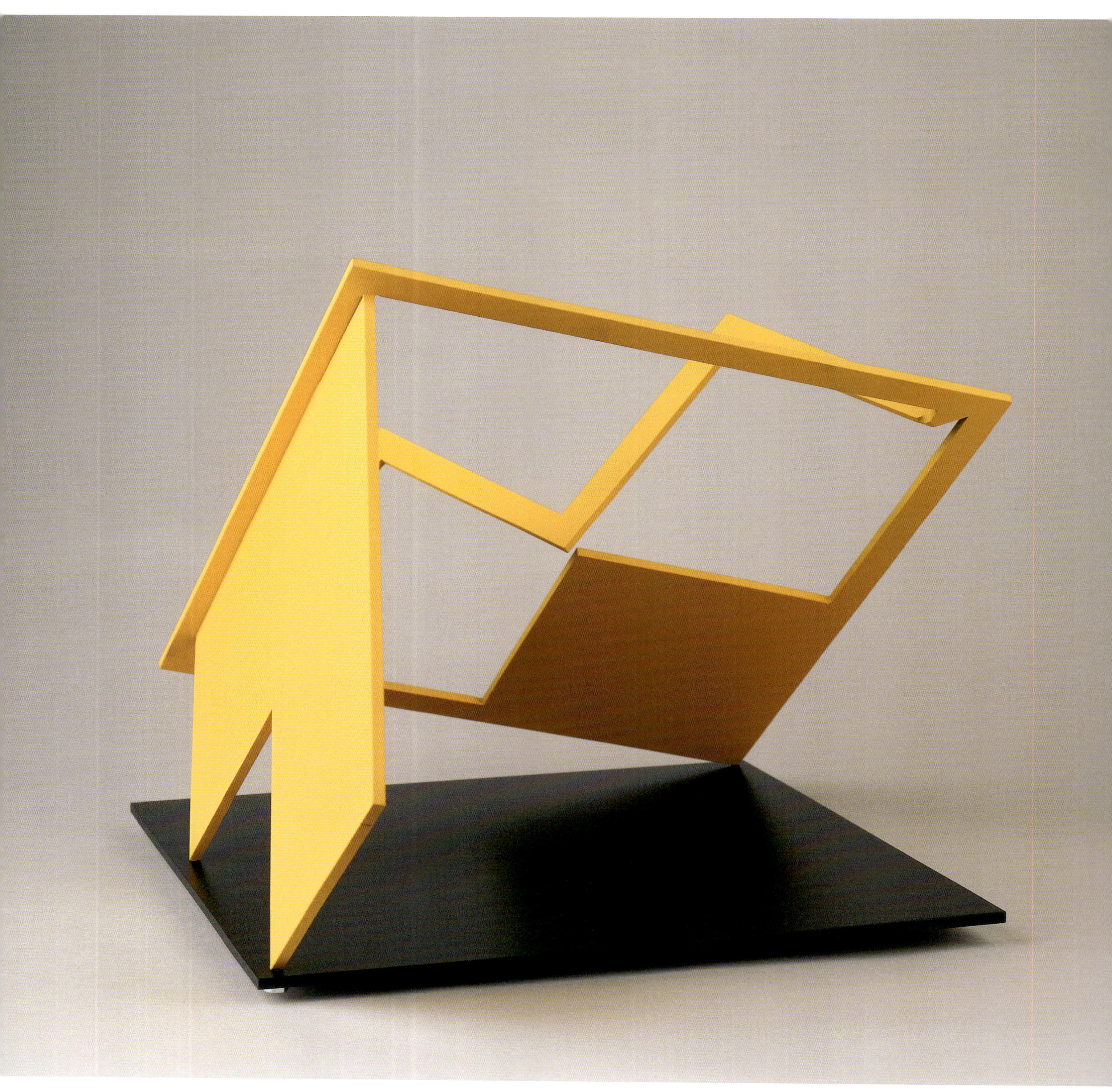

Folded Square Alphabet M

2004, painted steel
12 x 12 x 12 inches
30 x 30 x 30 cm

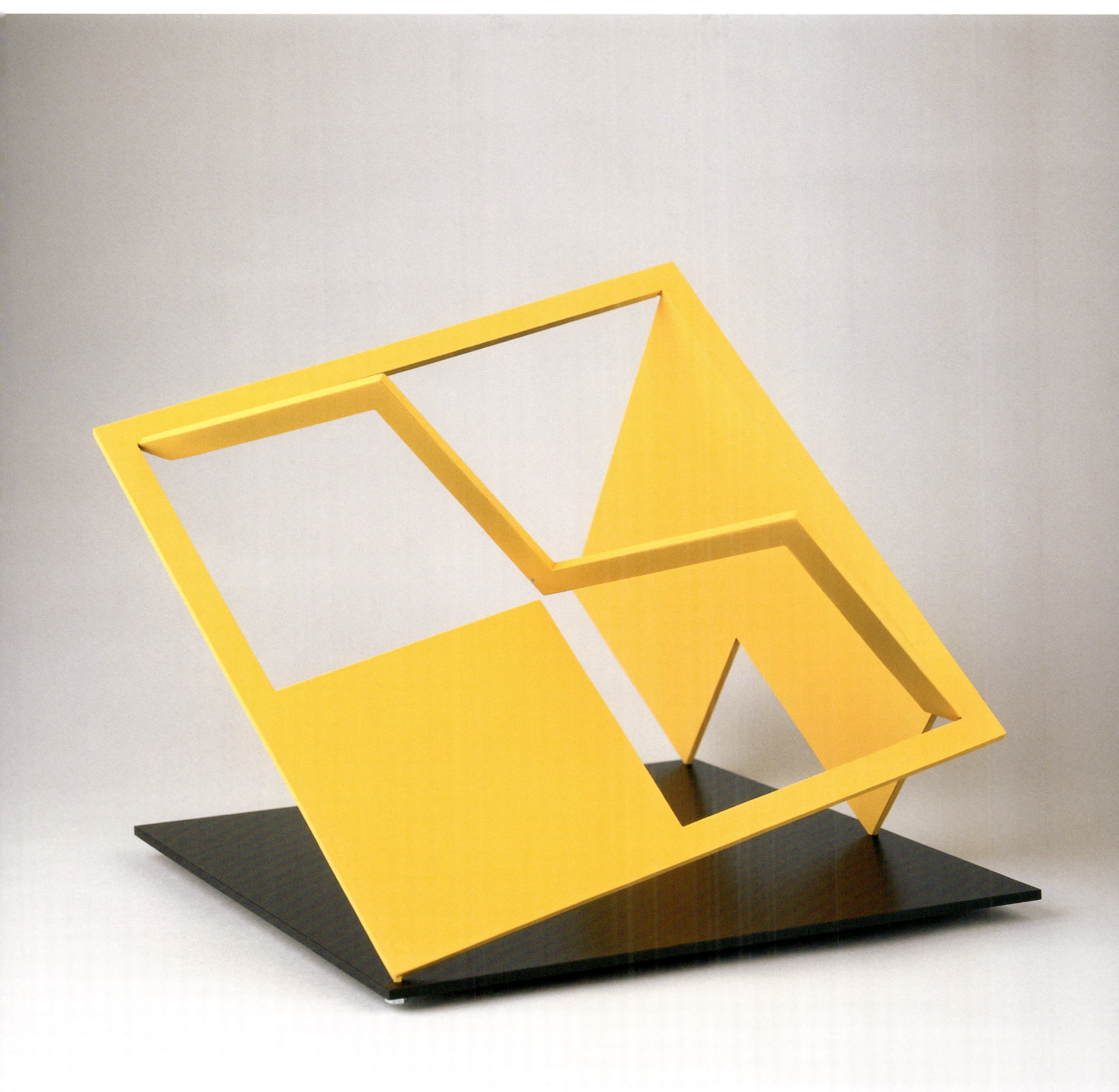

Folded Square Alphabet M

2004, painted steel
12 x 12 x 12 inches
30 x 30 x 30 cm

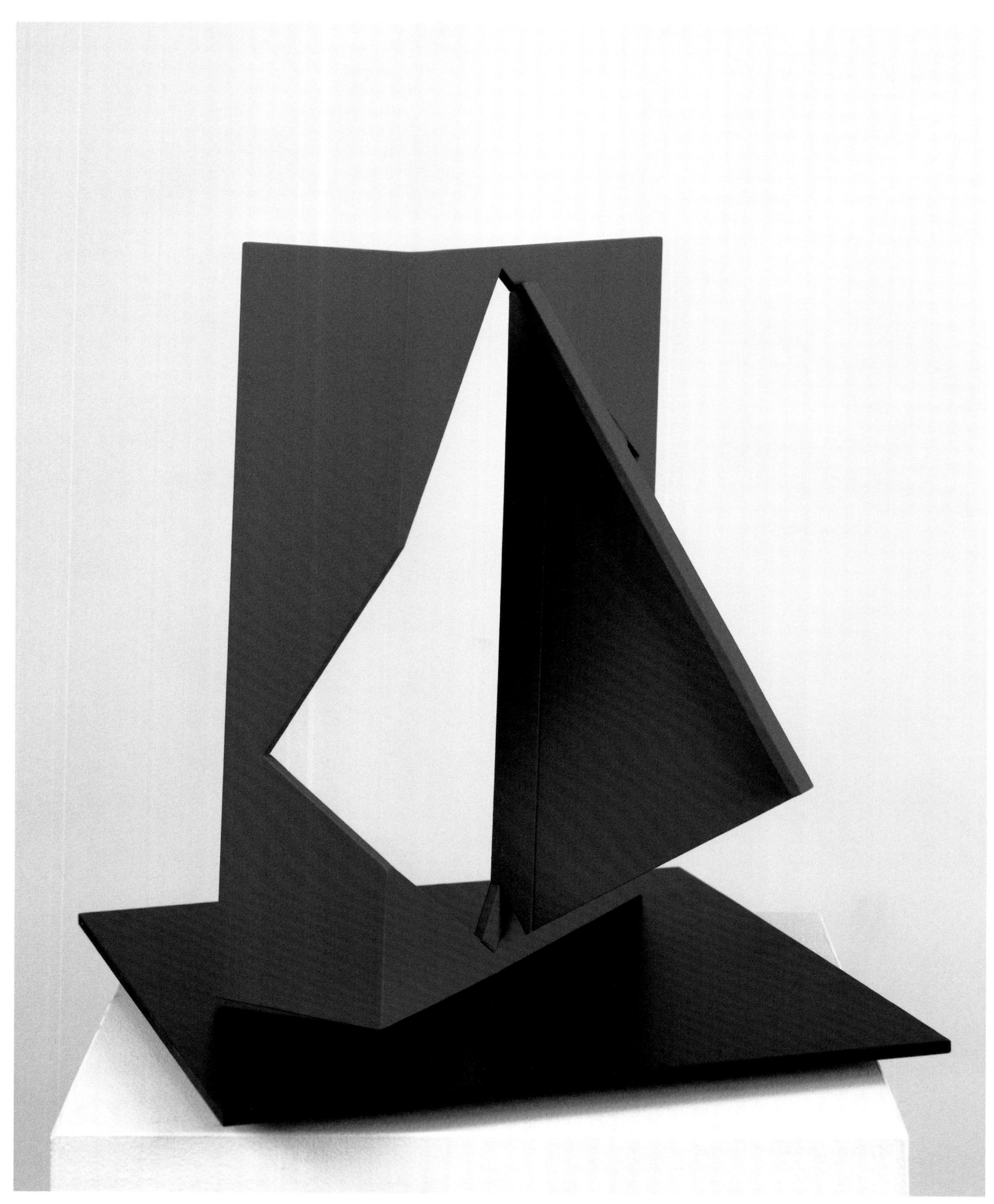

Folded Square Alphabet N

2004, painted steel
12 x 12 x 12 inches
30 x 30 x 30 cm

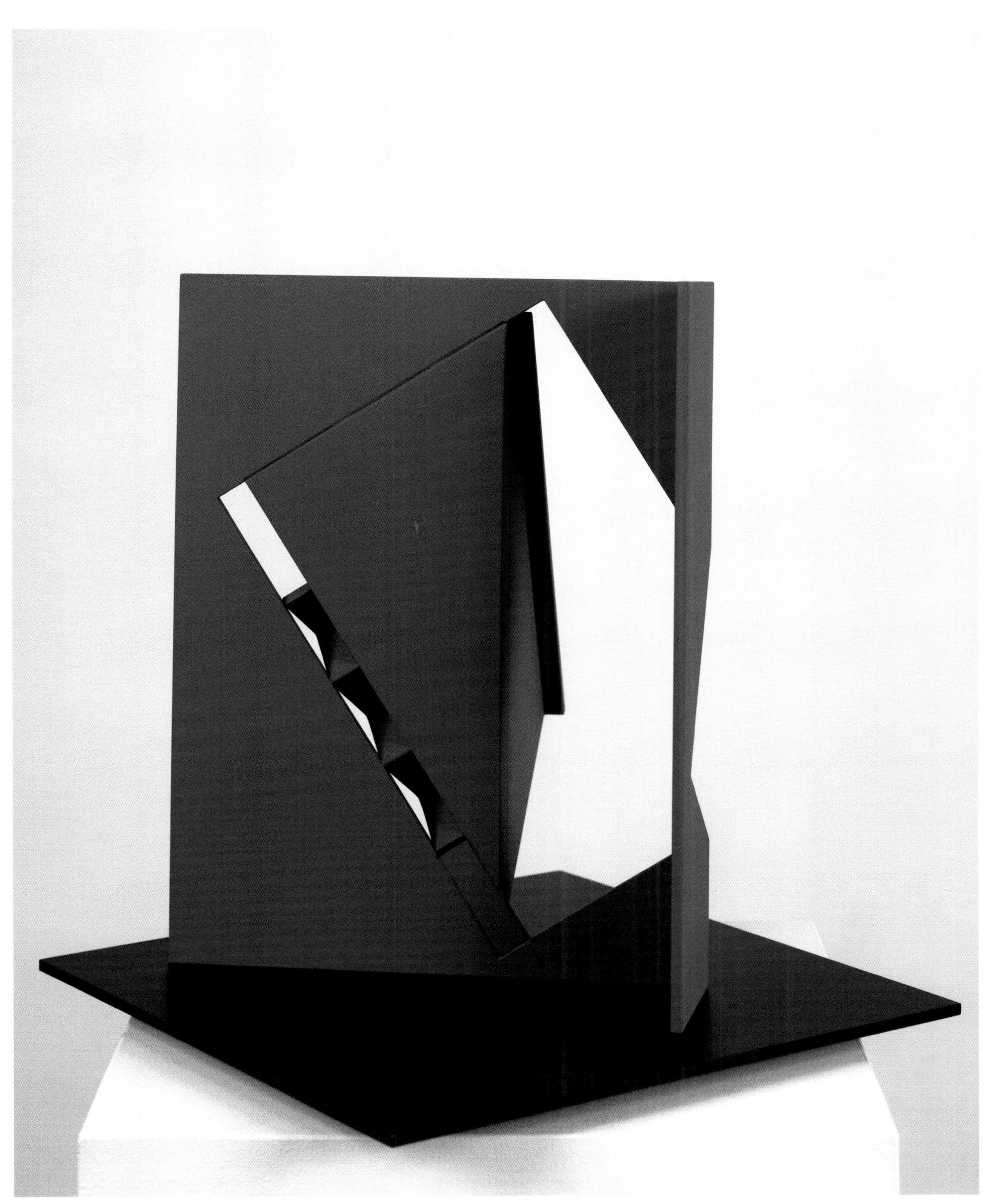

Folded Square Alphabet N

2004, painted steel
12 x 12 x 12 inches
30 x 30 x 30 cm

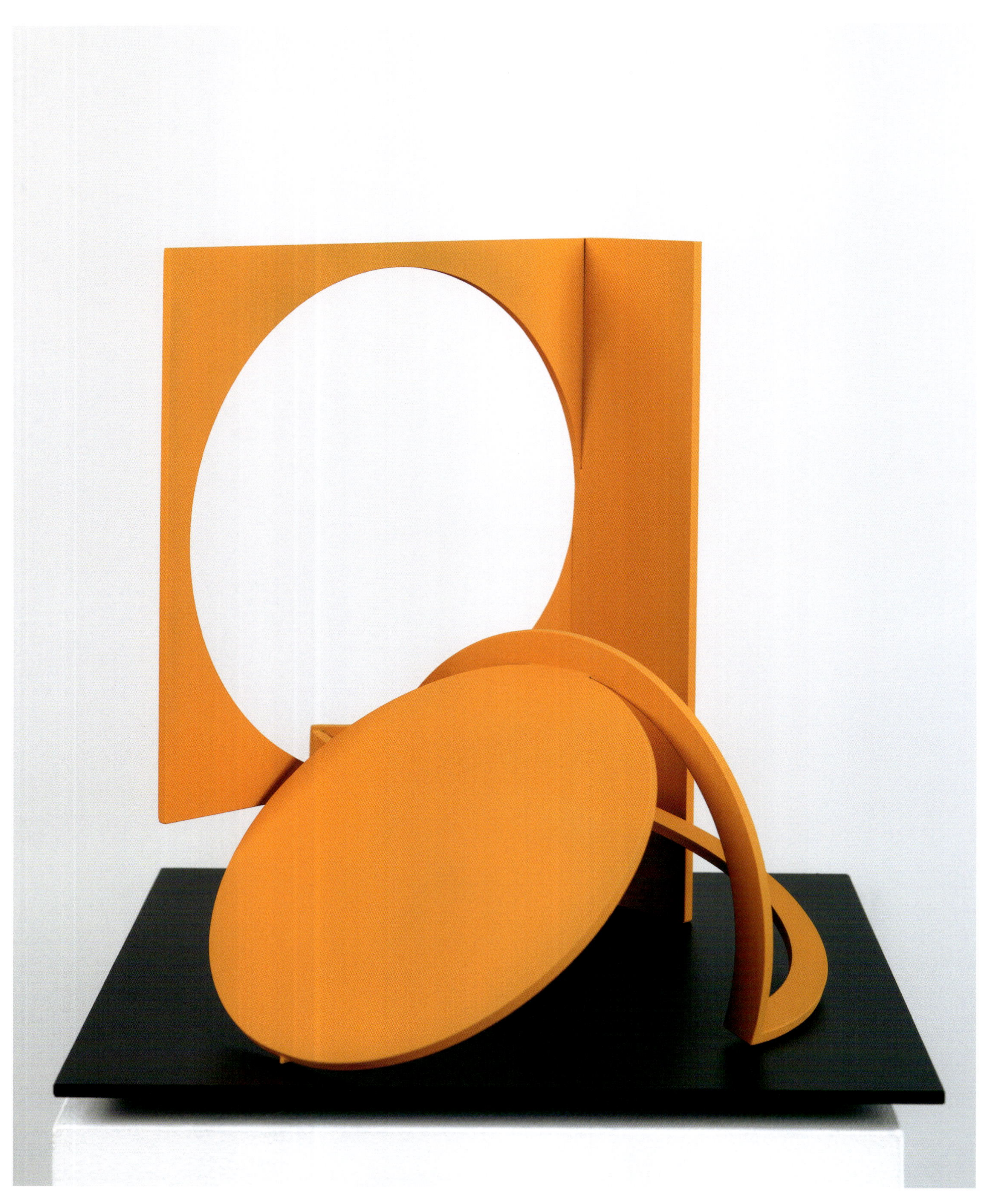

Folded Square Alphabet O

2004, painted steel
12 x 12 x 12 inches
30 x 30 x 30 cm

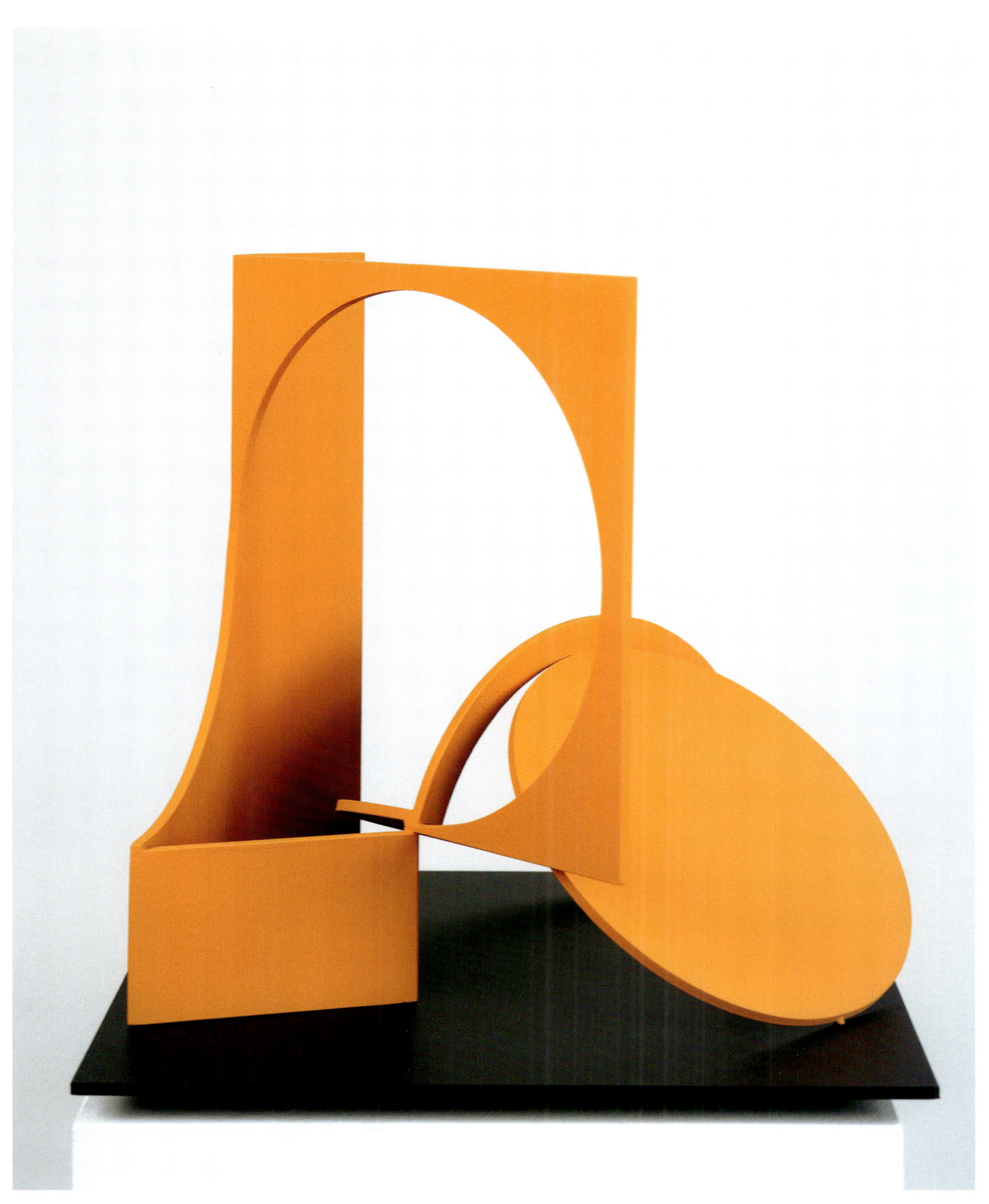

Folded Square Alphabet O

2004, painted steel
12 x 12 x 12 inches
30 x 30 x 30 cm

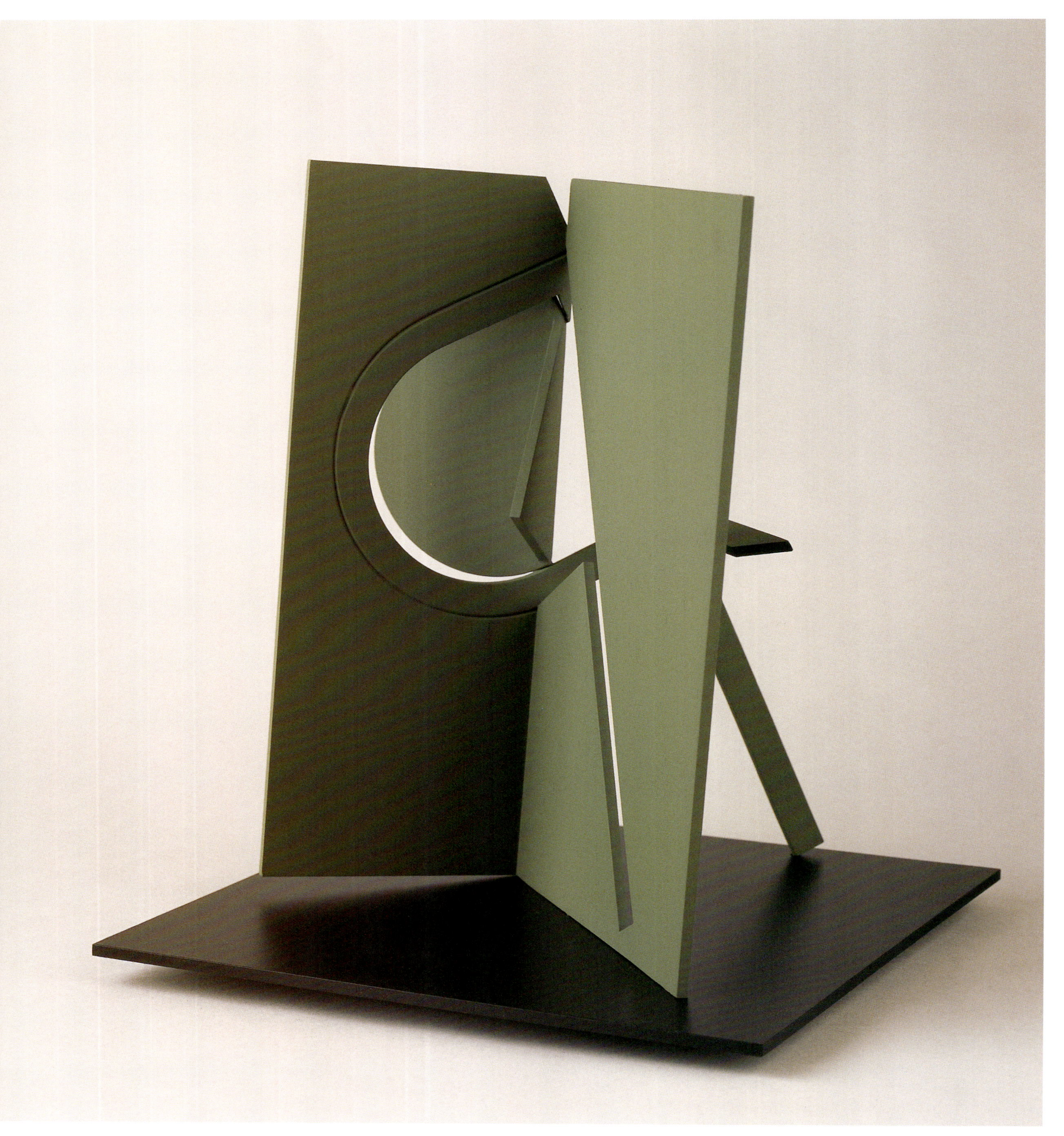

Folded Square Alphabet P

2004, painted steel
12 x 12 x 12 inches
30 x 30 x 30 cm

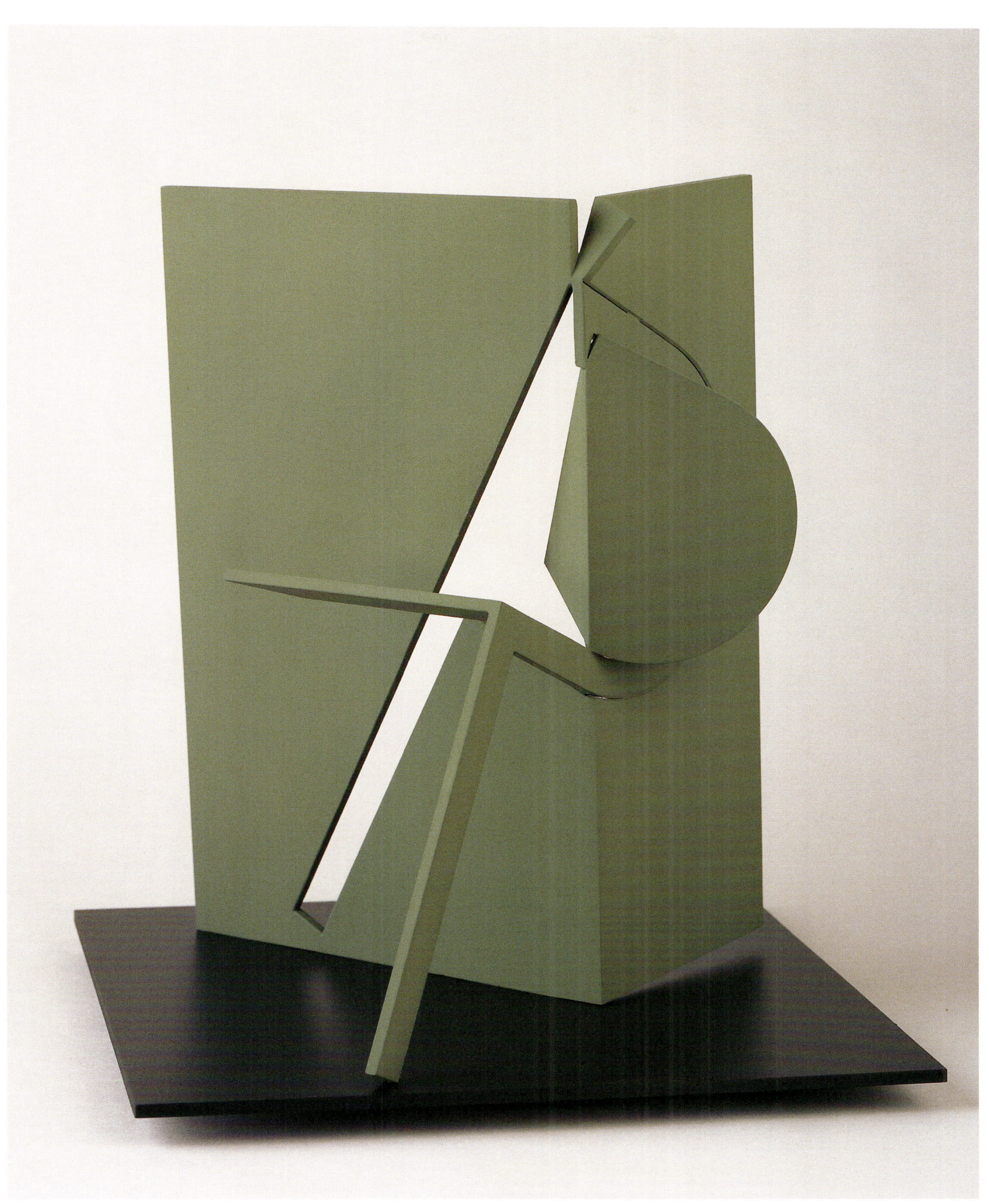

Folded Square Alphabet P

2004, painted steel
12 x 12 x 12 inches
30 x 30 x 30 cm

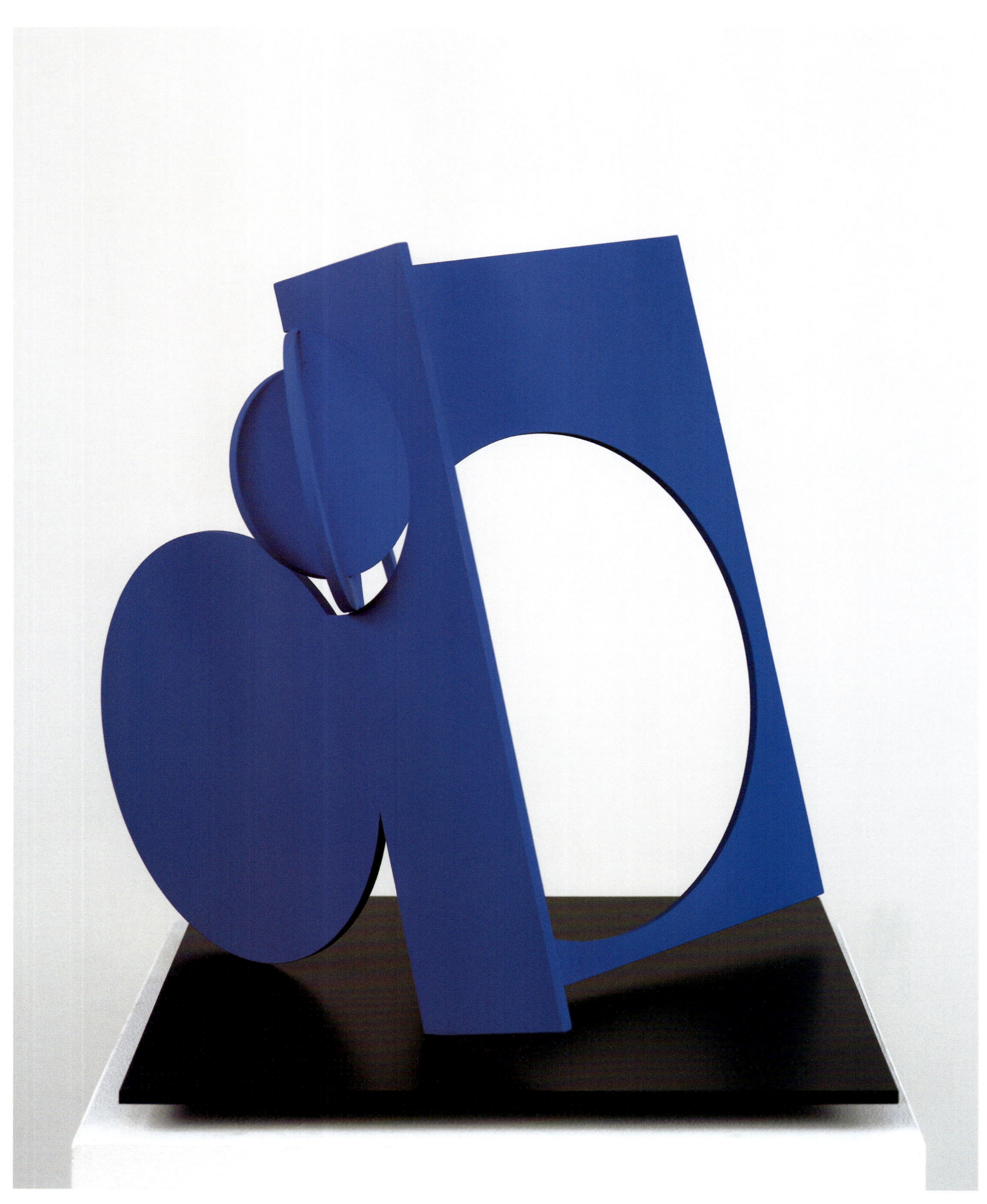

Folded Square Alphabet Q

2004, painted steel
12 x 12 x 12 inches
30 x 30 x 30 cm

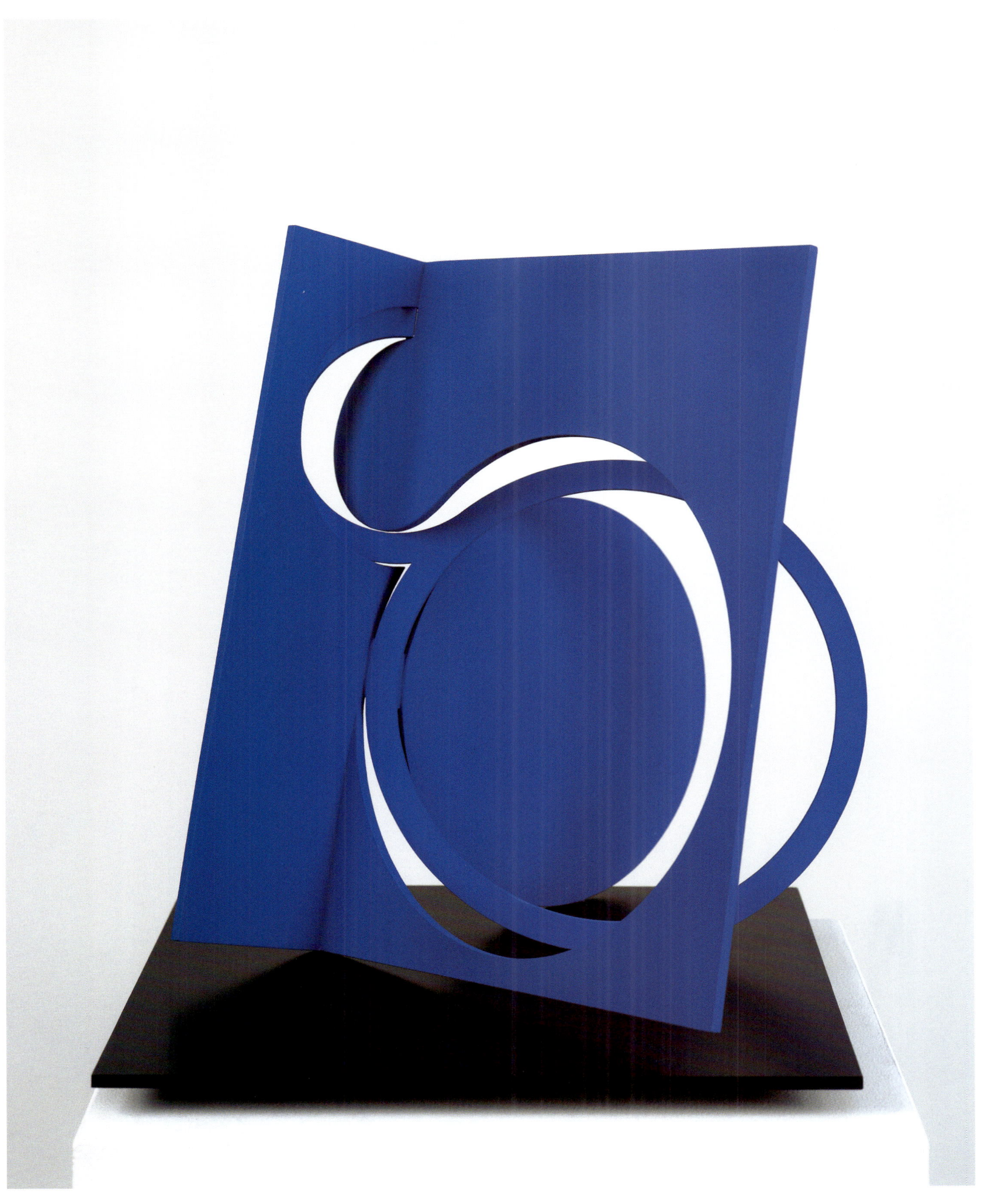

Folded Square Alphabet Q

2004, painted steel
12 x 12 x 12 inches
30 x 30 x 30 cm

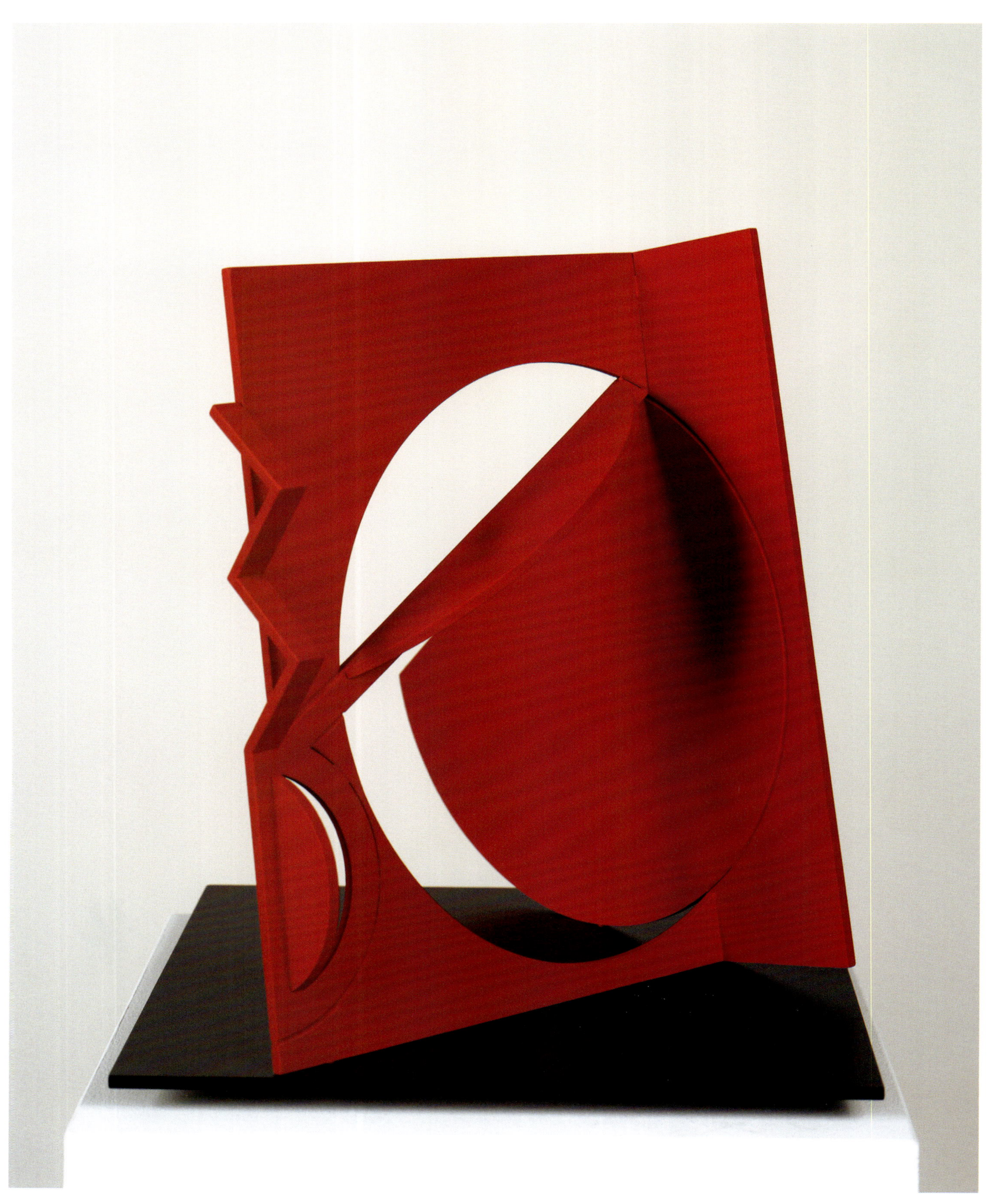

Folded Square Alphabet R

2004, painted steel
12 x 12 x 12 inches
30 x 30 x 30 cm

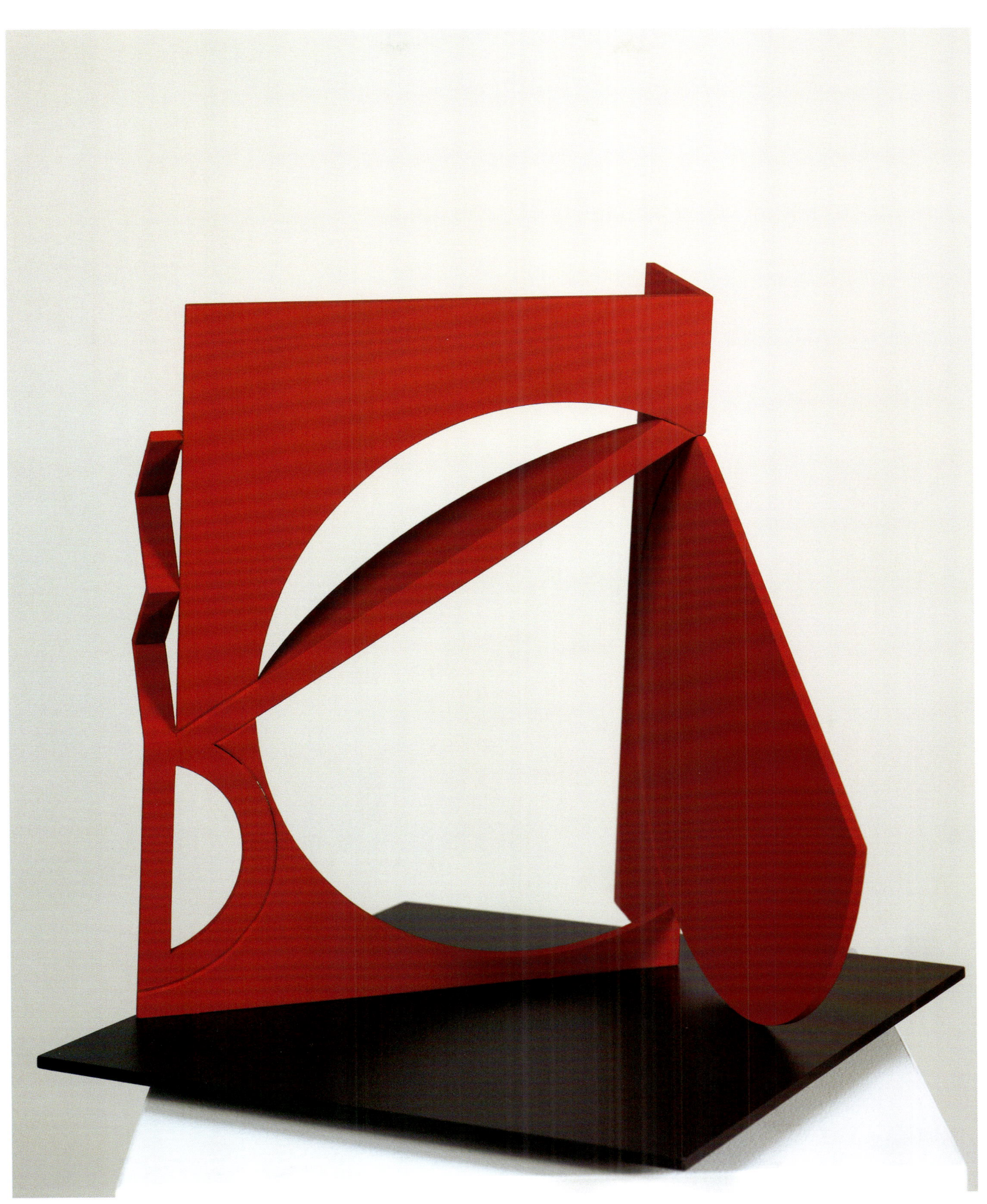

Folded Square Alphabet R

2004, painted steel
12 x 12 x 12 inches
30 x 30 x 30 cm

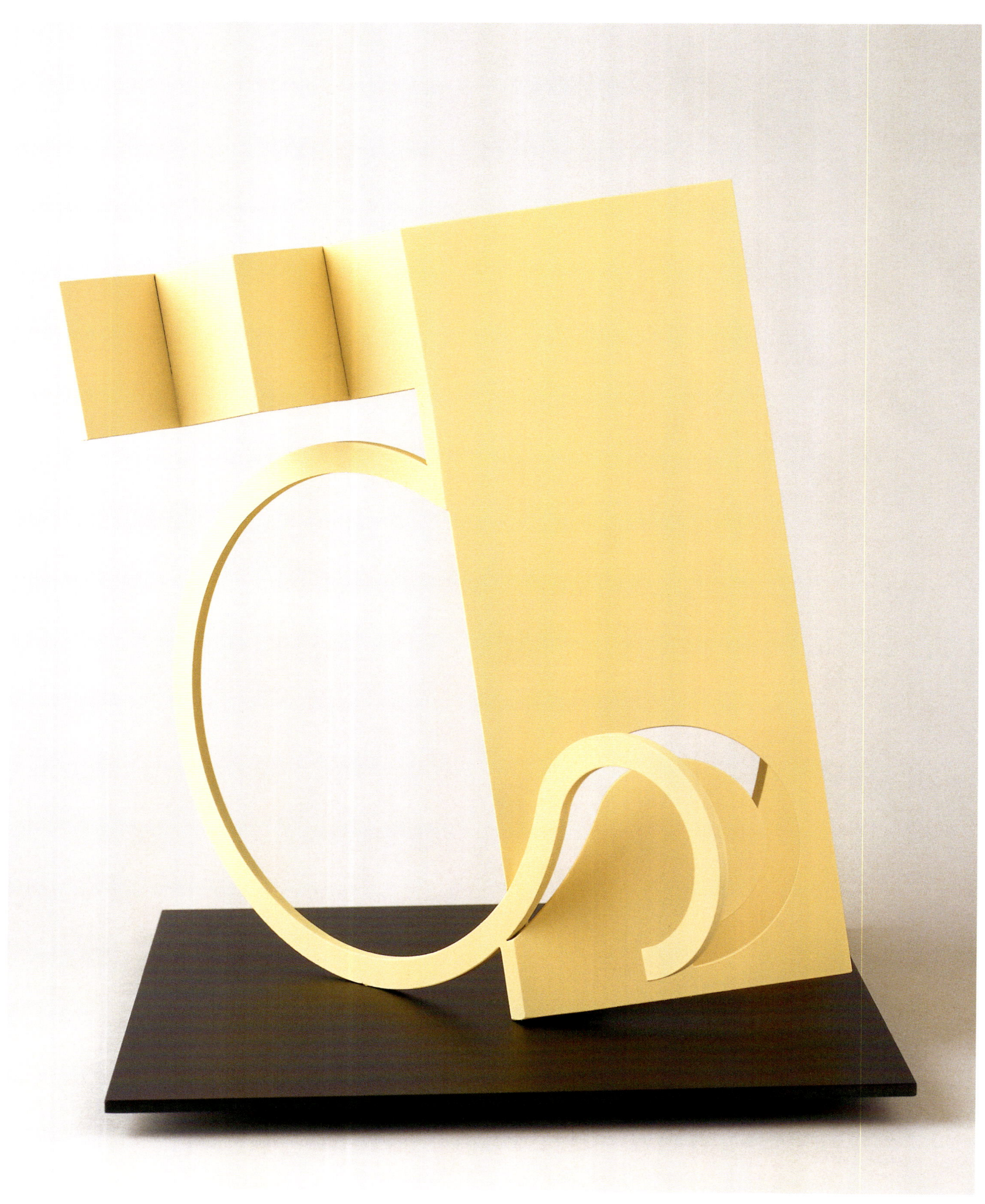

Folded Square Alphabet S

2004, painted steel
12 x 12 x 12 inches
30 x 30 x 30 cm

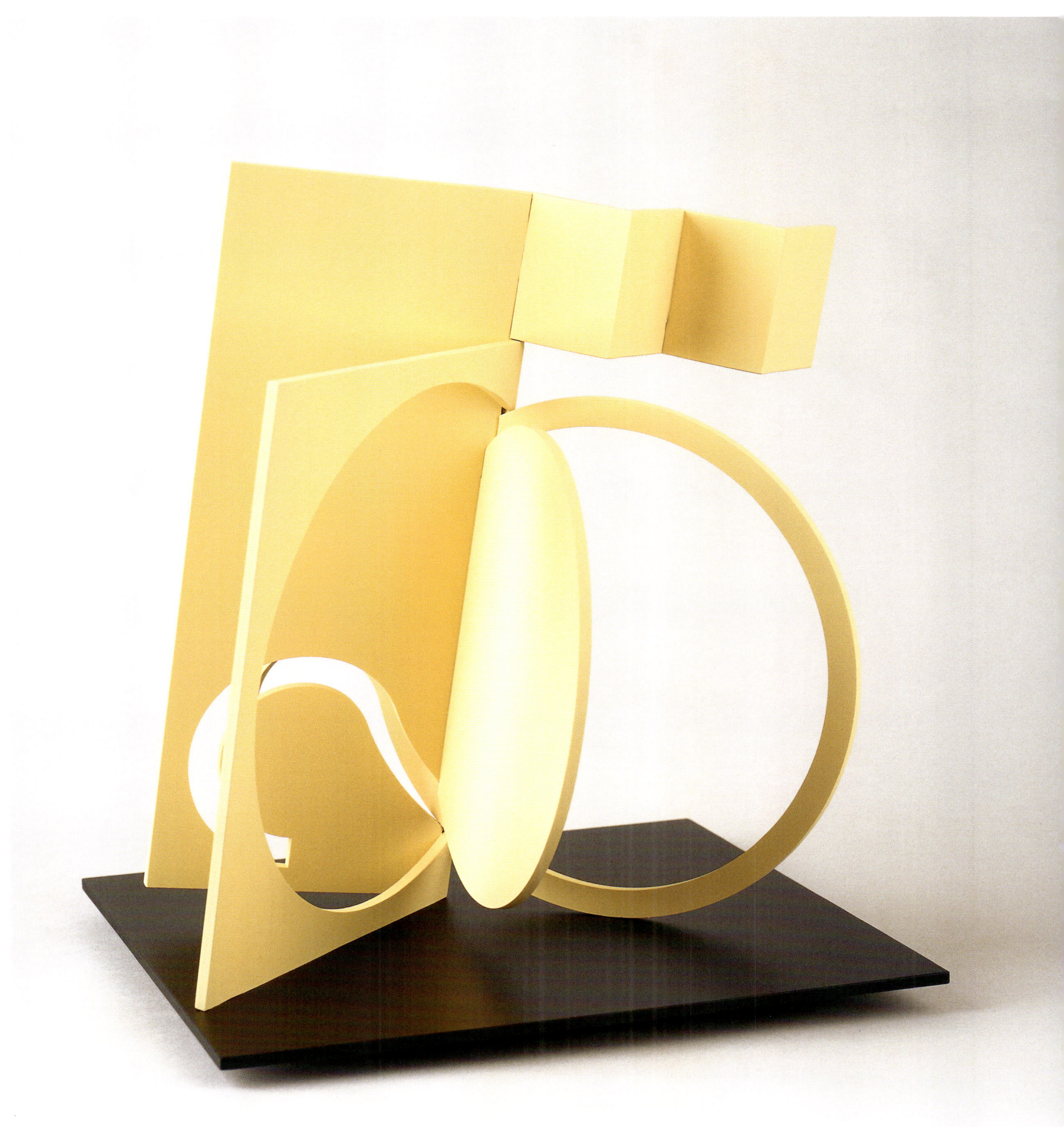

Folded Square Alphabet S

2004, painted steel
12 x 12 x 12 inches
30 x 30 x 30 cm

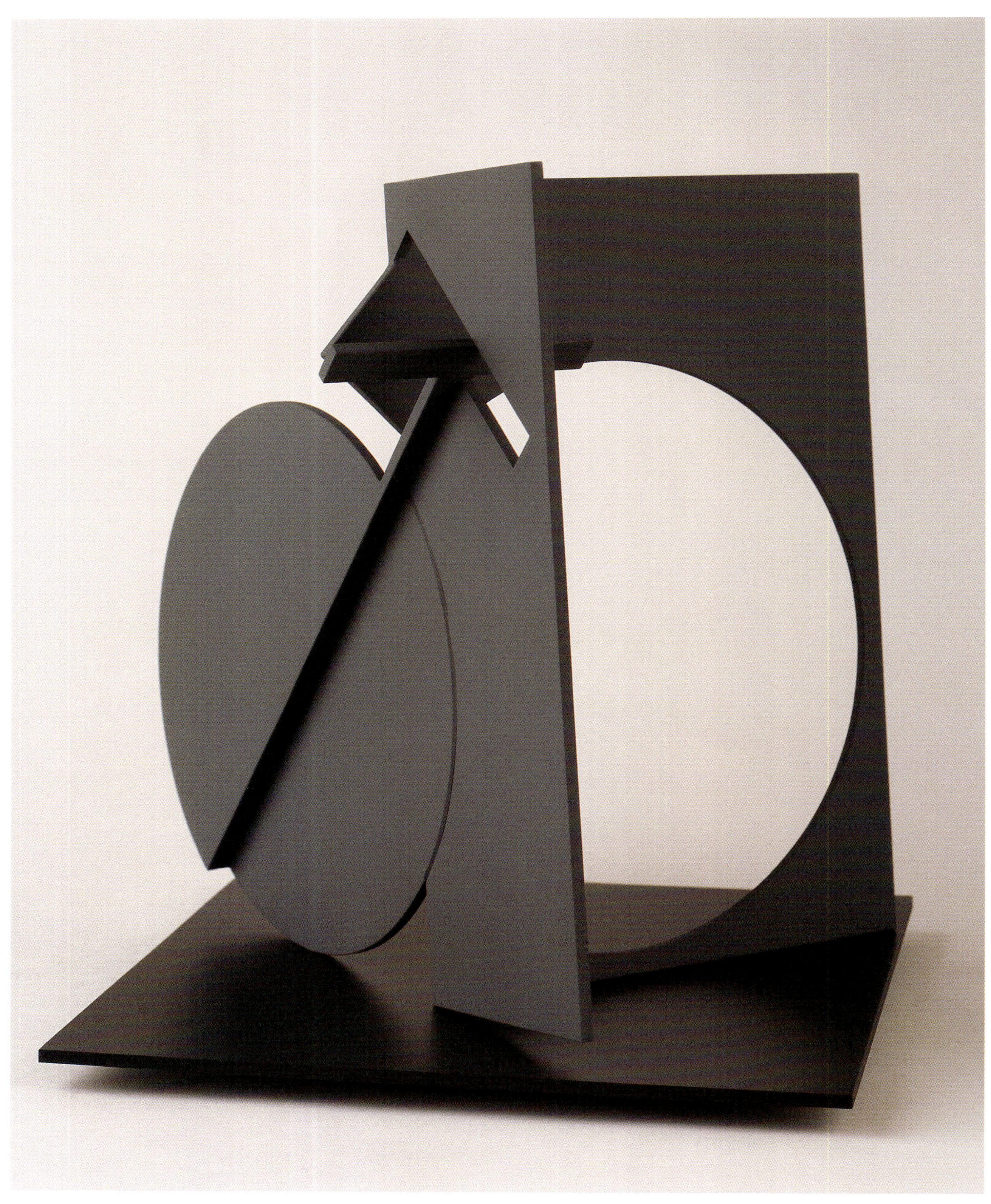

Folded Square Alphabet T

2004, painted steel
12 x 12 x 12 inches
30 x 30 x 30 cm

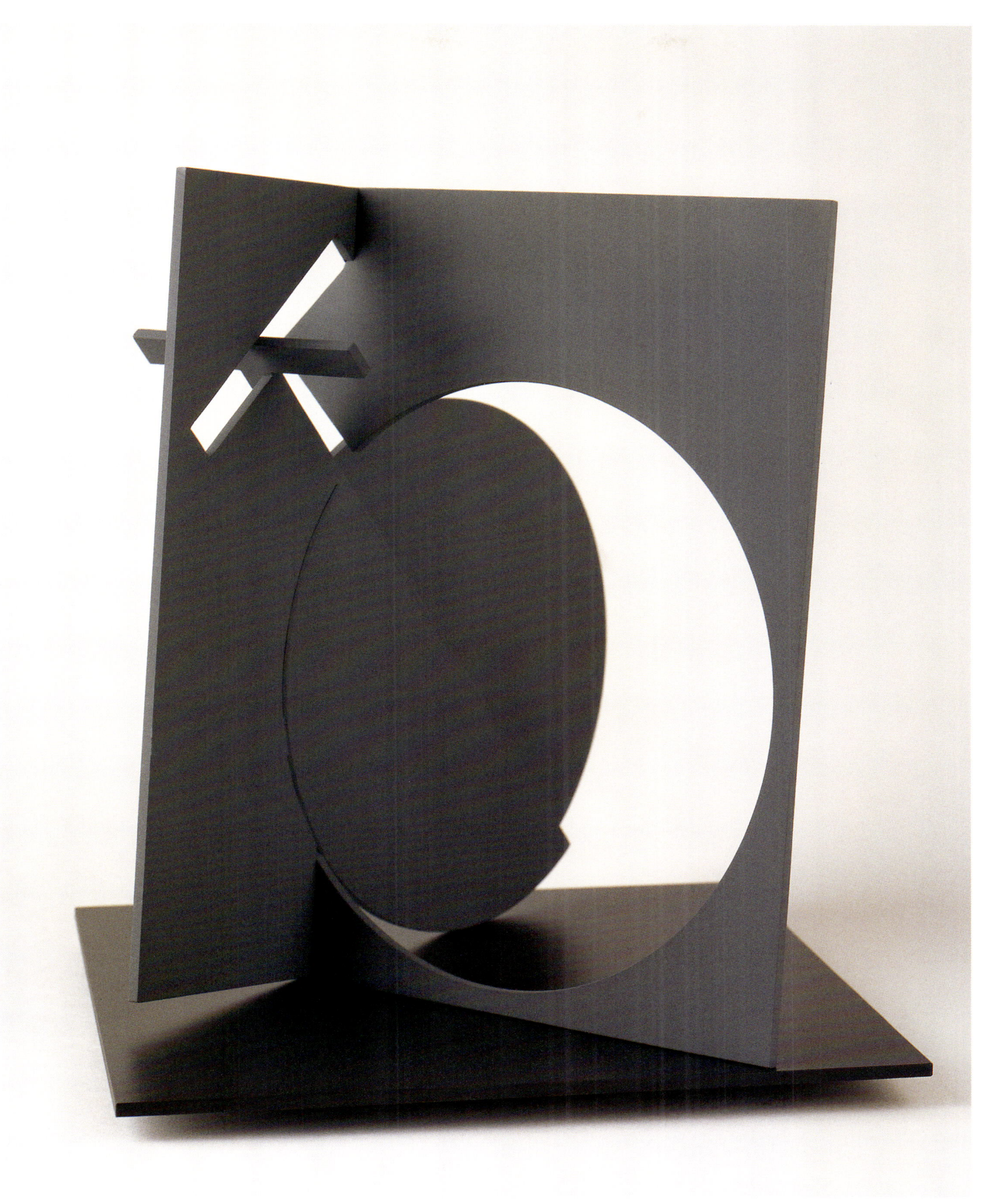

Folded Square Alphabet T

2004, painted steel
12 x 12 x 12 inches
30 x 30 x 30 cm

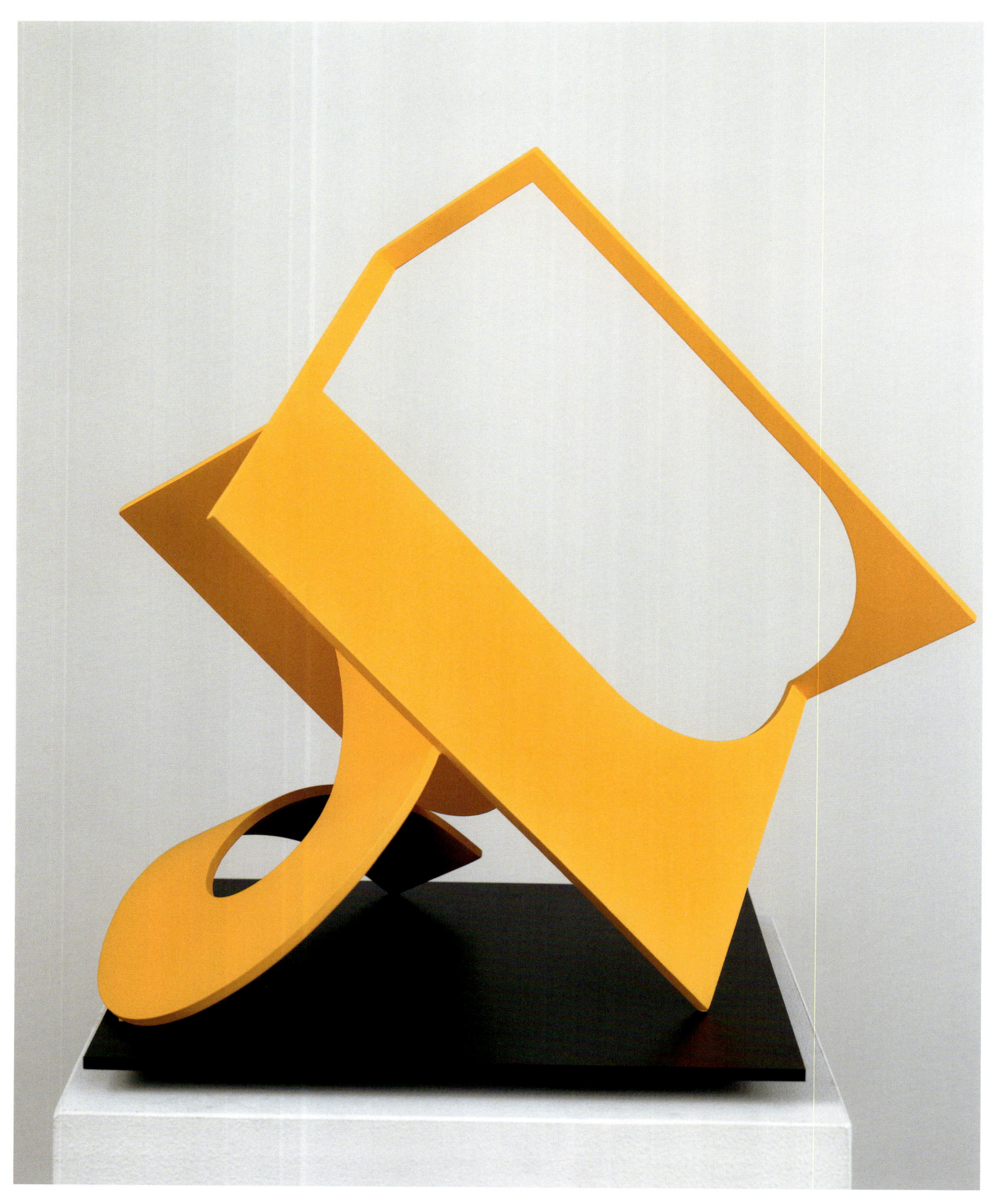

Folded Square Alphabet U

2004, painted steel
12 x 12 x 12 inches
30 x 30 x 30 cm

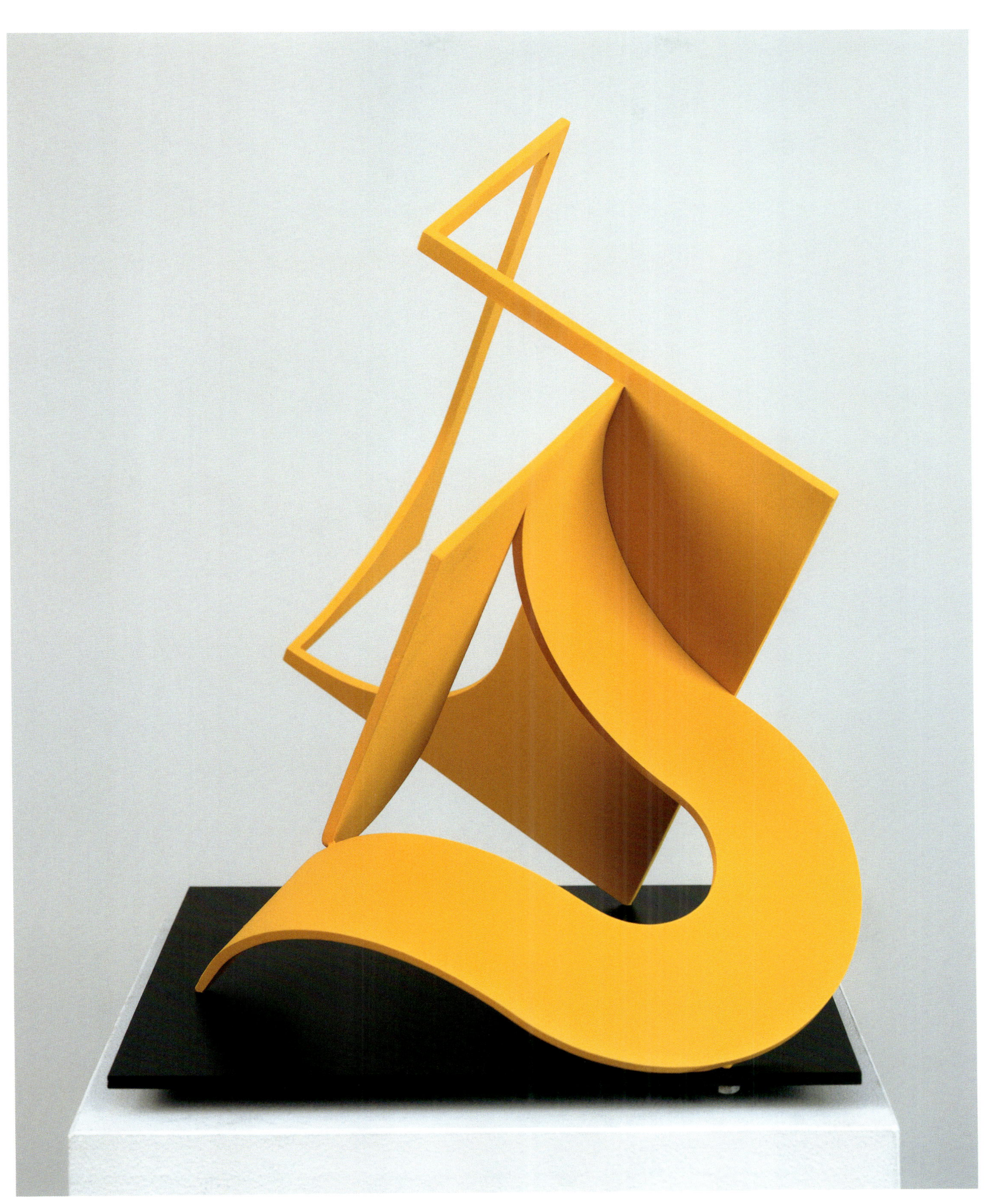

Folded Square Alphabet U

2004, painted steel
12 x 12 x 12 inches
30 x 30 x 30 cm

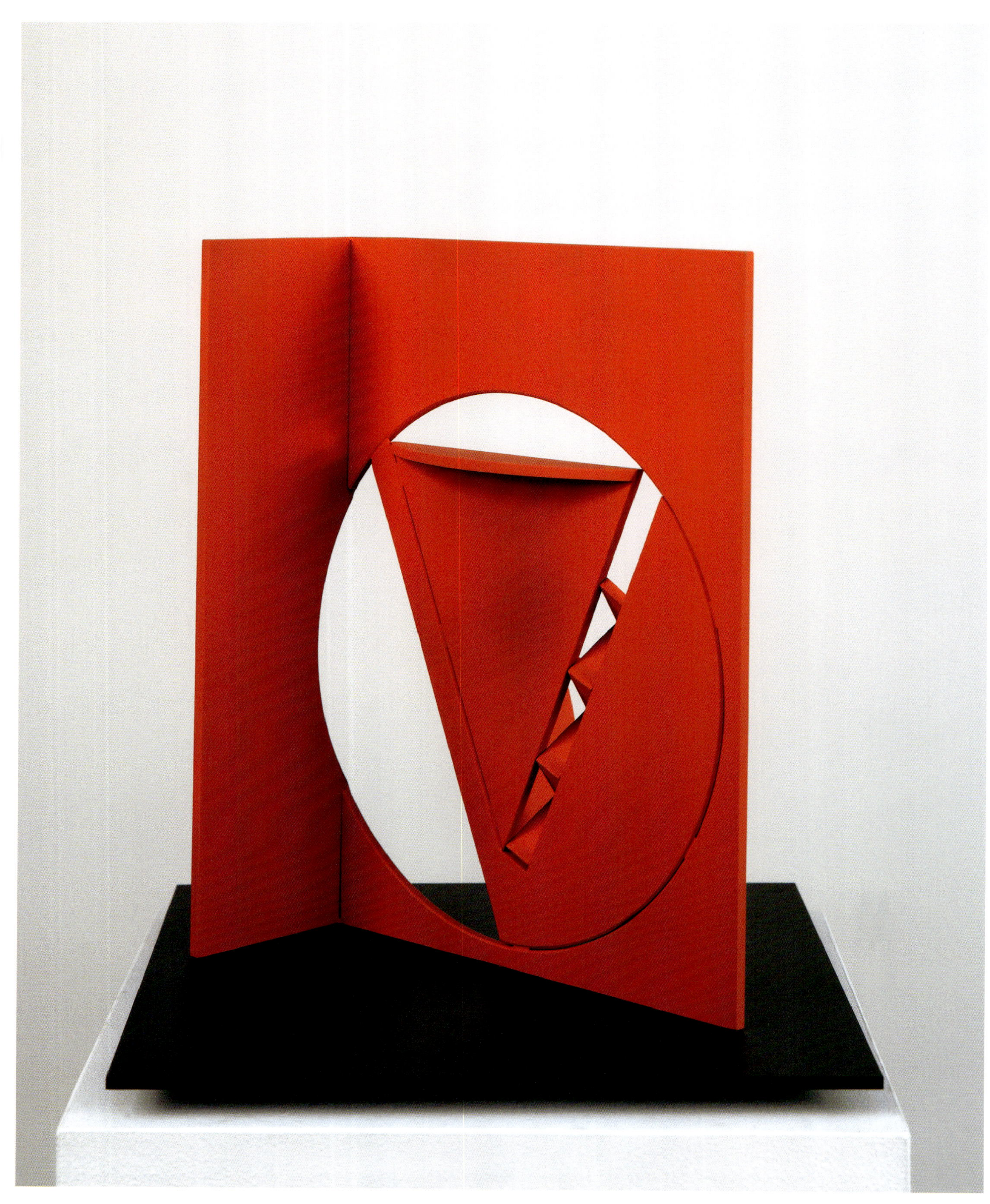

Folded Square Alphabet V

2004, painted steel
12 x 12 x 12 inches
30 x 30 x 30 cm

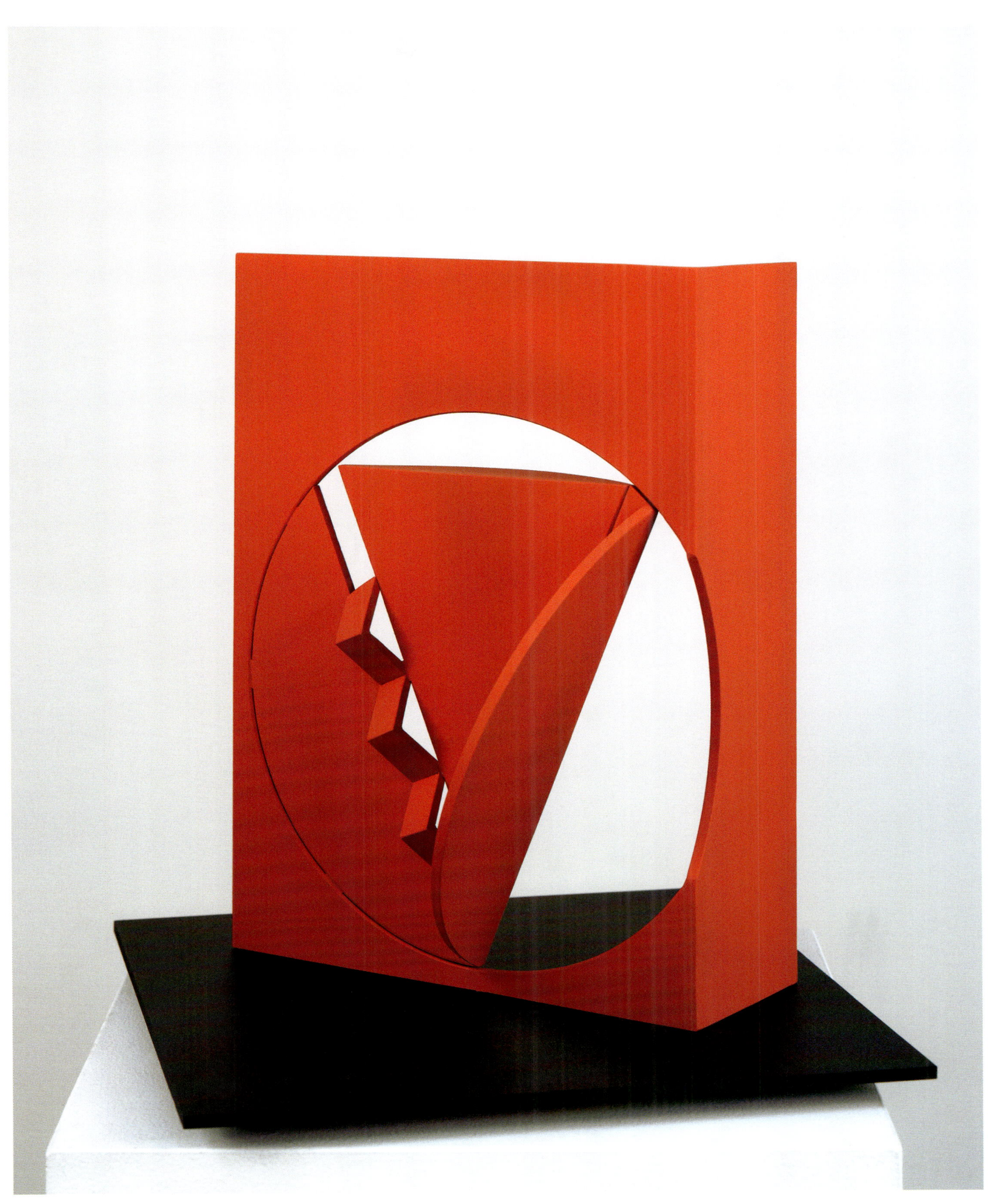

Folded Square Alphabet V

2004, painted steel
12 x 12 x 12 inches
30 x 30 x 30 cm

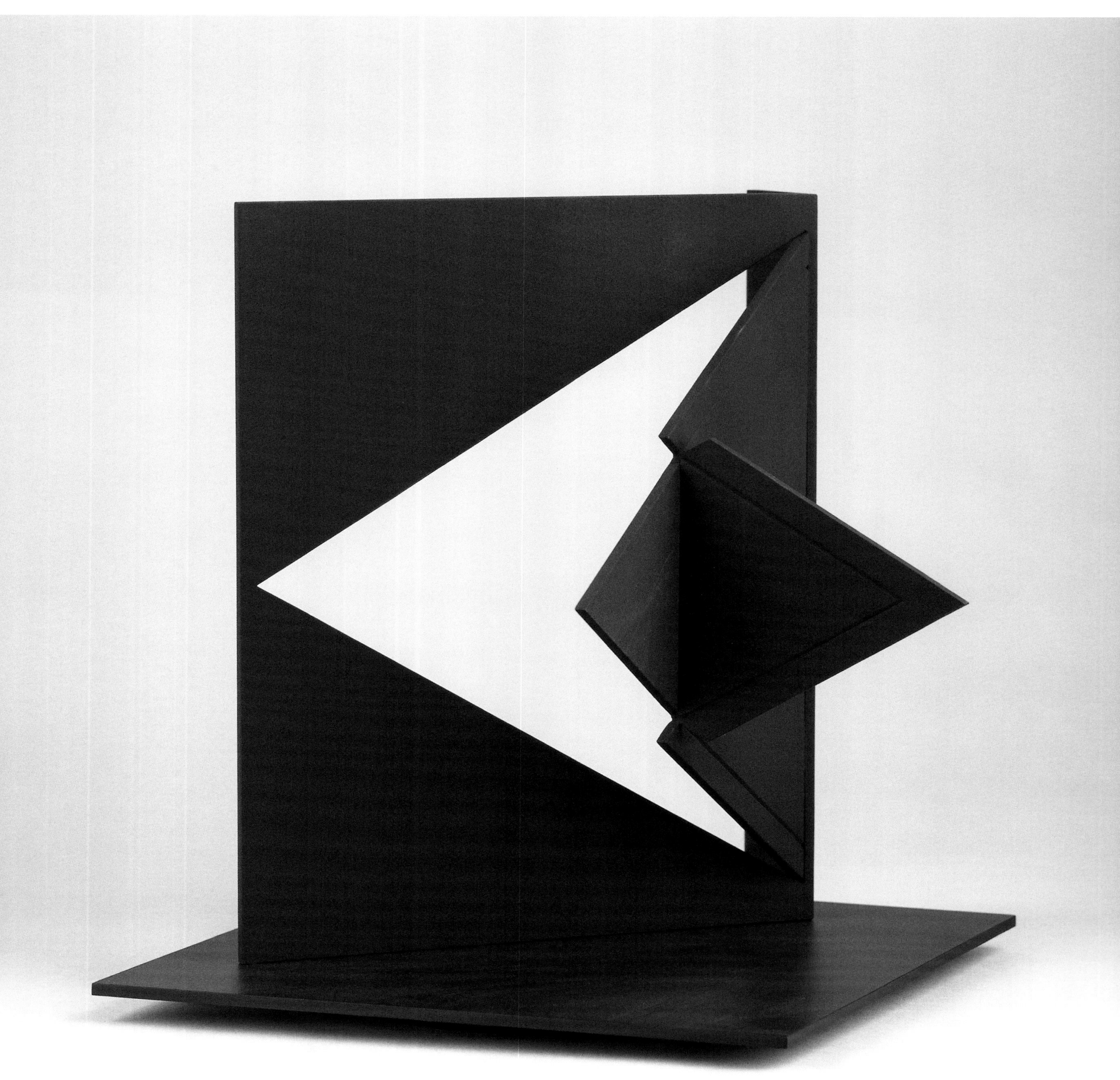

Folded Square Alphabet W

2004, painted steel
12 x 12 x 12 inches
30 x 30 x 30 cm

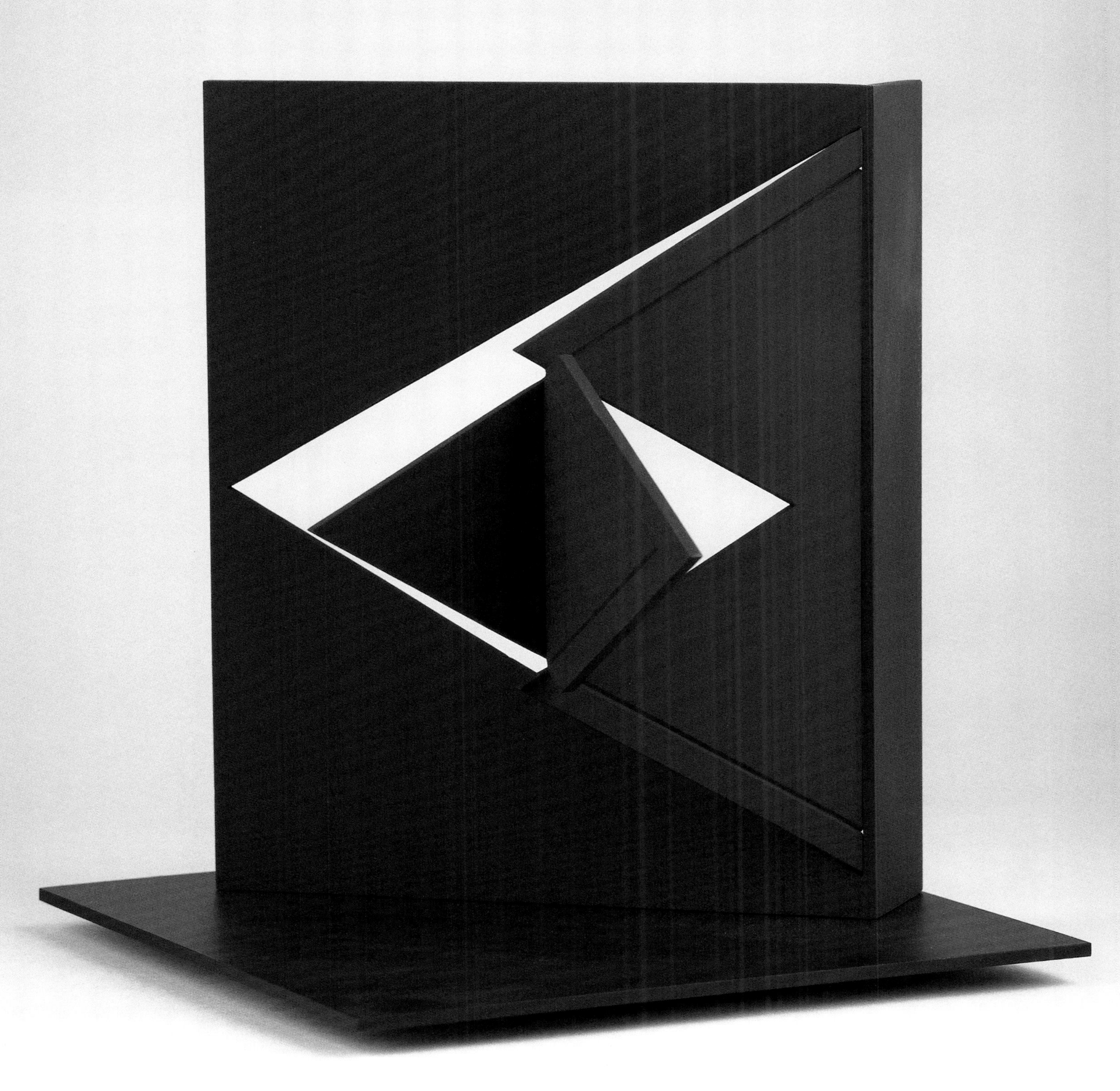

Folded Square Alphabet W

2004, painted steel
12 x 12 x 12 inches
30 x 30 x 30 cm

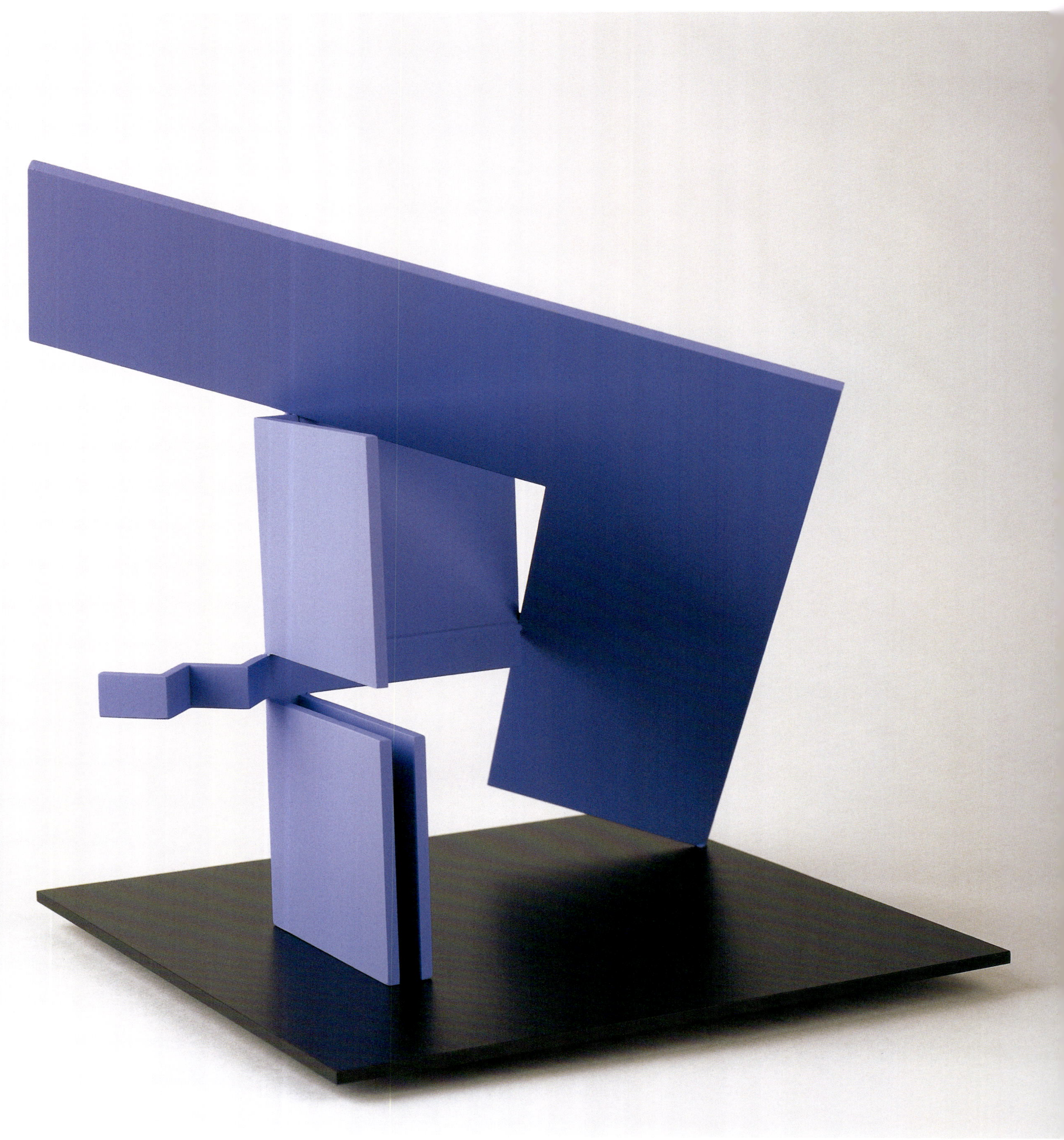

Folded Square Alphabet X

2004, painted steel
12 x 12 x 12 inches
30 x 30 x 30 cm

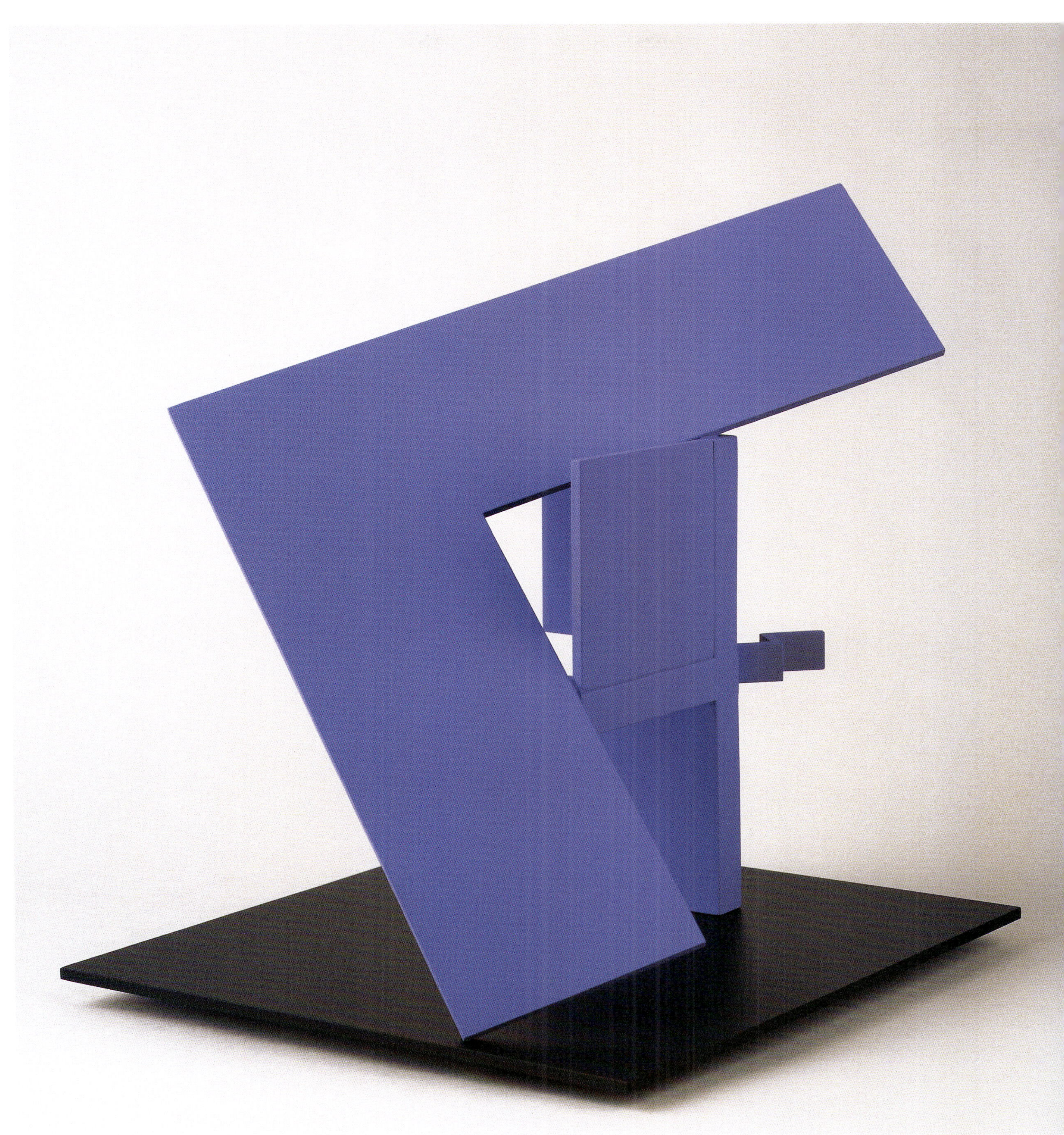

Folded Square Alphabet X

2004, painted steel
12 x 12 x 12 inches
30 x 30 x 30 cm

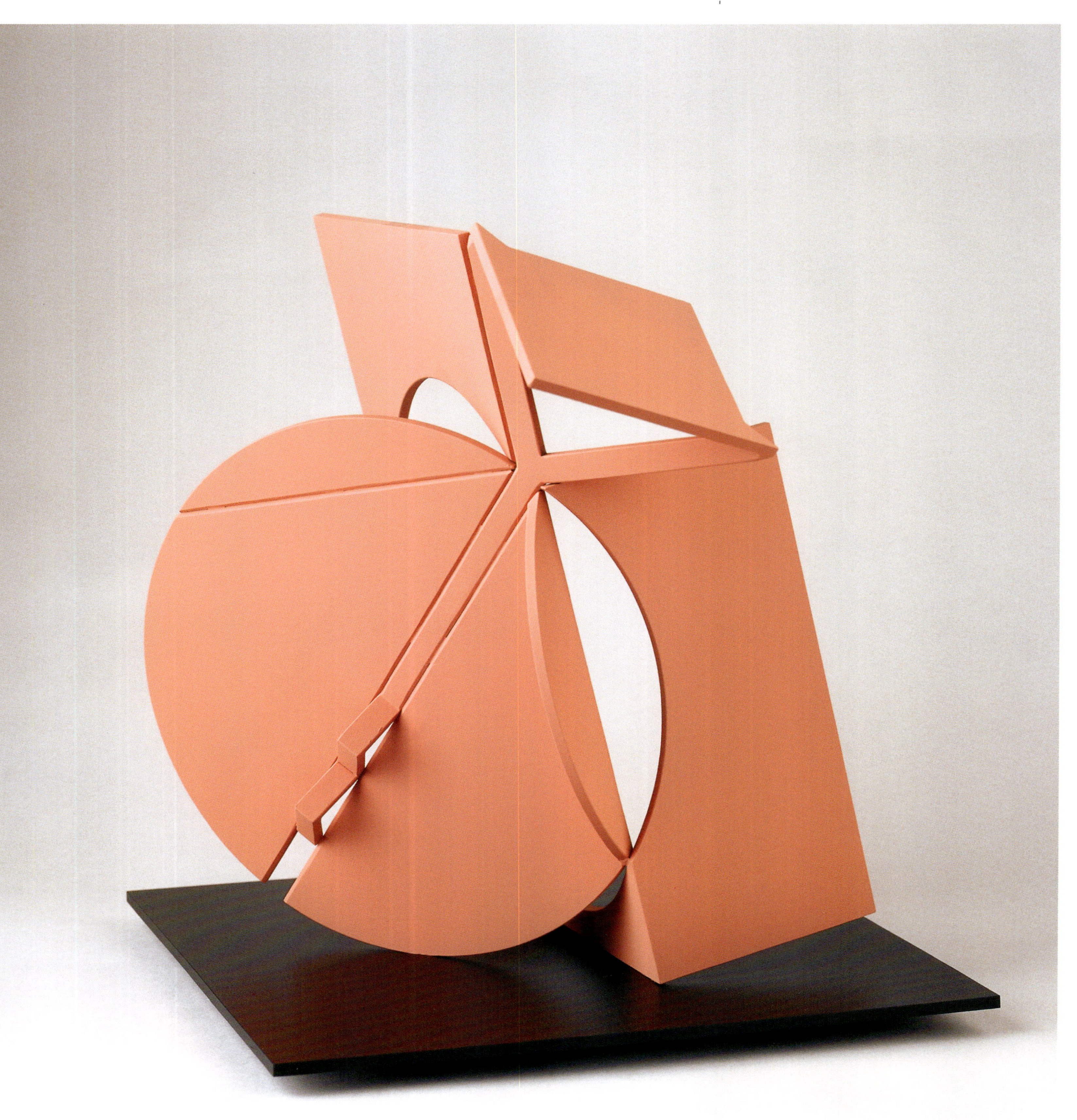

Folded Square Alphabet Y

2004, painted steel
12 x 12 x 12 inches
30 x 30 x 30 cm

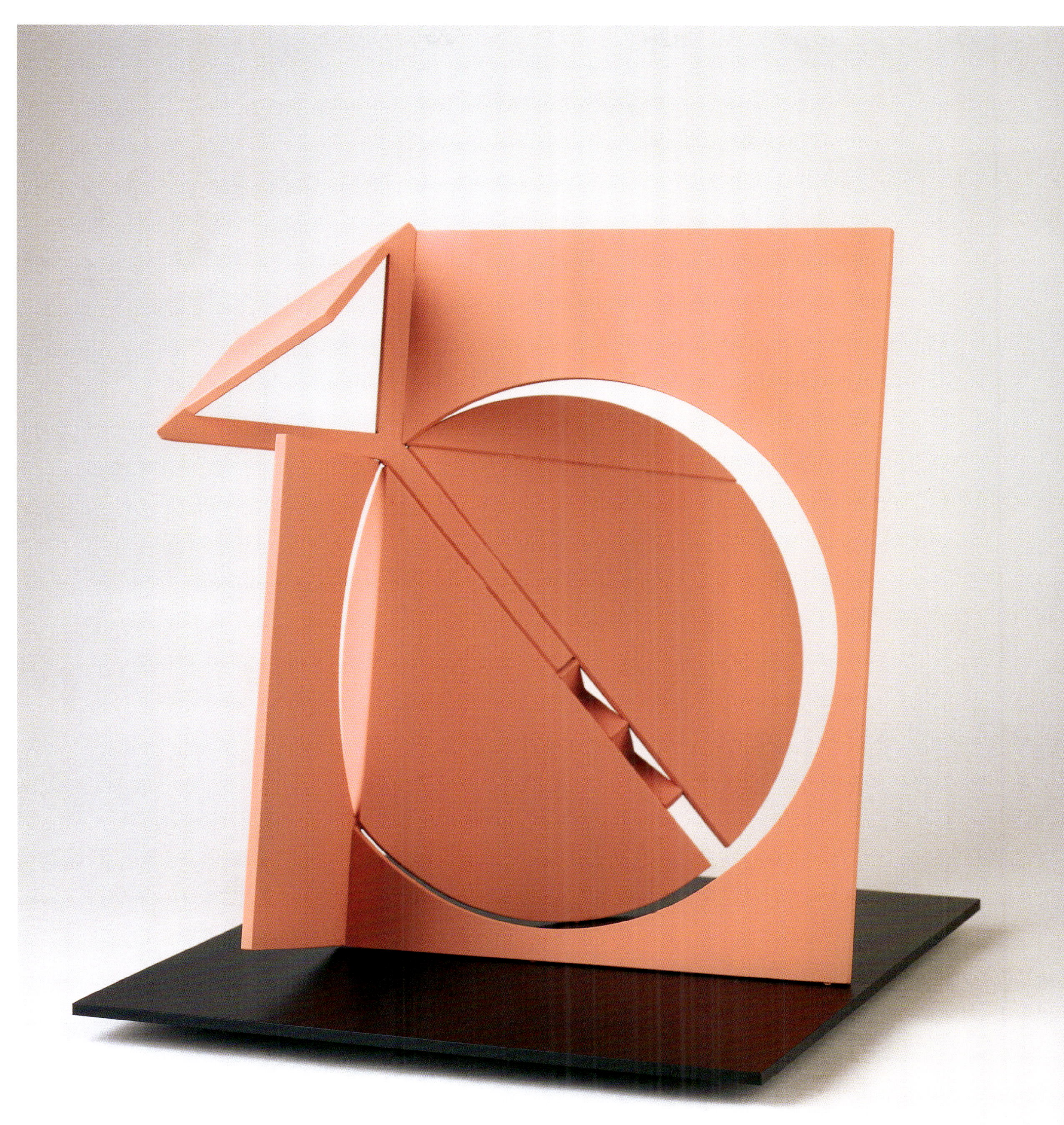

Folded Square Alphabet Y

2004, painted steel
12 x 12 x 12 inches
30 x 30 x 30 cm

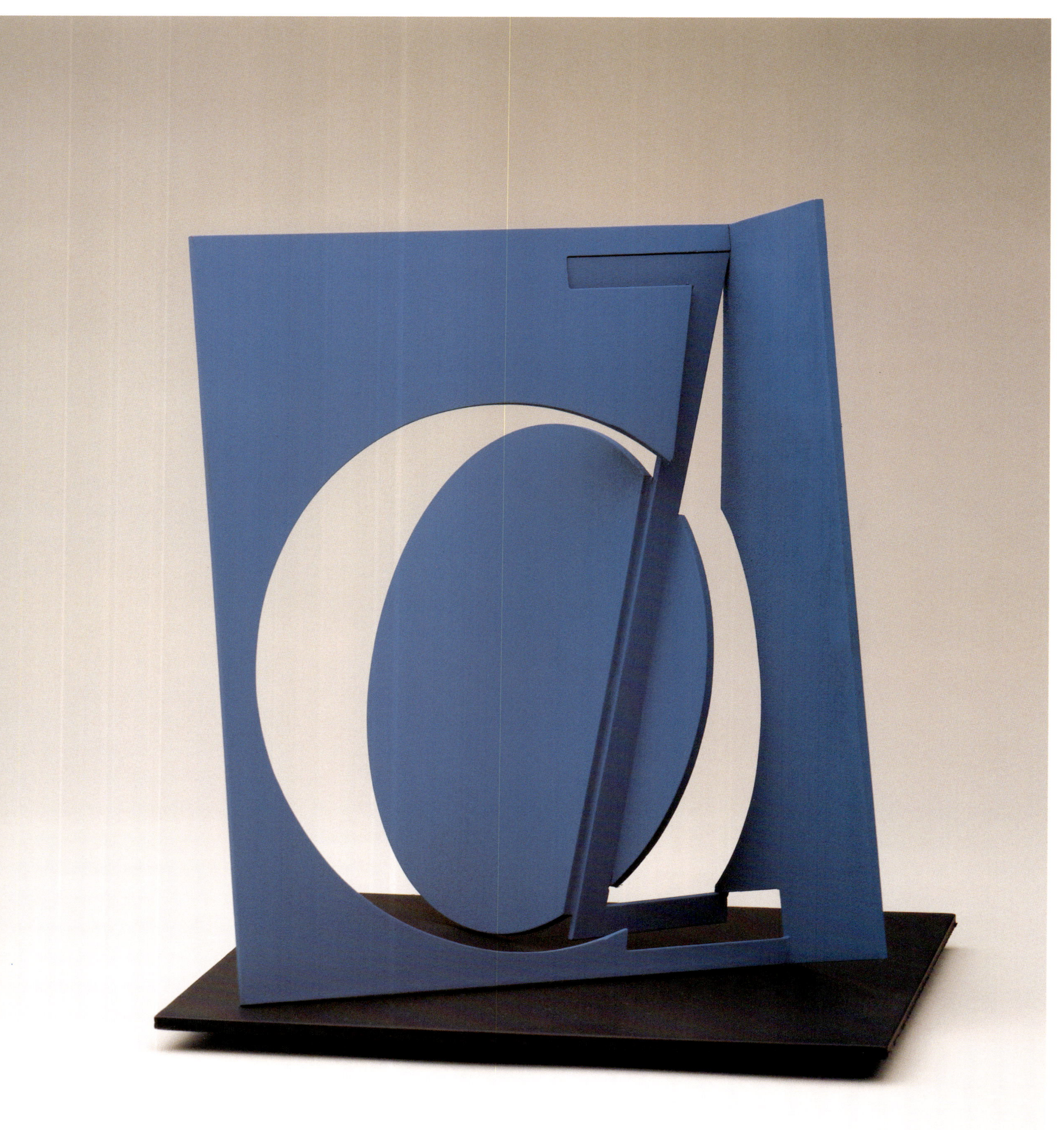

Folded Square Alphabet Z

1986, painted steel
8 x 8 x 8 inches
20 x 20 x 20 cm

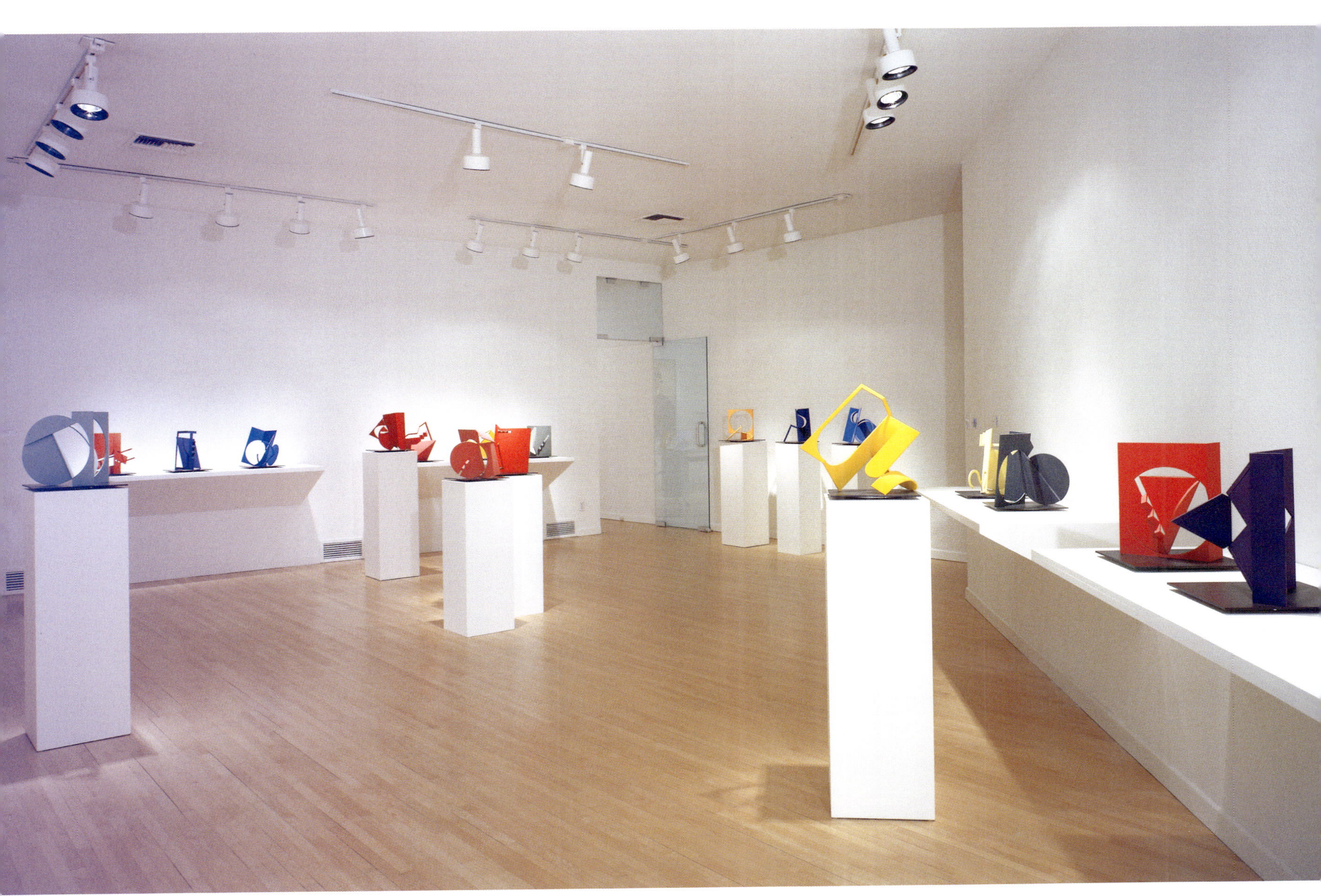

Folded Square Alphabet and Numericals

Installation view of Benton solo exhibition at Riva Yares Gallery, Scottsdale, Arizona 2006

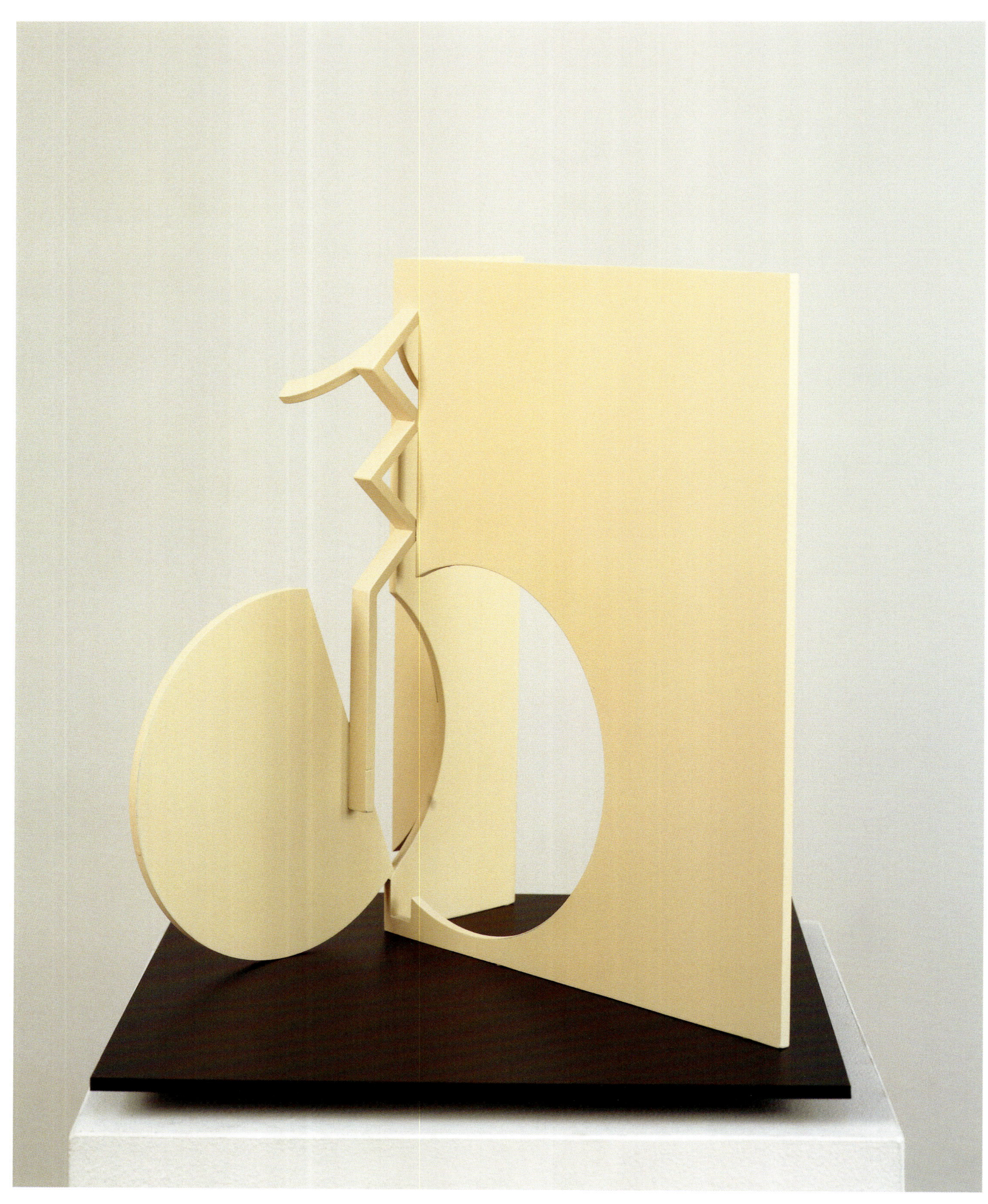

Folded Square Numerical 1

2004, painted steel
12 x 12 x 12 inches
30 x 30 x 30 cm

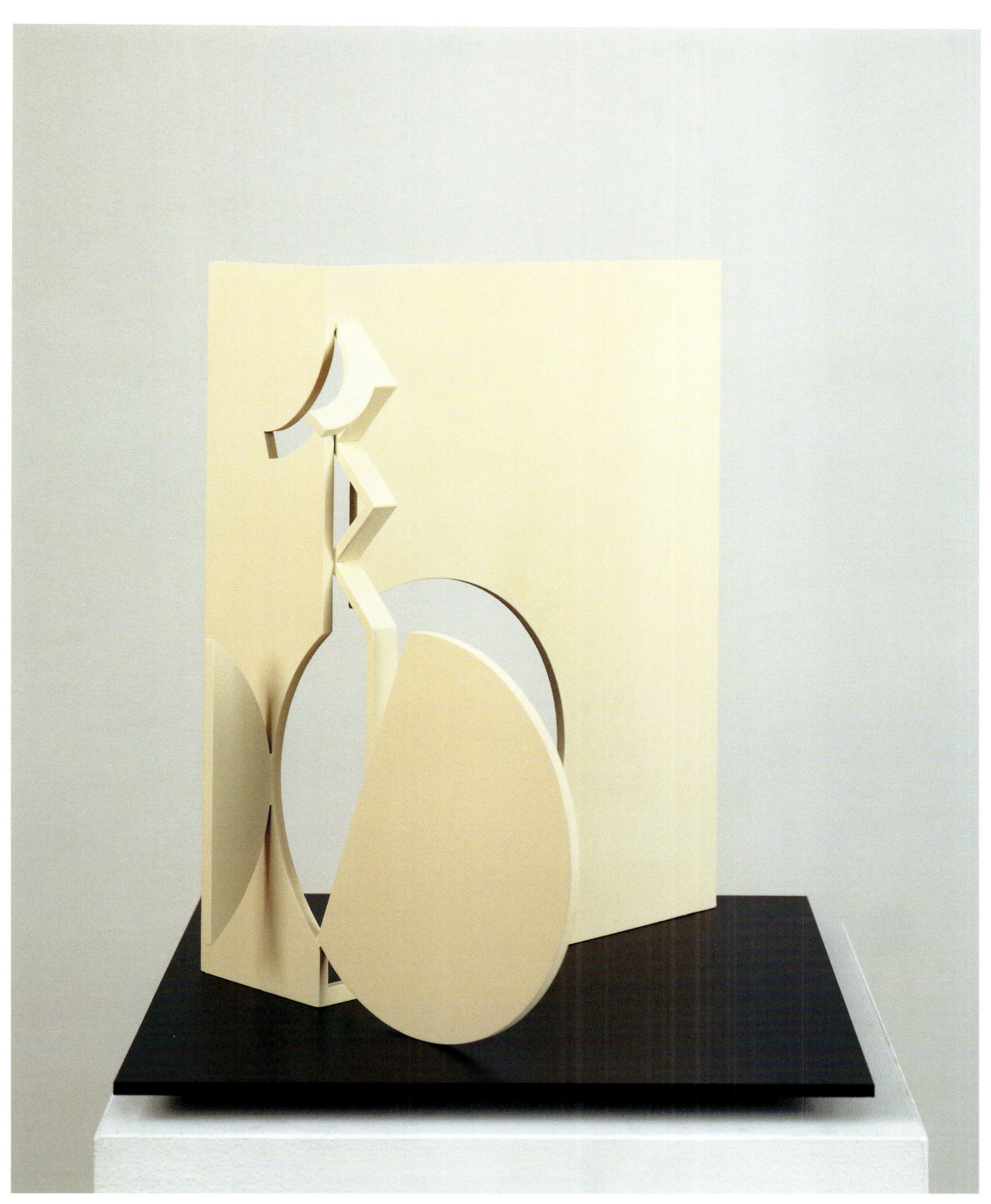

Folded Square Numerical 1

2004, painted steel
12 x 12 x 12 inches
30 x 30 x 30 cm

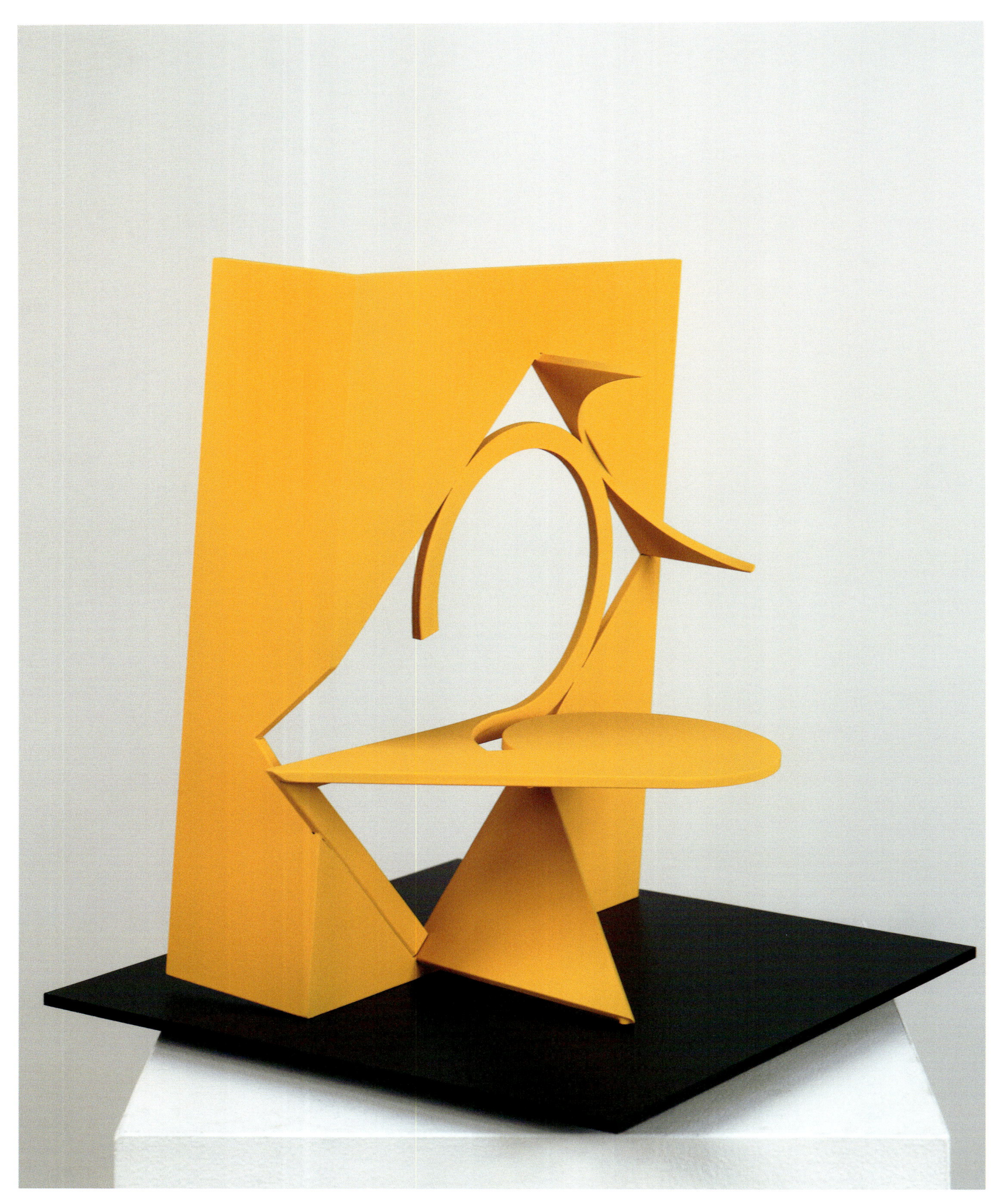

Folded Square Numerical 2

2004, painted steel
12 x 12 x 12 inches
30 x 30 x 30 cm

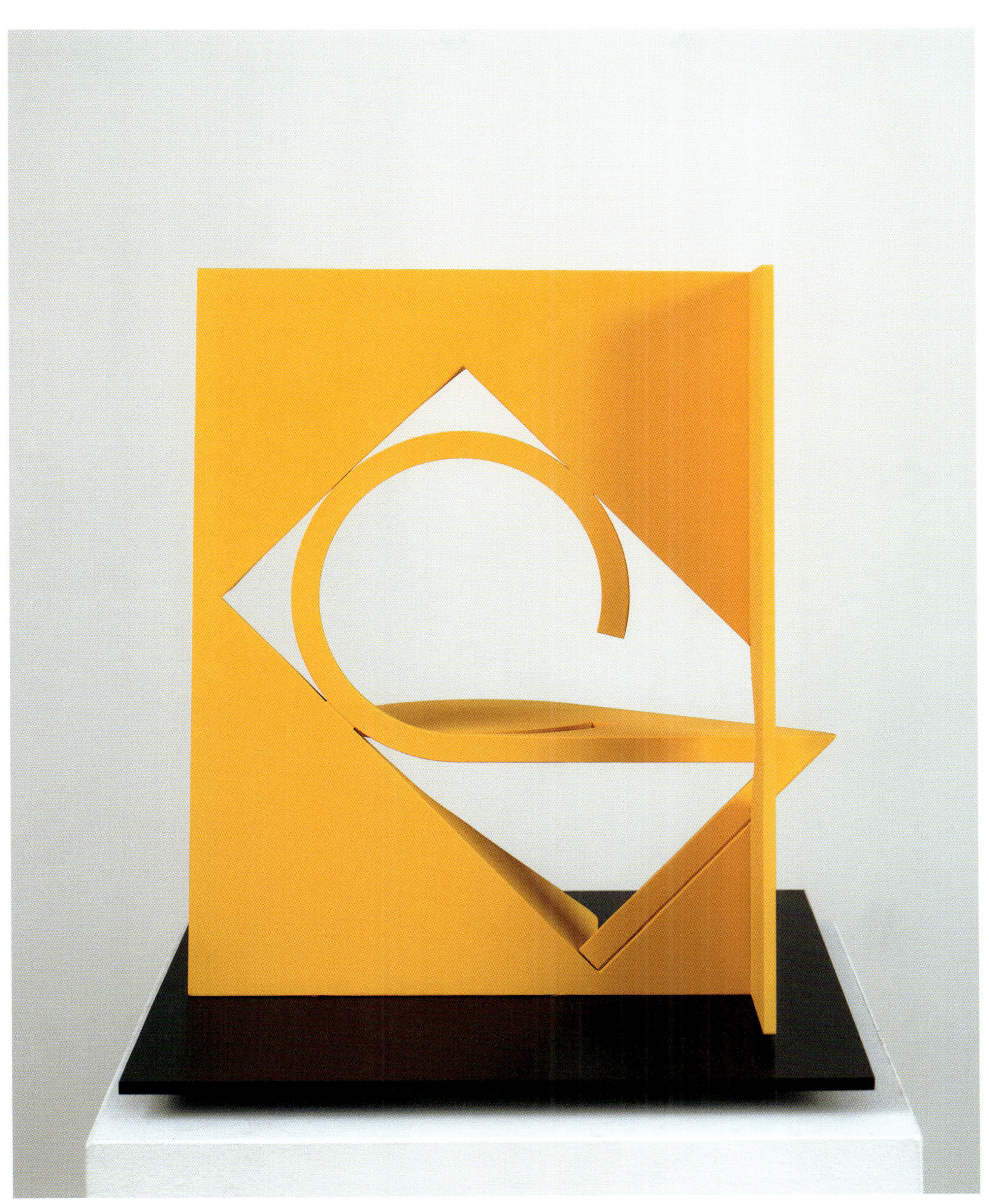

Folded Square Numerical 2

2004, painted steel
12 x 12 x 12 inches
30 x 30 x 30 cm

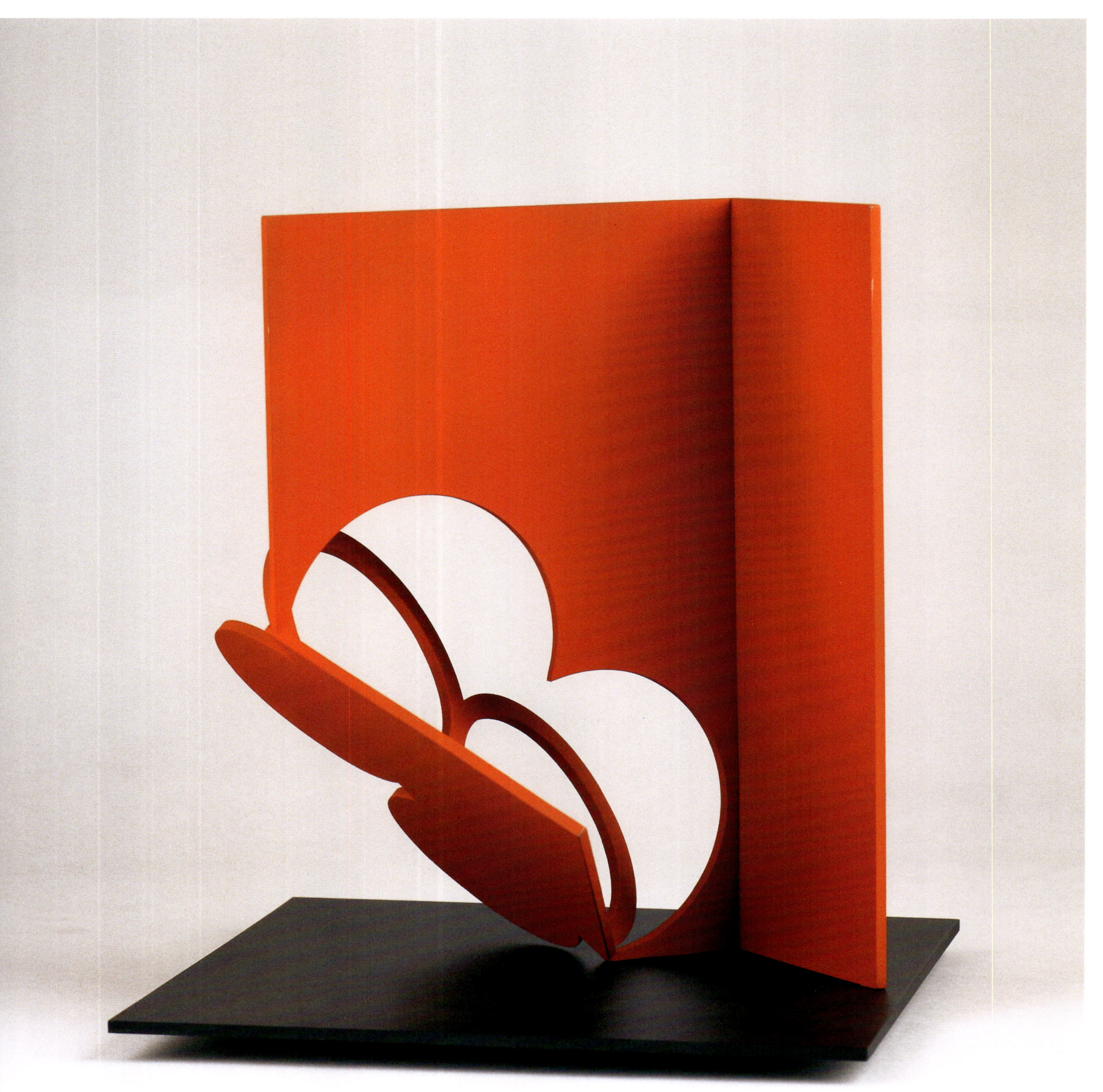

Folded Square Numerical 3

2004, painted steel
12 x 12 x 12 inches
30 x 30 x 30 cm

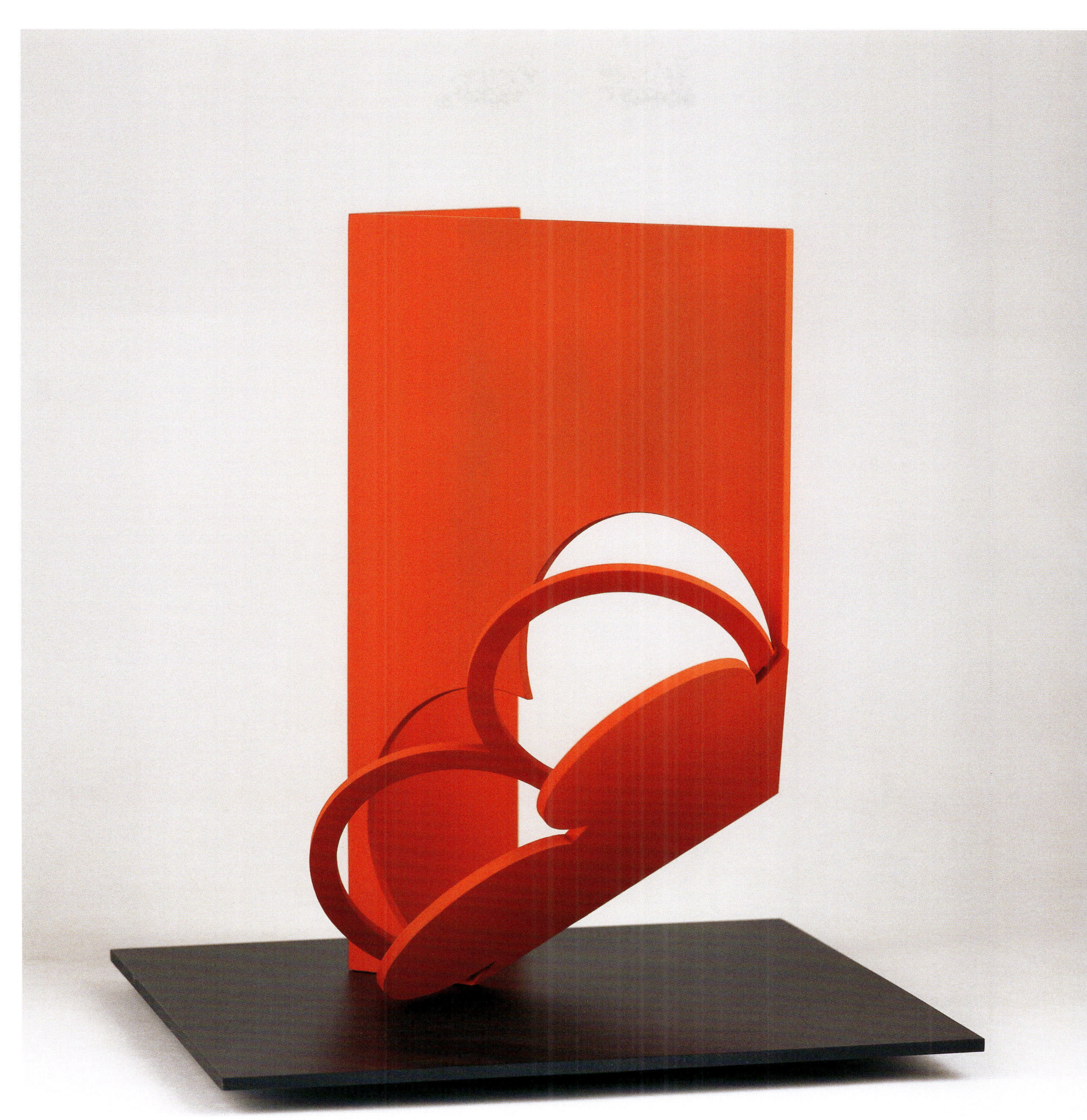

Folded Square Numerical 3

2004, painted steel
12 x 12 x 12 inches
30 x 30 x 30 cm

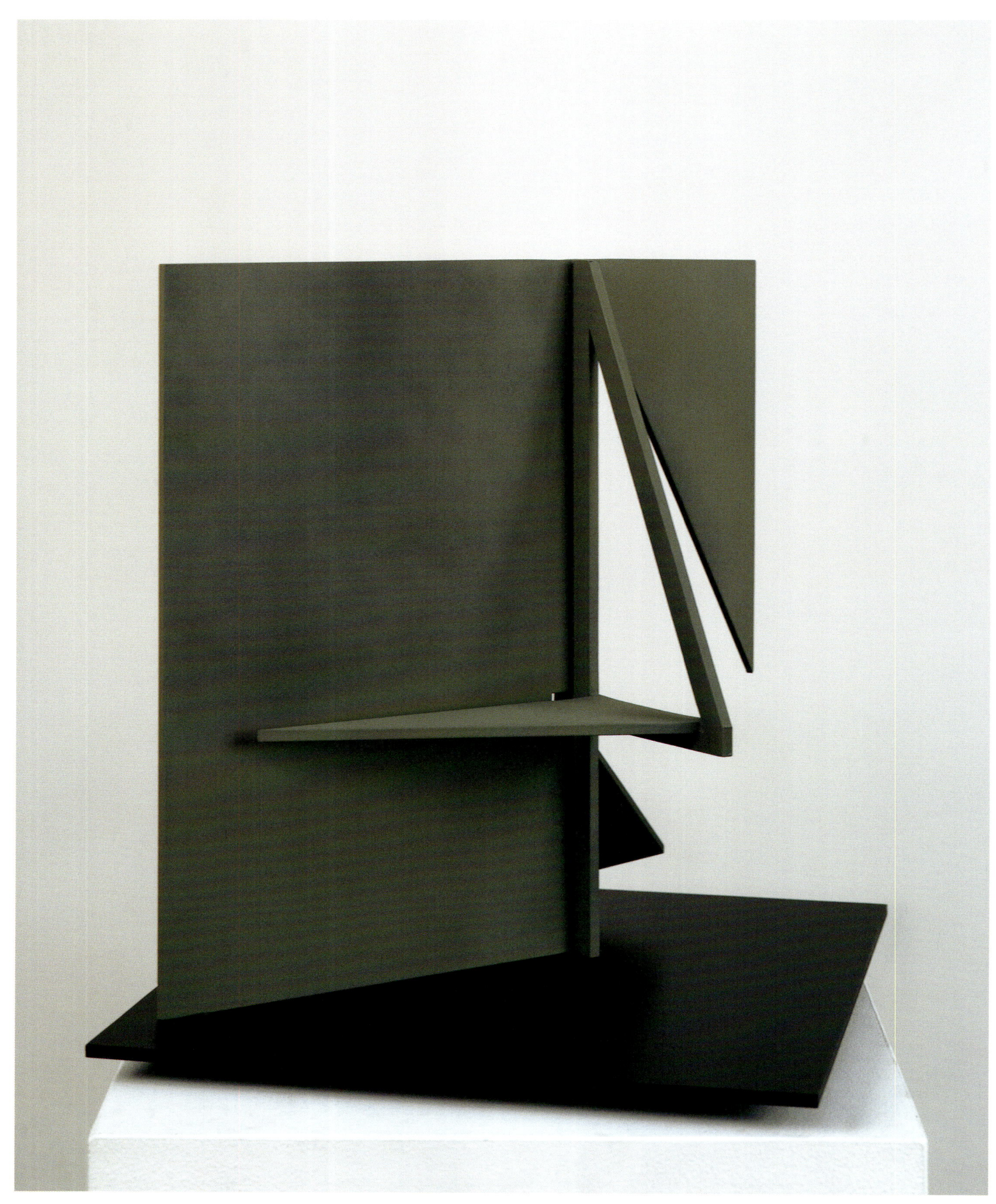

Folded Square Numerical 4

2004, painted steel
12 x 12 x 12 inches
30 x 30 x 30 cm

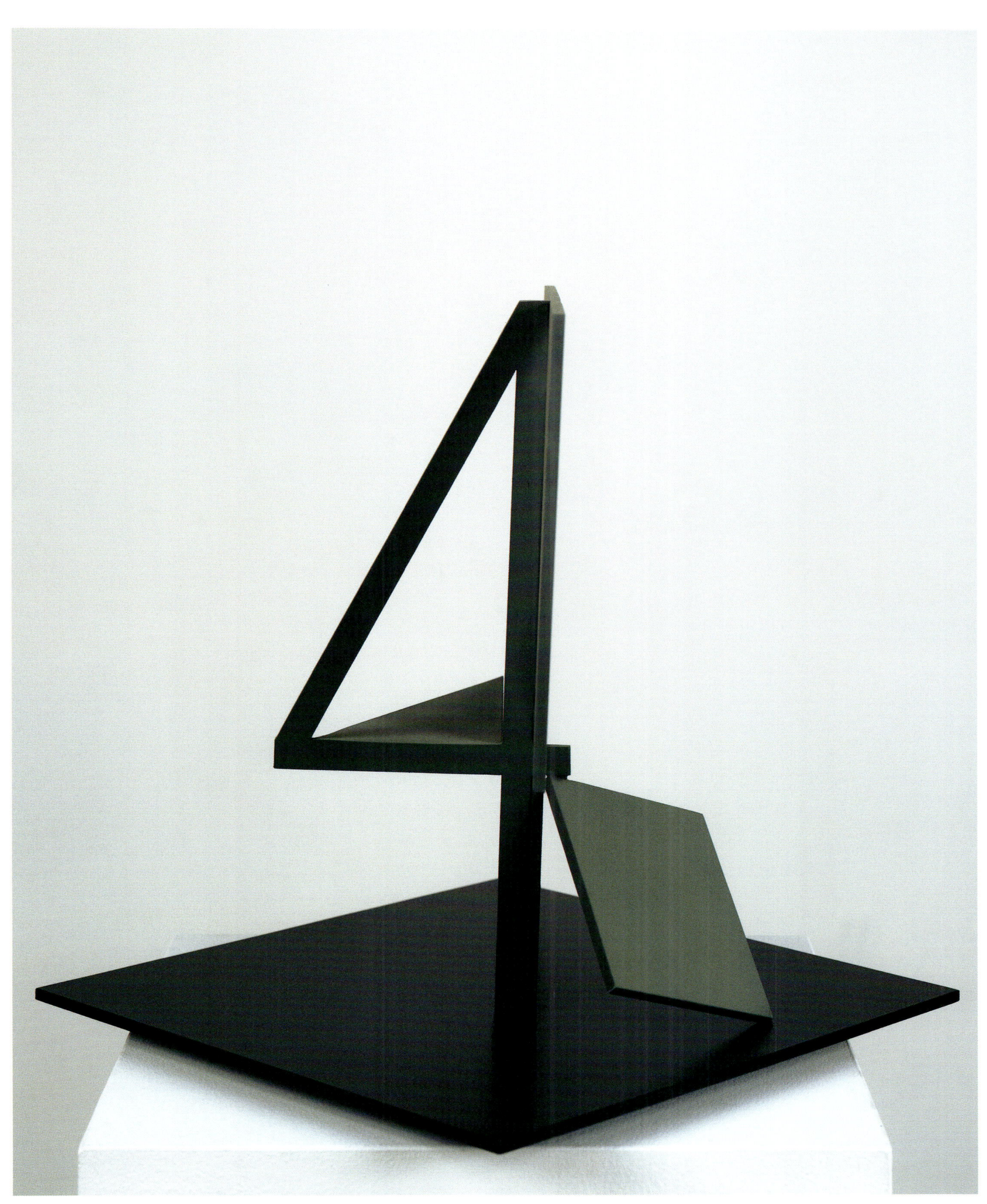

Folded Square Numerical 4

2004, painted steel
12 x 12 x 12 inches
30 x 30 x 30 cm

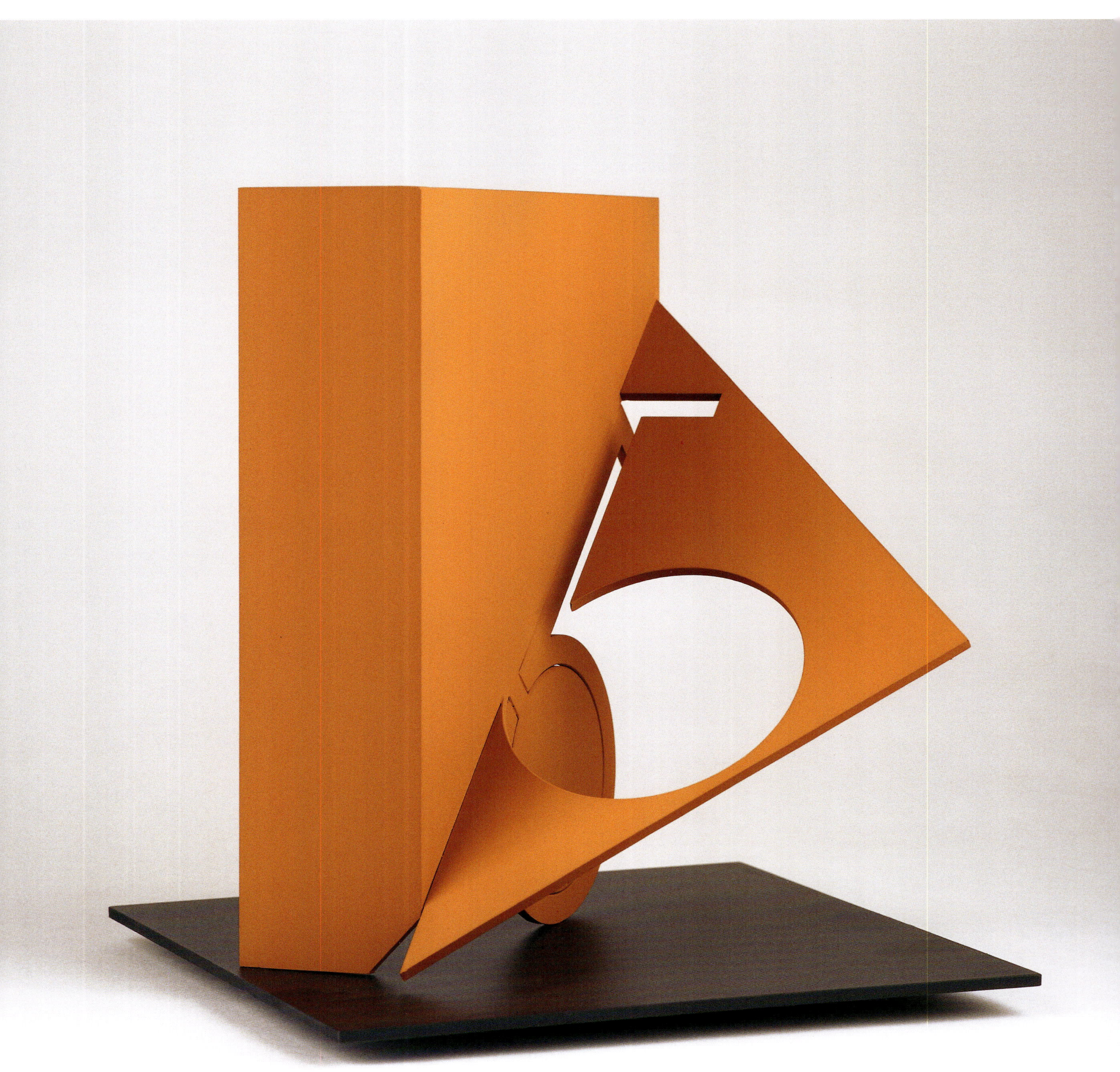

Folded Square Numerical 5

2004, painted steel
12 x 12 x 12 inches
30 x 30 x 30 cm

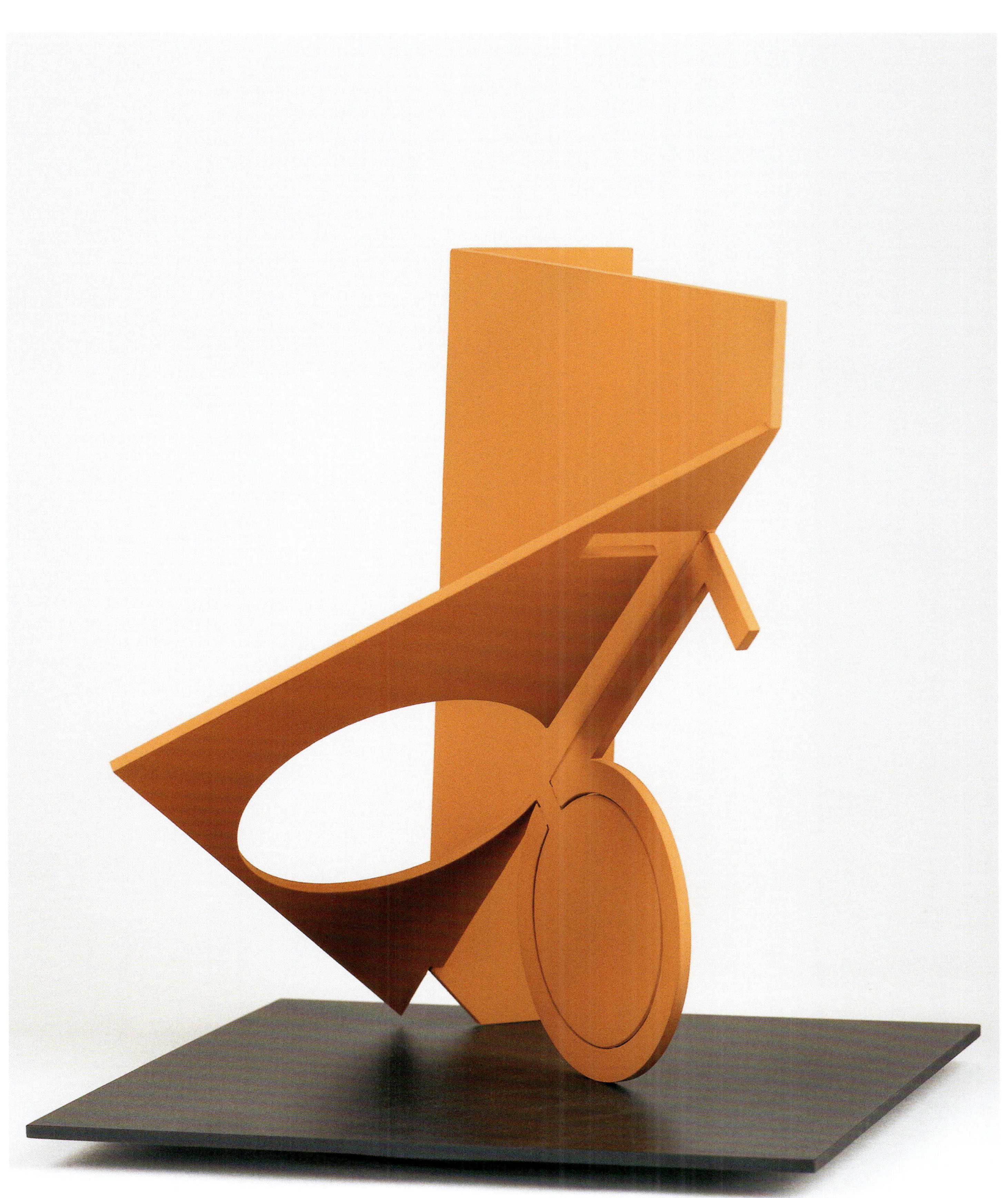

Folded Square Numerical 5

2004, painted steel
12 x 12 x 12 inches
30 x 30 x 30 cm

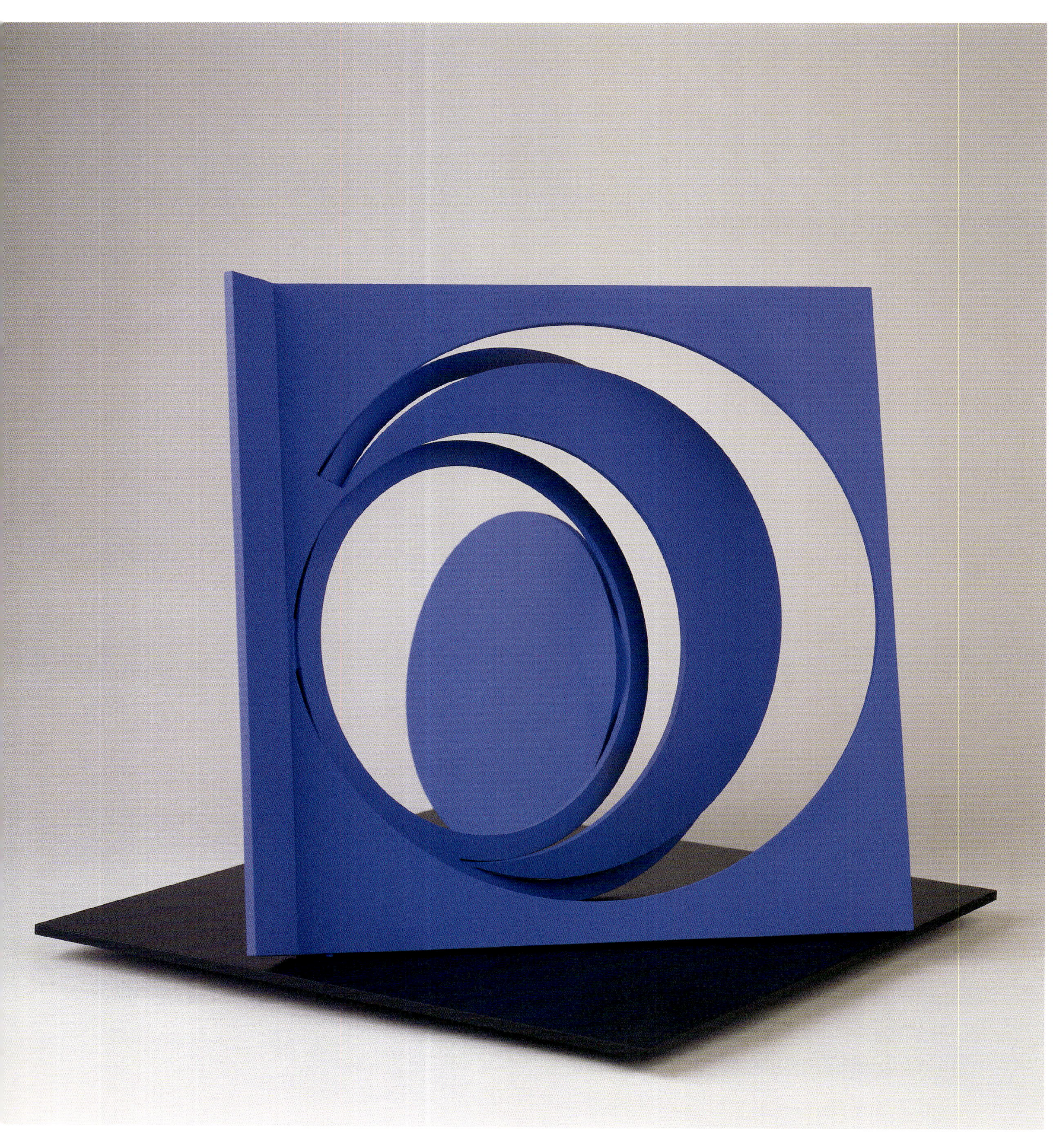

Folded Square Numerical 6

2004, painted steel
12 x 12 x 12 inches
30 x 30 x 30 cm

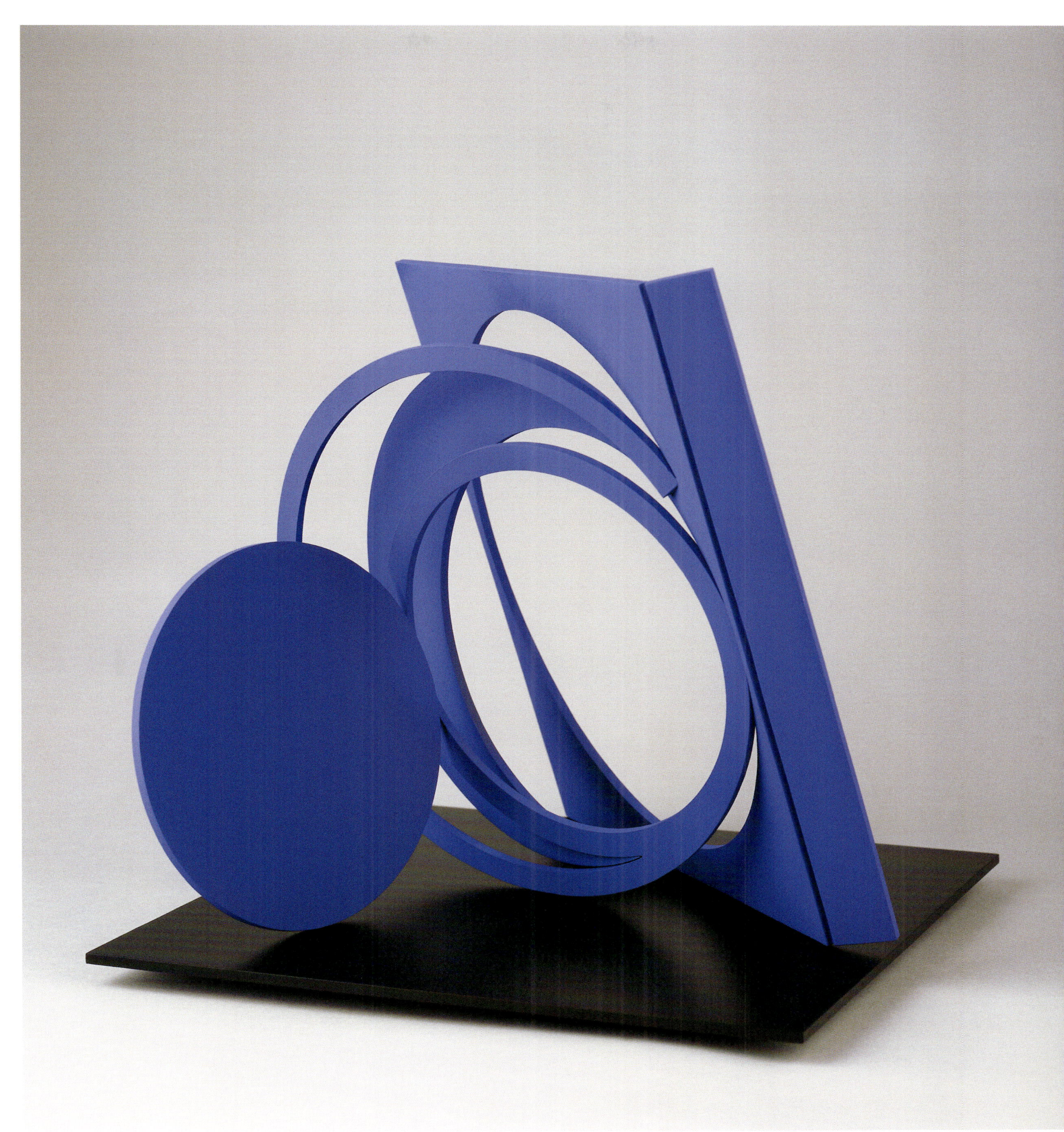

Folded Square Numerical 6

2004, painted steel
12 x 12 x 12 inches
30 x 30 x 30 cm

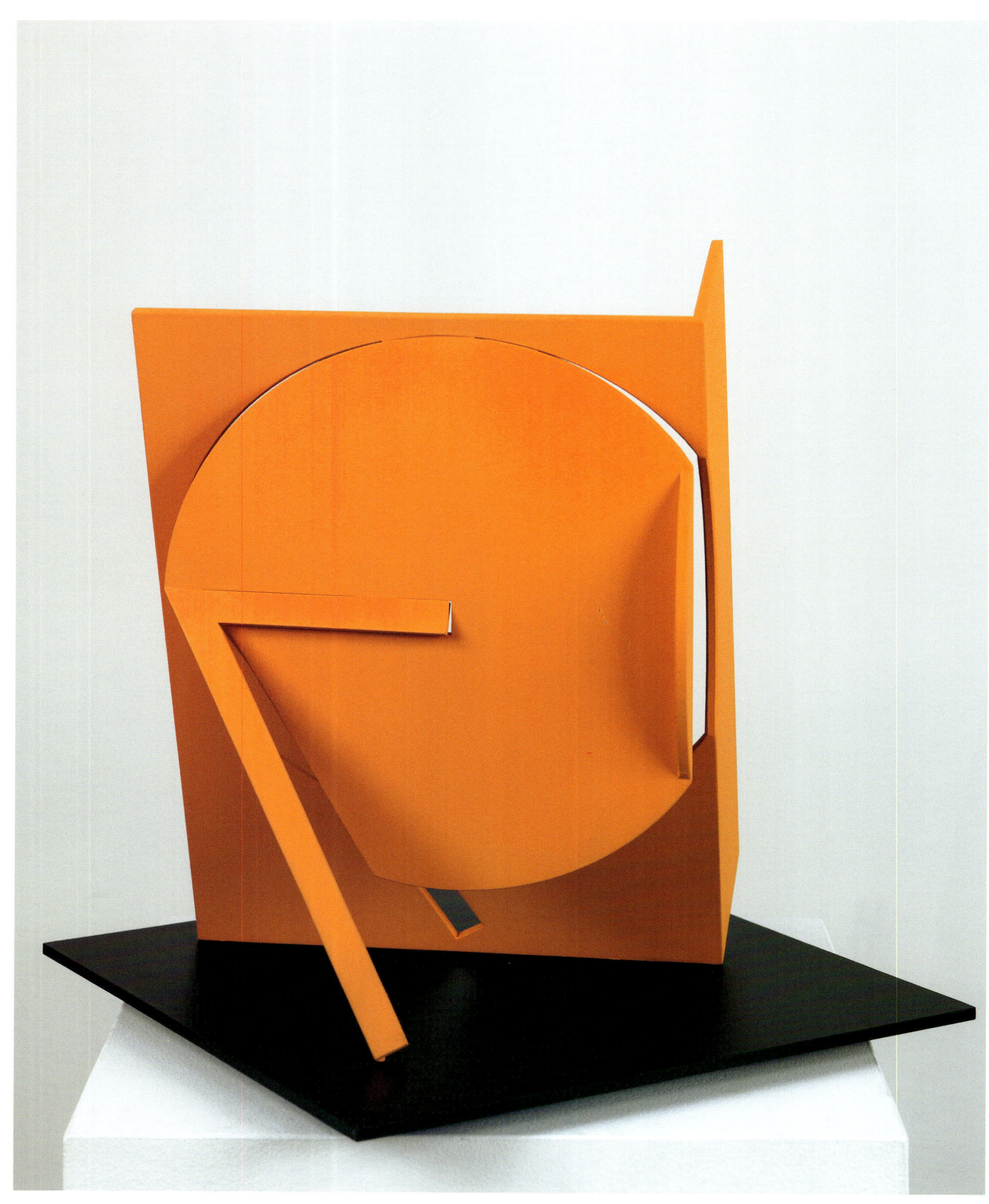

Folded Square Numerical 7

2004, painted steel
12 x 12 x 12 inches
30 x 30 x 30 cm

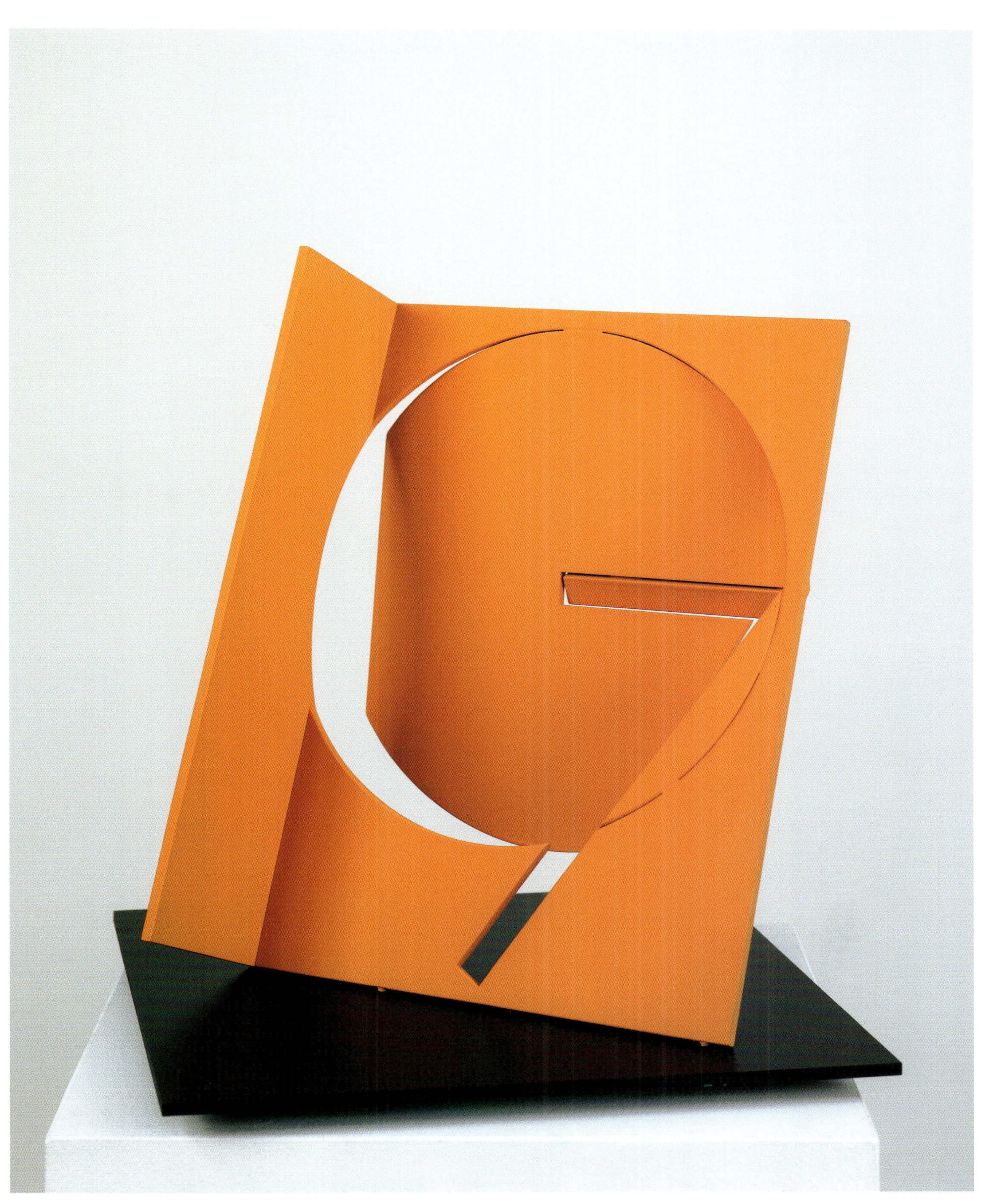

Folded Square Numerical 7

2004, painted steel
12 x 12 x 12 inches
30 x 30 x 30 cm

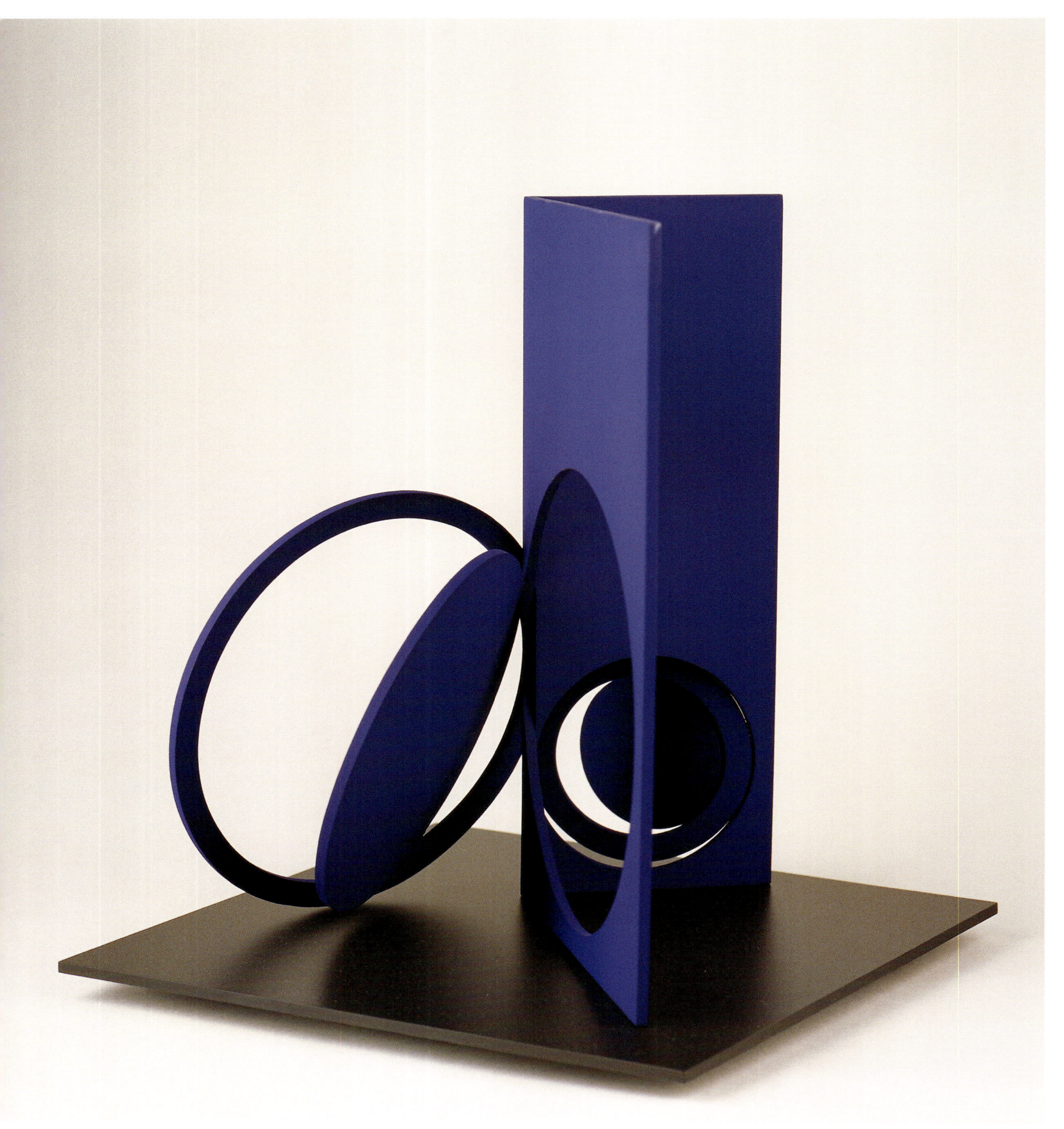

Folded Square Numerical 8

2004, painted steel
12 x 12 x 12 inches
30 x 30 x 30 cm

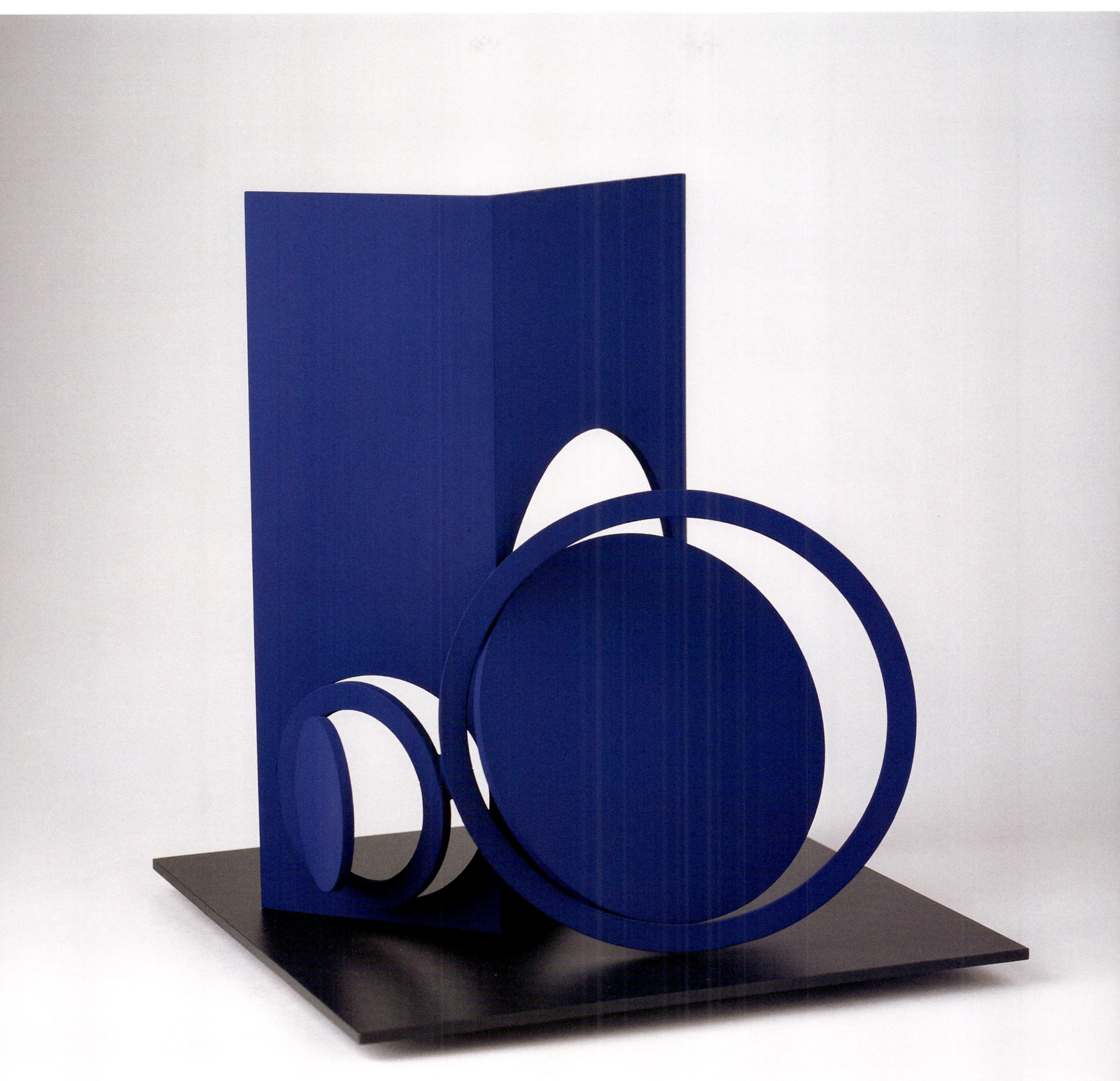

Folded Square Numerical 8

2004, painted steel
12 x 12 x 12 inches
30 x 30 x 30 cm

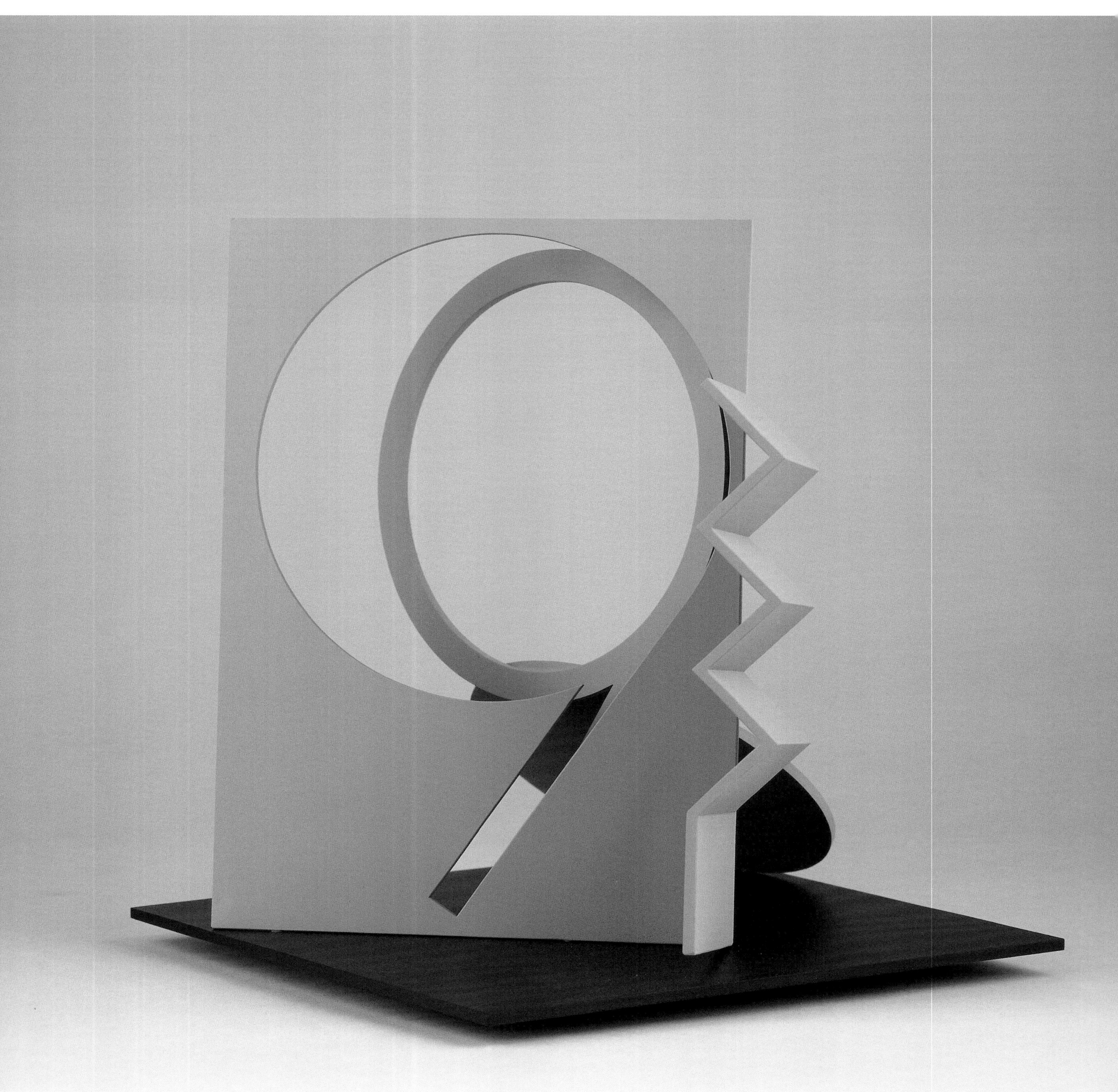

Folded Square Numerical 9

2004, painted steel
12 x 12 x 12 inches
30 x 30 x 30 cm

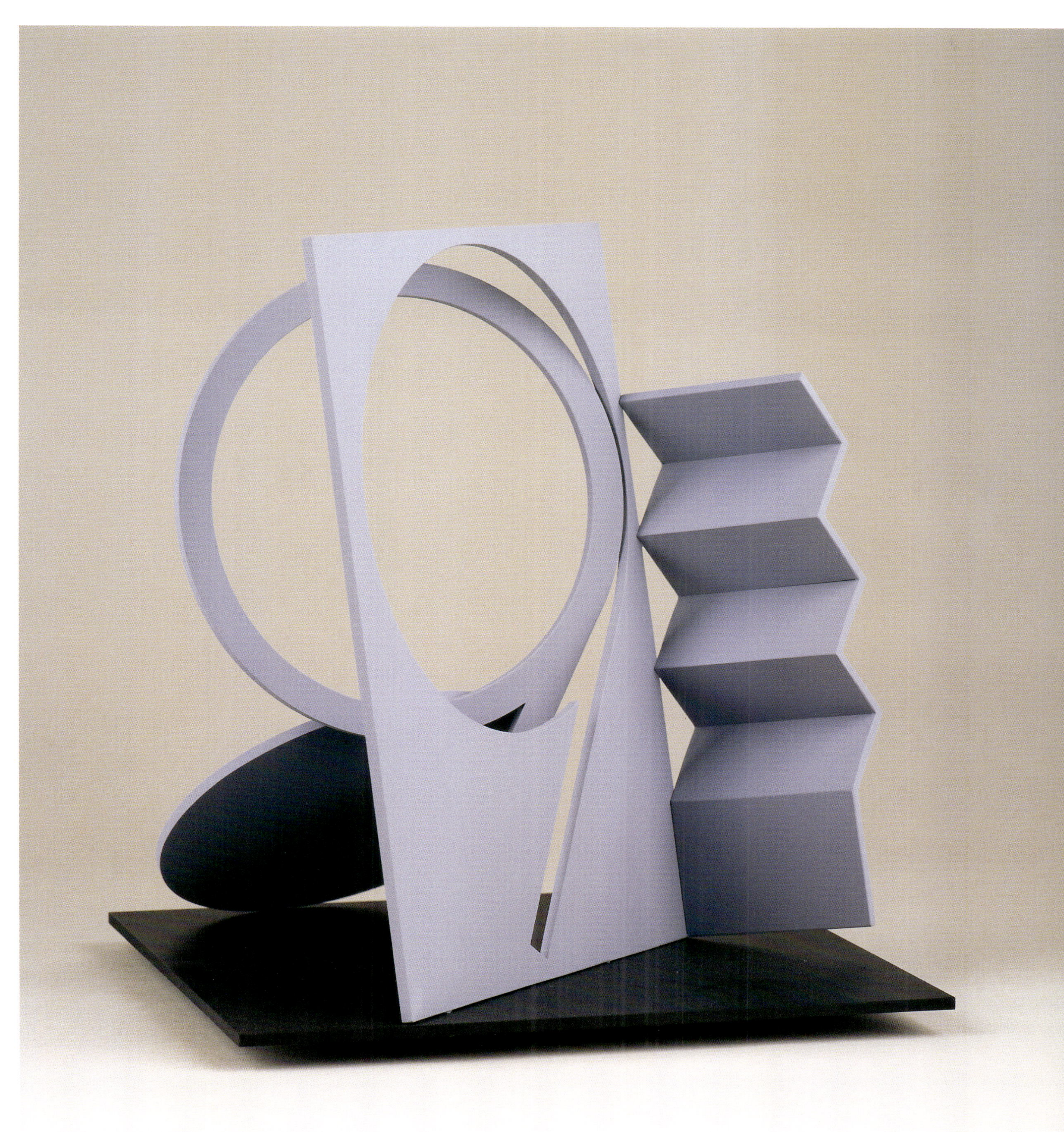

Folded Square Numerical 9

2004, painted steel
12 x 12 x 12 inches
30 x 30 x 30 cm

Installation view of Benton solo
exhibition at Imago Galleries
Palm Desert, California 2004

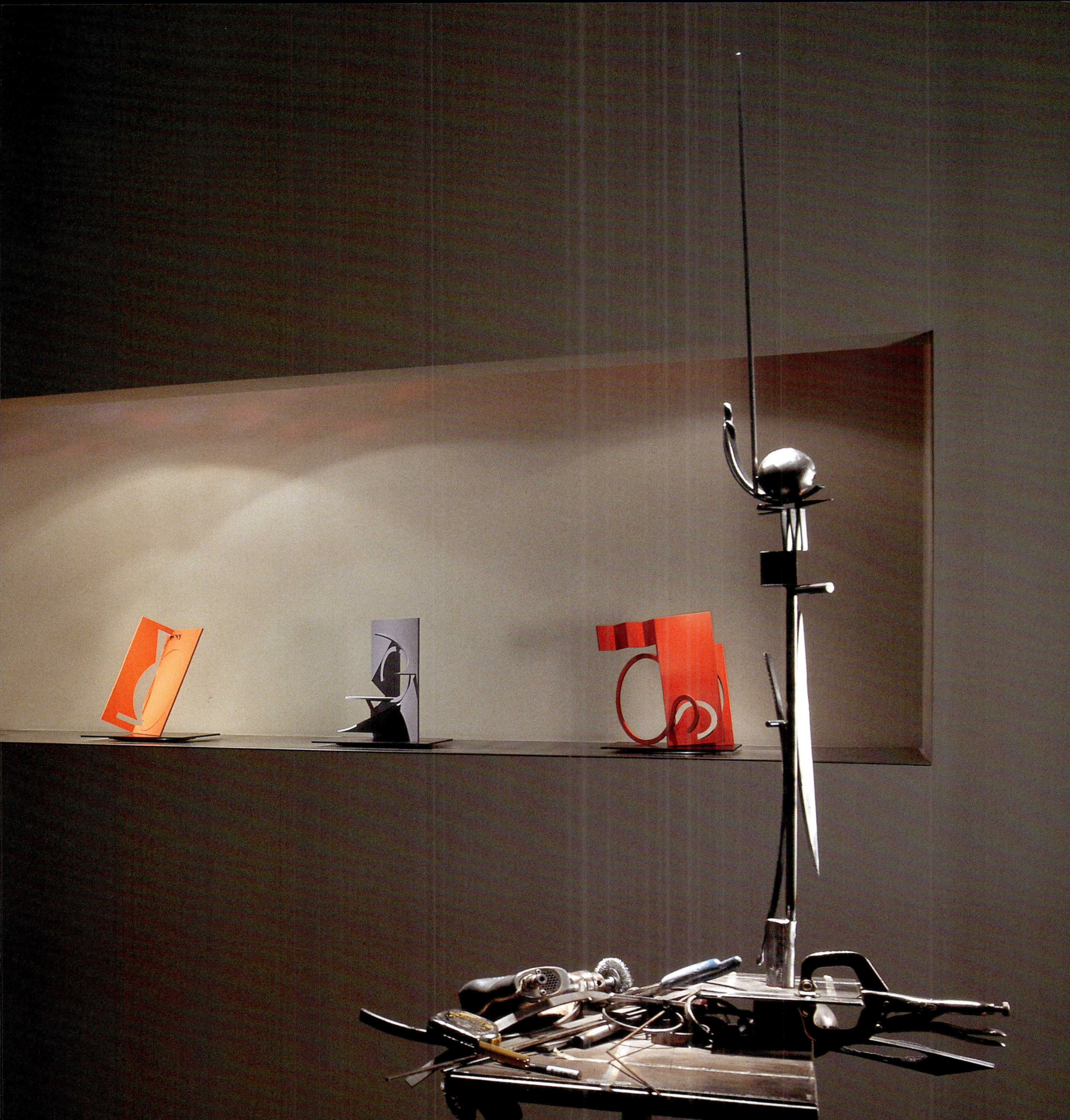

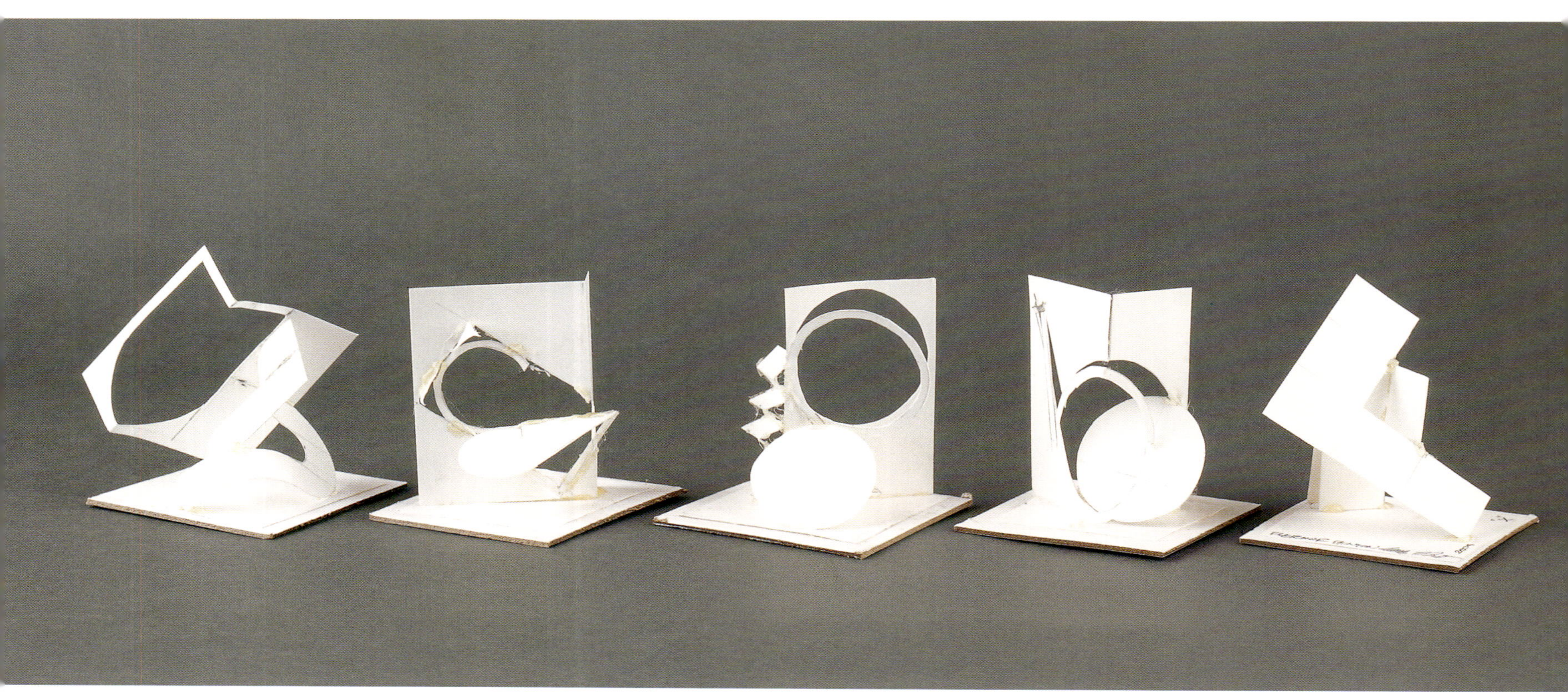

Folded Square Alphabets & Numericals

U, 2, 9, J & X (from left)
1978/2004, paper
3 x 3 x 3 inches (each)
8 x 8 x 8 cm

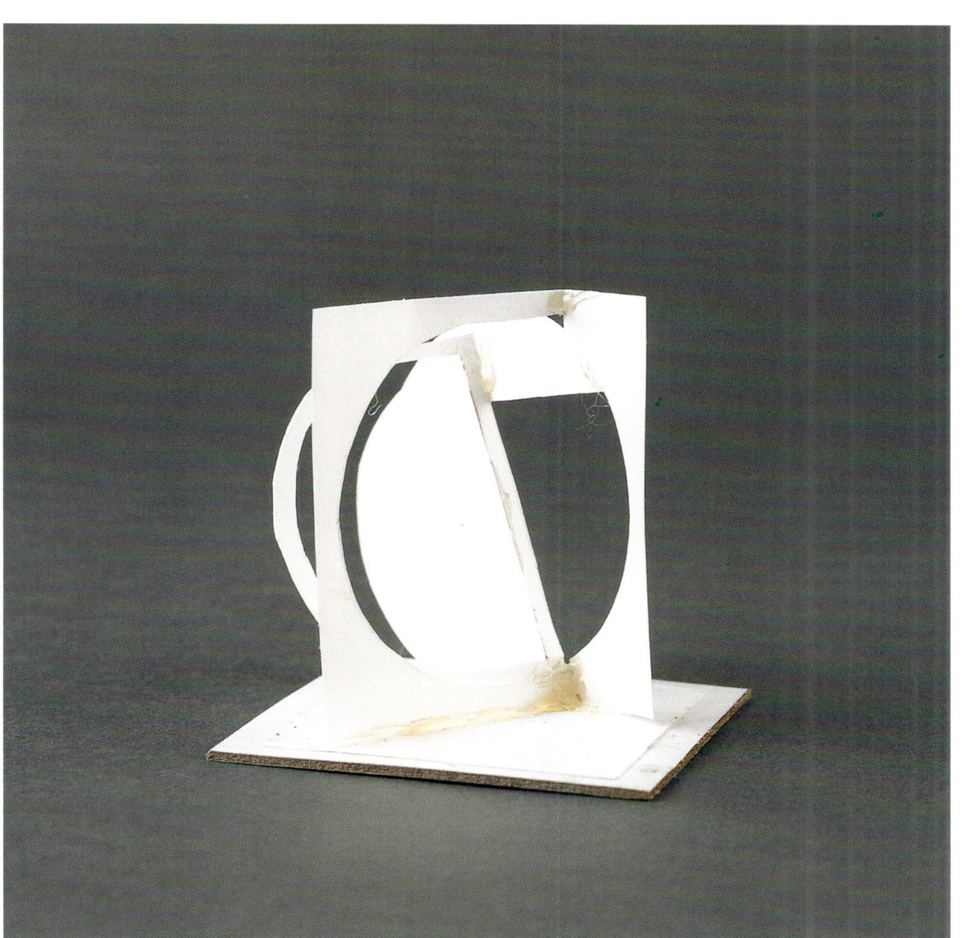

Folded Square Alphabet D - study

1978/2004, paper
3 x 3 x 3 inches
8 x 8 x 8 cm

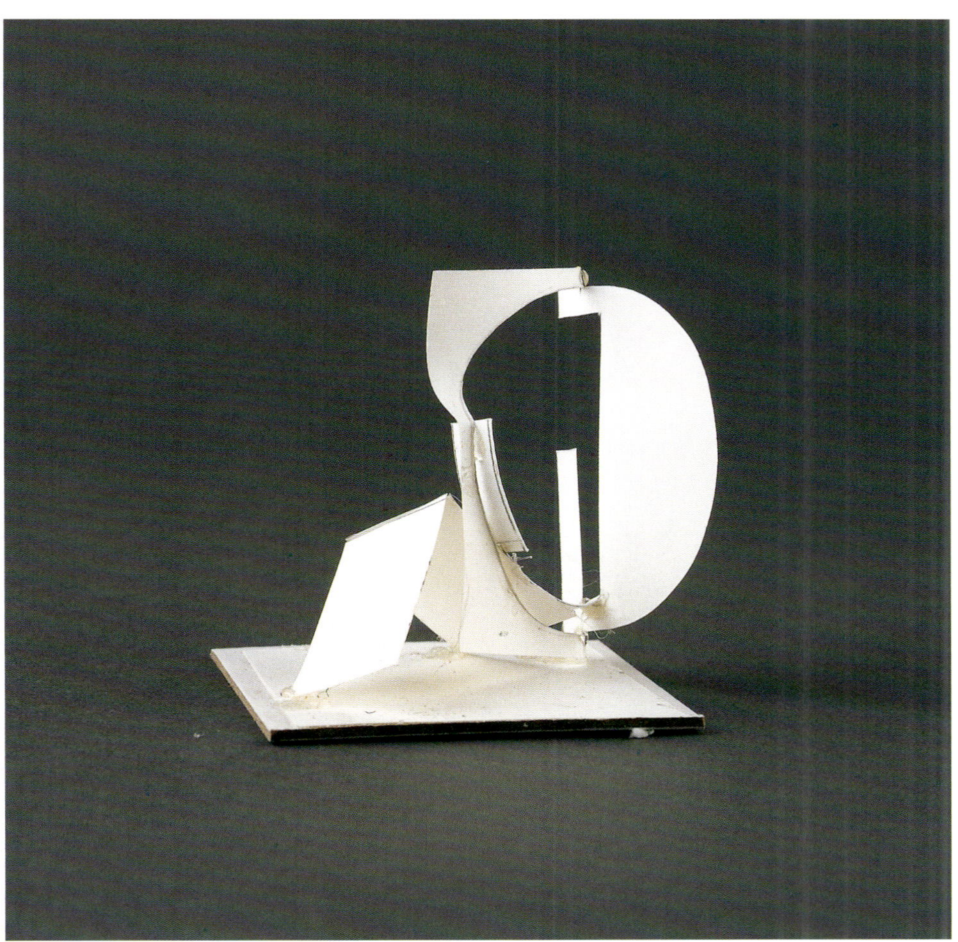

Folded Square Alphabet G - study

1978/2004, paper
3 x 3 x 3 inches
8 x 8 x 8 cm

Folded Square Alphabet J - study

1978/2004, paper
3 x 3 x 3 inches
8 x 8 x 8 cm

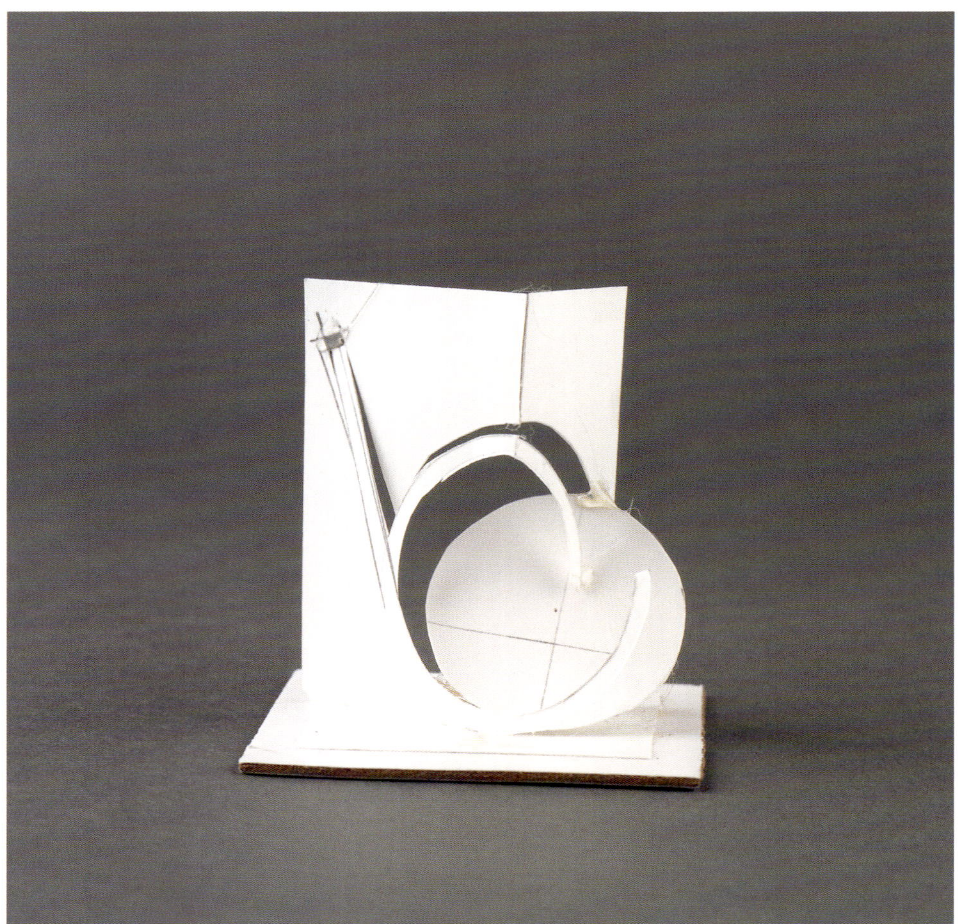

Folded Square Alphabet K - study

1978/2004, paper
3 x 3 x 3 inches
8 x 8 x 8 cm

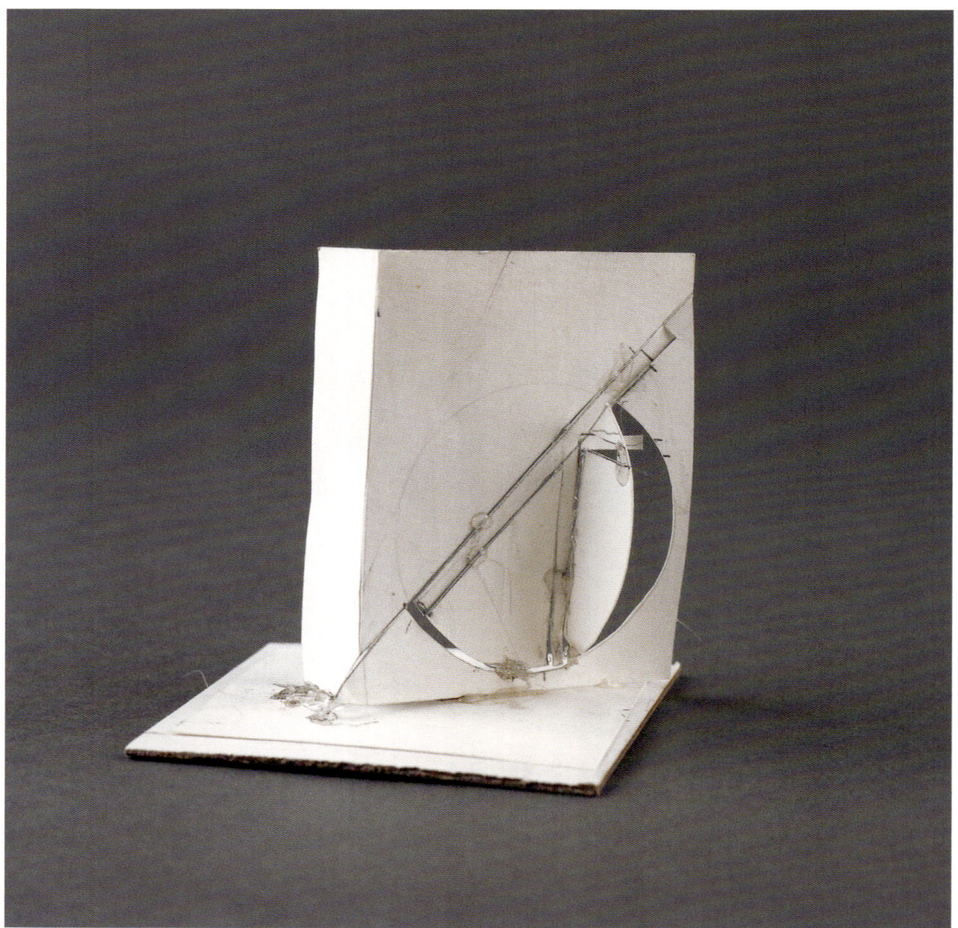

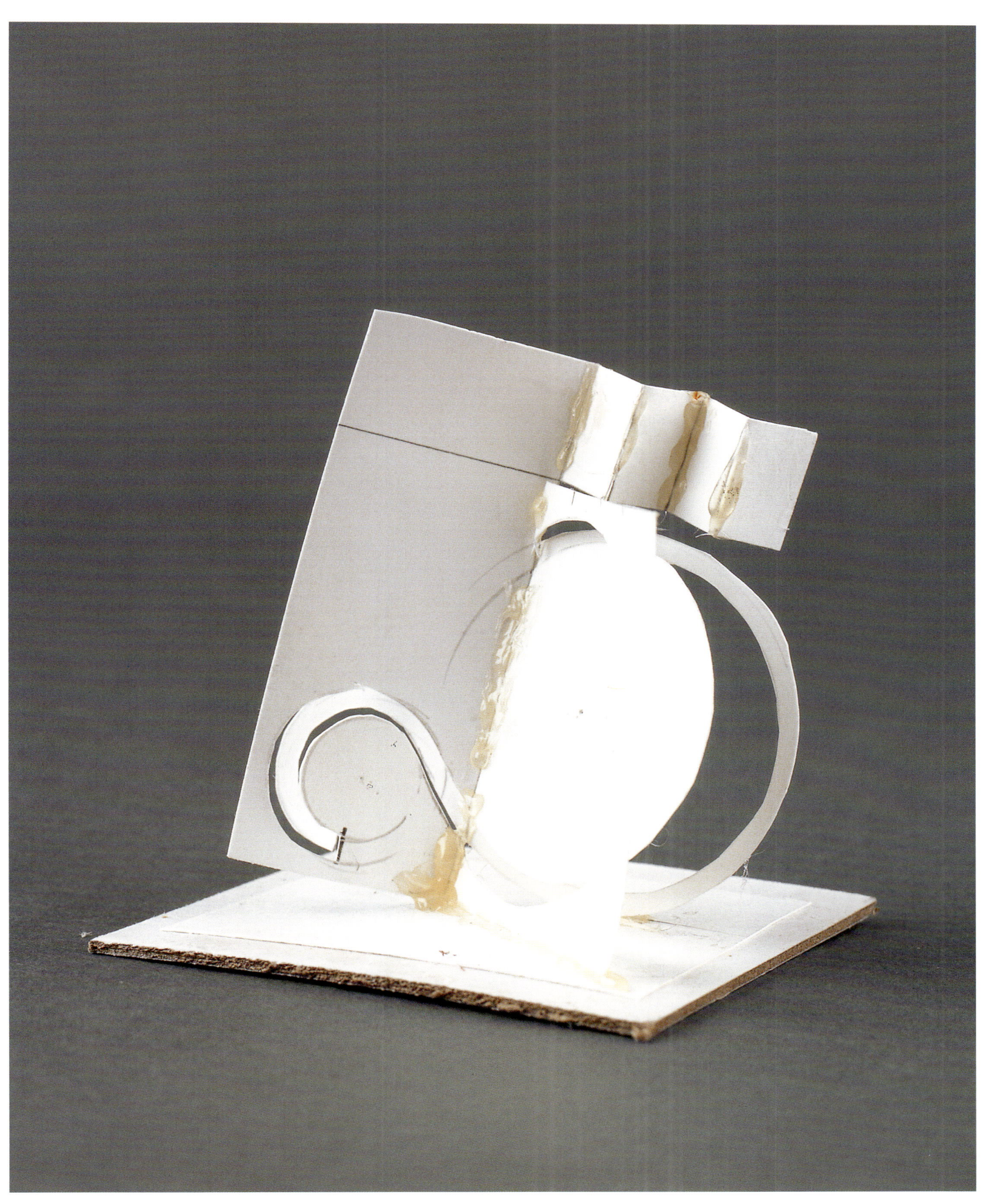

Folded Square Alphabet S - study

1978/2004, paper
3 x 3 x 3 inches
8 x 8 x 8 cm

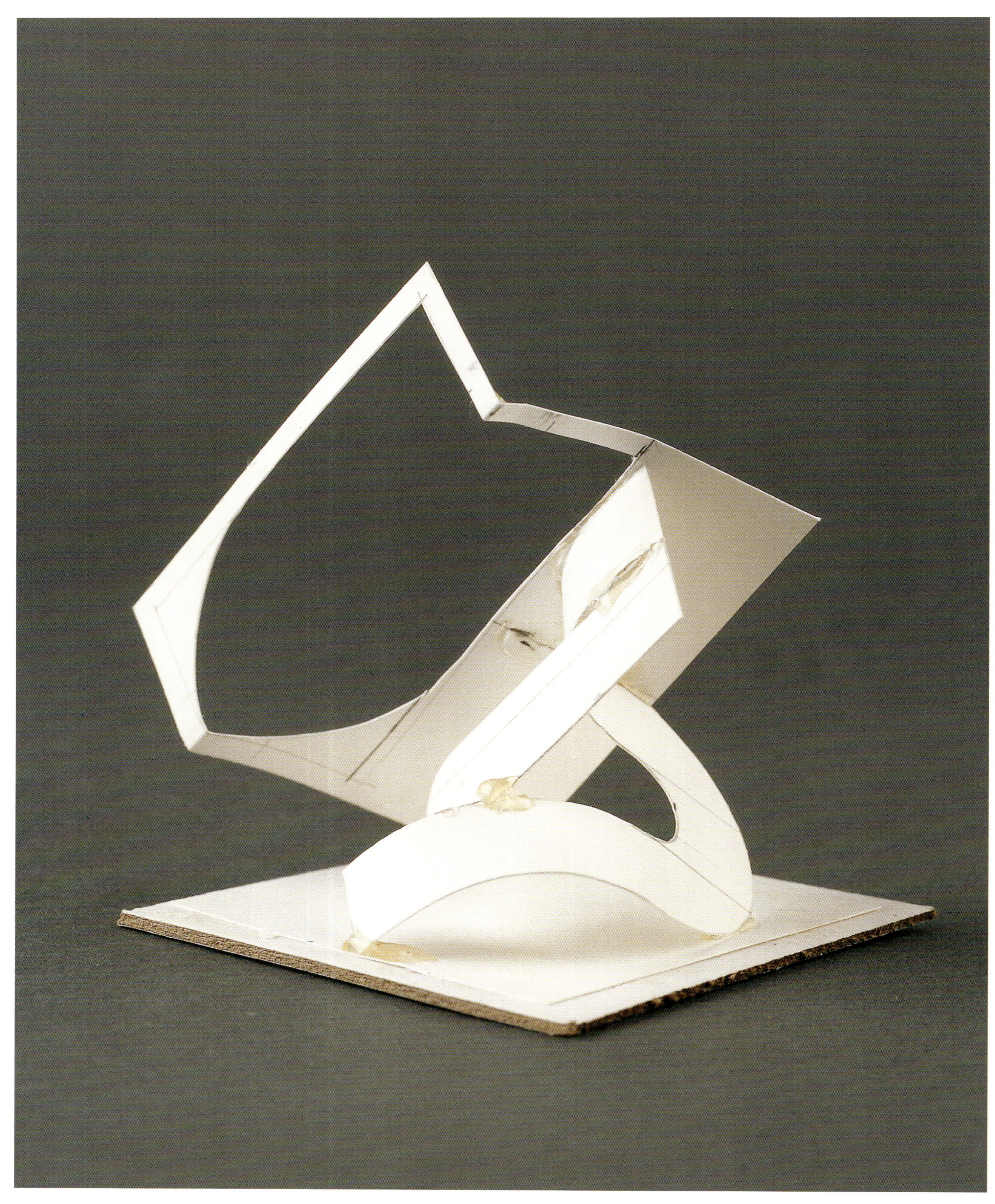

Folded Square Alphabet U - study

1978/2004, paper
3 x 3 x 3 inches
8 x 8 x 8 cm

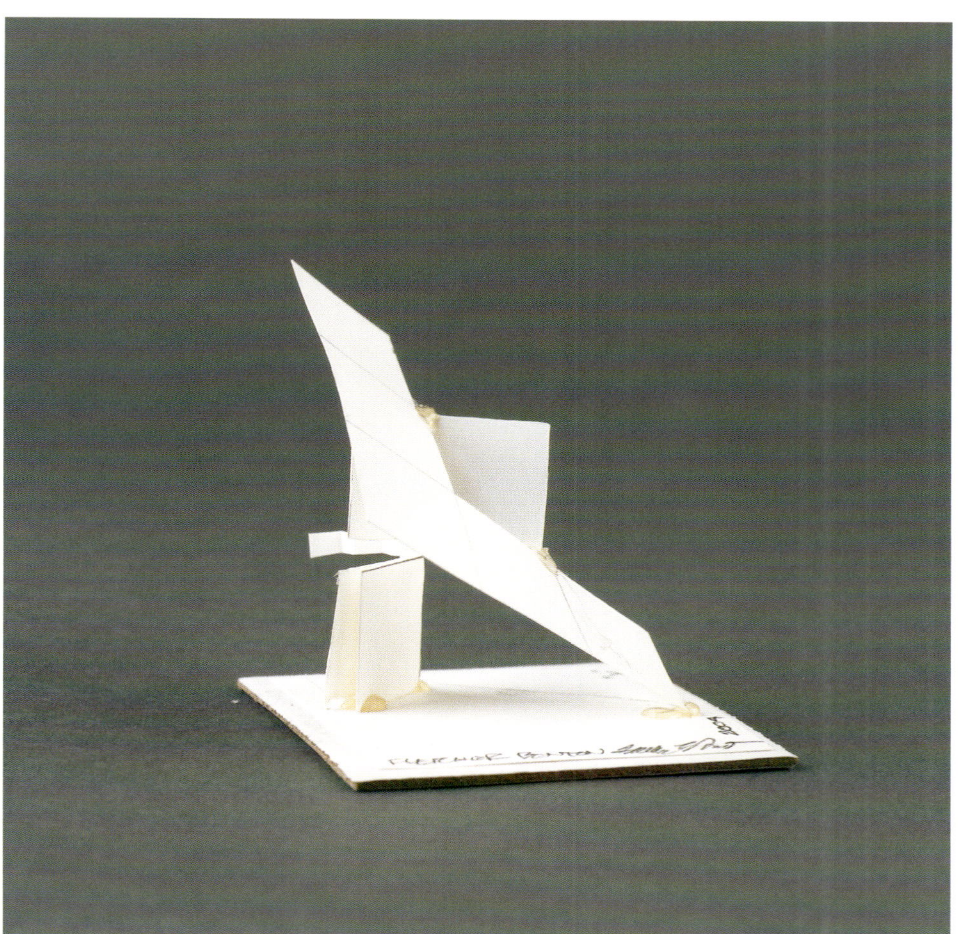

Folded Square Alphabet X - study

1978/2004, paper
3 x 3 x 3 inches
8 x 8 x 8 cm

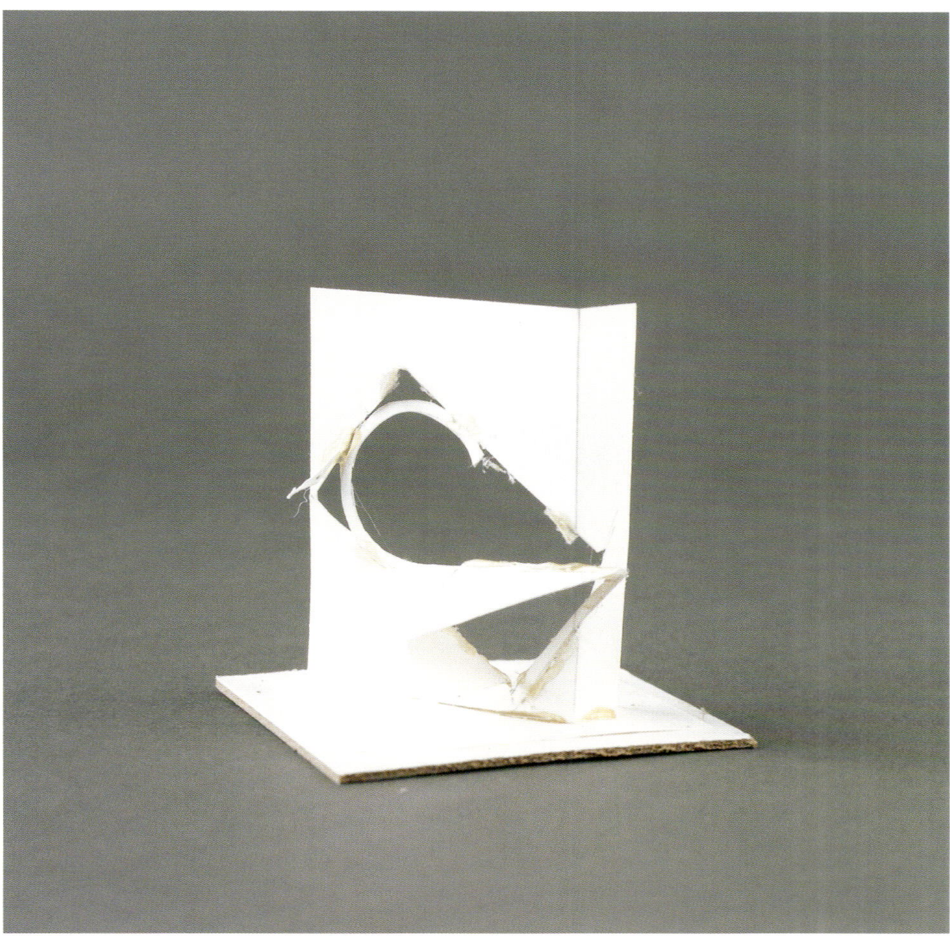

Folded Square Numerical 2 - study

1978/2004, paper
3 x 3 x 3 inches
8 x 8 x 8 cm

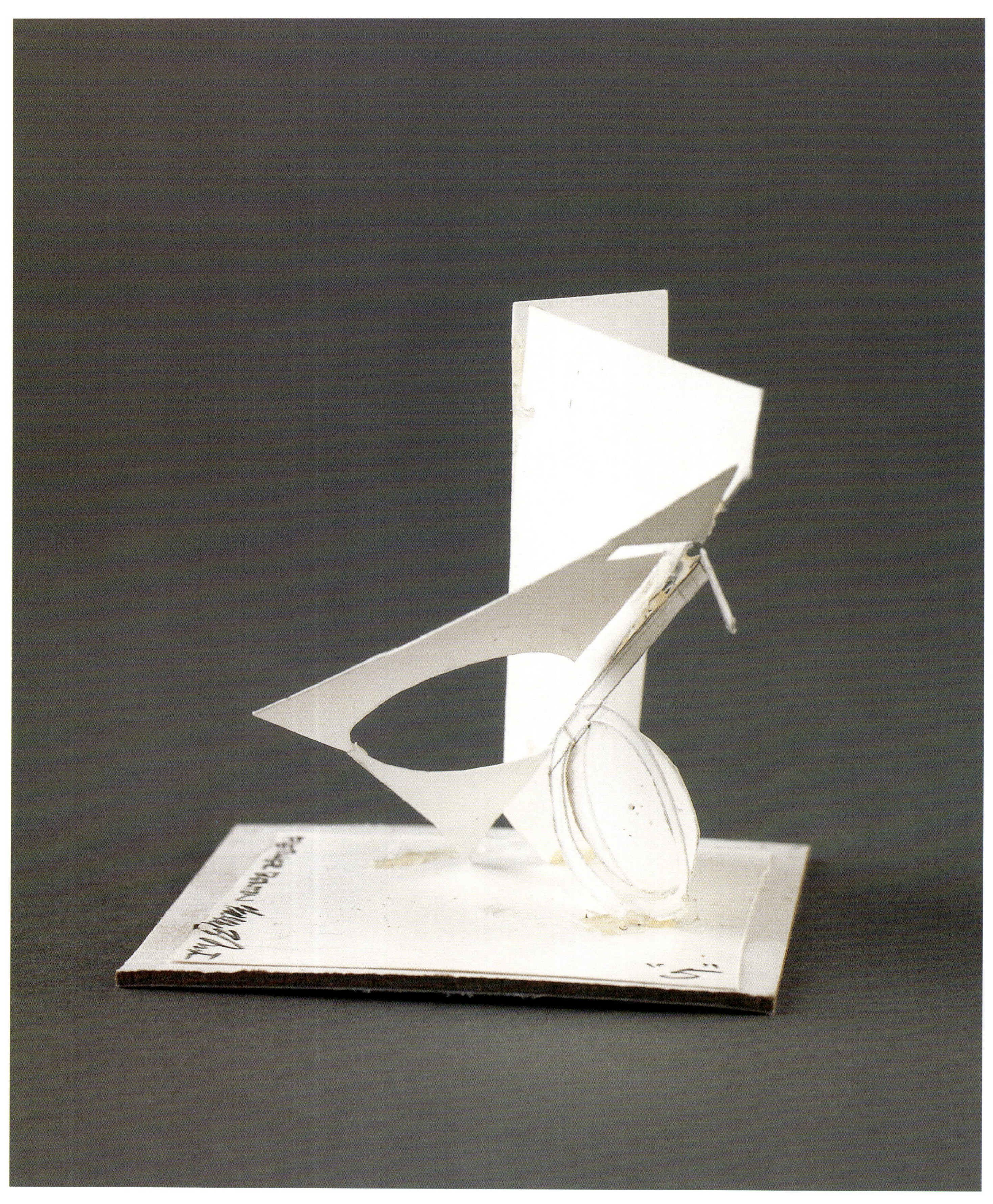

Folded Square Numerical 5 - study

1978/2004, paper
3 x 3 x 3 inches
8 x 8 x 8 cm

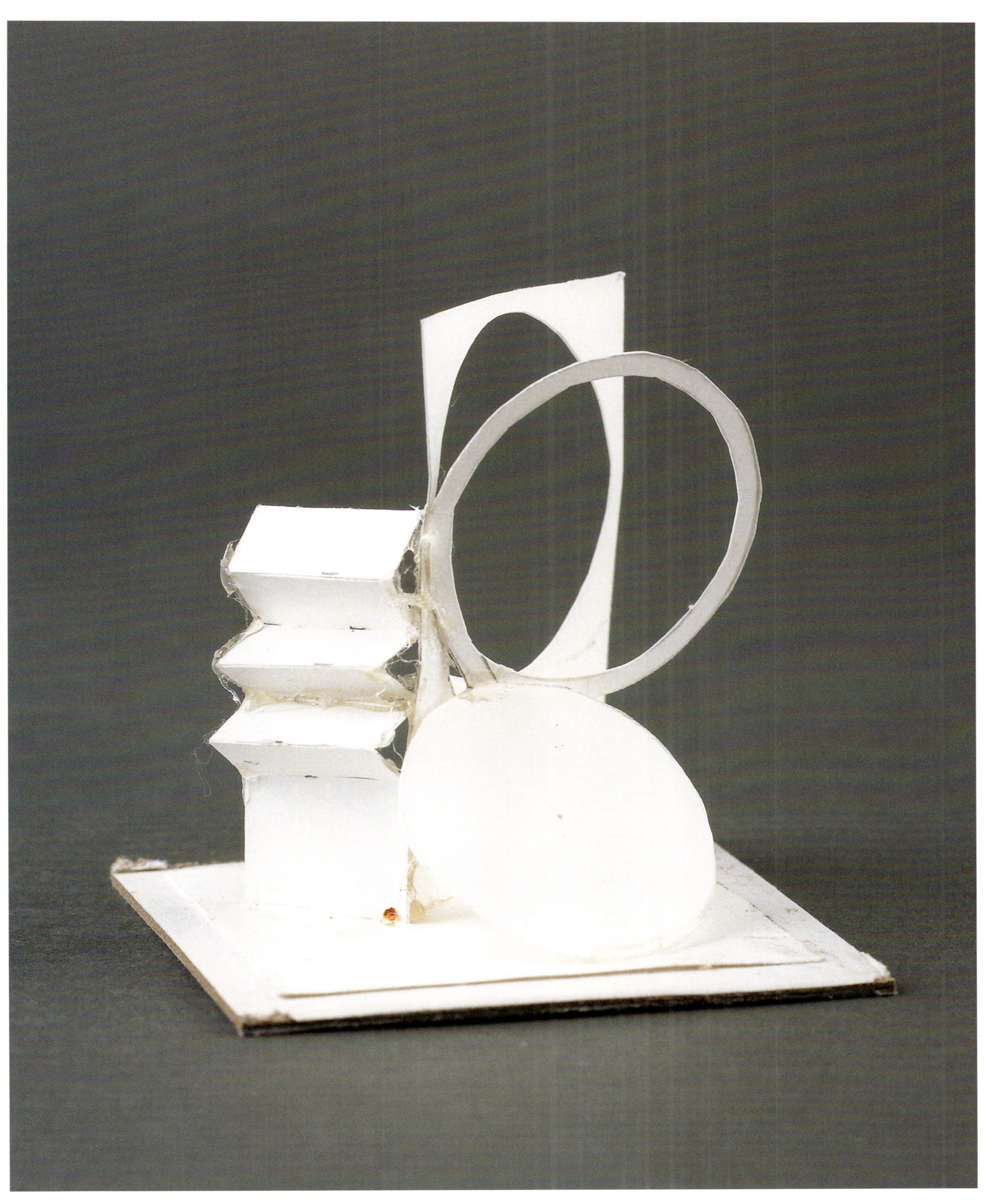

Folded Square Numerical 9 - study

2004, paper
3 x 3 x 3 inches
8 x 8 x 8 cm

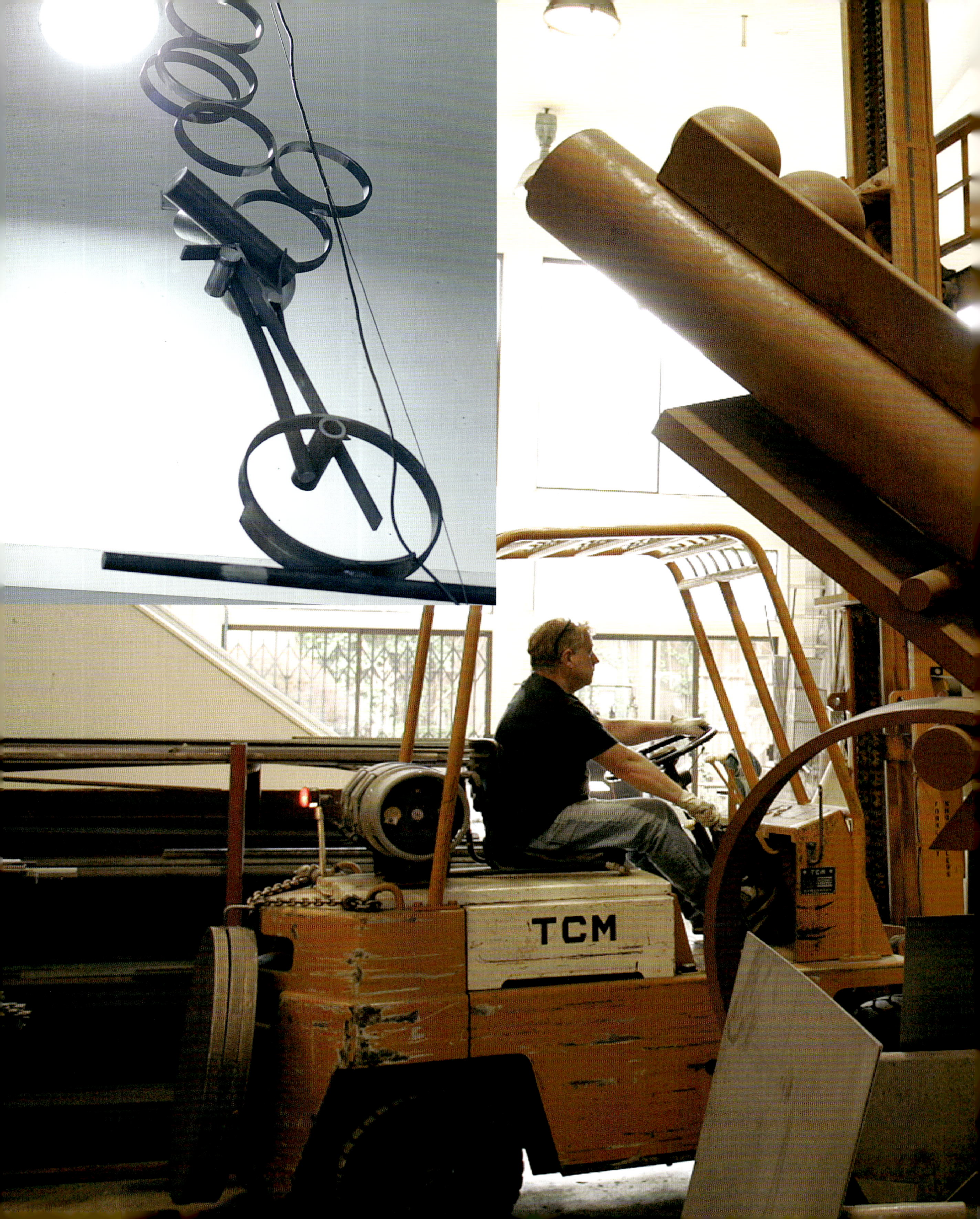
TCM

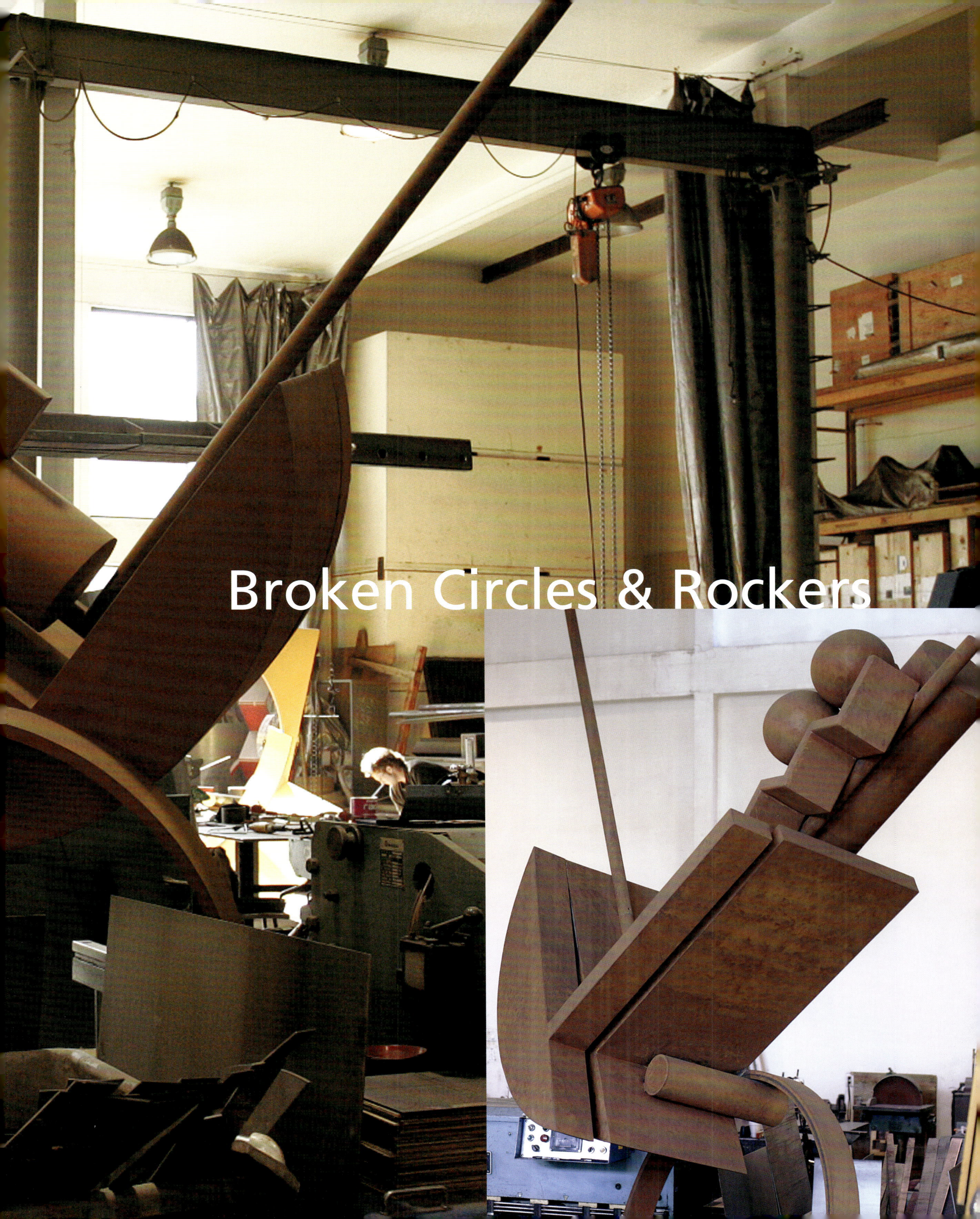

Broken Circles & Rockers

Rocker with Balls and X

2003, steel with patina
18 x 12 x 8 feet
549 x 366 x 244 cm

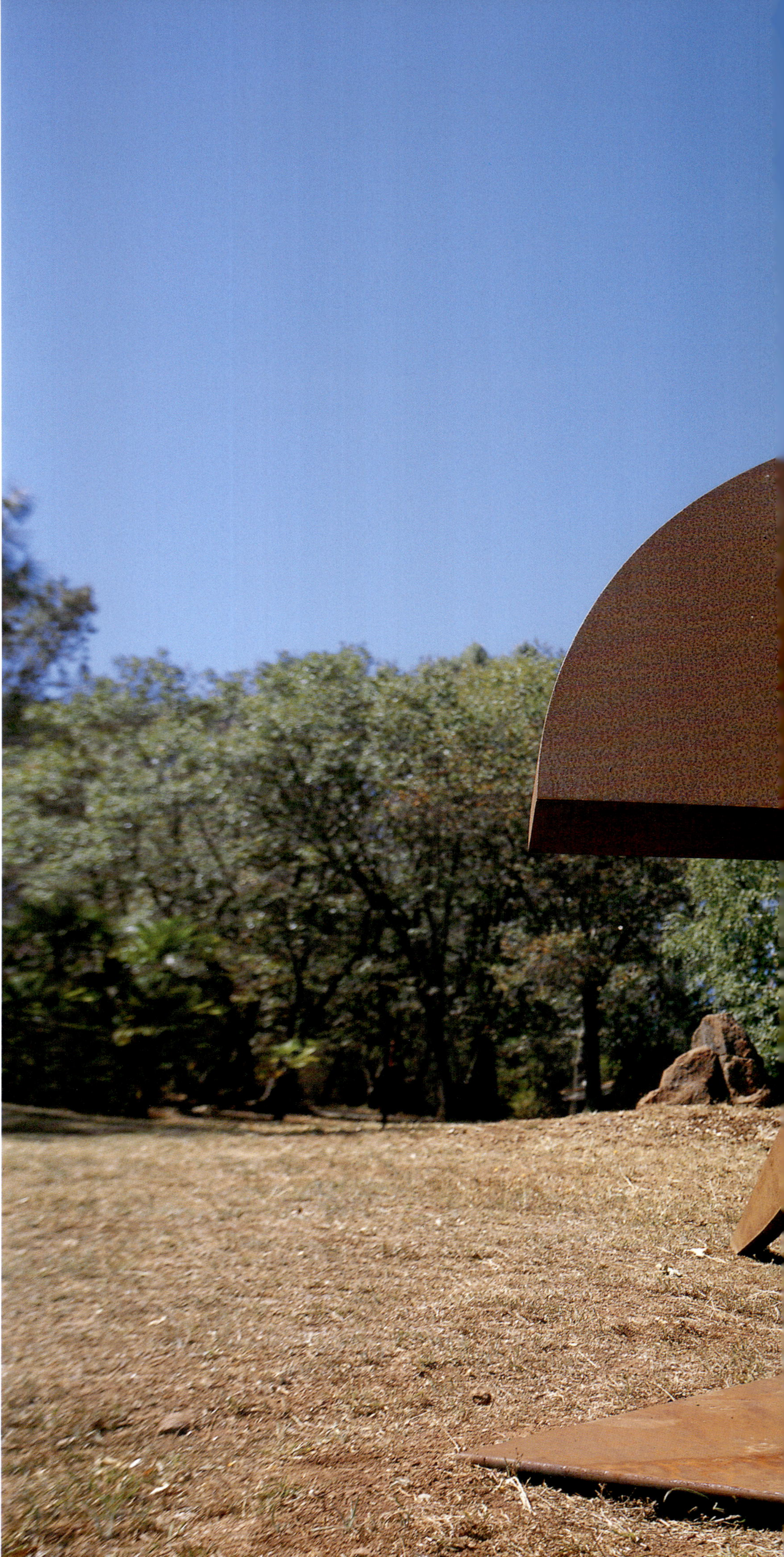

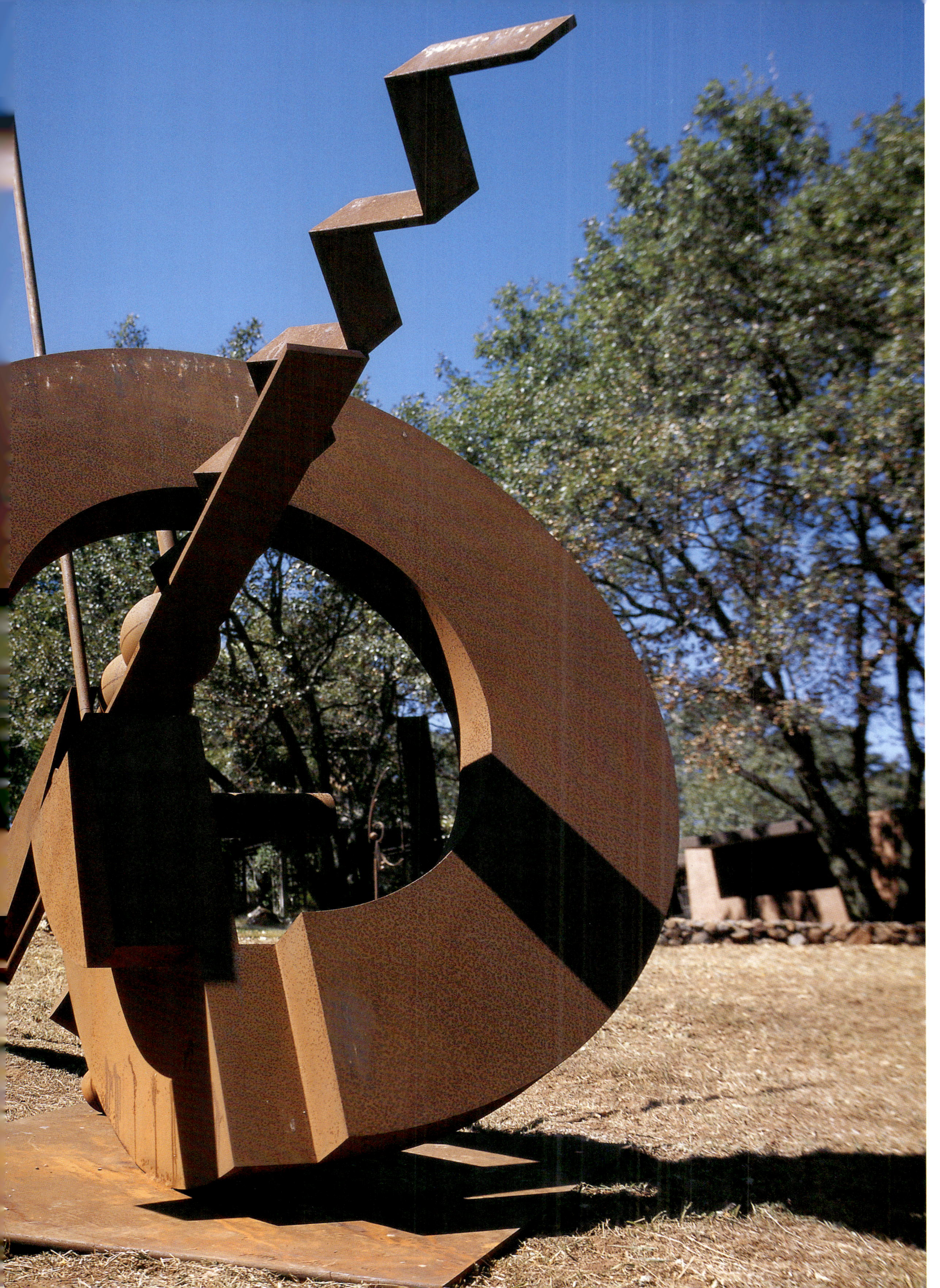

Broken Circle 11

2004, steel with patina
17½ x 16 x 14 inches
44 x 41 x 36 cm

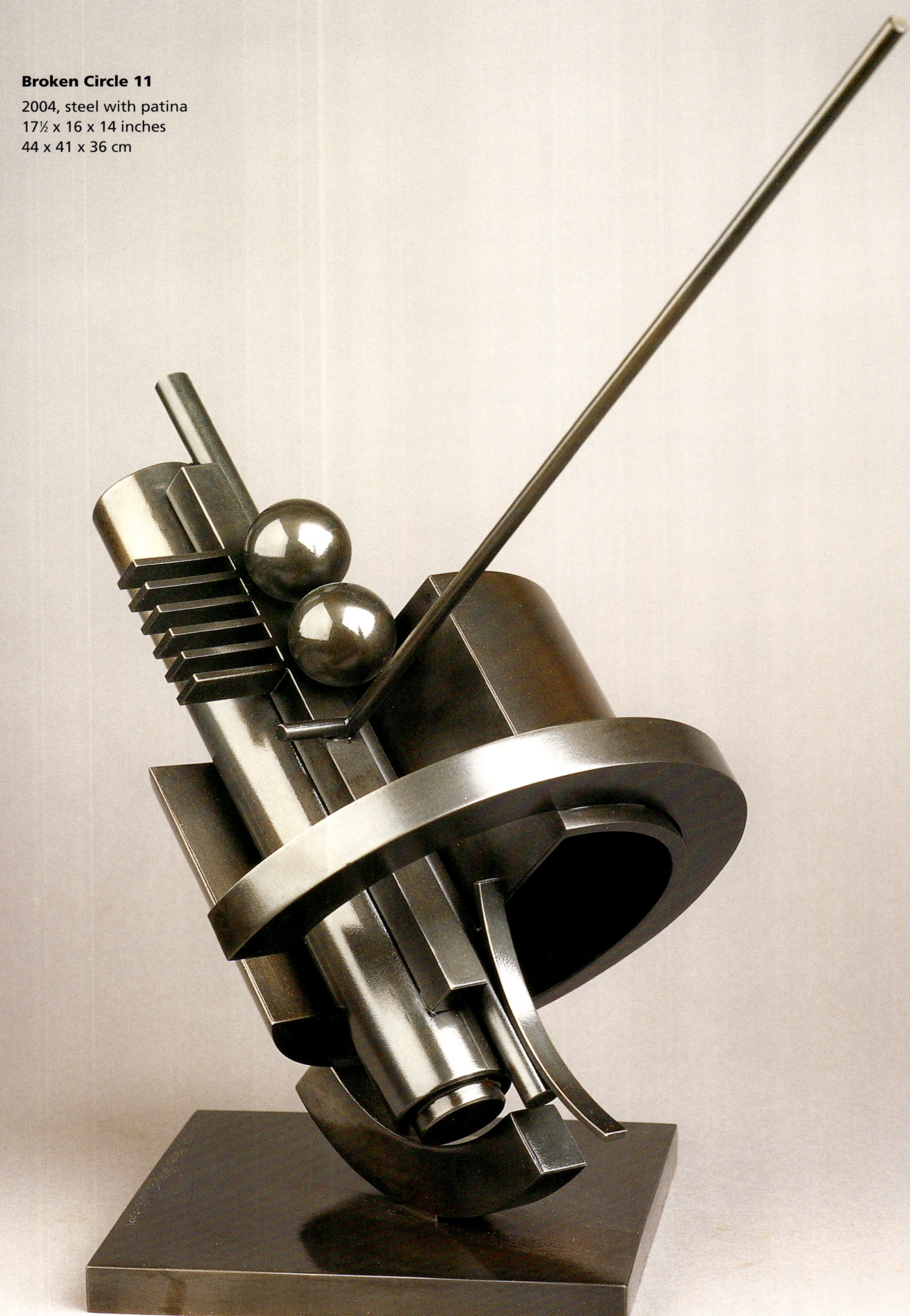

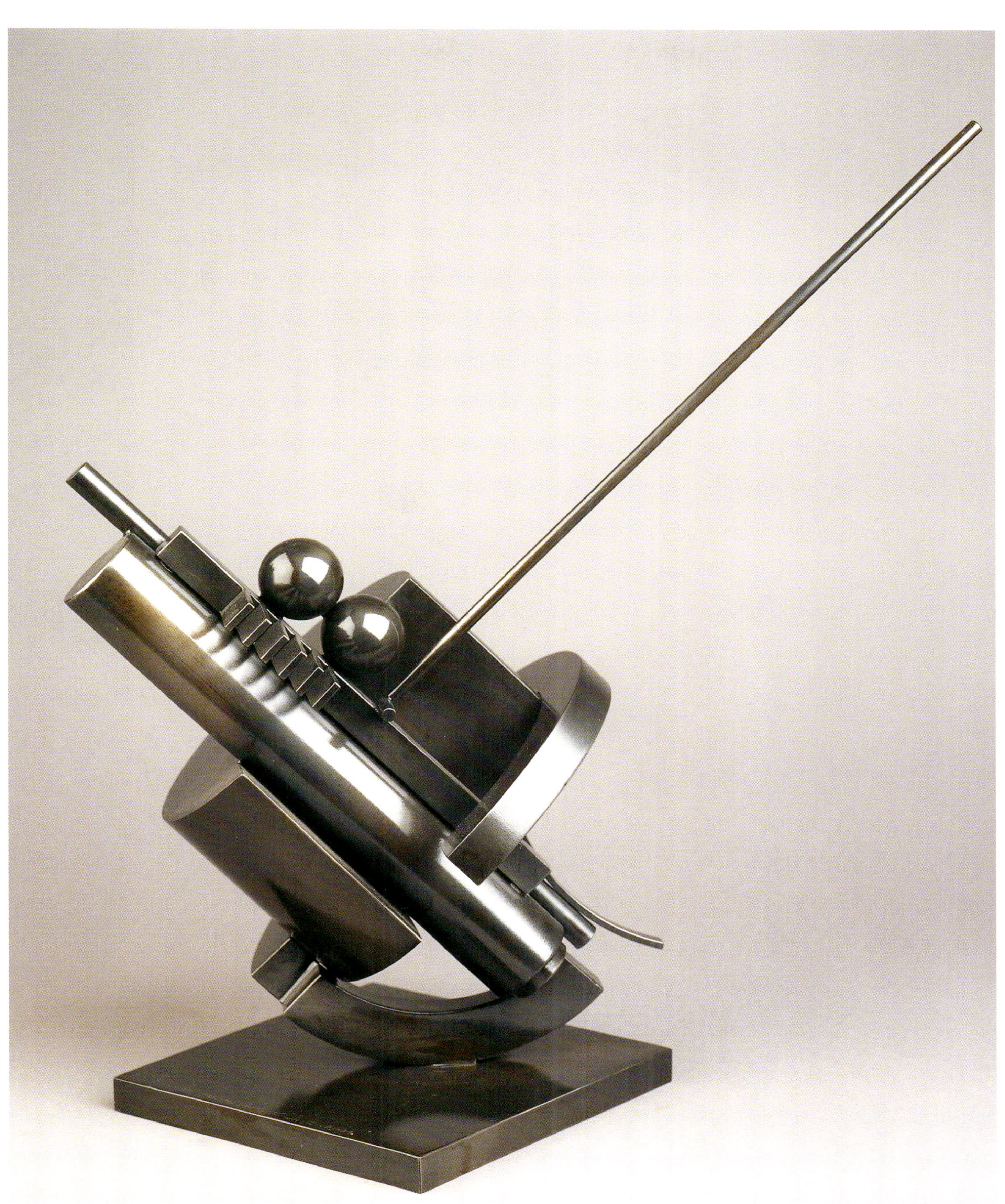

Broken Circle 11

2004, steel with patina
17½ x 16 x 14 inches
44 x 41 x 36 cm

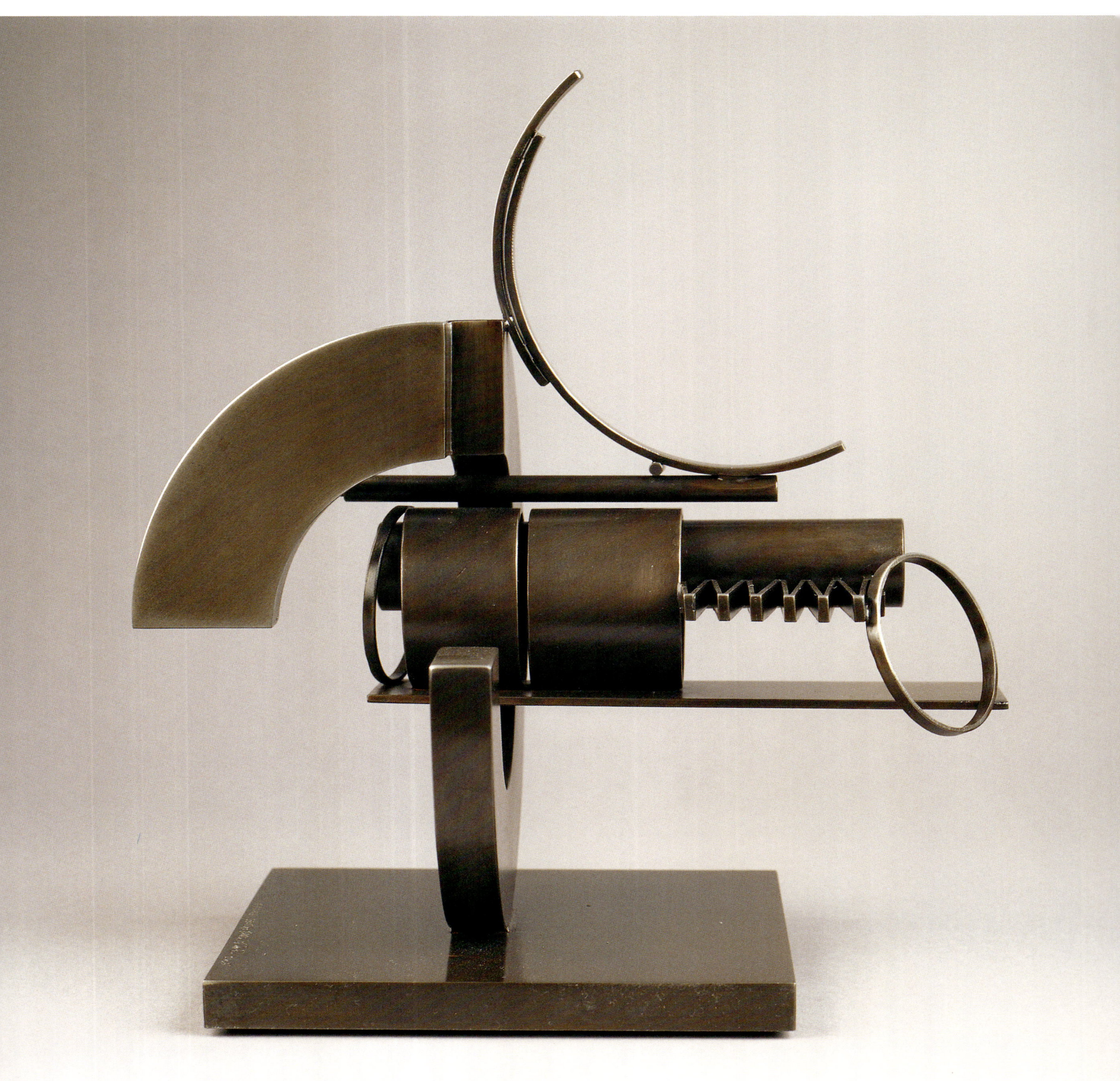

Broken Circle 16

2005, steel with patina
12½ x 11½ x 8 inches
32 x 29 x 20 cm

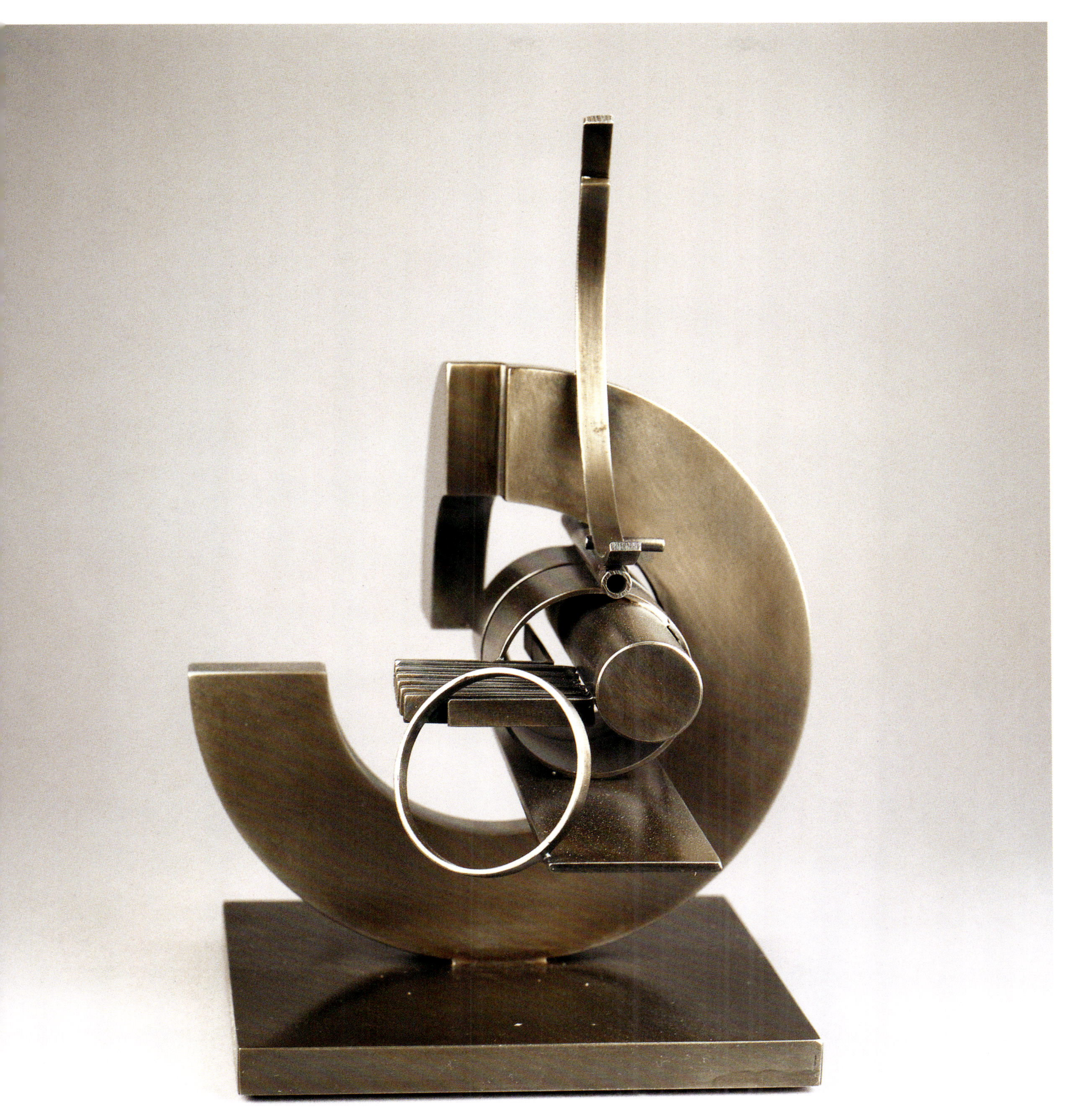

Broken Circle 16

2005, steel with patina
12½ x 11½ x 8 inches
32 x 29 x 20 cm

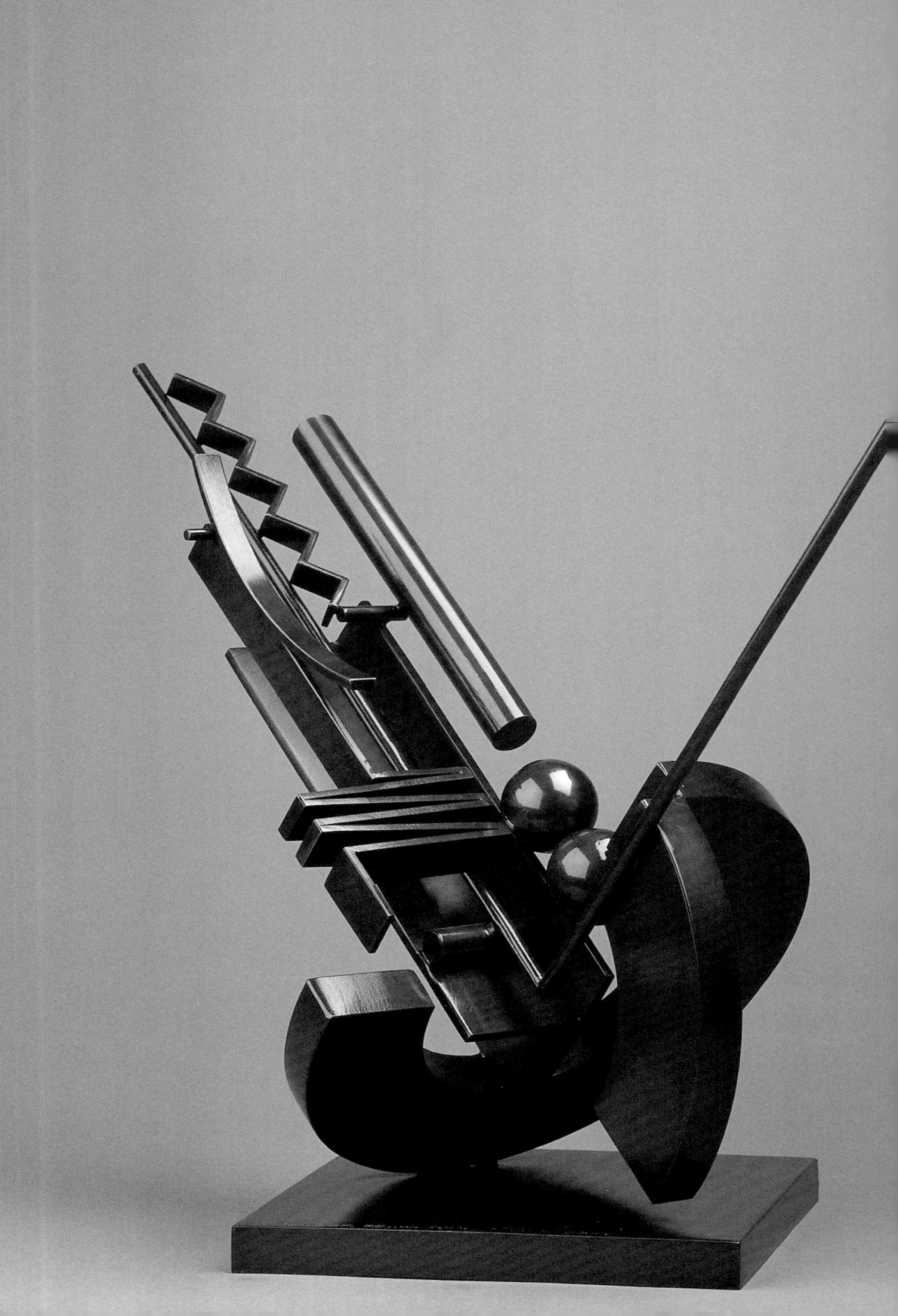

Broken Circle 3

2004, steel with patina
22 x 15 x 13 inches
56 x 38 x 33 cm

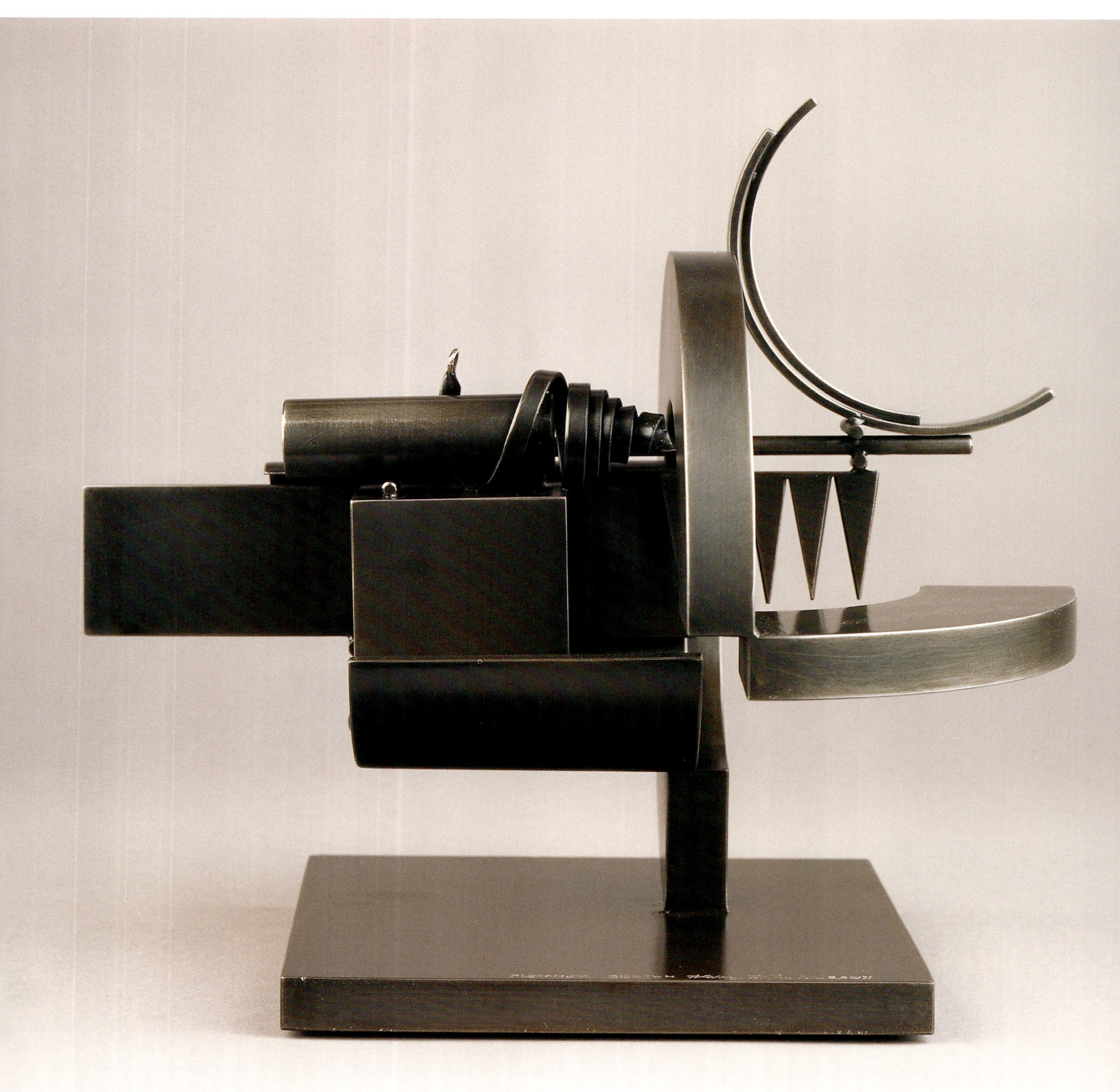

Broken Circle 17

2005, steel with patina
11 x 12 x 8 inches
28 x 30 x 20 cm

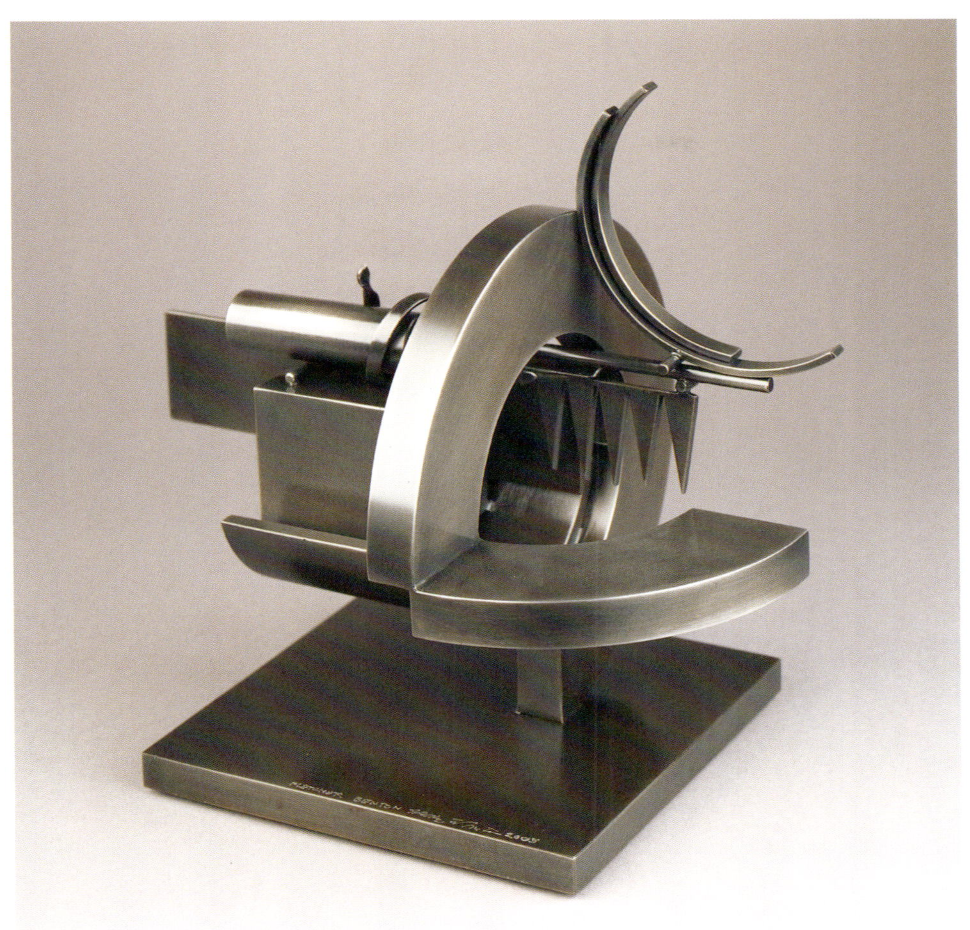

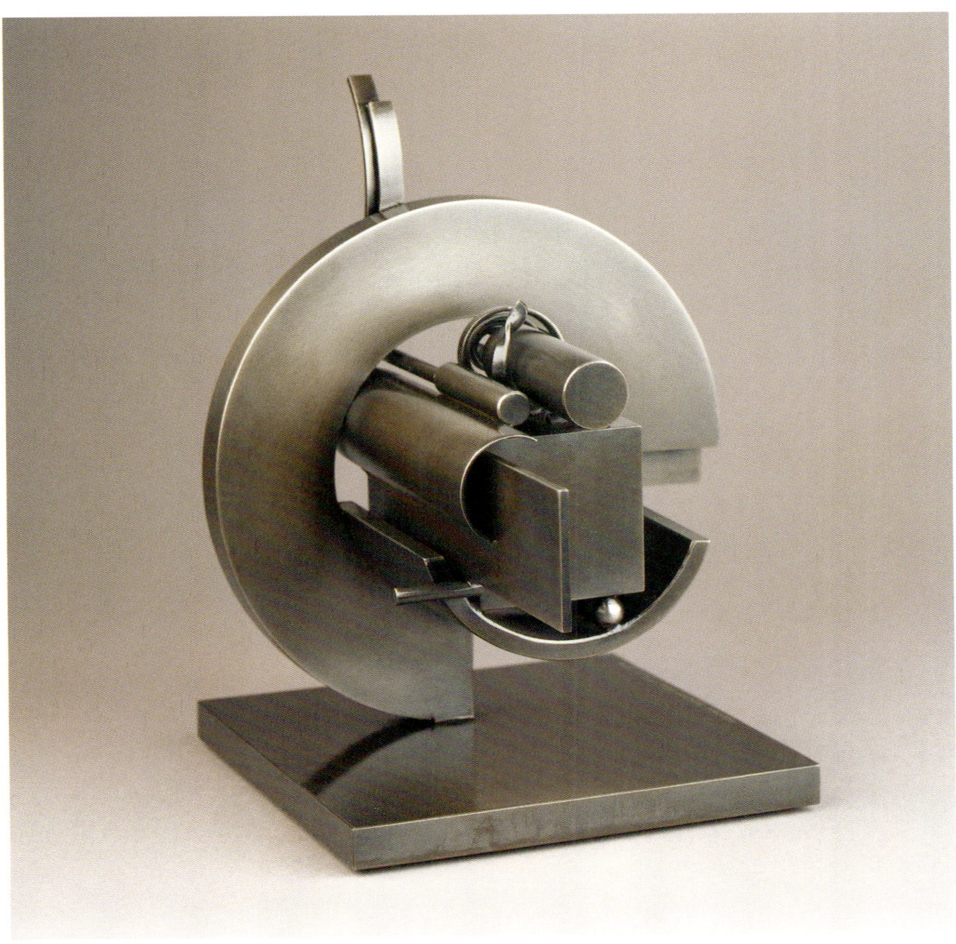

Broken Circle 17

2005, steel with patina
11 x 12 x 8 inches
28 x 30 x 20 cm

Broken Circle 18

2005, steel with patina
12½ x 12 x 8½ inches
32 x 30 x 22 cm

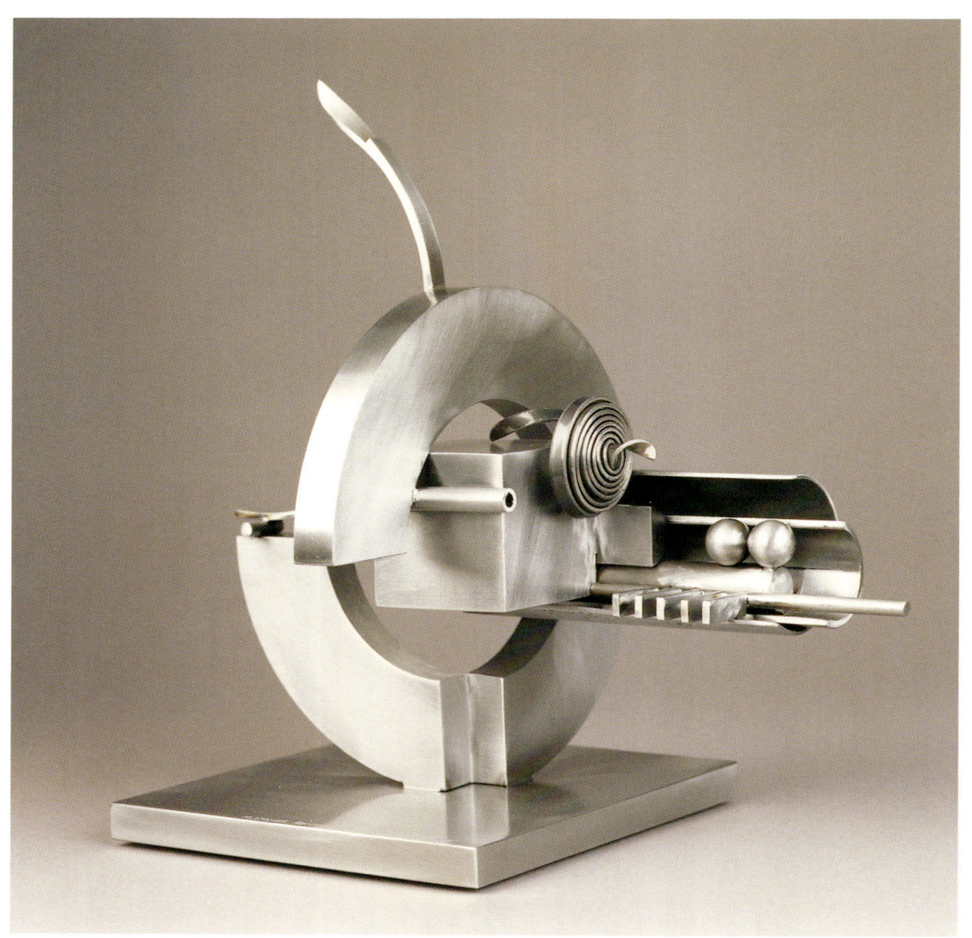

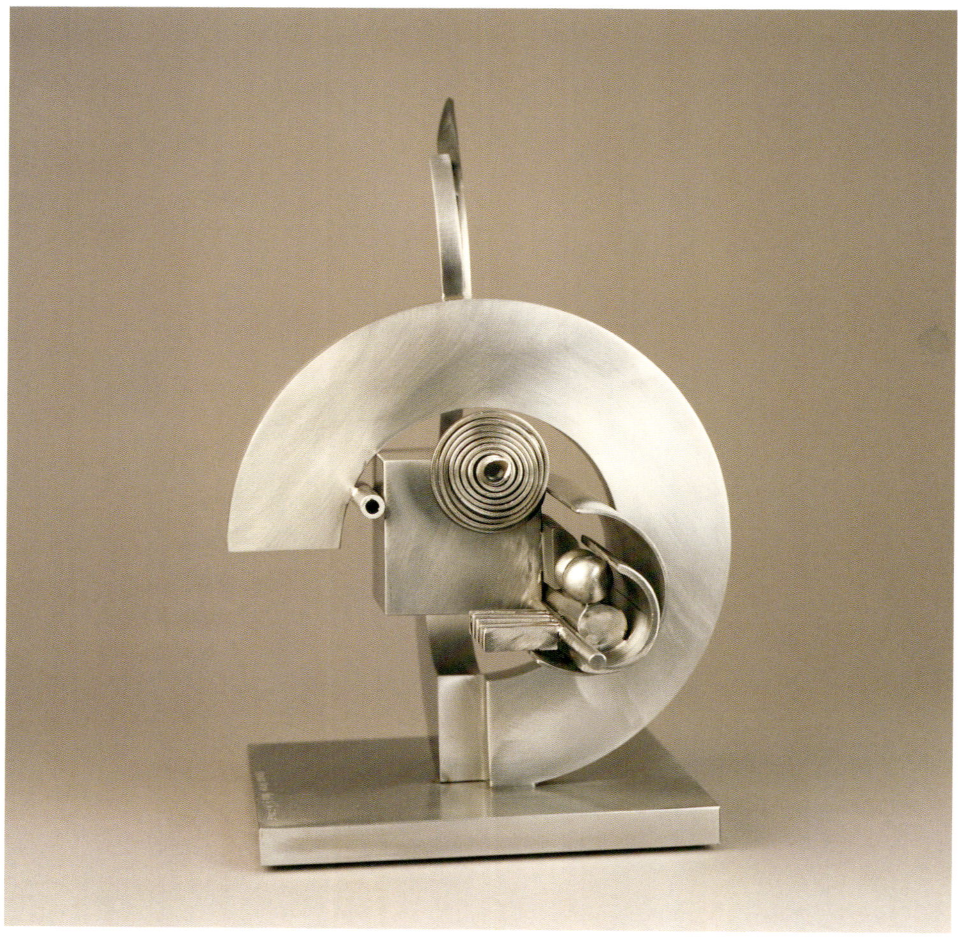

Broken Circle 18

2005, steel with patina
12½ x 12 x 8½ inches
32 x 30 x 22 cm

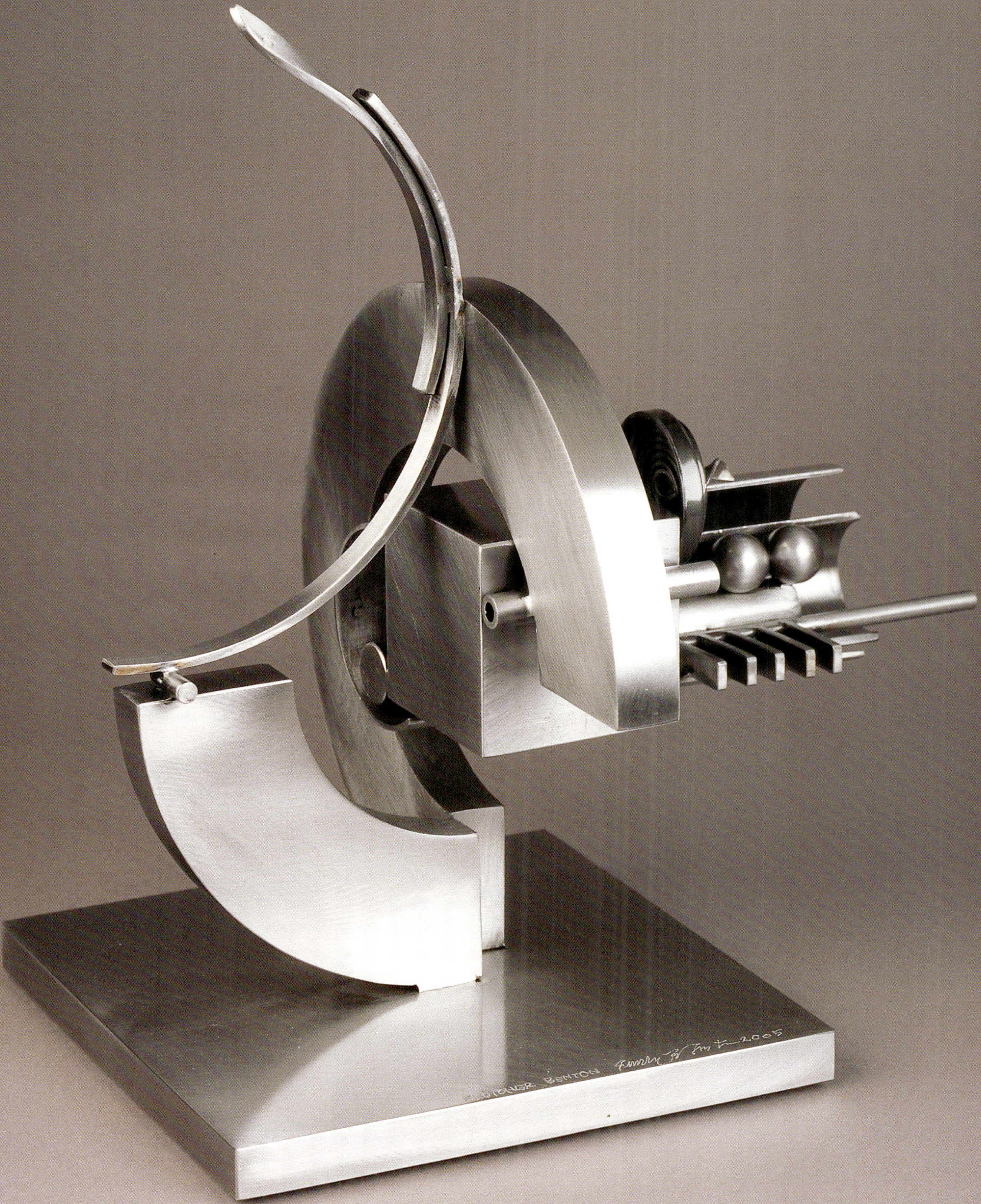

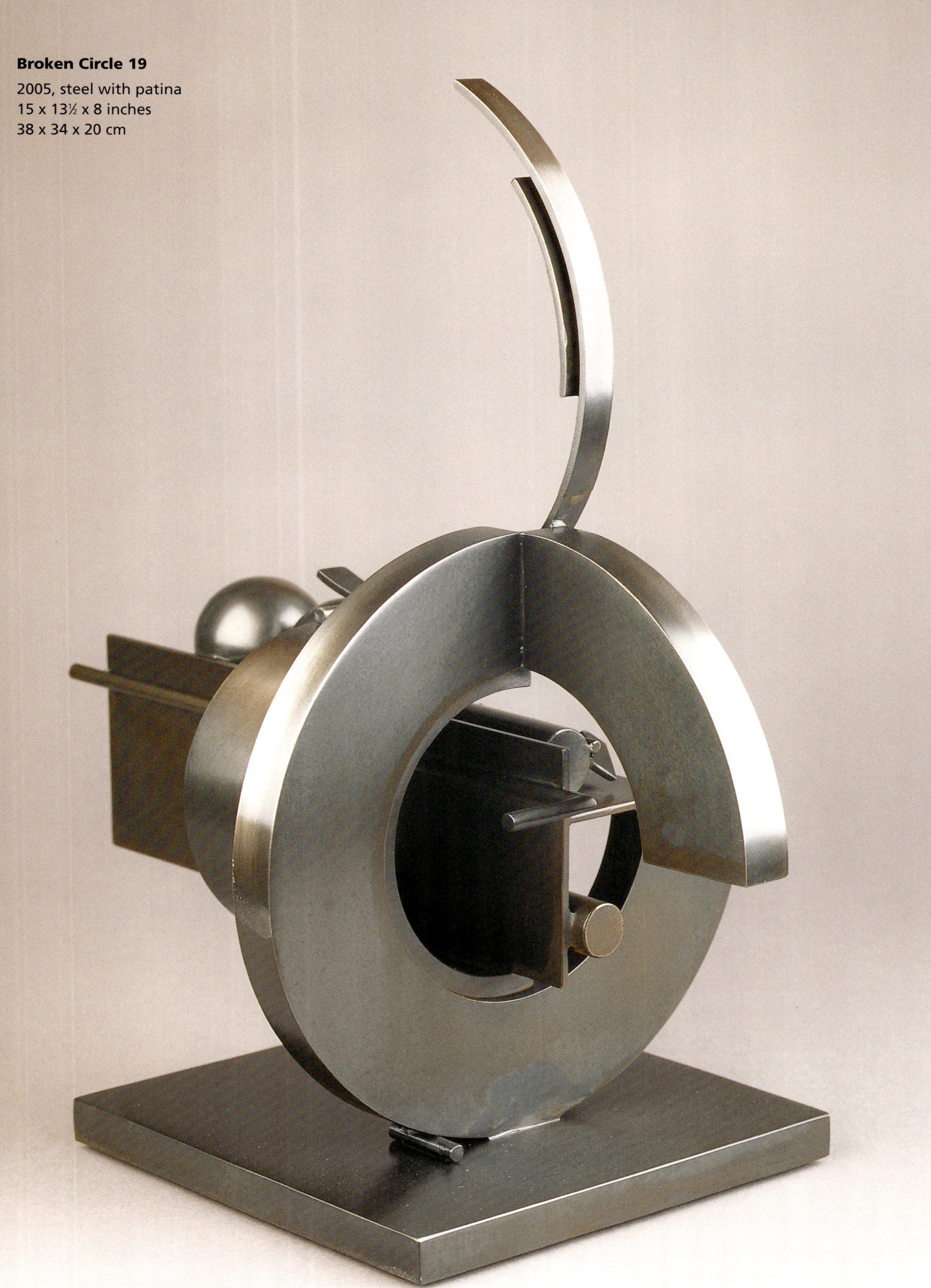

Broken Circle 19

2005, steel with patina
15 x 13½ x 8 inches
38 x 34 x 20 cm

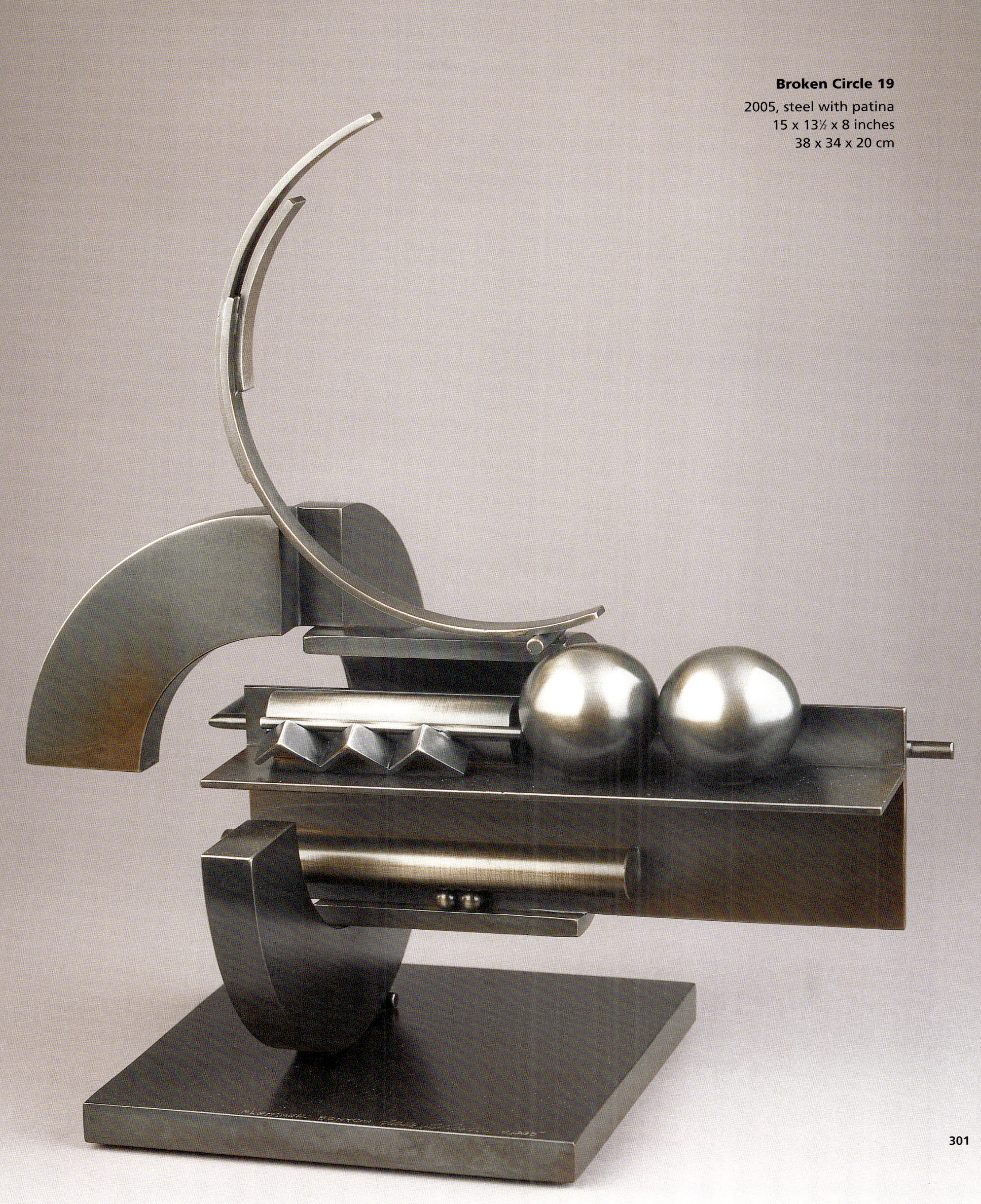

Broken Circle 19
2005, steel with patina
15 x 13½ x 8 inches
38 x 34 x 20 cm

Broken Circle with Two Balls, II

2004, bronze
19 x 10 x 10 inches
48 x 25 x 25 cm

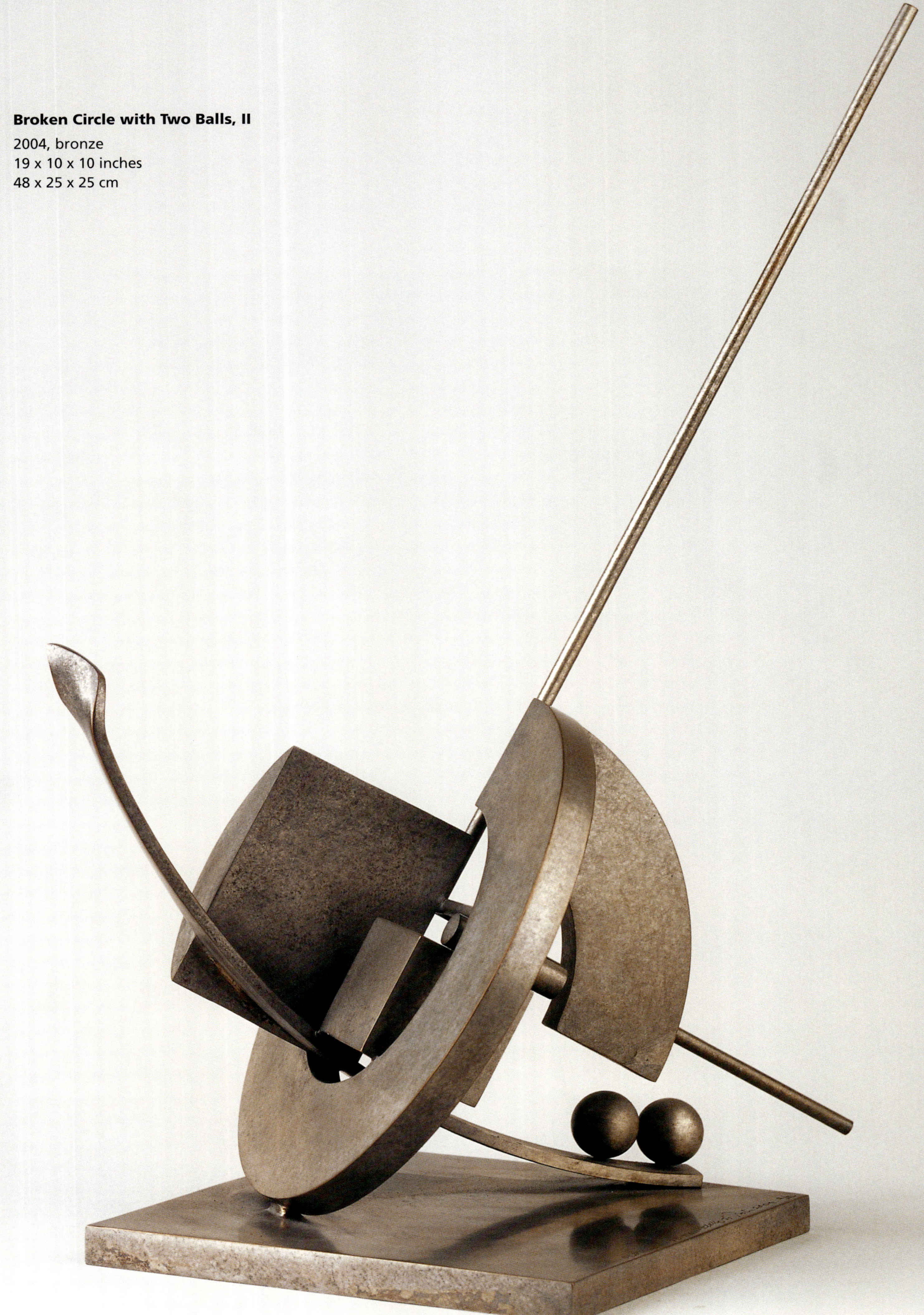

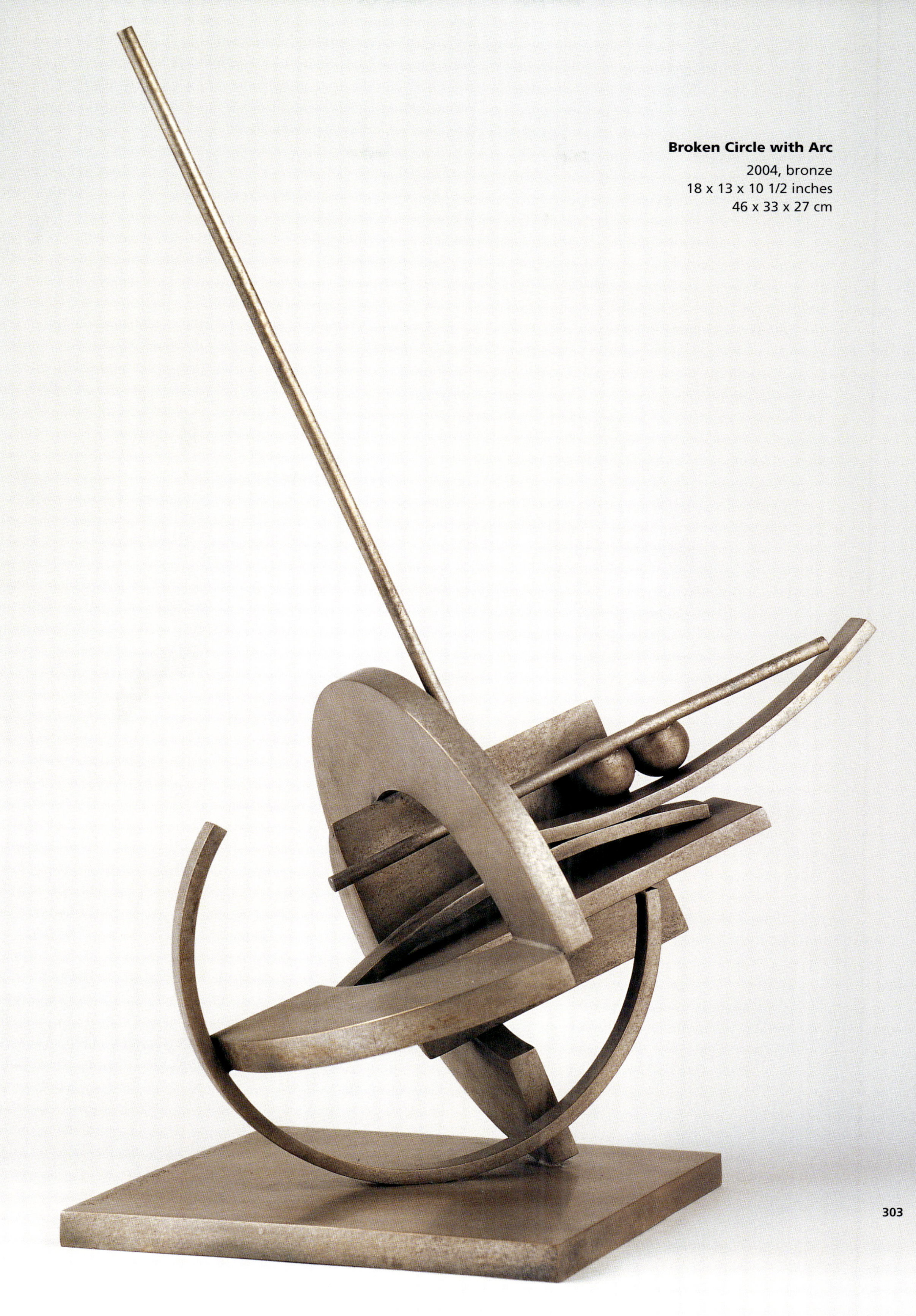

Broken Circle with Arc
2004, bronze
18 x 13 x 10 1/2 inches
46 x 33 x 27 cm

Broken Circle with Ring

2004, bronze
14 x 16 x 11 inches
36 x 41 x 28 cm

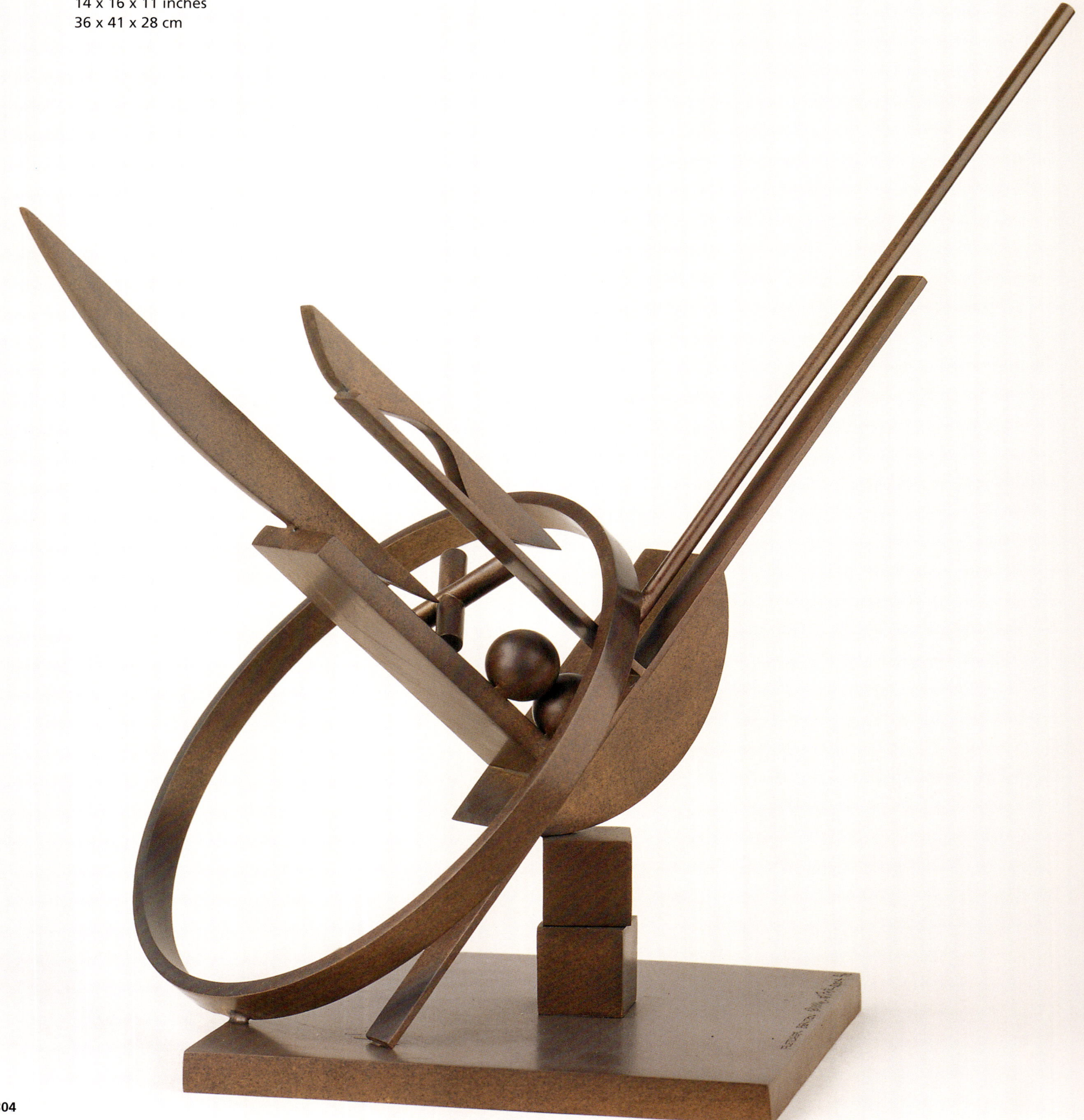

Broken Circle with Ring

2004, bronze
14 x 16 x 11 inches
36 x 41 x 28 cm

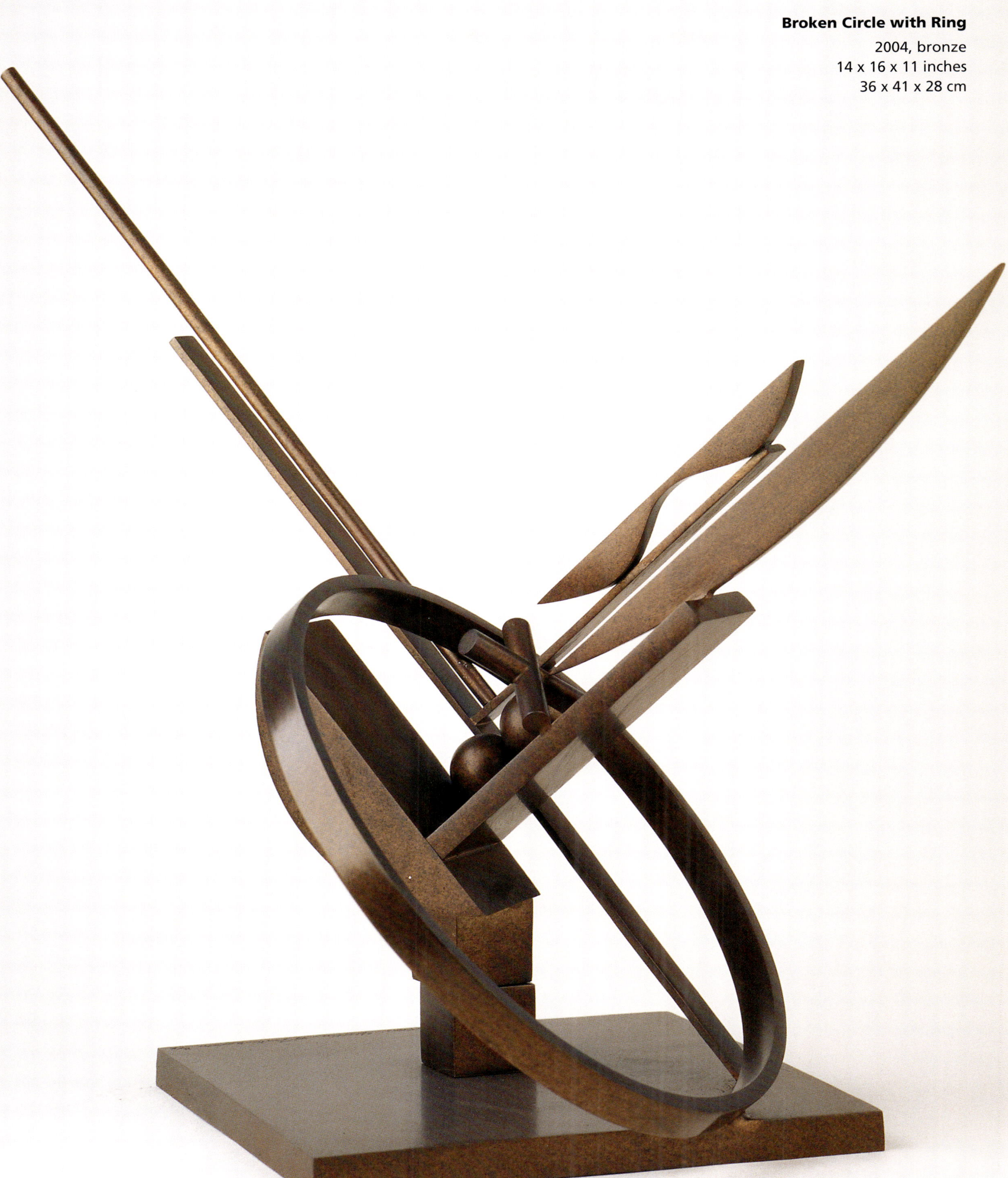

Rocker with Balls 6

2003, steel with patina
25½ x 26 x 10 inches
65 x 66 x 25 cm

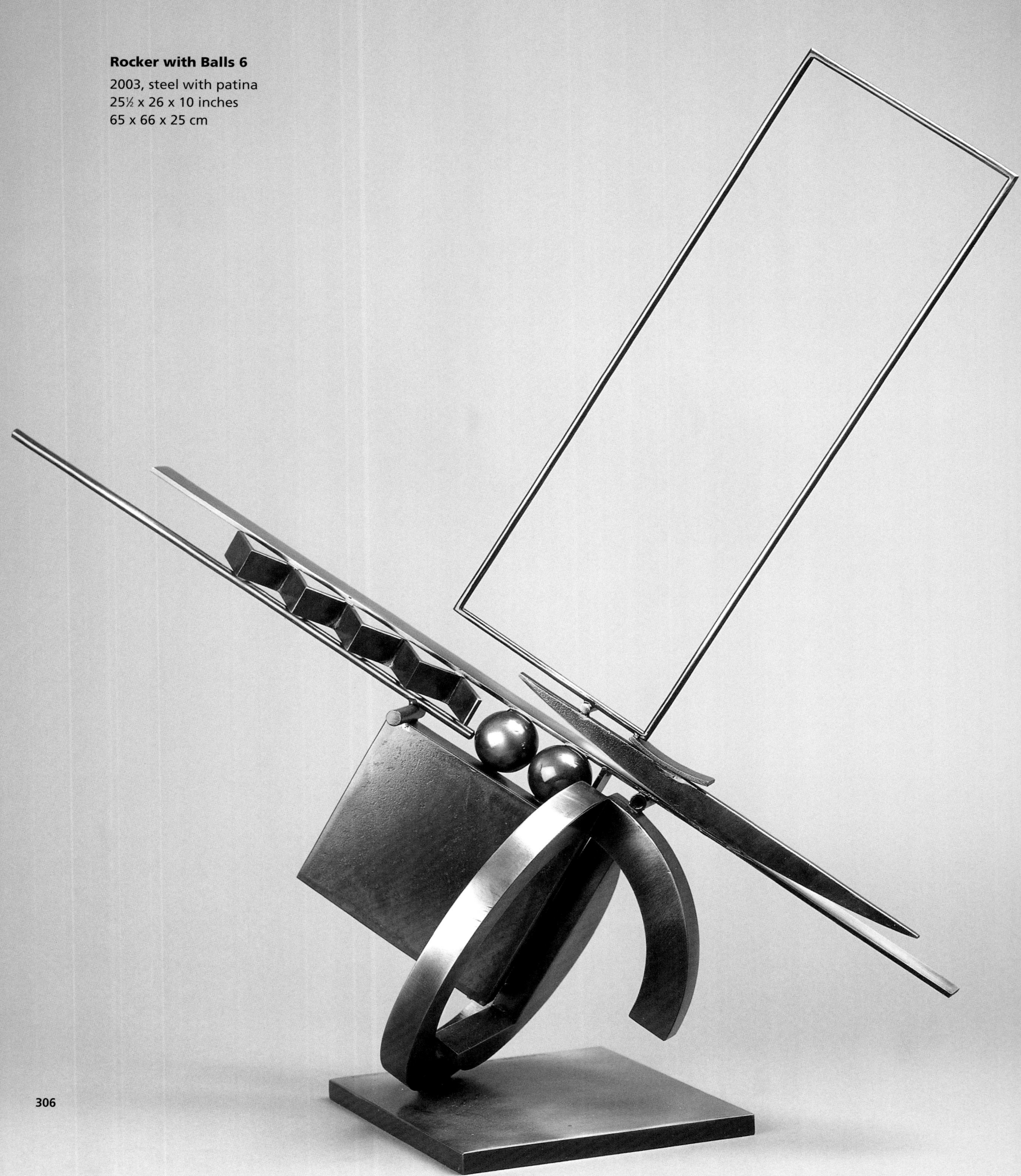

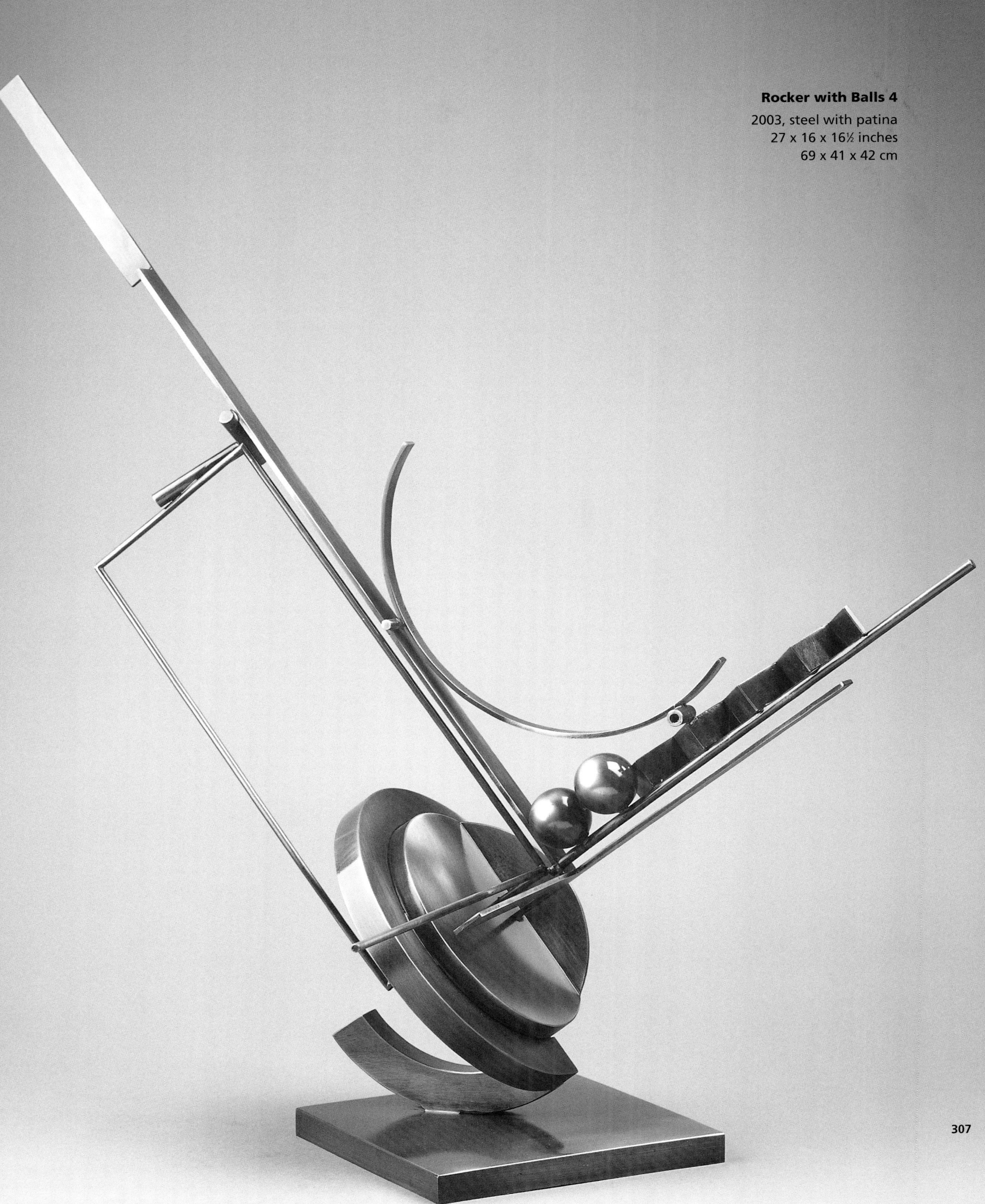

Rocker with Balls 4

2003, steel with patina
27 x 16 x 16½ inches
69 x 41 x 42 cm

Three Broken Circle sculptures
Dore Street Studio, 2006

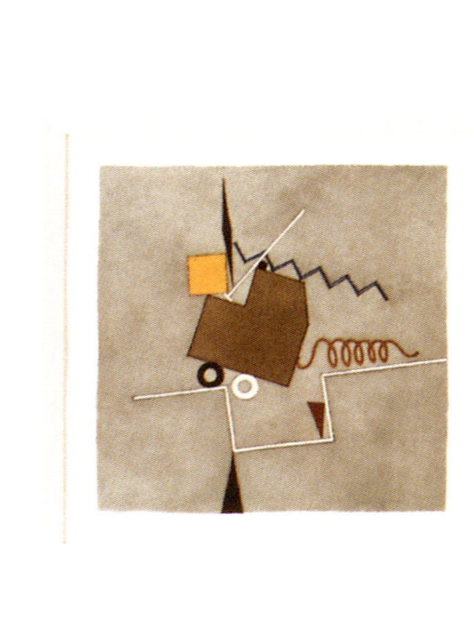

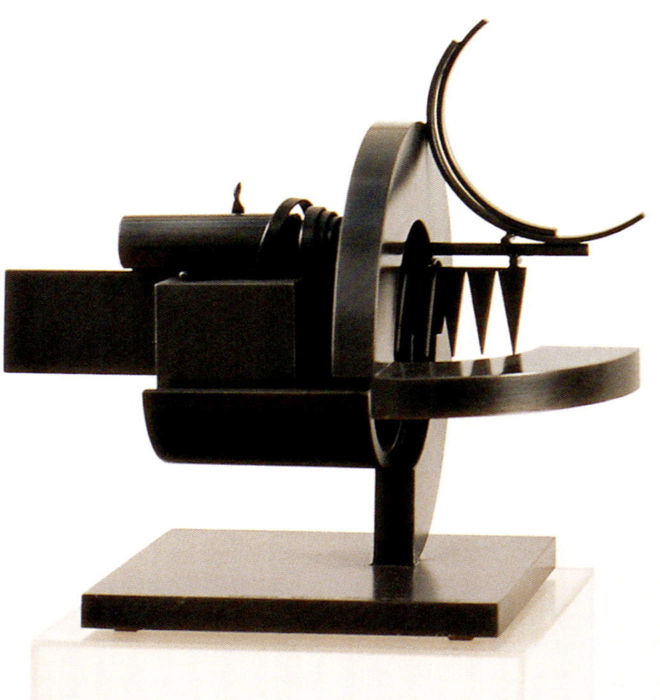

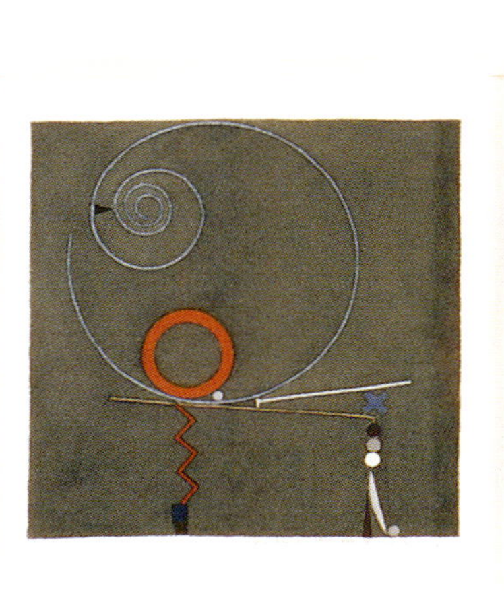

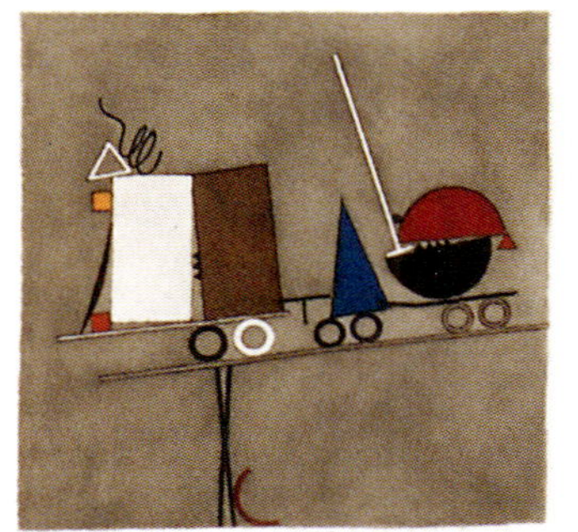

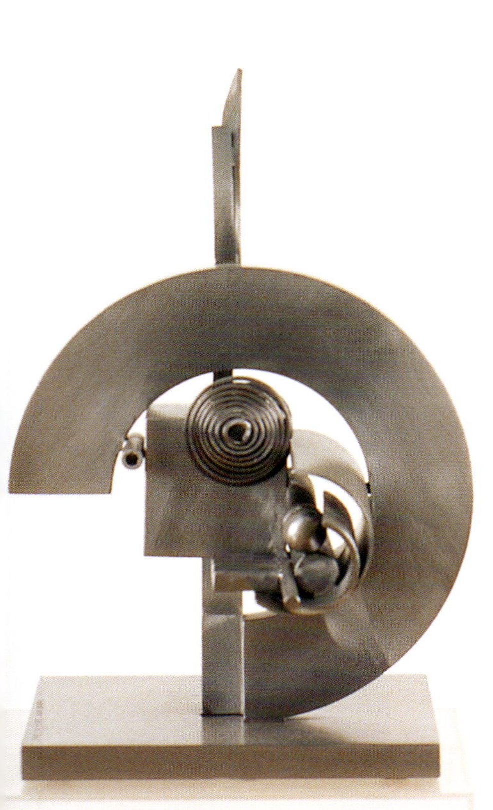

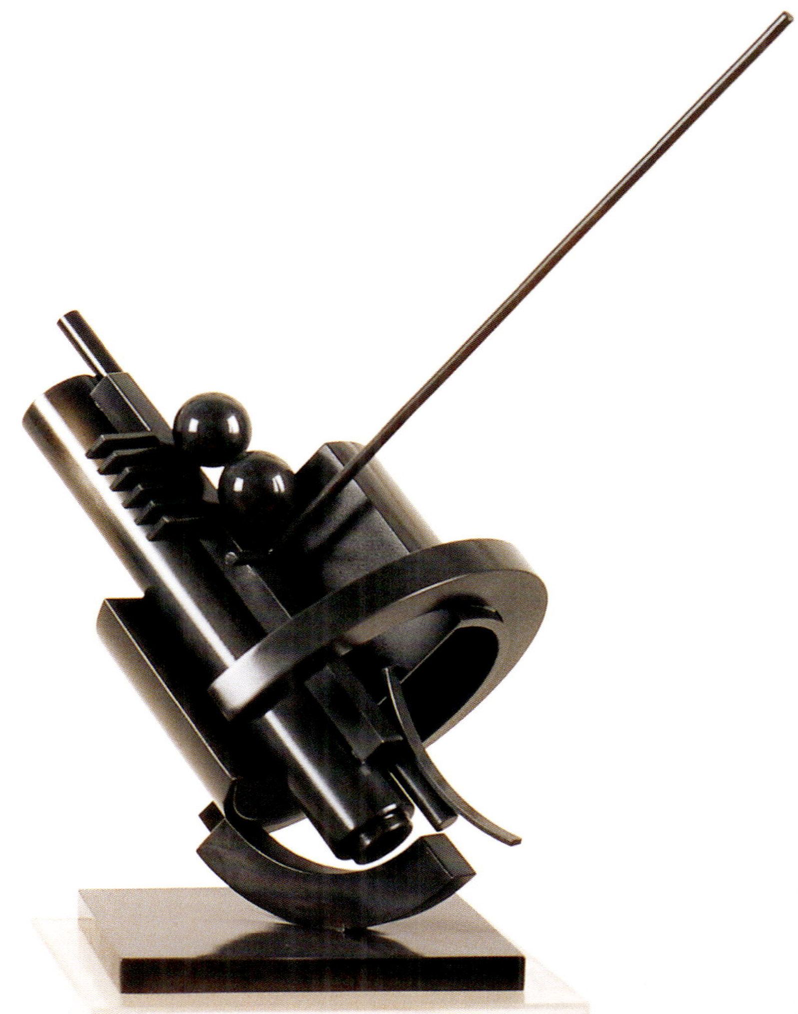

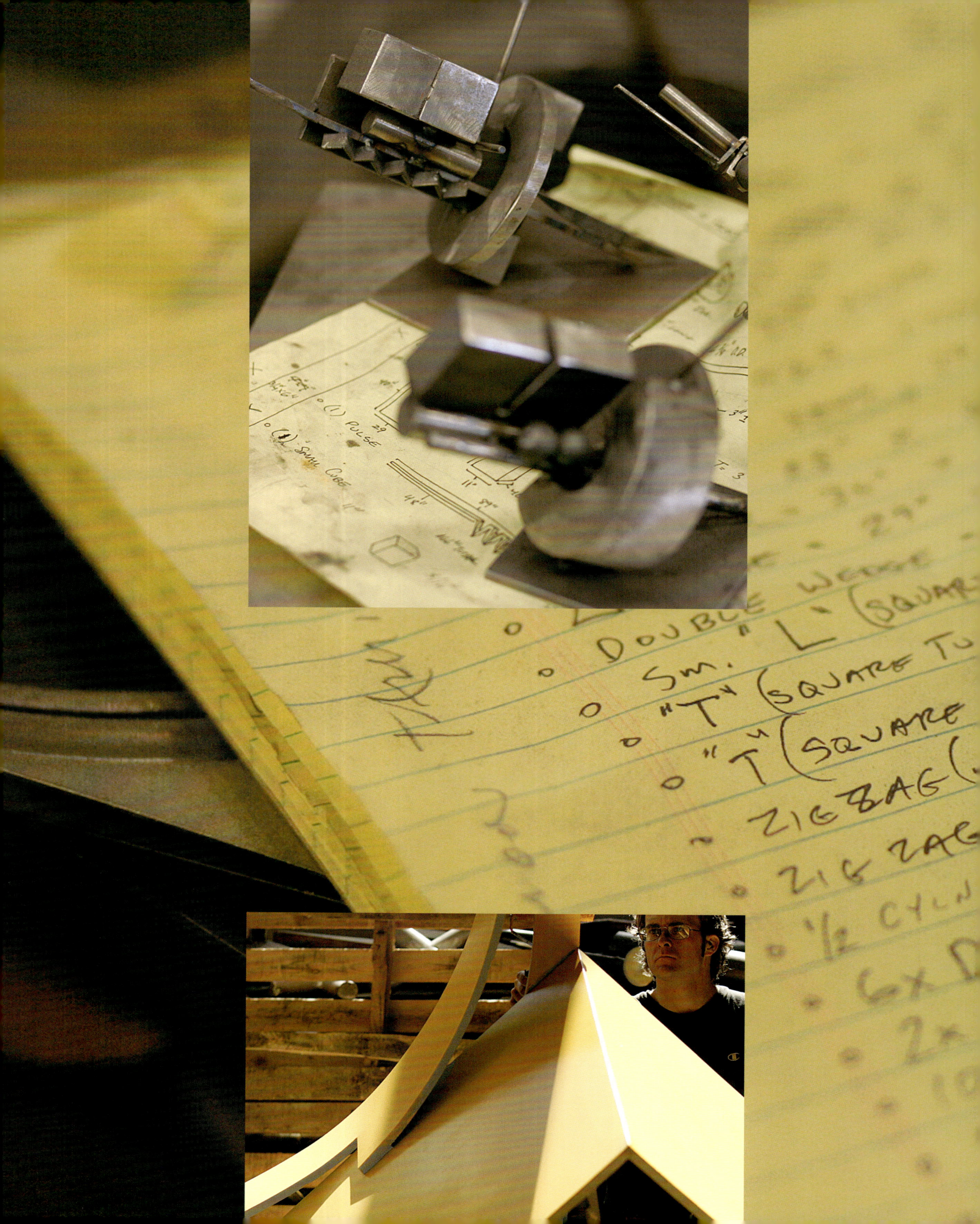
(1) PULSE
(1) SMALL CUBE
DOUBLE WEDGE
Sm. "L" (SQUAR
"T" (SQUARE TU
"T" (SQUARE
ZIGZAG(
ZIG ZAG
½ CYLN
6 X D

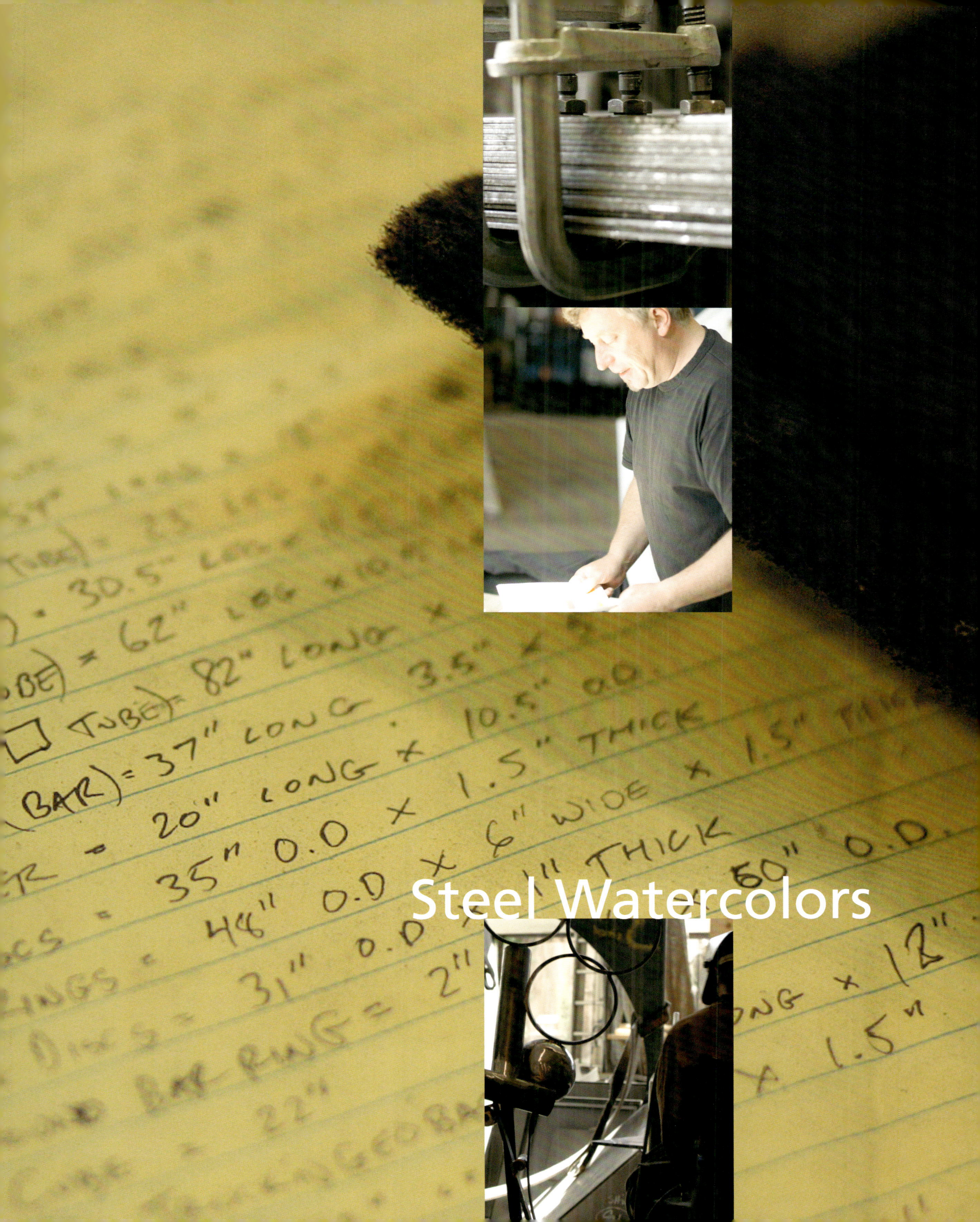

Steel Watercolors

▷
Steel Watercolor 81, Phase III

1985, steel with patina
16 x 5 x 3 feet
488 x 152 x 91 cm

▷ ▷
Truckin Jumbo Geo

2001, painted steel
H: 17 feet
H: 518 cm

▷ ▷ ▷
One-Legged Table 3

1989, painted steel
120 x 48 x 46 inches
305 x 122 x 117 cm

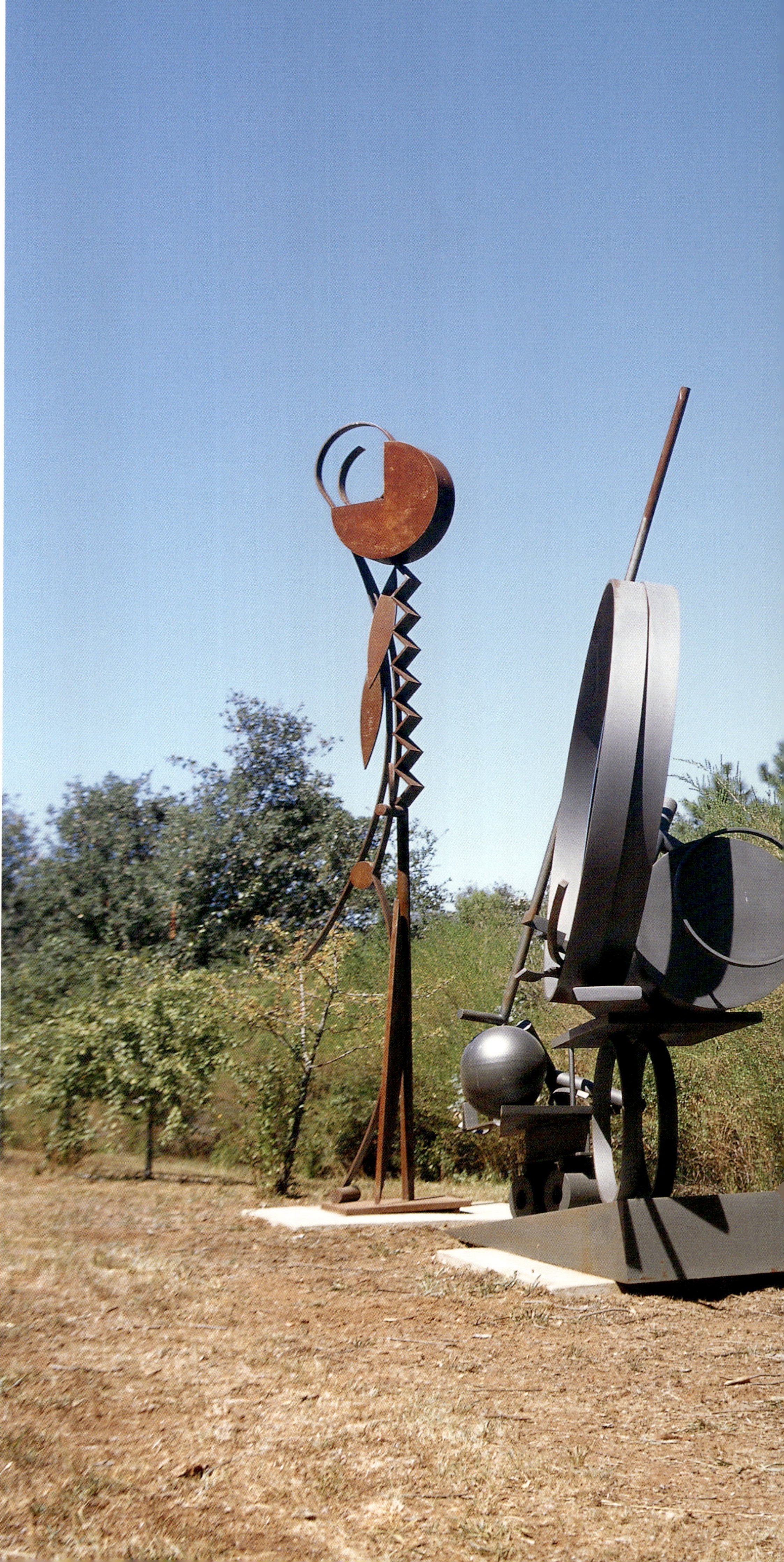

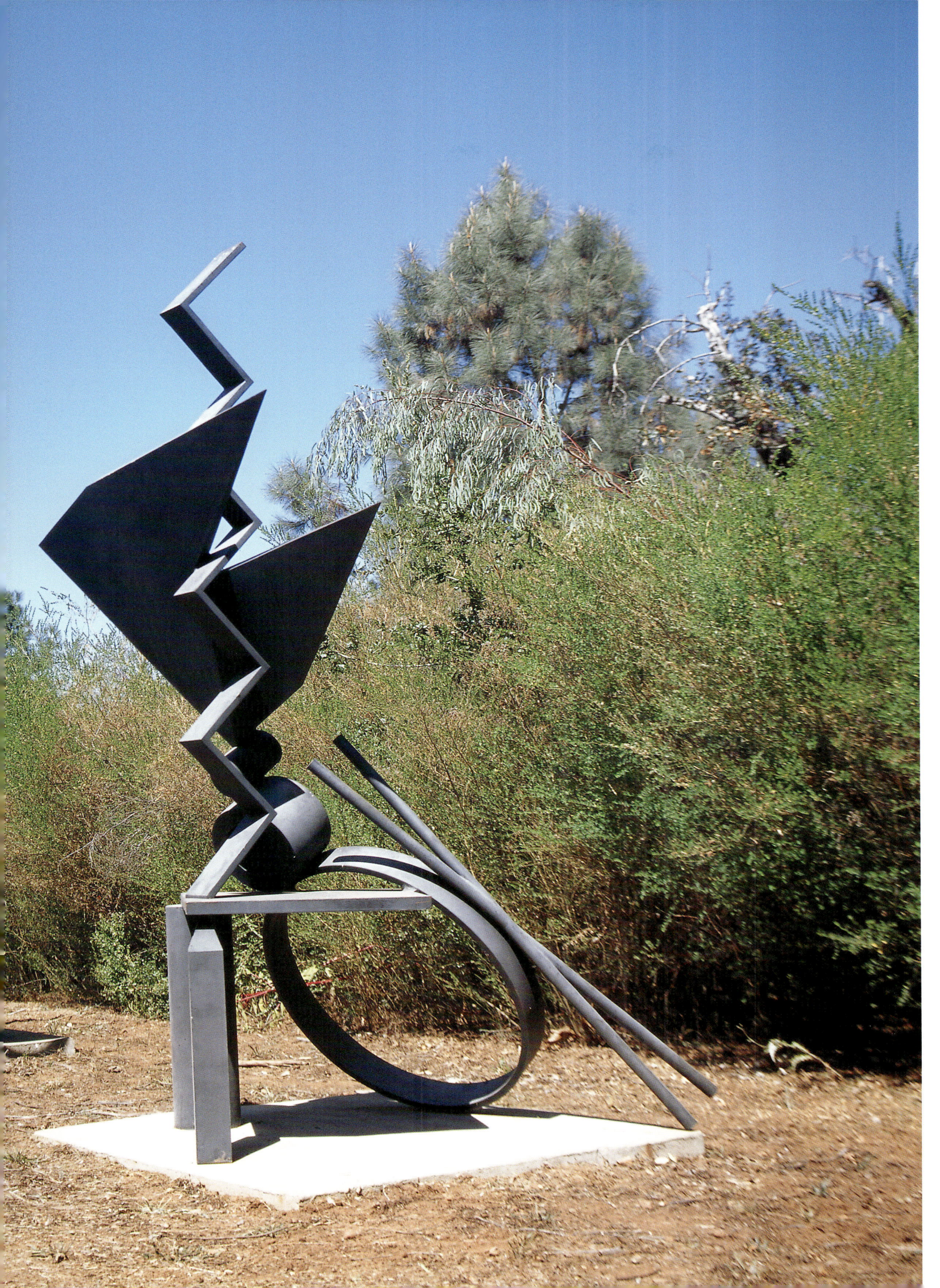

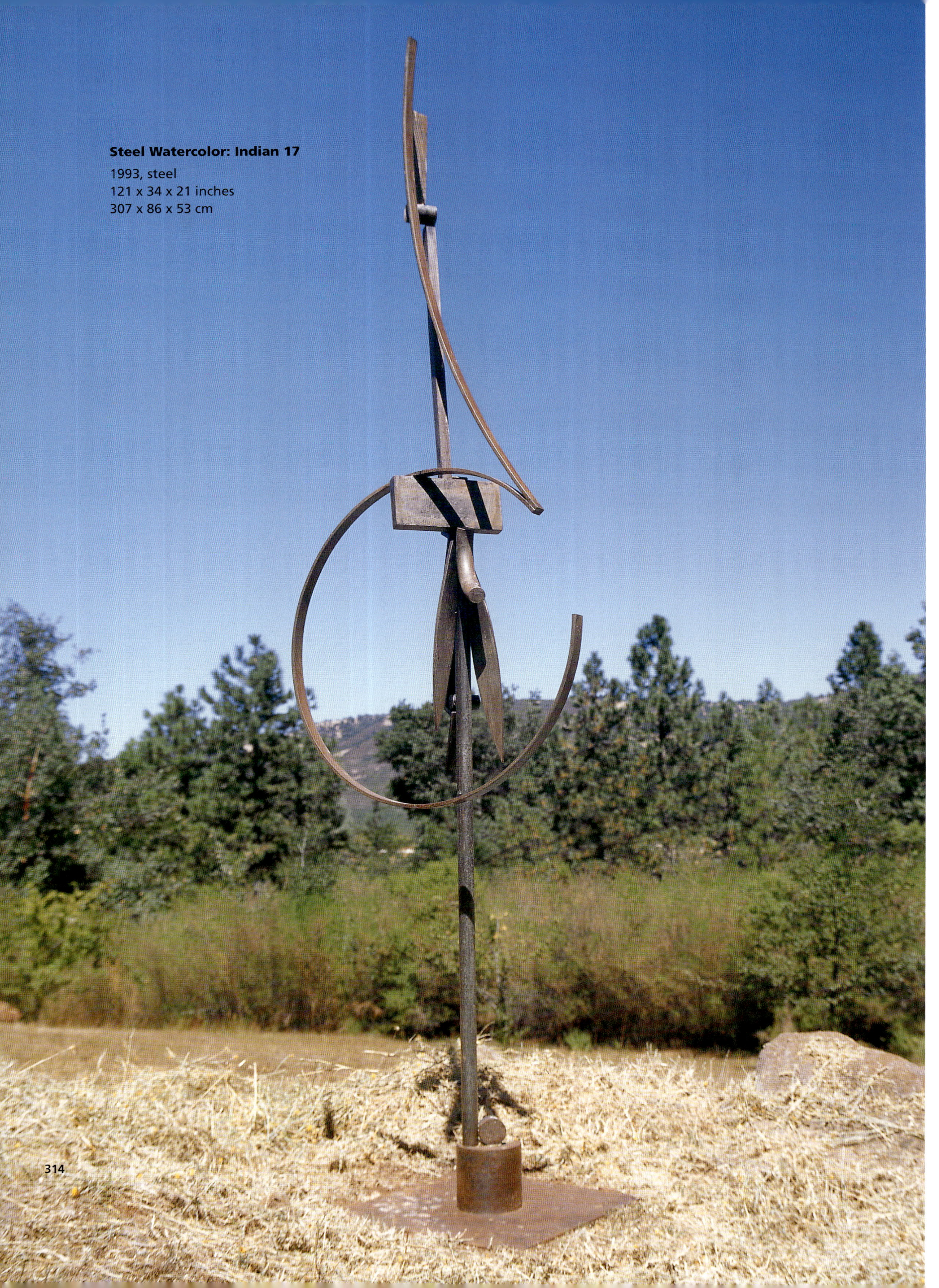

Steel Watercolor: Indian 17

1993, steel
121 x 34 x 21 inches
307 x 86 x 53 cm

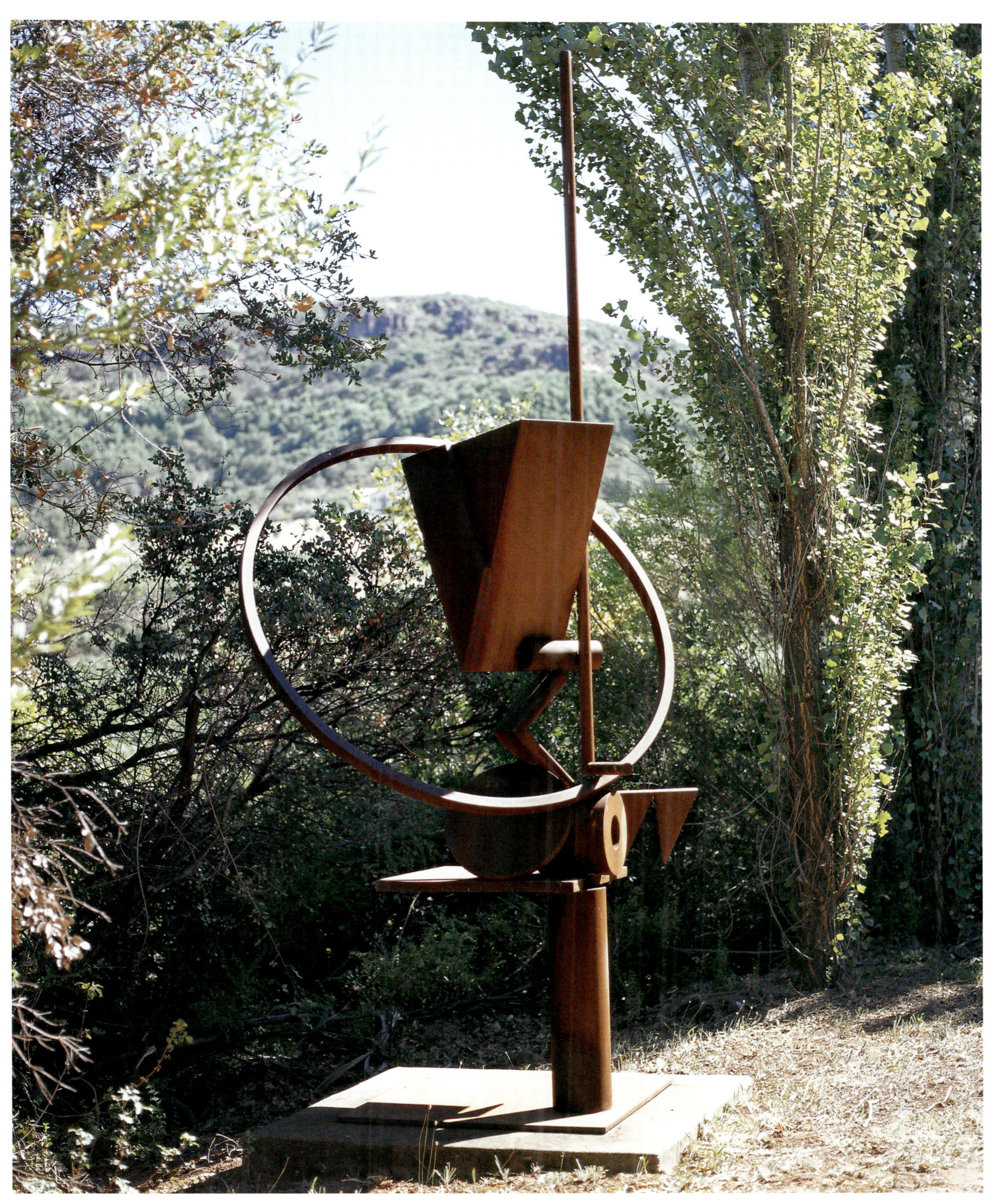

One-Legged Table with Triangle

1993, steel with patina
132 x 68 x 68 inches
335 x 173 x 173 cm

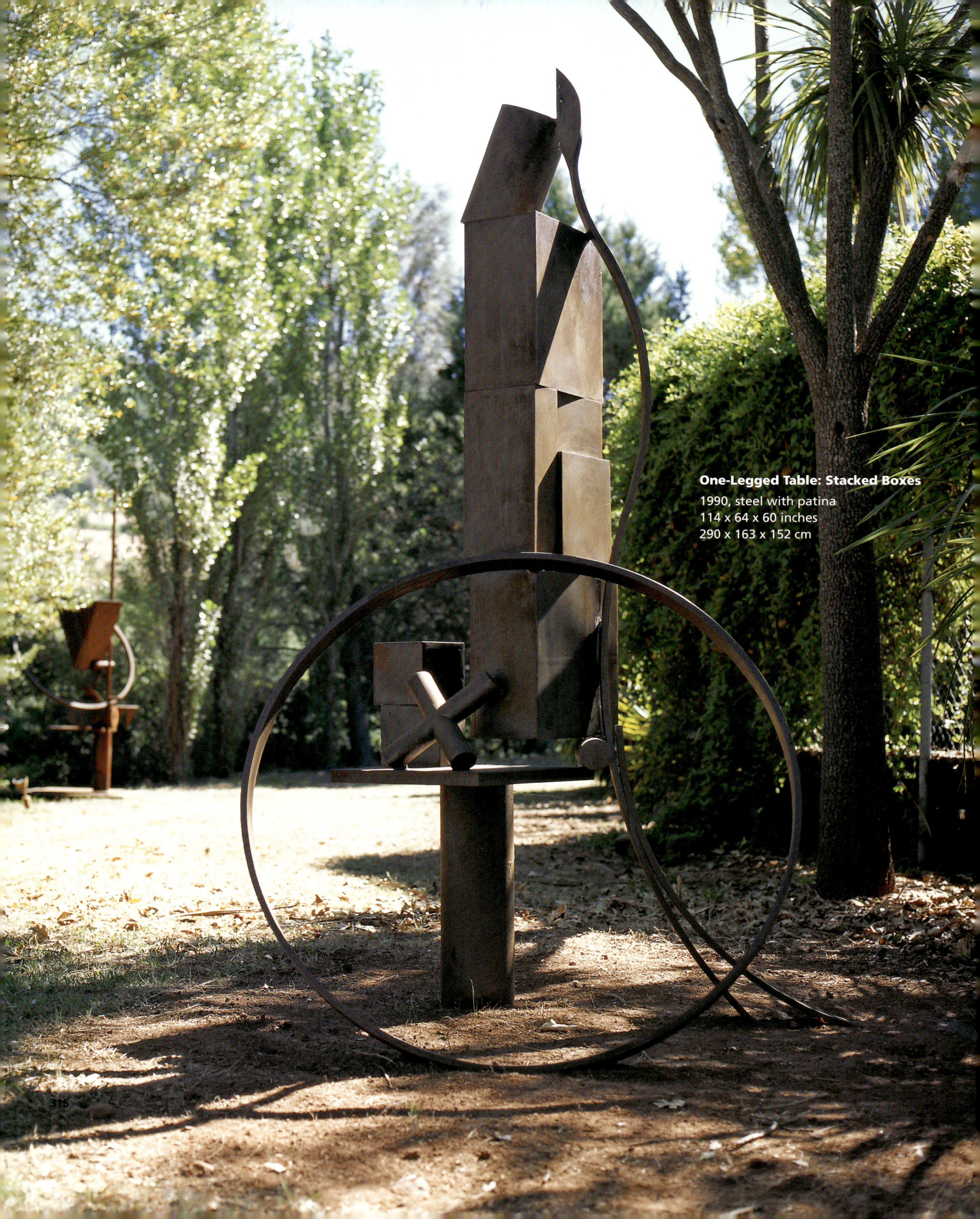

One-Legged Table: Stacked Boxes
1990, steel with patina
114 x 64 x 60 inches
290 x 163 x 152 cm

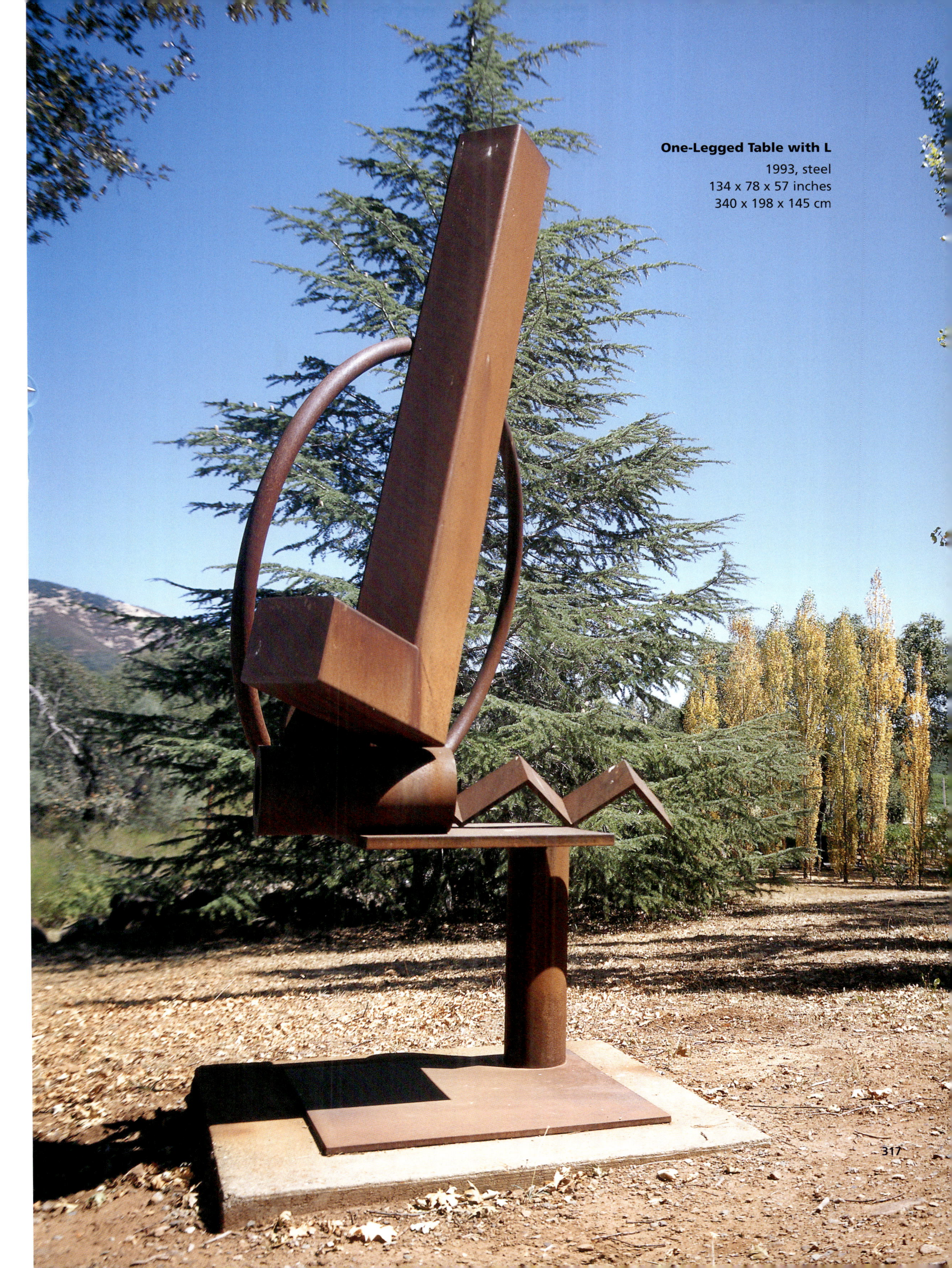

One-Legged Table with L
1993, steel
134 x 78 x 57 inches
340 x 198 x 145 cm

Wedge Arc

1998, steel
26 x 8 x 13 feet
792 x 244 x 396 cm

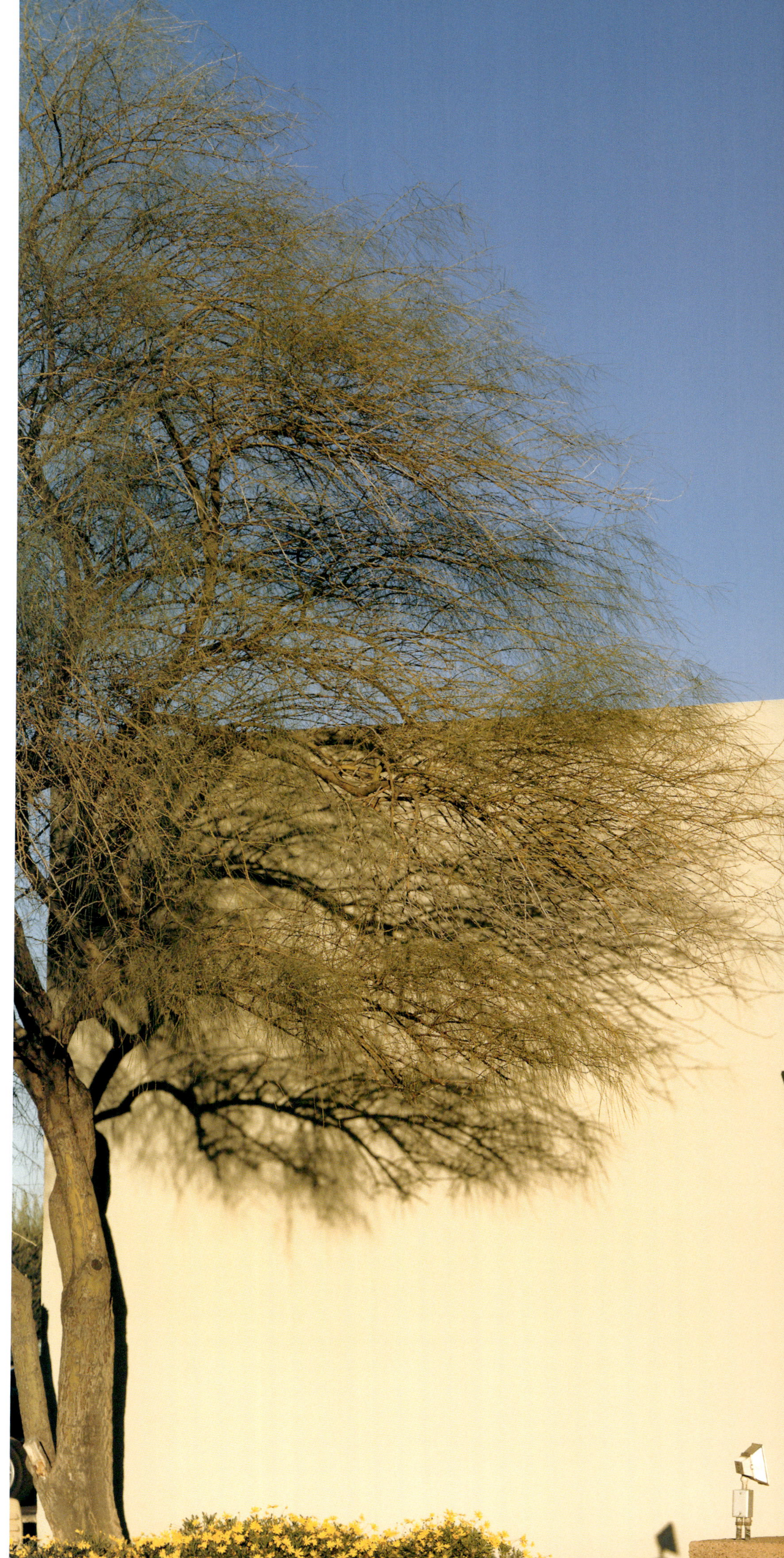

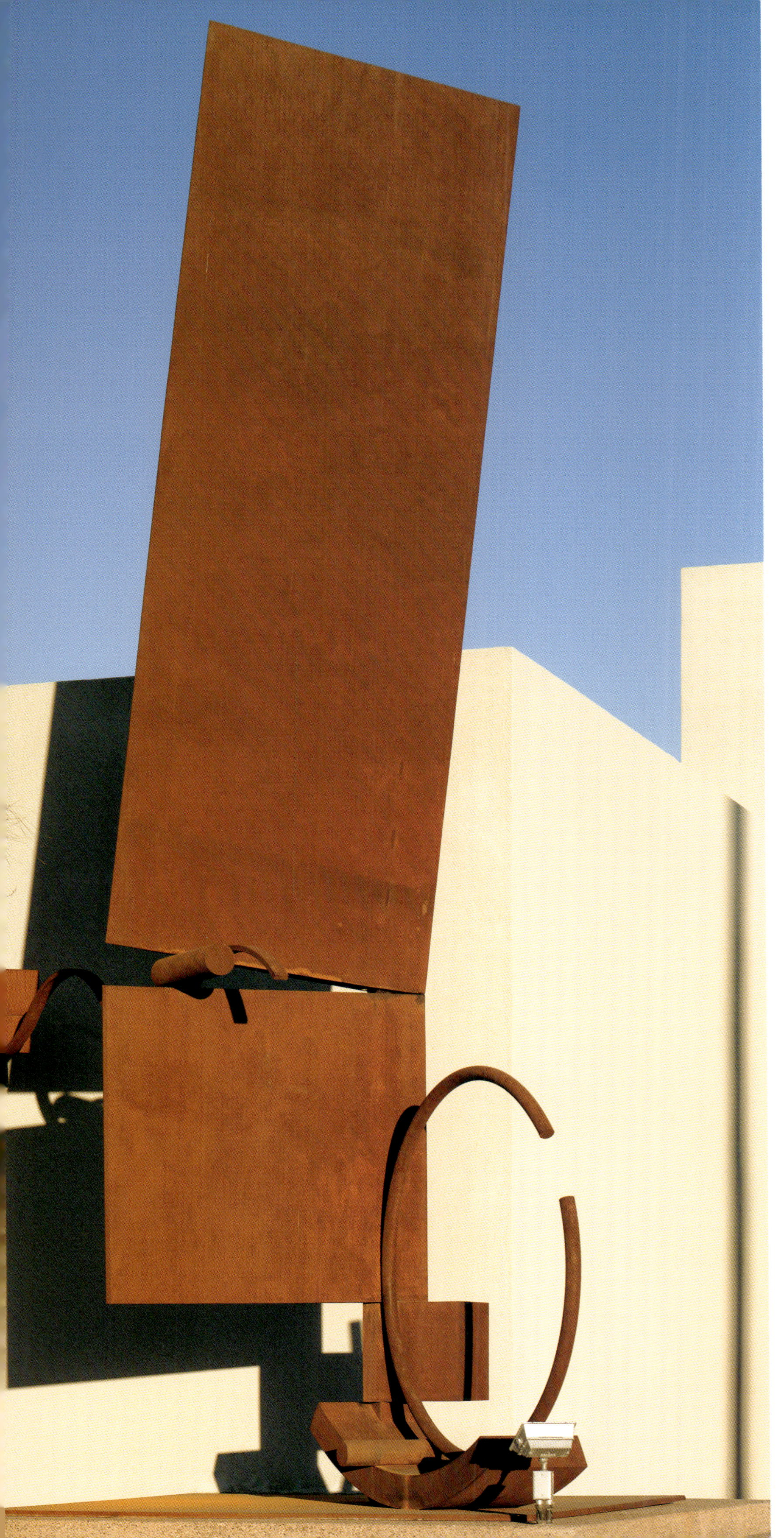

Truckin Jumbo Geo

2001, painted steel
H: 17 feet
H: 518 cm

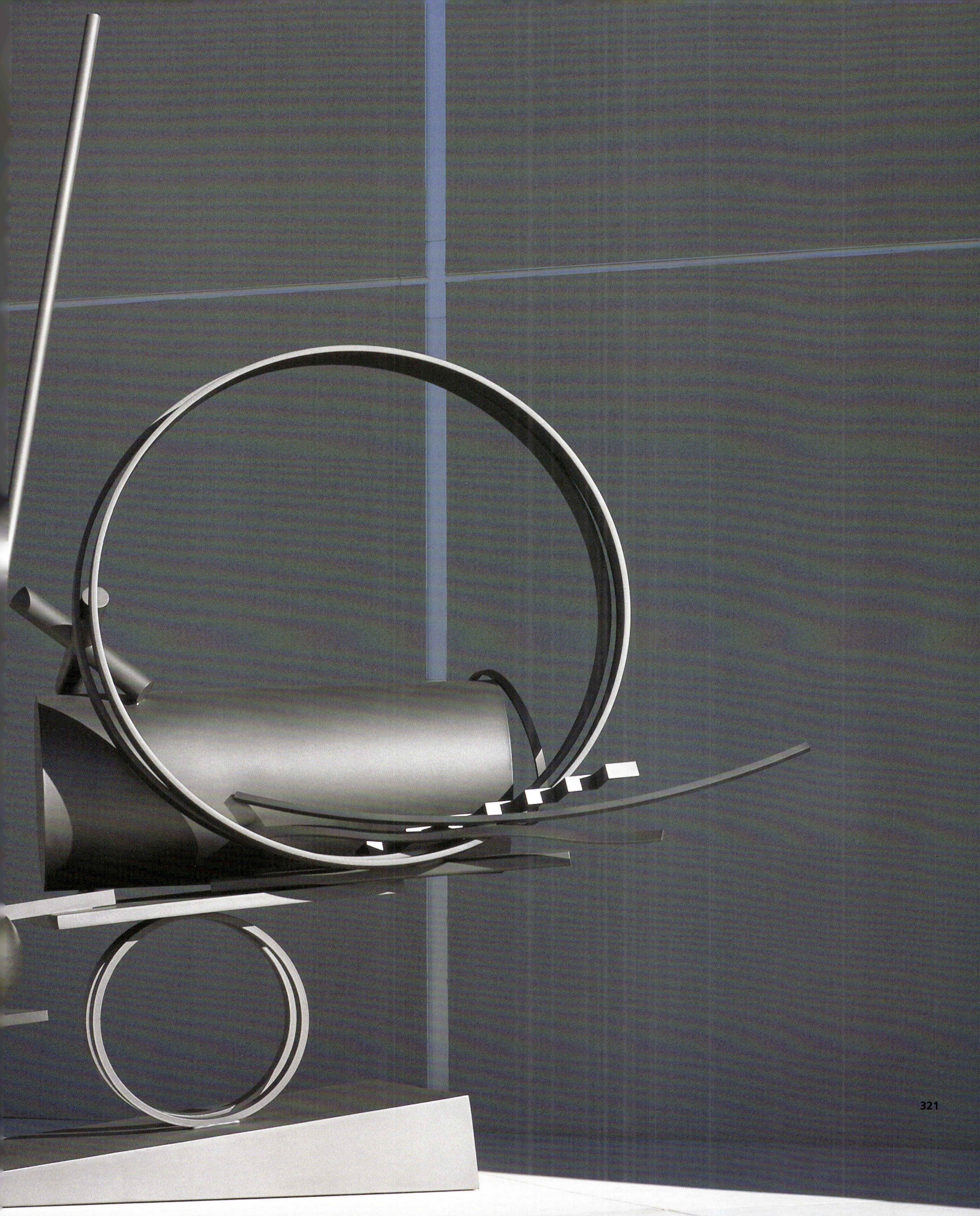

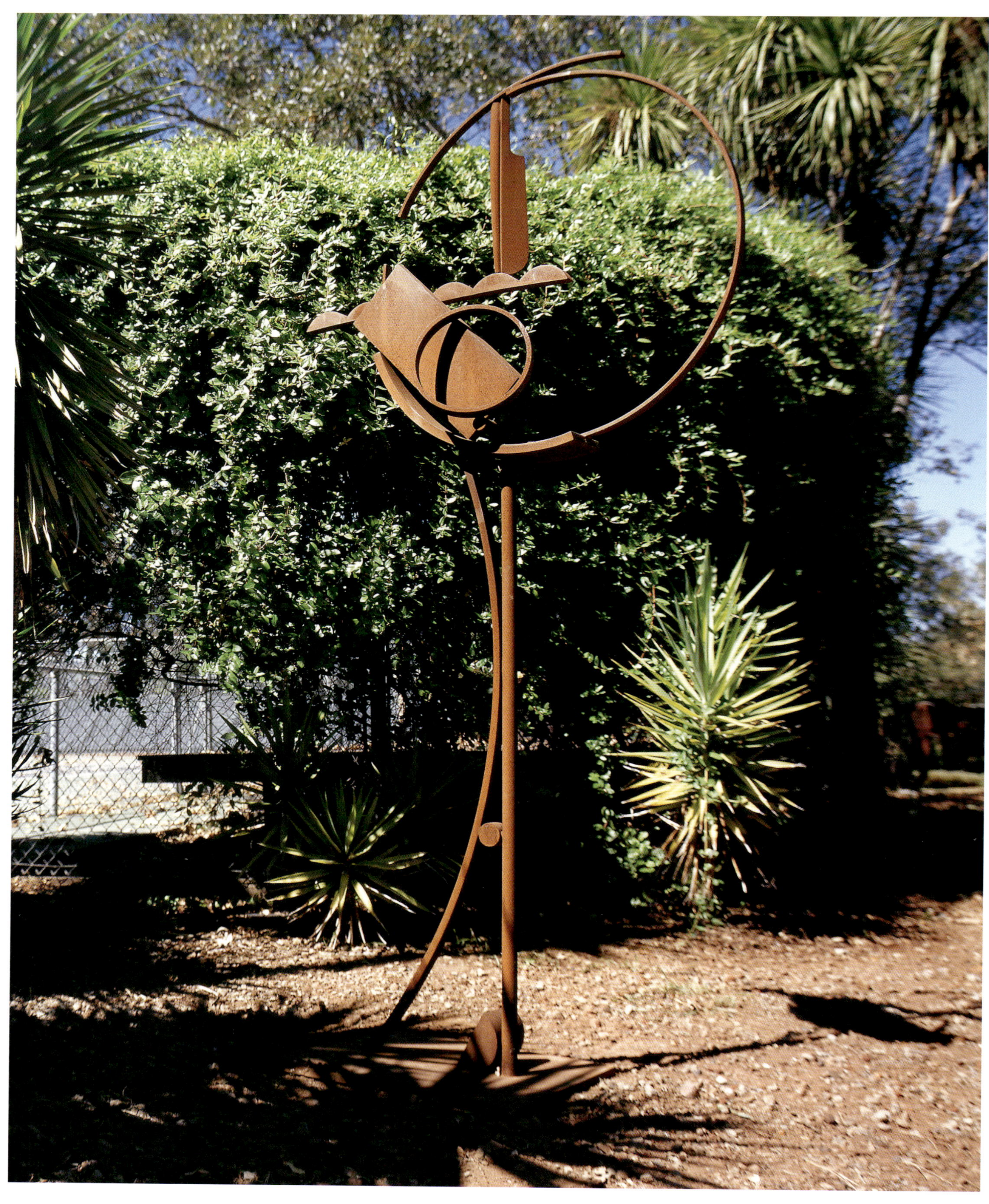

Steel Watercolor: Indian 15, Phase II

1992, steel
107 x 51 x 21 inches
272 x 130 x 53 cm

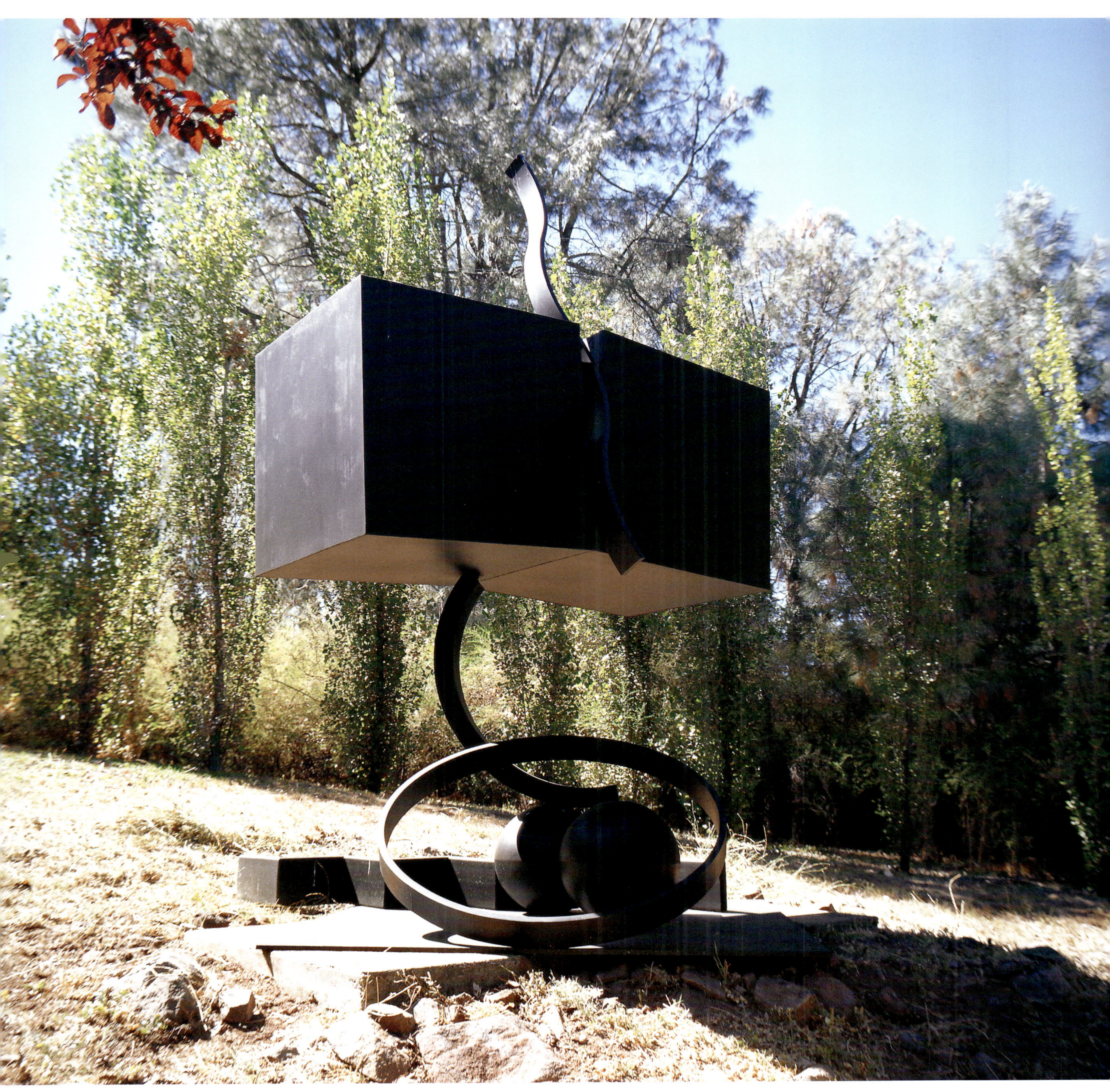

It's Harder To Do It with Balls, Wave

1999, steel
15 x 8½ x 8½ feet
457 x 259 x 259 cm

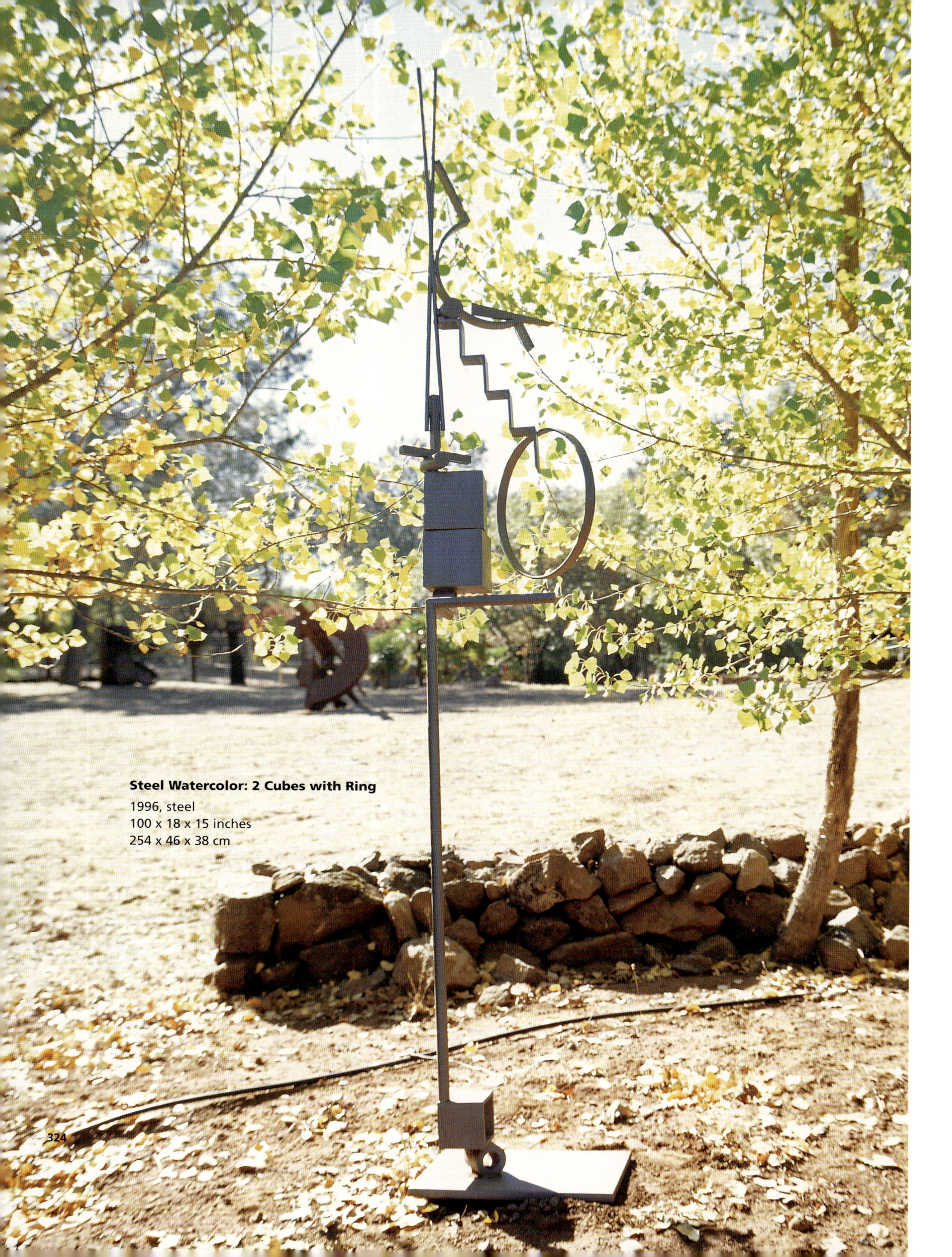

Steel Watercolor: 2 Cubes with Ring
1996, steel
100 x 18 x 15 inches
254 x 46 x 38 cm

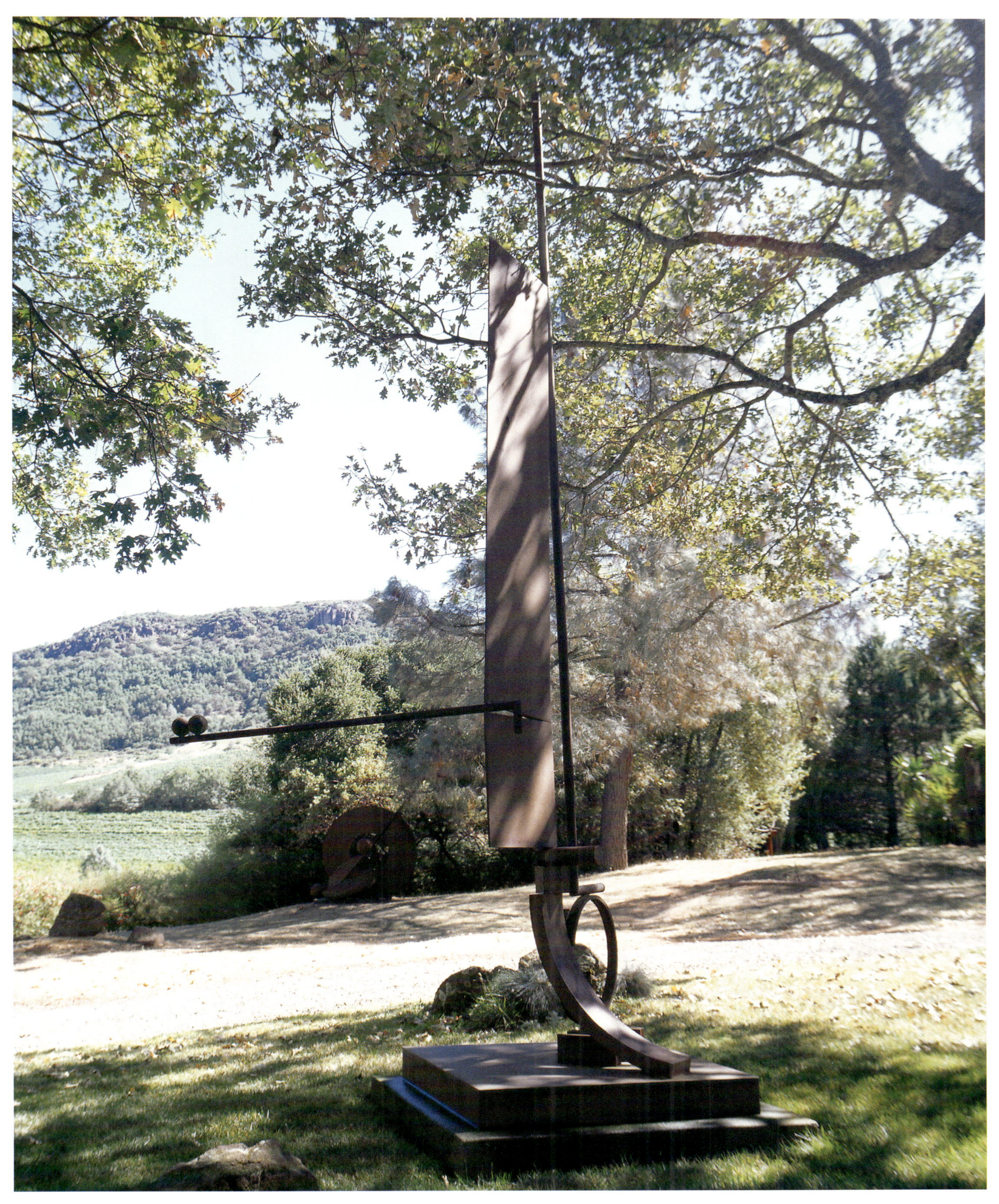

Plane to Edge: Wedge

2003, steel with patina
H: 14½ feet
H: 442 cm

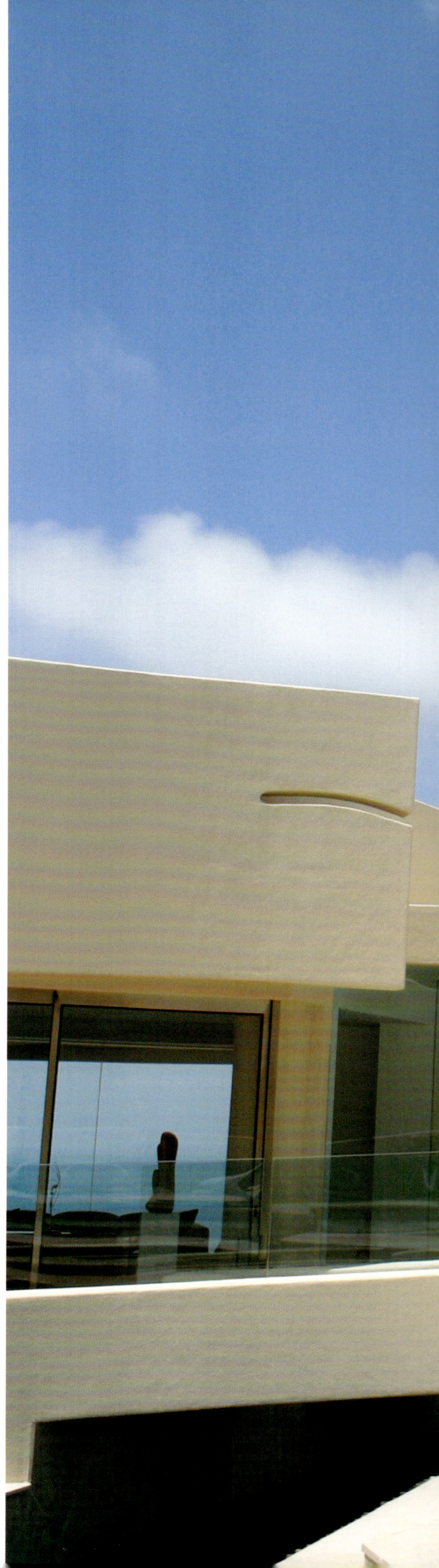

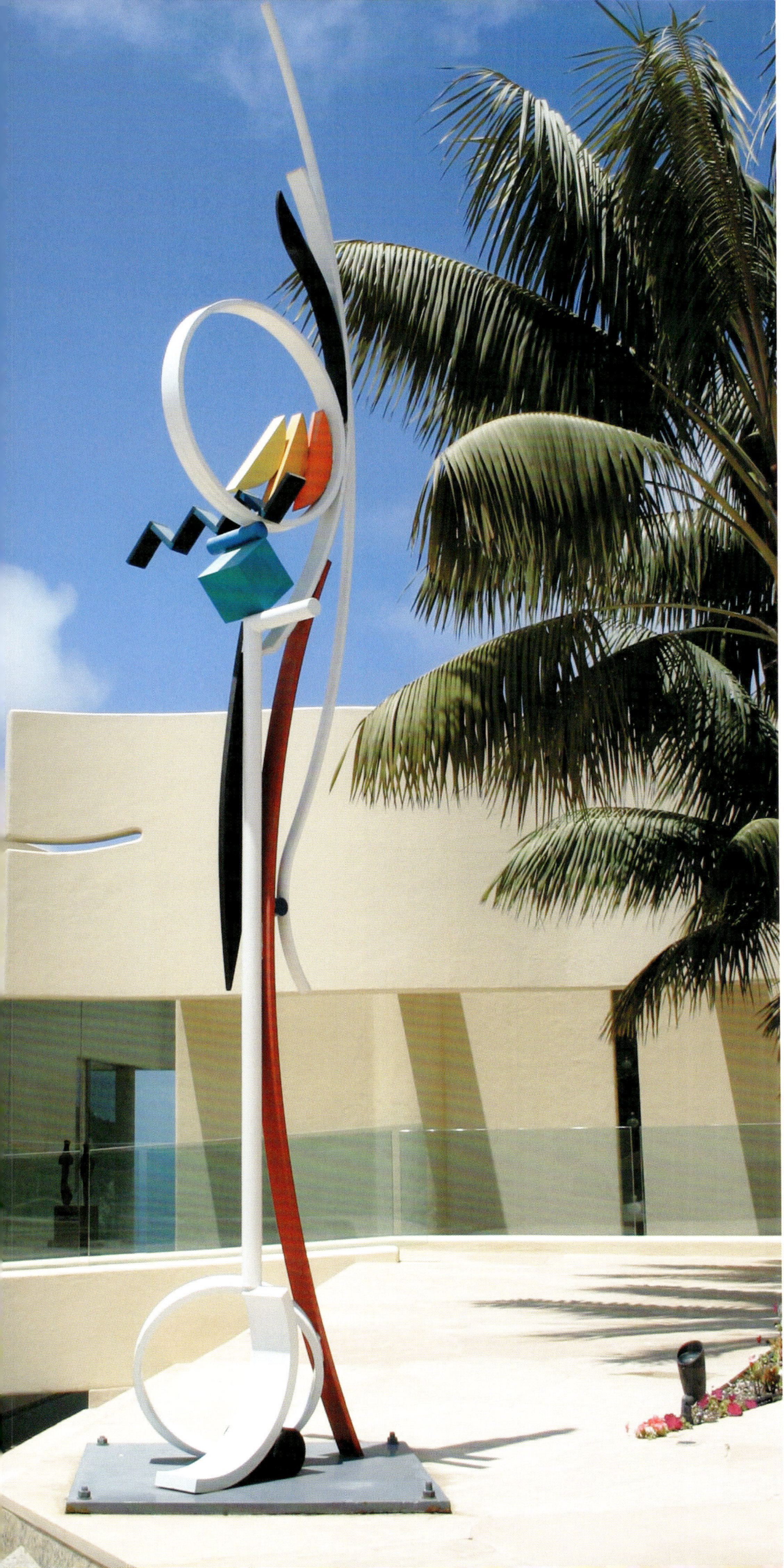

Steel Watercolor: Yellow Lilly

1991, painted steel
H: 14 feet
H: 427 cm

Straight-Up with Ball

2002, Cor-ten steel
32 x 4½ x 4½ feet
975 x 137 x 137 cm

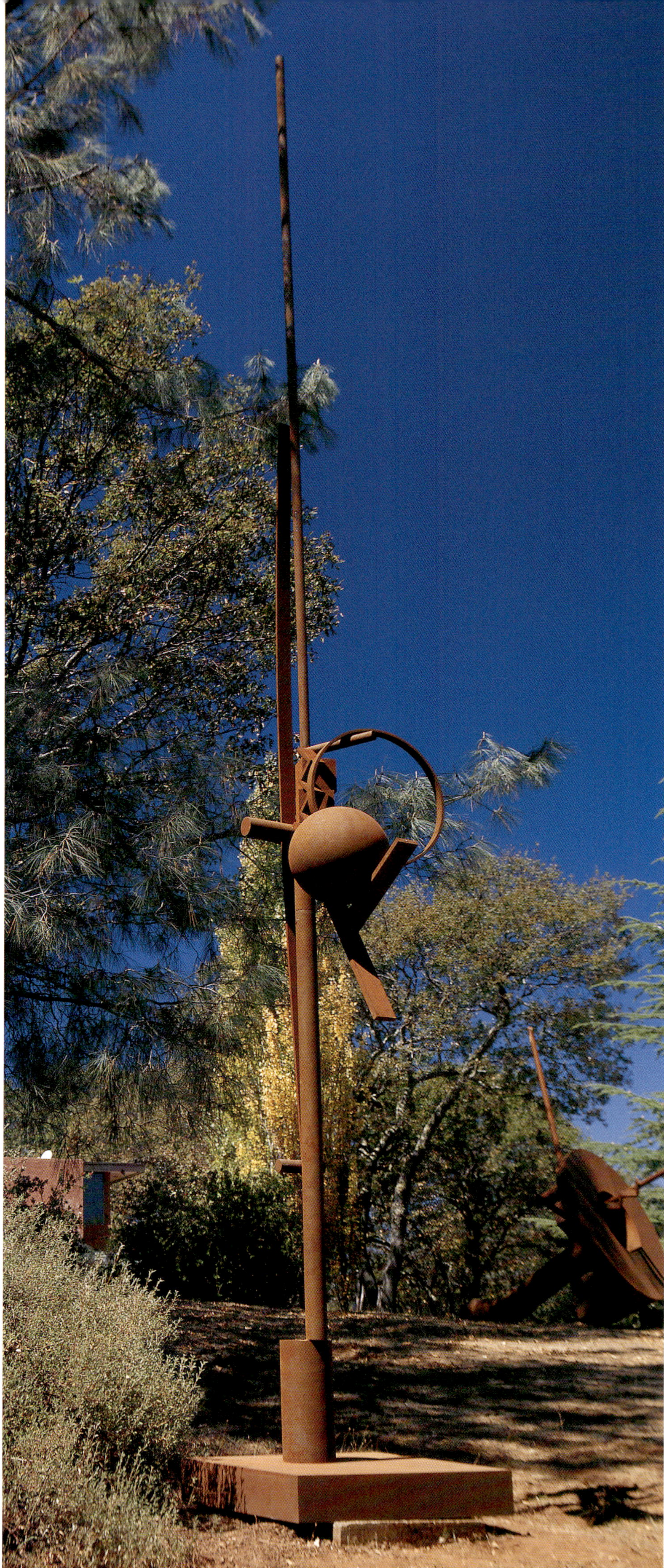

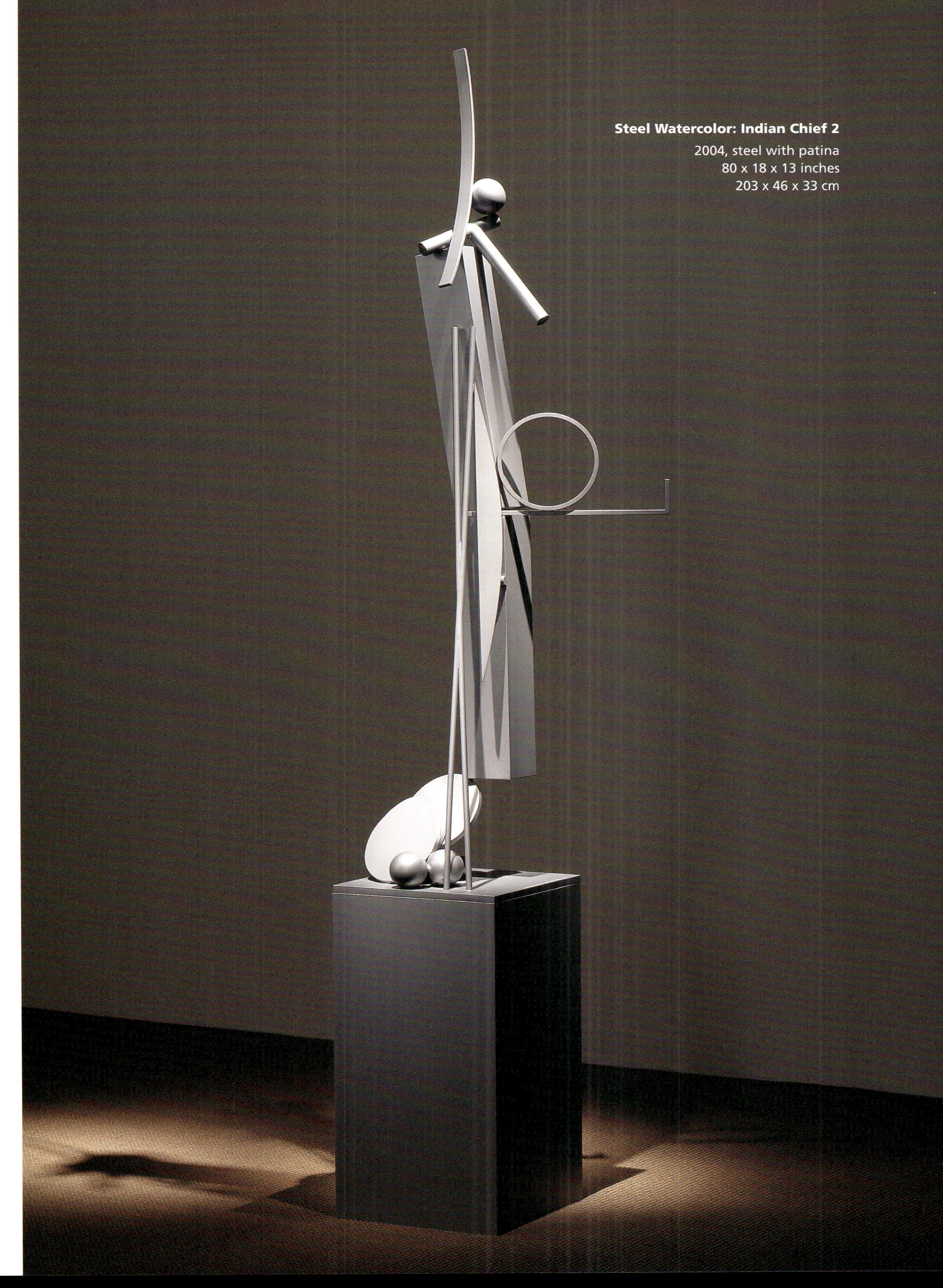

Steel Watercolor: Indian Chief 2

2004, steel with patina
80 x 18 x 13 inches
203 x 46 x 33 cm

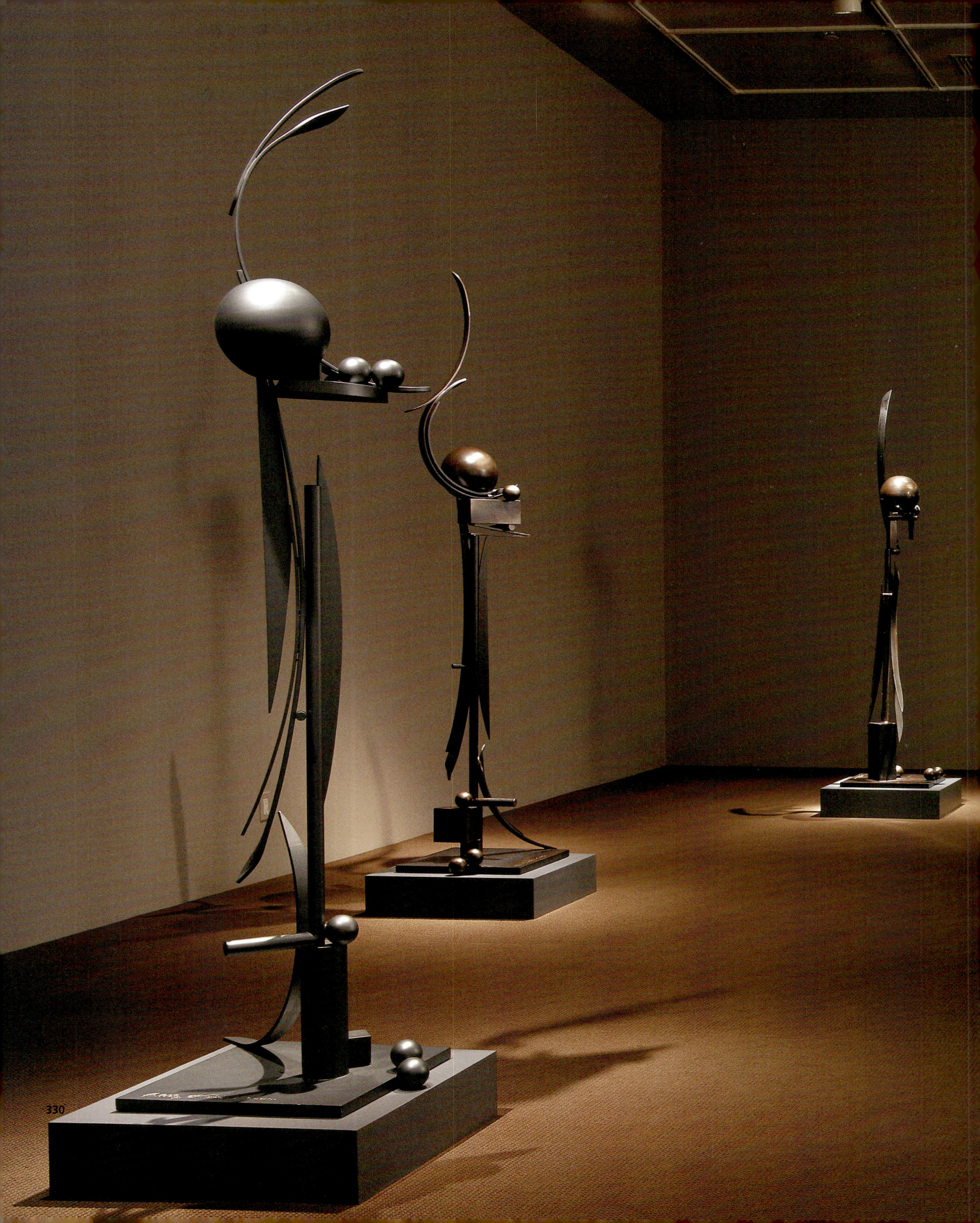

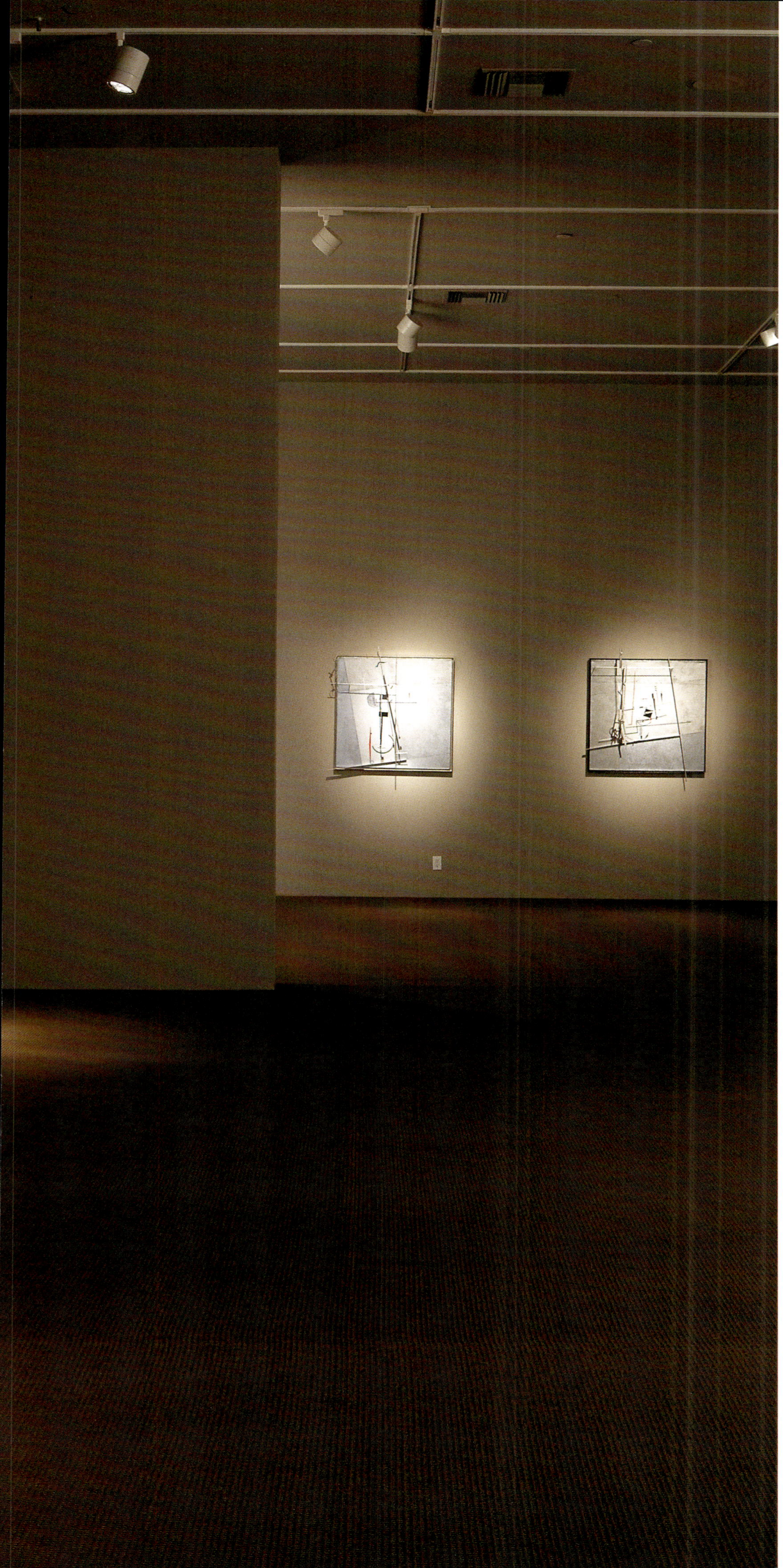

Installation view of Benton solo
exhibition at Imago Galleries
Palm Desert, California 2005

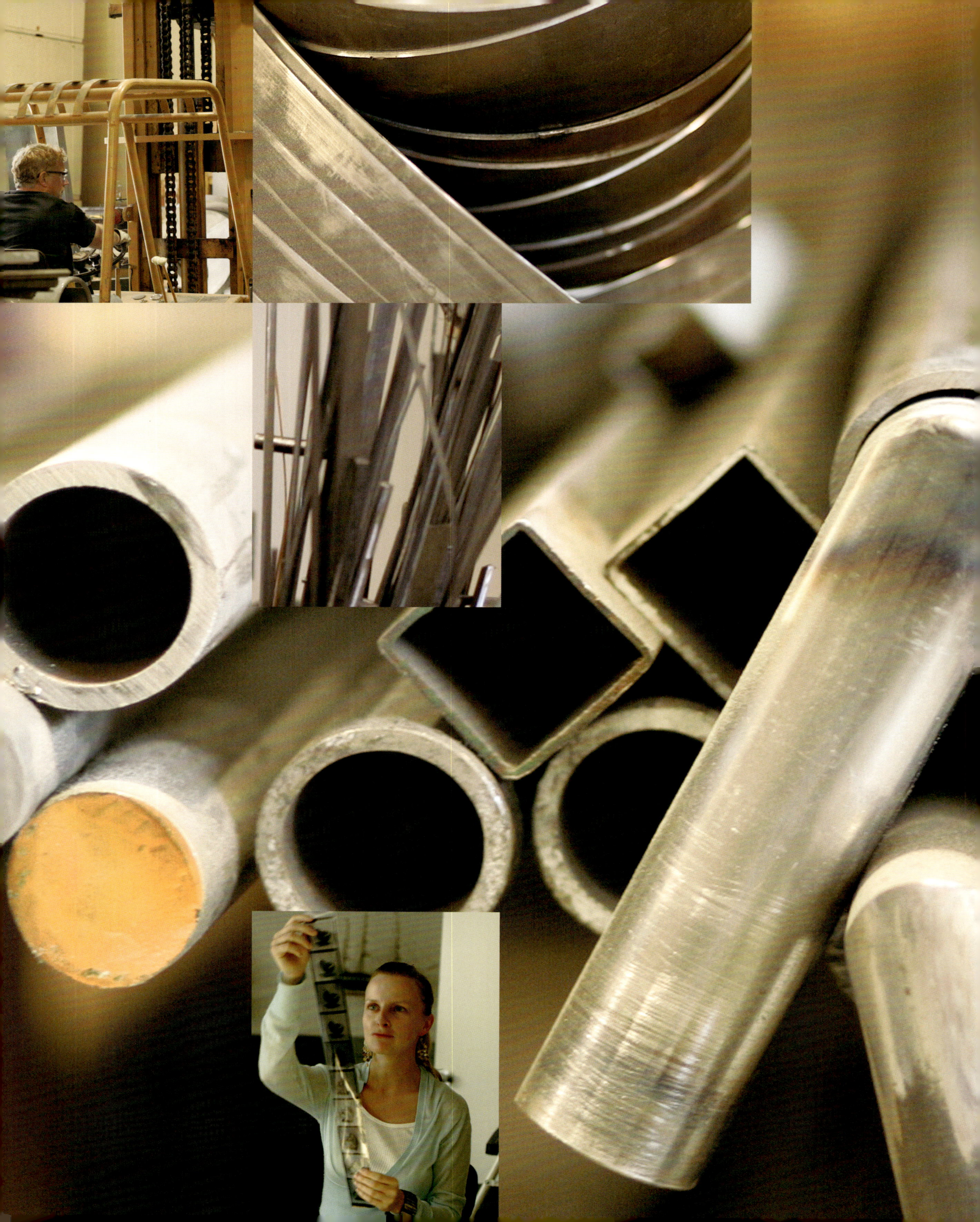

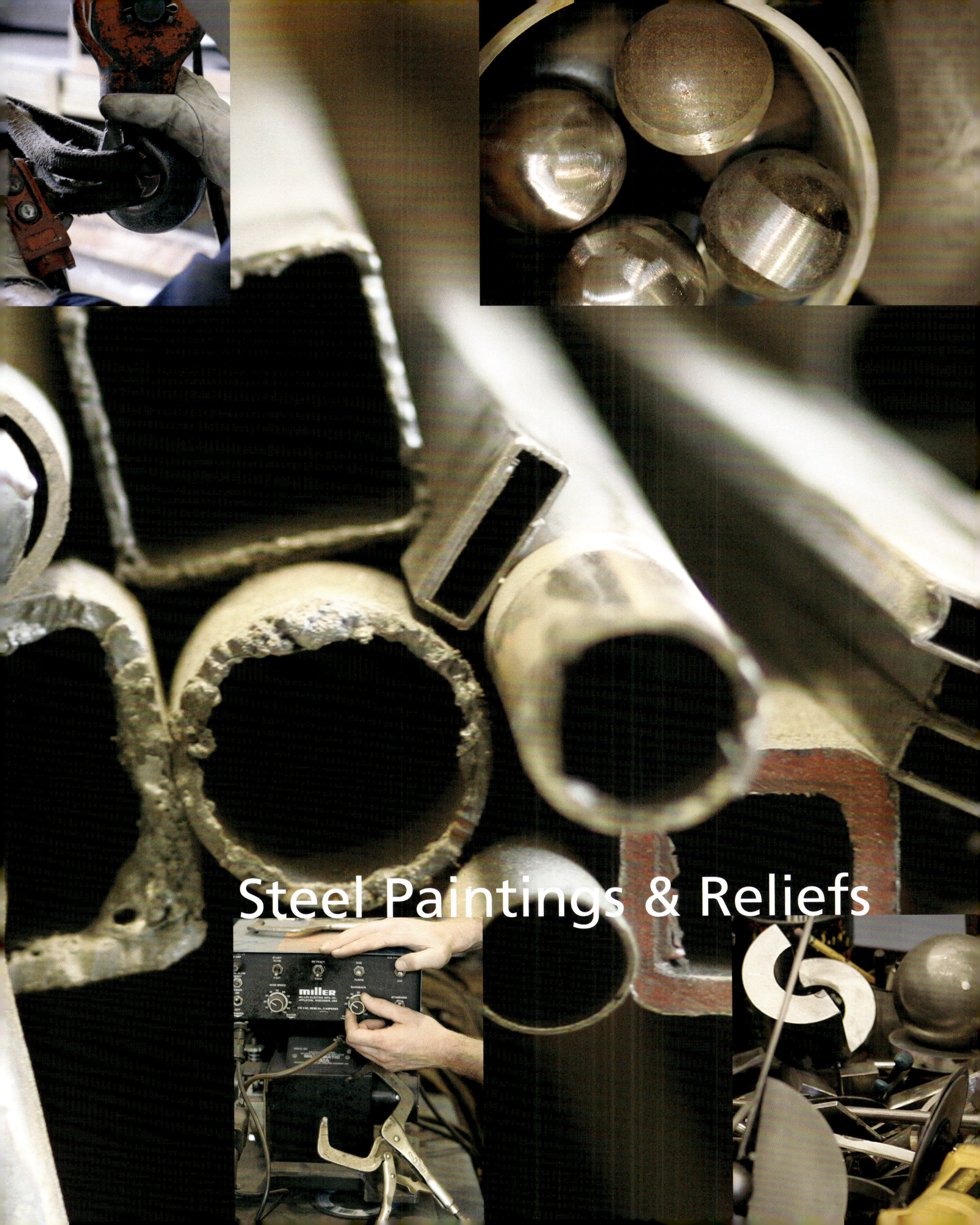

Steel Paintings & Reliefs

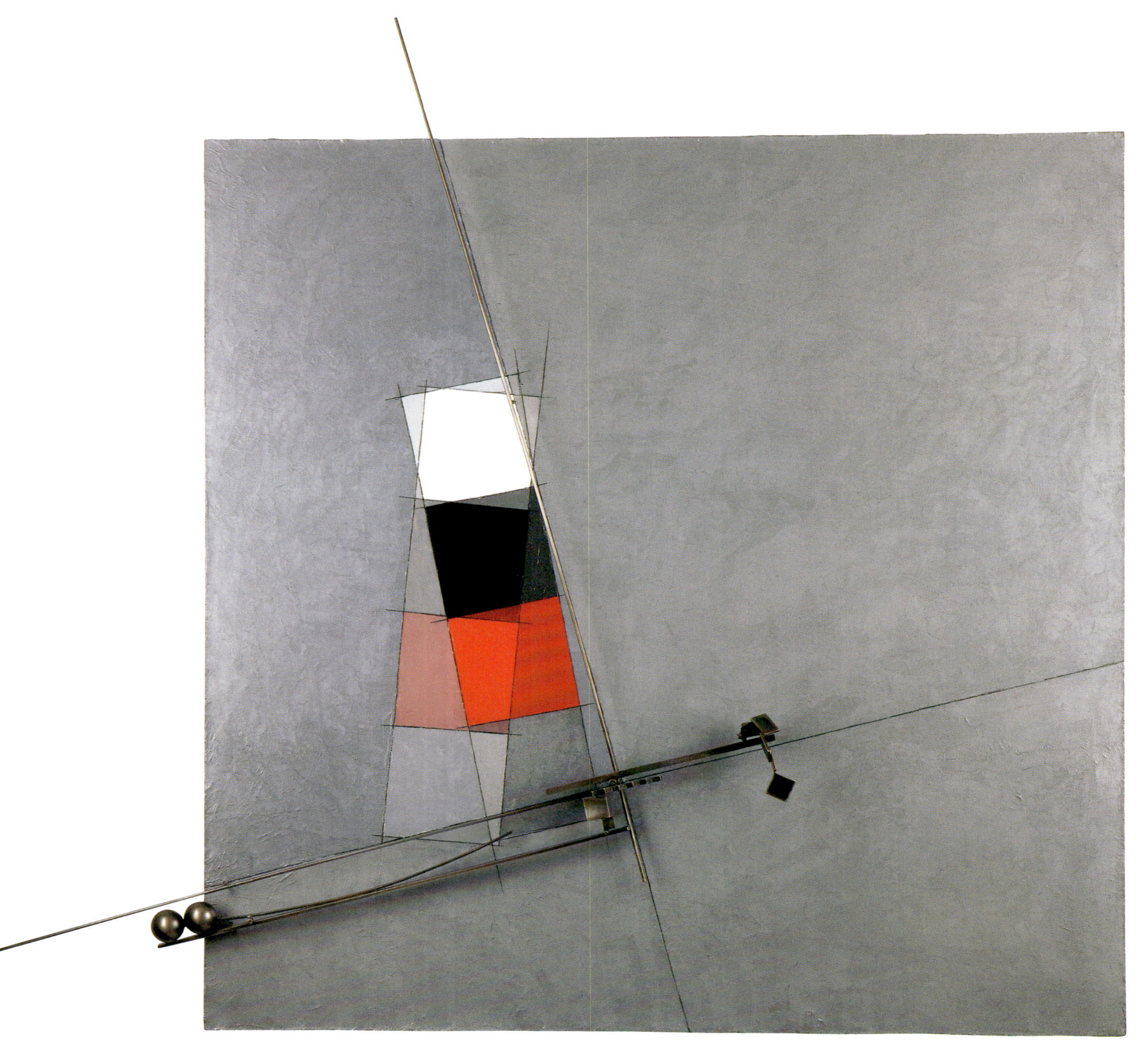

Construct Falling 14

2005, steel and acrylic on canvas
58 x 60 inches
147 x 152 cm

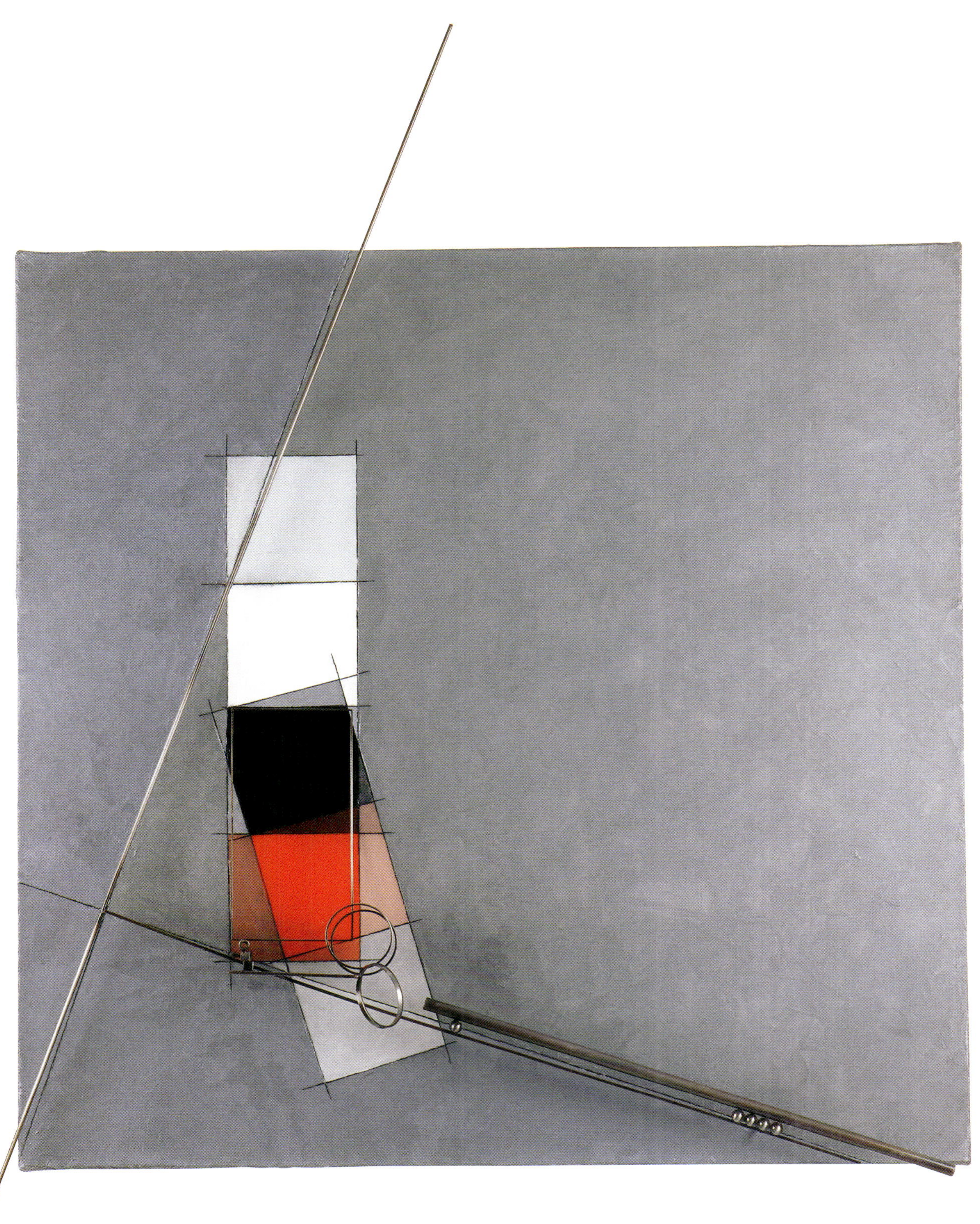

Construct Falling 15

2005, steel and acrylic on canvas
58 x 50 inches
147 x 127 cm

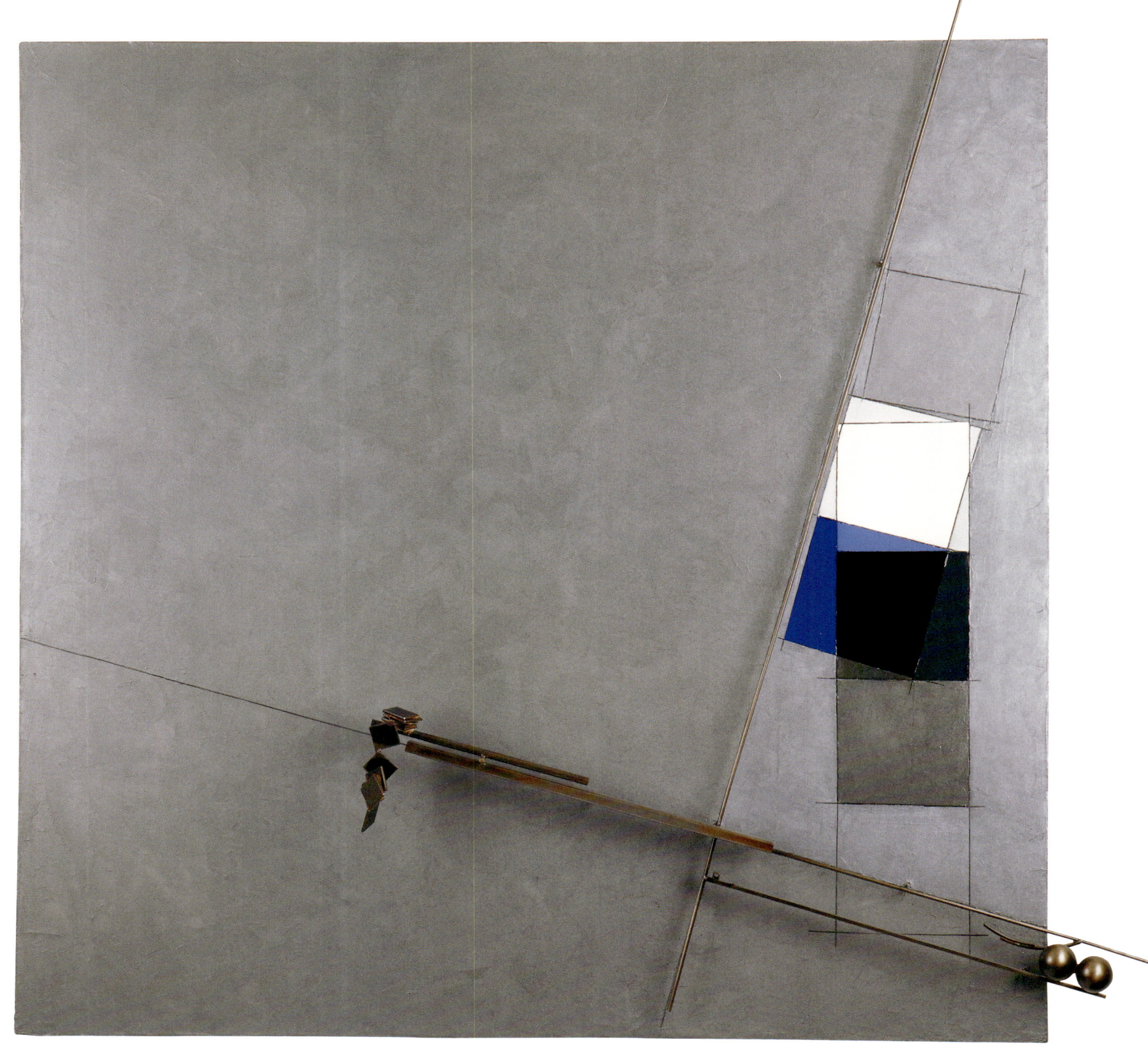

Construct Falling 12

2005, steel and acrylic on canvas
56 x 55 inches
142 x 140 cm

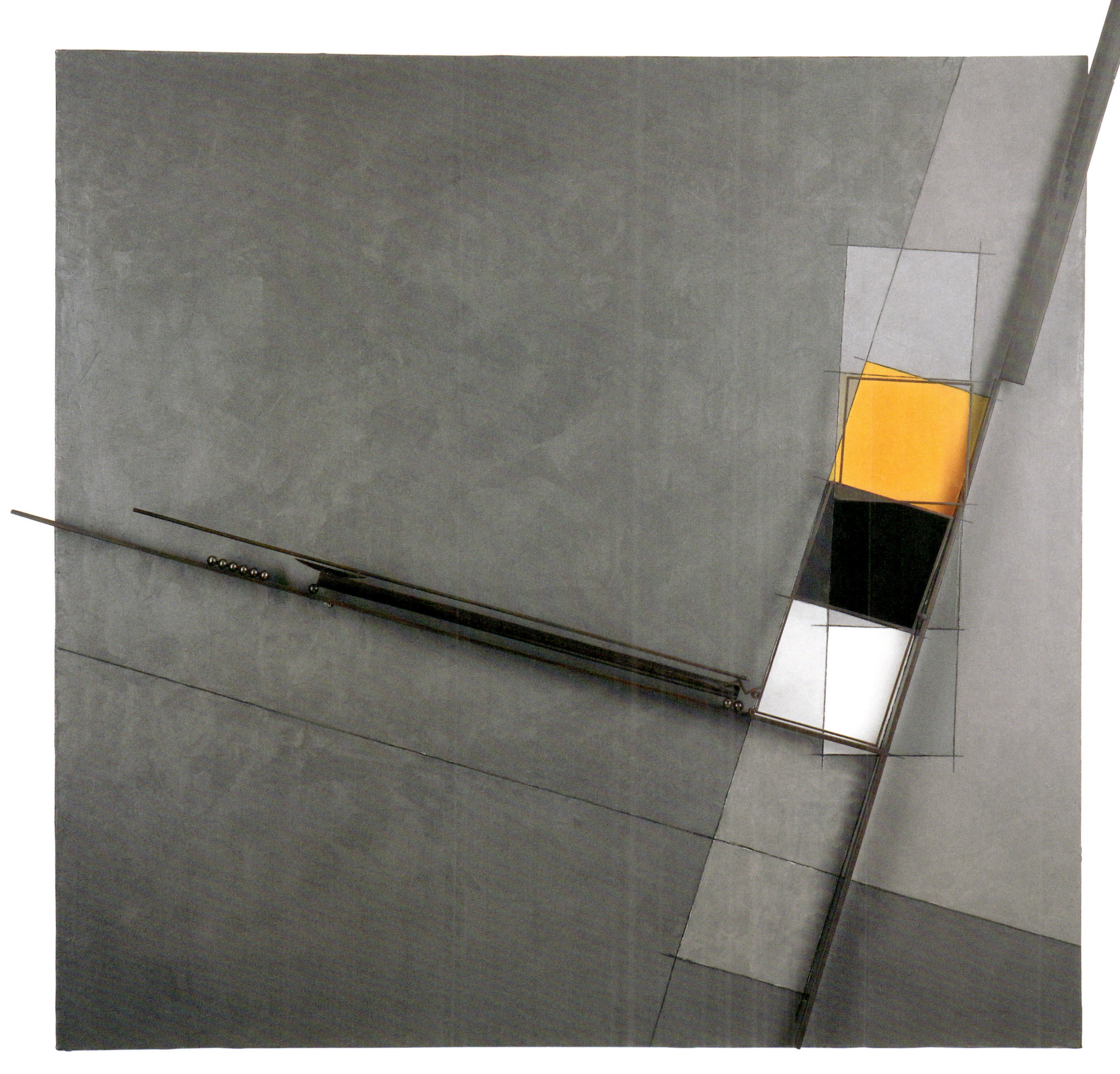

Construct Falling 16

2005, steel and acrylic on canvas
50 x 50 inches
127 x 127 cm

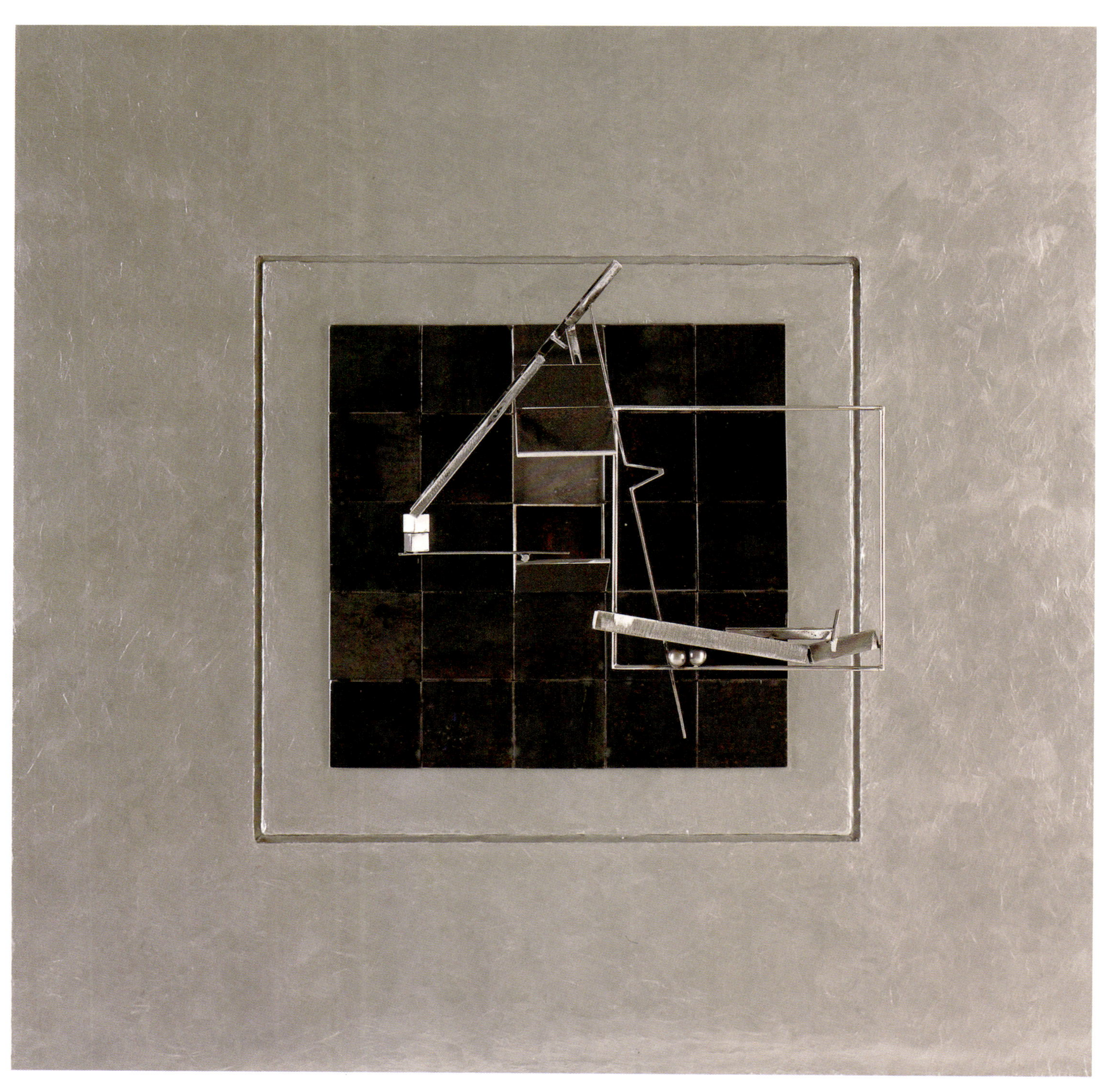

Grid Construct: 25 Squares – No. 4

2000, steel and acrylic on canvas
22 x 22 inches
56 x 56 cm

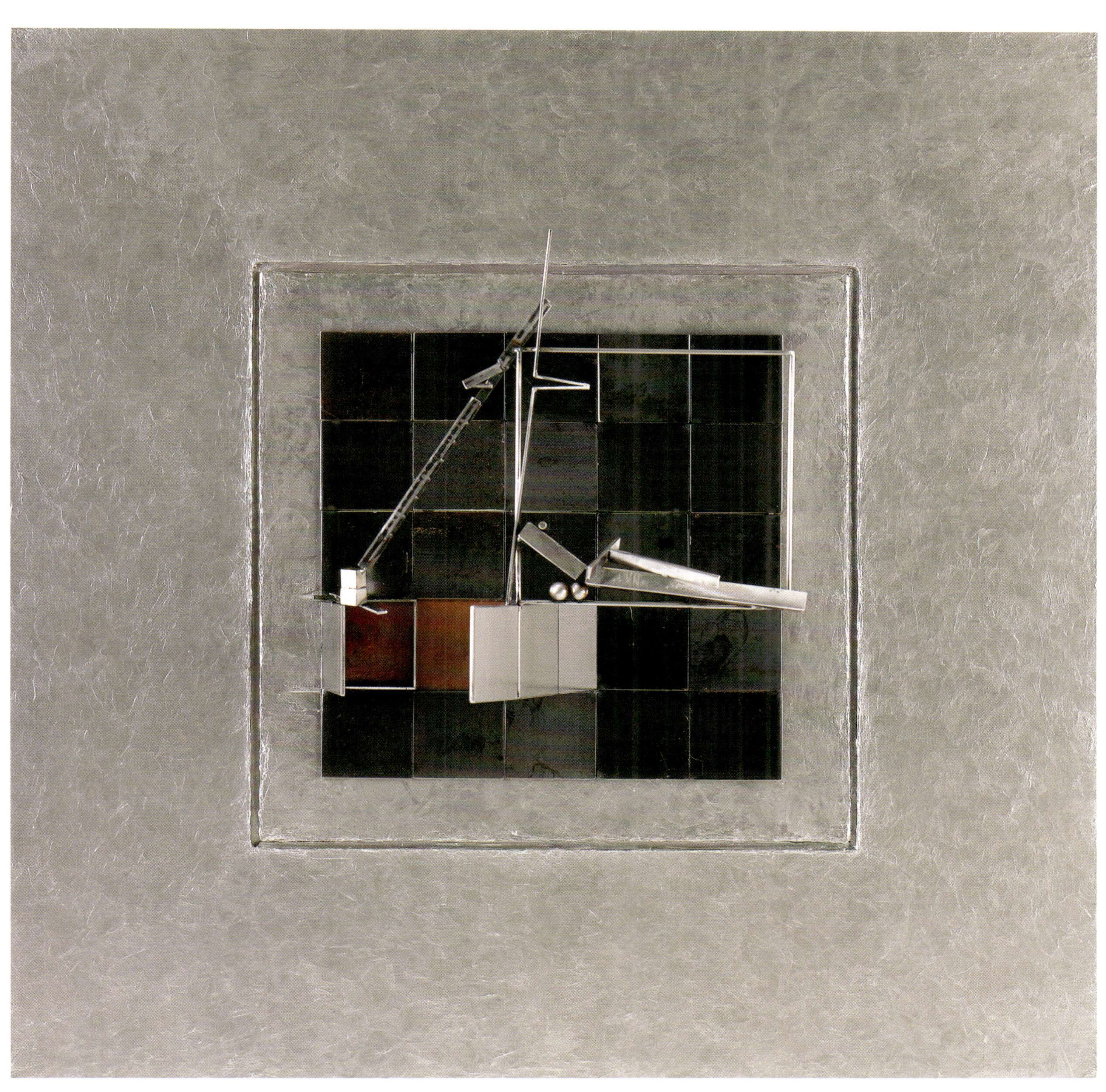

Grid Construct: 25 Squares – No. 1

2000, steel and acrylic on canvas
22 x 22 inches
56 x 56 cm

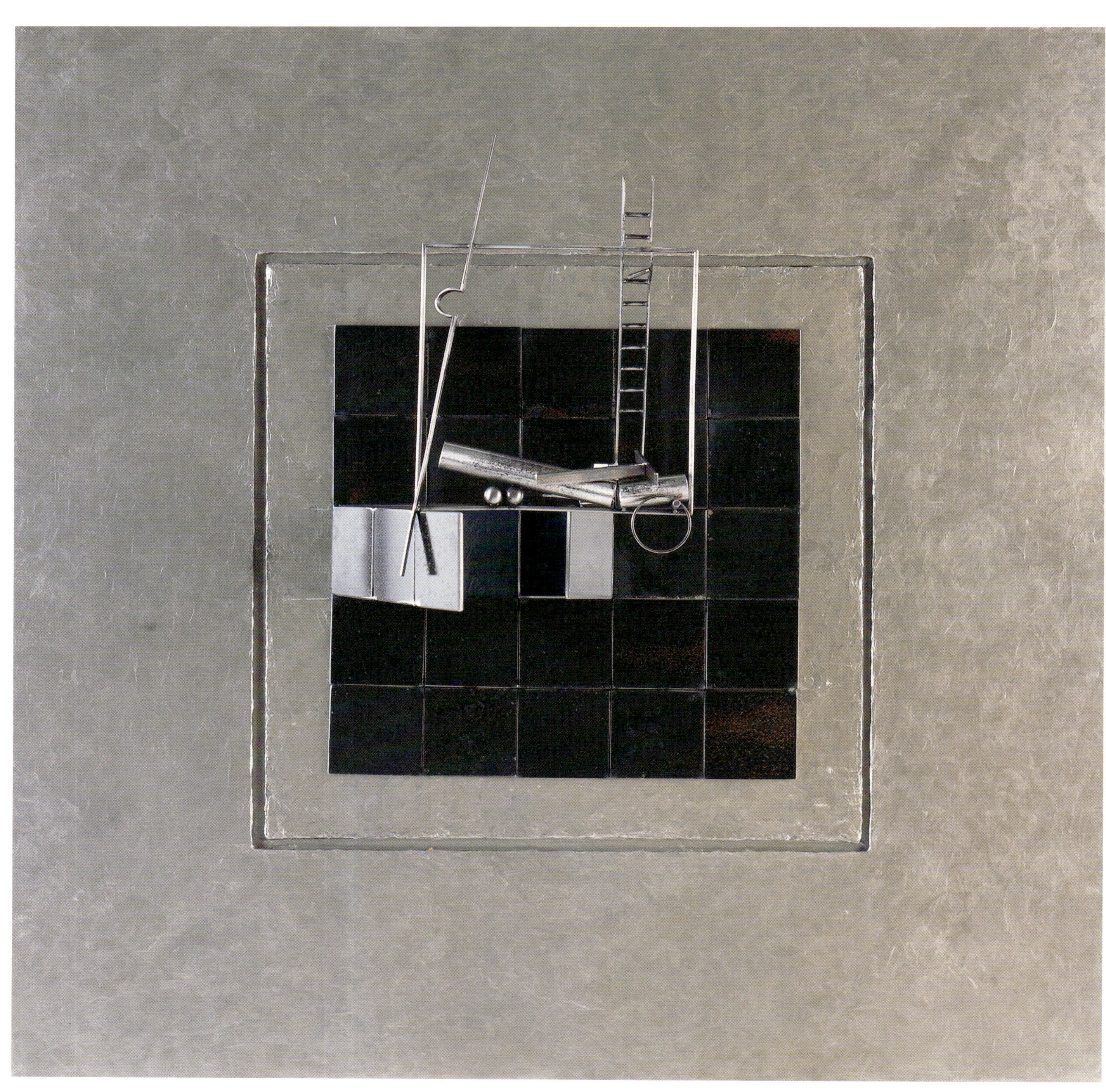

Grid Construct: 25 Squares – No. 2

2000, steel and acrylic on canvas
22 x 22 inches
56 x 56 cm

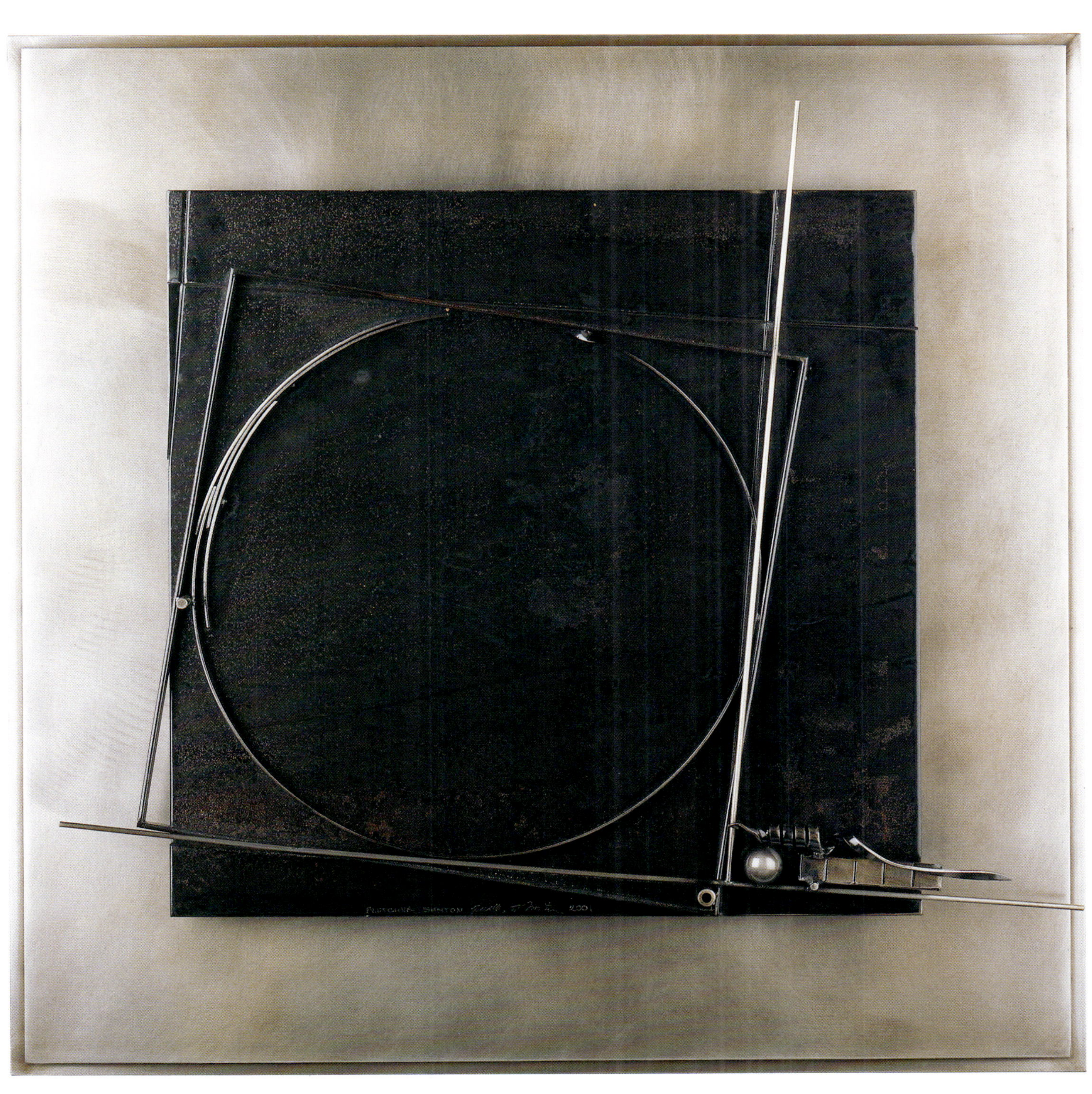

Construct M – No. 3

2001, steel with patina
24½ x 24½ inches
62 x 62 cm

Construct M – No. 4

2001, steel with patina
24½ x 24½ inches
62 x 62 cm

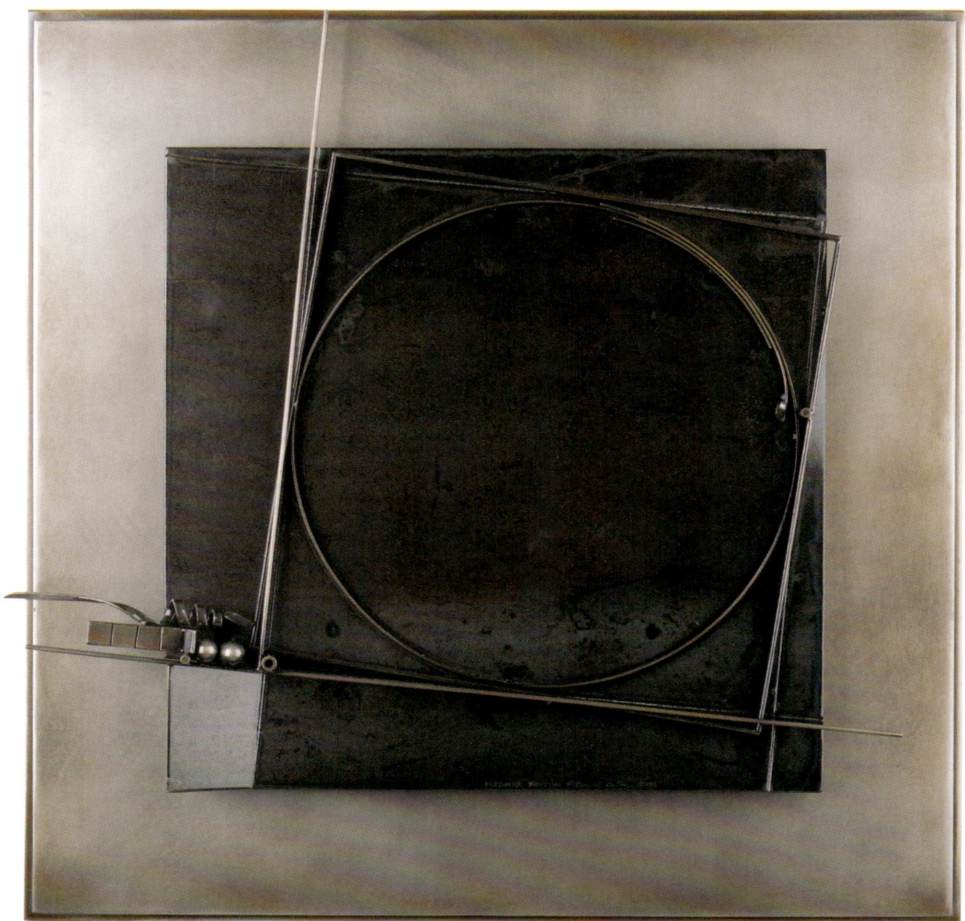

Construct M – No. 5

2001, steel with patina
24½ x 24½ inches
62 x 62 cm

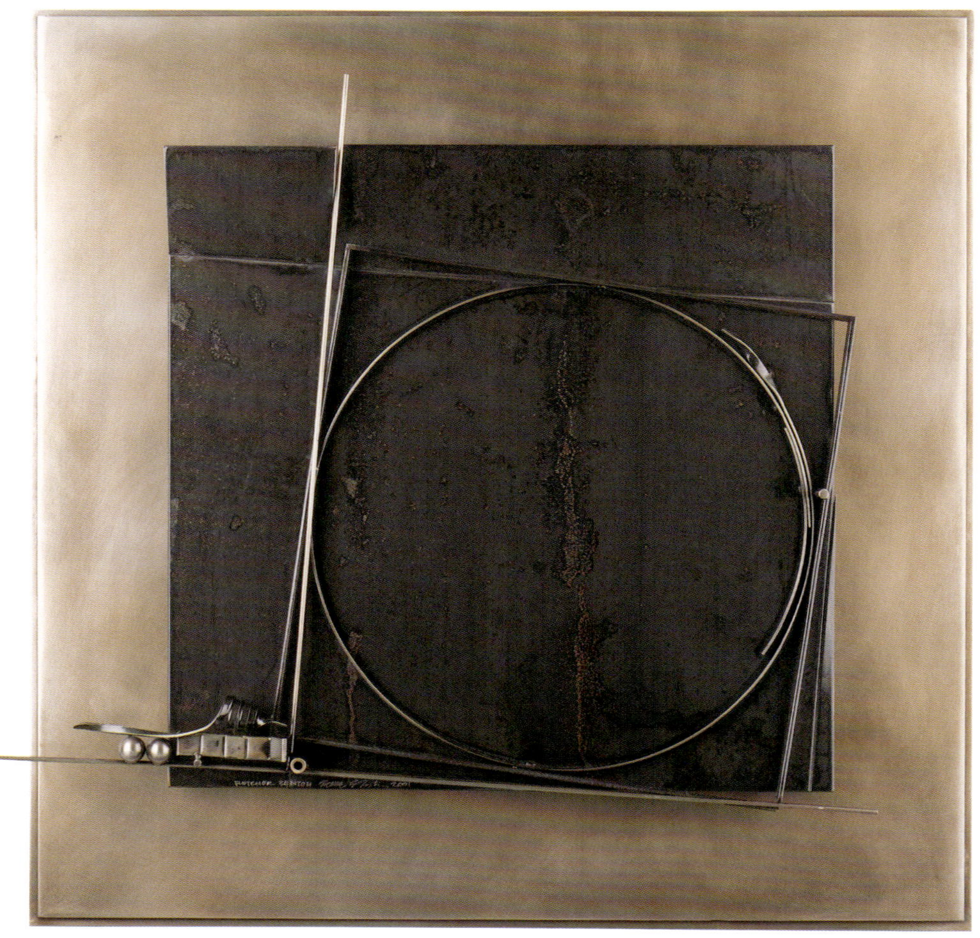

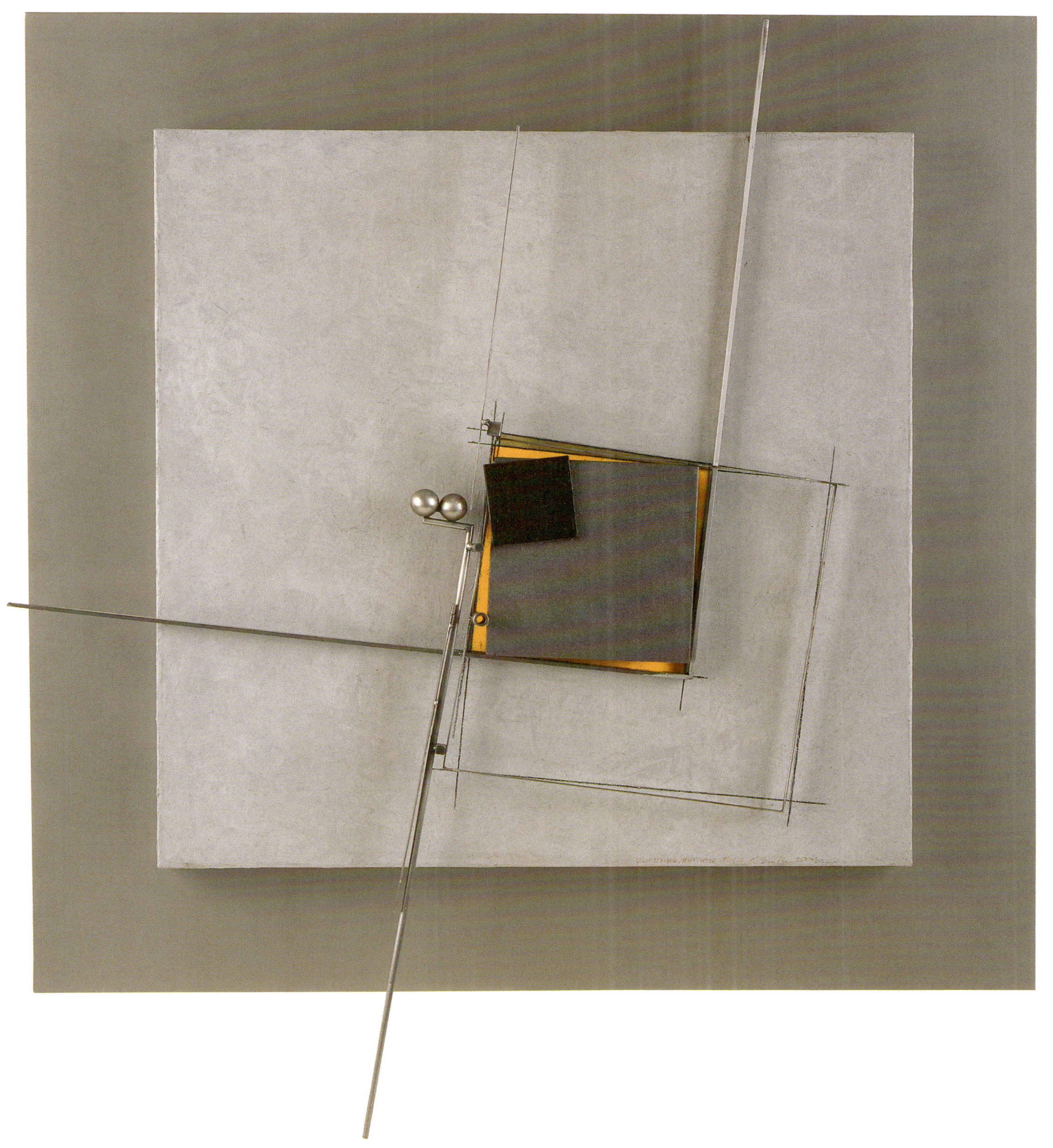

Dynamic Rhythms 22

2004, steel and acrylic on canvas
32 x 28 inches
81 x 71 cm

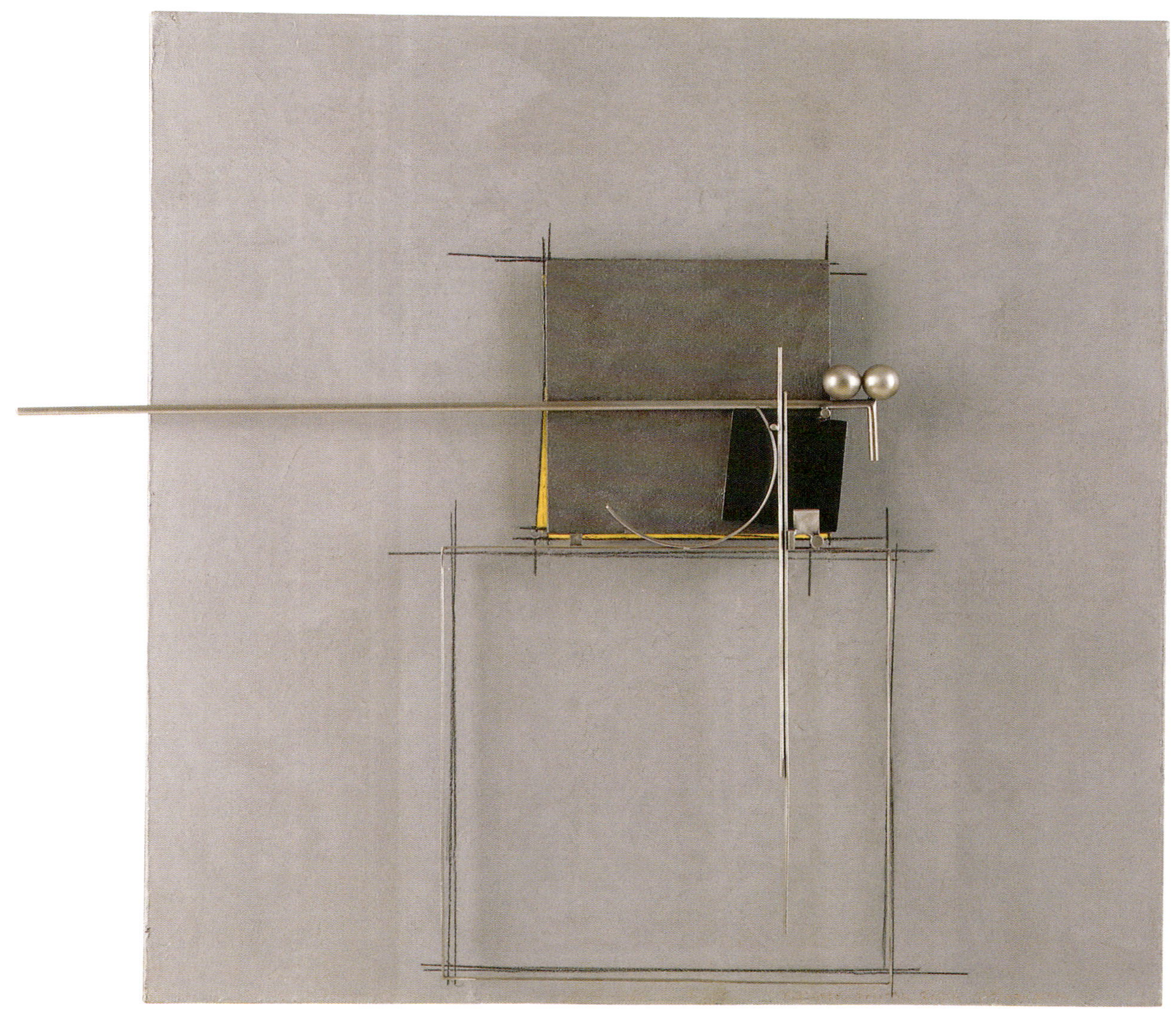

Dynamic Rhythms 21

2004, steel and acrylic on canvas
27 x 27 inches
69 x 69 cm

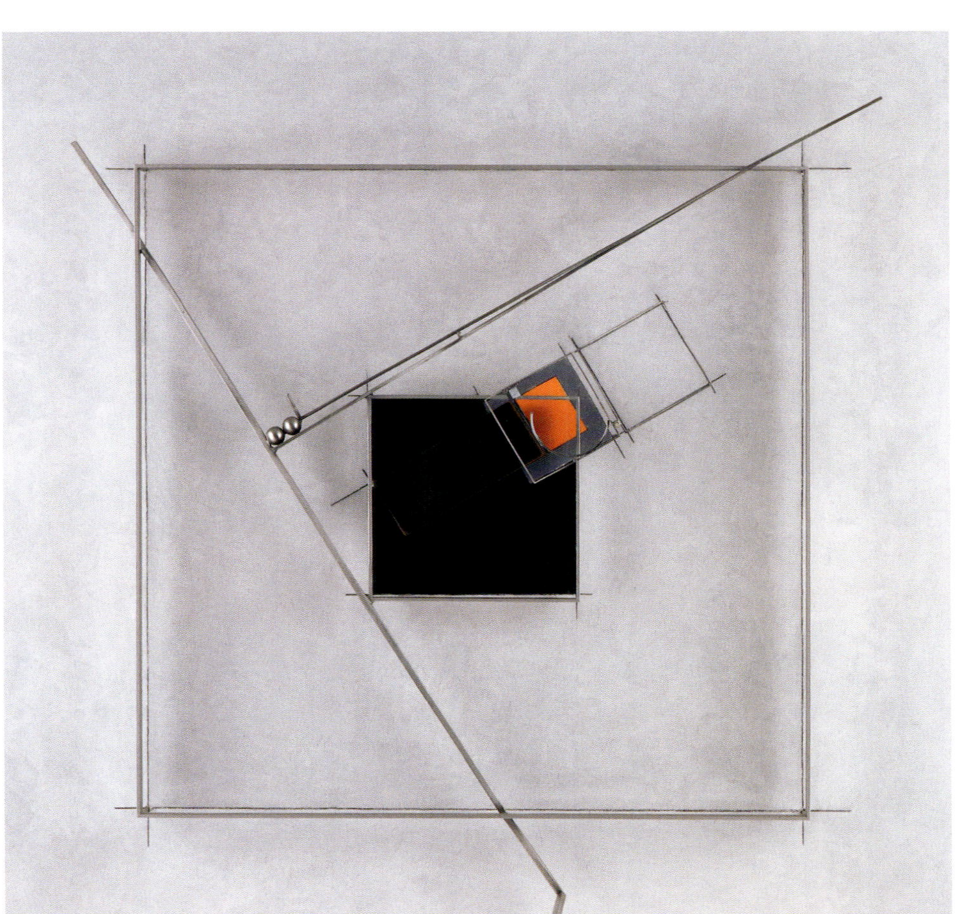

Dynamic Rhythms 11

2004, steel and acrylic on canvas
36 x 36 inches
91 x 91 cm

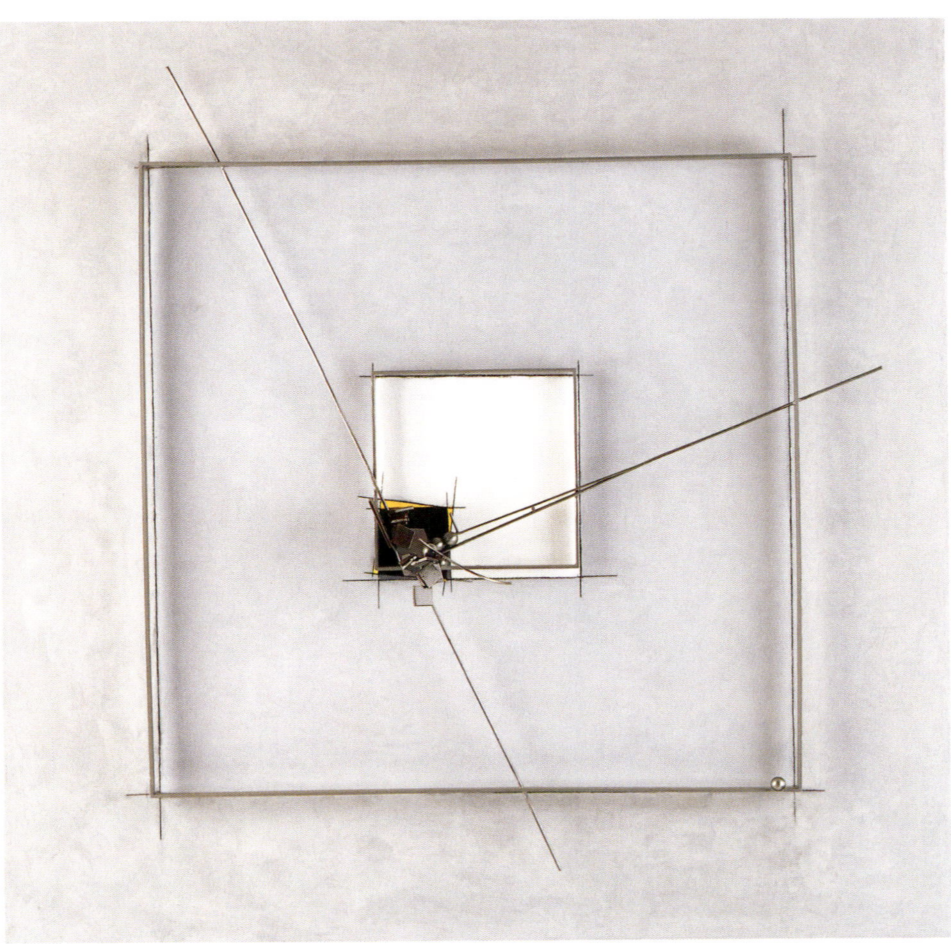

Dynamic Rhythms 20

2004, steel and acrylic on canvas
36 x 36 inches
91 x 91 cm

Dynamic Rhythms 12

2004, steel and acrylic on canvas
36 x 36 inches
91 x 91 cm

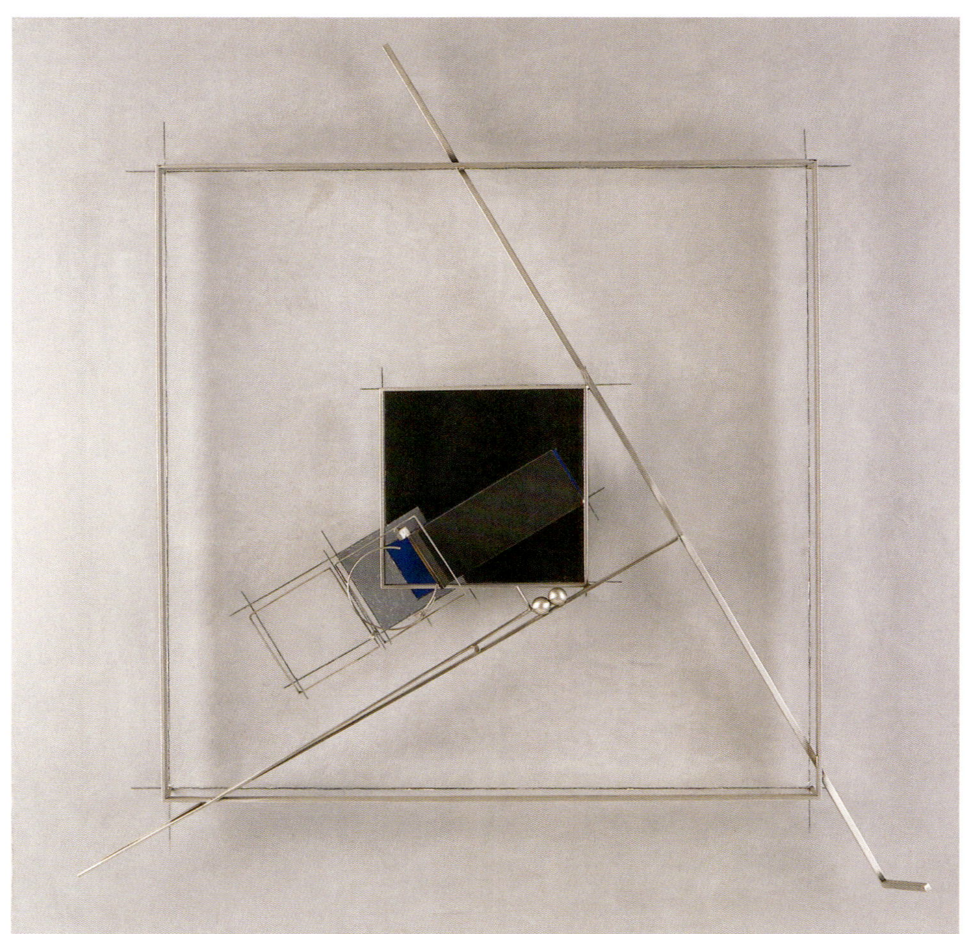

Dynamic Rhythms 13

2004, steel and acrylic on canvas
36 x 36 inches
91 x 91 cm

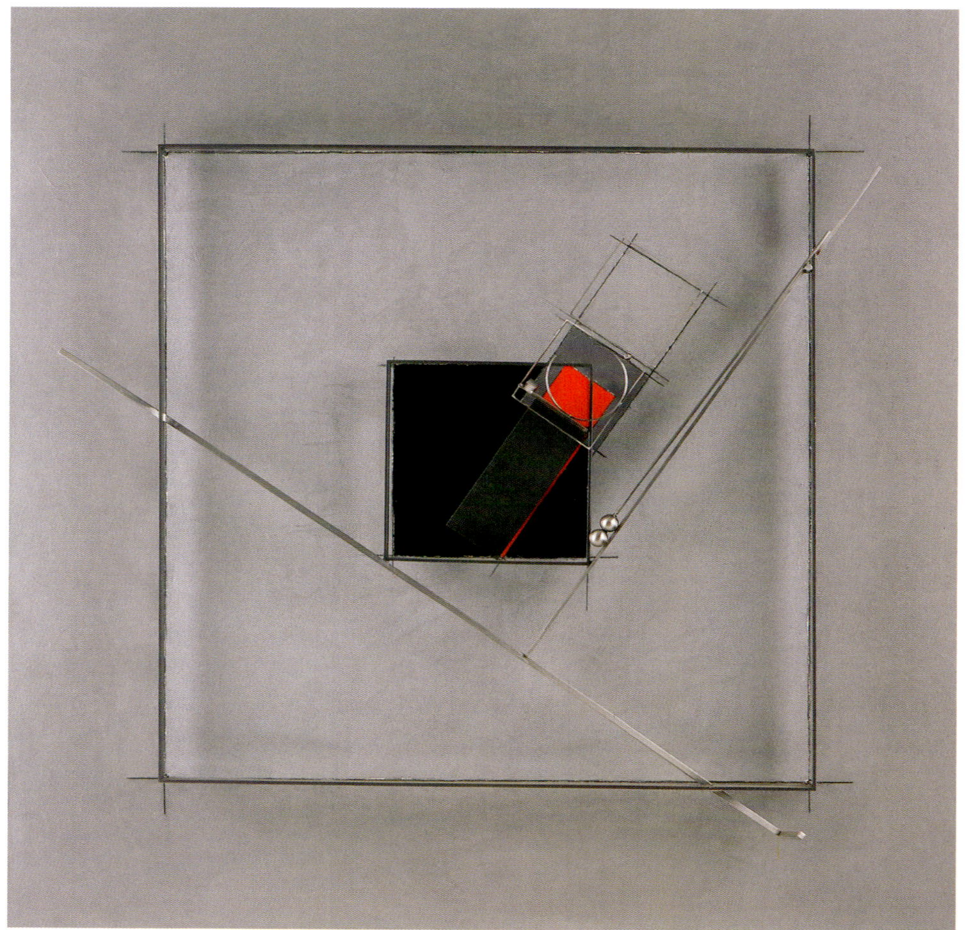

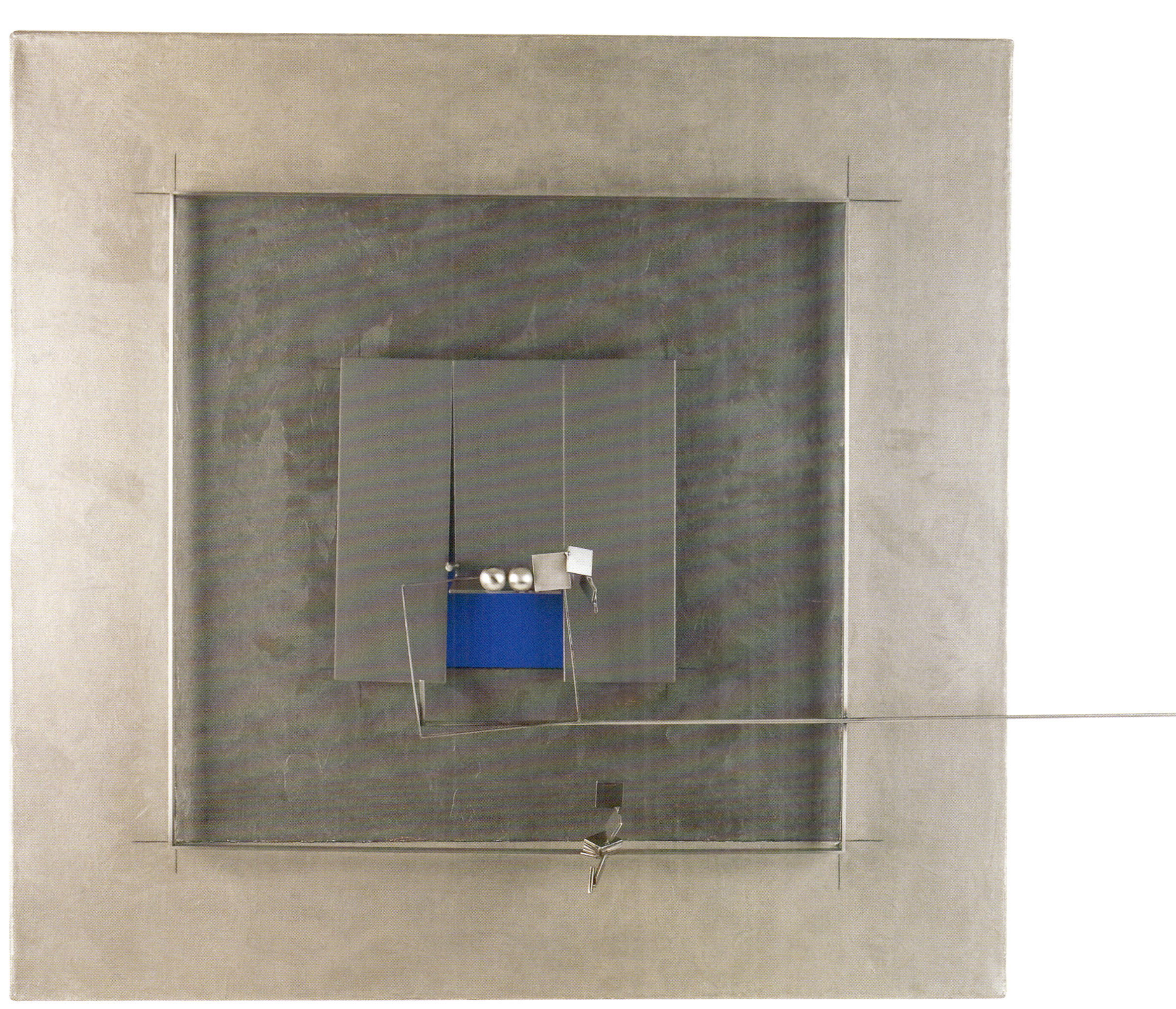

Dynamic Rhythms 4

2004, steel and acrylic on canvas
36 x 42 inches
91 x 107 cm

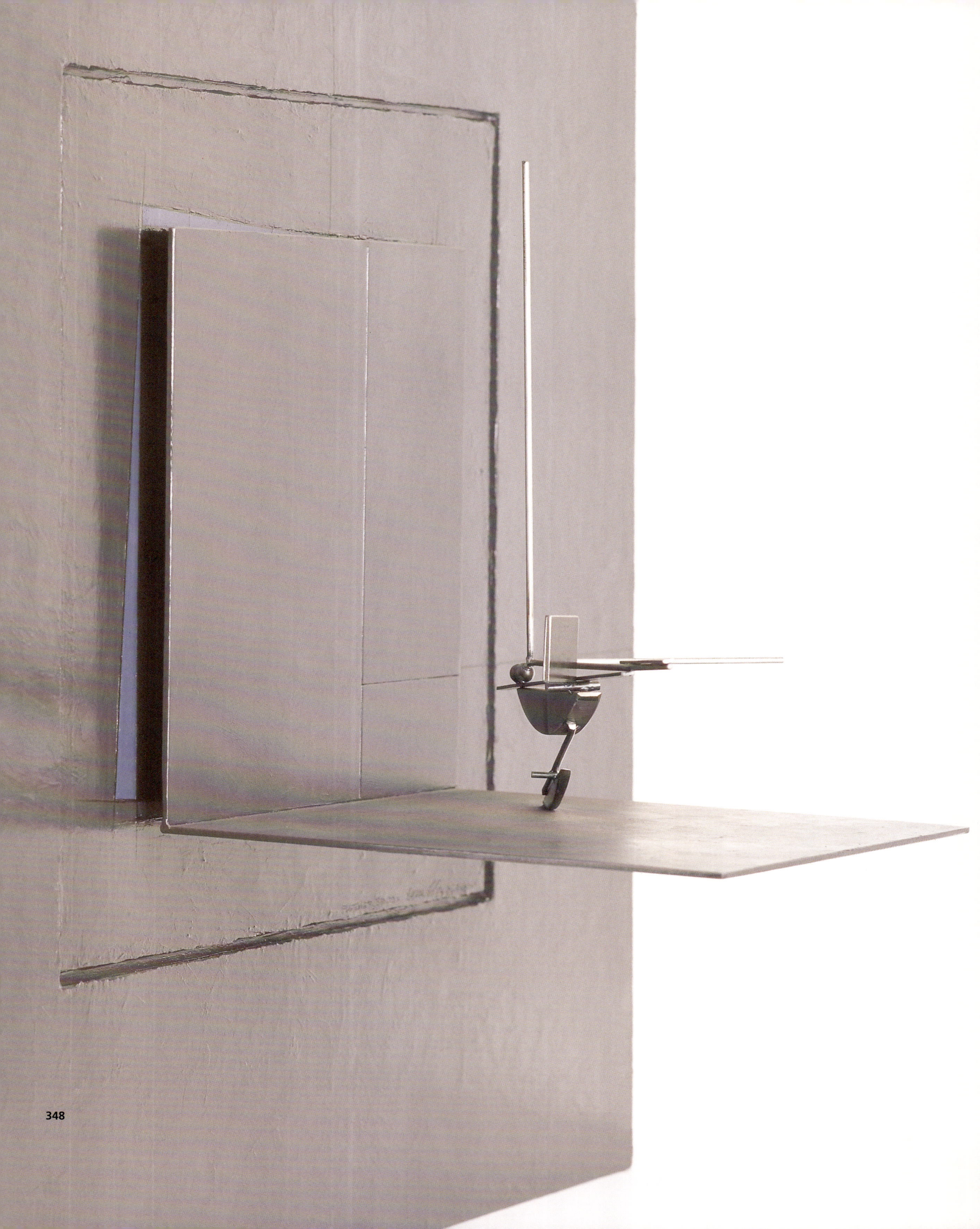

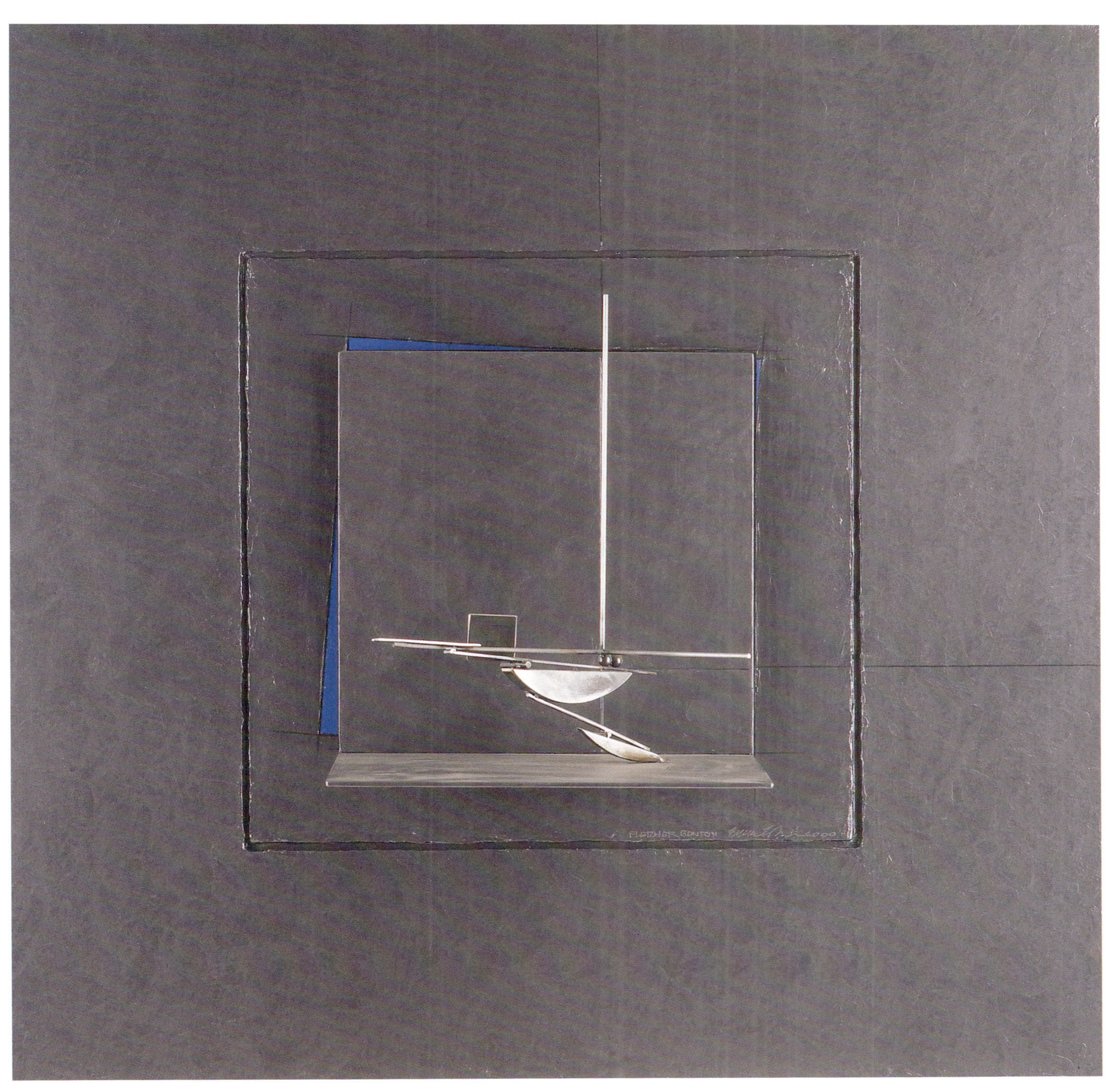

◁△

Meridian Lines, Phase II, Composition 7

2002, steel and acrylic on canvas
29½ x 29½ x 14 inches
75 x 75 x 36 cm

Meridian Lines, Phase II, Composition 3

2002, steel and acrylic on canvas
29½ x 29½ x 14 inches
75 x 75 x 36 cm

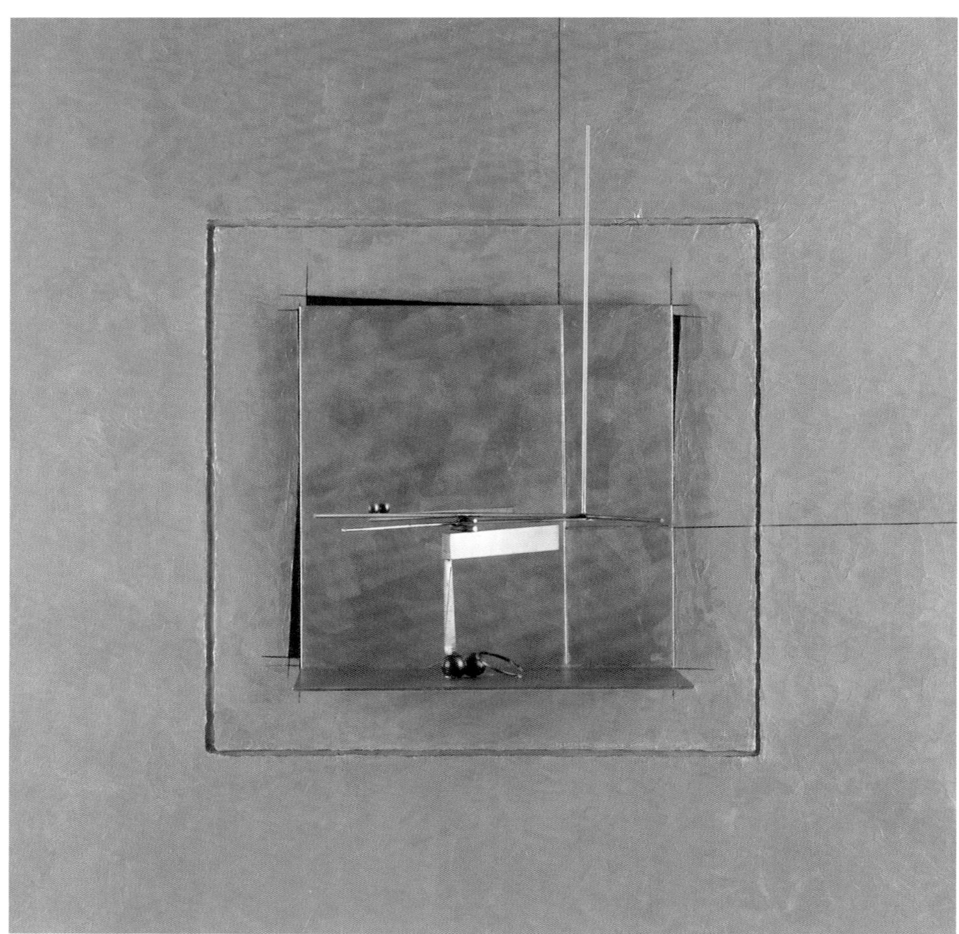

Meridian Lines, Phase II, Composition 5

2002, steel and acrylic on canvas
29½ x 29½ x 14 inches
75 x 75 x 36 cm

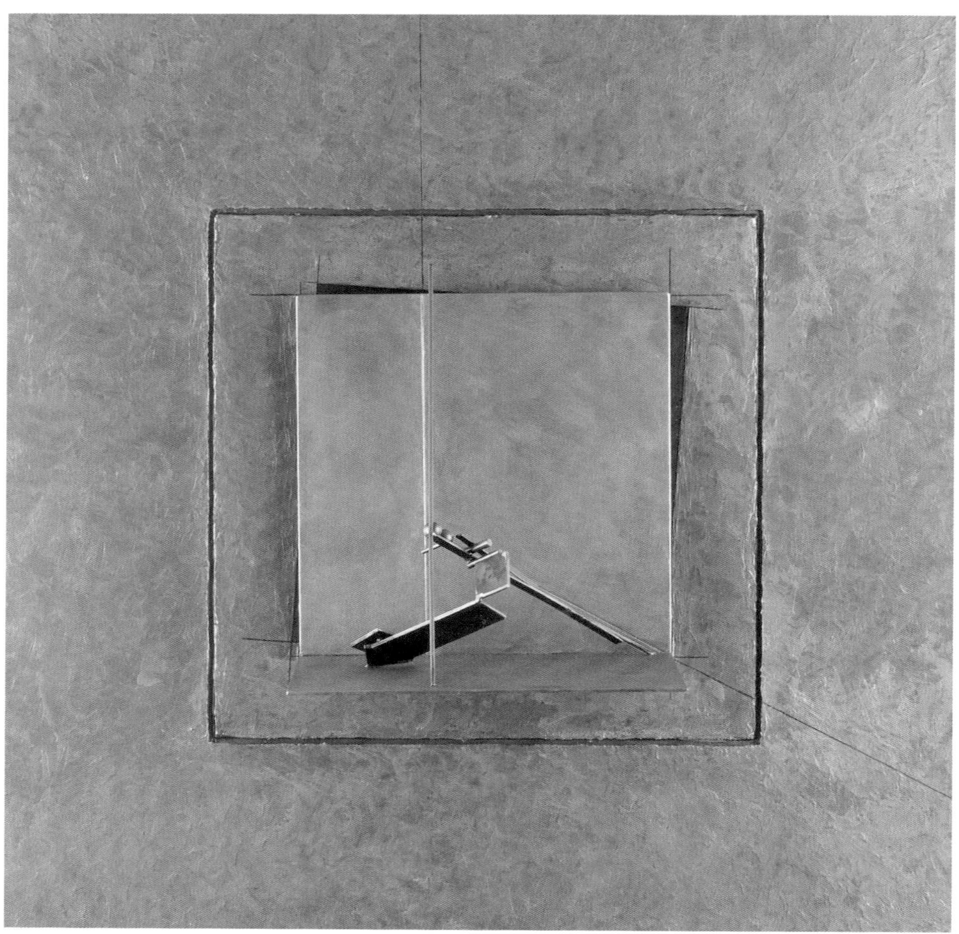

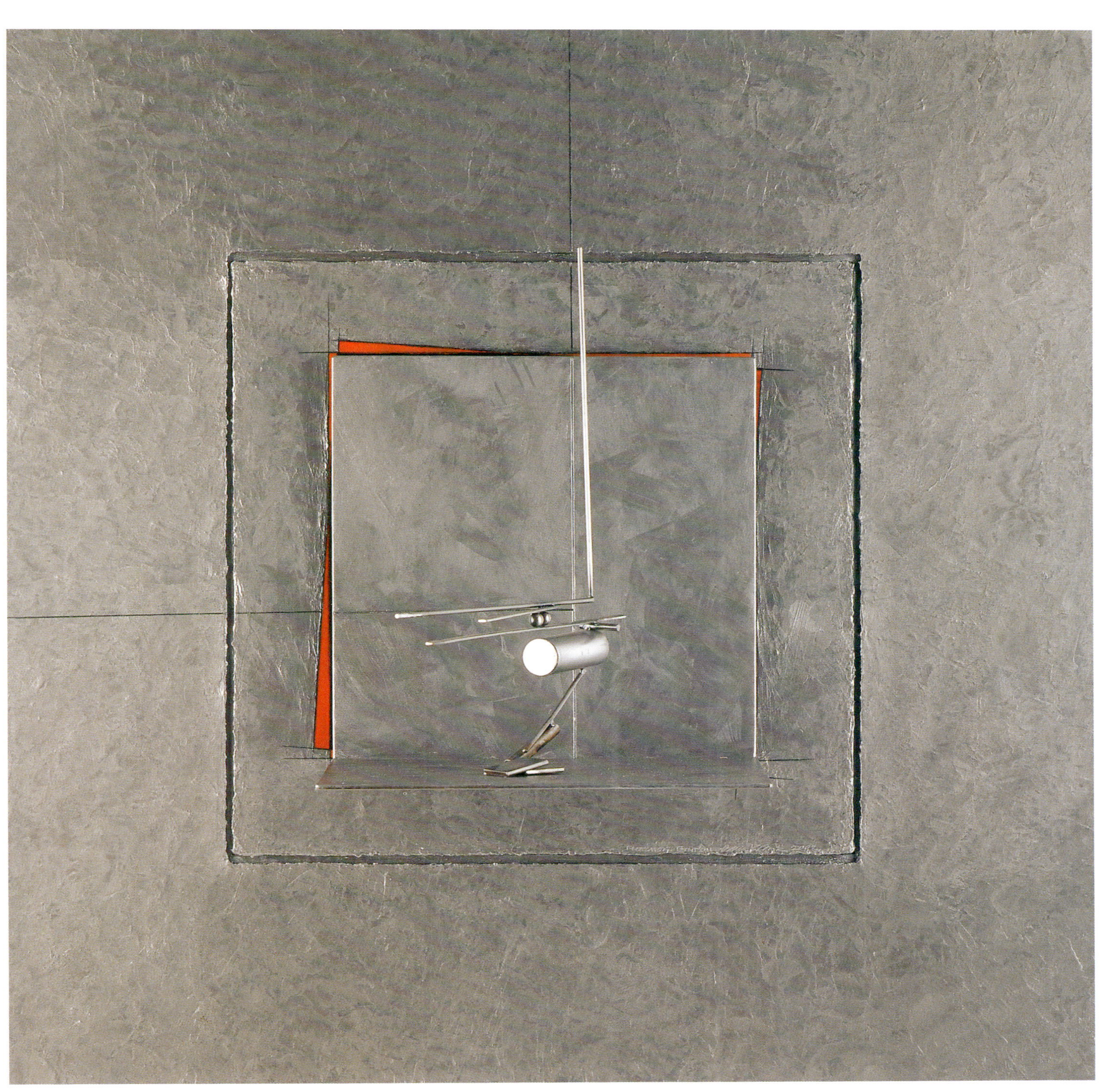

Meridian Lines, Phase II, Composition 8

2002, steel and acrylic on canvas
29½ x 29½ x 14 inches
75 x 75 x 36 cm

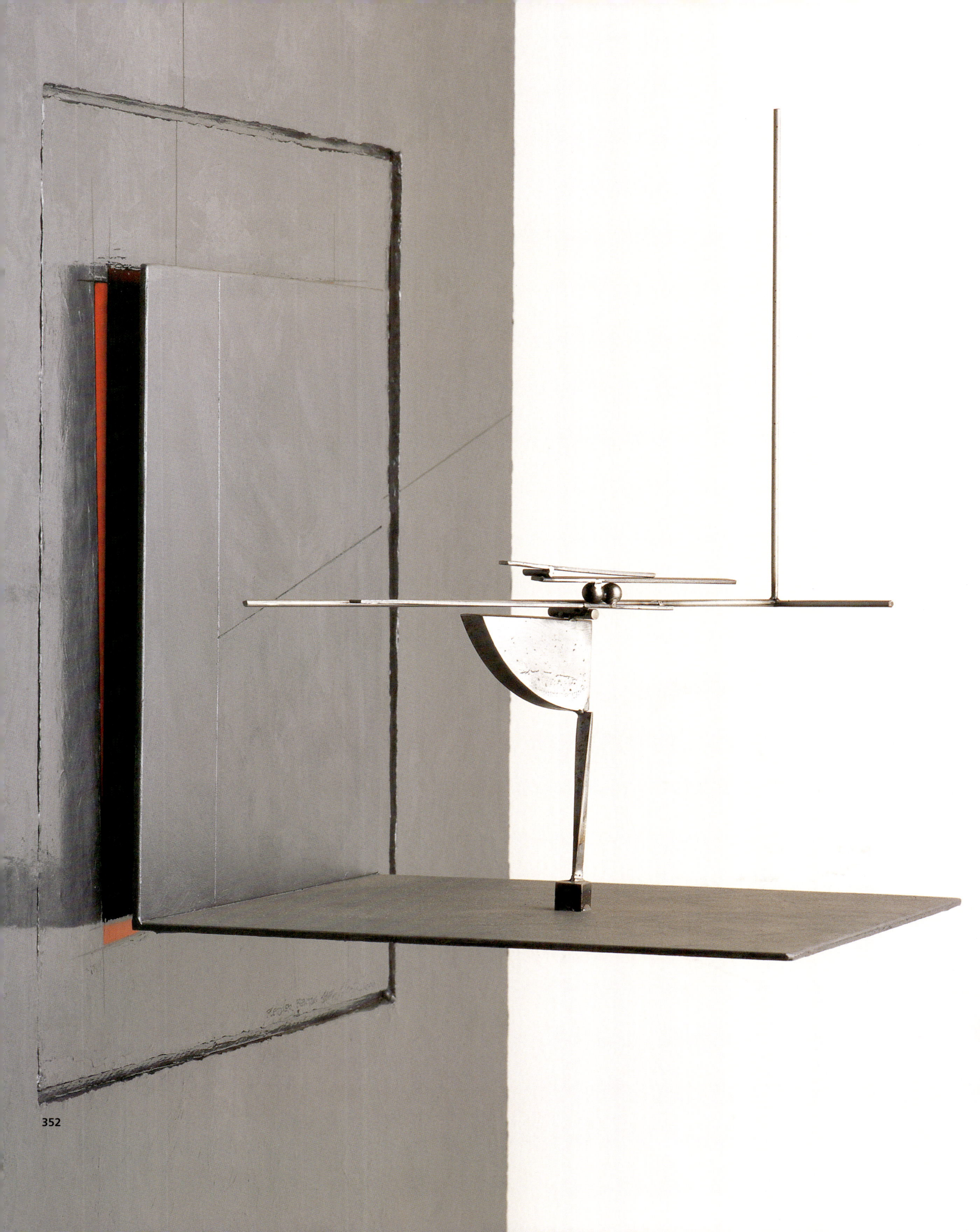

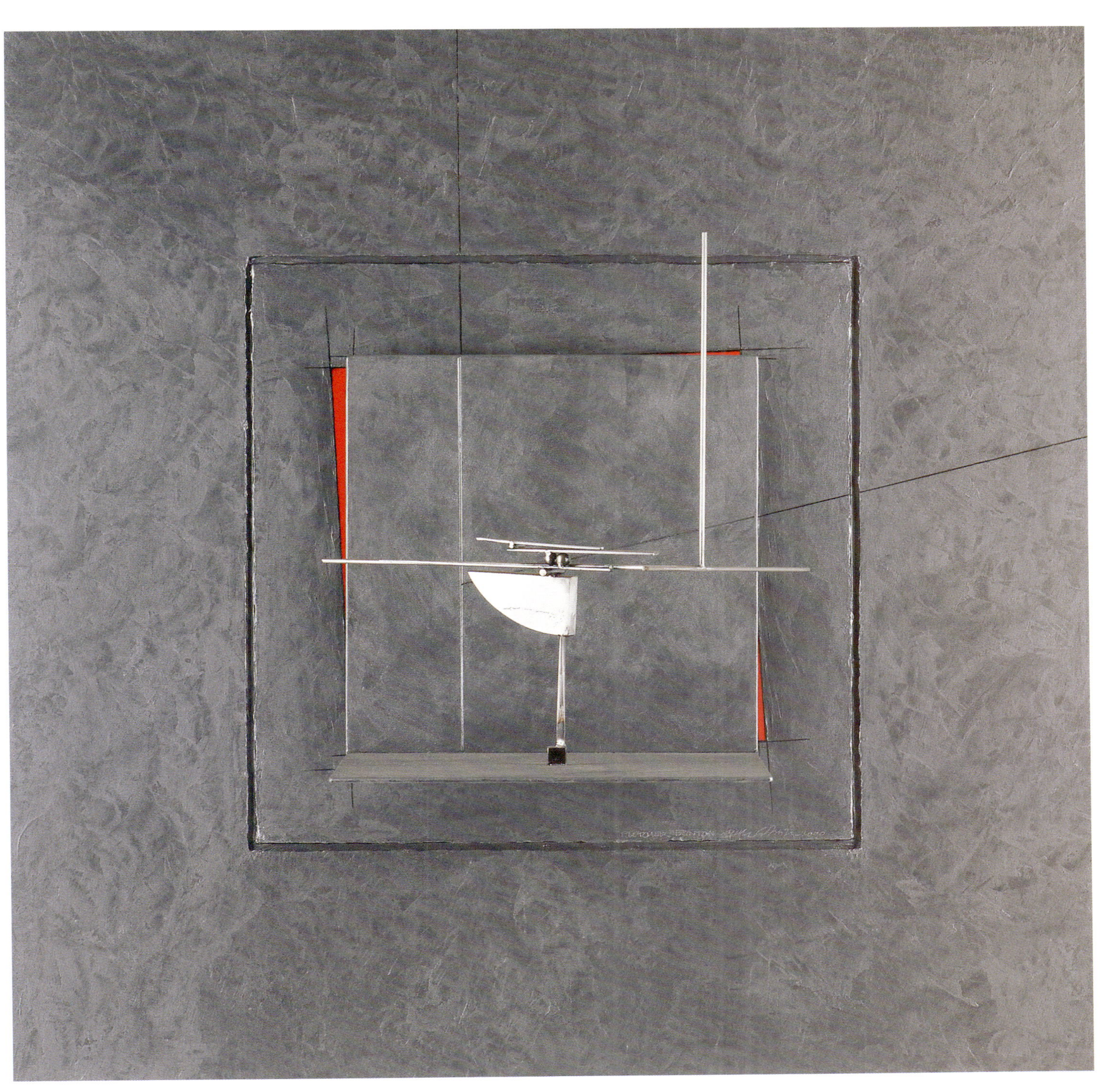

◁△

Meridian Lines, Phase II, Composition 6

2002, steel and acrylic on canvas
29½ x 29½ x 14 inches
75 x 75 x 36 cm

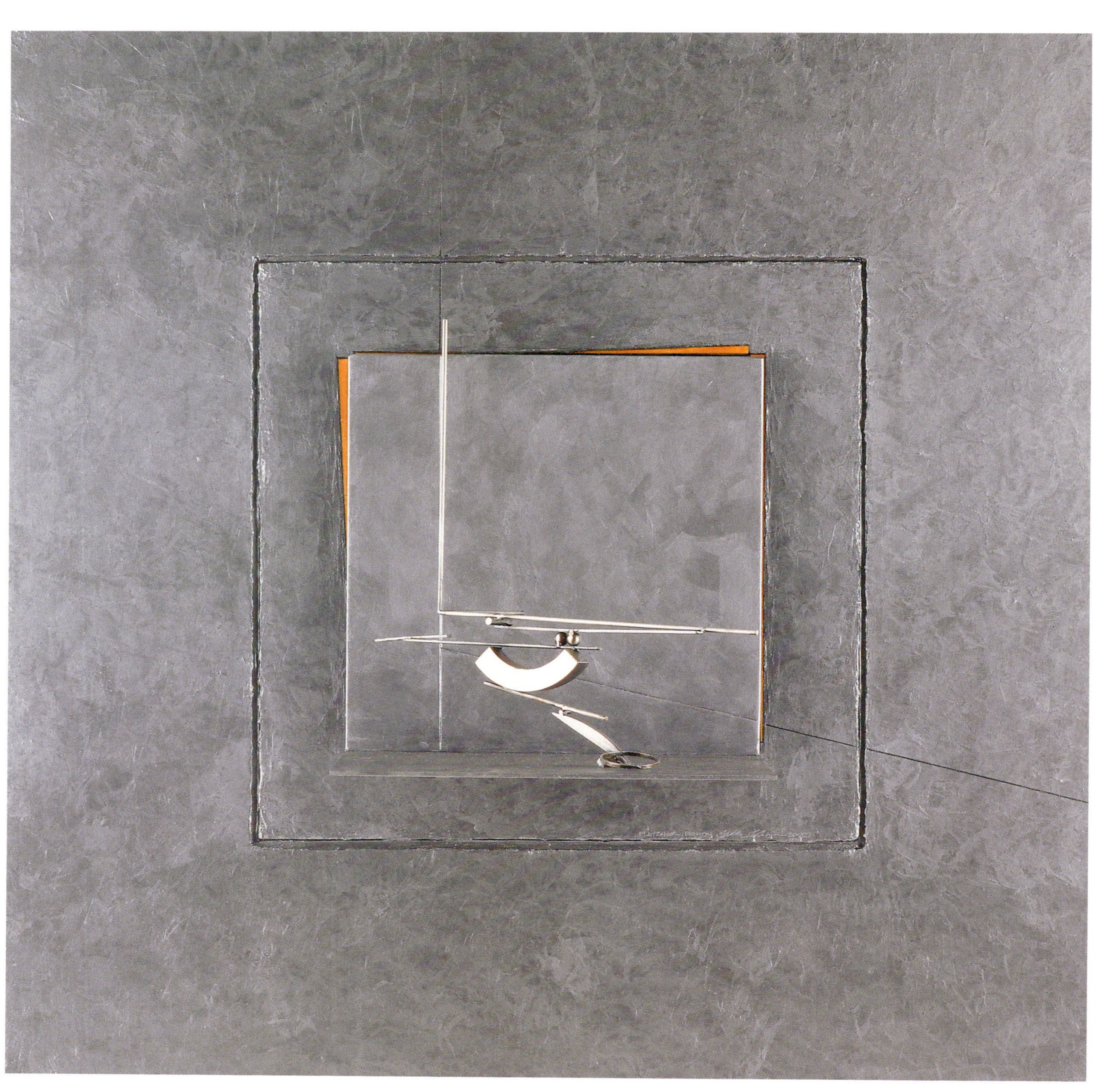

Meridian Lines, Phase II, Composition 2

2002, steel and acrylic on canvas
29½ x 29½ x 14 inches
75 x 75 x 36 cm

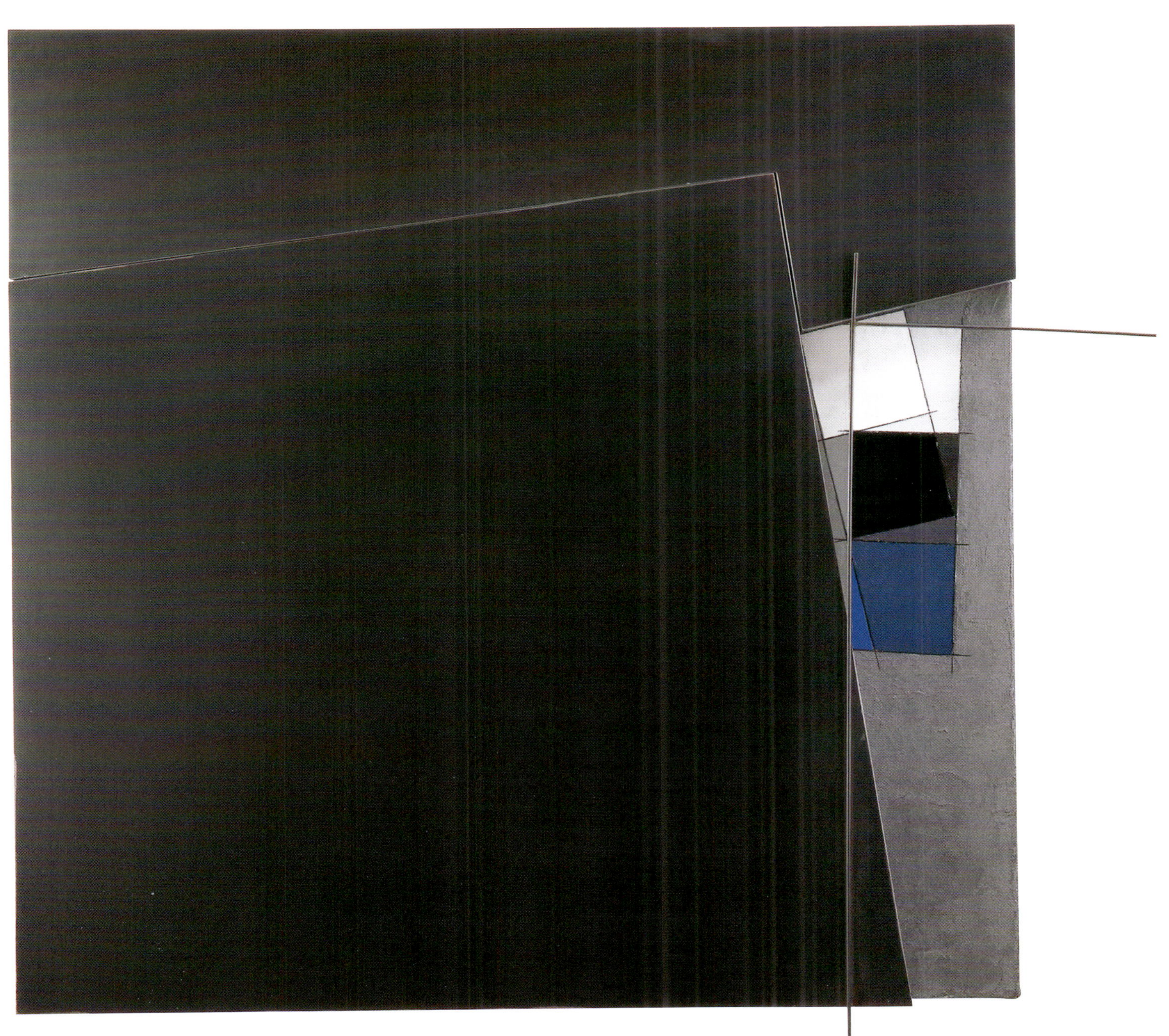

Plate Construct 8

2005, steel and acrylic on canvas
41 x 45 x 4½ inches
104 x 114 x 11 cm

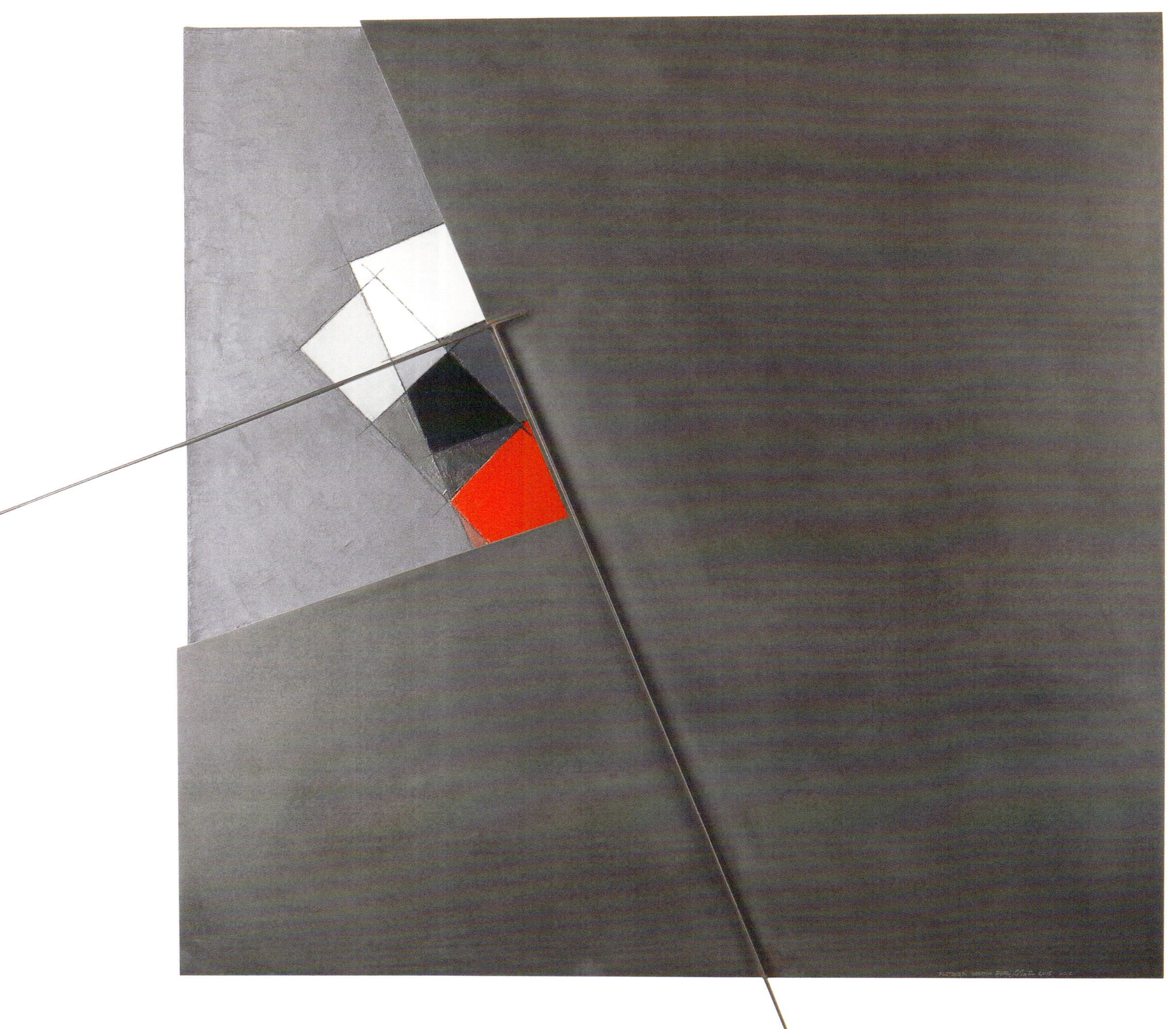

Plate Construct 1

2005, steel and acrylic on canvas
44 x 43 x 4½ inches
112 x 109 x 11 cm

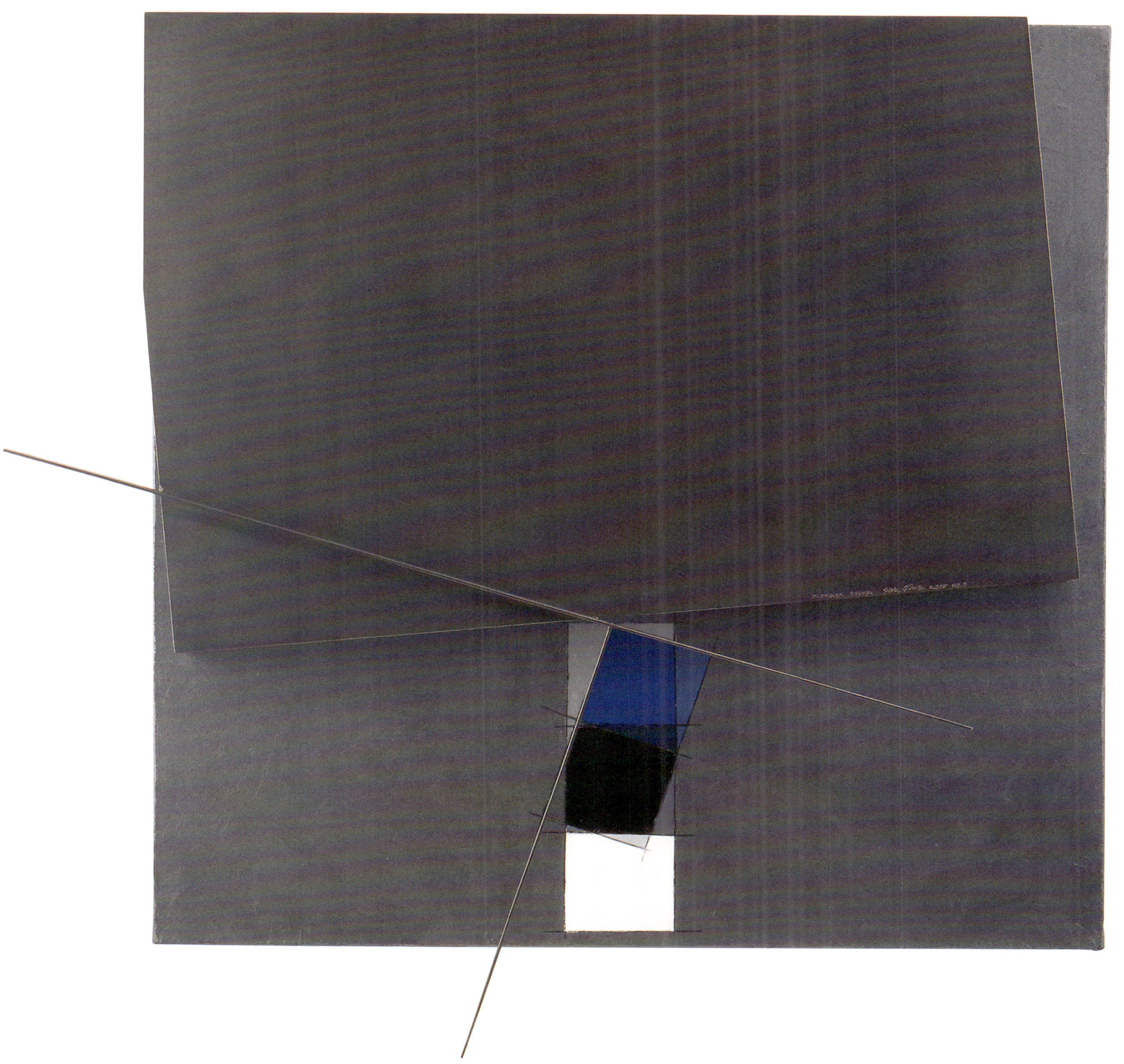

Plate Construct 3

2005, steel and acrylic on canvas
40 x 40 x 4½ inches
102 x 102 x 11 cm

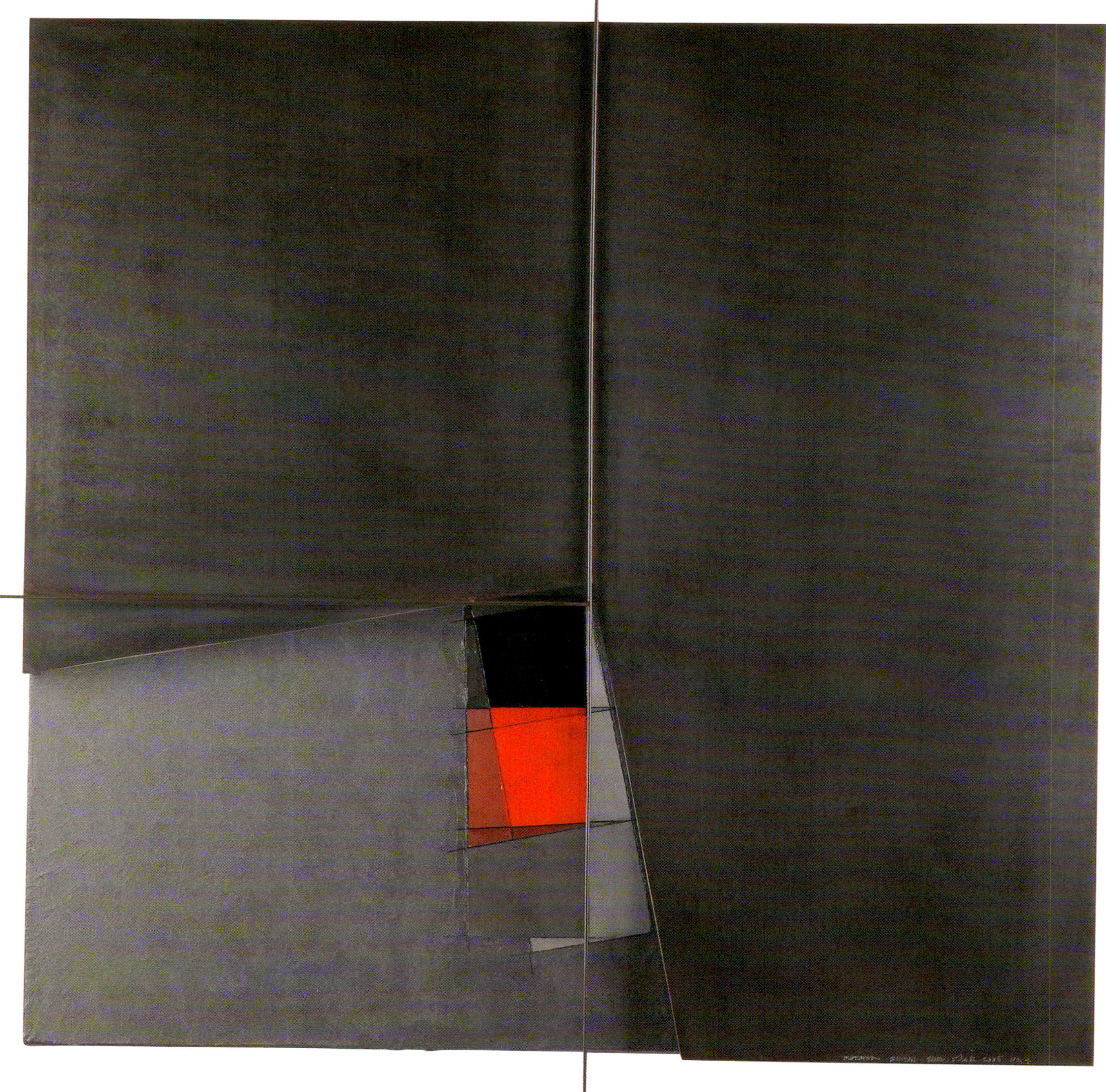

Plate Construct 4

2005, steel and acrylic on canvas
42 x 45 x 4½ inches
107 x 114 x 11 cm

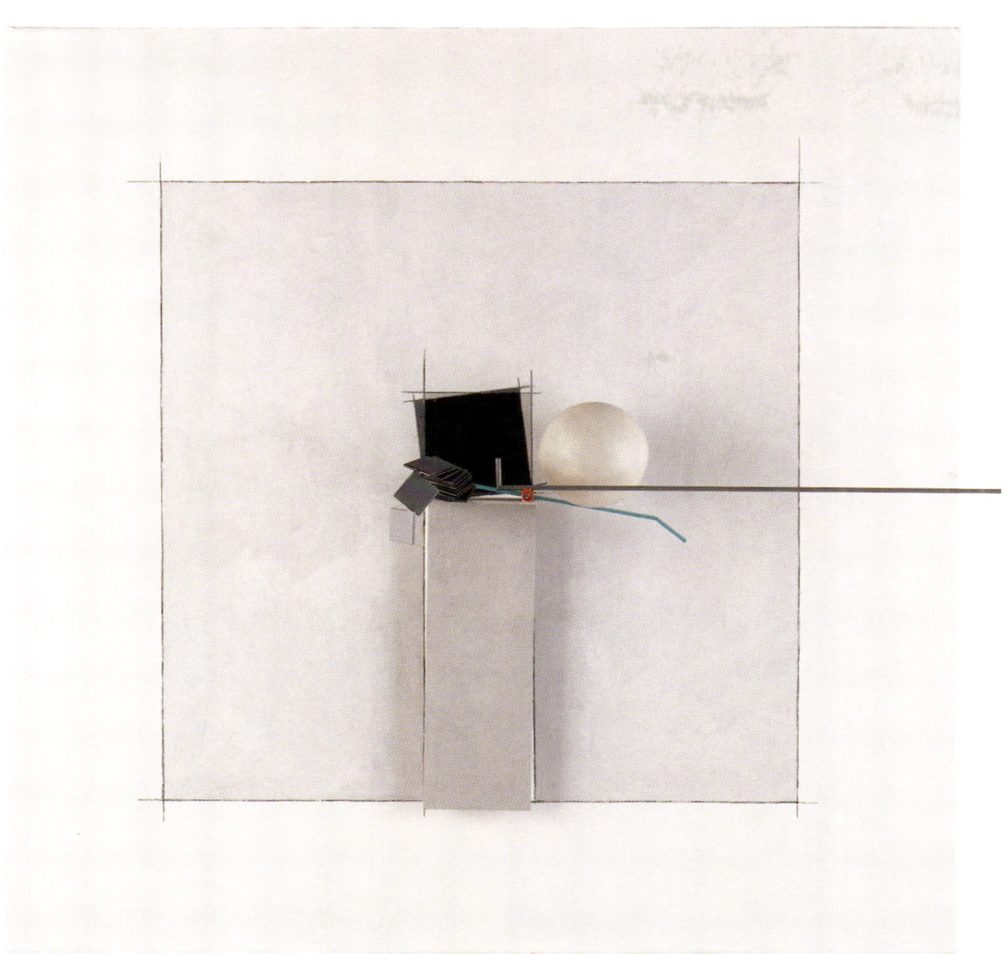

Quiet Rhythm 9

2005, steel and acrylic on canvas
20 x 20½ inches
51 x 52 cm

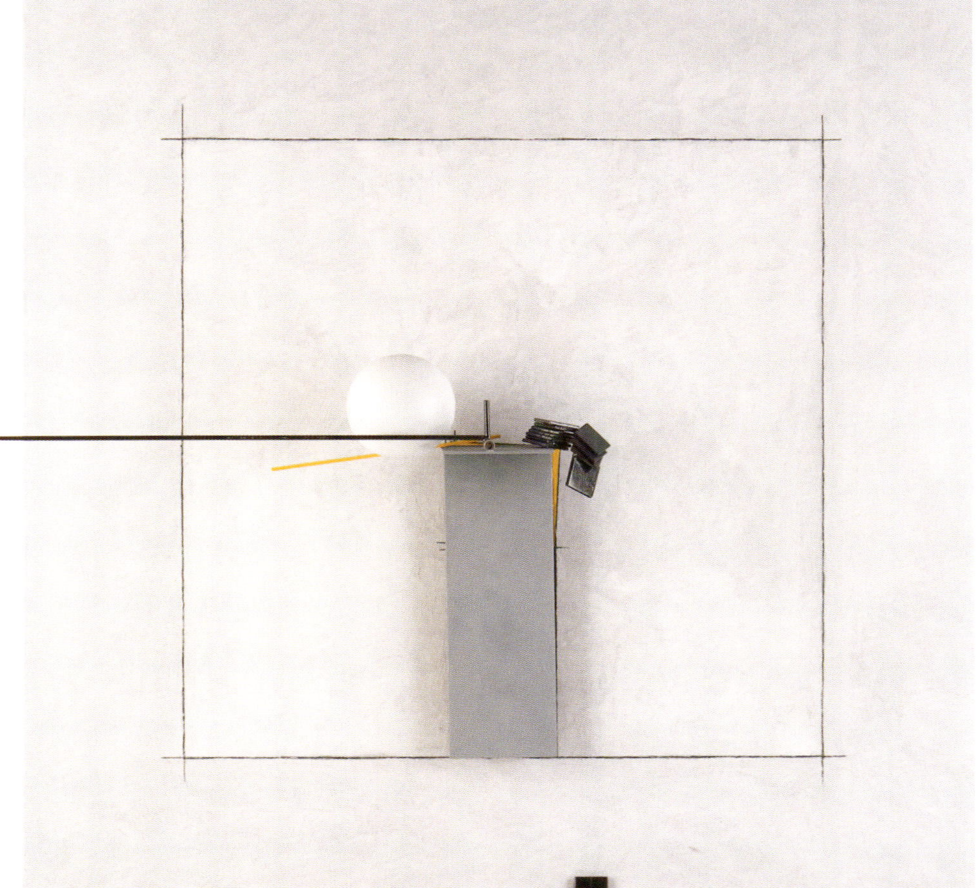

Quiet Rhythm 8

2005, steel and acrylic on canvas
22 x 20½ inches
56 x 52 cm

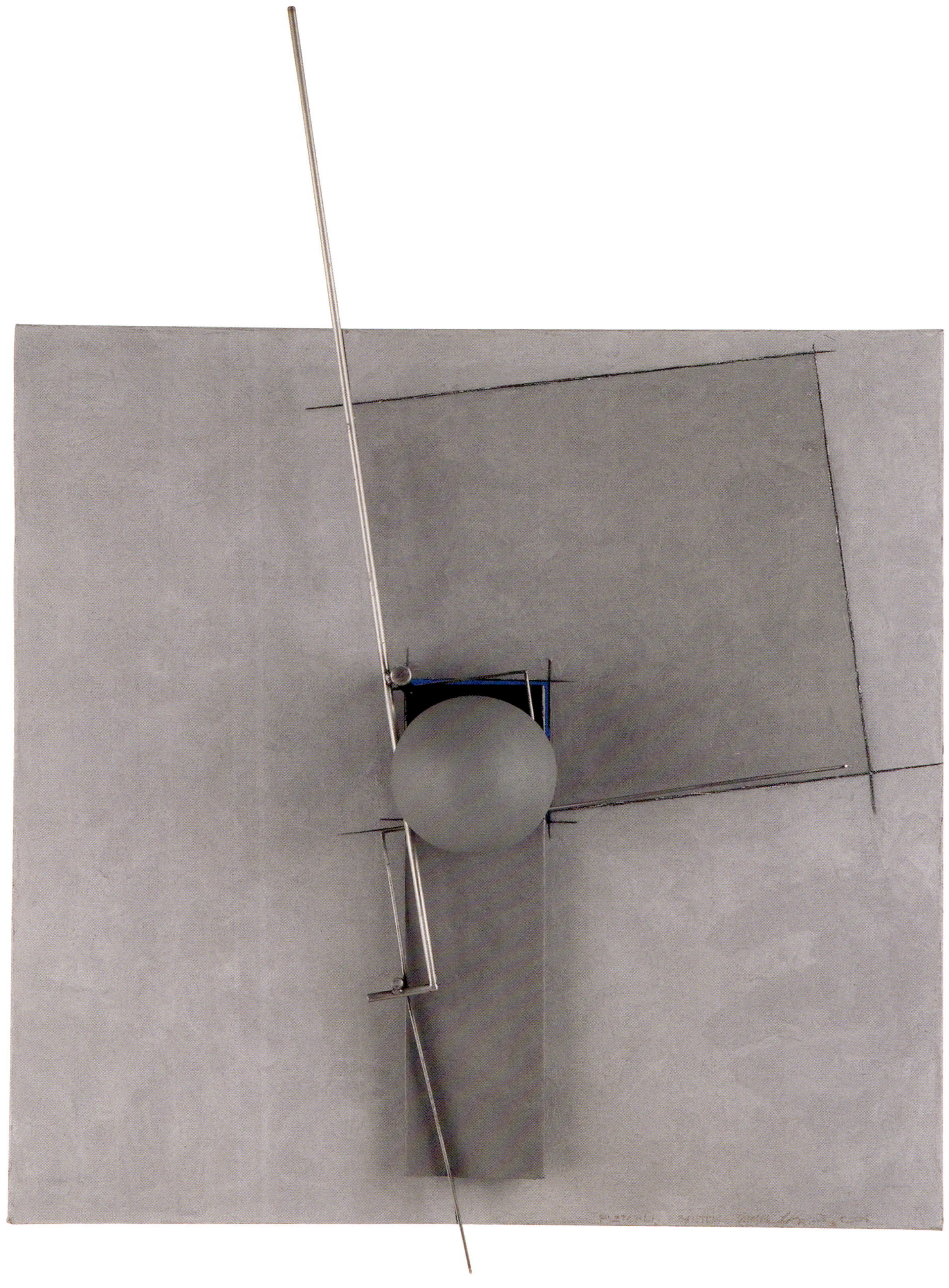

Quiet Rhythm 4

2004, steel and acrylic on canvas
28½ x 20 inches
72 x 51 cm

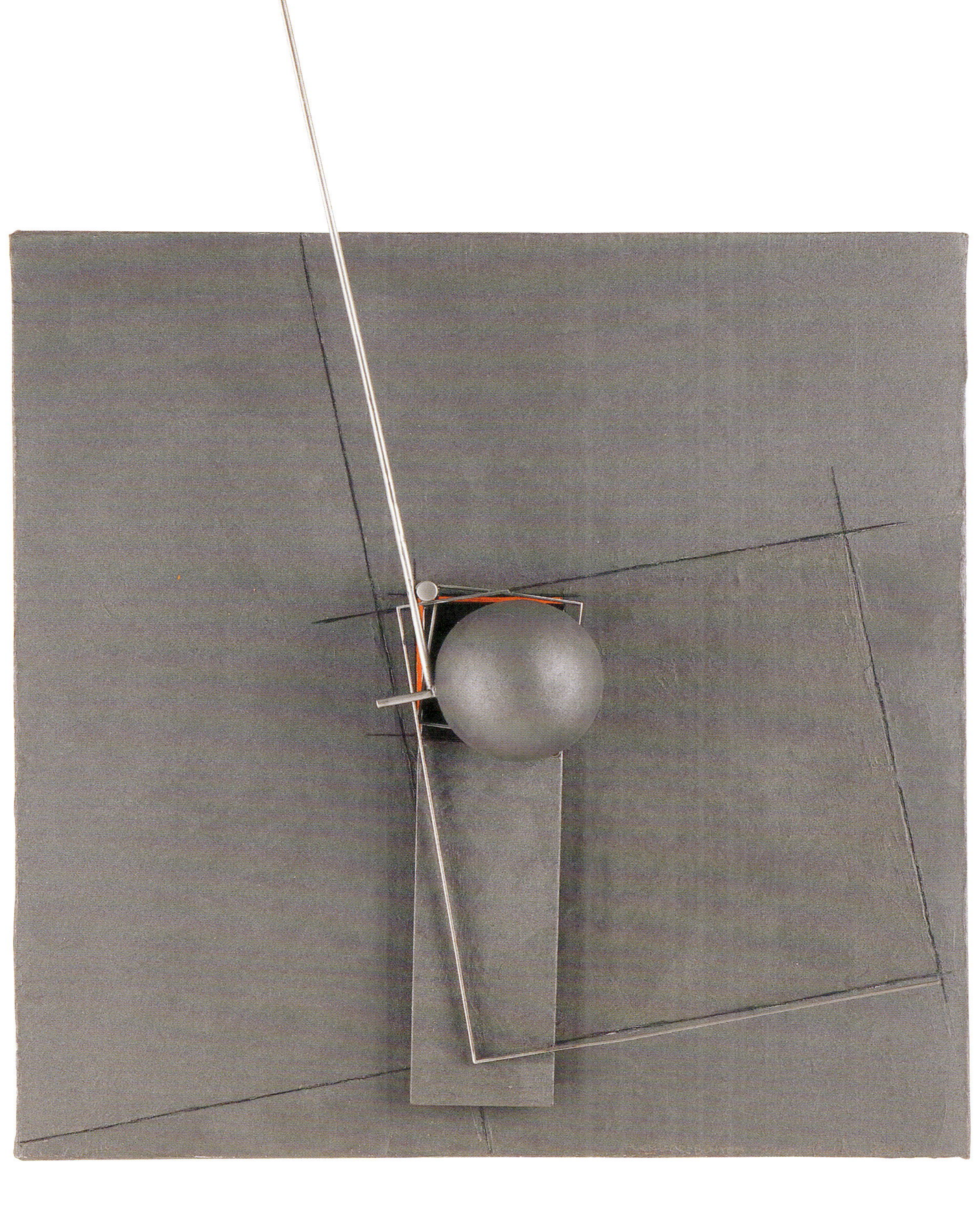

Quiet Rhythm 6

2004, steel and acrylic on canvas
29 x 20 inches
74 x 51 cm

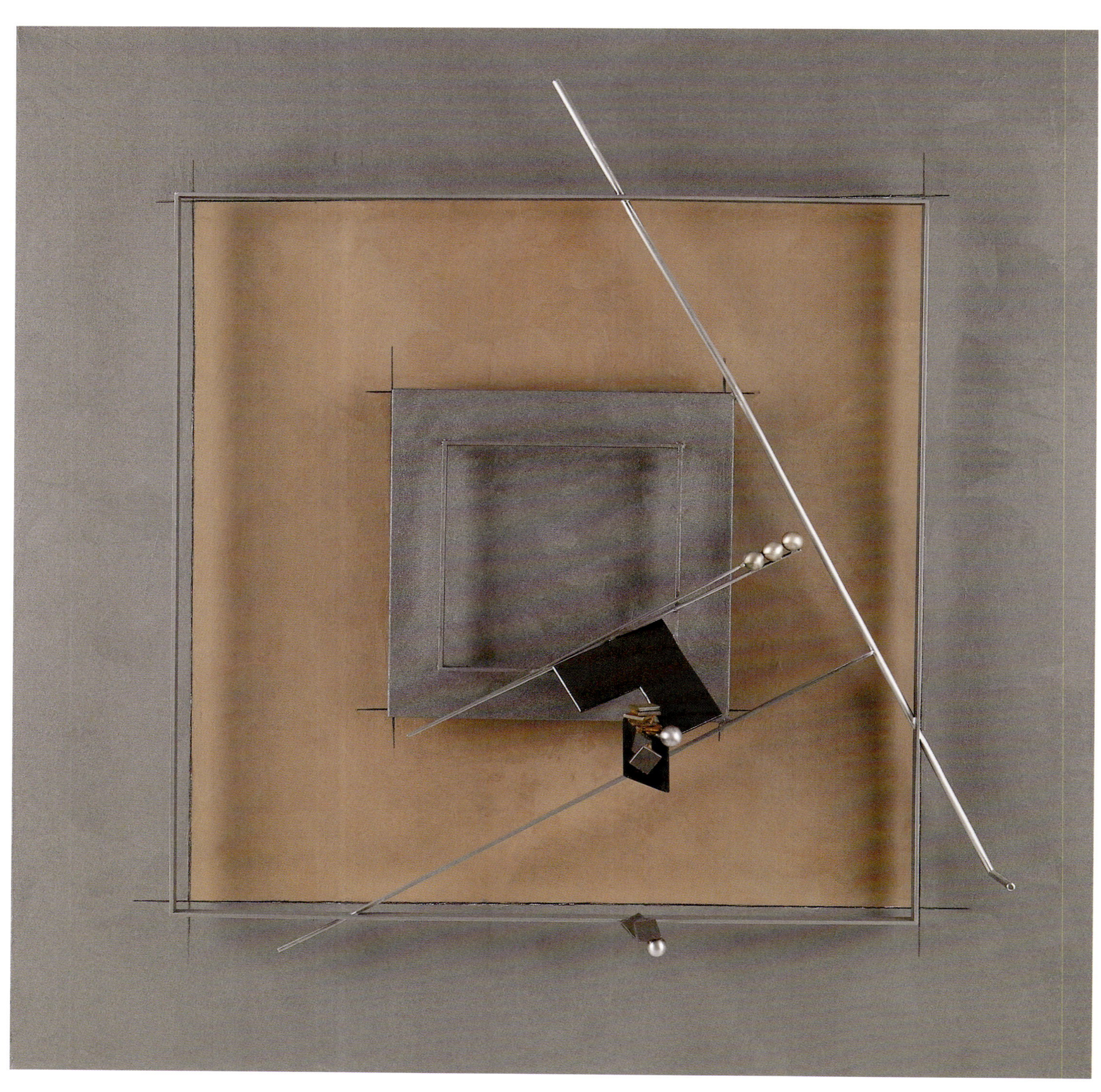

Red Rhythm Construct 3

2004, steel and acrylic on canvas
36 x 36 inches
91 x 91 cm

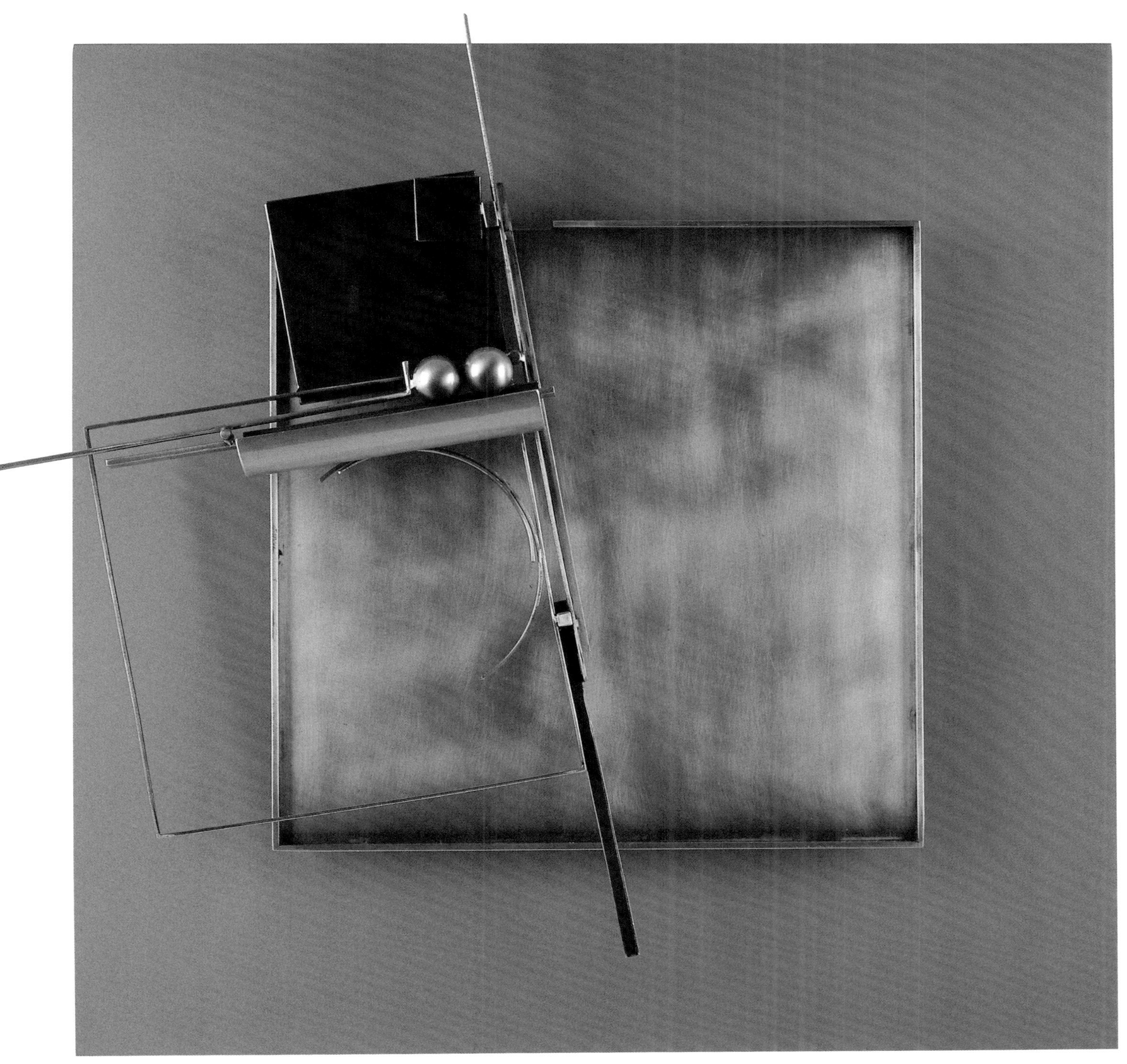

Steel Construct 27

2004, steel
20½ x 23 x 4 inches
52 x 58 x 10 cm

Steel Construct 11

2004, steel
20 x 20 x 4 inches
51 x 51 x 10 cm

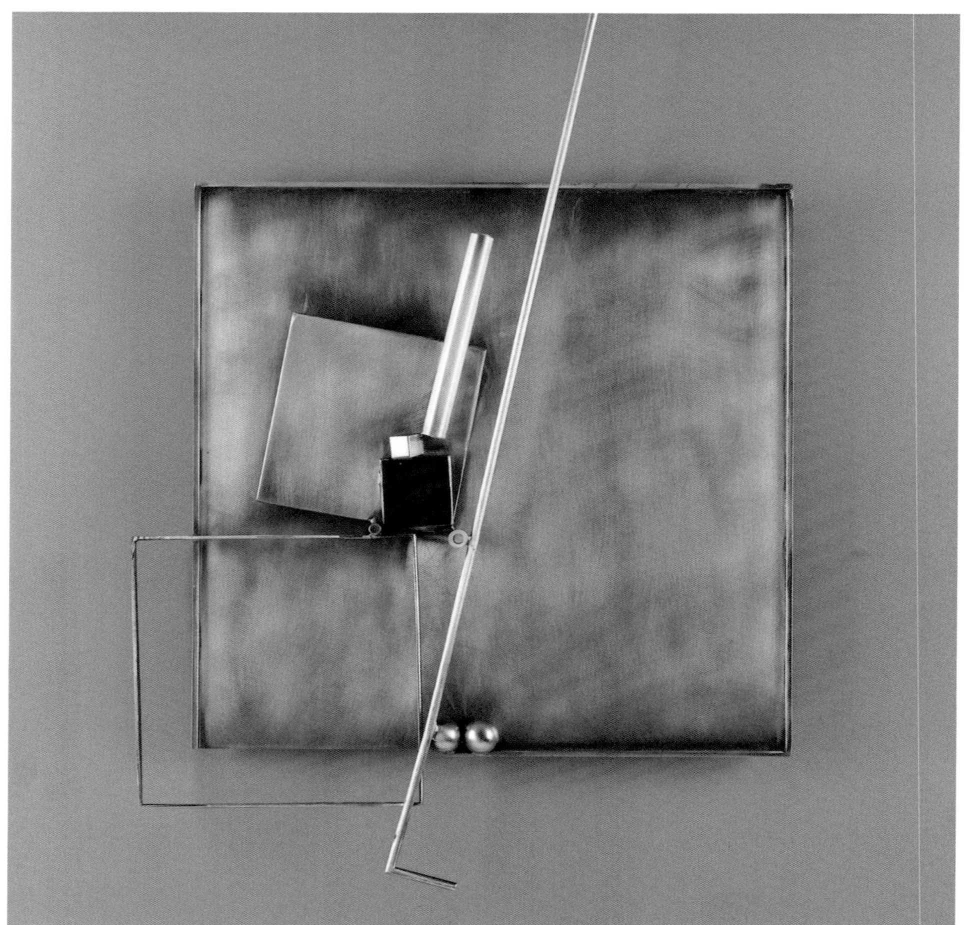

Steel Construct 16

2004, steel
20 x 20 x 4 inches
51 x 51 x 10 cm

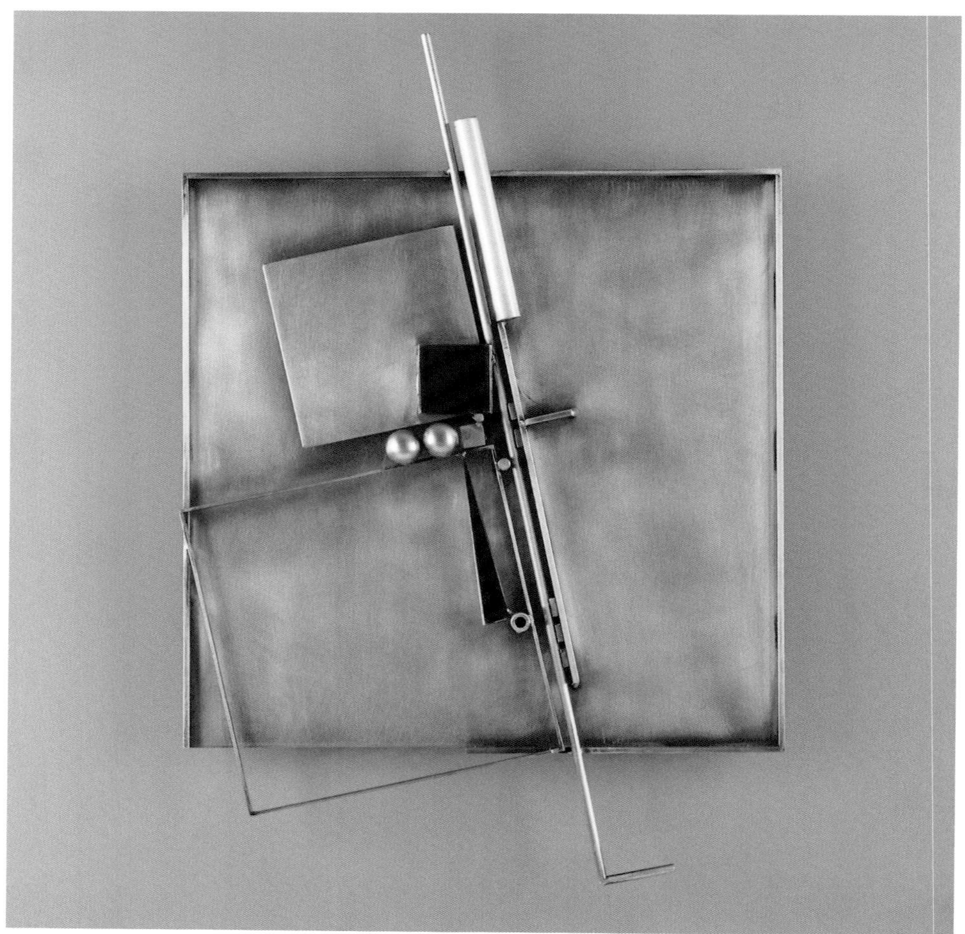

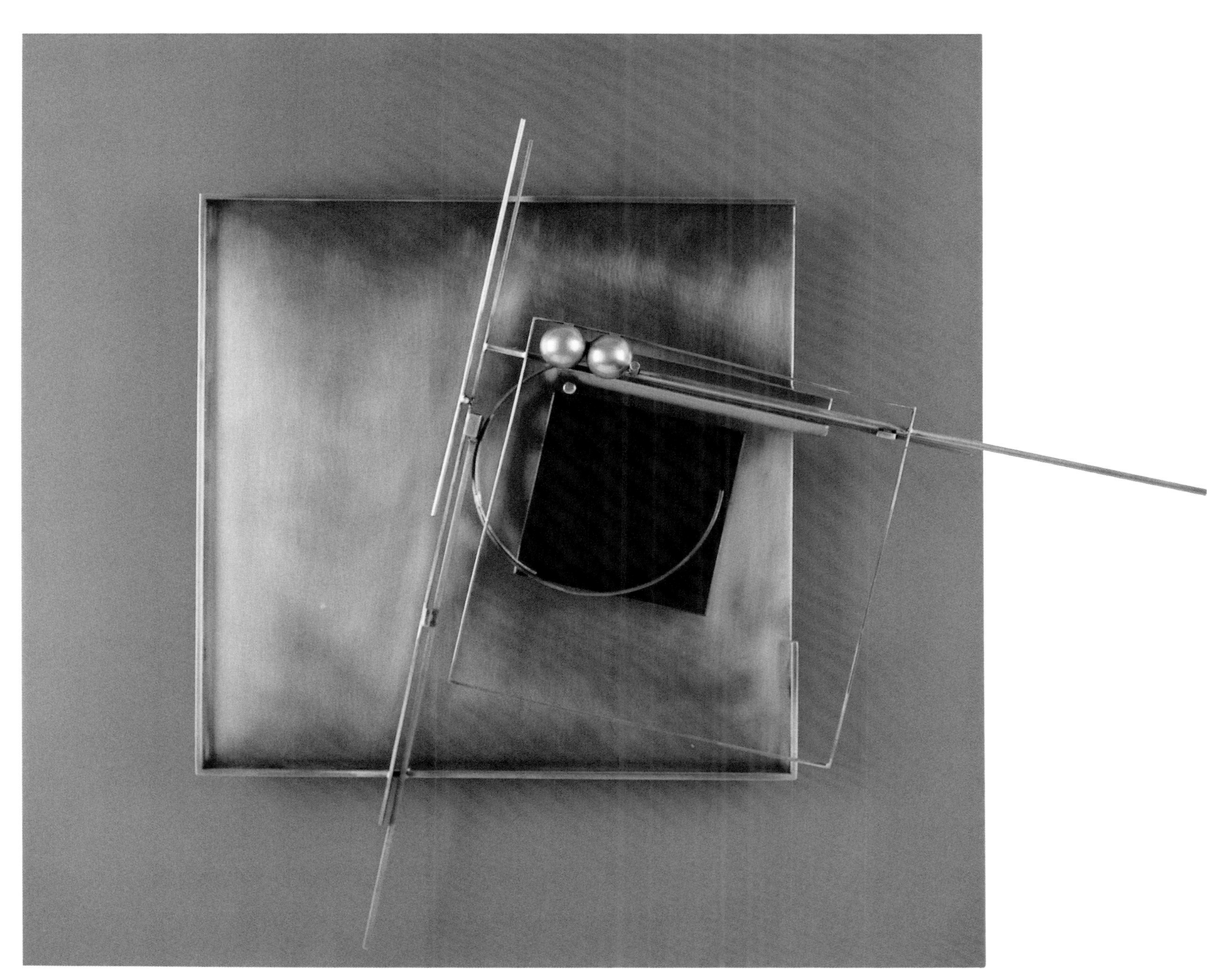

Steel Construct 20

2004, steel
20 x 24 x 4 inches
51 x 61 x 10 cm

Steel Painting 37

2001, steel and acrylic on canvas
29½ x 29½ inches
75 x 75 cm

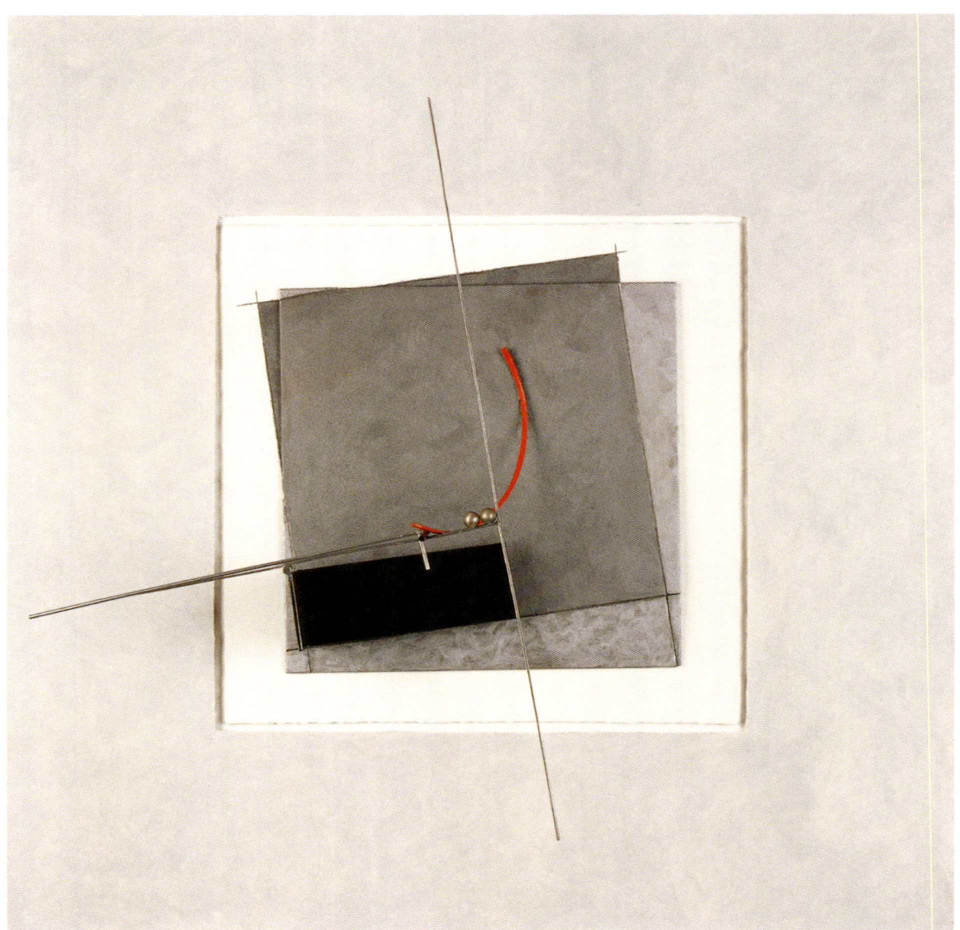

White Rhythm Construct

2004, steel and acrylic on canvas
36 x 36 inches
91 x 91 cm

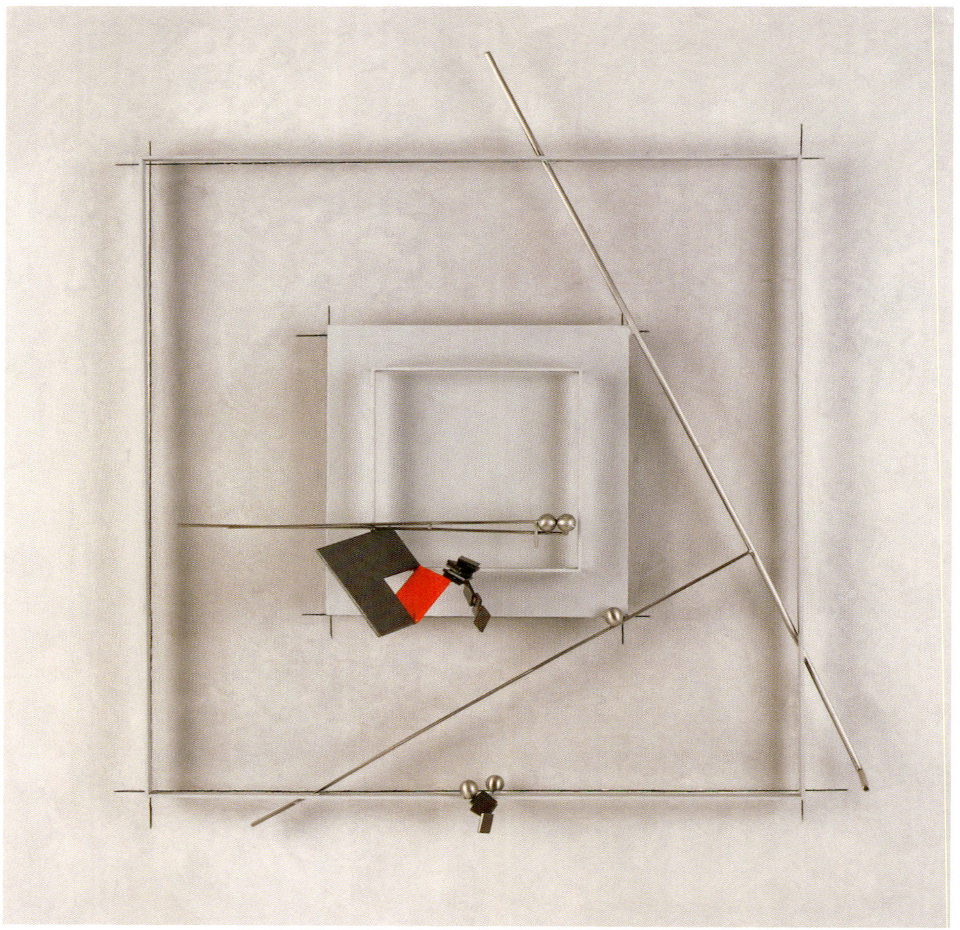

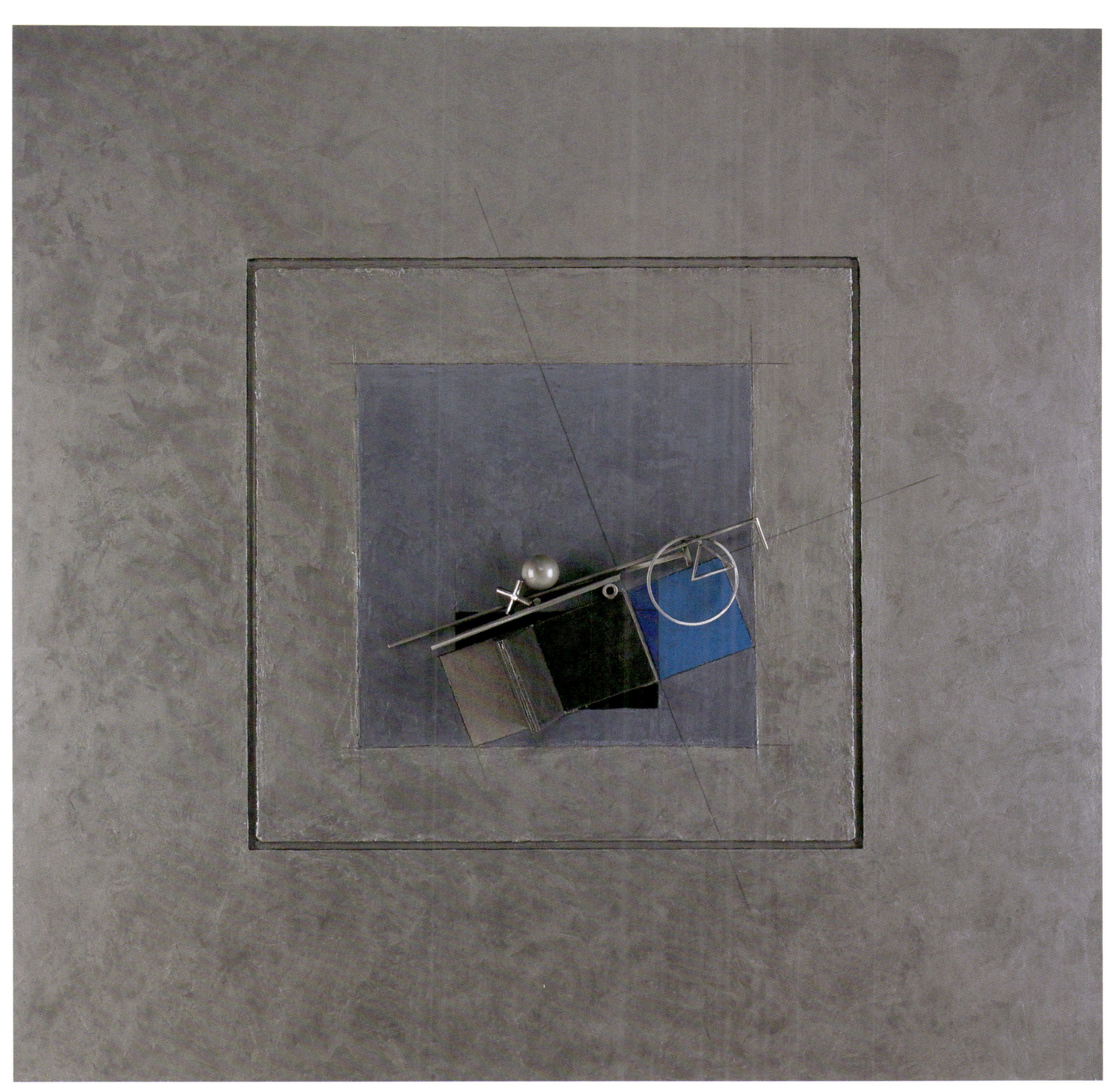

Steel Painting No. 17, Blue Square

2000, steel and acrylic on canvas
29½ x 29½ inches
75 x 75 cm

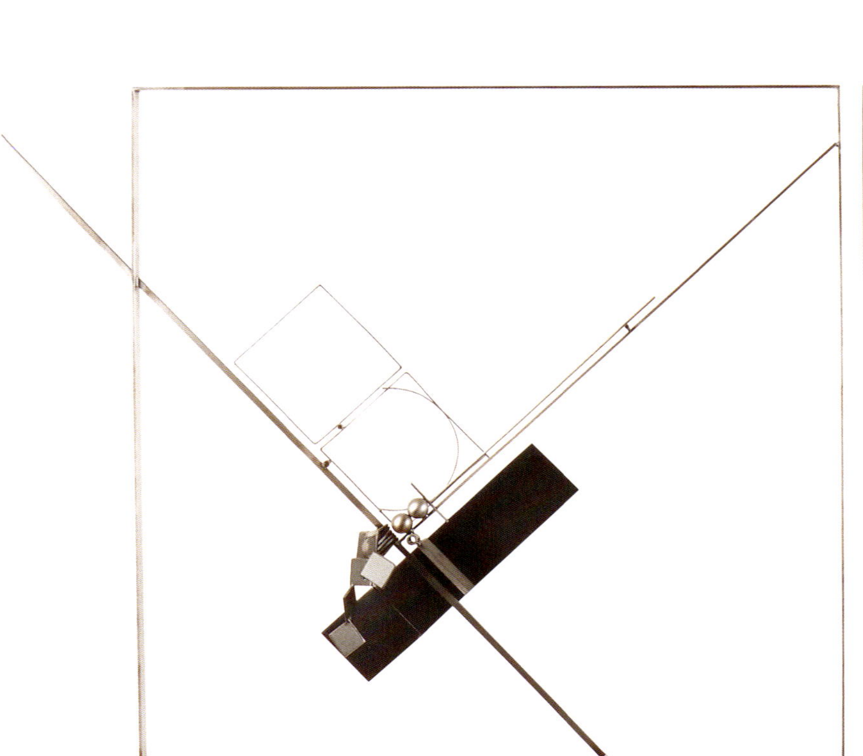

Open Construct T - No. 3

2003, steel
24 x 28½ inches
61 x 72 cm

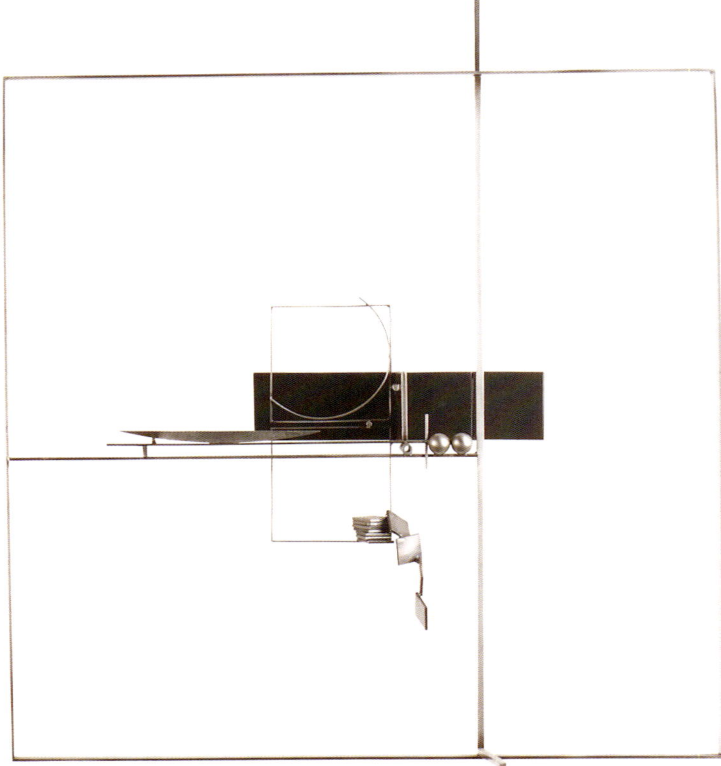

Open Construct T - No. 2

2003, steel
28 x 24 inches
71 x 61 cm

AFTERWORD

Geometric Sculpture in Equilibrium: Fletcher Benton

Peter Selz

Fletcher Benton's workplace is located in the light industry district of San Francisco. The busy 6,000-square-foot space is 23 feet high and can easily hold the forklift needed to assemble his large sculptures. It is filled with the noise of hammering, cutting, and welding—work performed by Benton's assistants. It is amidst all this commotion that, working on a small metal table, he makes his steel maquettes. On a lucky day, intuition—Benton calls it his "Magic Man"—comes into play, and he will be able to finish a maquette, a process in which precision is guided by inspiration.

Benton loves precisely made models and has placed his own in a sparsely appointed, meticulously arranged room above his work space, which houses, in addition to his works, a fine collection of World War II American, British, German, and Japanese fighter and bomber aircraft, made to 1:48 scale by an ex-U.S. Marine and a German biochemist turned model makers. Among the models is a Ju-52, which was the German warplane that bombed Guernica during the Spanish Civil War: "My homage to Picasso," Benton says. He also commissioned models of famous sailing ships such as the *Cutty Sark*, the *Constitution*, and the H.M.S. *Victory*, all crafted to scale with consummate skill. An elaborate electric railroad travels around close to the ceiling of one room, to the delight of the artist and his visitors. One senses the grown-up boy's delight in these model planes, trains, and ships. His living room, in the penthouse of the building, is furnished with vintage Bauhaus furniture by Ludwig Mies van der Rohe and Marcel Breuer, as well as recent work by the noted Oakland craftsman Gary Bennett.

Born in the coal- and iron-producing district of southern Ohio, Benton was a successful sign painter as a youth. He attended college at Miami University in Oxford, Ohio, after mustering out of the Navy, and he moved to San Francisco in 1956. He began as an instructor at the California College of Arts and Crafts and then went to Europe, traveling by his motorcycle through Scandinavia, Holland, and France; he spent some time in Paris and then in New York. Back in San Francisco in 1961, he had a solo exhibition at the California Palace of the Legion of Honor, showing his portraits of fellow artists like David Simpson and William Morehouse.

Benton, however, is rarely seen as a Bay Area Artist. His mature work as a sculptor is in the Constructivist tradition and differs entirely from mainstream Bay Area sculpture. Sculptors here have transformed ceramics into sculpture, made Funk pieces, and, as exemplified by Robert Arneson,

Manuel Neri, and Stephen de Staebler, made figurative sculpture. This is not the tradition in which Benton seems to fit. He speaks highly of Peter Voulkos, among California Artists, but it is the achievement of dynamic equilibrium within the stability of geometry in John McLaughlin's paintings that Benton most admires. Among his elders in American sculpture, he esteems David Smith and George Rickey, with whom he formed a friendship when his work was shown in the first international exhibition of kinetic sculpture at the University Art Museum in Berkeley. (In the interest of full disclosure, I curated this exhibition.) Here, Benton's work was shown with that of the Movement's leaders: artists such as Rickey, Pol Bury, Len Lye, Takis, and Jean Tinguely. In January 1966, Benton was featured with some of these artists in *Time* magazine's article on the Movement movement. And Benton, heretofore known only locally, came to international attention.

His work at the time consisted of motorized paintings, and he was fascinated by being able to use movement—time—to make art. He soon found, however, that pieces such as *Yin and Yang* (1965) showed their repetitive cycles too clearly, and, although he was showing at the Whitney Annual and the International Exposition in Osaka, he decided to risk his substantial reputation as a painter and to begin working in three dimensions, bending flat pieces of paper or cardboard into three-dimensional figurations in the early series *Folded Circles* and *Folded Square Alphabets* that occupied him during the 1970s. Made of bronze, aluminum, or steel, they were frequently painted in primary colors. By the 1980s, in the *Balanced/Unbalanced* series, he began to play with gravity, working with cubo-geometric forms—squares, circles, triangles, rods, and rings. He clearly had fun making these sculptures, large and small, often adding playful elements to offset the severe Euclidean geometric forms. In 1993 he received a major commission to build a gigantic sculpture in Cologne. Awkwardly named *Steel Watercolor Triangle Ring*, this elegant red tower, 66 feet high, points skyward in fluent grace. While putting this tower in place in Cologne's Barbarossaplatz, he saw an exhibition of Malevich at the Ludwig Museum and a model of Tatlin's *Monument to the Third International* in Düsseldorf. He became convinced of something he had only assumed before: he was a disciple of Constructivism. He knows that true originality is not a matter of the "innocent eye," but that artistic identity is established in relation to the artist's antecedents. Malevich and Kandinsky became paradigmatic to his work. Many of the early abstract artists felt that their new art had great potential power, and Malevich had postulated that Suprematism could "make the world into a true model of perfection." Such utopian faith is not available to artists today, and, for an artist like Benton, the forms developed by these masters of early abstraction are sufficient unto themselves. The tilted square in Malevich's monochrome paintings finds an echo in Benton's three-dimensional steel paintings. The circles, semicircles, triangles, bars, and checkerboards in Kandinsky's paintings of the early 1920s are imported into contemporary aesthetics in Benton's *Construct Reliefs*. His *Odes to Kandinsky* (1995–97) are steel reliefs that consist of rods set at right angles with rings, triangles, and staggered grids in balanced compositions that renew the viewer's understanding of the almost inexhaustible possibilities offered within the framework of geometric construction. When Benton feels he has achieved his objective in a work, he speaks of its "inherent rightness," reminding us of Kandinsky's "inner sound," except that for Kandinsky this concept had express spiritual significance.

Benton's next step was to fashion steel paintings in which the rods, rectangles, and metal squares, falling downward, are not set into steel frames. These works are meant to hang on the wall with no backing, so that the steel construction seems to float freely in space. They are indeed to be seen in pairs: *Open Constructs T* (2003) exemplifies this innovative series.

The *Folded Square* concept continues to be a central form in Benton's work. It appears again on the campus of the University of California, Berkeley, as *Folded Circle Trio* (1999). When the Haas Business School, the last building designed by the renowned architect Charles Moor, was completed, a work by Benton was selected for one of its courtyards. As suggested by its title, the piece consists of circular, square, and oblong forms. They are engaged in a dynamic, rhythmic interaction with each other and with the negative space suggested by the solid forms; the void, which echoes the large open arches of the building, is a vital element of the sculpture.

In 2000 Benton began his *Donut* series, finding "inherent rightness" in works such as *Tilted Donut with Zig and Balls* (2003), in which balance appears to defy gravity. Having worked with circular forms for decades, he now achieved a remarkable illusion. As the viewer moves and different aspects of donut, poles, semicircle, balls, zigzags come to the fore, the sculpture appears to change so strikingly as to be almost a different work from each perspective. The balls and zig, being smaller elements, lend import to the large circular form, informing the work with monumental presence. *Donut with 3 Balls* (2001), captured by the eminent photographer of sculpture David Finn on Benton's property in the Napa wine country, illustrates how placing this geometric steel structure into the rolling hills and vineyards makes for an eloquent contrast between nature and man-made artifact.

Previous writers on Benton's work—Paul Karlstrom, Carter Ratcliff—have noted that it is marked by duality: palpable sculpture and illusionary painting, the slim and the blocky, the circle and the square, emotion and restraint. In his finest recent work, Benton, now in his 70s, seems to have found harmonious resolution.

AFTERWORD

Fletcher Benton: Indifference to the Absolute

Carter Ratcliff

For more than three decades, Fletcher Benton has been refining and redefining geometric sculpture. The result is one of the major oeuvres of our era. In art, geometry is almost always an appeal to timeless absolutes. Benton's brilliance shows in his indifference to the absolute—or, to put it positively, in his tireless responsiveness to the contingencies of experience. For him, geometric form is not so much abstract as immediate, resourceful, alive. From blunt simplicity, he generates buoyancy. From disparity, unity.

Benton calls himself "a builder." His material is steel. His forms are geometric: planar, angular, circular. This material and these forms imply modernity. Steel, after all, did not become a common industrial material until the middle of the 19th century. Geometric forms, on the other hand, provide the structural premises of just about every building ever built, including the simplest hut. Over the millennia, however, layers of ornamentation have obscured the builder's geometry of plane and rectangle and occasional circle. Not until the Industrial Revolution, with its demand for strictly utilitarian interiors, did builders allow geometric form to stand forth in all its stark clarity. A warehouse from the early 1800s can have the look of a square building block topped by a triangular one.

These developments did not affect the art of sculpture until the early decades of the 20th century. Prompted by the quasi-abstractions of the Cubist painters, certain European sculptors dismissed the ancient understanding of sculpture as the representation of familiar forms, chiefly the organic articulations of the human body. Their sculpture would acknowledge—it would be built of—the blunt, geometric forms that modern technology and building practices had made increasingly visible during the previous century. Still a place of cathedrals and marble statues, the landscape of Western culture now included vast, unadorned factories and mills, as well as bridges with the look of Euclidian theorems demonstrated in beams of steel.

Liberated from old forms and materials, these new sculptors—often called Constructivists—felt free to redefine art and its purposes. They would produce no easily recognized images. Yet they did not completely eradicate representation. Perhaps that was not their aim. In any case, Naum Gabo and a few other Constructivist sculptors set the elements of their works in motion with small motors. The resemblance to industrial machinery was unmistakable. In retrospect, it looks entirely intentional. There was something compelling about the idea of a sculpture as a nonutilitarian machine: an engine for generating aesthetic experience. As the decades went by, a few geometric sculptors kept this option quietly alive. Then, in the 1960s, it exploded into an international movement: kinetic sculpture.

As fresh as Op or Pop or Minimalism, kinetic sculpture quickly found an enthusiastic audience. Among the movement's most prominent members was Fletcher Benton, then in his early 30s. For more than a decade, he produced geometries that move. His inventiveness increased from year to year and then, in 1973, came to a sudden halt. As a kinetic sculptor, he had brought one implication of Constructivism into sharp, brilliant focus. Stepping back and taking up the tools of a builder in steel, he reinvented the full implications of Constructivism—of constructed metal sculpture—on his own terms. As I've suggested, this new beginning led to one of our era's major bodies of work.

Benton's sculptures tend to be large, even monumental. But large or small, their meanings are boundless. Each work begins with a series of practical decisions. The initial premise might be a single sheet of steel. Or it might be impossible to say which of several forms we are to consider as the first—a circle, a ball, or one of several long, elegantly curving strips. I am thinking of *Botanical Rose* (see page 9), a tall, slim sculpture from 1993. You could say that the ball is primary, the circle provides it with its immediate support, and the strips are like limbs and spine—a body supporting a head. A less figurative reading might rearrange these priorities. Wherever interpretation might lead, one arrives at a sense of a configuration having emerged over time, as disparities were induced to complement one another. Benton persuades geometric elements to operate in unison, having worked through their differences—and few differences are more salient than the ones that distinguish flatness from volume, straight line from curve.

Of course, we can never know the steps that brought a sculpture to its final form. Still, Benton makes it possible to imagine the conflicts that animated the struggle. From a sense of the whole, we intuit what was at stake in the placement of each part. Seeing the finished work as a unity at the quiet center of the present we share with it, we sense the history of its coming into being. This history gives it an aura—a light and an atmosphere—distinctively its own.

In the 1920s and '30s Benton's Constructivist predecessors tried to give their works the look of rarefied machinery—industrial forms freed from the exigencies of industry. At its most highly conceptualized, a Constructivist sculpture might allude to a physicist's model of the atomic structure of matter. Guided less by concept than by feeling, Benton is more in tune with music than with science and industry. Treating his forms as notes, he composes "with timing, with repetition, with beat, with all the things that go into music."

This comment of Benton's helps us to see a work like *Steel Watercolor: 2 Cubes with Ring* (1996) as an intricate riff, its circular curves modulating into a zigzag that turns into a curve of a different, less enclosed kind. Yet there is a danger in concentrating too exclusively on the musical complexities of Benton's art. Music verges on immateriality. Benton works with the obdurate materiality of steel. He is an engineer, as he must be if his sculptures are to stand rather than collapse. Yet his engineering is as improvisational as a jazz musician's treatment—reinvention—of a standard melody. Even his monumental works ask for an immediate response. Not a quick response, but one that is immediate by virtue of staying in the present, alive to the object of contemplation. Ideally, our response would extend the present as long as necessary for a sculpture in all its complexity to become as familiar as the simple geometries from which the sculptor built it. The grand intricacies of Benton's art are not intended to overawe us. They are intended to make sense—sculptural, gestural, musical sense—and to encourage us to be aware of what it is to find meaning in our experience.

Within a single sculpture, there can be great differences in scale. For example, small wedges, cylinders, or blocks sometimes mark the intersection of major forms. Though these elements sometimes look like structural necessities, Benton could get by without them—but only if he were a designer, not a sculptor. The necessities that matter to him are visual, not utilitarian, and he can never know in advance what they are, for sculptural imperatives cannot be stated as axioms. The sculptor must discover them experimentally, as he works. Once he has settled on a few large forms—a sculpture's basic premises—Benton looks for the overall structure that will bring them into harmony. Smaller forms can have the function of exclamation points, emphasizing some subtlety of organization. Slowing vision, so that the sense of resolution doesn't arrive too quickly, these elements work like commas or even semi-colons.

Staking out extremes of scale and form, Benton implies every gradation in between. Thus he presents a precise invocation of all the disparity, all the difference, there is. Having invoked the world, he finds equally concise ways to suggest the reconciliation of its differences. Concision is a form of wit, and Benton's is endlessly resourceful. His placements of small elements often have the tone of elegant insightful one-liners. When medium-size forms assemble, one thinks of fast-moving repartee. And when he ascends to monumentality, he becomes a logician finding new and surprising solutions to long-standing problems.

From physical contingencies, Benton builds aesthetic necessities. What keeps his sculptures alive is his refusal to let necessity look ponderous, or smugly resolved. Because he allows hints of chaos and disintegration to infiltrate his configurations, we see balance teased with the possibility of unbalance. We see large forms at the mercy of much smaller forms. He plays sober, weighty blocks off thin, soaring—even flighty—curves and zigzags. Thus he shows us that there is nothing inevitable about sculptural necessity. It must be won from the forces of mundane disorder, and once the victory is achieved in one sculpture, it must be achieved anew in the next one. Each of Benton's sculptures finds its own balance, at once solidly resolved and alive with a sense of precariousness just barely overcome. Thus he suspends his forms between two states: levitation and collapse, defiance of gravity and submission to it.

Weightless and weighty, monumental and intimate, abstract and obliquely figurative, his sculptures reconcile opposites—or, it might be better to say, seeming opposites, for our immediate experience is of an intricate unity. To look further is to see conflict, to see it resolved, and to sense a work's power to engage its surroundings. Despite the complexity of their internal relations, these sculptures are not self-involved—or not entirely, though a Modernist ideal of autonomy, of absolute purity, hovers in their background. Constructivism understood abstraction as a means of severing art's connection with ordinary life, of giving form the power to transcend familiar meanings and concerns. Place a Benton sculpture against that historical backdrop, and it will look as autonomous, as disengaged, as a work by Gabo, or Antoine Pevsner, or any other proponent of Constructivist purity. If, however, we take a larger view, we will see Benton's art finding its way into the world, into the space of down-to-earth experience. There, its abstract purity takes on a new and richer meaning. Its autonomy gives up its narrowly aesthetic significance and becomes an invocation of an abiding ideal: the self-sufficiency of the individual. Benton celebrates individuality itself, the self-reliance that makes it possible for him to be an artist and for all of us to realize, in some degree, our best hopes for ourselves.

At the beginning of his career, Benton was swept up in the excitement of the 1960s. As a kinetic sculptor, he contributed to that excitement. Then he rediscovered the traditional—the perennial—stasis of sculpture. He taught himself, through experiment, that the movement of the sculptural object is more powerful when it is not actual but virtual. Not literal but imagined. For that is the power of Benton's works—to activate the imagination and to keep it in motion, in ever-widening patterns. From an appreciation of his formal wit, his command of structural possibility, we advance, sooner or later, to larger meanings. In an interview with Paul Karlstrom, of the Archives of American Art, Benton said, "I think artists become artists—those who stick it out—because they want to be . . . 100 percent responsible for their actions . . . responsible from beginning to end for every single decision." Thus, as I suggested, his sculptures become emblems of the independent, fully realized individual. Benton's ideal of the completely responsible self may be utopian but it is not irrelevant. It is by such ideals that we measure and thus come to know ourselves.

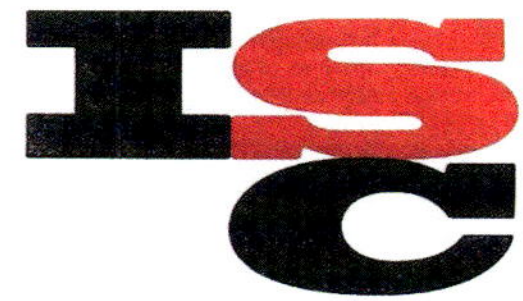

27 July 2007

Fletcher Benton
250 Dore Street
San Francisco, CA 94103

Dear Fletcher,

On behalf of the Board of Directors of the International Sculpture Center (ISC) I would like to congratulate you on being selected as the winner of the ISC's 2008 **Lifetime Achievement in Contemporary Sculpture Award**. We are delighted to be honoring such a well deserving recipient!

The International Sculpture Center's Board of Directors established the Lifetime Achievement Award in 1991 to recognize individual sculptors who have made exemplary contributions to the field of sculpture. Candidates for the award are masters of sculptural processes and techniques who have devoted their careers to the development of a laudable body of work, as well as to the advancement of the sculpture field as a whole. When nominating, and subsequently selecting, the Lifetime Achievement Award winners guidelines for assessing the recipient include the quality of a sculptor's work, the impact and influence of their work, their sense of dedication and commitment to the field of sculpture in general, and their generosity of spirit with other sculptors.

International Sculpture Center

Publisher of Sculpture Magazine
www.sculpture.org

14 Fairgrounds Rd.
Suite B
Hamilton, NJ
08619-3447 U.S.A
609.689.1051 tel
609.689.1061 fax

Past recipients of this prestigious award include **Manuel Neri, Magdalena Abakanowicz, Louise Bourgeois, Sir Anthony Caro, Elizabeth Catlett, John Chamberlain, Eduardo Chillida, Christo and Jeanne-Claude, Mark di Suvero, Claes Oldenburg and Coosje van Bruggen, Nam June Paik, Gio' Pomodoro, Robert Rauschenberg, George Rickey, George Segal and Kenneth Snelson**.

As the recipient you will be honored and presented with your award at the 2008 **Lifetime Achievement Award Gala** which will be held in the Spring of 2008 in San Francisco, California (date and location to be announced soon). We will invite ISC patrons and collectors as well as your friends and supporters to attend this fundraising gala where we will celebrate your career and lifetime of accomplishments in the field of Sculpture.

Once again congratulations on receiving the 2008 International Sculpture Center's Lifetime Achievement Award. I look forward to talking with you soon as we plan this momentous occasion to honor your dedication and contributions to the field and celebrate your excellence in sculptural achievement.

Sincerely,

J Hutchison

Johannah Hutchison
Executive Director

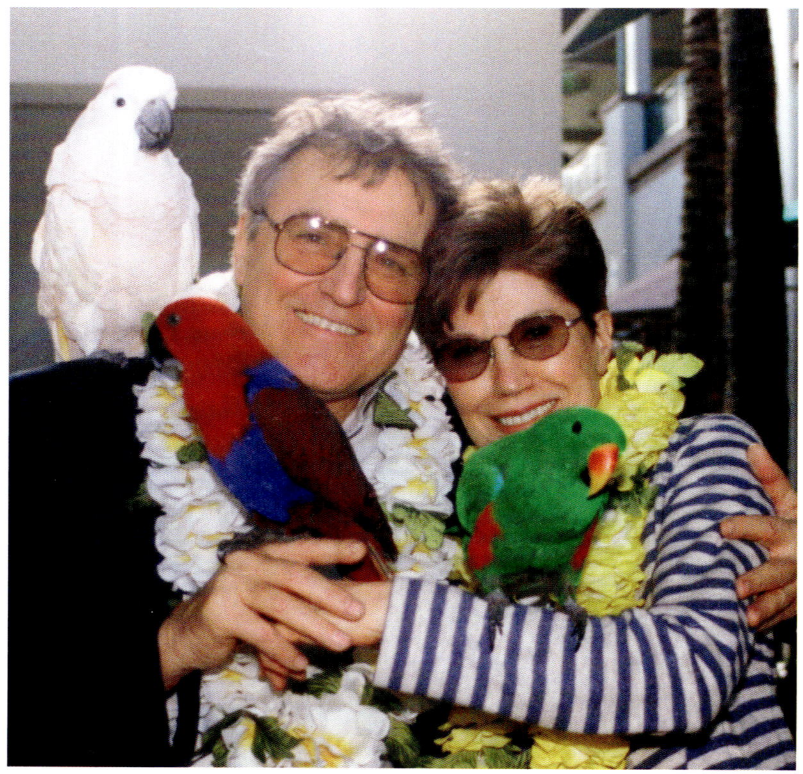

Fletcher and Bobbie Benton, Hawaii, 1998

Chronology

Born

1931 Jackson, OH

Education

1956 B.F.A., Miami University, Oxford, OH

Teaching

1959 California College of Arts and Crafts, Oakland, CA

1966–67 San Francisco Art Institute, California

1967–86 California State University, San Jose, CA

Awards and Honors

1979 Award for Distinguished Service to the Arts, American Academy of Arts and Letters, New York, NY

1980 President's Scholar Award, California State University, San Jose, CA

1982 Award of Honor for Outstanding Achievement in Sculpture, San Francisco Arts Commission, California

1993 Honorary Doctor of Fine Arts, Miami University, Oxford, OH

1994 Ohioana Career Award, Ohioana Library Association, Columbus, OH

Honorary Doctor of Fine Arts, University of Rio Grande, Rio Grande, OH

2008 Lifetime Achievement in Contemporary Sculpture Award, International Sculpture Center, Hamilton, NJ

Solo Exhibitions

1959 Gump's Gallery, San Francisco, CA

1961 California Palace of the Legion of Honor, San Francisco, CA

1962 Dintenfass Gallery, New York, NY

1964 Esther Robles Gallery, Los Angeles, CA

Gump's Gallery, San Francisco, CA

1965 San Francisco Museum of Modern Art, California

Hansen Gallery, San Francisco, CA

1966 Esther Robles Gallery, Los Angeles, CA

Hansen Gallery, San Francisco, CA

1967 Esther Robles Gallery, Los Angeles, CA

Sonoma State College, Rohnert Park, CA

San Francisco Art Institute, California

1968 Galeria Bonino, New York, NY

Humboldt State College, Arcata, CA

1969 Milwaukee Art Center, Wisconsin

Galerie Françoise Mayer, Brussels, Belgium

Galeria Bonino, New York, NY

1970 San Francisco Museum of Art, California

Albright-Knox Art Gallery, Buffalo, NY

London Arts Gallery, Detroit, MI

California State University, Chico, CA

Berkeley Arts Center, Berkeley, CA

Reed College, Portland, OR

Galeria Bonino, Buenos Aires, Argentina

Estudio Actual, Caracas, Venezuela

1971 John Berggruen Gallery, San Francisco, CA

Stanford University Museum of Art, California

1972 La Jolla Museum of Art, California

Esther Robles Gallery, Los Angeles, CA

Landry Bonino Gallery, New York, NY

1973 Phoenix Art Museum, Arizona

University of California, Davis, CA

Galeria Bonino, Rio de Janeiro, Brazil

1975 de Saisset Art Gallery and Museum, University of Santa Clara, Santa Clara, CA

Smith Andersen Gallery, San Francisco, CA

1977 Fresno State University Gallery, California

John Berggruen Gallery, San Francisco, CA

1978 Tortue Gallery, Los Angeles, CA

San Jose Museum of Art, California

1979 Art Club of Chicago, Illinois

John Berggruen Gallery, San Francisco, CA

Grossmont College, El Cajon, CA

American Academy of Arts and Letters, New York, NY

1980 San Jose State University, California

Newport Harbor Art Museum, Newport Beach, CA

Oakland Museum, Calfornia

Portland Art Museum, Oregon

John Berggruen Gallery, San Francisco, CA

Miami University Art Museum, Oxford, OH

Suermondt-Ludwig Museum, Aachen, Germany

Muscatine Art Center, Muscatine, IA

Milwaukee Art Center, Wisconsin

1981 Klingspor Museum, Offenbach, Germany

Riva Yares Gallery, Scottsdale, AZ

John Berggruen Gallery, San Francisco, CA

1982 San Jose Museum of Art, California

1984 Thomas Babeor Gallery, La Jolla, CA

Fresno Arts Center, California

John Berggruen Gallery, San Francisco, CA

1985 Harcus Gallery, Boston, MA

Fresno Arts Center, California

1986 California International Arts Foundation, Los Angeles, CA

Thomas Babeor Gallery, La Jolla, CA

John Berggruen Gallery, San Francisco, CA

Laguna College of Art, Laguna Beach, CA

Transamerica Redwood Park, San Francisco, CA

1987 Galerie B. Haasner, Wiesbaden, Germany

Harcus Gallery, Boston, MA

1988 Dorothy Goldeen Gallery, Santa Monica, CA

1989 John Berggruen Gallery, San Francisco, CA

1990 Galerie Simonne Stern, New Orleans, LA

1991 Riva Yares Gallery, Scottsdale, AZ

Sung Dam Fine Arts, Seoul, South Korea

1992 Galerie B. Haasner, Wiesbaden, Germany

1993 Miami University Art Museum, Oxford, OH

Dorothy Goldeen Gallery, Santa Monica, CA

Gothaer Kunstforum, Cologne, Germany

Galerie Simonne Stern, New Orleans, LA

1994 University of Rio Grande, Rio Grande, OH

1995 Dorothy Goldeen Gallery, Santa Monica, CA

1996 John Berggruen Gallery, San Francisco, CA

Klingspor Museum, Offenbach, Germany

Gallery Camino Real, Boca Raton, FL

Galerie B. Haasner, Wiesbaden, Germany

1997 Galerie Simonne Stern, New Orleans, LA

Frankfurt Art Fair, Germany

Hall's Gallery, Kansas City, MO

Galerie B. Haasner, Wiesbaden, Germany

1998 Riva Yares Gallery, Scottsdale, AZ

Tasende Gallery, West Hollywood, CA

Tasende Gallery, La Jolla, CA

Jean Albano Gallery, Chicago, IL

1999 Sheldon Memorial Art Gallery and Sculpture Garden, University of Nebraska, Lincoln, NE

Strategic Air Command Museum, Omaha, NE

2000 Imago Galleries, Palm Desert, CA

2001 Robert McClain Gallery, Houston, TX

Tasende Gallery, West Hollywood, CA

Tasende Gallery, La Jolla, CA

The Art Show, 7th Regiment Armory, New York, NY

Galerie B. Haasner, Wiesbaden, Germany

Art Cologne 2001, Cologne, Germany

2002 Galerie B. Haasner, Wiesbaden, Germany

San Antonio Museum of Art, Texas

2003 Tasende Gallery, West Hollywood, CA

Heidi Neuhoff Gallery, New York, NY

2004 Riva Yares Gallery, Scottsdale, AZ

Imago Galleries, Palm Desert, CA

2005 Tasende Gallery, West Hollywood, CA

Imago Galleries, Palm Desert, CA

Gallery Camino Real, Boca Raton, FL

2006 Tasende Gallery, La Jolla, CA

Riva Yares Gallery, Scottsdale, AZ

Galerie B. Haasner, Wiesbaden, Germany

Group Exhibitions

1960 Gump's Gallery, San Francisco, CA

1961 *Third Winter Invitational Exhibition,* California Palace of the Legion of Honor, San Francisco, CA

1963 *Bay Area Artists,* Santa Barbara Museum of Art, California

1964 *Twenty Bay Area Artists,* San Francisco Museum of Art, California

Polychrome Sculpture, San Francisco Art Institute, California

Fifth Winter Invitational Exhibition, California Palace of the Legion of Honor, San Francisco, CA

1965 *2 Dimensional Sculpture–3 Dimensional Painting,* Richmond Art Center, California

Some Aspects of California Painting and Sculpture, La Jolla Museum of Contemporary Art, California

Sculpture from San Francisco, San Francisco Art Institute, California

Art '65: Young American Sculpture–East to West, New York World's Fair, Flushing, NY

84th Annual, San Francisco Art Institute, California

1966 *Obelisk without an Eye,* Walker Art Center, Minneapolis, MN

Directions in Kinetic Sculpture, University of California, Berkeley Art Museum; Santa Barbara Museum of Art, California

Kinetic Currents, San Francisco Museum of Modern Art, California

2D/3D Sculpture and Painting, Richmond Art Center, California

California '66–Painters and Sculptors, Crocker Art Gallery, Sacramento, CA

Annual Exhibition 1966, Sculpture and Prints, Whitney Museum of American Art, New York, NY

1967 *The Whitney Review,* Whitney Museum of American Art, New York, NY

Contemporary American Painting and Sculpture, Krannert Art Museum, University of Illinois, Urbana-Champaign, IL

West Coast Now, Portland Art Museum, Oregon; Seattle Art Museum, Washington; M. H. de Young Memorial Museum, San Francisco, CA; Los Angeles Municipal Art Gallery, California

American Sculpture of the '60s, Los Angeles County Museum of Art, California; Philadelphia Museum of Art, Pennsylvania

Kinetic Art Invitational, University of Hawaii, Honolulu, HI

Pittsburgh International Exhibition of Contemporary Painting and Sculpture, Museum of Art, Carnegie Institute, Pittsburgh, PA

Light and Movement, Flint Institute of Arts, Flint, MI; Worcester Art Museum, Worcester, MA

California Art Festival, Lytton Center of the Visual Arts, Los Angeles, CA

1968 *The West Coast Now,* Portland Art Association, Oregon

Light and Kinetic Sculpture, University of Nevada, Las Vegas, NV

Hemisfair, U.S. Pavilion, San Antonio, TX

Plastics, Light, and Movement, Esther Robles Gallery, Los Angeles, CA

Highlights of the 1967–68 Art Season, The Aldrich Contemporary Art Museum, Ridgefield, CT

28th Annual Exhibition, Art Institute of Chicago, Illinois

Options, Walker Art Center, Minneapolis, MN; Museum of Contemporary Art, Chicago, IL

Art from California, Janie C. Lee Gallery, Dallas, TX

Two Exhibitions, Sonoma State College Art Department Gallery, Rohnert Park, CA

Park Synagogue Art Festival, Cleveland, OH

Art for Your Collection VII, Rhode Island School of Design, Providence, RI

1968 Annual Exhibition, Contemporary American Sculpture, Whitney Museum of American Art, New York, NY

Plastics, Hansen Gallery, San Francisco, CA

Kinetic and Mechanical Devices, Lytton Center of the Visual Arts, Los Angeles, CA

Selection 1968/University of California, Berkeley, University of California, Berkeley Art Museum, CA

New Canaan Library, New Canaan, CT

1969 *Contemporary American Painting and Sculpture,* Krannert Art Museum, University of Illinois, Urbana-Champaign, IL

Inaugural Exhibition, New School Art Center, New School for Social Research, New York, NY

50th Anniversary Commemorative Art Exhibit, Members Gallery, Albright-Knox Art Gallery, Buffalo, NY

Impressions de USA, Galerie Françoise Mayer, Brussels, Belgium

American Report on the '60s, Denver Art Museum, Colorado

2nd Flint Invitational, Flint Institute of Arts, Flint, MI

Spaces. Civic Art Gallery, Walnut Creek, CA

Electric Art, UCLA Art Galleries, University of California, Los Angeles, CA; Phoenix Art Museum, Phoenix, AZ

1970 *Fletcher Benton, Jerry Ballaine, Sam Richardson,* San Francisco Museum of Modern Art, California

Contemporary Trends, Expo Museum of Fine Arts, Osaka, Japan

Berggruen at Art Center, Art Center College of Design, Pasadena, CA

4th Annual Invitational, Kent State University, Kent, OH

Collectors Choice X, Philbrook Art Center, Tulsa, OK

Kinetics, Hayward Art Gallery, London, England

Looking West, 1970, Joslyn Art Museum, Omaha, NE

Crocker Museum Invitational, Crocker Art Gallery, Sacramento, CA

The Japan Art Society. Traveled: Municipal Art Galleries, Yokohama and Sendai, Japan; Kawatoku Gallery, Morioka, Japan

The 73rd Western Annual, Denver Art Museum, Colorado

Constructivist Tendencies, Art Galleries, University of California, Santa Barbara, CA; University Art Museum, University of New Mexico, Albuquerque, NM; Fine Arts Gallery of San Diego, CA; Minnesota Museum of Art, St. Paul, MN; Art Gallery, University of Alabama, Birmingham, AL; Akron Art Institute, Akron, OH; Andrew Dickson White Museum of Art, Ithaca, NY; Indiana University Art Museum, Bloomington, IN; Museum of Art, University of Iowa, Iowa City, IA; Art Gallery, State University of New York at Albany, NY; De Cordova Museum, Lincoln, MA

Painting and Sculpture Today, Indianapolis Museum of Art, Indiana

1971 *Kinetic Art,* Hudson River Museum of Westchester, Yonkers, NY

Constructivist American Art, Denver Art Museum, Colorado

A Decade in the West, Stanford University Museum of Art, California; Santa Barbara Museum of Art, California

Painting and Sculpture Today, Indianapolis Museum of Art, Indiana

Summer Series, Albright-Knox Art Gallery, Buffalo, NY

1972 Stanford University Museum of Art, California

Looking West, ACA Gallery, New York, NY

Galeria Bonino, Buenos Aires, Argentina

1973 *1973 Biennial Exhibition: Contemporary American Art,* Whitney Museum of American Art, New York, NY

Sculpture Invitational, Palo Alto Cultural Center, California

The Product as an Object, Ohio, Akron Art Institute, Ohio

Kinetic Exhibit, University of California, Berkeley Art Museum, CA

Art Is for the People, San Diego Museum of Art, California

Acquisitions, '73, The Aldrich Contemporary Art Museum, Ridgefield, CT

1974 *Pioneering Printmakers,* Fine Arts Gallery of San Diego, California

Neuberger Museum of Art, State University of New York at Purchase, New York

Public Sculpture/Urban Environment, Oakland Museum, California

Inaugural Exhibition, Hirshhorn Museum and Sculpture Garden, Smithsonian Institution, Washington, D.C.

Acquisitions, Denver Art Museum, Colorado

Arte-Contacto, Estudio Actual, Caracas, Venezuela

1975 *Experimental Printmaking Institute Group Exhibition,* Polly Friedlander Gallery Seattle, Washington; Cleveland Art Institute, Ohio

The First Artists' Soap Box Derby, San Francisco Museum of Modern Art, California

Sculptural Directions in the Bay Area, Esther Robles Gallery, Los Angeles, CA

1976 Elvehjem Museum of Art, University of Wisconsin–Madison, WI

University Art Gallery, University of Minnesota, Minneapolis, MN

Rice University, Houston, TX

Martha Jackson Gallery, New York, NY

Wenger Gallery, Inverness, CA

James Willis Gallery, San Francisco, CA

Santa Barbara Museum of Art, California

Invitational, University of North Dakota, Grand Forks, ND

Painting and Sculpture, San Francisco Museum of Modern Art, California; Renwick Gallery, National Collection of Fine Arts, Washington, D.C.

1977 *The California Artists,* Huntsville Museum of Modern Art, Alabama

The Aldrich Contemporary Art Museum, Ridgefield, CT

Thomas H. Segal Gallery, Boston, MA

1978 *Northern California Artists,* University Art Gallery, Sonoma State University, Rohnert Park, CA

20th–Century Sculpture, John Berggruen Gallery, San Francisco, CA

Art Center College of Design, Pasadena, CA

California 3 by 8 Twice, Honolulu Academy of Arts, Hawaii

1979 *Art Contact,* Miami, FL

Prospectus: Art in the Seventies, The Aldrich Contemporary Art Museum, Ridgefield, CT

John Berggruen Gallery, San Francisco, CA

University Art Gallery, University of California, Santa Cruz, CA

Aspects of Abstract, Crocker Art Museum, Sacramento, CA

Sculpture Invitational, Crocker Art Museum, Sacramento, CA

Spaces Civic Arts Gallery, Walnut Creek, CA

1980 Tacoma Art Museum, Washington

Miami University Art Museum, Oxford, OH

Syntex Outdoor Sculpture Show, Syntex Corporation, Palo Alto, CA

American Paintings and Drawings, John Berggruen Gallery, San Francisco, CA

1981 Amerika Haus, Frankfurt-am-Main, Germany

Project Sculpture, Oakland Museum, California

Chicago Arts Fair, Navy Pier, Chicago, IL

Sculptors' Works on Paper, Quay Gallery, San Francisco, CA

20th–Century American Art: Highlights of the Permanent Collection, Whitney Museum of American Art, New York, NY

Polychrome, Hansen Fuller Goldeen Gallery, San Francisco, CA

1982 *San Francisco Arts Festival,* The Moscone Center, California

Forgotten Dimension . . . A Survey of Small Sculpture in California, Fresno Arts Center, California

20 American Artists: Sculpture 1982, San Francisco Museum of Modern Art, California

Sculpture Conference, Smith Andersen Gallery, Palo Alto, CA

Chicago Arts Fair, Navy Pier, Chicago, IL

Inaugural Exhibition, John Berggruen Gallery, San Francisco, CA

Aspects of Sculpture, John Berggruen Gallery, San Francisco, CA

100 Years of California Sculpture, Oakland Museum, California

Northern California Art of the Sixties, de Saisset Museum, University of Santa Clara, Santa Clara, CA

Bay Area Sculpture, University of California, Berkeley Art Museum, CA

Project Art, Claremont Hotel, Berkeley, CA

California Sculpture, 1982, John Berggruen Gallery, San Francisco, CA

Brook House Sculpture Invitational, Kaiser Center, Oakland, CA

1983 *Bay Area Collects,* San Francisco Museum of Modern Art, California

Chicago Arts Fair, Navy Pier, Chicago, IL

CCAC: 75 Years Resource/Reservoirs, San Francisco Museum of Modern Art, California

The Planar Dimension: Geometric Abstraction by Bay Area Artists, Civic Arts Gallery, Walnut Creek, CA

Selected Works, Thomas Babeor Gallery, La Jolla, CA

Metal and Stone, Five Sculptors, Riva Yares Gallery, Scottsdale, AZ

1984 *Chicago Arts Fair,* Navy Pier, Chicago, IL

California Sculpture Show, Olympic Arts Festival; Fisher Gallery, University of Southern California, Los Angeles and California/International Arts Foundation; traveled through 1986: C.A.P.C., Musée d'Art Contemporain, Bordeaux, France; Städtische Kunsthalle, Mannheim, Germany; Yorkshire Sculpture Park, West Bretton, England; Sonja Henies Og Niels Onstads Stiftelser, Høvinodkodden, Norway

Recent Acquisitions, John Berggruen Gallery, San Francisco, CA

California Deluxe, Gloria Luria Gallery, Bay Harbor Islands, FL

Works in Bronze: A Modern Survey, University Art Gallery, Sonoma State University, Rohnert Park, CA

1985 *Chapman College Sculpture Acquisition Program,* Chapman College, Orange, CA

The Art of the 1970s and 1980s, The Aldrich Contemporary Art Museum, Ridgefield, CT

Going Public, Civic Arts Gallery, Walnut Creek, CA

Art in the San Francisco Bay Area, Oakland Museum, California

Teachers and Their Pupils, Anna Gardner Gallery, Stinson Beach, CA

Aspects of Constructivism, Atrium Gallery, New York, NY

Artists Forum, Fine Arts Gallery, California State University, Los Angeles, CA

1986 *Chicago International Art Exposition,* Navy Pier, Chicago, IL

Seven Artists in Depth: The Creative Process, San Francisco Museum of Modern Art, California

Art in the Aluminum Vein, Kaiser Center, Oakland, CA

Artists Forum, Fine Arts Gallery, California State University, Los Angeles, CA

Thanks for the Memories, Harcus Gallery, Boston, MA

San Jose Museum of Art, California

San Jose Biennial, San Jose State University, California

John Berggruen Gallery, San Francisco, CA

San Francisco Arts Commission Festival, Civic Center Plaza, California

San Francisco Landscape Garden Show, Fort Mason Center, California

1987 *Arts Irvine '87,* Irvine, CA

International Working Symposium of Open Air Sculpture in Steel, Kleinewefers, Krefeld, Germany

Summer Exhibition, Scott Hanson Gallery, New York, NY

American Artists in Jewelry, Dorothy Goldeen Gallery, Santa Monica, CA; Fuller Gross Gallery, San Francisco, CA; Harcus Gallery, Boston, MA; Nancy Hoffman Gallery, New York, NY

1988 *Summer Selections,* Thomas Babeor Gallery, La Jolla, CA

Steel Sculpture Exhibition, Yorkshire Sculpture Park, West Bretton, England

Bay Area Sculpture: Metal, Stone, Wood, Palo Alto Cultural Center, California

In the Beginning: Maquettes, Syntex Gallery, Palo Alto Cultural Center, California

Paper Thick: Forms and Images in Cast Paper, Erie Art Museum, Pennsylvania

American Artists in Jewelry, Nancy Hoffman Gallery, New York, NY

Harcus Gallery, Boston, MA

1989 *5x5: Five Artists, Five Works,* Conley Gallery of Art, California State University, Fresno, CA

American Pop Culture Today, Laforet Museum, Tokyo

1990 *Outdoor Sculpture at Esprit,* John Berggruen Gallery, San Francisco, CA

Picasso, Gravuren, und Fletcher Benton, Skulpturen, Einladung in das Mathias Spital, Rheine, Germany

American Artists in Jewelry, Gilman Baker Gallery, Boca Raton, FL

1991 *Florence–Santa Clara: Two Schools of Sculpture,* Triton Museum of Art, Santa Clara, CA

Summer Exhibition, André Emmerich Gallery, New York, NY

Constructivism: Past and Present, Ersgard Gallery, Santa Monica, CA

1992 *Two Schools of Sculpture,* Academia, Florence, Italy

Foire Internationale d'Art Contemporain, Paris, France

Objects of Affection, John Berggruen Gallery, San Francisco, CA

American Artists in Jewelry, Rhona Hoffman Gallery, Chicago, IL

The Endowed Chair, Franklin Parrasch Gallery, New York, NY

1993 *Out of Town,* Krannert Art Museum, University of Illinois, Urbana-Champaign, IL

In the Sculptor's Landscape, Wight Art Gallery, University of California, Los Angeles, CA

Malibu International Sculpture Exhibition, Malibu, CA

Recent Acquisitions, John Berggruen Gallery, San Francisco, CA

American Artists in Jewelry, Palm Springs Desert Museum, California

The George and Edith Rickey Collection of Constructivist Art, Neuberger Museum of Art, State University of New York at Purchase, NY

Table Sculpture, André Emmerich Gallery, New York, NY

1994 *Twenty-six Artists: Selections from John Berggruen Gallery,* Friesen Gallery, Seattle, WA

1995 *XXV Years,* John Berggruen Gallery, San Francisco, CA

1996 Galerie B. Haasner, Wiesbaden, Germany

Chicago Arts Fair, Navy Pier, Chicago, IL

California '97, Susan Rush Fine Arts, Sag Harbor, NY

Made in Ohio, Miami University Art Museum, Oxford, OH

California Art from the Frederick R. Weisman Collections, Pepperdine University, Malibu, CA

1997 *2x2,* Galerie Simonne Stern, New Orleans, LA

Theater of Art, Riva Yares Gallery, Scottsdale, AZ

1998 *The Art Show,* The Seventh Regiment Armory, New York, NY

Floating Forms, Miami University Art Museum, Oxford, OH

Summer Exhibition, Tasende Gallery, West Hollywood, CA

Figuration and Abstraction, John Berggruen Gallery, San Francisco, CA

The Art of Collaborative Printmaking, Nevada Museum of Art, Reno, NV

Carl Schlossberg Exhibitions, Inc., Malibu, CA

Theater of Art II, Riva Yares Gallery, Santa Fe, NM

Theater of Art III, Riva Yares Gallery, Scottsdale, AZ

San Francisco International Art Exposition, California

Beverly Hills International Art and Antique Fair, Los Angeles, CA

McClain Gallery, Houston, TX

1999 *The Foundry Fifty,* Foundry Art Gallery, Sacramento, CA

Exhibition of ISC Collection II, International Sculpture Center, Chicago, IL

San Francisco International Art Exposition, California

Winter Exhibition, Tasende Gallery, West Hollywood and La Jolla, CA

Chicago Arts Fair, Navy Pier, Chicago, IL

The Museum Collects: Treasures of Twenty Years II. Miami University Art Museum, Oxford, OH

The Grosvenor House Art & Antiques Fair, Grosvenor House, London, England

2000 *Art Miami 2000: International Art Exposition*, Miami, FL

Inagural Show, Imago Galleries, Palm Desert, CA

The Art Show, The Seventh Regiment Armory, New York, NY

Carl Schlossberg Exhibitions, Inc., Malibu, CA

May in New York, Carl Schlossberg Fine Arts, New York, NY

San Francisco International Art Exposition, California

Celebrating Modern Art: The Anderson Collection, San Francisco Museum of Modern Art, California

Galerie B. Haasner, Wiesbaden, Germany

Riva Yares 2000 – The First 35 Years, Riva Yares Gallery, Scottsdale, AZ; Santa Fe, NM

Welded! Sculpture of the Twentieth Century, Neuberger Museum of Art, New York, NY

Made In California, Los Angeles County Museum of Art, California

Art/Science – Line/Design, Miami University Art Museum, Oxford, OH

2001 *artpalmbeach: Modern & Contemporary Art Fair*, West Palm Beach, FL

spektrum kunstlandschaft, Kunsthalle Darmstadt, Germany

Sculptures, Drawings and Works In Relief, John Berggruen Gallery, San Francisco, CA

San Francisco International Art Exposition, California

Reflections: Fifteenth Anniversary Show, Jean Albano Gallery, Chicago, IL

Galerie B. Haasner, Wiesbaden, Germany

2002 *San Francisco International Art Exposition*, California

Spring Forward: New Work from the Studio, John Berggruen Gallery, San Francisco, CA

Chicago Arts Fair, Navy Pier, Chicago, IL

art bodensee 2002: 'San Francisco Bay Area' – Künstler aus Kalifornien, Dornbirn, Austria

On Ramps: Transitional Moments in California Art, Pasadena Museum of California Art, Pasadena, CA

Sculpture 2002, Foundry Art Gallery, Sacramento, CA

The 30th Anniversary Exhibition: Sculpture, Paintings, Prints, Drawings and Photographs, Carl Schlossberg Fine Arts, Sherman Oaks, CA

Wired: Art that Moves, Miami Art Museum, Florida

2003 *San Francisco International Art Exposition*, California

New Beginnings, Tasende Gallery, West Hollywood, CA

Art Chicago, Navy Pier, Chicago, IL

Navy Pier Walk, Chicago, IL

Beyond the Surface 2, Art and Cultural Center at Fallbrook, Fallbrook, CA

Art Cologne 2003, Cologne, Germany

Art Santa Fe 2003, Santa Fe, NM

Art Basel Miami Beach, Miami Beach, FL

2004 *San Francisco International Art Exposition*, California

Palm Beach Contemporary 2004, Palm Beach, FL

Art Karlsruhe, Karlsruhe, Germany

The 179th Annual: An Invitational Exhibition of Contemporary American Art, National Academy Museum, New York, NY

Made of Steel, McClain Gallery, Houston, TX

Los Angeles Art Show, Santa Monica, CA

Art of the 20th Century, The Seventh Regiment Armory, New York, NY

Art Basel Miami Beach, Miami Beach, FL

Carl Schlossberg Exhibitions, Inc., Malibu, CA

Dovetailing Art & Life: The Bennett Collection, San Francisco Museum of Craft & Design, California

2005 *San Francisco International Art Exposition*, California

Paint on Metal, Tucson Museum of Art, Tucson, AZ

Art Karlsruhe, Karlsruhe, Germany

Art of the 20th Century, The Seventh Regiment Armory, New York, NY

Art 36 Basel, Basel, Switzerland

Highlights: New Acquisitions, John Berggruen Gallery, San Francisco, CA

Art Basel Miami Beach, Miami Beach, FL

2006 *Five Centuries of Art: The 11th Annual Los Angeles Art Show*, Santa Monica, CA

Art of the 20th Century, The Seventh Regiment Armory, New York, NY

Art Karlsruhe, Karlsruhe, Germany

Art Basel Miami Beach, Miami Beach, FL

Breaking Out! Sculptural Explorations in Metal and Wood, Palm Springs Art Museum, Palm Springs, CA

John Berggruen Gallery, San Francisco, CA

McClain Gallery, Houston, TX

Theater of Art VII, Riva Yares Gallery, Santa Fe, NM

Selected Bibliography

Books

Albright, Thomas. *Art in the San Francisco Bay Area, 1946–1980.* Berkeley, CA: University of California Press, 1985.

Blank, Chotsie, and Ann Seymour. *California Artists' Cookbook.* New York, NY: Abbeville Press, 1982.

Busch, Julia. *A Decade of Sculpture*. Philadelphia, PA: Art Alliance Press, 1974.

Davis, Douglas. *Art and the Future.* New York, NY: Praeger, 1973.

Finn, David. *Fletcher Benton: The Alphabet*. New York, NY: Ruder-Finn Press, 2005.

Hennum, Gerd. *På sporet av beat-bohemene.* Oslo, Norway: H. Aschehoug & Co., 1998.

Hopkins, Henry, and Mimi Jacobs. *50 West Coast Artists: A Critical Selection of Painters and Sculptors Working in California.* San Francisco, CA: Chronicle Books, 1981.

Jenkins, Jim, and Dave Quick. *Motion Motion: Kinetic Art.* Salt Lake City, UT: Gibbs Smith, 1989.

Lucie-Smith, Edward. *Constructivism: Origins and Evolution.* New York, NY: Braziller, 1967.

———. *Art in the Eighties.* Oxford: Phaidon, 1990.

———, and Paul Karlstrom. *Fletcher Benton.* New York, NY: Harry N. Abrams, 1991.

McCarthy, Jane, and Laurily K. Epstein. *A Guide to the Sculpture Parks and Gardens of America.* New York, NY: Michael Kesend Publishing, Ltd., 1996.

Mendelowitz, Daniel Marcus. *History of American Art.* New York, NY: Holt, Rinehart and Winston, 1970.

Mogelon, Alex, and Norman Laliberte. *Art in Boxes.* New York, NY: Van Nostrand Reinhold, 1974.

Neubert, George, Peter Selz, Gerhard Kohlberg, and Phyllis Tuchman. *The New Constructivism of Fletcher Benton.* Lausanne, Switzerland: Editions Acatos, 2001.

Newman, Thelma. *Plastics as Sculpture.* Radnor, PA: Chilton Book Co., 1974.

Plagens, Peter. *Sunshine Muse: Contemporary Art on the West Coast.* New York, NY: Praeger, 1974.

Radfort, Warren and Georgia. *Outdoor Sculpture in San Francisco.* Gualala, CA: Helsham Press, 2003.

Ratcliff, Carter, and David Finn (photographer). *Fletcher Benton.* New York, NY: Ruder-Finn Press, 2003.

Strauss, Anselm. "Three Related Frameworks for Studying Artistic Production." *Sociologie de l'Art.* Paris, France: Documentation Française, 1986, pp. 183–90.

Exhibition and Collection Catalogues

Acquisitions, '73. Ridgefield, CT.: The Aldrich Contemporary Art Museum, 1973.

American Academy of Arts and Letters. New York, NY, 1979.

American Paintings and Drawings. San Francisco, CA: John Berggruen Gallery, 1980.

American Sculpture of the '60s. Los Angeles, CA: Los Angeles County Museum of Art; and Philadelphia, PA: Philadelphia Museum of Art, 1967.

Anderson, Wayne, and Brian O'Doherty. *Art '65: Lesser Known and Unknown Painters/Young American Sculpture–East to West.* New York, NY: Star Press, 1965.

Annual Exhibition 1966, Sculpture and Prints. New York, NY: Whitney Museum of American Art, 1966.

Art in Public Places. A Self-Guided Tour through the City of Brea. Brea, CA: 1975.

Art Miami 2000, International Art Exposition. Miami, FL: Miami Beach Convention Center, 1999.

The Art of Collaborative Printmaking. Reno, NV: Nevada Museum of Art, 1998.

Art/Science – Line/Design. Oxford, OH: Miami University Art Museum, 2000.

artpalmbeach. West Palm Beach, FL: International Fine Art Exposition, 2000.

Aspects of Abstract. Sacramento, CA: Crocker Art Museum, 1979.

The Atlantic Richfield Collection. New York, NY: Atlantic Richfield Company, 1969.

Bellezza, Elaine. *Art at Santa Teresa Laboratory.* San Jose, CA: IBM Santa Teresa Laboratory, 1978.

Berggruen, John. *XXV Years.* San Francisco, CA: John Berggruen Gallery, 1995.

Beyond the Surface 2. Fallbrook, CA: Art and Cultural Center at Fallbrook, 2003.

Bishop Ranch. San Ramon, CA: Sunset Development Company, 2001.

Bolomey, Roger. *Forgotten Dimension . . . A Survey of Small Sculpture in California.* Fresno, CA: Fresno Arts Center, 1982.

Burke, Diane, and Diane Ghirardo. *Fletcher Benton: Selected Works, 1964–74.* Santa Clara, CA: de Saisset Art Gallery and Museum, University of Santa Clara, 1975.

Butterfield, Jan. "Sculpture Is Realer Than Painting." *California Sculpture Show.* Los Angeles, CA: California/International Arts Foundation, 1984.

———. *Fletcher Benton.* Seoul, South Korea: Sung Dam Fine Arts, 1991.

California '66–Painters and Sculptors. Sacramento, CA: Crocker Art Gallery, 1966.

CCAC: 75 Years Resource/Reservoirs. San Francisco, CA: San Francisco Museum of Modern Art, 1983.

Cedarhurst Sculpture Park. Mt. Vernon, IL: Mitchell Museum at Cedarhurst/Cedarhurst Sculpture Park, 1999.

Celebrating Modern Art: The Anderson Collection. San Francisco, CA: San Francisco Museum of Modern Art, 2001.

Chicago International Art Exposition. Chicago: Chicago International Art Exhibition, Navy Pier, Chicago, IL, 1986.

Constructivist Tendencies. Santa Barbara, CA: University of California, Santa Barbara, 1970.

Contemporary American Painting and Sculpture. Urbana–Champaign, IL: Krannert Art Museum, University of Illinois, 1967.

Contemporary Trends. Osaka, Japan: Expo Museum of Fine Arts, 1970.

Demetrion, James T. *The Hirshhorn Collects: Recent Acquisitions.* Washington, D.C.: Hirshhorn Museum and Sculpture Garden, Smithsonian Institution, 1997.

Dickson, Joanne. *Project Sculpture.* Oakland Museum, California: Cal Central Press, 1981.

Electric Art. Los Angeles, CA: UCLA Art Galleries, University of California, Los Angeles, 1969.

Elsen, Albert E. *A Decade in the West.* Stanford, CA: Stanford University Museum of Art, 1971.

Fall/Winter Exhibition. Hamilton, NJ: Grounds for Sculpture, 1998.

Fletcher Benton. New York, NY: Galeria Bonino, 1968.

Fletcher Benton. New York, NY: Galeria Bonino, 1969.

Fletcher Benton. Brussels, Belgium: Galerie Françoise Mayer, 1969.

Fletcher Benton. Fresno State University Gallery. Fresno, CA: California State University at Fresno, 1977.

Fletcher Benton. San Jose, CA: San Jose Museum of Art, 1982.

Fletcher Benton. Scottsdale, AZ: Riva Yares Gallery, 1991.

Fletcher Benton. Wiesbaden, Germany: Galerie B. Haasner, 1997.

Fletcher Benton. Los Angeles, CA: Tasende Gallery, 2001.

Fletcher Benton. New York, NY: Heidi Neuhoff Gallery, 2003.

Fletcher Benton: Escultura Cinética. Rio de Janeiro, Brazil: Galeria Bonino, 1973.

Fletcher Benton: In Southern California. Los Angeles, CA: Tasende Gallery, 2005.

Fletcher Benton: New Sculpture. San Francisco, CA: John Berggruen Gallery, 1979.

Fletcher Benton: Recent Sculpture. San Francisco, CA: John Berggruen Gallery, 1981.

Fletcher Benton: Sculpture and Watercolors, 1980–1986. Los Angeles, CA: California International Arts Foundation, 1987.

Fletcher Benton: Skulptur und Raum. Cologne, Germany: Gothaer Kunstforum, 1993.

Foley, Suzanne. *Fletcher Benton, Jerry Ballaine, Sam Richardson.* San Francisco, CA: San Francisco Museum of Modern Art, 1970.

Foster, James W. *California 3 by 8 Twice.* Honolulu, HI: Honolulu Academy of Arts, 1978.

Gaugler, William M. *Florence–Santa Clara: Two Schools of Sculpture.* Santa Clara, CA: Triton Museum of Art, 1991.

Ghirardo, Diane. *Fletcher Benton, 1975: Paintings, Watercolors, Sculpture.* San Francisco, CA: Smith Andersen Gallery, 1975.

Gregg, Richard N., and Leroy Butler. *Looking West, 1970.* Omaha, NE: Joslyn Art Museum, 1970.

Griffen, Rachel, Henry Hopkins, and Alvin Balkind. *The West Coast Now.* Portland, OR: Portland Art Association, 1968.

Hemisfair. San Antonio, TX: U.S. Pavilion, 1968.

Highlights of the 1967–68 Art Season. Ridgefield, CT: The Aldrich Contemporary Art Museum, 1968.

Holland, Katherine Church. *The Art Collection: Federal Reserve Bank of San Francisco.* San Francisco, CA: Federal Reserve Bank of San Francisco, 1986.

———. *The Bay Area Collection: Works from The Anderson Collection.* Santa Clara, CA: Triton Museum of Art, 1996.

Inaugural Exhibition. New York, NY: New School Art Center, New School for Social Research, 1969.

In the Sculptor's Landscape. Los Angeles, CA: Wight Art Gallery, University of California, Los Angeles, 1993.

The Japan Art Society. Japan: Municipal Art Galleries, Yokohama and Sendai; Kawatoku Gallery, Morioka, 1970.

Kinetics. London, England: Hayward Art Gallery, 1970.

Kunst in der Fabrik. Krefeld, Germany: Kleinewefers Intern, 1987.

Light and Movement. Flint, MI: Flint Institute of Arts, 1967.

Lytton, Barbara. *California Art Festival.* Los Angeles, CA: Lytton Center of the Visual Arts, 1967.

Made In California: Art, Image, and Identity 1900–2000. Los Angeles County Museum of Art, California, 2000.

McClain, Malcolm A. *Artists Forum.* Los Angeles, CA: California State University, Los Angeles, 1986.

Minschew, William E. *5x5: Five Artists, Five Works.* Fresno, CA: Conley Gallery of Art, California State University, 1989.

The Museum Collects: Treasures of Twenty Years II. Oxford, OH: Miami University Art Museum, 1999.

Navy Pier Walk 2002: The Chicago International Sculpture Exhibition. Navy Pier, Chicago, IL, 2002.

Navy Pier Walk 2003: The Chicago International Sculpture Exhibition. Navy Pier, Chicago, IL, 2003.

Neubert, George W. *Public Sculpture/Urban Environment.* Oakland, CA: Oakland Museum, 1974.

———. *Brook House Sculpture Invitational.* Oakland, CA: Kaiser Center, 1982.

1968 Annual Exhibition, Contemporary American Sculpture. New York, NY: Whitney Museum of American Art, 1968.

1973 Biennial Exhibition: Contemporary American Art. New York, NY: Whitney Museum of American Art, 1973.

Nordland, Gerald. *Franklin D. Murphy Sculpture Garden.* Los Angeles, CA: University of California, Los Angeles, 1978.

———. *Fletcher Benton: New Sculpture.* Milwaukee, WI: Milwaukee Art Center, 1979.

———. *New Sculpture by Fletcher Benton II.* San Jose, CA: San Jose State University, 1980.

———, and Thomas H. Garver. *Fletcher Benton: Recent Sculpture, Folded Circle Series.* San Francisco, CA: John Berggruen Gallery, 1977.

Northern California Art of the Sixties. Santa Clara, CA: de Saisset Museum, University of Santa Clara, 1982.

100 Years of California Sculpture. Oakland, CA: Oakland Museum, 1982.

Options. Minneapolis, MN: Walker Art Center, 1968.

Out of Town. Urbana–Champaign, IL: University of Illinois, 1993.

Paint on Metal: Modern and Contemporary Explorations and Discoveries. Tucson, AZ: Tucson Museum of Art, 2005.

Painting and Sculpture Today. Indianapolis, IN: Indianapolis Museum of Art, 1970.

Perlman, Raymond. *Contemporary American Painting and Sculpture.* Urbana–Champaign, IL: University of Illinois, 1969.

Pittsburgh International Exhibition of Contemporary Painting and Sculpture. Pittsburgh, PA: Museum of Art, Carnegie Institute, 1967.

The Product as an Object, Ohio. Akron, OH: Akron Art Institute, 1973.

Riva Yares 2000, The First 35 Years. Scottsdale, AZ: Riva Yares Gallery, 2000.

Salzmann, Siegfried. *Steel Sculpture.* Krefeld, Germany: Park der Burg Linn, 1987.

2nd Flint Invitational. Flint, MI: Flint Institute of Arts, 1969.

Selection 1968/University of California, Berkeley. Berkeley: University of California, Berkeley Art Museum, 1968.

Selz, Peter. *Directions in Kinetic Sculpture.* Berkeley: University of California, Berkeley Art Museum, 1966.

———. *Fletcher Benton.* New York, NY: Landry Bonino Gallery, 1972.

———. *Fletcher Benton: Recent Work.* La Jolla, CA: La Jolla Museum of Art, 1972.

———. *Sculpture, Drawings: Fletcher Benton.* Los Angeles, CA: Esther Robles Gallery, 1972.

———. *Fletcher Benton.* Rio de Janeiro, Brazil: Galeria Bonino, 1973.

———. *Pioneering Printmakers.* San Diego, CA: Fine Arts Gallery of San Diego, 1974.

The 73rd Western Annual. Denver, CO: Denver Art Museum, 1970.

Smith, Howard Ross. *Third Winter Invitational Exhibition.* San Francisco, CA: California Palace of the Legion of Honor, 1961.

———. *Fifth Winter Invitational Exhibition.* San Francisco, CA: California Palace of the Legion of Honor, 1964.

Some Aspects of California Painting and Sculpture. La Jolla, CA: La Jolla Museum of Art, 1965.

Story, Ada. *Constructivist Tendencies.* Goleta, CA: Triple R, 1970.

Sujo, Clara Diament. *Fletcher Benton.* Caracas, Venezuela: Estudio Actual, 1970.

Swig, Roselyne, and Henry Hopkins. *San Francisco Arts Festival.* San Francisco, CA: The Moscone Center, 1982.

Ten Touring Exhibitions, 1965/66. San Francisco, CA: Art Bank of the San Francisco Art Institute, 1965.

20 American Artists: Sculpture 1982. San Francisco, CA: San Francisco Museum of Modern Art, 1982.

28th Annual Exhibition. Chicago, IL: Art Institute of Chicago, 1968.

2 Dimensional Sculpture–3 Dimensional Painting. Richmond, CA.: Richmond Art Center, 1965.

Two Exhibitions. Rohnert Park, CA.: Sonoma State College Art Department Gallery, 1968.

Welded! Sculpture of the Twentieth Century. New York, NY: Neuberger Museum of Art, 2000.

The Whitney Review, 1966–67. New York, NY: Whitney Museum of American Art, 1968.

Works in Bronze: A Modern Survey. Rohnert Park, CA: University Art Gallery, Sonoma State University, 1984.

Worth, Carl. *Spaces.* Walnut Creek, CA: Civic Art Gallery, 1979.

Wortz, Melinda. "Sensuous Constructivism in California Sculpture." *California Sculpture Show.* Fisher Gallery, University of Southern California, Los Angeles and California/International Arts Foundation, 1984.

Articles and Reviews

"A quarta dimensaõ do movimento." *O Globo* (Rio de Janeiro, Brazil), Oct. 16, 1973.

Ahlgren, Calvin. "Setting up the Soap Box Derby Was a Loving Plot." *San Francisco Chronicle,* California, May 21, 1978.

Albright, Thomas. "Stowing Sail and Beeping. 1968." *San Francisco Chronicle,* California, Aug. 18, 1968.

———. "Three Masterful Artists." *San Francisco Chronicle,* California, Jan. 15, 1970.

———. "Benton at the Oakland Museum." *Artweek* (San Francisco, CA), Jan. 17, 1970.

———. "Fletcher Benton at the San Francisco Museum of Art." *Artweek* (San Francisco, CA), Jan. 17, 1970.

———. "Benton's Kinetic Sculpture." *San Francisco Chronicle,* California, June 12, 1970.

———. "Fletcher Benton's Subtle Sculptures." *San Francisco Chronicle,* California, Mar. 10, 1980.

———. "The Innocuous Flavor of Art School Art." *San Francisco Examiner,* California, Aug. 8, 1982.

Aldrich, Larry. "New Talents USA." *Art in America,* no. 54 (New York, July 1966): pp. 22–23.

Amy, Michaël. "Fletcher Benton at Neuhoff." *Art in America,* no. 5 (May 2004): p. 163.

"An Artistic Look at West Coast Artists." *Ross Valley Reporter,* California, Nov. 18, 1981.

"Art Alley." *Berkeley Gazette*, California, Sept. 30, 1961.

"Art Cologne." *Weltkunst moderne – ein Sonderheft der Weltkunst* (Munich, Germany), Oct. 15, 2001.

"Art in Corporate Use." *Artweek* (San Francisco, CA), Oct. 20, 1973.

Auer, James. "He Likes to Metal in 'A' to 'Z'." *Milwaukee Journal*, Wisconsin, Dec. 2, 1979.

Ayala, Walmir. "Arte e Tecnologia." *O Jornal* (Rio de Janeiro, Brazil), Oct. 7, 1973.

Bachmann, Stephen R. "Fletcher Benton." *New Orleans Art Review* 8: 5 (Louisiana, May–June, 1990): pp. 6–7.

Baldwin, Nick. "Sculpture for Muscatine." *Des Moines Register*, Iowa, Aug. 27, 1980.

"Benton begleitet seinen Stahlkoloss." *Kölnische Rundschau* (Germany), Nov. 12, 1993.

"Benton–Plastik an neuem Standort." *Frankfurter Allgemeine Zeitung* (Germany), Aug. 22, 1996.

"Benton Sculpture Presented to Museum." *Oxford Press*, Ohio, June 19, 1980.

Bentzrud, Inger. "Skulptur fra California." *Dagbladet* (Norway), Sept. 3, 1985: p. 21.

Benzig, Gerhard. "Kolorierte Stahlkörper modellieren den Raum." *Wiesbadener Kurier* (Germany), Nov. 30, 1992.

"Bewegungs Variation." *Frankfurter Allgemeine Zeitung* (Germany), Dec. 5, 1992.

"Big Sculpture Coming to University of Iowa." *Des Moines Register*, Iowa, Aug. 23, 1981.

Bittencourt, Francisco. "Escultura Cinetica." *Tribuna da Imprensa* (Rio de Janeiro, Brazil), Oct. 26, 1973.

———. "Esposicoes no Rio de Salaõ do Farana." *Tribuna da Imprensa* (Rio de Janeiro, Brazil), Nov. 10, 1973.

Blair, Kim. "1,000 View American Sculpture Exhibit." *Los Angeles Times*, California, Apr. 29, 1967.

Bloomfield, Arthur. "Brush Strokes Do Most of the Talking." *San Francisco News Call Bulletin*, California, Jan. 11, 1960.

———. "The Figuring Is Good at the Legion." *San Francisco News–Call Bulletin*, California, Oct. 5, 1964.

———. "Art in Slow Motion." *San Francisco Examiner*, California, Jan. 16, 1967.

———. "UC Museum Shows Enviable Acquisitions." *San Francisco Examiner*, California, Aug. 6, 1968.

———. "Three Sculptors Play It Cool." *Oakland Tribune*, California, Jan. 31, 1969.

———. "The Square That Unfolds into Circles." *San Francisco Examiner*, California, Oct. 27, 1977.

Bøe, Bjørg. "Premiere på Wennesland-filmen" *Fædrelandbvennen* (Norway), Feb. 14, 2001.

Borsick, Helen. "Art and Artists." *Plain Dealer* (Cleveland, OH), Nov. 3, 1968.

Bratten, Dawna. "Heart of steel: Benton brings 40 works to Tasende." *La Jolla Village News*, California, June 6, 2001.

Brehm, Kyle. "Geometric Sculpture Displayed." *Spartan Daily* (San Jose State University, California), May 8, 1980.

Brown, Carol. "Portrait of Two Artists." *KQED Focus* (San Francisco, CA), Mar. 1975: p. 15.

Brumfield, John. "The Olympics California Sculpture Show." *Artweek* (San Francisco, CA), July 28, 1984.

Bruner, Louise. "Shows at Flint, Dayton Are Worth the Trip." *Blade* (Toledo, OH), Nov. 9, 1969.

Burke, Diane. "Fletcher Benton: Selected Works." *San Jose Mercury News*, California, Mar. 13, 1975.

Burkhart, Dorothy. "Sticks and Stones." *San Jose Mercury News*, California, Aug. 8, 1982.

———. "The Fletcher Benton Boom." *San Jose Mercury News*, California, Aug. 29, 1982.

"Business Park Attracts Some Big–Time Clients." *Tri–Valley Herald* (Livermore, CA), Sept. 24, 1983.

Butterfield, Jan. "An Interview with Fletcher Benton." *Art International* 24, no. 26 (Oct.–Nov. 1980): p. 43.

Cebulski, Frank. "Sculpture as a Mirror for Life." *Artweek* (San Francisco, CA), Aug. 14, 1982.

Chappelow, Tracy. "Starving for Art's Sake: Sculptor Fletcher Benton." *Miamian* (Oxford, OH) 4: 2 (Jan. 1986): pp. 14–18.

Chattopadhyay, Collette. "Reviews: Los Angeles; Fletcher Benton." *Sculpture*, no. 7 (Sept. 2001): p. 20.

"Children Learn All About Time." *Minneapolis Star*, Minnesota, June 23, 1966.

Cortright, Barbara. "Fletcher Benton Sculpture." *Artweek* (San Francisco, CA), Apr. 27, 1974.

Craig, Pat. "Oakland Hosts 'Joan of Art'." *Oakland Tribune*, California, Mar. 16, 1980.

Cross, Miriam D. "Pioneer of 'The Movement'." *Oakland Tribune*, California, Mar. 27, 1966.

———. "U.S. Art Renaissance Is in Full Bloom." *Oakland Tribune*, California, Aug. 4, 1968.

———. "Kinetic Sculpture Enchants All Eyes, All Ages." *Oakland Tribune*, California, June 21, 1970.

Curtis, Stephanie. "Conceptual Art Changes." *San Jose State University News*, California, Oct. 19, 1972.

D'Agostino, Bill. "Birth of a sculpture." *Palo Alto Weekly*, California, Aug. 3, 2005.

D'Agostino, Bill, and Patricia Bass. "Everyone's a Critic." *Palo Alto Weekly*, California, Aug. 3, 2005.

Daugherty, Charles. "How Do You Know What You Like?" *Famous Artist Magazine* 17, no. 1 (autumn 1968): pp. 17–20, 38.

Davis, Mary Kaye. "An order to chaos." *Register–News*, Mt. Vernon, IL, no. 268 (Aug. 11–12, 2001): pp. 1a, 3a.

Del Parker, Marjorie. "Benton's Small-Scale Sculpture." *West Art* (Auburn, CA), 23: 8 (Jan. 11, 1985).

Dickson, Joanne. "San Jose Museum Showcases Art Work of Faculty Members." *Palo Alto Times*, California, Jan. 27, 1978.

Dittmar, Peter. "Am liebsten mit Rost." *Die Welt* (Krefeld, Germany), Sept. 17, 1987.

"Drei Künstler stellen aus." *Offenbach-Post* (Frankfurt, Germany ed.), June 23, 1981.

Drohojowska, Hunter. "California Sculpture for the World to See." *Los Angeles Herald Tribune*, California, June 8, 1984.

"Ein fallendes D." *Offenbach-Post* (Frankfurt, Germany ed.), June 21, 1981.

Emanuel, Jerry. "San Francisco." *Artscan* (San Francisco, CA), Mar. 1967.

Emerson, Paul. "Exhibit Features Art in Form, Color." *Palo Alto Times,* California, June 25, 1971.

———. "Kinetic Sculpture Display Merges Several Elements." *Palo Alto Times,* California, Oct. 1, 1971.

"Erstarrte Bilder und Skulpturen mit Bewegung." *Wiesbadener Tagblatt* (Germany), Apr. 18, 1997.

"Exhibition of Kinetic Art by Fletcher Benton Opens Sunday at Estudio Actual." *Daily Journal* (Caracas, Venezuela), Sept. 6, 1970.

"Exposición de Fletcher Benton." *Imagen* (Caracas, Venezuela), Sept. 15, 1970.

"Exposiciones y Expactaculos Para Hoy." *La Verdad* (Caracas, Venezuela), Sept. 6, 1970.

Fagan, Beth. "Sculptor Says Public Art Important." *Oregonian* (Portland, OR), Feb. 28, 1980.

"Favoriten auf der Art Cologne." *Weltkunst Sonderheft* (Munich, Germany), Oct. 2001.

Field, Michael. "From California to West Bretton." *Star* (West Bretton, England), May 27, 1985.

Filho, Paulo Serrado. "Fletcher Benton Luz e Movimento em Formas Geometricas." *Jornal de Brasil,* Oct. 10, 1973.

"Fletcher Benton." *El Universal* (Caracas, Venezuela), July 9, 1970.

"Fletcher Benton." *Daily Journal* (Caracas, Venezuela), Sept. 13, 1970.

"Fletcher Benton Art Exhibit at UC Davis." *Appeal Democrat* (Davis, CA), Nov. 23, 1973.

"Fletcher Benton at Neuhoff Gallery." *New York Gallery Guide,* Nov. 2003.

"Fletcher Benton Bild am Barbarossaplatz." *Kölner Stadt-Anzeiger* (Germany), Nov. 12, 1993.

"Fletcher Benton: Ein Amerikaner in Wiesbaden." *Wiesbaden International* (Germany), June 1987.

"Fletcher Benton for the First Time in Germany." *Stadt und Kreis* (Frankfurt, Germany), June 15, 1981.

"Fletcher Benton: Sculpture at UC Davis Fourth Floor Gallery." *Artweek* (San Francisco, CA), Dec. 8, 1973.

Flick, Verena. "Fletcher Benton." *Art International* 10: no. 10 (Dec. 20, 1966): p. 53.

———. "Rationalitat und Geheimnis: Ausstellung." *Wiesbadener Kurier* (Germany), June 3, 1987.

———. "Aquarelle aus Stahl im Raum: Plastiken von Fletcher Benton in der Kunsthandlung Haasner." *Wiesbadener Tagblatt* (Germany), June 4, 1987.

———. "Interesting Imports from the California Art Scene." *Der Kunsthandel* (Germany), Feb. 1997.

Fowler, Carol. "Sculpture Goes Public." *Contra Costa Times,* California, Aug. 20, 1982.

Frankenstein, Alfred. "Kinetic Forces." *San Francisco Examiner–Chronicle,* California, Jan. 12, 1965.

———. "Art's Most Moving Moments." *San Francisco Examiner–Chronicle,* California, Mar. 27, 1966.

———. "The 85th: A Gamble against Time." *San Francisco Examiner–Chronicle,* California, Oct. 30, 1966.

———. "A Little Corner of Kinetic Sculpture." *San Francisco Examiner–Chronicle,* California, Aug. 11, 1968.

———. "Impressive Sculpture Show." *San Francisco Chronicle,* California, Nov. 25, 1970.

———. "Some Technical Marvels." *San Francisco Chronicle,* California, Sept. 30, 1971.

French, Palmer. "Exhibition in San Francisco." *Artforum* 8 (Mar. 1970): pp. 86–88.

Fried, Alexander. "Sculpture in Motion." *San Francisco Examiner–Chronicle,* California, Mar. 20, 1966.

Glaze, Rick. "Thirty Years of Recent Sculpture Represented in Syntex Exhibition." *Palo Alto Weekly,* California, Dec. 6, 1979.

Golonu, Berin. "Fletcher Benton's Art of Geometry." *Artweek* (San Francisco, CA), July/Aug. 2000: Vol. 31, pp. 7–8.

Grauvogl, Ann. "Sculptor Won't Let Circle Stay Unbroken." *Quad City Times* (Muscatine, IA), Sept. 13, 1980.

Green, Roger. "Artfully Entertaining." *New Orleans Times–Picayune,* Louisiana, Apr. 18, 1990.

"Grossplastik als Verbeugung vor Schrift–Stadt Offenbach." *Offenbach–Post* (Germany), Aug. 22, 1996.

Guevara, Roberto. "Dinasmo Cromatico en Fletcher Benton." *El Nacional* (Caracas, Venezuela), Sept. 8, 1970.

———. "Arte en los Espacios del Hombre." *El Nacional* (Caracas, Venezuela), Feb. 21, 1971.

Hagberg, Marilyn. "Benton's Moving Paintings." *Artweek* (San Francisco, CA), Apr. 29, 1972.

———. "The City Is for People." *Artweek* (San Francisco, CA), Sept. 1, 1973.

Hakanson, Joy. "Very Moving Pictures." *Sunday News* (Detroit, MI), Mar. 29, 1970.

Hale, David. "Fletcher Benton's 'Moving Paintings'." *Fresno Bee,* California, Mar. 27, 1977.

———. "New Exhibits at Fresno Art Center Include Benton's Painting, Sculpture." *Fresno Bee,* California, Nov. 18, 1984.

Heinrichs, Kirk. "Art Prof's Work Style: Sculpting on a Grand Scale." *San Jose Mercury News,* California, Nov. 30, 1977.

Helfand, Glen. "National Reviews: Fletcher Benton." *ARTnews* (Mar. 2001): p. 161.

Hildebrand, Martin. "Spiele eines Malers mit Stahl." *Wiesbadener Tagblatt* (Germany), Nov. 15, 1988.

———. "Mehr als nur die Mindestform." *Wiesbadener Tagblatt* (Germany), Dec. 4, 1992.

———. "Der Amerikanische Bildhauer." *Wiesbadener Leben* (Germany), Jan. 1993.

Huther, Christian. "Art Frankfurt." *Weltkunst* (Germany), Apr. 15, 1997.

Ianco-Starrels, Josine. "Art News." *Los Angeles Times,* California, May 21, 1978.

Imm, Val. "Art and the Lively." *Dallas Times-Herald,* Texas, Oct. 17, 1968.

"In der Nacht kam der Stahlriese an." *Kölnische Rundschau* (Germany), Nov. 10, 1993.

Jacobs, Jay. "The Neuberger Museum." *Art Gallery (*Purchase, NY), May 1974.

Jaszi, Jean. "Fletcher Benton Kinetic Sculpture." *Artweek* (San Francisco, CA), June 13, 1970.

Jensen, Dean. "Fletcher Benton." *Milwaukee Sentinel,* Wisconsin, Nov. 23, 1979.

"Joan Mondale Has Busy Day in Bay Area." *San Francisco Examiner,* California, Mar. 17, 1980.

Johnson, T. "Abstract Sculpture Installed at Hospital." *Daily Iowan* (Iowa City, IA), Aug. 27, 1981.

Kino, Carol. "Special Supplement: The Art Show." *Art & Auction* (Feb. 2001): pp. 41–46.

Kramer, Hilton. "Sculpture: A Stunning Display of Radical Changes." *New York Times,* Apr. 27, 1967.

Krautter, Martin. "Weit schweifender Blick auf aktuelle Kunstwetterlage." *Offenbach–Post* (Germany), Apr. 1997.

Krisch, Nora Louise. "Invitation to a Kinetic Hanging." *Houston Post,* Texas, Oct. 20, 1968.

Langsner, Jules. "Benton Hypnosis; Vasa." *ARTnews* (summer 1967): p. 62.

Ledbetter, Les. "Coast Artists Draw Crowd in Soapboxes." *New York Times,* May 22, 1978.

Leisegang, Joachim. "Tatort San Francisco." *Die Waage* (Germany) 18:3 (1979/80): p. 114.

Leopold, Michael. "Los Angeles." *Art International* (Jan. 1974).

Levine, Melinda. "Where Sculpture Hangs Out." *Berkeley Gazette,* California, Aug. 13, 1982.

Lewinson, David. "More to See." *Muscatine Journal,* Iowa, Dec. 4, 1980.

———. "Benton's Art Holds Strength." *San Diego Union,* Feb. 26, 1984.

Lien, Tor Martin. "En happening om beat-kunst." *Agderposten* (Norway), Feb. 15, 2001.

Lorenzelli, Tiziana. "Fletcher Benton's Note-Free Harmony." *Habitat Ufficio 45* (Italy), 47 (Dec. 1991): p. 20.

Martin, Fred. "Art in the San Francisco Bay Area, Early Winter 1965." *Art International* 10: 2 (Feb. 1966): pp. 76–83.

Maves, C. E. "Polished World of Fletcher Benton." *Palo Alto Times,* California, Mar. 1975.

McCann, Cecile N. "Fletcher Benton Color Flow." *Artweek* (San Francisco, CA), Oct. 23, 1971.

McDonald, Robert. "Artist Lives in His Sculpture." *Habitat* (Cleveland, OH) (Dec. 13, 1985): p. 6.

Melten, Brigitta. "Papiermöbel und Steinbücher." *Allgemeine Zeitung Mainz und Wiesbadener Tagblatt* (Germany), Nov. 1, 2001.

Metcalf, Katherine. "Kinetic Sculpture: An Exhibition Assembled by Peter Selz." *Arts and Architecture* 83 (June 1966): p. 30.

Mitchell, John L. "In Beverly Hills Building Is Art." *Los Angeles Times,* California, Aug. 1, 1985.

Monte, James. "Fletcher Benton: Studio Exhibition." *Artforum* 2: 11 (Apr. 1964): p. 45.

Morch, Al. "Bronzing the Alphabet." *San Francisco Examiner,* California, Mar. 24, 1980.

"The Movement Movement." *Time* 87: 4 (Jan. 28, 1966): p. 64.

Muchnic, Suzanne. "Fletcher Benton Retrospective." *Artweek* (San Francisco, CA), Apr. 2, 1977.

Neubert, George. "Taking It to the Limits." *Oakland Museum Newsletter,* California, 8: 2 (Mar.–Apr. 1980).

Newhall, Edith. "Bauhaus Echoes." *ARTnews* (Feb. 1988): p. 14.

"Oakland Sculpture Hubbub." *San Francisco Chronicle,* California, Sept. 1, 1974.

"Offenbacher Denkmal für den Buchstaben D." *Frankfurter Allgemeine Zeitung* (Germany), Oct. 31, 1996.

Olvera, Jennifer. "Art for art's sake Public sculpture blooming in the 'burbs." *Daily Herald* (Chicago, IL), May 24, 2002.

"Picasso-Originale und Benton–Skulpturen im Krankenhaus." *Westfälische Nachrichten* (Germany), Nov. 17, 1990.

Porges, Maria. "New Orleans, Louisiana." *Sculpture* (May–June 1994): p. 71.

"Provocative Sculptures at Stanford." *Palo Alto Times,* California, June 23, 1972.

Reeves, Jean. "Two 'Organic' Sculptors Put Beauty in Motion." *Buffalo Evening News,* New York, Jan. 20, 1970.

Regalia, Ron. "Art Provides 'Free Way of Life,' Prof. Says." *Spartan Daily* (San Jose State University, San Jose, CA), Apr. 30, 1980.

"Renowned Artist Commissioned for Orbanco Building." *Orbanco Newsletter* (Portland, OR), Jan. 1980.

Rickey, George. "Kinesis Continued." *Art in America* 53 (Dec. 1965–Jan. 1966): pp. 45–55.

Rico, Diana. "California Sculpture Show: Really Tubular." *Los Angeles Daily News,* California, June 2, 1984.

Robbeloth, DeWitt. "San Francisco." *ArtScene,* Feb. 1970.

Roder, Sylvie. "A Sampling of Sculpture." *Palo Alto Weekly,* California, Mar. 2, 1988.

Rogers, Marcia. "Art Is Subjective." *Muscatine Journal,* Iowa, Oct. 8, 1980.

———. "Benton's Bent." *Quad-City Times* (Muscatine, IA), Nov. 23, 1980.

———. "Benton Art Shown in Muscatine." *Des Moines Register,* Iowa, Dec. 5, 1980.

Saeks, Diane. "Home for Sculpture." *Nob Hill Gazette* (San Francisco, CA), Mar. 1986: p. 24.

Sampaio, Ruy. "A Laranja Antimecanica de Fletcher Benton." *O Jornal* (Rio de Janeiro, Brazil), Oct. 14, 1973.

"Scenes from S/12." *Sculptors International* 1: 4 (fall 1982).

Schumann, Manfred E. "Geschnitten, geschweist, gebogen." *Frankfurter Rundschau* (Frankfurt, Germany), July 18, 1981.

"Sculpture—It's Everywhere." *Montclarion* (Oakland, CA), Aug. 4, 1982.

"Sculpture of the Sixties." *San Francisco Art Institute News,* California, May 1967.

Seldis, Henry J. "U.S. Sculpture Exhibit Looks beyond the '60s." *Los Angeles Times,* California, May 7, 1967.

Selz, Peter. "Geometric Sculpture in Equilibrium: Fletcher Benton." *Sculpture*, June 2004: Vol. 23, No. 5.

"Seregrafias de Vasarely." *El Nacional* (Caracas, Venezuela), Sept. 6, 1970.

Seymour, Ann. "Art for Art's Sake, Sculpture of Fletcher Benton: Color in Motion." *Centervoice* (San Francisco, CA), Oct. 1981.

———. "Constructivist Sculptures and Paintings." *Artweek* (San Francisco, CA), Sept. 29, 1984.

———. "Fletcher Benton's Creative Space." *Centervoice* (San Francisco, CA), Mar. 1985.

"Shades, Forms, Daring Colors." *Offenbach Post* (Germany), June 1981.

Shere, Charles. "Two Exhibits Show Constructivists." *Oakland Tribune*, California, Mar. 18, 1980.

———. "Fletcher Benton's Poised Sculpture." *Oakland Tribune*, California, Mar. 30, 1980.

Sheridan, Jan. "Balanced Tension Gives Sense of Motion to Fixed Structure." *Arizona Republic* (Phoenix, AZ), Aug. 18, 1985.

Sherman, Ann Elliott. "Bay Area Art Beats." *Metro*, Dec. 21–27, 1995.

Sherman, Lola. "Golfers See Red over Sculpture in Rancho Santa Fe." *San Diego Tribune*, San Diego, CA, May 8, 1989.

Smith, Starla. "University of Iowa Gets 'Folded Square D'." *Iowa City Press Citizen*, Iowa, Aug. 26, 1981.

Stiles, Knute. "Fletcher Benton at John Berggruen." *Art in America* 68: 6 (June 1980): p. 163.

Sullivan, Meg. "Malibu Sets up Waves of Art." *Los Angeles Daily News*, California, June 28, 1993.

Tall, William. "Exploring the Mystery of Kinetic Art." *Detroit Free Press*, California, Apr. 5, 1970.

Temko, Allan. "Benton's Unexpected Spatial Treasures." *San Francisco Examiner*, California, Mar. 30, 1980.

———. "Sculptural Fun and Games." *San Francisco Chronicle*, California, Mar. 20, 1981.

"10 Meters by 10 Meters Alphabet Sculpture." *Frankfurter Rundschau* (Germany), June 15, 1981.

Thorson, Alice. "Fletcher Benton." *New Art Examiner*, Dec. 1979.

Tomidy, Paul. "Fletcher Benton: New Sculpture." *ART* 8: 2 (Mar.–Apr. 1980): pp. 8–9.

"Un Cinetico en la Estudio Actual." *El Nacional* (Caracas, Venezuela), Sept. 7, 1970.

"Vanishing Circus Nudes." *San Francisco Chronicle*, California, Apr. 17, 1974.

Van Tongeren, Herk. "Fletcher Benton at the Oakland Museum." *Sculptor's News Exchange*, Apr. 1980.

"Viel Raum für Skulpturen." *Sonderveröffentlichung des Kölner Stadt–Anzeiger* (Germany), Oct. 30, 2001.

Waddington, Chris. "Graceful Forms from an Unwieldy Substance." *New Orleans Times–Picayune*, Louisiana, Dec. 10, 1993.

———. "San Francisco Artist Twists, Bends, Impresses." *Lagniappe* (New Orleans, LA), Sept. 19, 1997.

Wallace, Dean. "Polychrome Sculpture Says 'Please Touch'." *San Francisco Chronicle*, California, Aug. 24, 1964.

———. "Art: Hard-Edge and Electronic." *San Francisco Chronicle*, California, Nov. 23, 1964.

Walls, Jim. "Experimental Artist Explores New Domain." *San Francisco Chronicle*, California, Jan. 20, 1960.

Walsh, Tom. "Gift to University of Iowa Isn't Cost Free." *Cedar Rapids Gazette*, Iowa, Aug. 22, 1981.

Weaver, Gay M. "Sculpture '72." *Artweek* (San Francisco, CA), July 29, 1972.

———. "Sculpture Show One of the Finest Ever Held at Palo Alto Center." *Palo Alto Times*, California, Jan. 19, 1973.

Weimers, Leigh. "A Rather Involved Slice of Real Life." *San Jose Mercury News*, California, Sept. 26, 1980.

Wilson, Pete. "Benton Sculpture in Main Lobby of Columbus Bank." *Jackson Journal*, Ohio, Dec. 6, 1976.

Wilson, William. "Air of Pageantry in Banner Art." *Los Angeles Times*, California, July 26, 1965.

———. "Benton's Sculpture Shines." *Los Angeles Times*, California, May 6, 1966.

———. "Sculpture: California Dreaming." *Los Angeles Times*, California, Aug. 29, 1982.

———. "A Potpourri of California Sculpture." *Los Angeles Times*, California, June 17, 1984.

Younger, Carolyn. "Elegance and balance–Thinking outside the box: The art of Fletcher Benton." *St. Helena Star*, June 3, 2004.

Films and Videos

Dore Street Studio–Fletcher Benton. Color video. Producer: Dave Hatch, 1984.

Dr. Wennesland: An Icon Among the Beats. Color video. Producer: Roald Jørgensen. Director: Gerd Hennum and Svein Tallaksen, Norway: Media Service As and NRK Kultur., 2001.

Fletcher Benton. Color video. Chico: Library, California State College, Chico; San Jose, CA: California State University, 1973.

Fletcher Benton. Color video. Producer: Michael J. Parsons. Director: Morgan Cavett. Baguio City, Philippines: Duntog Foundation, Inc., 1997.

Fletcher Benton: Dedication of Brussels Sculpture. Color video. Brussels, Belgium: Morgan Guaranty Trust, 1993.

Fletcher Benton: Homage to WWII Fighter and Bomber Aircraft. Producer/Director: Morgan Cavett, 1997.

Fletcher Benton: Selected Works, 1964–1974. Color video. Narrated by Gerald Nordland. de Saisset Museum, University of Santa Clara, CA, 1975.

Fletcher Benton's Studio. Library, California State University, San Jose, CA, 1969.

It's a Good Time to Be West. California/International Arts Foundation. Producer/Director: Robin Lough, British Broadcasting Corporation. Executive Producer: Lyn Kienholz, 1984.

The Shape of Change. San Jose, CA: Library, California State University, San Jose, CA, 1973.

Two Artists—Fletcher Benton and Marva Cremer. Color video telecast, March 2, 1975, KQED, San Francisco, CA.

Selected Collections, Commissions & Material in Archives

Achenbach Foundation for Graphic Arts, California Palace of the Legion of Honor, San Francisco, CA

Agder College, Kristiansand, Norway

The Aldrich Contemporary Art Museum, Ridgefield, CT

American Republic Company, Des Moines, IA

Anderson Collection, University of California, Los Angeles, CA

Banque Lambert, Brussels, Belgium

Berkus Outdoor Collection, Santa Barbara, CA

Bishop Ranch, San Ramon, CA

Capital Research, Los Angeles, CA

Cedars-Sinai Medical Center, Los Angeles, CA

City of Offenbach, Germany

City of Palo Alto, Stanford University, California

City of West Bend, WI

Civic Arts Gallery, Walnut Creek, CA

Columbia Savings and Loan, Beverly Hills, CA

Corcoran Gallery of Art, Washington, D.C.

Crocker Art Museum, Sacramento, CA

Louise M. Davies Symphony Hall, San Francisco, CA

De Cordova Museum, Lincoln, MA

de Saisset Art Gallery and Museum, University of Santa Clara, Santa Clara, CA

Denver Art Museum, Colorado

Eunji Corporation, Seoul, South Korea

Federal Reserve Bank of San Francisco, CA

First National Bank, Dallas, TX

First National Bank of Ohio, Columbus, OH

Grounds for Sculpture, Hamilton, NJ

Guggenheim, Las Vegas, NV

Haas School of Business, University of California, Berkeley, CA

Hare, Brewer and Kelley, Mountain View, CA

Hartwood Acres Sculpture Park, Pittsburgh, PA

Hibernia Bank, San Francisco, CA

Highland Court, Orange, CA

Hilton Hotels, Seoul, South Korea

Hirshhorn Museum and Sculpture Garden, Smithsonian Institution, Washington, D.C.

Hughes Aircraft Company, Sunnyvale, CA

IBM Corporation, Boca Raton, FL

IBM Corporation, Los Angeles, CA

IBM Corporation, New York, NY

IBM Corporation, San Jose, CA

Kleinewefers, Krefeld, Germany

Klingspor Museum, Offenbach, Germany

Koll Company, San Jose, CA

Krannert Art Museum, University of Illinois, Urbana–Champaign, IL

Kröller-Müller Museum and Sculpture Garden, Otterlo, The Netherlands

La Jolla Museum of Contemporary Art, California

Laumier Sculpture Park, St. Louis, MO

Metropolitan Museum of Art, New York, NY

Miami University Sculpture Garden, Oxford, OH

Milwaukee Art Center, Wisconsin

Mirabella Corporation, Los Angeles, CA

Mitchell Museum at Cedarhurst, Mt. Vernon, IL

Modernes Köln, Cologne, Germany

Morgan Guaranty Trust, Euroclear Headquarters, Brussels, Belgium

Mount Zion Hospital, San Francisco, CA

Franklin D. Murphy Sculpture Garden, University of California, Los Angeles, CA

Museum Ludwig, Cologne, Germany

National Bank of Commerce, Lincoln, NE

Neiman Marcus Group, Dallas, TX

Nestle USA, Inc., Glendale, CA

Neuberger Museum of Art, State University of New York at Purchase, NY

New Orleans Museum of Art, Louisiana

Newport Harbor Art Museum, Newport Beach, CA

Oakland Museum, California

Orbanco Corporation, Portland, OR

Pacific Mutual Life Insurance Company, Newport Beach, CA

Phoenix Art Museum, Phoenix, AZ

John Portman Collection, San Francisco, CA

Pratt Institute, Brooklyn, NY

Prudential Life and Casualty, Merrillville, IN

Pyramid Hill Sculpture Park and Museum, Hamilton, OH

Nelson Rockefeller Collection, New York, NY

San Francisco Museum of Modern Art, California

San Jose State University Sculpture Garden, San Jose, CA

Sheldon Memorial Art Gallery and Sculpture Garden, University of Nebraska, Lincoln, NE

Singer Company, New York, NY

Smalley Sculpture Garden, University of Judaism, Los Angeles, CA

Stanford University Museum of Art, Stanford, CA

Stanley Associates, Muscatine, IA

Summa Corporation, Las Vegas, NV

Taubman Corporation, Ann Arbor, MI

Taubman Corporation, Fair Oaks, VA

Taubman Corporation, Reno, NV

3-D Chicago, IL

Thurman Arnold Building, Washington, D.C.

Trizec Western Inc., Los Angeles, CA

University of California, Berkeley Art Museum, CA

University of California, Irvine, CA

University of Iowa, Iowa City, IA

University of Miami, Florida

University of Michigan, Ann Arbor, MI

University of Northern Iowa, Cedar Falls, IA

University of Rio Grande, Rio Grande, OH

Victoria and Albert Museum, London, England

Whitney Museum of American Art, New York, NY

Material in Archives

Archives of American Art, Smithsonian Institution, Washington, D.C.: *The Fletcher Benton Papers*. The Archives contain an exceptionally large number of business correspondence, magazine and newspaper clippings, exhibition catalogues, brochures and fliers, photographs, books, and audiovisual material.

Photography Credits

Ben Blackwell
Page 90

Turner Davis
Page 172

M. Lee Fatherree
Pages 213, 256

David Finn
Pages 1, 2, 3, 6, 7, 9, 10

David Glomb (Photographs courtesy of Imago Galleries)
Pages 80, 81, 82, 100, 101, 173, 276, 277, 320, 321, 329, 330

Brigitte Haasner
Page 83

Wayne Hoy
Page 76

Stephen Joseph
Pages ii, iii

Monja Merkel
Pages 72, 73, 94, 104, 105, 355

Roger Paperno
Pages vi, 12, 18, 22, 23, 24, 25, 26, 27, 28, 29, 30, 31, 32, 33, 34, 35, 36, 37, 38, 39, 40, 41, 42, 43, 44, 45, 46, 47, 48, 49, 50, 51, 52, 53, 54, 55, 56, 57, 58, 59, 70, 71, 86, 87, 88, 92, 93, 95, 96, 97, 98, 99, 102, 103, 106, 107, 110, 111, 112, 113, 114, 115, 116, 117, 120, 121, 122, 123, 124, 125, 126, 127, 128, 129, 130, 131, 132, 133, 134, 135, 136, 137, 138, 139, 142, 143, 144, 145, 146, 147, 148, 149, 150, 151, 152, 153, 154, 155, 156, 157, 158, 159, 160, 161, 162, 163, 164, 165, 166, 167, 168, 169, 170, 171, 174, 175, 182, 183, 184, 185, 186, 187, 188, 189, 190, 191, 192, 193, 194, 195, 196, 197, 198, 199, 200, 201, 202, 203, 204, 205, 206, 207, 208, 209, 210, 211, 214, 215, 216, 217, 218, 219, 222, 223, 226, 227, 230, 231, 236, 237, 242, 243, 244, 245, 250, 251, 252, 253, 254, 255, 262, 263, 266, 267, 268, 269, 272, 273, 274, 275, 278, 279, 280, 281, 282, 283, 284, 285, 286, 287, 288, 289, 290, 291, 292, 293, 294, 295, 296, 297, 298, 299, 300, 301, 302, 303, 304, 305, 306, 307, 308, 309, 310, 311, 312, 313, 314, 315, 316, 317, 322, 323, 324, 325, 328, 332, 333, 334, 335, 336, 337, 338, 339, 340, 341, 342, 343, 344, 345, 346, 347, 348, 349, 350, 351, 352, 353, 354, 356, 357, 358, 359, 360, 361, 362, 363, 364, 365, 366, 367, 368

Francee Ricarte
Jacket

Michael Roby
Pages 74, 75, 176

Craig Smith (Photographs courtesy of Riva Yares Gallery)
Pages 89, 91, 118, 119, 140, 141, 318, 319

Bob Springate (Photographs courtesy of Riva Yares Gallery)
Pages 212, 220, 221, 224, 225, 228, 229, 232, 233, 234, 235, 238, 239, 240, 241, 246, 247, 248, 249, 257, 258, 259, 260, 261, 264, 265, 270, 271

Aitor Tasende (Photographs courtesy of Tasende Gallery)
Pages 60, 61, 62, 63, 64, 65, 66, 67, 68, 69, 108, 109, 172, 173, 177, 178, 179, 180, 181, 326, 327, 331

Mark Wilson
Page 84, 85

Unknown
Pages 77, 78, 79, 376